BIBLE "MYSTERIES" EXPLAINED

Understanding "Global Societal Collapse" from The "Science" in The Bible

What Every Scientist, Bible Scholar and Ordinary Man Needs to Know!

Charles S. Brown.

BIBLE "MYSTERIES" EXPLAINED

Understanding "Global Societal Collapse" from The "Science" in The Bible

What Every Scientist, Bible Scholar and Ordinary Man Needs to Know!

Charles S. Brown.

http://www.crystalbooks.org

This Edition published in **NEW ZEALAND**
by: —
CRYSTAL PUBLISHING.
P.O.Box 60042, Titirangi, West Auckland,
NEW ZEALAND.

Revised Second Edition 2011.
First Edition 2007.
Copyright © 2007 – 2011 Charles S. Brown.

ISBN 978-0-9582813-6-2

DEDICATION

This Work, *unequivocally and unashamedly; recognises and confesses*:

The:

* * * * *

"I AM!"

THE ALMIGHTY!

For it is **HIS** Eternal Beneficence, Grace and Power which ever offers *all* humankind the **True** and **Pure**:

DIVINE LOVE!

* * * * *

With very deep gratitude, therefore: All is offered **'UPWARDS'** to **"THE SOURCE"** for the *sure Guidance* which *Graciously* permitted the *recognition* of **'Perfect Truth'** inherent in:

DIVINE WILL!

For only *with* the necessary, clarifying, insights that *such* recognition *humbly permits* was it so possible, through this Work, to disseminate for global humankind the crucial help increasingly fragile and 'collapsing societies' sorely need: The **Key Knowledge** which clearly and *logically* elucidates so-called **Bible 'Mysteries'**.

Foreword

*   *   *   *   *

"In his latest work, **Bible "Mysteries" Explained**, Charles S. Brown explores in an open-minded and scientific manner, the nature and meaning of a number of the core teachings of the Bible; from the creation of the world in seven days versus evolution, to the resurrection and the virgin birth, as well as a number of broader spiritual issues such as rebirth, the relationship between Christian teachings, other religions and modern scientific thought.

Brown offers a deeper spiritual understanding of our place in the cosmos, both as a group and individually. Any scholar who enjoys the cut and thrust of spiritual discourse of a Biblical nature will find this book well worth reading."

Graeme Beals Publisher (Managing Director)
Zenith Publishing Group Ltd.
New Plymouth, NEW ZEALAND.

*   *   *   *   *

Contents

Acknowledgements

Crystal Publishing is extremely grateful to certain key people whose vital contribution helped bring this Work to light!

To Mr. R. M. Duraisamy (M.E. Hons.), author of "From India to the Truth: Towards a New Knowledge for the Reformation of Indian Spirituality" and other publications. For his kind permission to use the major part of his published essay on the phenomenon of Stigmata – "Stigmatised! A Necessary Clarification of the Phenomenon of Stigmata" – for Chapter 6 herein.

For his crucial support in helping to bring to fruition the publication of the various works of **Crystal Publishing**. And, not least, for encouraging this writer to learn and use *seemingly complicated software* which, however, was not as daunting as first appeared and entirely appropriate for the purpose.

To (Dr.) Stephen Lampe (author of "The Christian and Reincarnation" and "Building Future Societies: The Spiritual Principles") for his very kind permission to use essential material from his publications. His succinct collation of **The Spiritual Laws of Creation** — CREATION-LAW — form the essential core of the primary works of **Crystal Publishing**.

Also to Jacques Imbeau D.M.D., FACNEM (Dent), NZDREX: for applying his analytical skills to reviewing certain key parts of this book – particularly the Chapter: *"The Origins of Man, Genesis and Science Agree!"* His assistance there has resulted in greater clarification of perhaps the most important revelatory segments of that Chapter for both science and Christian orthodoxy. The correct knowledge of our Origins forms part of the primary foundation of the main works of **Crystal Publishing**.

Especially, however, to **Ferrar Fenton** – long deceased from the physical world – yet whose monumental work of re-translating **The Bible** finally permitted the centuries-old controversy between science and religion i.e., – **Creation** versus **Evolution** – to be perfectly reconciled. Through his intuitively-correct translation of **The Book of Genesis**, particularly **Chapters 1 and 2**, he has singularly rendered *every other* Genesis 'Bible translation' – that does not accord with his powerfully-guided, correct insights – irrelevant. Future events will unequivocally bear out the truth of this statement.

His crucial spiritual insights have therein returned to **The Creator** that which is **His – the Majesty and Power of The Pure Truth of His stupendous and humanly-incomprehensible Creation**. Fenton has therewith bequeathed to the worlds of science and religion the ordained foundation upon which to build, within their Disciplines:

The 'Harmonising Truth' about Creation and Evolution; and thus the True Origins of Man!

Author's Note

In the present, academic achievements and intellectual sophistry are lauded virtually above all else. These two 'cornerstones' of world and 'worldly' education hold powerful sway in probably most Universities, and thus strongly drive the 'learning paradigm' in many countries.

A book titled: **BIBLE "MYSTERIES" EXPLAINED**
Understanding "Global Societal Collapse" from The "Science" in The Bible:
What Every Scientist, Bible Scholar and Ordinary Man Needs to Know!
– would surely have the average reader keenly searching for the author's *"academic qualifications"*.

Anyone writing 'theologically', as it were, is invariably expected to have at least some "University letters" after their name. On that basis with regard to this Work and the subject matter it examines, one *could* therefore *perhaps* dismiss it without any examination whatsoever for, *on the surface*, it evidences not even a hint that the author possesses any kind of *educationally-suitable*, and thus *intellectually-acceptable*, 'qualifications'.

However, in the many and, *seemingly*, irreconcilable points of disputation between science and religion, in this case the Christian religion and around **one question, especially**; *this* Work provides a particular and **decisive** insight that cuts completely across long-held yet totally divisive scientific and religious notions to *clearly reveal* **how** and **why** *we arrived*. And we do so without the need for "letters" and/or "educational titles".

Despite the very large numbers of well-educated and "many-lettered" University-authors on each side of this unfortunate science/religion divide, that divisive difference nonetheless represents a truly strange and illogical mindset which manifestly *affects* each camp like some kind of incurable disease. For earth-science holds to its "eternal doubt" paradigm, whilst the Christian religion embraces a kind of "blind-faith" doctrine.

So, centred on exactly that one single key question we allude to: If it *were* truly *recognised* in its *truthful* yet *utterly profound* simplicity, it would provide – **from that seminal moment on** – the answers to so many more *seemingly inexplicable* "life-questions". Quite logically, the answers would be absolutely relevant for **both** science **and** religion. For the idea that science and religion should be mutually exclusive and irreconcilable is, in the final analysis, a foolish one anyway. In the case of the key question we allude to, **it is singularly and crucially so.** What is that key question, exactly? Quite simply, our **Origins**.

It is an affront to simple, common-sense logic to believe or proclaim that we cannot *precisely know* our Origins; our human "make-up". Why should that be so? What is the point of being on Earth in an *aware* state, yet still say "we cannot know for sure"? The endless debate that has raged for centuries over this issue certainly proclaims to the world that science and religion do not **definitively** know – otherwise there would not be present within those key Disciplines such serious division.

The crucial nature of that singular question is very evident by the fact that two of the primary Documentary Channels: **The History** and **The National Geographic**; both addressed it in relevant documentaries in 2008.

National Geographic queried *exactly* this question in two separate Documentaries: "**Birth of Life**", and "**Human Ape**". The associated and most relevant point asked was:
"**How did *non-living* material come to life?**"

The History Channel, too, seeks the same kind of definitive answer. The series, "**How Life Began**", asks:
"**Where did [this] life come from? What IS life, exactly?**"

And in a *space* of perhaps *insightful prescience*, the Series further and crucially queries:
"***Is it chemical, spiritual, or a combination of both?***"   (All emphases mine.)

On the basis of that crucial question, how does the so-called 'great scientific breakthrough' of 2010 by scientist Dr Craig Venter in *creating* 'artificial life' in a laboratory test tube rate? The world headlines read: "Giant leap for science..." What does the word, *creation*, really mean anyway? In this case, of course, the building blocks required to *produce* this 'new life form' were already available to science. So it is not a question of truly **creating**, as such; but, with the aid of a computer, more *assembling* the various components – albeit to a precise configuration under strictly-controlled conditions.

To some degree in their crass sensationalism, the hype that journalistic jingoism gave to this new 'life-form' may perhaps have stemmed from envisioning all sorts of 'creatures' developing from *it*. However, in a Q. and A. session, Dr Venter quashed that 'possibility'.

> **Question**: 'So is this new form of life a replicating, free-living organism.'
>
> **Answer**: "That is correct, only it is free-living in the sense that it grows *in the laboratory* in a very rich culture media **so it wouldn't survive in the outside environment**. Given the right nutrients *in the laboratory* it is self-replicating on its own."
>
> (All emphases mine.)

So this new thing will never even develop to the level of just a common garden slug – a real and mobile life-form animated by a real **life-force** – let alone anything higher. Human science can only *assemble*, not truly create. For we, ourselves, are simply a *species* of, and *in*, Creation!

With regard to *my* 'qualifications': In Truth, I possess no such academic refinement from any worldly "Institution of Higher Learning". What I do have *in the first instance*, however, is simple *common sense* coupled with a very logical-thinking mind. For the necessarily-deep analyses of the subjects that this book examines, the *logical-thinking* aspect is perhaps brutally so. But therewith, precisely the '*right stuff*' to strip away **inexcusable errors and distortions** strongly present in the too-long-held 'sacrosanct' cornerstone beliefs of Christendom – and the later, now equally-strong, views of earth-science – to thereby provide simple and logical *reconciliation* of our **How** and **Why**.

Over millennia, countless generations of Christians have been "conditioned" to "accept without question" the official tenets of the once all-powerful Church. In former times by brutal suppression of any deviation from the official view if need be.

The long life of that "religious" institution saw those official tenets eventually come to be regarded as almost 'absolute' truths. Yet a simple, logical and keen examination of **The Bible** of just the *primary* sacrosanct tenets, absolutely-clearly and brutally-unequivocally reveal that what the Christian Church, its noted theologians and its two billion global adherents seemingly *accept without question*, is simply *not there* in The Scriptures they constantly refer to.

In the pages of ***this*** book, therefore; you, the reader, ***will discover this clear fact for yourself.***

0.1 The Mandate For This Work: — Through Paul The Apostle

So, do I possess *any* mandate at all? Yes, I most certainly do! But not from a University or similar. For this work, I accept the mandate given by Paul, The Apostle of **Jesus: The Son of God!** Regarded as a noted intellectual thinker and scholar by Christian academics throughout history to the present day, let us all take note of Paul's clear admonition to the academic elite of his time and apply it to the *present*, and thus to the *author* of *this* Work.'

From Paul, founder of "The Church": For University academics, for Christian theologians and for the reader of this book; I accept as *my* clear mandate the directive *he* gave to *his* followers. From "The Holy Bible in Modern English" – Ferrar Fenton's seminal Work – in Corinthians 1:26-29, we read:

> "For, contemplate your vocation brothers: that not many philosophers, not many powerful, not many high-born – on the contrary, God has ***chosen*** the ***foolish of the world***, so that He might ***shame the philosophic***..."
> "Therefore none can boast in the presence of God."
>
> "...how many of you were wise in the ordinary sense of the word, how many were influential people, or came from noble families? No, it was to ***shame the wise*** that God ***chose what is foolish by human reckoning***..."

> (The same from The Jerusalem Bible.
All emphases mine.)

Since I have no academic mandate from a "Theological College" or similar I will, for this Work – which greatly derives from The Bible and Teachings of Jesus – therefore accept without boast, the *greater mandate* from Paul, the appointed Apostle of that time. For with the Works I have been ***directed*** to write, I surely count myself blessed in being one of **His** "foolish".

And as Pope Benedict has made a logical plea to scientists that science and religion [or spirituality] should not be mutually exclusive, we should therefore also include here two very relevant texts *for* earth science: One from "historical science"; the other from The Bible.

The problem for science and scientists is that the current "standard scientific viewpoint" fails to take into account or even *acknowledge* that *all* scientific endeavour must also embrace the *non-material aspect* of **Creation** that ***its concomitant "Laws"*** unequivocally attest to. Only with that crucial recognition will earth-science *ever* be able to offer *complete and meaningful* answers to the never-ending questions it [science] continually finds itself faced with. In his book, The Sacred Balance [p.19], Dr. David Suzuki points out:

> "Scientism, the aura of authority carried by scientists, has made us believe that knowledge obtained by scientists is the ultimate authority, that as we accumulate information, our capacity to understand, control and manage our surroundings will grow correspondingly. But the basic principle of scientific exploration contradicts this faith: knowledge comes from empirical observations, which are "made sense of" by hypotheses, which in turn can be experimentally tested. All information is open to being disproved. As Jonathan Marks has pointed out":
> "...the vast majority of ideas that most scientists have ever had have been wrong. They have been refuted; they have been disposed of. Further, at any point in time, most ideas proposed by most scientists will ultimately be refuted and disposed of... Science, in other words, undermines scientism."

The message that the Prophet Isaiah gave millennia ago [Ode 44: Book 1, The Fenton Bible] clearly foresaw the quandary that would develop for earth-science and scientists if the higher knowledge of Spiritual Law was not taken into account. Preceding the above scientific reality by thousands of years, the following ode could almost be called: **"The Scientists' Lament"**.

Denunciation of Hypocrisy.

Now the Almighty demands,
"Why do this people approach
With their mouth and their lips,
To pay honour to Me,
While their heart is far off?
Their reverence is worthless to Me:-
It teaches the doctrines of men!

"So on this race I lay wonders,
Add wonders to wonders,
Destroying its scientists' science,
And baffling its scholars' researches."

We should further note that the "The great Prophet's" visions of a "Reeling Earth" far in the future from *his* viewpoint can *now* be understood as the simple reality of **Plate Tectonics** – something once ridiculed by science and therefore *exactly illustrating* **"The Error of Scientism"**. Notwithstanding our complete agreement with Isaiah's crucial message for earth-scientists, we certainly do not denigrate science, per se; not at all. Despite the fact that there is far too much "bad science" today, there is also very much very good science in the world, from which humankind has benefited hugely. We unequivocally support that kind of science.

In concert with the subject matter of this Work, the reader must understand that it is, by design and contents, very different to other publications. The subject matter and its associated structure places it in a specific category of its own. In "edit-speak", moreover, the Work would ordinarily be considered too "dense" and too repetitious. Accepting that such a categorisation is very probable, without apology it thus occupies a singular place outside standard editing/publishing parameters.

The nature of the analyses centred on the various topics examined nonetheless offer a serious challenge to beliefs and theories current in academia. In order to *fully explain* the revisionist and spiritually-radical concepts herein it is most necessary to constantly and regularly reinforce those very concepts throughout. It is exactly that radical aspect, however, which permits the revelation and clarification of some specific and contentious, so-called, "Bible Mysteries".

To that end, the comprehensive **Preface** to the main text very broadly outlines certain historical events where the *religious/spiritual thought* contained in The Bible brought it into serious contention with powerful Nations and individuals who sought to impose their religious stamp of authority on the known world of their times. The fact that many attempts over millennia failed to achieve the obliteration or expunging of that *elevated Biblical thought* from wider dissemination into an enlarging "known world" – facilitated through the emergence of certain Peoples and Empires – meant that a "disaster" was *potentially* averted.

Why a "disaster averted"? And why the inclusion of the word, *potential*, in this case? There are two very decisive reasons associated with those key questions. The first is the fact that within that especial Book, **The Bible**, are *the actual keys* to the **what, where, how and why of human existence.** So, had a different thought been imposed upon the world for all time, those *golden keys* would not now be here to show humankind the true direction forward. That is the "disaster averted" in the first instance.

The second reason – the "potential" aspect – unfortunately refers to the fact that despite **The Bible** not suffering total suppression or even obliteration from history, the *golden keys* to our ***what, where, how and why*** are today suppressed by a modern tyranny. It takes the form of *elitist intellectualism* emanating from the Universities of the world – the West especially. Instead of recognising the clear and unequivocal Truths that **actually <u>are</u> in The Bible** – and the *greatest* Truth of all that it clearly points to – academics of science and religion *endlessly debate* points of disputation that ultimately do not even *begin* to gravitate towards those stupendous Revelations.

Masquerading as the apex of educational excellence in critical analyses and so called "intellectual insight", the whole thrust of current earth-science and theological theory hold the Western world in thrall to its rather strange paradigm of "just theory" and ultimately more theory. ***Ultimate Truths****, accessible to all, seem not to have all that many champions anywhere in religious and scientific academia.*

Precisely centred around what is supposed to be **The Critical Knowledge** for the human race – our ***what, where, how and why*** – Western academia seeks reasons/answers from a foundation solely thought out by the human intellect. The higher connective-element inherent in all human beings that the Pope challenges science to recognise and thus utilise is, in the most enigmatic paradox, not actually recognised by "intellectual science" at all – hence its ***failure*** to see the greater horizon.

Chapter 1 of this Work, **"The Crucial Imperatives"**, itemises certain key realities exactly about that "greater horizon" for the serious attention of "Western academia", yet still primarily centred around the Judaeo/Christian ethos in any case. If that "learning-industry" is ever to proclaim actual and definitive Truths about our ***what, where, how and why***, it will not ever do so until it seriously engages with exactly that list of "Crucial Imperatives" to begin with.

The clear answer to our ***what, where, how and why*** – *especially including* **the <u>real</u> human/chimp split** – can actually be found ***in just a few very key sentences*** in Chapters 1 and 2 of The Book of Genesis. [Fully and logically *elucidated* in **Chapter 2: "The Origins of Man: Genesis and Science Agree!"**]

Unfortunately, however, and zealously perpetuated by the Christian Church, earthly science and committees of Ph.D and degree-toting Bible "scholars"; this "triune" of earthly power persistently continues to *intellectually debate* this foolish divide. Unsound teachings and theories – to begin with – in diametric opposition to each other can never ever find harmonious reconciliation; let alone lead to Truth. Riding on the back of so-called "expert" translations and opinions, the main Bible Publishers continue to reproduce the same appalling error – a completely wrong interpretation of the actual processes of Creation and Evolution that really ***are explained*** in **The Book of Genesis**.

Despite this dreadful suppression of The Truth about Creation by the "educational elite" of the "Christian" part of global humanity, ***this Work nonetheless reveals those processes that facilitated our [human] entry into*** <u>***life***</u> ***on Earth***.

In terms of the many so called "Bible Mysteries" accepted as such by Theology and certain scientific Disciplines, I have concentrated mainly on those that either receive the most attention and are hotly debated, and/or are so-called "mysteries" that have become "sacrosanct tenets" of the global Christian Church. However, with the aid of the knowledge of **The Laws of Creation** – explained herein – along with explanations about key processes and experiences that all human beings must go through in any case, the reader is offered the means by which he can *thereby* understand why there are no real "Bible Mysteries" – with regard to what we are ***meant to know and understand***.

The *true* mysteries are centred on events, processes and inhabitants that The Bible alludes to but which lie far above our human Origins. By virtue of their incomprehensible [for the human spirit] height and nature, *they* will forever be the actual "Mysteries". The academic reader, particularly, should therefore strive to "absorb" the explanations of the many diverse elements that make up the complete interconnected picture. This Work should not be rushed through.

I believe it important to *once more restate the fact* that because the explanations and concepts examined in this book are so vastly different to what is currently accepted and taught in Universities and Theological Colleges throughout Western academia, the Work thus stands well outside standard, perhaps currently accepted, "educational" parameters. Quite logically, therefore, that is *exactly* its rightful place! The literary style, in its repetitive aspect of constant reinforcement of the concepts examined, similarly also stands in its correct place too.

The prophetic fulfilment of the most **"Crucial Imperative"** of all – perhaps the greatest "Bible Mystery" explained further on in the Work – will, in the future, sheet home for the academic world the *sure statements* contained herein!

May the **collective spirit** of *intellectual academia* be sufficiently open to intuitively recognise the clear Truths inherent in this Work!

Charles S. Brown.

Pope Benedict's Regensburg Address

0.2 The Call to Science

On September 13th 2006 in Regensburg, Germany; Joseph Ratzinger – Pope Benedict XVI – in an address at the university where he was once a professor, established the basis for dialogue between cultures and religions; **in effect a new relationship between faith and reason.**

He said that in a world characterised by the coexistence of cultures and religions, dialogue will be successful;

> *"...only if reason and faith come together in a new way, if we overcome the self-imposed limitation of reason to the empirically verifiable, and if we once more disclose its vast horizons."*

> "Only thus do we become capable of that genuine dialogue of cultures and religions so urgently needed today." The Pope pointed out that modern scientific reason "...bears within itself a question which points beyond itself and beyond the possibilities of its methodology."

> *"Modern scientific reason quite simply has to accept the rational structure of matter and the correspondence between* **our spirit and the prevailing rational structures of nature as a given**, *on which its methodology has to be based. Yet the question why this has to be so, is a real question, and one which has to be remanded by the natural sciences* **to other modes and planes of thought** *– to philosophy and theology."*

> "For philosophy and, albeit in a different way, for theology, listening to the great experiences and insights of the religious traditions of humanity, and those of the Christian faith in particular, is a source of knowledge, and to ignore it would be an unacceptable restriction of our listening and responding."

> *"The West has long been endangered by this aversion to the questions which underlie its rationality, and can only suffer great harm thereby."*

> "The courage to engage the whole breadth of reason, and not the denial of its grandeur – this is the program with which a theology grounded in biblical faith enters into the debates of our time."

Comments of the Bishop of Rome

> "In the Western world it is widely held that only positivistic reason and the forms of philosophy based on it are universally valid."

"Yet the world's profoundly religious cultures see this exclusion of the divine [The Divine] from the universality of reason as an attack on their most profound convictions. A reason which is deaf to the divine [The Divine] and which relegates religion to the realm of subcultures is incapable of entering into the dialogue of cultures."

This address by the Pope and the concomitant statements by the Bishop of Rome are most timely given that certain earth-sciences are digging themselves deeper and deeper into paths that carry them further and further from the connection to natural truth set in place by the natural processes of Creation itself. The very Title of this work and the foundation of the subject matter within resonate perfectly with the truths expressed by Pope Benedict XVI.

For, as we state unequivocally throughout this work – and indeed in *all* publications of Crystal Publishing – there should be no contradiction between science and religious truth, and that **science cannot supersede any such truths.**

The great scientist, Einstein, though noting the demarcation between science and religion, nonetheless understood the strong reciprocal relationships and dependencies between the two. He stated:

"Though religion may be that which determines the goal, it has, nevertheless learned from science, in the broadest sense, what means will contribute to the attainment of the goals it has set up. *But science can only be created by those who are thoroughly imbued with the aspiration toward truth and understanding.*"

Einstein summarises his view of the relationship between science and religion thus:

"Science without religion is lame, religion without science is blind."

(Albert Einstein, "Ideas and Opinions", p 42-3.
All Emphases mine.)

Thus, the SCIENCE in The Bible is the "Crucial Imperative" for ALL of humankind!

Preface

0.3 The Bible! A Primary Work of "Foundational-Science"

> "Above all, *the pure light of revelation* has had an influence [***powerful impact***] on mankind, and *increased the blessings* of society. It is ***impossible*** to <u>**rightly govern**</u> the world <u>**without God and the Bible**</u>."

(George Washington.
Emphases and parenthetic addition mine.)

Now: Why would Washington so emphatically cite **The Bible** as a necessary medium by which, and with which, leaders and rulers should govern their societies? The answer is brutally simple. Of all so-called *religious* Works, ***only The Bible*** comes closest to explaining the knowledge of **The ONE-LAW – CREATION-LAW** – decisive for the life of ***all*** men.

For aside from all else that **The Bible** teaches, contained within it [from as far back as the eighth century B.C.] is – from out of **THE LAW** – the *one sentence*[1] of ***absolute prophecy*** that unequivocally explains ***why all*** global societies of Planet Earth are not just *failing*, but will ***fall utterly***. Isaiah – the "Great Prophet" – even then *foresaw* the path that we of Planet Earth *would take*. His warning, though brutal in its Truth, has never really been heeded by we humans. For we know better – *don't we*?

> "The earth also is *defiled* under the *inhabitants* thereof; because they have
> <u>*transgressed*</u> *the laws*,
> <u>*changed*</u> *the decrees*,
> <u>*broken*</u> *the everlasting covenant*."

(Isaiah 24:5, Fenton. Emphases mine.)

President George Washington – whom many Americans regard as their *great* President – would surely be appalled at present-day American society. Perversely demanding the so-called "freedom-rights" of the Constitution, its citizens, through the visual, written and electronic mediums, have flooded not just their own society but also much of the rest of the world with [to name just two] spiritually-foolish and totally unnecessary excesses – foul language in music, and explicit sexual deviancy and pornography in numerous forms. Much of the world has followed – if not actually embraced – America's absolutely non-spiritual, non-beneficial, societal *example*.

---

[1]Because Isaiah's prophecy encapsulates the ***real*** reason for ***all*** of humankind's problems and failings, where relevant in this Work, it is repeated.

A small example from America – land of the free!

> When Minister Joe Wright was asked to open the new session of the Kansas [USA] Senate, everyone was expecting the usual generalities, but they heard a very different kind of prayer.
> The response was immediate. A number of legislators walked out during the prayer in protest.
> In 6 short weeks, Central Christian Church, where Reverend Wright is Pastor, logged more than 5,000 phone calls, with only 47 of those calls responding negatively.
> The church is now receiving international requests for copies of this prayer from India, Africa and Korea.
> Commentator Paul Harvey aired this Prayer on his radio program, "The Rest of the Story", and received a larger response to this program than any other he has ever aired.
> With the Lord's help, may this Prayer sweep over our nation and wholeheartedly become our desire so that we again can be called: "One Nation Under God!"
> If possible, please pass this prayer on to your friends.
> "If you don't Stand for something, you will fall for everything."

Minister Joe Wright's **"Prayer of Truth"**!

> "Heavenly Father,
> We come before you today to ask your forgiveness and to seek your direction and guidance.
> We know your Word says: "Woe to those who call evil good", but that is exactly what we have done.
> We have lost our spiritual equilibrium and reversed our values.
> We have exploited the poor and called it the lottery.
> We have rewarded laziness and called it welfare.
> We have killed our unborn and called it choice.
> We have shot abortionists and called it justifiable.
> We have neglected to discipline our children and called it building self-esteem.
> We have abused power and called it politics.
> We have coveted our neighbour's possessions and called it ambition.
> We have polluted the air with profanity and pornography and called it freedom of expression.
> We have ridiculed the time-honoured values of our forefathers and called it enlightenment.
> Search us, O God, and know our hearts today; cleanse us from every sin and set us free.

> Amen.

Many voice doubts about the existence of God, and/or that God – or a God – is irrelevant for modern, technological, intellectual man. Past publications have carried Titles such as: "Does God Exist?", or asking, "Is God Dead?", or stating, "God is Dead". The associated age-old question about whether Creation came about by accident or Divine Plan is thus hardly surprising. The "accident" notion must pre-suppose no God, whilst a Divine Plan scenario will mean the existence of a God of humanly-incomprehensible power.

The three major monotheistic religions, all of which name Abraham as their founding Patriarch have, as their very foundation, primary books of "God's Law". A One-God, All-powerful and All-knowing. In basic terms for probably most of the followers of those three religions; One determined to save us from our own folly too. In short, a God for all seasons and reasons. What about a God of immovable Justice and Law, however? For a "Divine Plan" God would surely set such in place. Where might man stand in transgression of such Laws? For The Laws of The Creator must surely be Perfect, and we certainly would not want to have our personalised God imperfect, would we?.

Such a strange relationship so many humans have with their God. Everyone wants Him to be on *their* side. Everyone wants Him to destroy *their* enemies. Yet opposing sides of the same faith have often prayed to the same God for victory over the other. The First World War produced one of the most remarkable wartime episodes ever when opposing British and German Units simply stopped fighting and joined together to exchange Christmas greetings and gifts and sing the time-honoured Christmas Carols. Technically, it was a mutinous act by both groups of soldiers and the British High Command soon put a stop to it by directing an artillery barrage toward that part of the "line".

Bob Dylan, troubadour, contemporary and often quite insightful, socially-influential bard and songwriter, over his career has produced lyrics that have literally changed perceptions and galvanised groups globally.

Perfectly tailored for our current analysis, his song, "With God on Our Side", exactly illustrates the strange relationship humans have with their God. Verse four:

> "Oh the First World War, boys
> It closed out its fate
> The reason for fighting
> I never got straight
> But I learned to accept it
> Accept it with pride
> For you don't count the dead
> When God's on your side."

During the Second World War, major Units of the German Army carried, as part of their uniform, the engraving "Gott Mit Uns" (God with us) on their belt buckle. Could a Just and Perfect God support something as horrific as Hitler's megalomanic rampage of death and destruction? Surely only a distorted mind would think so. The compelling verse five from Dylan's same composition tells it succinctly.

> "When the Second World War
> Came to an end
> We forgave the Germans
> And we were friends
> Though they murdered six million
> In the ovens they fried
> The Germans now too
> Have God on their side."

On a much smaller scale we humans on occasions will give thanks to a deity for good things that come our way, but may also rail against the fates and the same deity when we suffer tragedy. Does this indicate that we expect the God of *our* choosing to provide good things for us *all* the time, no matter what *we* do or how *we* behave? Surely such a mind-set is akin to petty childishness. Or does it actually show that, for the most part, we humanity of earth have little or no understanding of the God we pray to, particularly in times of great distress.

Unfathomable disasters often trigger such debates, as in the case of the 2004 Indian Ocean tsunami tragedy. Now, if one is *genuinely* true to one's stated belief that one has "found Truth" in one's religion, then such terrible tragedies should produce **compassionate understanding** of it, *not* non-understanding.

Deriving from the inherent truth of that perception, one of the strangest ironies to emerge from that catastrophe were comments from the, then, Archbishop of Canterbury. The most senior clergyman of one of the world's major Christian denominations publicly questioned his own faith over the issue of so many tsunami deaths. All the training for that position, the very reason for being the head of his chosen Church, must surely have presupposed the very strongest belief in God, or at the very least a God – even if only to set an example in guiding and leading 'the flock'.

To publicly state, however, that such a tragedy "...should make all Christians question the existence of God...", perfectly illustrates how so many on Earth want a "personalised God" – even Church 'leaders'. Thus a God Who only produces what *we* think He should. This pre-eminent clergyman's query: "How can you believe in a God who permits suffering on this scale?", perfectly portrays the classic assumptive question. On the one hand is the **totally unrealistic belief** that such things **should never ever happen**.

On the other, the only reason that it did happen is, perversely, '**because God let it**'. "What other reason could there possibly be...", seems to be the dangerously-fundamentalist mindset here. It is almost medieval in its particular brand of reasoning. Paradoxically, both views reveal **this** clear fact, also stated by the Archbishop: "...*most of the stock Christian answers to human suffering do not go very far in helping us*, one week on, with the intolerable grief and devastation in front of us." (Italics mine.)

And therein lies the true answer. Religions – all religions – whilst *professing* to understand The Laws of God, stand uncomprehending before disasters of this magnitude. If the followers of the various religions were brutally-honest they would admit that such questions are asked at such times simply because they possess no real answers. Just the same tired old standard, hackneyed, phrases. So we must never question the obvious in the case of any and all tsunami waves; i.e., the logical fact that they do not distinguish between adults and children, or coral reefs and animals. A very silly idea, indeed.

Affecting millions in various religions over a relatively large portion of the globe, the most devastating natural disaster to hit the world in a long time would surely have tested the faith of the sufferers in a way not perhaps ever experienced before. The peoples bordering the Indian Ocean are mainly Hindus, Buddhists and Muslims; with some Countries supporting quite large Christian populations as well.

Newsweek Magazine reported how the different religions of the area would generally regard the visitation of a major natural disaster upon them. A key observation; "No survivor of a disaster of this magnitude can long avoid asking the 'Job-like' questions, 'Why us, why here, why now?' "

Hindus: Hard-hit by the tsunami, Hindu fishing communities along the coast of south India relate strongly to various local deities who exert a powerful influence on their everyday life. "Local deities possess the power to create or destroy". "The ocean itself is a terrible god who eats people and boats, but also provides fish as food." According to Richard Davis, "a specialist in South Asian Hinduism at Bard College in New York", "Hindus explain happenings like the tsunami as destructive acts by the gods". "Relating to the local deity and cooling her anger through propitiation is more important than thinking about personal or collective guilt for what has happened."

Buddhists: Donald Lopez, professor of Buddhist studies at the University of Michigan, states: "Buddhists will look to the idea of karma and ask what they did, individually and collectively, that a tragedy like this happened." Generating good merit to transfer to the deceased as a positive force in their next lifetime would be a primary concern. Monks would be employed to act as intermediaries in the transfer of merit.

Muslims: The Muslim view – as explained in this particular source – is especially revealing. "Like the Bible, the Koran recognises no natural laws independent of God's will. All that happens is Allah's doing, and nature itself – wind, rain, storms, – constitute signs of his mercy and compassion. Even the destructive tsunami, therefore, must have some hidden, positive purpose". According to Akbar Ahmed, chair of Islamic Studies at American University: "Ninety per cent of Muslims will understand a tragedy like this in this way. On the individual level they also have this notion that God is testing them by taking away a child or a spouse. Will you lose your faith, or will you continue to believe?" Ahmed says this idea of testing, and the patience it requires, gives an "in-built psychological cushion which allows Muslims to absorb a tragedy of this scale."

Christians: Christians in the affected area had to try to make sense of it all too. "Although the acceptance of suffering is embedded in the Christian world view, the death of so many innocent children alone was an excruciating test of the Christian belief that their God is a God of Love." Little wonder that from Sumatra to Madagascar, voices cry out to God.

The closing observation is one that many more than just those affected might also wonder at. "The miracle, if there is one, may be that so many still believe". Perhaps the greater degree of understanding, however, was that voiced by Syed Abdullah, "a local imam of Nagapattinam", a port where Muslims, Hindus and Christians have lived together for centuries. "In this kind of tragedy there is no religion", he said. "Let the dead be buried together. They died together in the sea. Let their souls get peace together."

Four *different* religions espousing four *dissimilar* views. Which of the four, if any, *correctly* describes the why of the tragedy? Obviously, each will avow that it has the answer. Logically, however, without agreement or consensus, uncertainty remains. Yet could all of the stated views hold at least *some* measure of truth, even if to varying degrees about the why? If so, could all those truthful elements be culled and somehow combined to give a more comprehensive answer than the subsequent fragmented anguish? And what if the actual reason *why* such an event occurred on the scale that it did were to have some degree of resonance and answer in **all** of the main religions, as should be considered?

Could the powerful, controlling, Christian West, in its drive to democratise other Nations, accept the possibility that perhaps other religions might offer at least *some* element of the ultimate reason why? In the present climate of global power-politics and fragmenting world religions, probably not.

In the tsunami aftermath, former US Presidents, George Bush Snr. and Bill Clinton, interviewed on CNN's "Larry King Live", offered insights from their own personal-faith aspect. Bill Clinton, however, presented an understanding that really explained it more simply and truthfully than perhaps any other commentator from the main global news players over the two weeks of intensive coverage. His simple but profoundly truthful observation resonates well with the whole tone and message of *this* work. The sense of his statement was, basically: "We are not in charge here. The earth is an organism that has its own [dynamics]. We have to remember that we are not in charge." Our acceptance of the view that "...we are not in charge..." certainly runs to the Earth and the cosmos and beyond.

In terms of *personal fate*, however, we would absolutely state that yes, we *are* in charge. The Chapters herein will explain both parts of that 'quandary'. Bill Clinton went on to say that 'rather than diminishing his faith', in the face of such adversity 'the courage of the human spirit strengthened it'.

In the final analysis what took place in the Indian Ocean, indeed, whatever transpires anywhere, does so under the outworking of inviolable Laws – **CREATION-LAWS**. The very nature of Planet Earth, in terms of its "life-dynamics", means that what we call disasters and catastrophes must, and will, always continue to happen. An objective viewpoint, therefore, will logically note that "Mother Nature" is simply bringing about *necessary change* within the body of the Earth – albeit huge changes from *our* perspective. Such events are **not** caused by some kind of all-powerful, vengeful finger coming out of the sky to *arbitrarily* destroy communities on a capricious whim.

Were that the case it would mean that we are nothing more than puppets dangling on the end of a string at the constant mercy of a super-deity who possesses no logic, and no love. What, then, would be the point of being on earth at all if we could not determine our own fate? Only illogical superstition and human-religious belief systems could invent such foolish notions.

CREATION-LAW, in its Immutable and thus Perfect outworking, could never do so.

In concert with that **Inviolable Truth**, the Title page of this work unequivocally states that understanding **"Global Societal Collapse"** from the *"Science"* in **The Bible** is crucial for every scientist, Bible scholar and ordinary man. That, of course, is a position that a large proportion of global humanity would not necessarily accept. We may note now, however, that Pope Benedict's crucial and keynote speech of September 13th, 2006, in Regensburg, Germany, reveals that *he* has recognised the debilitating and problematic divide that currently exists between science and religion. It is one, moreover, that needs to be *immediately* addressed and resolved so that we may *finally begin to understand* **why** "societal collapses" **are** increasing globally.

His insights and statements have cut to the heart of the matter for earth-science. This work spells out in detail, for both science and religion, the timely and very salient crucial points that Pope Benedict XVI has now courageously delivered to the world, in particular to science.

> He, however, as the Pope of the very large numbers that make up the global Church he heads, should therefore be the **primary** religious leader to **recognise and embrace** the *actual* Truths contained in **The Bible** – clearly explained herein. Moreover, he, **especially**, should shepherd his church towards the crucial Revelation to which **this Work** points! For that revelation **decisively-resonates** with the **choice** of the **Life** and the **Death** – The **Blessing** and the **Curse** – of the following Scripture!

> "Bear witness to me, now, Heavens and Earth! I place *Life and Death* before you, – the *Blessing and the Curse*! Therefore **choose** for yourselves **the Life**, – that **you** and **your posterity** may **live**!"

> (Deuteronomy 30:19, Fenton.
> Emphases mine.)

The foundation of our explanations is strongly based on The Bible, in which that "science of life" the Pope alludes to is very clearly revealed. Apart from that The Bible is obviously a key Work anyway, for the current time-line of the whole world is centred round the B.C/A.D [B.C.E/A.C.E] paradigm of the central figure in it: **Jesus Christ!**

Since the importance of The Bible cannot be denied, why is that especial book not accepted by all? The fact that The Bible is not held in high regard universally must presuppose the conclusion that followers of other religions believe their faith to be equal in value to Christianity or perhaps Judaism. Current global events of inter-religious warfare certainly show that to be the case, i.e., that both the Founders of the great religions and the very religions themselves are promoted and defended by their adherents as inviolable and equal to the Teachings of The Bible and its central figure. So perhaps for those religions that do not accept The Bible, the historical time-frame associated with Jesus Christ is little more than a "calendrical" point of convenience.

Yet are we, as human beings inherently endowed with a thinking, reasoning faculty, meant to simply accept the religious framework which we seemingly inherit at birth, without question? Should we meekly, or perhaps fearfully, just go along with what we are told by religious leaders, even to the point of long periods of "head-nodding" whilst parroting the standard mantras of those religions where such practices seem to be the norm? No, we should not!

Are we not, therefore, all enjoined to seriously question all aspects of all religions? Indeed we are! For by doing so we not only begin the very necessary process of fulfilling the primary purpose of our "earthly reason for being" but, more crucially, *of our complete existence*. We are not then numbered among the many hundreds of millions who, for the most part, are simply automatons content to accept a religious or *culturally-religious* life-interpretation paradigm thought out by others.

Through serious study of the time-line whereby the great religions emerged, and the study of the cultures and key historical events surrounding the founding of them therein, we may note a precise and key thread which powerfully endorses our unequivocal premise: **That The Bible is crucially important for all of global humanity, and the scientific knowledge contained in it is fundamental for all current religions and science.**

Since that is a provable reality – *which we will reveal and outline in this Preface and detail through the individual Chapters* – who within those very religious and scientific establishments today should be the primary catalysts/s for such a crucial awakening? As most people are just followers of one thing or another, the major responsibility for such an awakening thus lies with the current crop of religious and academic leaders worldwide.

The **"Crucial Imperatives"** that we note as being key to the **RECOGNITION** of what we state – for that is the precise and necessary requirement for any kind of awakening: **THE RECOGNITION** – are also those that science, too, must ultimately recognise and accept. For they stand on and are the primary foundation for all scientific direction and endeavour as well.

Therefore, from the moment of its very inception around the beginnings of recorded history, that "sacred" Work – initially in the form of The Torah – thrust itself inexorably and relentlessly into the affairs of men and Nations where it originated, and subsequently onto the global stage in the enlarged form of The Bible.

Notwithstanding what we have already noted about those religions that do not accept The Bible as their founding premise, and since the ramifications of what we state are clearly momentous and far-reaching, let us revisit our central premise and ask the key question/s:

> "What exactly *is* in that 'Book' for it *to impact so decisively upon the affairs of men*? And *why* has it shaped the history of the world to the *degree* that it has *in such a powerfully-delineated and definitive way*?"

Is it a history book? Yes, it is certainly that. Is it a religious book? Yes, it is also that. But there are many ancient works that can claim to possess those two aspects. In themselves, those particular characteristics are unremarkable. So what does The Bible possess that other similar kinds of Works do not; to the point of moving the very spirit of man toward the good, noble and altruistic, and yet others towards the opposite pole; towards destruction, depravity and all manner of evil?

Perhaps in the final analysis there is inherent in that document a singularly powerful feature that the spirit of man inherently perceives, but without actually recognising "consciously". Perhaps this "unknown quantity" resides in the deepest recesses of man's inner self – his spirit – but lies there suppressed by that part of the human entity which we now laud above all else as the greatest thing to aspire to; intellectual sophistry and sagacity. In a word – *intellectualism*! If we continue this analytical thread, we next need to ask the question:

"What, then, *is* that crucial aspect of and within The Bible that *the spirit* might understand and *recognise*, but the too-strongly developed *intellectual part* of Western man, particularly, simply *does not want to openly or consciously recognise* and thus *acknowledge*?"

For the two billion odd Christians worldwide, the answer as to what is inherent in The Bible is generally quite clear. The Bible provides the story/history of The Creator and His Creation. It thus naturally teaches His Laws and Commandments and also traces our origins and entry onto the Earth. It also offers the opportunity for "believing Christians" to have "everlasting life". "Everlasting life" in the Christian ethos, however, can only be granted through accepting in the first place the Person of The Son of God, Jesus, and similarly accepting the very prevalent belief among them that He died to save *us* from *our* sins. That is the basic Christian view; singular and loyal, to the point of being simplistic. Just believe, have faith, do not question, listen to the numerous church-leader/s interpretation/s and be assured of – "a place in heaven".

If only it were that simple!

Despite this basic belief being a more or less unifying principal among most Christian denominations, what we do not have and have never had among the thousands of different belief-systems therein is one single and unanimous cry from them all that jubilantly proclaims to the world: "Here is the complete thing. Now we are all in agreement, because it is all so clear and correct."

What do we have instead? We have dissension, disagreement, split factions and argument, and historically much violence, even between Christian factions. True unity in the Christian Church is the great historical myth and a "forever-fallacy".

What, then, is our viewpoint? If we claim to be able to shed light on the so-called "Bible Mysteries" but question and challenge the overall Christian Church paradigm, do we by inference disagree with the overall content of The Bible? The short answer is no; we do not.

What we actually and unequivocally claim is that The Bible is very much *more* than the Christian world of the laymen and general believer presently understands. It is even more than either the Christian/Bible scholar and/or Theologian would currently accept. We should not forget the world of science and scientists here either, for what we reveal within the pages of this work would advance the knowledge of virtually all of the scientific Disciplines – if those practitioners possess the inner (spiritual) greatness of humility to *at least consider the ramifications of what we state*. In any case, *that is the way it is*. And the strongly-fostered intellectual ethos and framework under which science itself believes it must operate *cannot change that simple and profound truth*.

What, then, is The Bible, actually? Strange as it may sound **The Bible is, *essentially*, a book of Science!** But science on a "foundational-scale" and concept that mightily transcends our present brand of earth-science, yet nevertheless permits that very Discipline to develop to heights and depths of knowledge thus far undreamed of. So whilst it is clearly an historical document and a religious one for the three great monotheistic faiths – and certainly reveals the very Laws of life for *all* of humankind – **it is the primary and therefore foundational-book of, and for, all the earth-sciences!**

In the final analysis science can only truly thrive where it has the correct foundation upon which to begin its necessary work in the first place. Without a solid and true foundation of the actual lawful processes that brought all things into existence – *both the material and the non-material* – science can only theorise around possibilities and probabilities. The correct foundation of truth would thus free earth-science of much unnecessary expense and time-wasting on research projects of dubious value or on projects that appeared to hold promise but which finally led to dead-ends, and certainly on the kinds of projects that produce nightmarish outcomes. Had the scientific community collectively recognised "The Crucial Imperatives" that decisively impact upon "true life" and its inviolable laws, the dangerous or spiritually unethical or socially untenable projects currently "on-stream" around the world would never have gotten off the ground.

Since a major feature of this work is to *reconcile* particular, so-called, sacrosanct tenets of science and religion from **the Science** in **The Bible**, the two key points for scientists that were stated in **Author's Note** therefore find resonance here too. So, if science is ever to find complete and meaningful answers to the never-ending questions it continually finds itself faced with, it must embrace the *reality* of the *non-material* aspect of **"The Law"** in Creation. Unfortunately, however, the current "standard scientific viewpoint" fails to take into account or even *acknowledge* such a thing.

On page 19 of his book, The Sacred Balance, well-known environmentalist and biologist Dr. David Suzuki points out:

> "Scientism, the aura of authority carried by scientists, has made us believe that knowledge obtained by scientists is the ultimate authority, that as we accumulate information, our capacity to understand, control and manage our surroundings will grow correspondingly. But the basic principle of scientific exploration contradicts this faith: knowledge comes from empirical observations, which are "made sense of" by hypotheses, which in turn can be experimentally tested. All information is open to being disproved. As Jonathan Marks has pointed out":
> "...the vast majority of ideas that most scientists have ever had have been wrong. They have been refuted; they have been disposed of. Further, at any point in time, most ideas proposed by most scientists will ultimately be refuted and disposed of... Science, in other words, undermines scientism."

Ultimately, therefore, the notion that **Truth** should be discovered, perhaps re-discovered and *proved* by every individual for our own selves through personal experience – and perhaps even produce a cry of 'eureka' in the process – is not so simple to implement. Much like the experience of Higher Planes that cannot easily be described by people in words here on Earth [i.e., "In My Father's House are many mansions."]: We must simply use our *intuition and conscience* to *recognise* Truth. That key *recognition should* then simply lead one on to *living* **It**, and *thereby* fully experiencing **It** as *absolute conviction*!

Since science generally subscribes to the ethos of "...not proven unless proven *empirically*", the message that the Prophet Isaiah gave millennia ago clearly foresaw the quandary that would develop for earth-science and scientists if the higher knowledge of Spiritual Law was not taken into account. Preceding the scientific reality of "The Error of *Scientism*" by thousands of years, the following ode could almost be called:

"The Scientists' Lament".

At this critical time in man's tenure on Earth, it is, unfortunately, now exactly that. Ultimately, only *correct* science will prosper; all wrong science will be brought to an end.

Denunciation of Hypocrisy.

Now the Almighty demands,
"Why do this people approach
With their mouth and their lips,

To pay honour to Me,
While their heart is far off?
Their reverence is worthless to Me:-
It teaches the doctrines of men!

"So on this race I lay wonders,
Add wonders to wonders,
Destroying its scientists' science,
And baffling its scholars' researches."

(Isaiah. Ode 44: Book 1, Fenton. Emphases mine.)

Despite the fact that "The Great Prophet" proclaims a strong and crucial message for earth-scientists, we should understand that his words certainly do not denigrate science in its broad sense. Good and beneficial science is obviously correct for humanity.

A clear example of "good and beneficial science" wringing change in the consciousness of those who have attended the presentation in various countries, or have seen the same in cinemas now; is the documentary: **"An Inconvenient Truth"**. The brainchild of American Senator, Al Gore, this very powerful and thought-provoking documentary places earth-science in its absolutely correct role. It is that kind of science, moreover, which gives the documentary its raw power and thus reinforces its incontrovertible message to the world.

Notwithstanding the fact that without such science, that key and timely documentary could not have been produced at all, earth-science yet needs to recognise and then work with the overarching "natural-force" power which produced the material world of Earth and the universes in the first place. That power, inherent in what we loosely call "nature", is the actual aegis under which earth-science can exist and make its discoveries. Its proper role, therefore, is to firstly recognise the true nature of that power, incorporate it into the fundamental structure of all earth-sciences and, from that recognition and knowledge, then set about explaining and educating the wider mass of humanity about the greater wonders *they would discover* via that course.

The great scientist Isaac Newton understood the *non-empirical aspect* of earth-science, for that is what he evidently sought to discover for much of his life. ***And no scientist today would dare say he was a deluded dreamer.***

During his time with the Anglican Church the great mathematician directed his monumental talent of genius to analysing The Bible, trying to discover the secret knowledge he believed lay hidden there. He further believed that some of the ancients – in particular the Greek mathematicians – had known this secret. If he could find it, he would know it too; the 'Plan' – of the 'World'. Two major points lay at the heart of Newton's unshakeable belief:

1. "A rational God made a rational universe".

2. "All wisdom lay in the knowledge of numbers".[2]

Of special interest to Newton was The Book of Daniel with its mathematical time-line, and The Book of Revelation. Because Newton believed that only: ***"A few natural laws apply to the whole universe"***, he regarded those natural laws as ***"...proof of the existence of a great and Almighty God"***. Since he was both a Theologian and Scientist – and regarded by scientists today as one of the greatest of all (even NASA readily acknowledges that its space

---

[2]In terms of the wisdom Newton sought in the 'knowledge of numbers" we should recognise that *that knowledge of numbers* is actually more **The Law of Numbers**.

programme is based on "Newtonian physics") – he is the perfect example of one whom we might regard as "a complete man", vitally interested in apparently all things.

Let us therefore take our lead from that remarkable Scientist, Astronomer and Theologian, go a step further, and state that The Bible also possesses both the keys and the foundational-knowledge to such diverse and "modern" scientific Disciplines as Anthropology and Palaeontology, and the many sub-branches of both. The true Origins of man are thus revealed therein, and the forever and contentious issue of Creation versus Evolution is shown for the totally pointless debate that it actually is.

The scientific reality of Plate Tectonics is also alluded to, particularly in the prophecies of Isaiah. The "shaking of the Earth" at the decisive point in the human spiritual/evolutionary journey – this present era – has now been experienced by scientists, and thus also by global humanity. The unprecedented earth movement that spawned the recent and catastrophic "Indian Ocean tsunami", though large by human experience, should nevertheless be recognised as just a small but crucial indicator – a 'precursor' – to the greater "Plate movements" that Isaiah's prophecies clearly state are yet to occur.

The keys to Astronomy and Cosmology lie within that especial Book as well, and scientists engaging with these two "space" Disciplines can actually know "the extent of the *total number* of universes". That is not the same knowledge as the *size of it all*, for in the final analysis that can only be *very broadly* calculated mathematically. We are not just simply talking here about the universe we see and *think we know*, but something far more stupendous. An entity that cosmology, as a scientific Discipline overall, does not yet know about. (Chapter 11 in this Work explains the details of that momentous revelation.)

It is exactly that which Newton sought.

What that great scientist and theologian believed about The Bible is therefore true.

It actually does ultimately reveal: 'The "Plan" of the World'.

Newton, however, was not able to find the key in his particular time in history. Some of the answers he sought could not have been resolved around his time anyway for they needed, paradoxically, the input of certain aspects of scientific knowledge only available today. However, they could not have been resolved *at all* without the complete and detailed knowledge inherently and *solely* contained within **The Laws of Creation**. That is a level of knowledge so comprehensive and far-reaching in its import that it was reserved for this latter and closing point in our evolutionary journey to be revealed.

This work is thus primarily directed to the academics of the Western world; to those whose views and teachings on religion and science determine, for the most part, the broad, educational path of basic belief inherent in the Judeao/Christian ethos that underpins Western "civilisation". The work is also offered to help the wider Christian community to a greater understanding of the age-old, contentious questions that mankind have puzzled over for millennia and which **"still confound the wise today"**.

Numbering close to somewhere around two billion, Christians make up between one quarter and one third of global humanity. Divided into innumerable sub-churches, religious organisations, associations and sects, the primary text book of this large group – The Bible – has similarly undergone many changes, sometimes specifically to suit the particular interpretation of the individual group/s concerned.

Much of that change has been wrought in the Universities of the Western world. For the global Christian Church numbers among its many hundreds of millions of believers very many academics, all of whom strive to push their particular interpretation of the so-called "Bible Mysteries" to world attention. This practice can result in two key things:

1. The particular interpretation arrived at might become the primary "signature-theology" of the University or College concerned; and:

2. That specific "distillation" might thereby translate into the basic "belief-paradigm" of the student body receiving instruction.

Any specific interpretation arrived at would logically set that particular school apart from every other. The promotional direction that each key Western educational facility might thus adopt would naturally provide the academic impetus to possibly differentiate it from other institutions. Yet all must ultimately derive their individual interpretations from the overall "storyline" contained in that One Book – notwithstanding the fact that other historical writings can obviously greatly add to "Bible history".

If we include Islam and Judaism as the other two monotheistic religions that claim a connection with or to The Bible – or at least a connection back to Abraham and/or The Old Testament – then we have a truly strange and lamentable situation of many more sects and groups marching to very different drums. The nightly news items on TV screens worldwide testify to a kind of perverse human madness ultimately centred around this book of clearly great power called The Bible. The current stupidity of it all is probably without parallel historically, for it reveals not only the increasing polarisation and "splintering-effect" of inter-religious rivalry, but also the factional destruction of the individual religions from within of once previously-broad support bases.

It is a strangely lunatic situation, for it cannot possibly be described as sane. Moreover, it is one without resolution if human thinking and/or interpretation is set as the sole benchmark by which we believe we will find answers. Despite the fact that constant attempts at peace overtures, resolutions and unifying proposals rarely work anywhere anymore, *we* are able to conclusively say that the splintering or fragmentation process driving it all to its obvious outcome can be traced to the NON-RECOGNITION of "The Crucial Imperatives" that we unequivocally state are clearly outlined in the key Work for **ALL** of humankind: **THE BIBLE!**

Since the current destructive course will run itself to its inevitable end, it is perhaps appropriate to state here a sure fact of **The Law** for all of global humanity. It is short, blunt and, for every person – irrespective of religious belief and/or scientific bent – primed with either promise or perdition. It states simply:

"All can see if they are really willing to see!"

Thus the long line of many books written to *seemingly answer* some of the great questions to life – but which rarely do – probably parallels that peculiar trend in Universities, Theological Colleges, Seminaries and other "Institutions of higher learning" that we "intellectual humans" tend to give far too much credence to. The thousands upon thousands of Degree and PhD-toting Theologians, Bible scholars and various miscellaneous academics who cannot conclusively determine the actual answers to those very questions – much less come to any kind of clear and *collective agreement* about them – clearly reveals that they and the Universities they represent *do not have the answers*.

The Documentary Channels of "Discovery", "National Geographic", "History" and "Biography" etc., produce and screen very many varied and absorbing programmes about so-called Bible "Mysteries" and related religious questions. To add credibility to the research and hypotheses of the documentaries themselves, however, the opinions of numerous academic experts from very many Universities and Colleges of intellectual and/or religious bent are sought. In the visual medium of the Documentary Channel; the programmes – whilst wonderfully researched and very informative – invariably close with the requirement for the viewer to decide for himself the conclusions he may wish to draw from the presentation. Whilst some documentaries are able to draw conclusions around a particular question from the purely historical perspective, the more important religious or spiritual dimension is usually *inconclusive.*

The whole *"religious-documentary industry"* therefore reveals two key things:

1. The fact that there is a growing, perhaps even exponential, interest in these kinds of subjects.

2. And its related aspect that conclusive answers to the most contentious questions *are simply not there.*

There are many theories and opinions, of course, but that is all. The avid viewer may also note a kind of "competition-mentality" among the main Documentary Channels around not only the key questions to life and history in the religious/spiritual sense, but in the screening times of similar kinds of documentaries on those different channels. Part of the problem surrounding this vital aspect of life called Truth stems from a strange side to the human condition. Perversely, we prefer **mystery** to truth!

With a mystery, human beings are free to indulge their theories, notions and even fantasies unchecked. After all, who can challenge it? With the **Truth** of a particular thing *recognised as such*, however, that is no longer possible.

For The Truth simply Is! And all men must bow to It.

On the matter of greater and greater interest developing over religious questions, Time Magazine has regularly Cover-featured key issues. e.g.; – a small but nonetheless telling number:

1. March 23, 1987: .... Bang! [The Big Bang; Origins of the universe]

2. December 18, 1995: ...... Is The Bible fact Or Fiction?

3. April 8, 1996: .... The Search For Jesus.

4. November 4, 1996: .... And God Said...

5. March 24, 1997: .... Does Heaven Exist?

6. July 1, 2002: .... The Bible & The Apocalypse.

7. April 12, 2004: .... Why Did Jesus Have To Die?

8. August 15, 2005: .... Evolution Wars.

9. October 9, 2006: .... How We Became Human.

10. November 13, 2006: ..... God Vs. Science.

Whilst it can be said that *elements of the truth* of a particular thing can be logically arrived at or theorised about, it cannot be definitively stated that that elusive and constantly sought-after academic goal of **The Truth** is taught or revealed in any 'Institution of higher learning' anywhere on the globe. Yet it should be precisely those very 'schools' that, historically, should always have taught **The Truth**.

The very Truth of the sage observation of the Danish philosopher, Kierkegaard i.e.,: **"It is not the Truth that lies with the masses, but the untruth!"** should resonate constantly within the walls of Universities and Churches throughout the world.

That is not to say that analyses of certain Bible aspects in the Disciplines, particularly, of Archaeology, Anthropology and even Cosmology, do not or could not offer their vital contribution to conclusively permit the final pieces of the jigsaw to fit together to thus reveal exactly that which we state is waiting to be recognised. Science can, should and could – if it were not so blind – *do exactly that*. It could, **at this very moment**, marry the knowledge **that it already possesses** with the beliefs of Christian theology/religion to finally reveal what is, paradoxically, the ultimate goal of both science and religion; the clear vision of **The Truth** of *our origins*. That is Pope Benedict's rational and very correct plea.

Time Magazine, issue Oct. 9, 2006 – "How We Became Human" – probably *believes* it has achieved precisely that in its featured article about the human genome. Unfortunately, however, the "science" used to "explain" our origin has only looked at just the **materiality** of humans and monkeys in the idea that *that* is all we consist of and thus what we ultimately *are*.

Since human-science chooses not to accept the truth of our origins, then, as previously stated and no doubt will be said again in this Work, "we" will reveal that very science within the pages of The Bible. For it really does unveil the key connections between science and religion to show that there is, indeed, one marvellous and wonderful, stupendous and harmonious whole that actually describes our origins. As previously stated, completely divorced from the ongoing religious and intellectual foolishness driving the Evolution versus Creation versus Intelligent Design debate to nowhere, the Truth of it all – **which can be read in just the first two Chapters of Genesis** – is so perfect and sublime we yet contend that even such sublime simplicity as we will reveal **will still not be recognised by most**. And, moreover, that the thrust of Western academic thought and Christian religious teachings therefore actually **lead away from** that very necessary recognition and goal.

So how can this lone book claim to be able to **definitively reveal the actual truth of our origins** when thousands upon thousands of academic publications have not?

After all, as stated in **"Author's Note"**, I am not "trained" in Theology, and I certainly cannot claim to be recognised, "academically" or otherwise, as any kind of "Bible Scholar". And I am definitely not a scientist. What, then, can I claim as a mandate for the unequivocal and unapologetic content and nature of this Work?

Apart from the Mandate of Paul the Apostle, I further claim – and thus possess – two further primary mandates. The most basic one is that of simple and clear recognition that the current situation of endless academic debate and **theorising** about the great questions of life *cannot possibly produce* any kind of final resolution. That unfortunate state of affairs exists purely because the whole thrust of academic debate does not rest on a sufficiently strong or correct foundation to begin with. The second and more telling Mandate is The Source from which this book ultimately derives its knowledge and which therefore permits the so-called 'Mysteries' of The Bible to be revealed.[3]

The Bible, the foundation for science, too, has exerted and continues to exert, it could be argued, disproportionate 'pressure' on human affairs historically. So perhaps there resides within many human beings a still, small warning voice that strives to make itself heard above the clamour and pontificating of the much-lauded intellectualism blaring forth from the singular University path that now drives the only officially-accepted educational paradigm for all matters spiritual and temporal in present-day Western society.

How many millions of litres of blood have been spilt historically for causes that were thought out by prominent men in positions of great power, even to the point of invoking the very Name

---

[3]Information about the Source is stated further on in the work.

of The One Whom they believed they served? And, of course, Whom they similarly believed mandated and even sanctified their bloodthirsty adventures. The same kinds of invocations were, in various reversals of fortune, uttered by those groups who spilt the blood of others, and by opposing groups who spilt their blood at another time.

While there is not that literal bloodletting in Western academia today; played out in the corridors of academic power from time to time there are, nevertheless, educational power-politics that sometimes surface so strongly that they spill out beyond carefully nurtured and protected boundaries into the glare of media coverage for public consumption. That kind of "bloodletting" is invariably centred on wounded pride and ego.

The concepts and conclusions outlined in this book ultimately represent a major challenge to most present-day cultural, philosophical, academic, medical, religious and spiritual beliefs. As an amateur writer who possesses no religious, scientific or academic qualifications, can I claim any other mandate to at least *"academically-strengthen" those previously stated*? Such a mandate is certainly defined by the sage observation: **"The Proof of the Pudding is in the Eating!"** Therefore, despite the zealously-guarded educational parameters of Western society; under the aegis of precise **Creation-Law**, the concepts and *conclusions* herein will be found to be *inviolable*, and thus *immutable*.

"Lone voices in the wilderness" who dare to challenge the status quo inevitably clash with the current academic thought of their particular generation. However, the historic reality is such that *every generation of academics must re-learn Kierkegaard's great truth* – reinforced here once more – *especially* with regard to the Spiritual Truths contained within the great Religions:

That it is not The Truth that lies with the masses, but the untruth!

Historically, it is the lone voice or small group that holds, in lonely constancy, to the kernel. Very often that lone voice or small group will not possess that level of education or erudition which the "establishment" deems necessary for the retention, understanding and dissemination of such "elevated concepts" as religious or spiritual Truth. Out of the Prophets, Apostles and Disciples in The Bible, the very same "establishment" of Christian-religious academia generally laud Paul the Apostle as a key intellectual thinker and scholar, which he certainly was.

The story of Saul in the New Testament provides, for the University academic, the perfect example of how a singular, particularly powerful trait – if wrongly directed – could so easily produce the opposite of what the owner might actually desire. As a member of the Jewish Religious Authority, his relentless persecution of the first believers in Jesus eventually led to the stoning to death of Stephen, who became the first Christian martyr. Whilst believing he zealously protected and defended the letter of the Law of Moses, he failed to apply compassion to it in the "Spirit of the Law".

Possessing an exceptionally keen intellect, Saul's implacable conviction about the correctness of his beliefs and the methods he employed to enforce them were shattered and transformed when he was struck blind during a journey to Damascus. The event we know as the "Conversion of Saul" resulted in a far more spiritually-powerful ministry by this man of intensely strong convictions. The powerful trait was still there, but now utilised for a vastly different purpose and directed towards a very different outcome than he could ever have foreseen under the domination of his previous volition – a volition driven by the *soulless intellect* and not that of his *living spirit* in the **'Power of Love'**. Despite campaigning savagely against the Disciples and early Christians as **Saul**, after his "Conversion" **Paul** tirelessly travelled through many countries evangalising and baptising until his death in Rome. He became the greatest of the Apostles of Jesus.[4]

---

[4]Notwithstanding Paul's correctly elevated position today in certain Christian Churches and among

The "Conversion of Saul" perfectly illustrates how any individual or whole peoples – or even **an entrenched education system** – *can transform* certain particularly strong but unhelpful traits and utilise that *transformed energy for a higher, more powerful cause.*

Since Theological Colleges and Religious Studies Departments of the Universities of the West, particularly, tend to centre much of their educational content on the central figure of Jesus, a curious element emerges here. It is the insufficiently-debated fact that of all those He **could** have chosen to **be** His Disciples, the one group that He chose **not to approach** were the learned, the scribes, the "intellectuals" of His day.

He selected, instead, simple men – *men who did not have to struggle with the false belief that The Truth required or requires large Universities, Theological Colleges and intellectually-derived educational degrees to recognise and understand it.*

Like the Catholic Church of old where Latin was the medium by which The Word of The Bible was spoken to effectively deny the ordinary man personal access to Bible Scripture, so is it generally the same today in "Institutions of higher learning".

The words of Jesus to the Pharisees of His time resonate today around those who control the academic and religious education of the world through those Universities and/or Theological Colleges and Churches that seek to promote and strengthen the long-protected status quo. In terms of the **greater knowledge that would lead to real answers** via that regime, these words of Jesus thus apply equally well to the latter-day Pharisees in the Educational Institutions of the present time:

> *"...you enter not yourselves, and you allow no others to enter."*

In the final analysis it is all about ego, power and control. It is not about the real and very necessary true education for the peoples of the world. True education will only come when those who control education *in all cultures* **become truly seeing**, as Paul did, or when 'untruth' and educational deceit have outlived their pointless time of existence.

Thereby have I thus firmly established a clear mandate to so state what needs to be stated. However, we have yet to assess the historical events that might precisely determine whether or not it *was* ordained that The Bible was to be the foundation upon which **all peoples and all cultures** were, by this present time, to have broadly based their societal rules and religious beliefs.

0.3.1   The Entry of The Bible into Europe and Around the Globe

Therefore, was The Bible, this pivotal Book in human affairs, **always** destined to become the main religious base of the Western Nations, or could particular historical factors have possibly prevented that outcome? And if it was to be the primary foundation there, was it also destined to be the same for **all** peoples of the world, irrespective of their traditional cultural or religious beliefs then and now?

If it **was** so ordained that The Bible would be the foundation for all the world's peoples, and if it **was** similarly ordained that it **was** because of the person of Jesus and His Mission as

---

some theologians, we should nevertheless note quite marked differences between Paul's teachings **as they are now interpreted** and that of "James the Just", the earthly brother of Jesus, then leader of what was known as the 'true Church of Jerusalem'. Those *differing interpretations* have produced strong debate among Bible scholars and theologians for a very long time, e.g., the 'Faith Vs Works' debate.

the central figure and reason, then the very fact that it is **not** embraced by some would clearly presuppose that those religions and cultures that did not or do not accept it, quite logically *oppose that specific ordination*. And what might that mean in the final analysis? By the same token, however, those cultures and religions that **do** broadly embrace the general tenor and ethos of The Bible but **distort** that very ethos, by definition also place themselves **in opposition** to that same, specific, ordination.

The entry of The Bible into the West can be broadly traced to the emergence of Christianity in Roman-occupied Palestine around 2,000 years ago. Proclaimed by His Disciples after His death as the Messiah or deliverer of His people, this claim about Jesus repudiated the need to accept Jewish Law completely to gain salvation and led to the final rift between Christians and Judaism. Although rooted in the Old Testament, Christianity developed in the crucible of the Graeco-Roman world, which largely determined its thought and culture.

The primary catalyst for the more rapid spread of Christianity throughout the Roman Empire was Constantine the Great (c 285-337) who ruled the Western Empire (312-24) and became sole Emperor (324-37). He adopted the Christian faith (312), suspended the persecution of Christians and rebuilt Constantinople (modern Istanbul) as the new Rome. Christianity subsequently took root as the primary religion throughout Europe and was later exported to the New Worlds.

In just two short paragraphs we have very broadly outlined the history of The Bible's entry into much of the world. But was it that simple and clear-cut? To determine that, we need to look at events preceding even the emergence of the Roman Empire, for the time-line of The Bible stretches back to early recorded history. Was there, then, a key event – or perhaps a series of relatively closely related key events – that:

1. ultimately cleared the way for the Roman Empire to emerge in the first place? – or:

2. could possibly have brought about a world where The Bible was actually prevented from evolving to become a primary force at all? – and/or:

3. where it might even have been largely expunged from history?

Firstly, in order for there to have been a Bible to begin with, there had to have been one race of people whose path would carry them beyond the beliefs and religious thought-processes that virtually all other races were mired in, to a point of divining the fact that far more existed than just the material world, and even more than the world of the immediate 'beyond'. The religious evolutionary path of the Jewish race was strongly moulded through the hardships they brought upon themselves – *precisely through the outworking of the very Laws given to them and from which they still claim Divine mandate even today*. Their long period of suffering provided a purification process that finally seeded the longing for something better; a spiritual path and life that would offer a stronger connection to the Higher Source that their emerging Prophets were proclaiming.

The chronological time-line of some of the primary figures of the Old Testament shows the long preparatory process required for the Jewish people to be sufficiently spiritually-matured for the entry of The Bible's central figure, Jesus, into their midst. That it was the Jewish race into which He was born *exactly reveals an inviolable outworking of precise and lawful processes that cannot be circumvented*. An incarnation into a tribe of idol worshippers would thus be a totally pointless exercise in this case and could not possibly achieve anything worthwhile, let alone leave any lasting legacy.

That chronology of those crucially-important Jewish Patriarchs/Prophets who occupied particular time-frames, B.C., strengthens *our* key premise that certain critical historical events helped The Bible to *eventually* make its way into lands then undreamt of.

Samuel, one of the "Judges" of the Old Testament, lived in the 11th century B.C. The 15 named Prophets of the same Work spanned 300 odd years; from Isaiah in the 8th century, to Malachi in the 5th. These dates are important for understanding where the primary series of events, to which we are leading, fit, in order for our key premise to be *"recognised"*. The entry of The Bible and Christianity into Europe through the Roman Empire does not stand alone and in isolation, however. That was the last major act of an Empire and its people and culture for this "Divinely-ordained" purpose. It is important to also understand that, for centuries, the Romans succeeded the Greeks as the major and dominating force and culture in that part of the world.

Prior to the emergence of the Greek Empire, a greater one held sway in the known world – that of Persia. Greece was not a single, unified Nation or people. It consisted of a number of more or less independent city-states in loose coalitions or alliances which could, and did, shift with the prevailing political situation.

Xerxes the 1st, son of Darius the Great and Atossa, the daughter of Cyrus the Great, was appointed King of Persia by his father. In October, 485B.C, he succeeded to the throne. A major military campaign left to him by Darius was the task of punishing the Athenians, Naxoans and Erectrians for their interference in the Ionian revolt and the victory of Marathon. From 483 Xerxes prepared his expedition with great care. His military force comprised a large naval and supply convoy and numerous soldiers. (Herodotus, the Greek historian, had claimed that there were over 2,000,000.) Latter-day military historians have concluded that his army, though very large for the time, probably numbered no less than 250,000, and possibly up to as many as 500,000. In the spring of 480 Xerxes set out from Sardis.

Xerxes had concluded an alliance with Carthage and thus deprived Greece of the support of the powerful monarchs of Syracuse and Agrigentum. Many smaller Greek states, moreover, took the side of the Persians, especially Thessaly, Thebes and Argos. Initially Xerxes was victorious everywhere. With the Greek navy beaten at Artemisium, Thermopylae stormed – albeit with huge losses – and Athens conquered, the Athenians with Sparta were driven back to their last line of defence at the Isthmus of Corinth and the Gulf of Saron.

> The Battle of Thermopylae has gone down in the annals of warfare as arguably the greatest deed of bravery and necessary sacrifice ever. Led by the Spartan King, Leonidas, a total force of between four and five thousand Greeks – but with the legendary 300 Spartans as the core fighting group – held the pass at Thermopylae for around three days. Incredible fighting skill and stamina against Xerxes' overwhelming military might saw literally tens of thousands of Persians slaughtered in the battle. However, upon being informed they had been betrayed by a fellow Greek, the bulk of that force returned to their homelands. (The betrayer led a large force of Persians over a secret mountain pass, defeating the small contingents of Greek soldiers sent to guard against just such a possibility, to take the rear of the Spartans and cut off their line of retreat.)
>
> Despite that betrayal, Leonidas and his 300 chose to stay and fight. Other Greek soldiers also stayed, and all fought to the end. The Battle of Thermopylae is far more than just one battle in countless thousands during man's bloody tenure on Earth. It is, without doubt of course, an especially impressive one. The decision of those to stay, fight and die in that Battle is pivotal to our story of why The Bible would not ever be expunged from history, for the courage and sacrifice of all the Greeks who died at Thermopylae provided the catalyst and rallying point for the disparate Greek City-States to field a combined Army – led by a Spartan General – to defeat the Persian Army that Xerxes left behind in Greece.

Despite his initial success, Xerxes was induced to attack the Greek 'task force' under unfavourable conditions. The Battle of Salamis (September 28th, 480) was won by the Athenians.

Having lost communication by sea with Asia, Xerxes was forced to retire to Sardis, leaving behind in Greece an army of around 50,000 under its Commander, Mardonius. He was defeated at Plataea in 479 suffering huge losses in the battle. The defeat of the Persians at Mycale roused the Greek cities of Asia. The victory of the Greeks threw the Empire into a state of slow decline, and the once great Persian Empire could not rise to its former glory.

The period of the Greco-Persian Wars or Persian Wars were a series of clashes between the Greek city-states and the Persian Empire that started about 500 B.C. and lasted until 448 B.C. The two Persian invasions of the Greek mainland in 490 B.C. and in 480-479 B.C. saw the Greeks unite successfully to defeat both invasions. Persia, in its weakened state, was not able to ever again pose a serious threat to Greece.

The Greeks, however, were still not united. The unification of the diverse city-states under a single ruler had its genesis under King Philip II of Macedon. Born in 382 B.C., he ruled Macedonia from 359 until his death in 336. The birth of Greece as a single entity perhaps really began with Philip's defeat of a Greek coalition at Chacronea (338). He achieved a peace settlement in which all states except Sparta took part.

Final unification, however, was only realised when Philip's son – who later became known as Alexander the Great – twice fought coalitions of southern Greeks who rebelled after the death of Philip. Alexander went on to rule both Macedon and Greece. After conquering Persia, then ruled by King Darius III, he built an Empire that was to spread Greek culture from Egypt to India. He integrated foreigners (non-Macedonians, non-Greeks) into his Army and administration, and encouraged marriage between his soldiers and foreigners. He practised it himself, ensuring the retention of Greek thought and culture for a longer period after his death than might otherwise have been the case.

After twelve years of constant Military campaigning, Alexander died. His life (July 21st, 356 B.C. – June 11th, 323 B.C.) and his remarkable conquests ushered in centuries of Greek settlement and rule over distant lands. That period, known as the Hellenistic Age, is widely regarded as the height of Greek culture.

Alexander permits us the luxury of recognising that his legacy strongly anchored a "secure foundation" for The Bible to journey forward into human history. From that point onwards, therefore, we may note a certain and strong guidance that, step-by-inexorable-step, ensured that specific civilisations and Empires emerging in parallel with the evolving Jewish religion – though not sharing exactly the same beliefs – would nevertheless tolerate Jewish thought within those Empires. Thus the Greek and Roman Empires, philosophically and religiously incompatible for the most part with Judaism, were nonetheless more open to such an accommodation.

A comprehensive defeat of the Greeks by Xerxes 1st, therefore, could well have set in place centuries of expanded Persian rule over the whole region and the possible suppression of the evolving new thought of "an Unknown God" – which Paul the Apostle discovered among the Athenians – emerging from Greek philosophy. Paul, however, though familiar with Greek thought and culture, was raised in a land ruled by Rome.

Rome – one of the greatest of all Empires, and the **key one** in our premise. Founded in 753 B.C., the Roman Empire lasted centuries. Greece was conquered in 168-146 B.C. Rome itself fell to the Goths in the 5th century A.D., to the Byzantines in 552, was later sacked by the Arabs in 846 and Normans in 1084. Gradually it came under Papal control; its fortunes followed those of the Papacy until it was annexed to Italy.

The two great Empires of Greece and Rome had served their spiritual purpose. Their Military might, open cultures and willingness to accept and tolerate other religious beliefs within their borders, ensured that the teachings of The Bible would be protected. Even though thousands of "Christians" suffered cruelly under certain Roman Emperors, the overall thought could not be stemmed, even in Rome itself.

During the twilight years of Rome's ebb as the world's superpower, different peoples emerged to deliver successive and ultimately crippling blows to Rome's long reign and thus its continuity as an Empire. In 477 A.D., the Vandals under Gaiseric sacked Rome. The tribe was Arian and dealt severely with Orthodox Christians. Their power began to decline at Gaiseric's death, however. Justinian 1, Christian Emperor of Eastern Rome, sent his Byzantine General, Belsarius, against them, and in 534 they were defeated.

The 4th and 5th centuries saw the Huns make repeated incursions into the Roman Empire. Under Attila, the most renowned of its leaders and perhaps the most feared, the series of wars brought both parts of the Roman Empire, East and West, to the verge of destruction. Attila extended his domain to as far as Gaul – where he was defeated in 451 – and into Italy. After Attila's death in 454, the power of the Huns was broken and they no longer played a part in European History.

The Huns and the Vandals emerged as powerful Military forces sufficiently strong to dominate history for the time of their supremacy and seriously threaten Rome and Christendom. Their motivating purpose was not the foundation of The Bible or any connection to it, but simply to conquer. The next major incursion into Christian Europe was made by an Army that was technically "non-Christian". Like Christians, the men of Abd-ar-Rahman, the Muslim King from Spain, also claimed *descent* from the Patriarch, Abraham.

Seeking to extend Islamic control further into Western Europe, Abd-ar-Rahman invaded France in 732. His nemesis and undoing, however, was the Frankish King, Charles "Martel", Carolingian ruler of the Frankish kingdom of Austrasia – North-eastern France and South-western Germany. Undisputed ruler of all the Franks, his greatest achievements in battle were against the Muslims from Spain.

Charles defeated them in a great battle near Poitiers in which the Muslim leader, Abd-ar-Rahman, was killed. The progress of Islam, which had filled all Christendom with alarm, was checked for a time. Charles drove the Muslims out of the Rhone valley in 739, when they had again advanced into France as far as Lyon. His unrelenting and valiant determination earned him the surname, Martel, meaning "hammer". History thus records his title as "Charles the Hammer".

Had he not prevailed, a new and different thought emerging from Islam – even though tracing origins back to Abraham – at that point would have suppressed the "Primary Truth" contained in The Bible. The, then, Christian Europe, if not permanently changed, would surely have been continually racked thereafter by religious revolution and dissent.

The conquests of the Mongolian Emperor, Genghis Khan (c. 1162 -1227), into Iran and as far as southern Russia produced great disquiet in Christian Europe. The later, almost similar "re-run" by the Mongol conqueror, Tamerlane (1336-1405), who overran vast areas of Persia, Turkey, Russia and India, also posed a threat to the Europeans.

Yet despite the free-will decisions made by many warlords, Emperors and Kings throughout recorded history, the "path of guidance" we have broadly outlined – though seriously threatened at times – nevertheless continually strove to ensure that this crucial Book, The Bible, would *not be lost* for global humanity. Moreover, not only was that need vital for humankind, but its journey to the present ensured that its true significance might be finally understood. That is the crucial aspect that neither science nor Christianity yet truly understands, for neither Discipline *has really listened to the key and serious admonitions and warnings from the central figure of that most important Work.*

The argument could be raised that the ordination or providence guiding the path of The Bible – whereby it was intended that it be made known to all of humankind – could not be conclusively linked to the failure of the Persians to defeat Greece. Whilst that is a possibility, the opposite is equally true; that had Persia conquered Greece and extended control further, then Alexander might not have emerged to eventually conquer Persia. And perhaps Rome might not have emerged as the power that would disseminate Bible thought in the way it eventually did – notwithstanding the fact that other warring groups seriously threatened that subsequent outcome.

For had Persia achieved its aim and conquered and controlled lands and peoples beyond Greece, it would probably not have been as magnanimous or accommodating as Greece or Rome were in allowing their conquered subjects to continue worshipping their "own gods". So suppression of culture and/or religion by the Persians in this scenario might ultimately have suppressed or expunged Bible thought as a consequence. And thereby concomitantly ensured that it did not enter Europe and journey to distant lands courtesy of the Maritime Nations of Europe as ordained, as is our sure contention and thus our absolute premise.

Yet, even if Persia had achieved such a goal, a "paradox of religious evolution" – another thread of ordained guidance – also plays a major part in this Bible story and history. It, too, roughly parallels the basic time-line of our overall analysis.

0.3.2   Distortions of The Teachings Given to Enlighten Humankind

That "religious evolution" was the emergence of those different religions that sprang up at various times in history from diverse areas of the world out of different peoples. Each founded by one Called for the purpose, the different "Teachings" were nevertheless anchored by a similar basis of beneficial law, the recognition of a "giver" of that law, tolerance toward others and the requirement to strive for the betterment of oneself and the particular society concerned.

It would be safe to say that the general estimation today concerning the different religions is that they *are* different because that was the *intended purpose* of the Founders of them. But were they ***actually different*** religions insofar as the ***Spiritual Principles*** that ***anchored the original beliefs*** were concerned? Given the parlous state of religious intolerance today, one could quite easily believe that the aim of the Founders of the main teachings was to set up ***singular religions*** that would stand for that particular people and culture ***for all time***. If that were the case, intolerance and bigotry would surely have *eventually* resulted from such singular, religious entrenchment.

However, since the *main tenets* of the "great religions" clearly reveal only spiritual virtues as their foundation, we can readily deduce the fact that *that outcome* was ***not*** the intention of the Founders. The unfortunate conclusion we must then draw is that we, the various groups of human followers, have distorted their clear ***spiritual*** legacy. We, the followers, the adherents, are too blind, intolerant and immature to even begin to emulate the high level of spirituality shown by all the great "Spiritual Teachers of Mankind". In short, we are "a spiritually-destitute" humankind. We have allowed those original and beneficial Teachings to degenerate, for the most part, into what is really aspiritual behaviour in our societies today.

In place of their sacred and ordained mission to bring the substance of spiritual enlightenment to all of humanity, we have, instead, generally defiled those very Truths with base and opposite outcomes to that envisioned by those highly advanced men. The proof of this particular pudding can be readily observed depressingly frequently on the television screens and in the newspapers every day.

We have designated those "Founders": **Teachers of Mankind!** Was there, then, a higher plan ordained for humankind under the leadership of those men through careful guidance from Above? If we studiously examine the times of their emergence and balance that against the particular level of spiritual maturity of the people concerned we can, indeed, readily observe a precise pattern whereby Nations and peoples could be taken, step by careful step, to the final recognition of *all* Spiritual Truth. That **"All-Truth"** – stated by Jesus to one day emerge, and for humankind to therefore be awake to recognise it – **was reserved for this present time!**

That this carefully guided process did not happen as intended can be placed squarely upon our shoulders. The responsibility for that failure is ours alone. Through our arrogant and foolish belief that *we could know it better than the ones who were carefully prepared and ordained to bring the respective teachings to humankind*; we are the root cause of all religious strife throughout history and today. By virtue of the Founders' far higher level of spiritual maturity, it is ludicrous *for any of their followers today or any other time in history to believe* that **they could know more, or be greater, than the Teachers!**

Because Truth is Eternal and unchangeable, it must forever remain the same. It is therefore recognisable to us in The Spiritual Laws of Creation, including The Laws of Nature which are equally unchangeable. By extension, the recognition of these inviolable Laws leads without deviation to God because His Will is revealed to us in The Spiritual Laws. Through them we learn what He Wills. The "Teachers of Mankind", to whom all this was known, were "Forerunners for The Truth".

We can identify the key ones as:

1. **Krishna:** for India at a very early time.

2. **Moses:** and the Old Testament Prophets.

3. **Lao-Tse:** in China (6th Century B.C.)

4. **Zoroaster:** in Persia (c.628-551B.C.)

5. **Buddha:** in India (c.563-483B.C.)

6. **Mohammed:** in Arabia (c.570-632.)

Their appointed task was to mediate the knowledge of the truth *exactly adapted to their peoples and countries, and formed according to their spiritual maturity for that time.* The symbols of some of the different teachings, which are still in use today, possess precise spiritual meanings.

The lotus blossom of Buddhism symbolises the necessary requirement to strive for purity. In its place in water it exemplifies the need for a strong connection with the stream of life. The Star of David is the sacred symbol of Judaism where the two triangles symbolise the inseparable connection between the *visible material* and the *invisible non-material* worlds. The crescent moon of Islam is linked with the sacred obligation to honour women at all times.[5]

In the beginning, all the teachings were pure in their origin. Moreover, had mankind kept them pure and not distorted them over thousands of years for their own base ideas and selfish ends, those individual teachings *would have long since converged and today be recognised as only transit and concomitant teachings to* **The One Truth!** Unfortunately, the paths which the individual teachings illuminated **came to an end** in the temple or church **of the particular religion**. Through the non-understanding of the followers of those various religions, the teachings did not, and could not, then lead on to **the final Temple of Truth**.

Those "Teachers for Mankind" thus brought that unchangeable Truth in a form understandable to their particular people. Mankind was therefore meant to be carefully guided step-by-step over thousands of years to the recognition of Truth, and thus eventually into *one single acknowledgement of Divine Truth* – the **"All-Truth"** that The Son of God Himself warned to watch for around this present time. Unfortunately for most, however, it would, in its Pristine and Inviolable Perfection, be the very same **"All-Truth"** about which He also stated **only the few** would ultimately **recognise**.

---

[5] *Naturally, however, if women wish to be so honoured, they should ensure that in their everyday manner and activity they live and behave honourably.*

In summary, what was ordained and set in place was a careful, step-by-step process whereby there would have been only one single, unified Truth permeating the very consciousness of all the world's peoples right across the whole Earth today. *It was meant to be that simple.* Man, however, *perversely converts Truth to just religion.*

Thus, the path that religious expansionism did take globally, which can be traced quite clearly, did not permit that simple course to evolve. As exploration and trade increased, The Bible and Christianity did reach many of the new lands via the European Maritime Nations. Even in New Zealand among the Maori people – once a group of disparate and constantly warring, cannibalistic tribes – The Bible holds a place of special importance today.

Journeying to the 'bottom of the world' – about as far from European Christendom as it is possible to go – its introduction to Maori by Missionaries seeded a powerful and fundamental change culminating in a line of "Religious Prophets" who helped to quickly lead Maori away from their former, more savage, practices. From a tentative, early emulation of the British Monarchy, a King Movement gradually evolved to become an established "Maori Monarchy" in New Zealand. Spiritually and symbolically underpinning key protocols within this Monarchy is a special Bible handed down through the generations within the King Movement. At the death of the Maori Queen in 2006, it was brought out for the protocols involved in the necessary succession proceedings.

Other religions were transported to the different countries too. Some prospered as the mainstream belief, others became isolated pockets. Some, of course, did not take root at all. Those that made a considerable impact in countries other than that of their origin are mainly Hinduism, Buddhism, Judaism, Islam and Christianity. Unfortunately, the end result of so many different beliefs sharing the same geographical space has resulted in a kind of "competition-mentality" between the proponents of the different beliefs. As previously stated, its particular excrescence is too often translated into the visual images of brutal reality that are shown almost nightly on television screens. It is that of bombs, bullets, suicide-terror and all its associated destruction. And, curiously, *in complete opposition to the tenets of the original Founders of those vital Teachings.* Yet nevertheless set in motion by narrow and rigid fundamentalism where interpretations are so far removed from the original texts that it is difficult to comprehend the inner workings of the minds of such interpreters.

That reality, however, offers a key clue as to the reason for such intractable views of intolerance toward others. Whilst such intolerance may clearly mirror the religious bent of the particular groups involved in their sometimes desperate struggles, it also invariably reveals their personal and/or political agendas. Such incorrect interpretations surely cannot be solely religious, and they most certainly *do not* derive from anything *genuinely* Spiritual.

Therefore, in accordance with the very tenets of the Truths that the "Teachers of Mankind" brought to the Earth's peoples, it naturally follows that all races and religions *should have lived* both the spiritual duty and responsibility of them. To thus ensure that their beliefs encompassed the true essence of what are the actual Laws of Creation, for that was the foundation upon which all the great Teachings were unequivocally anchored in the first place.

Through such correct spiritual choices we would have *gifted to ourselves a present experiencing of a true blossoming of spiritual harmony under the outworking of those Eternal Laws.* In its place, however, is an opposite and potentially terrifying kind of world which we can all plainly see. The very evidence of our eyes simply precludes denial.

Despite that obvious reality, the sole foundation for any kind of genuine awakening must, at the very least, *yet still symbolically follow the Truths contained in the Teachings of Zoroaster, Lao-Tse, Buddha, Moses and the Prophets, Mohammed, and finally through the more complete Teachings of Jesus.*

With virtually all of the primary religions emerging prior to the "Age of Reason", there was not such a thing as hard science to really challenge the religious ideas of the main teachings before that time. Before the so-called "Age of Enlightenment", the churches or main religions were the dominant force ruling all thinking and providing all answers. Paradoxically, whilst the age of science and reason was an obvious and beneficial step forward and did provide enlightenment to all manner of questions, the pendulum effect actually swung too far with the result that the scientific community became almost too afraid to revisit the Spiritual question – or totally dismissed it as a meaningless aspect of life altogether.

> *Yet it should be a simple and fundamental recognition that integration of the Spiritual and the material as was originally ordained, is not, nor should it be, a denial of one or the other – precisely as Pope Benedict XVI has also stated!*

The unfortunate consequence of this one-sided aspect of "science and reason" is that too many people are afraid, even against their own "gut-feelings" and personal experiences, to admit there is anything other than the material world. It might almost be described as a new dark-age – a retrograde step backward to before the much-vaunted "Age of Enlightenment". It is thus timely that Pope Benedict XVI has now brought this crucial notion to the attention of science and scientists.

In the statement; "I come not to overthrow the Law but to fulfil It", the belief permeating the Christian world would probably deem that utterance of Jesus to relate to the religious laws of The Bible. Science on the other hand would probably deem it totally irrelevant to all scientific thought and practice. But there science would err terribly. Science, especially, needs to understand that *that* statement of Jesus is precisely about "the whole of The Law", and not just about religion – which is a foolish idea anyway. His reference to The Law describes one of "The Crucial Imperatives" – explained in Chapter 1 of this work.

Despite the possibility that The Bible **could** therefore have been lost to humankind, the very fact that it was not validates our assertion that the *more complete knowledge* brought by Jesus and recorded therein was an 'Ordination' assisted by powerful guiding forces. For His entry into The World of Matter fixed certain key knowledge *for all time*; **knowledge which all science and all religions would have to bend knee to.**

So even the largest Armies of the ancient world, led by ambitious Kings and Emperors, ultimately were not able to expunge or even suppress this especial and remarkable Book with the simplest of titles: **The Bible**. That is not to say, however, that religious activities of adherents cannot or will not be suppressed, for that is an entirely different matter, for the adherents of any religion are not the religion itself. In diverse ways the final outcome allowed at least *the knowledge* about The Bible to thus reach virtually every corner of the globe. To recognise the gift of that Divinely-guided path for humankind and to strive to embrace it completely was, and is, *our primary purpose in life*, for it opens the way to the answers to life itself – in both the material and the *non* material worlds. Both have their origin in the "whole of The Law" which was "not to be overthrown", and therefore "cannot be circumvented"!

However, since it is also a strong human trait to cling at all costs to one's academic achievements – *for that is the measure by which men display their <u>intellectual</u> prowess and knowledge to the world* – then it is a simple matter to confidently predict a clear outcome for the academic world.

Embedded as it is in solidly entrenched and rigid systems encompassing all religions and all sciences, it will, despite the clear logic inherent in our absolute and unequivocal premise, continue to drive the present educational direction to its unfortunate yet obvious conclusion.

Thus: *The Light Above gives the Truth to men, and men then convert it to just a religion.*

That being our sure contention, we should complete this introductory phase with the reiteration that:

ALL CAN SEE IF THEY ARE REALLY WILLING TO SEE!

1

THE CRUCIAL IMPERATIVES!

Why the term, *crucial imperative*? Well, the word, **imperative**, means very important, vital, essential, urgent, of the essence, necessary – and *crucial*. The word, **crucial**, means vital, critical, central, decisive, key, essential, fundamental, important, necessary – and *imperative*. Taken together, the two words underline the importance of this Chapter in the strongest possible way, and concomitantly demonstrates the serious nature of this Work. The very tone of the words should make very plain to those to whom this Work is directed – the academics of science and religion of all races and cultures – that the information and explanations offered herein are precisely those that "will lead" both those primary Disciplines in the "right" direction.

However, before we can even begin to talk about genuinely understanding the "great questions of life" – particularly those euphemistically termed the "Bible Mysteries" – we must first recognise a number of key, and thus crucial, Imperatives. For only with that recognition might we then start to truly understand why there is so much dissension and argument around questions that we are obviously meant to know the answers to. For without the knowledge of the correct answers we are actually blind and ignorant to our true "purpose for being".

Theory, supposition and religious faith, therefore, should have no place in any frame of reference regarding the search for answers, for theory, supposition and just simple faith of any kind will always be and remain just that. They cannot ever be transformed into genuine knowledge of Truth despite claims that faith can be just as relevant for a meaningful life-path. By their very nature, theory, supposition and faith are tenuous and amorphous, and therefore not "solidly grounded".

What is required to go beyond faith, theory and supposition to a point of sure and knowledgeable conviction is a firm anchorage that allows no gaps in the particular premise or premises examined, and no gaps between any, and/or every, other premise. The "Crucial Imperatives" that we outline inherently possess that exact quality. Each one stands in its own right, yet each connects to every other to permit the whole to emerge. These "Crucial Imperatives" apply to all Disciplines, right across the complete scientific and religious spectrum that humanity might seek to look at, research and/or perhaps finally embrace. Here, too, there are no gaps when the "Imperatives" are employed. And neither should there be.

The unfortunate fallacy that science and religion are mutually irreconcilable effectively prevents the **necessary marriage** of both. The self-imposed divide driving the opposing and entrenched views thus hold **real enlightenment** at bay. Current notions from both Disciplines therefore leave little common ground for meaningful accommodation and transformation. Yet we are enjoined by the very Laws of Life to discover, to recognise and understand, every facet that each of us as an individual human being inherently possesses. And that clearly cannot be achieved through dissension, uncertainty and diametrically opposing views to the questions to life itself.

The *ostensible* "Bible Mysteries" certainly have very many interpretations about what they are supposed to mean, with many more supporters and detractors for each interpretation. But the very fact that there **are** so many diverse views centred on the great questions to life clearly illustrates the huge amount of confusion that surrounds this "search for truth". However, despite our strong and unshakeable position on this matter, we should state at the outset that we do not question, *for example*, the scientific fact that science can and has identified huge genetic similarities between humans and primates. That must be materially correct in any case, purely because the focus of such research centres on **just the physical form. So that is precisely what science <u>would</u> find.**

Exegesis and eisegesis, two leading "methods of interpretation" that Bible Scholars and Theologians use for critical explanation, analysis and exposition of the Scriptures; whilst certainly permitting a broad range of interpretative analyses are, in the final analysis, just two more ways to argue and debate.

Exegesis: Basically arriving at a theory or perhaps even conclusion about a particular point of Scripture using more the empirical aspects such as the historical record, for example, about a particular notion or event.

Eisegesis: The same kind of critical analysis, again usually of Biblical texts, using, however, one's own ideas. These two methods appear to be the standard and perhaps only viable system of analysis of Bible Scripture for the academic world at this time.

Notwithstanding the probable merits of such a technique, we must surely all recognise that, in the final analysis, it is ludicrous to believe that there are not, or there cannot be, true and definitive answers to 'the great questions to life'. That is a ridiculous belief. Of course there must be answers. So to be content with a mindset that states in essence; "we may never ever know", and then continue to endlessly debate and pontificate about those very questions – particularly within hallowed walls of so-called "Institutions of higher learning" – reveals the foolishness of that belief. It also displays the incredible degree of collective fear and ego that seems to be incapable of looking beyond the self-imposed limitations set by the very people who should be *most open* to Truth.

What, then, are these "Crucial Imperatives" which would permit those very "Institutions of higher learning" recognition of the answers to the great, primary questions of life and human existence – and therefore about Creation Itself? Whilst there are probably many that could be given name, the search for answers require us to recognise just a few key ones. **Truth!**

1.1   Crucial Imperative No 1:   "The Scientific Bible..."

That "**The Bible**" should not be regarded as simply a religious work. The Bible should be *recognised* as a **scientific Work** for all of humanity, for it is a **Book of Spiritual and scientific Truth and Law**!

For example – Anthropology: The pointless argument between Creationists and Evolutionists – or between Christian fundamentalism and scientific fundamentalism – is completely destroyed by just two sentences **in just the first two Chapters in the Book of Genesis**. There we find the correct explanations for a perfect marriage between science and religion. Using three different Bibles for our particular assessment in the later Chapter explaining our origins offers a broader picture of translation and interpretation where even subtle changes in word meaning either greatly expand the scale of Creation – thus the concomitant and associated knowledge for our necessary edification – or greatly reduce it.

Only *one* of our *four* reference Bibles gives the correct understanding of the Creative Process. [Purposely not featured among the many Bibles on the Cover.] The single author of the particular translation we allude to — **The Holy Bible in Modern English** by **Ferrar Fenton** — offers an insightful glimpse into an event that we could never ever grasp in its stupendous, unfathomable nature. However, the recognition that it really does fit, that it actually marries the separating views of science and religion and that there are no gaps, permits the spirit to soar in exultation and gratitude that one has finally found that crucial answer. This revelation is as sublime as it is stupendous, unequivocally illustrating with crystal-clarity that the petty bickering "down here on Earth" is as pointless as it is puerile! The harmonising of the Science of Creation and Evolution is thus explained in detail in the Chapter:

The Origins of Man – Genesis and Science Agree.

Mathematics: Actually the **Law of Numbers**; is more fully explained in the Chapter:

The Spiritual Laws – The Crucial Knowledge.

1.2 Crucial Imperative No 2: "The Duality of Man..."

That we, the human beings of planet Earth, are not solely a physical entity, but also necessarily possess a *non-material* inner animating core: *For the physical **cannot** – and therefore **does not** – animate the physical!*

Without that Truth as a key foundation, it is simply not possible to provide satisfactory answers to the primary scientific, religious and spiritual questions that beset those Disciplines and thus ultimately all of humankind. The exact same paradigm must especially be applied to virtually all earth-science research and analysis, *particularly in medical research*. Medical science needs this recognition more than any other Discipline, for certain "conclusions" arrived at therein seriously transgress the very Laws of Life and therewith endanger the actual life-force of the particular patients concerned. A number of Chapters in the Book address various aspects of current medical 'knowledge' to offer serious Creation-Law clarification for particular, contentious, 'medical-science' issues that polarise communities in many countries.

For Medical science is not divorced from the rigid ethos and thus subsequent direction that the "human-science" paradigm overall – solidly entrenched around genetics and the study of comparative DNA percentages between human life and various other life forms – is now pursuing with gusto. The so-called rapid advances in new knowledge concentrated on those two "cornerstones" – that biological scientists and evolutionary anthropologists now pat each other on the back about – paradoxically reached its *nadir* with the photograph and accompanying text on the Time Magazine cover of October 6th, 2006.

Featuring a photograph of a cherub-faced and beautiful human baby alongside a baby chimpanzee, the "Feature-cover" reads: "HOW WE BECAME HUMAN – Chimps and humans share almost 99 percent of their DNA. New discoveries reveal how we can be so alike – and yet so different...”

And the grand discovery in the feature article:– **3 billion – number of base pairs in the human genome. 1.23 percent – that are different in the chimp genome.**

Perhaps the most amazing aspect of the Time-cover illustration is **_not_** the scientific community's so-called revelation of new knowledge that identifies 99 percent of our genetic make-up is shared with chimpanzees, but the **indisputable evidence of one's own eyes** that **_that_** 99 percent of so-called *sameness* **does not at all translate to anything resembling physical and thus future 'life-path' similarities between the human baby and the chimpanzee.**

It is the **_1 percent of difference,_** not the **99 percent supposed similarity**, that *actually* and *incontrovertibly* shows **how far apart we really are.** There is a precise and far more powerful and logical reason why that is, and why it will *forever remain so.* Moreover, it is infinitely *more* than any earth-science theory could *ever* formulate.

As we stated in the "lead-in" to the actual "Crucial Imperatives" and need to strongly restate here again; despite our strong and unshakeable position on this matter, **we *do not* question the scientific fact that science can and has identified huge genetic similarities between humans and primates.** That must be *materially correct* in any case, **purely because the focus of such research centres on *just the physical form*.** Quite obviously, then, that is precisely what science **_would find._**

What we are therefore saying very, very loudly to all such researchers is: – *"Wake up, look at the evidence of your own eyes."* Such a clear and huge *unbridgeable difference* **between** the 'monkey' and the human child quite obviously means **that <u>another</u> more <u>powerful</u> factor is present in the <u>human baby</u>** which is clearly *not present* in the *animal*!

Unfortunately, to make it all fit, or perhaps be more palatable to the 'awed layman', genes and DNA provide the perfect "scientific explanation" to the "human-origin" quandary and therewith a supposedly "conclusive answer" for our beginnings. And by such *supposedly* 'incontrovertible' and 'unassailable' scientific logic and knowledge, we are all craftily enjoined to accept that *that* beautiful human baby can be **99 percent *the same* as an animal** even if, genetically-speaking, a 'closely related' monkey. **It is ludicrous in the extreme!**

It is often said that "science doesn't lie". In this case, however, and regardless of what anthropological science may claim, the eyes recognise the *deeper reality* and thus the *clear Truth* surrounding the human/chimp split. **It is not that which science states it to be!**

One noted scientist, however, has publicly stated what we unequivocally affirm; that Evolution and Creation are mutually inclusive; that they are virtually two sides of the same coin.

Francis S. Collins, M.D., PhD, director of the National Human Genome Research Institute and author of the book, "The Language of God: A Scientist Presents Evidence for Belief", in a recent interview on "Anderson Cooper 360°" (CNN), had this to say:

> "As the director of the Human Genome Project, I have led a consortium of scientists to read out the 3.1 billion letters of the human genome, our own DNA instruction book. As a believer, I see DNA, the information molecule of all living things, as God's language, and the elegance and complexity of our own bodies and the rest of nature as a reflection of God's plan. I did not always embrace these perspectives. As a graduate student in physical chemistry in the 1970's, I was an atheist, finding no reason to postulate the existence of any truths outside of mathematics, physics and chemistry. But then I went to medical school and encountered life and death issues at the bedside of my patients. Challenged by one of those patients, who asked: "What do you believe, doctor?", I began searching for answers. I had to admit that the science I loved so much was powerless to answer questions such as: "What is the meaning of life?" "Why am I here?" "Why does mathematics work, anyway?" "If the universe had a beginning, who created it?" "Why are the physical constants in

the universe so finely tuned to allow the possibility of complex life forms?" "Why do humans have a moral sense?" "What happens after we die?"

Dr. Collins was also asked questions by others, such as:

"Can you both pursue an understanding of how life works using the tools of molecular biology, and worship a creator God?" "Aren't evolution and faith in God incompatible?"

Dr. Collins continues:

"Actually, I find no conflict here ... evolution by descent from a common ancestor is clearly true. If there was any lingering doubt about the evidence from the fossil record, the study of DNA provides the strongest possible proof of our relatedness to all other living things."

Proceeding from his remarkable statements, Dr. Collins's following insights are precisely those which are inherently imbued with precise Truth, and which unequivocally concur with the explanations offered in this Work.

"But why couldn't this be God's plan for creation? I have found there is a wonderful harmony in the complementary truths of science and faith. **The God of the Bible is also the God of the genome.**"

(Emphasis mine.)

The key to understanding our assertions, and thus the spiritual/scientific insights of Dr. Collins, lies in the following "Crucial Imperative", which offers the logical and thus spiritually/scientifically correct paradigm in broad outline. The greater detail, however, will be found, as previously stated, in The Chapter:

The Origins of Man – Genesis and Science Agree.

1.3 Crucial Imperative No 3: "The Spirit Within..."

That being more than just a physical body means we naturally and *inherently* possess a *separable entity* **within** the material form. And that *that* is the *actual* life-force, the *animating* core, that is *actually each individual!*

Since that is the actual Truth, we can readily deduce the sure fact that the heart as the pump and the brain as the computer are there solely as *physical* necessities for a *physical* form performing *physical* functions. But only for as long as the actual life-force – *the animating power within* – permits it, or the physical form itself suffers irreparable damage and/or is destroyed.

This is a notion not officially acceptable to the scientific community involved in human-science research. Notwithstanding what we have already stated in **"Crucial Imperative No 2"** about genetics and DNA, researchers involved in the human genome research project identifying all our genes firmly believe that the various genes are the primary controller/s of everything connected with the human condition, and thus hold the key to all health problems and disorders.

The discovery of the "human genome", now academically and intellectually lauded as the breakthrough discovery that will offer cures and a better life for all forever, labours under a false and thus ultimately fatal error, for it is *solely* about the *physical body only*. The physical body is just that, nothing more; necessary for life on physical Earth of course but, having served its purpose, **simply rots away**. Referred to in The Bible as "the deadly carcase", the author of that statement clearly understood what modern medical and anthropological science equally clearly does not. Notwithstanding what should be a logical recognition anyway, National Geographic and IBM, two world leaders in education and technology, are currently engaged in a study of man. It is referred to as: "The Genographic Project – The Physical Origins of Man".

It, too, will not get anywhere near the truth of mans' real substance and origins, but it will certainly provide reams of "scientific material" that all manner of academics will pore over, comment on and generally laud as vital for "increasing our knowledge of our origins". And, of course, millions of dollars will be spent on the whole pointless exercise!

A case in point is the Time cover-feature mentioned in **Crucial Imperative No 2.** The feature writers' note:

> *"...tiny differences, sprinkled throughout the genome, have made all the difference. Agriculture, language, art, music, technology and philosophy – all the achievements that make us profoundly different from chimpanzees and make a chimp in a business suit seem so deeply ridiculous – are somehow encoded within minute fractions of our genetic code."*

They go on to state the standard scientific line, which is also science's quandary:

> *"Nobody yet knows precisely where they are or how they work, but somewhere in the nuclei of our cells are handfuls of amino acids, arranged in specific order, that endow us with the brainpower to outthink and outdo our closest relatives on the tree of life. They give us the ability to speak and write and read, to compose symphonies, paint masterpieces and delve into the molecular biology that makes us what we are."*

And there we have it. That is how it works for human beings – according to the sciences and scientists who study animals **to try to determine why they are not human.**

Anthropologist, C. Owen Lovejoy of Kent State University has hit upon the key point. He says:

> *"Take the genes involved in creating the hand, the penis and the vertebrae. These share some of the same structural genes. The pelvis is another example. Humans have a radically different pelvis from that of the apes. It's like having the blueprints for two different brick houses. **The bricks are the same, but the results are very different.**"*

(Emphasis mine.)

Inadvertent yet incontrovertible Truth! The bricks [*the material genome*] are the same. The results, however – *"which derive from the respective non-physical inner animating power"* – are different. And that is precisely why *there can never ever be* any kind of "convenient scientific solution" around the "human/chimp split" problem.

However, it is only a problem for science so long as the simple truth is not realised that:

It is <u>not</u> the *physical* that <u>animates</u> the physical!

Were that truly the case here, then there would **not be** the great and unbridgeable divide between humans and our supposedly closest relatives, the chimpanzees. Since there obviously is – which even the most obtuse can readily see – then something far more stupendous has occurred to bring that difference into such sharp and obvious focus. (We reiterate once more that the process and difference is explained in Chapter 2: **The Origins of Man – Genesis and Science Agree.**)

The relatively recent designation, **Neuroscience**, whilst not strictly concerned with the human/chimp split, is, in the same manner as Anthropology, nevertheless strongly locked to genes and the genome also. Currently, Neuroscience researchers are searching for a "happiness gene". This kind of research attempts to fatalistically pre-determine human make-up in some kind of "hard-wired" configuration, and therefore without any recourse to change. That is ridiculous. Millennia ago, Aristotle and his contemporaries *already understood* the truth of the human entity – that we possess a separable form *within the physical body*: **Crucial Imperative No 3.**

So the clear truth will forever be; that the so-called "life-force of the brain", with all its "gene-driven electrical 'pulsing' and 'computatory' activity", **all dies and rots away** when its host – the physical body – undergoes the physical death process. Therefore, to strongly repeat once more, genes and the genome **ARE NOT the Life-Force within!**

In summary, science, particularly medical science, dwells too strongly on the false delusion that humans (patients) are simply material forms activated by a pump and a computer. For all its apparent solidity, our human physical bodies are simply the forms or cloaks that *we* must *inhabit* if we wish to live on Earth The body, the physical shell, therefore, is not the actual you and me. If religion/theology and earth-science were to truly understand this vital Truth, embrace it and teach it, the very nature of global society would beneficially change, because further key recognitions would naturally follow.

Incorrect scientific views held as sure tenets of a particular Discipline will seed ideas and projects commensurate with the degree of error, even if not recognised as such. A wrong direction can then result in unfortunate outcomes. The non-recognition of the physical form as being just that – for, as previously stated, it rots away when the animating life-force vacates it – has long-created a virtual industry in which misguided science is devoted to "lengthening life". Yet scientists engaged in longevity projects have **not even recognised what this life actually is.**

It is patently clear, therefore, that this branch of science, with its huge budgets and many research scientists, will never prolong the life of any human being to the point it believes it can. Attempting to extend life beyond the boundaries set by precise and inviolable Natural Laws is not the main purpose or reason why we are on Earth in the first place anyway. The sci-fi idea of cyborgian-technology, long held by some scientists as a possible way of greatly extending life and perhaps for use in "space travel", now has actual practitioners in certain English Universities. Replacing natural body parts with the mechanical equivalent and/or marrying electronic control systems to increase human life and ability far beyond current parameters smacks of a kind of Frankensteinian madness. That is not to say that we should not repair or replace diseased joints to enhance the *natural span* of life.

In attempting to extend life far beyond that *natural span*, however; no matter how much hardware is replaced or how much software is embedded, the jigsaw that is then neither human nor machine will simply stop functioning when the *actual life-force within* so decrees. And that is *not* the hardware or the software. **The animating power within *all* mobile creatures is *not that* of its physical form!** That should be recognised as the *ultimate scientific fact.*

In the natural course of events, when the animating life-force within decrees that it must vacate the physical vessel, the ensuing process of separation between the physical form and the inner animating power takes place completely naturally, without any elements of religiosity whatsoever. Because it is a precise natural process for every human being, it could therefore be regarded as a scientific one since science – especially medical science – should be vitally interested in all natural processes regarding physical-life transition and transformation. This completely natural process, which we know as earthly death, is detailed in the two Chapters specifically about it.

1.4   Crucial Imperative No 4:   "The True Nature of The Forces of Nature..."

> That we, the human beings of planet Earth, must *fully understand* the true nature of **The Forces of Nature!**

A clash exists between various beliefs here too. Residual notions about the forces of the natural world deriving from ancient beliefs clash with religious fundamentalism which, in turn, clashes with science – specifically the sciences centred on meteorology. Vulcanology, 'plate tectonics' and even cosmology have their material genesis under the mantle of "Natural-force" Law. The key to it all lies in that wonderful Spiritual Law/scientific law Work, The Bible. The analyses and explanations about the Forces of Nature are derived *in part* from The Bible and elucidated in the Chapter:

'**Elemental Lore of Nature.**'

1.5   Crucial Imperative No 5:   "The Finite Universe..."

> That because the physical Universe is a *material* expanse, it is therefore *not* without end. **It is finite!**

The interesting belief which some hold that the physical universe might somehow be infinite fails to understand that *the very nature of its materiality* **must preclude** that possibility, for **all** material forms are finite. That is an inviolable law. The recognition of the Crucial Imperative that we as humans are more than just a material form applies equally to the universe in which we have our material home.

Cosmology. The Bible is a book about Cosmology also. In fact it reveals far more about the extent of the universe than even the Hubble Space Telescope could ever begin to see. The ongoing debates centred round the Big Bang versus the Steady State Theory etc., about the origins of the Universe pale into insignificance when the true picture is revealed. Whilst the immensity of the finite physical universes is answered in one part of The Bible, the end: the far more stupendous nature of Creation Itself is also revealed, as we have already noted, at the beginning. That process is analysed in the Chapter: **The Origins of Man – "Genesis" and Science Agree.**

And whilst the actual, incomprehensible size of the observable universe can only be approximated, the relative extent of the universes – and thus a clearer concept of an immensity that cosmologists are currently unaware of – is actually explained in The Revelation. The concept in its true cosmic reality is detailed in the Chapter:

The "Seven Churches in Asia Minor" – The "Revelation".

1.6   Crucial Imperative No 6:   "The Immutability of THE LAW..."

That there are certain and precise *Inviolable Laws* which govern *all life* and to which *all* human decisions and processes *are subject*. In their inherent Perfection these Laws are, in their perfect outworking, **Absolute**. And are therefore **Immutable**; and thus **Unchangeable**!

Tying all the Crucial Imperatives together are The Laws of Life. Science and all scientific research can only achieve **lasting success** through understanding and working with the knowledge of **Creation-Law**, and therefore *within the parameters* of those Laws. Good or correct decisions will produce beneficial outcomes. Bad or foolish decisions will therefore not bring about good outcomes, for the Power of **"The Law"** will drive all decisions to their full conclusion – thus exactly commensurate with the degree of beneficence or foolishness of the original idea or decision. Therefore the situation or circumstances that individuals, family groups, cultures, business corporations, churches, religions, scientific researchers might find themselves in at any given moment will always be echoed by the degree of compliance or non-compliance of *exactly* those Laws by the various groups concerned.

All human problems can thus ultimately be traced to a decision or decisions made somewhere by someone. Yet we grub about in ignorance whilst grandly believing we possess, if not, *all* the answers, then at least the right direction to find them. Unfortunately, without the recognition and knowledge of **"The One Law"**, that belief will always be found to be illusory. We, therefore, are not always the victims we too often *believe* we are. The consequential outworking for both good and bad decisions, however, will emerge at the appropriate time, for such Perfection in Inviolable Law could never be subject to the wishes or personal beliefs of men. A comprehensive explanation and assessment of the single Law for all mankind is detailed in the Chapter:

The Spiritual Laws – The Crucial Knowledge.

1.7   Crucial Imperative No 7:   "The Prophetic Bible..."

That **The Bible** is also a Book of clear and *sure* **Prophecy**.

The many ideas about the legitimacy or otherwise of Bible prophecy, and the myriad beliefs and interpretations surrounding it all anyway, miss the most crucial point. That crucial point understands **how** and **why** prophecy can *actually be* true and correct. We are not interested here in anything other than "Bible Prophecy". Since it is a subject that has exercised the minds of Theologians, Christian Scientists, other academics, believing Christians and many "everyday people" for a very long time now, it is surely time that a satisfactory explanation be offered.

Even though Bible Prophecy has in some cases probably derived from the gift of "visionary insight", **the key to understanding *how and why*** it can be fulfilled years, even many hundreds of years, after a prophetic proclamation, nevertheless rests in the operation of the "reciprocal outworking" of The Laws of Life: **"Crucial Imperative" No 6**. Because particular decisions must always produce the commensurate yet precisely lawful outcome for that decision, it is a simple matter to predict or prophesy the end result if one possesses the knowledge of those Laws.

Now, since the Laws that drive and govern all life are inviolable and unchangeable – and therefore ruthlessly consistent – collective decisions made by whole peoples that determine their very culture, religion and thus complete life-path, but made in opposition to those precise and inviolable Laws, will eventually bring the "lawful outcome", the "reaping". ·

If, then, the whole of global humanity follows paths opposed to those Laws for many thousands of years without deviation; then, depending on the overall degree of opposition, it is a simple matter to prophecy *the kinds of outcomes that must then occur*. For such opposition to The Laws of Life must one day bring about the commensurate return for that very collective – we human beings of planet Earth

So, whilst the great Prophets of the Old Testament probably saw the future for Earth-man of the present-day through Divine inspiration or via the gift of prophecy we, today, have access to a more complete knowledge of The Law and its outworking. By dint of that reality, we can now quite easily see and understand how and why such prophecies will come to pass.

1.8   Crucial Imperative No 8:   "Why We Possess Free Will..."

> That we, the human Beings of planet Earth, *inherently possess* the ordained attribute of "**free-will**". That *not understanding* the so-called inequities or injustices of life has its *genesis* in human *non-recognition* and thus *non-understanding* of this most "**Crucial Imperative**".

The publishing world has the spiritually-dubious distinction of having produced at least many hundreds if not thousands of books that have striven to make sense of the question: "Where lies free-will?" All those works were written, naturally enough, by human beings who, paradoxically, **actually possess** this very necessary quality. All humans, by virtue of their spiritual origin, have this aspect within as an essential element for life in the first place. Without free-will we could not live and work in a fully conscious and thinking way, and we would be little more than robots. We do not possess instinct as the primary component permitting us to actively engage with our environment; that is the interactive part that animals have and use. **We have free-will!**

Therefore, the ongoing struggle to understand why there are so many seemingly terrible injustices in the world and the associated treatises and theories from the academic world to attempt to explain it, must engage with the hard reality that *the very reason why* there are such terrible conditions suffered by millions globally *is precisely because the "forming-power" of human free-will has brought it about*!

The nauseous and servile belief that "**GOD**" causes all human suffering is totally absurd and an affront to simple logic. Why would **THE CREATOR** do that? What would be the point? That is such a cowardly way of attempting to divest humanity of its responsibility to live spiritually-correctly. Such an incredibly irresponsible belief not only very foolishly tries to apportion blame anywhere except to ourselves, but to **The Source** of our very life. That kind of very common "free-will" belief and decision held by billions of the world's peoples actually produces more hardship and suffering than would otherwise be the case. That is precisely *why* the planet and its myriad societies *are* in such a mess. Such a view reveals the cowardice of non-responsibility when we are *absolutely* responsible.

We are enjoined to live the admonition to 'do unto others' that which we would want them to 'do for us'. It is that simple. The sheer beauty of the natural world surely testifies to the simple Truth that **The Creator** Wills only joy to mankind. We human beings, *precisely because we possess free-will*, are thus the architects of *all* our miseries. Also, however, of whatever joy may fall to us.

There is no finger that comes out of the sky to arbitrarily "zap" unsuspecting individuals or groups. That is a positively silly notion, yet unfortunately seems to be the basis upon which even supposedly "highly qualified" academics build their skewed reasoning.

It is precisely the inherent aspect of free-will that permits Bible Prophecy to emerge **Crucial Imperative No 8** – for humans have set in place those predicted events through *not exercising their free-will for the good.* Knowledge and correct understanding of the precise and inviolable laws which govern all life and science – **Crucial Imperative No 7** – is the key to understanding what free-will is and how it works. We will once more mention the fact that *that* detailed knowledge is the subject of Chapter 3:

The Spiritual Laws – The Crucial Knowledge.

One of the most recent publications on this very subject is "The God Delusion" by Professor Richard Dawkins. He describes The Bible as "a weird volume" and, among other examples, cites the story of Noah as "appalling" in that so many children were destroyed in the ensuing deluge. The Archbishop of Canterbury said much the same thing publicly in the aftermath of the 2004 Asian tsunami. Professor Dawkins sub-titles his Chapter Eight: "What's wrong with religion? Why be so hostile?" He goes on to question why young British Muslims carried out suicide attacks in the London Underground. He asks: "Why did these cricket-loving young men do it?" Well, irrespective of motivation/reason, in the final analysis it was a free-will choice – their choice!

In the minds of academics and laymen alike, it all seems to come down to a standard question. It is very revealing in its *inherent foolishness* for it basically asks: "Why does God *allow* such things?" And because there *are* so many tragedies and catastrophes, an associated thought surfaces: "He therefore cannot be a God of Love..." ... if, and/or *because* – in the minds of such wrong-thinking people – He **permits** and/or perhaps even *'sanctions it'*.

How silly! Such a question/attitude shows the total lack of comprehension that there **really are** precise and absolutely inviolable Laws that we must know, learn and obey, and that there **actually are** severe consequences from transgressing them. No amount of intellectual theorising or debate can ever alter that one crucial immutable reality for all who live on Earth

So, rather than continually bleating about the so-called injustices in the world and inundating bookshelves with all their wrong theories, academics should set about learning these Laws of Life and teach *that* in their universities. If not, and they continue muddling on in disbelief then they, along with the rest of the world, will see many more so-called "injustices" occur.

For our part, we offer herein that very knowledge in the hope that the "learned" of the academic world might just be open enough to subjugate *academic vanity and ego* to at least objectively examine it – **without pre-conceptions.**

1.9   Crucial Imperative No 9:   "The Interconnectedness of All Events..."

That **all** is *interconnected*; that nothing stands *in isolation*!

The "Crucial Imperatives" we list here show this connection in broad association. The order of listing does not necessarily indicate any kind of religious, scientific or otherwise strategic prioritisation, however. That notwithstanding, the **'Imperatives'** nonetheless do follow a particular thread connecting revelation to revelation in a gradual build-up of knowledge. The individual Chapters that are strongly centred on the various **'Imperatives'** will reveal that absolute interconnectedness in clear detail.

The contentious nature of this book, coupled with the scientific ethos of "not true until proven empirically", drives the need for *constant reinforcement* of the **Principles** examined herein, and thus *very necessary repetition* of certain **Key Points** throughout – as stated in ***Author's Note***.

However, unlike other publications on this subject – academic or otherwise – this particular Work, through the outworking of ***Immutable and Inviolable Laws***, thereby derives its *very validity* from out of the knowledge *inherent in* those exact Laws to *therewith clarify* the great questions of life; for ***both*** science ***and*** religion. And through that mandate, therefore, so list the primary **"Crucial Imperatives"** necessary for that purpose.

All, however, under the Perfect and Inviolable aegis of: – **THE LAW!**

2

THE ORIGINS OF MAN: GENESIS AND SCIENCE AGREE!

"When we consider thy heavens, the work of *thy fingers*,
The moon and the stars, *which thou hast ordained*,
What is man, that *thou art mindful of him*?"

(The Gospel of the Essenes
E. B. Szekely, p.175)

"*...evolution by descent from a common ancestor is clearly true...*
The God of the Bible is also the God of the genome."

(Francis S. Collins. M.D. Ph.D.
Emphases mine.)

The above quote by Dr. Francis Collins – Doctor of Medicine, and scientist – was voiced when he was interviewed on "Anderson Cooper 360°" [CNN]. In a few very insightful words he captures the fundamental truth of a large measure of humankind's "whence", and therewith leads us into the concomitant and equally crucial question of our "whither and why".

Author of the book: **"The Language of God; A Scientist Presents Evidence for Belief"**, Dr. Collins's correct insights – which we included in the previous Chapter – in *this* particular one resonate perfectly with the following "Crucial Imperative":

Crucial Imperative No 2:

That we, the human beings of planet Earth, are not solely a physical entity, but also necessarily possess a *non-material* inner animating core: *For the physical **cannot** – and therefore **does not** – animate the physical!*

The Crucial Imperative which relates more precisely to our origins, however, is:

Crucial Imperative No 3:

That being more than just a physical body means we naturally and *inherently* possess a <u>separable entity</u> **within** the material form. And that <u>*that*</u> is the *actual* life-force, the *animating* core, that is *actually* <u>*each individual*</u>!

Even the National Geographic Documentary Channel, in two separate Documentaries decisive for human knowledge – **"Birth of Life"** and **"Human Ape"** – in essence queries *exactly* these two key **"Crucial Imperatives"**; respectively:

"How did *non-living* material come to life?"

And, in reference to the 98.4 percent of human DNA shared with chimpanzees:

"What is in the *less-than-two percent* that sets the two species *apart*?"

The History Channel, too, seeks the same kind of definitive answer. The series, **"How Life Began"**, asks:

"Where did [this] life come from? What IS life, exactly?" And in a 'space' of perhaps 'insightful prescience', the Series further and crucially asks:

"Is it chemical, spiritual, <u>or a combination of both?"</u>

(Emphases mine.)

In this Chapter we **reveal precisely** the spiritual/material processes surrounding those key 'scientific' queries. Thus that sequence of events which gifted to us conscious life. So, notwithstanding the very strong 'scientific mindset' that 'current education' holds to, in a curious paradox at exactly this crucial point in our evolutionary journey, science nonetheless still questions whether a 'possible' spiritual paradigm might also be present with the human entity. To *immediately* answer that question succinctly in terms of both scientific **and** spiritual 'Truth':

The ultimate and thus final answer <u>does not lie "in the genes"</u>!

Now, let us learn those exact processes.

Given the sometimes acrimonious history of the Creation versus Evolution debate, the clear and strong sub-title of this particular Chapter stating that "Genesis and Science" agree will, I am sure, cause many on either side of the debate to be derisively dismissive of such a claim. Nevertheless, the very fact that we human beings are actually living and breathing on the Earth unequivocally illustrates that irrespective of whichever view one might personally choose, the division itself is ultimately rendered irrelevant, **precisely because of our very presence here.** For we arrived, we are here.

So what is the debate really all about? Could it ultimately be about protecting ideas so long considered sacrosanct that pride and perhaps ego will no longer even consider any kind of accommodation whatsoever?

Obviously we should seek to know our origins, for such knowledge permits us not only the "where from", but also the why and the how! While all three aspects naturally offer the complete picture, the key, why, singularly allows us to focus on what we as a collective humanity have produced on our blue planet home over the many thousands of years of our tenure. The picture is not a good one, yet it is crucial to know the precise reason why.

It would be fair to say that for the most part science, particularly "Anthropological Science", would shy away from any notion that Creation, as it is currently accepted and promoted by the mainstream Christian Churches, could find accommodation with their views. Therefore, the solidly entrenched beliefs of Evolutionists and Creationists appear to be so diametrically opposed that attempting to show the opposite from The Book of Genesis would, on the surface at least, seem futile. Yet that is exactly what we can reveal, and therefore what we will do.

The key lies in reading Genesis very, very carefully line by line! A critical examination of the meaning of, and connection to, every other line is imperative for a complete understanding. Obviously, all assumptions and preconceptions should be discarded before undertaking such an analysis. One should also examine a number of different Bibles at the same time for there are translations which, in their interpretations, mask the great revelation and knowledge about the science behind Creation in Genesis.

Of course, we do not at all place human science before the great Creative Process. For the nature of the process as described in Genesis cannot ever be fully understood by either science or religion – simply because it describes an event utterly stupendous and incomprehensible, originating out of a very high non-material sphere or level, to its lowest precipitation in the material worlds of the physical universes. Incomprehensible as it is, however, it is nevertheless still the role of the earth-sciences to at least *strive* to understand them.

The time-frame that Creationism espouses is also clearly at odds with Evolutionism and probably represents the greatest sticking point in the whole debate. The 4.5 billion years that cosmology accepts versus the 6000 years of fundamentalist Christianity is clearly insurmountable. However, *either a thing is so, or it is not.* **It cannot be both at the same time.** It certainly cannot in terms of the huge unbridgeable difference in opposing views.

Notwithstanding such an obvious reality, is it possible for one key aspect of the debate to be immediately and perfectly reconciled? In other words, can Evolution actually be Creation? Thus, can the Creation Process, in its actual outworking to produce the great universes, at the same time also be the Evolutionary Process? If so, then the *apparently irreconcilable* and huge time difference is automatically resolved too.

This particular Chapter offers a very different look at a subject that, for many hundreds of millions, is simply intractable in its *seemingly* unbridgeable chasm. So, from that mini-introduction, let us examine in closer detail this *apparent* quandary.

> "Where does the world come from?"
> "She hadn't the faintest idea. Sophie knew that the world was only a small planet in space. But where did space come from?
> "It was possible that space had always existed, in which case she would not also need to figure out where it came from. But could anything have always existed? Something deep down inside her protested at the idea. Surely everything that exists must have had a beginning? So space must sometime have been created out of something else.
> "But if space had come from something else, then that something else must have come from something. Sophie felt she was only deferring the problem. At some point, something must have come from nothing. But was that possible? Wasn't that just as impossible as the idea that the world had always existed?"
>
> (Sophie's World, Jostein Gaarder, p.8, Phoenix Press.)

The questions that young Sophie finds herself faced with in Gaarder's International best-seller are the very same that men have asked since time immemorial. The fact that this particular publication was a "best-seller" illustrates the keen, ongoing interest to such ideas from far more than the scientific or philosophic community. For, quite logically, there should be a natural, inherent curiosity in each of us which brings forth these very same questions by virtue of the fact that we exist on planet Earth in the first place. Let us join Sophie as she asks more questions!

> "How was the world created? Is there any will or meaning behind what happens? Is there a life after death? And most importantly, how ought we to live? People have been asking these questions throughout the ages. *We know of no culture which has not concerned itself with what man is and where the world came from.* But history presents us with many different answers to each question."

> (Sophie's World, p.12, Italics mine.)

Sophie's second question is addressed further on in the book from the standpoint of The Spiritual Laws. This, in turn, provides the answers to the fourth question, namely how we should live. The third question on 'life' after death is also addressed further on. For if we do not know from where we originate, we cannot know who we are, what we are, or what our purpose is. That leaves only the first question to be answered, "How was the world created?" That question we examine here – **in this Chapter**.

The philosopher Plato believed that there had to be a reality behind what he termed the "world of ideas". He thought that we could never have true knowledge of anything that is in a constant state of change. We can only have true knowledge of things that we can understand with our reason. Plato also believed that man is a dual creature with a body bound to the world of the senses – which he thought were unreliable – and an immortal soul which is the realm of reason. He also believed that the soul existed before it inhabited the body.

Even though Plato wrote extensively about this dual concept, it was widely believed by many Greeks before him. Plotinus (ca. 205-270 AD) knew of similar ideas from Asia. Plotinus also believed that the world is a span between two poles with the Divine Light at one end, and absolute darkness at the other which receives none of the light. He believed that this darkness was simply the absence of light, without any existence. Thus the Divine Light becomes increasingly dimmer the further one travels from it. Finally, he believed, there is a point that it cannot reach. He believed, moreover, that the soul is both a spark from, and illuminated by, the Divine Light: a fascinating insight because this particular view contains much basic truth, as we will illustrate.

Whilst the philosophers have mulled over this question for millennia, the mainstream religions have generally not needed to do so. The acceptance of an immortal soul or spirit – whether it becomes "one with the universe" or retains its "personal self-conscious form" after earthly death – is part and parcel of most religious beliefs. Even within this field, however, there is no clear position either. Yet pre-dating the early philosophers and the main religions, we find that in some places "cave-men" buried their dead with plants in bloom, and other items that were probably personal possessions.

This indicates that the funeral ceremony was conducted with a certain ritualistic air, perhaps parallelling the first stirrings of a belief in the duality of man in the early progenitors of humankind. A degree of reverence for either the burial process or in the belief of a soul departing from the body is evident here. This offers a different perception of these early humans, once stereotypically depicted as brutish.

Democritus (ca. 450-370 BC), on the other hand, believed that people and animals were constructed solely of atoms, and that neither possessed immortal "souls". According to him, souls were built up of atoms that are dispersed to the winds when people die. In contrast to that particular view, The Spiritual Laws of Creation, the driving power of everything in

Creation – both the Eternal and the non-eternal material – decree that there are both animate and inanimate life-forms. The inanimate we may designate as that which is anchored in place such as trees and mountains. Rivers, lakes and glaciers etc., also come into this category. The animate is naturally the opposite and comprises those life-forms that are, in essence, *mobile*! They include the insects, birds, fishes, animals and, of course, man.

The "mobile group" is further divided into those forms that have free will and those that do not. In fact, only man possesses free will, as we have already stated. The *mobile life-forms* of the natural world do not. They do, however, possess instinct. The designation "mobile" means that all such creatures possess an "inner animating core" separate from their "physical form". We can picture that "inner core" as a "power pack"; the "battery in the machine", so to speak. However, because there is a huge and fundamental *inherent* difference between the *free will* of humans and the basic *instinct* of all other mobile life-forms, there is, similarly, the same great difference in the *respective kinds of animating power* contained within the "individual species".

For the greater understanding of this Chapter, the concept of free will needs to be thought about deeply. Because its nature has puzzled thinkers for centuries – free will being inherently necessary for any decision-making process – the non-understanding of what free will actually is and how it works, effectively prevents the understanding of the many problems that beset us. Problems appear which seem to have no causal reason at times.

Immanuel Kant, (1724-1804) a German idealist philosopher, Protestant and an ethical man, believed strongly in three things; that man has an *immortal soul*, that God *exists*, and that man has a *free will*. These aspects, he believed, were essential factors under which the necessary virtue of morality could grow. By exercising free will in his decision-making process, man moulds and shapes his individual personality in accordance with the strict outworking of certain immutable Laws, thereby determining his future. The subsequent "level of development" attained is then his alone. This simple yet absolute mechanism explains how inequalities occur – why men are not equal.

In order to fully understand our true nature as human beings, it is important to also understand what exactly constitutes the three main parts of the complete entity, earthman. In simple terms, they are the material or physical body, the soul, and the spirit. (The mind and emotions are part of the physical aspect because their contribution largely stems from the activity of the brain.) Unfortunately, the designations, 'soul', and 'spirit', either cause great confusion in the differences not being understood, or are thought to be the same thing.

Essentially, we can designate "spirit" as being the **innermost animating core** of man. His "spirit" is that "primary aspect" which inhabits the material body. *It is the actual animating power or force.*

The Spirit is thus the actual person!

The soul body and physical shell are respective *outer coverings* that *clothe* the "spirit". We may thus regard the soul as being composed of all the *"other-world" coverings* that *envelop* the **spirit** but is *not that* which is the **material** body. (In the Ethereal World of the *beyond*, however, it is the ethereal body that envelops the spirit, for the material body has now been vacated.)

So, whilst spirit and soul are closely linked together inside man's physical form as part of the complete entity, by virtue of their different origins they serve a slightly different purpose, even though still being animating aspects of that singular entity. Therefore, in addition to knowing the process by which we arrived here, what we also need to know is the how and why of our spirit, the how and why of our various "coverings" of the "soul-body", and finally how they all fit together.

Now, whilst man possesses *spirit* as his "innermost animating power", this is not the case with animals. Their "inner life force" may be designated as being *soul only*, because their ultimate place of origin stands at a *lower level* in Creation than man's *higher level* of Spiritual Origin.

Therefore animals do not possess the spiritual responsibility inherent with a free-will attribute as does humankind, and are thus not subject to the reciprocal outworking of particular, immutable Laws as humans are. Unfortunately for them, however, they *are* subject to every whim of mankind.

From those brief explanations it can be safely deduced that *inanimate objects* cannot therefore possess *either* soul or spirit. What is sometimes *perceived* or *felt* around great trees and around waterfalls or in mountains and forests is something entirely different, which in a sense can be called "soul" but is not of the same kind.

Having determined the nature of free will, soul and spirit – the origins of which we will discover in this Chapter – the next vital step is to address the question of the Creation-process itself. Since there has never yet been complete agreement about the "origin of the world" and all that it contains, let us add our voice to the debate and offer our explanations for mankind's beginnings to try to resolve that first question that Sophie is struggling to come to terms with. The reader should thus discover for himself that the following explanations do finally provide clear and logical enlightenment to this *seemingly* perplexing question.

Firstly, in concert with the discoveries of anthropological science, traditional, cultural and indigenous beliefs which state that ancestors were "things" or "beings" other than human, should be dismissed out of hand. Human beings are not descended from rivers or mountains or half-men or demi-gods that some indigenous beliefs allude to. Nor from any other form that superstitious conviction or legend has dreamed up, and neither are any races different with respect to the truth of this. Interestingly, this is not a religious truth, or even a "scientific" one. It is the Truth simply because the human form is the **only one** ordained for all of humankind under the outworking of **Creation-Law** – that Law which overrides and transcends all man-made beliefs.

Let us state here, therefore, an emphatic and bold statement! Those souls presently living on planet Earth have, as their common spiritual origin and therefore their true home:

The Spiritual Realm of Creation!

What do we mean by this, and what is the *Spiritual* Realm of Creation? Is there such a place? Can there be such a place? If there is, are we possibly "related" to all other races on Earth by virtue of our same place of origin? If so, were we once all there together as **different races** as is the case on Earth, or are those differences "recent developments" which permit reference points by which we can trace such natural, physical and regional differences? And do we all automatically return to our place of origin at earthly death as a member of "our own particular earthly race" as a matter of course – or are there other possibilities?

Where lies the answer to this most necessary of questions – our origins? For there is surely little point in journeying through life uncertain, confused, even angry at vexing questions such as race, racial mix and ethnic origins or whether one truly belongs to one race or country more than to any other. So, in the context of this particular composition, where should we begin?

We know that most races, cultures and religions have, as a common theme, a story of "Creation". The myriad views expressed in cosmology and Creation-theory etc., are as diverse and as numerous as the thought-processes that have spawned them. Yet very few of the many thousands of varying ideas completely agree with each other, and will therefore not be completely correct in their *entirety*. Certainly many aspects may be similar and have elements of The Truth contained within them. It would be equally true to also say that in the natural process of Evolution and development, certain races would have garnered insights which would have required previously accepted beliefs of "truth" to be discarded, in the sure knowledge that the "new" contained more "truth" than the "old".

The transition to the "new" was not necessarily without great travail and societal and religious upheaval, for man's precious ego does not easily allow him to "let go" what he considers to be his "great well of truth". Yet in the major issues relating to our origin and to our entry and exit from the Earth, collective humanity, for the most part, unfortunately remains just as ignorant and without real knowledge as it always has.

Through the great Wisdom contained within The Creative Will, however, certain especially chosen ones unveiled relevant aspects of The Truth to humankind in accordance with the developing spiritual maturity of the particular people into whose midst they were incarnated. Those teachings were given to mankind in a manner that could be understood by the race or Nation that had been specifically prepared to receive it from the particular "Truth-bringer" incarnated for that people at the appropriate time in their "spiritual" journey. This took place over many thousands of years. Man, however, could not leave them alone. He had to alter the original clarity of them.

In essence, the reluctance to discard precious pet beliefs reveals the inexplicable inability of mankind to leave such teachings in their pure and uncorrupted state. Rather than simply *living* the teachings as instructed, man chose to dissect them to suit his personal wants. This unfortunate fate has befallen all the great spiritual teachings – **without exception**. Even the setting up of the major religious institutions of so-called "higher-learning" has not advanced the cause of *Truth* a great deal.

In reality, its unfortunate "dissection" has been directly responsible for the incredible proliferation of so many *different religions*, with each generally purporting to be the only true one. After being offered the great Truths, man subsequently converted them all to "just religions". In a kind of perverse irony, if all the Teachings had been lived in a purely unadulterated way by those peoples to whom it was given, there would now only be *one single unified Teaching throughout the world today*. And that would have been **the complete Truth.**

Even though admitting to the existence of an "unattainable truth", The German philosopher, Hegel, (1770-1831) believed that "truth is subjective" and "all knowledge is human knowledge". He thus rejected the existence of any "truth above or beyond human reason". He believed, moreover, that because human ideas changed from one generation to the next, there could not be such a thing as "eternal truths" or "timeless reason". In his view history provided the only fixed point that philosophy could cling to. Since history in the philosophic sense is more or less constant 'contemplative-thought', Hegel believed that certain rules applied for this chain of 'introspective reasoning'.

Thus a thought is usually proposed on the basis of other, previously proposed, thoughts. However, the proposal of one thought is invariably contradicted by another, thereby producing tension between two opposing views. That is basically the current position with regard to the Creation versus Evolution debate. Hegel postulates a method whereby such entrenched positions can be "softened" so that the tension is resolved by the proposal of a third thought which accommodates the best of both points of view.

Hegel calls this a *"dialectic process"*.

Unfortunately, the belief still persists that science and religion will probably never be truly reconciled, and that perhaps they should not be. However, since our purpose is to move from a simple faith/belief position to genuine conviction as to the 'truth' of it all, the knowledge contained within **Creation-Law** perfectly permits a reconciling of the two viewpoints. We will therefore utilise Hegel's *"dialectic process"* to identify which of the respective main points of each argument can offer mutual accommodation without losing any genuine substance from either, thus merging the two into one complete and logical whole!

Classically, the subject of Creation has provided the perfect forum for completely opposing views – that of orthodox Christianity and Creationism against that of the scientific community generally tending toward Darwinism and/or Evolution. Galileo, Darwin and others whose findings challenged Church dogma were invariably branded heretics, and the polite way to reconcile 'Science' and 'Theology' was simply to agree that each would keep to one's own area. Basically, science would ask and answer the questions what, why and how empirically; and the church would do the same from the religious or spiritual standpoint.

In April 1997, what was billed as the Great Noah's Ark Trial was held in a Sydney court. Whilst not a case of an "Evolutionist" versus a "Creationist" in the classic sense, Dr Peter Pockley, a free-lance journalist, nevertheless reported that "...the trial had pitted the belief of many fundamentalist Christians in the literal truth of the poetry in Genesis against the conclusion of science for a 4.5 billion year old Earth."

In reality, there is no real discord between the two positions, as we will unveil and reveal. The disagreement exists only in the minds, and therefore in the *incorrect interpretations*, of the proponents of the respective points of view. Moreover, essentially *the same battle*, which we note later, was fought in an American State Supreme Court years ago.

So even with the current strong corporate-earth mindset today, the age-old question of "man or monkey" still produces passionate debate. Since this Chapter offers clarification of that debate, and with what we have at our disposal, let us now employ Hegel's *"dialectic process"* to determine where such truth lies in discovering an origin for ourselves that makes sense. The positions of science and religion should thus blend harmoniously, each supporting the other without disagreement as it obviously should be. For we human beings of Earth are the proof of this one simple reality.

We exist! We are here!

In the Evolutionist's corner, Charles Darwin (1809-1882) – once described as the most dangerous man in England because of the direct challenge to the teachings of Christian orthodoxy that his work of Evolution brought – proposed that "...all existing vegetable and animal forms were descended from earlier, more primitive forms..." via the simple mechanism of biological evolution. And that evolution was the result of "natural selection". Until quite recently science had "pushed back" and accepted a geological "birth-date" for our Solar System and the Earth as approximately 4.6 billion years. Darwin thought the age of the Earth to be about 300 million years. The age of the universe itself is believed to be around 14 billion years or so.

Historical anecdotes of Darwin's ideas possibly being correct actually sent shock waves through the "establishment", with even a distinguished scientist noting that it was "an embarrassing discovery", and "the less said about it the better". An "upper-class lady" expressed the hope that it was "not true", but if it was, then the further hope that it would "not be generally known".

> *"Much of the vitriol directed at Charles Darwin a century and a half ago came not from his ideas about evolution in general but from his insulting but logical implication that humans and the African apes are descended from a common ancestor. ... Along the way they [palaeontologists] learned, among other things, that Darwin, even with next to no actual data, was close to being right in his intuition that apes and humans are descended from a single common ancestor – and, surprisingly, that the ability to walk upright emerged millions of years before the evolution of our big brains."*

(Time Magazine, Oct. 9th, 2006.
"How We Became Human".)

In the opposite corner to Darwin stood the Creationists and Genesis "literalists". In Darwin's time, both the ecclesiastic and scientific views were virtually sacrosanct with regard to the doctrinal idea that all vegetable and animal species were created only once in each and every respective form. The views of Aristotle and Plato were not dissimilar to the Christian beliefs, since they basically thought that all animal species were patterned after "eternal ideas". This Creationist outlook, in concert with the Biblical, genealogical time-frame back to "Adam", postulated that the Earth was "created" about 6,000 years ago.[1]

In determining the various arguments for the "Creation versus Evolution" debate, and in the context of the subject matter in this Chapter, it is vitally important to know what evolution means – exactly. There is a view in some scientific circles that evolution means "selection by random chance", and not perhaps to a precise developmental path. British Astronomer, Sir Fred Hoyle, has stated that "...believing that the first cell originated by chance is like believing a tornado could sweep through a junkyard filled with airplane parts and form a Boeing 747". Professor N. Chandra Wickramasinghe, co-author with Sir Fred Hoyle of "Lifecloud: the origin of life in the universe", concurs with that view.

Overall, however, the science of astronomy believes it can trace the Evolution of the universe – "...on the assumption that matter is created; but just how it is created is another problem altogether, and no theory has given indication of how this came about." (The Atlas of the Universe, "Origin – or Evolution", p.214) Yet some scientist/theologians believe that Evolution provides clues to the very nature of God.

Plato, (428-347BC) who was basically concerned with what was eternal and immutable on the one hand and on what 'developed' on the other, found mathematics very absorbing because "...mathematical states never change". Much later in the seventeenth century Galileo observed that the book of nature "...was written in the language of mathematics". "Measure what can be measured, and make measurable what cannot be measured"; was his view.

The actuality of Immutable Laws, and therefore a Creator of those Laws which *automatically govern* "His Creation", negates the idea, for example, that life on Earth could ever have been the result of "random-chance" development. This image does not hold up because the **Creative-process**, under the aegis of **The Spiritual Laws of Creation**, translates that very mechanism into *precise mathematical formulae* in the material spheres. Thus the **"Spiritual Law of Numbers"** is also mathematical Law which can be noted in everything, everywhere.

Even the "primordial soup", produced at the birth of our planet aeons ago, had to have the appropriate formulae out of which eventually developed all the *physical* life forms and substances for planet Earth. Within each will be found their own *personal-species mathematical formula*. Change the formula and you change the substance or thing; if such change can be achieved within the bounds of scientific law which, in reality, is Spiritual Law.

Since this Law provides for development, but not for alteration outside of what is possible, science, therefore, *cannot actually create anything new at all*. It can only discover things not previously known, and produce new combinations, but only from substances that *already exist*. Even then, however, only within the parameters of what is scientifically and therefore spiritually possible under The Creative Will.

The Bible alludes to this mathematical precision in the exactness of The Laws of Creation by stating that everything is counted and nothing goes unnoticed. As a simple illustration of this lawful truth, scientific formulae decree that only a precise number and configuration of certain atoms can form molecules of a particular substance. Change the number and a different substance is produced, or the experiment may not work.

For example, one atom of copper, one of sulphur and four of oxygen will combine to produce $CuSO_4$, which will forever be copper sulphate. Copper sulphate, quite logically therefore, cannot ever be $CuSO_6$ or $CuSO_9$. In the same way common salt, mainly sodium chloride, will always be $NaCl$, not Na_2C_{16} or 8 or any another formula. And sodium bicarbonate, commonly used in the kitchen in the form of baking soda, can only ever be $NaHCO_3$, not Na_5HCO_7 or anything else.

Physicists have noted signs that the cosmos is custom-made for life and consciousness. It turns out that if the constants of nature – unchanging numbers like the strength of gravity, the charge of an electron and the mass of a proton – were the tiniest bit different, then atoms would not hold together, stars would not burn and life would never have made an appearance. John Polkinghorne, a former distinguished physicist at Cambridge University and now an Anglican priest, sagely observes: "When you realise that The Laws of Nature must be incredibly finely tuned to produce the universe we see, that conspires to plant the idea that the universe did not just happen, but that there must be a purpose behind it."

Charles Townes, who shared the 1964 Nobel Prize in physics for discovering the principles of the laser, goes further: "Many have a feeling that somehow intelligence must have been involved in the laws of the universe." And the authors of "The Mystery of Life's Origin", concluded that: a "...**Creator beyond the cosmos**..." *is the most plausible explanation of life's origins.* (Emphases mine.)

On the question of Evolution, other scientists sharing similar views to Fred Hoyle and N. Chandra Wickramasinghe include Colin Patterson, senior paleontologist at the British Museum who, after believing in evolution for more than 20 years, claimed he was "duped". Charles Darwin seemingly noted that not one change of species into another is on record, and he could not prove that a single species had been changed. In 1984, the former President of the French Biological Society, Professor Louis Bounovre, stated: "Evolutionism is a fairy tale for grown ups."

On the other hand, Arthur Peacocke, a biochemist who became a priest in the Church of England in 1971, has no quarrel with Evolution for he finds in it signs of God's nature. He infers from Evolution that God has chosen to limit His Omnipotence and Omniscience. In his apparent view, it is the appearance of chance mutations and the Darwinian laws of natural selection acting on this "variation" that bring about the diversity of life on Earth. Theologian, John Haught, founder of the Georgetown (University) Centre for the Study of Science and Religion, believes this process suggests a Divine humility, a God who acts altruistically for the good of Creation.

The sticking point in this whole debate is perhaps not actually that of Creation versus Evolution in any case, but probably more that of the time-frame required to produce either one, or both together! For if a time period for such a thing as "Evolutionary-Creation" can be logically established then both viewpoints can be accommodated in perfect harmony. In our view, therefore, the one key question in this debate that must be considered – yet rarely is – is:

"Can Creation also be Evolution?" And/or vice-versa?

Our reply is an unequivocal: — **Yes, it can. And, moreover, it is!**

However, to more *fully grasp* the *greater picture* that this long-contended issue demands, we need to seriously understand that whilst the Creative processes brought into being **the whole Creation**, the **Higher Realms** of the **Non-material World** were not subject to the *evolutionary processes* that we are familiar with *down here*. So it is vitally important to therefore set in place a demarcating barrier between the **Pure Creation** of those far Higher Realms — and **Creation** *and* **Evolution** *on Earth* in **The World of Matter**.

Evolution is thus a necessary and vital part of the Creative-process *down here*. Because the history of life on Earth *is* clearly one of aeons-long 'evolving' for *all* life-forms, *evolution **and** the Creative-process* are therefore inseparable — *down here*. That is simply because The Will of God must inherently be both natural and logical in **all** processes. That fact inherently stems from the Perfection of His Creative Will. Therefore, since it is vitally important to understand what we actually mean by "Evolution" – or what it is supposed to mean – from our particular standpoint we shall state it to mean, and also encompass and promote, "natural development"! We do not mean "random selection", or anything even remotely equating to any kind of "chaos theory" either.

Unfortunately, the respective default settings of science and religion presently seem to be so irreconcilable that there would appear to be no grounds anywhere for a meaningful merger of both realities. On the one hand science seems generally to hold to a kind of "eternal doubt" paradigm whilst the basic core of religion is faith. Since a major sticking point remains the possible time period necessary to accept both the scientific and religious or theological viewpoints, these two contentious aspects will nonetheless be drawn together to show that such a merger is not only possible, but is actually the true position – notwithstanding the many interpretations to the contrary from proponents of both Disciplines.

At this point in our analysis, we should revisit and clarify the question of exactly who and what we are. If we unequivocally state that our true origin is that of the Spiritual Plane of Creation, we logically imply that we cannot be purely physical in origin, just as the early Greek philosophers surmised. Therefore it may be presumed that the Earth Plane of the Material World is *not our true home* but a *material one* for the time that we are ordained to live on it. Yet the apparent obvious reality appears to indicate the opposite. We see, hear and feel everything around us as being solid and material. To all intents and purposes, it seems logical to believe that we are **solely** material beings. Should we expect that to be the last word if our "spiritual origin" is **not that** of The World of Matter, however? In this *seeming quandary* lies the key!

If we examine the Law of Gravity we observe that heavier objects sink whilst lighter substances rise. Whilst being obviously so, it is nevertheless important to stress this point. Thus, in the structure of Creation, a *material* object will occupy a lower level or plane than a *spiritual* one, simply because the higher the Plane of Creation, the finer and lighter is the substance of which it is composed. The same principle applies for the particular inhabitants of those respective Planes.

Therefore, only the Earth of the Material Plane is the home of blood and tissue. In this physical world we marvel in awe at the vast expanse that we see in the night sky. Astronomers speak of interstellar distances so incredibly immense that the human brain can scarcely even begin to comprehend such figures. We are reminded of the magnificence of such a work through the insights of the poets and philosophers in their attempts to understand our place in the universe:

"When we consider thy heavens ... what is man, that thou art mindful of him?"

A powerful question indeed and one that we should all ask of ourselves from time to time. For in the stupendous scale of things, it is vital to understand that the mind-numbing, incomprehensible immensity of just the physical universe alone can only be the **smallest and lowest part** of the **whole of Creation.** Our galaxy, on its own, contains something in the order of 100,000 million stars. The known universe, in turn, contains literally billions of such vast galaxies. The higher Spiritual Planes, by virtue of their far greater spiritually-expansive attributes, are therefore incomprehensibly and immeasurably far more immense.

If, then, our origin is out of The Spiritual, yet our earthly existence is obviously material, the only conclusion that we can logically draw here is that we must have both these aspects contained within us, i.e., the human being is both spiritual and physical. **And that is so!**

Only on the Earth, however, can this duality be so utilised. Indeed, it is the only way that humankind can meaningfully exist here at all.

> *For the spirit needs the material body to fulfil its purpose whilst on the Earth, and the body needs the power of the spirit to animate it here also – to give it life.*

Thus, as we stated at the beginning of the Chapter and reinforce here, two of the **Crucial Imperatives** necessary for earth-science – if that Discipline is ever to really recognise and understand the "origins of man" – find their place most pertinently in this part of our overall journey of revelation.

Crucial Imperative No 2:

That we, the human beings of planet Earth, are not solely a physical entity, but also necessarily possess a *non-material* inner animating core: *For the physical **cannot** – and therefore **does not** – animate the physical!*

And as a natural extrapolation of that human/spiritual reality-status:

Crucial Imperative No 3:

That being more than just a physical body means we naturally and *inherently* possess a *separable entity **within*** the material form. And that *that* is the *actual* life-force, the *animating* core, that is *actually each individual!*

Earthly death, therefore, is little more than the separating out, the drawing apart of the two; where also at this time the "spirit" *should* strive to free itself from the material world. The material shell then returns to the earthly components from whence it came in the normal process of decay that The Laws of Nature decree must take place. Hence the words of the Law: "Earth to earth, dust to dust" which we hear at funerals, and which only applies to the empty, discarded shell.

The process is simply outlined in The Book of Job:

> "Remember You made me from clay,
> That to dust You will make me return!
> And did You not curdle the milk,
> And fixed me together like cheese,
> Then clothed me with skin, and with flesh,
> And with bones and with muscles compact?
> And gave me my life and my reason,
> Then last, *fixed my Spirit in me*?"

(10:9-12, Fenton. Italics mine.)

Accompanying the process of establishing the physical/spiritual connection is the requirement to locate relevant reference points pertaining to the respective origins of both those parts to man in order to gain the necessary understanding. To thereby learn why, in the development of man and transition to human, (us) the spirit was fixed last – as Job states. (We will derive those points from certain mainstream writings.)

Therefore, of all the *religious works* that *purport* to have the Truth – insofar as most Western peoples are concerned anyway – The Bible is probably the best known and accepted by virtue of the fact that it is the one where the person of Jesus Christ is the key figure. Because of His particular Origin and pivotal role for humankind as documented in The Bible, we will therefore accept that especial Book – at least among the so-called *religious* works – as being *more able to provide* the answers we seek.

Thus, in one single, simple sentence from The Bible, **both our physical and spiritual origins are actually clearly revealed.** In its stupendously far-reaching yet stunning simplicity, it **completely destroys** the "great divide" that religion and science have constantly promoted and clung to. We ask why?

The King James Version of Genesis, Chapter **2**, Verse 7, states:

> "And the Lord God formed man of the dust of the ground, and breathed into his nostrils the breath of life; and man became a living soul."

Here has lain *one part* of the answer for centuries, unnoticed, unseen perhaps, but clearly not at all understood.

Now, if this particular Scripture is thought about in purely literal terms or from solely a fundamentalist viewpoint, a picture more or less naturally arises of The Creator, the Power of all that exists, descending to the Earth and building the shape of a man out of its substance – the mud of it. Then, what would effectively be a model of a *mud-man* would be instantly transformed into a living, breathing, walking, talking, internally-pulsating human being by the simple act of being *"breathed into"* in the literal sense.

Is that the method by which one could believe man was first formed? The crudeness of such an idea is difficult to reconcile with a Creative-Force responsible for the Creation of the immensity of the physical universes alone, never mind the far higher spheres spoken of in all religious works. With all that we have learned about our multi-faceted world today, is there any point in continuing to cling to such a preposterous idea?

Moreover, there is a major and insurmountable problem for literal fundamentalist thinking here in that The Bible alludes to the fact that God *cannot descend* to the Earth for it would be completely consumed by His Power. Immediately there is a contradiction, **if** we view it in a purely literal sense. Quite unequivocally, there can be **no** contradictions anywhere in the *actual Creation process itself.*

We should be very careful, therefore, not to apply any kind of heretical or blasphemous labels to an idea that may be markedly different to any current or Orthodox Church one. We should, instead, objectively allow the intuitive inner reason the spiritual freedom to determine the true nature of what is proposed here. Perhaps a wider vista might then suddenly open up offering the spirit the potential to "soar" instead of being shackled by too rigid an interpretation that refuses to allow even the "possibility" of such a thing as "Evolutionary-Creation".

The much-celebrated "Tennessee monkey trial" or "Scopes monkey case" of 1925 in Dayton, Tennessee, provided the key forum for exactly this debate. A high school biology teacher by the name of John T. Scopes who taught the theory of Evolution was accused of violating the Butler Act, a Tennessee law that forbade the teaching of Evolution because it contradicted the account of Creation in The Bible. The trial received worldwide publicity and was conducted in a circus-like atmosphere. And because of the popular belief that Evolution meant humans were descended from monkeys, the press dubbed it the "Monkey Trial".[2]

---

[2]The similarities between man and the anthropoid apes evidently caused Darwin to believe that both probably evolved from the same progenitor.

Because of its far-reaching educational implications, not least for many of the scientific Disciplines, the Education Department hired the famous criminal lawyer Clarence Darrow as their Defence Counsel, whilst a former US Secretary of State, William Jennings Bryan, appeared for the Prosecution. Clarence Darrow and his team argued for the scientific validity of Evolution and against the constitutionality of the Butler Act.[3] According to anecdotal reports, and after both views were aired, the case hinged on one crucial question which Darrow addressed to the opposition. The question concerned the existence of dinosaurs and the time frame in which they lived.

Since their existence could not be denied, the challenge and case could not be upheld. Had fundamentalism won that day, the State Supreme Court would have had no option but to order schools to teach only "the '6-days-of-Creation' belief". The concept of Evolution would then have been officially suppressed. The Butler Act remained on the State Statute books until 1967. Paradoxically, that court case need never have taken place simply because, as is our premise, the Evolutionary process is actually part of the Creative process, and naturally so. *Indeed it could not possibly be anything other than a natural union.*

Yet, even in this 21st century, the science of "biological anthropology" still persists with the totally incorrect belief that it is ***solely genetics*** that has determined the so-called "evolution" of "primate to human". Researchers from the Broad Institute of MIT and Harvard have evidently coined a new "anthropological term" – the "human-chimp split". Their ***basic*** hypothesis and time-frame *is* correct. An ancestral ape-species ***was*** the ancestor of the human race a very long time ago – **but only as the physical-form vessel, nothing more!**

Science must recognise and learn to understand the huge and fundamental difference between that ***physical/material-form of vessel/body***, and ***the animating life-force within it***; i.e., within ***every human being***. Only with that essential knowledge as the primary foundation for any further research – if it is deemed necessary – might the current, strong scientific emphasis on genetics and the human genome find its ***correct connection***. Rather than constantly needing to change hypotheses, this particular branch of science might, instead, begin to build *constant* upon *constant*.

So if we revisit our previous Genesis quote from the King James Bible, Chapter 2 Verse 7, the amazing revelation of the *"actual human/chimp split"* may be discovered therein.

That key Verse states:

> **"And the Lord God formed man of the dust of the ground, and breathed into his nostrils the breath of life; and man became a living soul."**

Therein lies the *overarching answer* to the most amazing evolutionary processes that, in the most natural and logical way, *separated out the first human beings from their physical-form progenitors.* Thus, The Bible described **the real human/chimp split** a very long time ago. *And human science has not yet caught up with this fundamental Truth.* The detail of this singularly-decisive event for humans more fully unfolds as we continue our journey, and clarifying explanations fill out the primary aspects.

Despite the incredible nature of what has been revealed here, it is still only a *part* of the complete process, albeit a stupendous one for human beings. A far greater revelation has been present in The Bible since its inception.

---

[3]Hollywood, too, played its part by producing the Movie, "Inherent The Wind". Broadly based on that celebrated case, it starred Kirk Douglas and Jason Robards in stirring performances as the two opposing Counsel.

2.1   The "First" Creation

That *greater* revelation is written in The Book of Genesis, most relevantly, of course, in Chapter 1. Verse 26 therein states:

> **"And God said, Let us make man in our image, after our likeness."**

Verse 27 continues:

> **"So God created man in his own image, in the image of God created He him; male and female created He them."**

Those two primary quotes from The Book of Genesis reveal, very clearly, what 'Science' and 'Theology' have not only **not understood**, but **missed completely**; *the second part of the answer*. And that is; that there are **two separate** "Creations of man". Thus, in Chapter **1**, we have **both** *male* and *female* beings *created*, **but not out of the dust of the ground**.

Conversely, in Chapter **2**, (our first quote) we initially have only man being formed, **but from** the *dust of the ground*. Later, after a plea for company, The Bible narrative describes the first *woman* as being *fashioned* from a rib of the first *earth-man*. All this, however, took place **AFTER** the **First** *Creation* of "man" i.e., male and female.

Is there a contradiction here? No there is not!

The Creation process, correctly described in Genesis, has simply not been understood at all.

This great degree of non-understanding has seeded the assumption for many that it all had to have taken place in the physical/material environment of the Earth. Such an assumption would be perfectly valid if we were *only and solely* physical substance. Since we are not, then other realities obviously need to be considered.

So, from the standpoint of general Christian thinking, the acceptance of a single Creation-concept for the formation of man is regarded as the norm. Yet the orthodox Bible, from which the Christian Church takes its teachings and spiritual substance, clearly states otherwise. Anyone can pick up *almost* any Bible and find the same for themselves. So what should we make of this?

What we should not fear to undertake is a keenly searching examination of a possibly contentious religious issue whereby the deepest and most wonderful revelations are missed. Moreover, it should be exactly the role of the Church in the first instance to **fearlessly** seek out the Truth, and to immediately discard any untruths discovered. That would be the right thing to do. With **bold courage and spiritual certainty**, that is what we will do here!

At this point in our search for answers, it is timely to examine a Bible that is not accepted as possibly being "church-standard" but is, nevertheless, one that comes closest to providing what we now know to be the **correct** interpretations to the answers we seek. The following comparative passages are taken from **"The Holy Bible in Modern English"** by **Ferrar Fenton**. The author of this remarkable Work heads the very first Chapter in The Book of Genesis with the words:

The First Creation of the Universe by God = Elohim.

This is clearly an exceptionally significant statement, and a radical departure from orthodox thinking in that Fenton *identifies* a **First Creation**. In a comparison of the relevant Verses it is patently clear that a complete and fundamental misinterpretation of Genesis regarding the Creation of man has entrenched itself in our thinking for the last two thousand odd years. And to the point, unfortunately, where we are now too afraid to even question this as just a *possibility*, thereby completely missing what is our rightful and ordained heritage – the actual "Truth of our Origins". So let us take the next steps boldly and examine, from Fenton's Bible, the two Creations of "man" in its *correct* sequence.

The *comparative* Verse 26 in Chapter **1** is preceded by the heading:

Creation of Man under the Shadow of God.

"GOD then said, *"Let Us make men under Our Shadow, as Our Representatives."*

Verse 27 continues:

"So GOD *created* men under HIS own Shadow, *creating* them in the Shadow of God, and constituting them *male* and *female*."

The actively-promoted notion by scholars and leaders of the three monotheistic religions that human beings – having transited through the earthly death-process – rise forthwith to 'heaven' to be in the very *immediate* presence of The Creator; in brutally-logical terms, *simply beggars belief.* How do they envision *their God*? Just as some kind of greater and stronger 'spiritual' or 'spiritualised' human being?

If we take the reality of just our Earth and Solar System as an example: It is powered by a small sun *so strong and bright* that its light will cause *immediate blindness* if we look directly at it. And that is a very small sun out of billions in just our galaxy alone. Our galaxy, as incomprehensibly immense as it is, is just *one* of billions in our universe in the Material Creation. [There is yet more, the extent and form of which we explain in Chapter 11.] That completely incomprehensible immensity, mind-blowing even in thought, is just the Material World only. By virtue of its materiality, therefore, it must inherently be; *and it is*: **The smallest and lowest part of the entire Creations!**

A life lived in a faith-belief doctrine that teaches *a close and convenient relationship* with a Power and Force that not only Created the vastness of the material Universes, but also the far greater Eternal Realms; at death is forced into the *shattering recognition* that we are not Created in the image of God at all. And, therefore, cannot *ever be* in His immediate Presence. The Bible states it very clearly.

To reinforce this Truth, an appropriate quote from John 1, Verse 18 of, respectively; the King James Bible and Fenton's Bible notes:

"No man hath seen God at any time."

"No one has ever yet seen God;"

The demarcating barrier is there for all to read; which we elucidate in this Chapter.

2.2   The "Subsequent" Creation for Earth-man

Now, very significantly, Verse 7 in Chapter 2 is also preceded by a relevant heading:

The Formation of Man from the Dust of the Ground by the Ever-Living God.

Thus we have clear and unequivocal clarification of a huge and fundamental difference – the *first* as an immediate **Creation**, close to The Creator. The *second* as simply a *forming*, very far from The Creator.

The actual Verse [some emphases mine] regarding *the forming of man* reads:

> "The EVER-LIVING GOD **afterwards** *formed* Man from the *dust of the ground*, and breathed into his nostrils the life of animals; **BUT MAN BECAME A LIFE-CONTAINING SOUL.**"

The last phrase of that Bible sentence should be marked well because it provides **the actual key** to a true understanding of this whole question of our origins. Significantly, **it is printed in bold capitals in Fenton's Work**. To state once more in reinforcement; the most significant aspect is the clear and unequivocal reference to the *first* happening; with man – both "male and female" – being directly *created*. That is in stark contrast to the second phase; with man being only **formed** – and from out of the "dust of the ground". The same relative Scriptures, moreover, appear in the same respective places in both the King James Bible and Fenton's, as it does in most.[4]

Thus far we have basically established that man is both a spiritual being and a physical one. And, moreover, further noted that only here on the Earth can these "two parts to man" co-jointly exist as a single, completely whole and integrated entity. What has not been explored yet is *how* they are co-joined. Again The Bible holds the key. Since the complete process naturally implies that there had to be a beginning for man and his earthly home, this is so stated.

Let us return once more to "Sophie's World" and join her on page 8 as she struggles to make sense of a concept that we may never be capable of grasping in its "living reality". That struggle to fully understand is due to the vast natural gulf existing between the Creative Power of all that exists, and us – the *lower* **formed** *entity* that is man. Such a notion is simply beyond our ability to even remotely comprehend.

> "They had learned at school that God created the world. Sophie tried to console herself with the thought that this was probably the best solution to the whole problem. But then she started to think again. She could accept that God had created space, but what about God Himself? Had He created Himself out of nothing? Again

---

[4]At this point in our journey it is probably pertinent to mention a few facts about the author of The Bible from which the last passages were taken. In 1853 Ferrar Fenton resolved to study The Bible in its original languages and to re-translate it completely into English. Fifty years later he had accomplished his task of translating the complete Scriptures of the Old and New Testaments from the original Hebrew, Chaldee and Greek. Whilst the general thrust of the recognised story of Genesis is obviously still present, there are seemingly small but extremely significant changes to some passages; changes which throw a whole new slant on some strongly entrenched beliefs. Throughout his work he explains translation errors, mainly in the Greek and Latin versions, by showing where and how they occurred. Most importantly, however, the "small changes" he identifies allow for a vast expansion of perception regarding the clarification of the problem of interpreting the *time* taken for the Creation-process, not to mention the whole concept of our relationship with The Creator. Ferrar Fenton's intuitive insight into a more logical and correct explanation of the *seven days of Creation* resulting from his re-translation of The Bible may well signal a note of warning to purveyors of the status quo and to more recent Bible translators whose own efforts may have been clouded by religious preferences rather than a purely objective and logical analysis. For the purposes of this discussion, if – and we use the word *if* only in terms of this essay being viewed as nothing more than an interesting hypothesis by some readers – *if* his re-translation of the Creation part of Genesis is correct, it might be wise to carefully consider whether this man's ordained spiritual purpose was to help bring clarification to those Christian Churches and Bible translators who still hold to the literal view of seven earth days for the Creation process. Fenton's re-translation of Genesis in this case clearly offers a more stupendously-correct interpretation, given its ability to accommodate both the viewpoints of scientific evolution and a Creation-process in a **logical** scenario and time-frame.

there was something deep down inside her that protested. Even though God could create all kinds of things, He could hardly create Himself before He had a "Self" to create with. So there was only one possibility left: ***God had always existed.***"

(Emphasis mine.)

Via this simple mechanism of logical elimination Sophie has hit on the only credible answer to the question – assuming, of course, that one accepts the belief of a Creator in the first place. Therefore, from the unequivocal acceptance of that premise – ***and that is the standpoint from which this Book is written*** – in order to have Planes of Creation to "fill the void", including the material worlds of the observable universe, there had to be set in motion a "Creation-process" to bring this about.

Hence, through the stupendous and humanly-incomprehensible process of Creation, driven by the Power of The Creator in the Divine Ordination and Command, **"Let There Be Light!"**, the Creation-process of the forming of all the worlds in all the various planes began. As the lowest and therefore last *precipitation* of all the levels in Creation – and under the outworking of The Spiritual Laws of Creation, particularly *The Law of Spiritual Gravity* – the vastness of the *material* universes also came to be. And contained within just that lower immensity, our earthly home. Thus the void was filled.

Because of the sheer impossibility of ever being able to picture or understand what is for human beings an inconceivable process anyway – for what words in the many languages of the world could one possibly use to even attempt to describe it – what kind of earthly example could we employ to *try* to explain *how* the separation between the respective Planes of Creation occurred? If we are able to arrive at some small degree of comprehension of *at least the mechanics of the process* and thus why this demarcation was necessary, we can gift to ourselves a large measure of inner awareness of our *true place* in Creation. That kind of recognition should also help in the understanding of what our *spiritual purpose and thus our actual reason for being* really is.

As a very basic and crude analogy, we can perhaps relate the main points of the Creation-process to that which occurs every hour of the day throughout the world in the numerous oil refineries of the petrochemical industry. This process is called distillation. It takes place in a "distillation column" whereby heat-generated crude petroleum vapour rises inside a tall metal column. At specific heights within the column, the vapour condenses to form various liquid petroleum products. Each ***different*** distillate ***will form itself*** from the condensing vapour ***at its appropriate condensing level as it cools.*** This will be determined by the ***weight and consistency*** of the particular distillate being condensed ***from the vapour at that level.*** The distilled product at ***each level*** will thus precisely configure itself to ***its own specific type of material substance***, and at its ***specific temperature.***

Particular terms in the previous paragraph have been highlighted in ***bold italics*** to help explain certain points that we will now outline. The explanations given here show the inviolable nature of one of the key Laws of Creation: The Law of Gravity. Whilst this one example is earth-orientated i.e., operating from below upwards, the process of Creation naturally works from the Highest Heights downward to the material worlds, but obviously still subject to that Law of Spiritual Gravity. Though we will never ever be able to even remotely understand this stupendous event – for even a combined distillation of the most ennobled aspects of all the world's languages could not even begin to offer a summary of words sufficient enough for the process – we should nevertheless strive to achieve at least some small insight. Even a diagrammatical picture in the mind would be of value, for that is better than having no picture at all.

In the actual Creation process, then, we might perhaps envisage something approximating an unfathomably vast, white-hot mass of "downwards-moving" substance suffused with the stupendous Power of: —

THE DIVINE

— vast enough to eventually form the humanly-incomprehensible immensity of just **The Worlds of Matter** – *after* – the far greater **First Creation** and then that of **The Higher Spheres**. And all driven from the immediate proximity of **The Light** and **Power** of **THE CREATOR** under the aegis of **HIS Creation-Words**:

"LET THERE BE LIGHT!"

Because of the obviously immense power and pressure in closest proximity to **GOD**, only the strongest and purest of beings could come to immediate consciousness there in the Planes of their sphere of activity – i.e., *closest to HIM*. Thus, at heights we could never comprehend, and certainly never ever reach in our spiritual form, occurred:

The Creation of Man in THE FIRST CREATION.

Man *created* in the **Image of GOD**, (Gen. 1:27, Fenton) – and **not** man *formed* later in the **second** Creation – from out of *the dust of the ground*. (Genesis 2:7, Fenton.)

Now, basically similar to the distillation process we examined earlier, the pressure of the Power of The Light drove the Creation-process to its completion. As each **different species within Creation** found its **appropriate level of consciousness** as determined by its **weight and consistency** – i.e., its own **specific gravity** so to speak – so, too, could the Planes for those inhabitants **form around them** in the **cooling-off process**.

This process was repeated all the way down to the material worlds. The governing factors which determined those levels of 'forming' were the same as in our oil-refinery example – the *lighter and finer* in the **Higher Spheres**, the correspondingly *heavier and coarser* toward the **lower levels**. Thus each Realm formed itself at its appropriate place, corresponding to a level or Plane whereby the *distance* from the Creative-Light permitted a *cooling off* and a *condensing* and thus an eventual *awakening to consciousness* there of that Plane's particular inhabitants.[5]

Only in the separating out and cooling off stage, roughly similar to the earthly process of *sedimentary deposition*, could worlds and landscapes form in which *all* the inhabitants of Creation would be able to fulfil their purpose, exactly as we must do here. For we should not suppose that only in the material sphere are there worlds of lands and rivers etc.. Again this difference is clearly alluded to in Genesis, Chapter 1, where worlds, animals and fishes were *created*, before the **first** *Creation* of *male* and *female* in the **Image of God**.[6]

---

[5]Each individual happening, each minute and incremental change in the cooling-off process clearly spans immense spaces and distances which, once again, we can never even begin to understand. The distances of interstellar space in the physical universes alone are simply too incomprehensible to grasp, never mind concepts of the vastly larger realms of The Spiritual – or the even greater Divine.

[6]By the Spiritual we do not mean the near-earth places that we generally associate with departed souls and occult or psychic activity, but a far greater spiritual reality. "In my Father's house are many mansions." John 14:2

And only in Chapter 2, in an incomprehensible time-frame representing the aeons-long evolutionary process concerned with the physical world of Planet Earth, do we then find the animals, fishes and birds being "...formed from the dust of the ground". Earth-man, "formed" the same way – "from out of the dust of the ground" – thus enters his new world. It is a world of incredible diversity and pristine beauty.

> "And out of the ground the LORD God *formed* every beast of the field, and every fowl of the air: ..."

> (Genesis 2:19, King James. Italics mine.)

The same Scripture in Fenton's work states:

> "Therefore the EVER-LIVING GOD, who had *formed*[7] out of the ground every animal of the field as well as every bird of the skies, took them to the man to see what he would name them. And whatever the man with the Living Soul called them, that was their name."

> (Italics mine.)

So the major difference between the lower and coarser physical worlds and the infinitely Higher and lighter Spiritual Realms is the *consistency* of the *substance* of which the *respective levels* are *composed*.

Thus the **First Creation** is of **Spiritual** substance whilst the *second*, out of the dust of the ground for the Earth and physical universes, is obviously *material*.

The key point to reinforce and understand here once again is that **each level represents a different consistency**, lightest and finest in the Highest Spheres – increasing incrementally with each subsequently formed level – until the heaviest and thus lowest in the material world. Such a far-reaching concept should not be all that difficult to understand. The statement of Jesus that: "*My Kingdom is not of this world*".; reveals the sure fact that His World ["*I came from The Father and I return to The Father*".] could not possibly be some kind of barren or filmy, amorphous expanse for He gives the strongest hint that His World is anchored in its infinitely more powerful and Eternal reality. Many of the great religions speak of an attainable paradise if one lives one's life **based on The Laws of God** (but not, however, according to the rules of Churches and Religions.) Every realm above the material would therefore become progressively more paradisiacal.

Quite logically, therefore, the consistency and substance of the various Planes of Creation must necessarily be the *same* as that of their inhabitants. This implies that each Realm must also feel, and be, very firm and *real* for those who reside there; exactly as with humankind on Earth. Any idea to the contrary is simply unrealistic. Nowhere in all the Spheres of Creation, therefore, do any of the inhabitants 'hover' aimlessly, as is sometimes depicted in religious interpretations or films. Every inhabitant and every thing in the various Planes is thus *anchored* into the *substance* of its particular "Realm" through the *consistency* of the level concerned.

The Eternal Laws operate throughout *all* of Creation, and the effects of The Law of Spiritual Gravity are felt in every sphere also. The Law of Movement, too, implies **activity** – everywhere. Thus we may note the perfect outworking of those Laws in the Creative process. Understandably, however, any sudden adjustment to this kind of conceptual perception may require a leap of quantum proportions. All we need do to achieve this, however, is to use the abilities of our inner

---

[7]The exact nature of the "forming" is of crucial import, for it reveals the science in the whole Creative process.

spiritual core, the life-force within. Abilities given to us precisely for this purpose; to understand our "Spiritual Origins" – explained in this Chapter.

So, let us look at our actual Spiritual Origins, our higher Spiritual Home. Because we are clearly only developed or *formed* beings (i.e., from *spiritual* **non-consciousness** to *personal* **self-consciousness** and not actually *Created Beings* as with man of the "First Creation" (as Fenton reveals), we did not therefore possess the inherent strength **to awaken to consciousness** *close to* **GOD**. Our level of *spiritual residence*, therefore, had to be *far lower* – in a kind of second-level Spiritual Realm. Yet even at that huge distance from **The Creative-Light Source**, we still did not possess sufficient strength to take on form and become conscious of self there either.

That state of *non-consciousness* therefore meant that we would require a home of transition – a material one – in which to acquire *self-consciousness*. Quite logically, any kind of material home could only be below that of "The Spiritual Realm". And only in that lower, material expanse would we be able to *develop to personal self-consciousness*.

Thus in our *non-conscious* state at the very lowest levels of The Spiritual Realm – our true home – we, the future spiritual human inhabitants of Planet Earth, awaited our time of *incarnation* in the Material World far below.

> We awaited the **completion** of the **evolutionary** developmental process that would **bring forth** the appropriate **physical** vessel – that of the **primate** – via *"...the forming of man* from out of the **dust of the ground"**. And **into which** the immortal **spiritual** aspect of man **could then be placed**. Thus; *"...the breathing into 'it' of the breath of life"*.

Therein lies *part* of the understanding of the Creation of man. And therein, also, *part* of the reconciliation of the Creation-versus-Evolution debate which is, in reality, a totally unnecessary argument since there is no actual reason for this division save that which the proponents of the two opposing views have "created" themselves. The complete process still requires further clarification, however.

So apart from the Earth being the place of transition for our awakening to self consciousness and spiritual awareness, was there a greater purpose for being permitted the opportunity for self-conscious life? Unequivocally yes! The material paradise of our earthly home was not only the place where we would *develop* to personal self-consciousness but, more importantly, **where we were to learn the truth of our origins**. We were also tasked to protect and nurture the Earth and its creatures given over to our stewardship as stated in Genesis and, having achieved *spiritual purity* through a *voluntary* adjustment to The Laws of Creation i.e., **The Rules**; we could then return, *ascend*, to our true home – The Spiritual Realm.

That particular sphere is the promised *Kingdom of GOD* for human spirits. Thus, we are not even beings who stand close to The Creator, but just *developed ones* far from The Light. In reinforcement of this Truth *once more*, the relevant quote from John 1, Verse 18 of the King James Bible states:

"No man hath seen God at any time."

Fenton writes:

"No one has ever yet seen God;"

For the purposes of spiritual clarity, the understanding that the level of our origin lies far below that of The Divine, the "Abode of The Creator", is imperative. This fact therefore forever *precludes* us from ever *personally knowing* the **All-Powerful CREATOR** we too loosely call

GOD. The Eternal Laws unequivocally impose the completely natural barrier that a creature can only possess "actual knowledge" as an "inherent part of itself", **up to** its "source of origin". It is clearly not possible for any creature to *fully understand* levels beyond, or *higher than*, its own beginnings.

A simple but pertinent illustration of that reality is the difference in the level of intelligence and "awareness" between animals and humans. How much greater must the difference naturally be between humans and He Who permitted us form and conscious life? To believe that we are at, or can attain to, the same degree of knowledge and power – as some scientists occasionally imply – is simply ludicrous and foolishly arrogant. Just as ludicrous is the belief among some eastern religious groups that they will one day become "one with God".

Whilst we cannot "consciously know" more than that which our level of origin would permit, we can, however, *perceive* things from above such a level – as in the case of the Jewish people's intuitive recognition of the one invisible God when most of the rest of the world at the time were worshipping a variety of idols. We also possess the capacity to perhaps roughly *visualise* levels above our origins if we are given this information from One Whose Origin is from a higher level. The tidings and knowledge of the Higher Spheres given to us by Jesus is such an example. To believe, however, that we have, or can achieve, the ability to absolutely "know" in this way is incorrect. It is simply beyond the capabilities of even our spirit, whose actual home is from a far higher point in Creation than this lower-level material Earth.

A "test" of this "truth" is to try to picture the concept of *infinity*, just as Sophie is attempting to do. To accept that there is a Creator logically means that there has never been a time when God did not exist. He has always existed. He will thus exist forever. We, on the other hand, need beginnings and ends as frames of reference to help in the understanding of everything connected with our existence and with time, and thus cannot even *begin* to grasp such a concept. The mind rebels and almost shuts down against such an alien thought because it has no affinity with such a far-reaching "idea". Only One who has no beginning and no end can logically "live" this kind of "infinite reality". For we human beings, with our very limited perceptive ability, it is simply an impossible thing to grasp. (This concept may sit uncomfortably with some, though might serve to inculcate a more realistic attitude in our self-perceived relationship to "The Creator of all the Worlds".)

For the moment, however, the problem of needing to completely reconcile the ongoing argument between orthodox science and fundamentalist religion as to the origin of man is not yet fully resolved. Some major points in previous paragraphs have offered many insights, but more explanations are needed As previously stated, the real tragedy here is that this great difference of opinion exists only in the minds of the proponents of the respective opposing views, for it *cannot actually exist in reality.*

In other words, the pointless arguments that have marred this path since the initial stirrings of scientific thought brought the first rumblings of disquiet into the previously sacrosanct Church view could not, quite obviously, have had *any bearing whatsoever* on the **actual** *forming* of the worlds in its stupendous scope and scale, however long ago it may have been. That reality will forever stand separate from all human opinion, as it obviously must.

To continue to rigidly and stubbornly hold to a personal or professional viewpoint at all costs, and sometimes even against the quiet warning of the inner intuitive voice, mirrors much of what is wrong with humankind. Yet for the sake of a clear, true picture of our Origins and for peace of mind, resolving this totally unnecessary debate is imperative. However, this can only be achieved with a completely open, fearless and enquiring mind and, most importantly, without preconceptions.

The Bible once more offers the final resolution to this *apparent* quandary. The question here is one of interpretation or, more precisely perhaps, *incorrect interpretation.* The standard view of fundamentalist Christianity is that the "7 days of Creation" scenario – applied to the complete Creation process including the emergence of man – is non-negotiable, and probably because of the view that The Bible itself *seemingly* states that this is so. So strong has been this belief that it is now an entrenched and apparently immovable cornerstone for many. However, rather than being recognised as correct "for all across the whole faith/belief spectrum", and therefore a sacrosanct anchor point for both the Church and society, it is one that clearly invites dissension thus resulting in much confusion.

Clarification of a previous key quote from Genesis should help to consign this division of opinion to its proper place in the sure relief of finally knowing the answer, thereby allowing the differences to be completely expunged. Hence, in the last phases of the great Creation, our world of the lower, material sphere could take on form too. As the last level of precipitation from out of the Creative-process, this vast world of matter took billions of years to coalesce into roughly the form we know.[8]

That long, slow, evolutionary progression which subsequently emerged from the initial Creative-process eventually allowed for all material life forms to emerge, including "...the formation of man from out of the dust of the ground" and the breathing into his nostrils "the life of animals". This is precisely what science has discovered. It was exactly that incredibly long evolutionary process which saw the emergence and preparation of the *physical vessel* – the development of the primate – the vessel which would ultimately house *spiritual* man.

The preparation of the physical vessel for man is clearly revealed in Fenton's work where that particular happening is separated from the formative process by its denotation in his key capitalised phrase. The two primary events are revealed in the following key Scripture:

> "The EVER-LIVING GOD afterwards formed Man from the dust of the ground, and breathed into his nostrils the life of animals, BUT MAN BECAME A LIFE-CONTAINING SOUL."

> (Genesis 2:7, Fenton.)

Now, if this "sacred Scripture" is separated into two parts and simple logic applied to both, we discover a crucial point. From the King James Version, the first part reads:

"And the Lord God formed man from the dust of the ground..."

To reinforce the key point once more; that small, seemingly innocuous, part-sentence actually holds one of the key components to resolving the Creation versus Evolution debate between Christian fundamentalism and science. In it is revealed the science of Creation that quite clearly equates to that aspect of the overall **Creation-process** denoting the long evolutionary development of the physical vessel – the primate – **formed from the dust of the ground** to one day house "spiritual man".

Now the second part states: ***"...and breathed into his nostrils the breath of life; and man became a living soul."*** Equally clearly, the "breath of life breathed into the nostrils" ***is the animating aspect for that physical vessel***. So simple yet so profound in concept, and so stupendous in scope and scale.

Perhaps many a reader may now recognise the correct picture with this explanation. For, as we state once more in reinforcement, the "...forming of man from the *dust* of the ground..." was simply the evolutionary journey by which all creatures developed *after* the formation and cooling of the material Earth. From the first minute microscopic life-forms out of the primordial

---

[8]The vast world of matter referred to here is infinitely more than that which cosmologists believe they know. Its true nature and size is explained in Chapter 11.

soup, to the fishes, insects, plants, birds and great lizards, and thence from mammals to the first primates. Thus did our **physical-form** ancestors slowly develop to their particular zenith – the refinement of form ordained for *Spiritual-man*. A marvellous and completely logical happening quite naturally divorced from any *fundamentalist* connotations when viewed *correctly*.

The associated aspect of the *time-frame* needed for evolutionary development, and how that could possibly be reconciled with a complete Creation time of just 7 days as depicted in The Bible requires clarification too. The 7 days account, though accepted by well-meaning Christians world-wide, is essentially rejected by the scientific community? Even the more recent "new and supposedly definitive translations" such as The Jerusalem Bible – compiled by committees of "learned" theologians – still persist with a literal 7 days Creation-time. The scriptural quote: "...and a thousand years are as one day..." (2 Peter 3:8) scarcely suffices to place even the smallest dent in the time period required for *evolutionary development*, given that the dinosaurs alone reigned for some 180 million years.

Why, then, do such a large slice of 'Christian' humanity still persist with the absurd belief that just 7 earth-days – *which equates to 7 earth-days of 24hr time* **as we experience it here on Earth** – accounted for **every single facet** of the **whole Creation-process**?

Do we really believe that just a few thousand years ago, dinosaurs marched into the Ark two by two, as some Creationists are desperately striving to promote?

The true answer in this case is one of *incorrect interpretation* and non-understanding, perhaps resulting from an incorrect translation of the original writings, or perhaps from simply accepting a symbolic "spiritual" term that was never meant to be so read, and applying to it a literal, earthly point of view. It is, in effect then, *an incorrect "Spiritual interpretation"*.[9]

WHAT, THEN, IS THE CORRECT INTERPRETATION?

The correct interpretation lies in recognising the fundamental differences between Chapter 1 and Chapter 2 of The Book of Genesis! The misinterpretation from Christian orthodoxy lies in attempting to ascribe two very different processes – one, **Creation**, the other, *primarily* **Evolution** – to a singular 7 earth-day Creation time-frame in Chapter 1, and attempting to also include in that time-frame *the completely separate processes that Chapter 2 explains*.

> **That includes the erroneous belief that the First Creation of Man – both male and female – refers to man on Earth.**

The scientific misinterpretation on the other hand lies in either completely disregarding the Creation aspect **as correctly outlined in The Bible**, and/or viewing Creation as a singular, material cosmological process out of which sprang the evolutionary developmental phase of the

---

[9]As stated earlier: The inexcusable errors about Creation and the Truth of our Origins **are actually perpetuated by the very people who should have long since recognised the logical reality of it all**. The Christian Church, earthly science and committees of Ph.D and degree-toting Bible "scholars" are the "triune" of **earthly power and defective education** which persistently clings to, and continues to *intellectually debate*, this foolish divide. Backing the so-called "expert" translations and opinions, the main Bible Publishers **continue to reproduce the same appalling error**. Despite this dreadful suppression of The Truth about Creation by the "educational elite" of global Christendom, the *primary Works* of Crystal Publishing, guided in the same way that Fenton surely was; with his essential contribution *together reveal – from The Bible –* the *actual processes* that facilitated our (human) entry into *'life'* on Earth.

various Earth creatures – including man – *through physical/genetic processes solely.* Fenton's Bible delineates yet *harmonises* both the earth-science and Christian fundamentalism points of view *so completely* that both are effectively *neutralised* in their **individual** positions, yet *conjoined perfectly* when **brought together.**

The "7 days of Creation" – **The First Creation** – described in Chapter 1 was therefore not immediately the Paradise of the human spirits, or the Earth. It describes actual spiritual happenings at heights and distances immeasurable and thus inconceivable to earthly humanity. We should therefore not become confused with the term, *earth,* used in the account of Creation in Chapter 1. That word **does not** refer to any kind of "local" association with our planet. It must be understood as a **"concept of Creation"** which applies to "dry land".

> "And GOD named the dry land *Earth*; and the accumulated waters He named *Seas*;..."

> (Genesis 1:10, Fenton. Emphasis mine.)

In "The First Creation", therefore, there are also mountains, forests, meadows, seas animals and men – as we have previously and strongly noted – but of inconceivable beauty and perfection as prototypes for all *subsequent* Spiritual Creations, all of which could only come into being **after** that First Creation.

Thus it is stated: "Let the Earth (the dry land) produce seed-bearing vegetation, as well as fruit trees according to their several species, capable of reproduction upon the Earth;" and that was done. The Earth (the dry land) produced the seed-bearing herbage according to every species, as well as the different species of reproductive fruit trees; and GOD saw that they were good. This was the close and dawn of the third **age.**

> (Genesis 1:11-13, Fenton.)

Now, what is this new and very different word – **age** – describing the Creation-process? A quick comparison of our two main reference Bibles reveals a vastly different contrasting picture with exactly that one small word making all the difference. The King James Version of Genesis 1:1 reads:

> "**In the beginning** God created the heaven and the earth."

This Bible, as with most others, goes on to state in Chapter 1 Verse 5:

> "And God called the light Day, and the darkness he called Night. And the evening and the morning were the **first DAY**."

And so on to Verse 31: "And God saw everything that he had made, and, behold, *it* was very good. And the evening and morning were the **sixth day**."

And thus to Chapter 2, Verses 1 and 2, which state:

> "Thus the heavens and the earth were finished, and all the host of them. And on the **seventh DAY** God ended his work which he had made; and he rested on the **seventh DAY** from all his work which he had made."

Surely we are able to acknowledge that this word **day** as used here is nothing more than a symbolic term for a particular "time-period", and was never ever intended to be taken literally. The example from *Verse 4* of the *same book* quantifies this premise because it states:

"These *are* the **generations** of the heavens and of the earth when they were **created**, in **the DAY** that the LORD God made the earth and the heavens."

As previously stated, the literal acceptance of the word day in the singular here for the complete Creation of both the heavens and the Earth, and the unequivocal and clear reference to the word **generations** in the *same* Creative phase, surely calls into question any such belief involving just 7 earthly days for the whole and complete Creative-process, for there is an immediate and obvious contradiction.

In stark contrast, Genesis 1:1 in Ferrar Fenton's re-translated Bible reads very differently:

"By Periods GOD created that which produced the Solar Systems; then that which produced the Earth." [10]

It is crucial to understand here that a vastly different conception of time must inherently exist in spheres that are obviously non-material. The diurnal rhythm we experience on Earth simply cannot apply to such Realms, for the passing of time can only be experienced in material worlds. In Realms that are Eternal, time, as we believe we know it, simply does not exist. Time, therefore, does not **pass** there. We on material and finite Earth, however, **experience its passing** every second of our earthly existence.

So in comparison with Verse 5, Chapter 1 of the King James Version, Fenton states:

"And to the Light GOD gave the name of day, and to the Darkness He gave the name of Night. This was the close and the dawn of the **first AGE**."

And so on to verse 31: "And God gazed upon all that He had made, and it was very beautiful. Thus the close came, and the dawn came of the **sixth AGE**."

And Chapter 2, Verses 1 and 2, comparatively state:

"Thus the whole Host of the Heavens as well as the Earth were completed. And GOD rested at the **seventh AGE** from all the works which He had made."

In similar vein, Verse 4 reads:

"These were the productions for the Heavens and the Earth during their Creation at the **'PERIOD of their organization'** by the LORD GOD of both the Earth and the Heavens."

(All bold emphases mine.)

And **only after** that *direct Creation Event* did God **then** subsequently *form* earthman – via a long evolutionary process – from "...out of the dust of the ground...", along with the animals and birds etc.. This scenario fits perfectly with the scientific view of a very long developmental phase for the Earth after its birth before even the ancestors of the very earliest primates could emerge.

---

[10] Fenton's translation of the word, "Periods", equates literally to, "By Headships". He writes: "It is curious that all translators from the Septuagint have rendered this word (- as -) B'reshitii, into the singular, although it is plural in the Hebrew. So I render it accurately. – F. F."

It is patently clear, therefore, that the difference between an "earth-day" and an **age** is immense indeed. Simple logic should suggest that the designation of an **age** to denote a **phase of Creation** utterly stupendous and incomprehensible to human thinking in its scope and scale makes eminently more sense than the literal acceptance of an earthly 24 hour time-period that Christian fundamentalism has perhaps interpreted as meaning a Genesis *"Creation-day"*.

And neither should the true and correct view clash with any religious interpretation regarding the awesome greatness of the Creation-process by The Creator Himself. Religious fear and blind faith do not supply answers. They only serve to perpetuate spiritually-wrong concepts with the resultant effect of producing adherents afraid to think for themselves. Perhaps the explanations outlined here may induce the tentative religious reader to become less afraid to question worrying uncertainties.

After all, how often do we hear the common phrase or variations of: *"It wasn't like that in my day!"* Generally used to compare an earlier time-period in a particular life to that of the present, the connotations are obvious to all. Such references do not refer to a single day.

2.3   The 'Real' Human/Chimp Split: The 'How' and The 'Why'

Even though the previous explanations offer solutions to some contentious questions, there is still the need to provide further clarification to particular points for our complete understanding. In one area at least, however, our discussions thus far should offer the clear recognition that we, in the *form of the complete entity* – man – *are not descended from the primates*. The physical body which we inhabit today is a refinement of form that developed from the very first primates during the long and natural evolutionary process that eventually *led* to upright man.

Therefore, let us re-state once more that this "body-form" is nothing more than *a physical vessel only*. It is, however, one we absolutely need in order to live in the material environment of the Earth. The *animating power* that separates itself out from the physical shell at earthly death, that some in the scientific community refer to as "the ghost in the machine"; *that* is the life-force within. It is our individual spiritual core whose home and origin is *not of the Earth*.

The above explanations may also answer the question as to what happened to the many varied species of primates that disappeared virtually overnight, and why the search for a so-called missing link is a difficult one. With the entry of the human-spiritual aspect into the most advanced species, all others *striving to develop to that same point* – but which *could not provide* the necessary *strength of attraction* for the *spiritual part of man then reaching the Earth plane* – simply died out. As a natural consequence of insufficient development and the inability to compete with this newly arrived spiritual "force" in the shape of early spiritual man, all other primate groups that *could have* developed to become *'that particular vessel'* were rendered redundant.

Now, whilst we have a resolution to both parts of this religious/scientific debate, further clarification of *how* the human-spiritual aspect could enter the appropriately developed primate species or group, and thence populate the Earth and develop into the world's peoples, is still needed.

We have established the premise that the human being is both spiritual and physical and possesses the attribute of *free will*. It is also clear that without the *spirit* as the *animating force* within the human body, the physical vessel has no life of its own i.e., it is naturally and necessarily dead. In this particular state, it follows the decree of The Laws of Nature and decomposes. It can thus be deduced that all other *mobile* life-forms of the Earth, such as birds, insects and fishes etc., must *similarly* have an inner animating core in order to have *life*. Their inner core is, however, not spirit, but **soul**, from which is derived the discernment of **instinct**.

As with man on Earth animals, too, have an original home above the material world from where they draw their life-force. However, because they do not possess the attribute of *free will* – which is synonymous with *personal spiritual responsibility* – their *place of origin* is **below** that of the human spirit. That plane of origin is designated as the Animistic, or Elemental Realm; which is that of the Nature Beings and the Elemental Forces of Nature.[11] Whilst these other *mobile* creatures of the Earth do not possess *free will*, they do have the driving power of the *instinct*. This inherent attribute allows all such creatures to develop to their ordained place and purpose too.

It is crucially important to therefore recognise that **up to** the incarnation or arrival of spiritual-man, *animal-man* [earthly primate] **possessed** <u>**soul**</u> **as his life-force**, and quietly developed the perfection of form that was ordained to provide the vessel via which the entry of the **human-spiritual** onto the 'Earth Plane' would be effected.

To this end, over the many millions of years of evolutionary development of the Earth's creatures to the perfecting of the form of *animal man*, the human spirits (we, us), existing in a state of non-consciousness in the lower levels of the *Spiritual Realm*, obeyed an *unconscious inherent urge* to develop to *personal self-consciousness*. Since this could not take place there and as a result of that "inner petition", the *non-conscious* spirit-seed – in terms of its individual journey – was *driven or expelled* from out of The Spiritual Realm – [*the true Garden of Eden*] downward towards the World of Matter.

> ***This is the mechanism whereby we ask to be born; precisely to develop to self awareness of who, what, and why we are!***

Now, as it traverses the *intermediate* levels *below* The Spiritual Realm all the way down to the Material Plane, the human "spirit-seed" – (Note: "A sower went forth to sow.") – is compelled to accept a covering or cloak of the *same consistency* as that of the level *through which* it is journeying. In the great immensity of what we refer to or understand as being "the beyond", there are "many mansions" too. Those "mansions" are the Realms or levels we must traverse to get here.

Thus, the closer the *now-stirring spirit-seed* gets to Earth, the *heavier* its outer coverings become. We may refer to them as the bodies or coverings that pertain to, and are of, the particular *consistency* of the *different Realms* traversed. Through this process, we become more than just an entity comprising a spiritual core (the real us) and a physical body. We possess a number of "cloaks" or coverings, each telescoped into the other, so to speak, with each having a different consistency exactly *commensurate* with the *Sphere* or *Plane* from which it is *derived*.

This *collective* covering is the *soul-body*, distinct from the inner spiritual core. The final cloak, of course, is that of the physical body, taken on when the *spirit*, with its enveloping "soul-coverings", *enters, incarnates*, into the growing foetus of a pregnant woman under the perfect outworking of The Law of Spiritual Attraction of Similar Species. This outer physical body becomes the earthly vessel for that "complete soul body" and its inner "enveloped spirit".

The processes that determine whether a male or female is born in this first incarnation will have been decided by the journeying spirit's *intuitive inclination* as it travels downwards toward the World of Matter and the Earth. From an initial *non-conscious* state, it gradually begins to slowly *awaken* the closer it gets to the world of the physical. During its transition downwards, it begins to sense the life-stream currents of the various levels through which it passes.

As it descends further, it becomes more and more firm *in its inclination towards the experiences it wishes to make its own*. With this increasing certainty comes the firm

---

[11]The origin, nature and purpose of those "Forces" are examined in the Chapter: Elemental Lore of Nature.

decision to choose either an **active** and, therefore, **male incarnation**; or a **passive** and, therefore, **female one**. (Passive in this context does not mean weakly submissive.) Thus, the *nature of the activity the entity chooses* **determines its body form**.

This explains the *mechanism* of *personal* choice that *determines* whether the entity's final form will be male or female. From that point onwards, in its successive incarnations, it *can* change its outer form depending on whether it changes its activity. Thus it is possible for a human spirit to incarnate in alternate male and female bodies which enables it to experience and develop both the male and female abilities inherent in the spirit. However, it can also happen that such a situation generates, for that individual, spiritual and emotional uncertainty as to its true ordained place.

> *In this explanation lies the key to the many emotional and/or psychological problems of humankind with regard to sexual orientation.*[12]

Now the stage is almost set for the entry of the human-spiritual into The World of Matter, therein to determine his future spiritual and material outcome. The earth, up to this point inhabited by prolific numbers of varied creatures, did not yet know spiritual man, nor the effect that this particular creature would exert on their natural, pristine world. Unknowingly awaiting the advent of this new stranger were the most highly developed species of primate quietly furthering their role as the chosen vessels through which this event would be fulfilled.

With the unnecessary quarrel between science and religion in **one** aspect of the "Creation versus Evolution" debate incontrovertibly resolved, let us complete the process by examining the **second** part of our wondrous yet contentious Genesis Verse to determine the final happening. This is tightly bound to our old friend, Verse 7, Chapter 2 in Genesis of the King James Version of The Bible. As previously stated, two distinctly separate parts to this Verse can be readily identified. Quoted in full once more, it reads:

> **"And the Lord God formed man of the dust of the ground, and breathed into his nostrils the breath of life; and man became a living soul."**

What we are now concerned with are the words:

> *"...and breathed into his nostrils the breath of life..."*

As previously refuted, this surely cannot be taken to mean that God Himself descended to Earth to literally blow His breath into a model of a mud-man. Though brief and simple, this part of the Scripture clearly depicts something else.

It depicts the **animating** of the future **physical vessels** for humankind, facilitated through **"...the forming of man from out of the dust of the ground..."**

That occurred quite naturally and logically during the aeons-long evolutionary process. Through those vessels – the especially prepared species of primate – man would eventually exert his new and far-reaching *spiritual authority* in the World of Matter at the ordained time for this to occur.

Now, in order to answer, from The Bible, the question of *how* the entry of the human/spiritual aspect into that species of highly developed primates prepared for its reception was effected i.e., those possessing a soul as their animating life-force – *animal man* – we need only re-visit Verse 7, Chapter 2, but *this time* using Ferrar Fenton's translation of Genesis to find the *true* connection. Fenton offers that actual revelation. It is one, moreover, which gives a far clearer understanding than we have thus far found in any other "scriptural writings". So, once again we read:

---

[12]Everything has its answer – its origin and end – under the immutable outworking of CREATION-LAW.

"The EVER- LIVING GOD afterwards formed Man from the dust of the ground, and breathed into his nostrils the **life of animals**; – **BUT MAN BECAME A LIFE-CONTAINING SOUL**."

(Bold emphases mine.)

The *difference* in wording here from commonly accepted Scripture represents a huge leap forward in our knowledge of the understanding of Creation and may well mirror Ferrar Fenton's *intuitive* grasp of the true happening to enable him to detail it *more* precisely, but without *actual* confirmed knowledge.[13]

The fact that the evolutionary development of the *primates* necessarily required the symbolic "*...breathing into the nostrils the life of animals...*", simply notes the creative and actual necessity *for all mobile creatures of the earth to have an inner animating core*, their actual *life-force*. Thus that which is referred to here as "*...the life of animals...*", is 'their' *inner life-aspect*, which all animals must possess in order to live.

It is that of soul.

As we have learned, man *also* possesses a soul – *but not as his innermost 'animating component'*. The primary life force of man – the actual person – is **spirit**. His **spirit** – *he* – is *enveloped* by his *soul*, the *multi-layered* outer cloak or *covering*.

Spirit is who and what man is **when all else is stripped away**.

So the reference to the word "soul" pertaining to man in this particular and *correct translation* of the Biblical account must be understood in its *true meaning*, since there is clearly a fundamental difference between the life-force inherent "*...in the man breathed into...*" and **what he then became** as a result of this **breathed-into process**. Moreover, there is a stated delineation with the use of the conjunction – **BUT!**

This can be further extended to logically mean "*...**but nevertheless became**...*" Fenton must have understood the crucial difference here because this key phrase is capitalised in *his* Bible: **"BUT MAN BECAME A LIFE-CONTAINING SOUL."**

We may perhaps better understand this most crucial difference which separates man from animal by examining Fenton's footnoted reference 1 immediately after the word, 'animals', in the Scripture: i,e., "*...and breathed into his nostrils the life of* **animals**1." Fenton's footnote states:

"1 Or reflective or intellectual life. See Cor. Ch ii.12. Ch iii.3."

We know, of course, that animals are not reflective or intellectual in the human sense, but that is not what is meant here.

So if we now look at Corinthians 2:12, we really do begin to understand what Fenton must surely have intuitively understood:

---

[13]Fortunately that new knowledge is available today, hence the unequivocal nature of this Chapter and, indeed, this whole Work. Fenton's clearer "spiritual insight" enabling him to clarify the terrible error/distortion about Creation – so long accepted without question – is revealed toward the end of the "Explanatory Note" of his remarkable work and sublime 'Calling'. It now finds voice here too. To those few of his assailants who 'sneered' that his work was 'not a translation but a mere paraphrase', he writes: "The remark shows that they do not know the difference between one and the other, or a perusal of my rendering of the Hebrew of the *two first chapters of Genesis*, and my note thereon, ...would show to them the purely philological basis of my translation." (Italics mine.)

"And we have *not* received the *spirit of the world*, but the **Spirit proceeding from God**; so that we can *distinguish* the gifts God has granted to us."

"...for you are animals still. For when there is *rage and strife and dissensions among you*, are you not rather like *animals*, than conducting yourselves like men."

(Corinthians, 3:3. All emphases mine.)

Note:

If there is still uncertainty regarding these explanations in the mind of you, the reader; here, now, is the final note on this *most crucial and necessary of revelations for **all** of earthly humanity*!

In reinforcement *once more*: We now know that the breathing "...into his nostrils the **life of animals**..." represented the entry — *__at the very beginning__* — of the *inner, animating life-force* into the very earliest *physical-form ancestors* of primates at *their* **forming** *from 'out of the dust of the ground'*, from which would *eventually develop* the most *highly evolved species* to exist on Earth And from that 'broad evolutionary spread', the *further development* of the *single primate branch* which would *subsequently produce* the "physical-form vessels" *human beings would require* for life on Earth

So the great and fundamental **unbridgeable difference** between primates and humans *is actually represented* – paradoxically for human science – *by the-__less__-than two percent of **DNA** __not shared__* with chimpanzees. For that vast and **unbridgeable primary difference inherent in human beings** centres on the fact that even though *we* also needed to use the basic physical form of the most *highly evolved* of the primate species for *our human* earth-life activity too, **we could not do so with just the 'inner, animating life-force' of the primate**. Thus the **absolute necessity** for an **actual** *human/chimp split*! For we are not animals, we are human. So we therefore could not simply *evolve* into humans *from* the animal primate.

Why not? Because, *once again*, that which gives human beings life *is not* the same inner life-force as that which the lower-level animal primates possess as *their* life-power. Thus, the capitalised reference to **"LIFE-CONTAINING SOUL"** reveals exactly that fact. That which is *contained in, and enveloped by, the 'soul'* in this crucial revelation, is **The Spirit – THE LIFE** – the __innermost__ animating core of the 'human being'.

The key phrase: **"BUT MAN BECAME A LIFE-CONTAINING SOUL."**, therefore reveals that the *quantum leap* from primate to human was *not one given life by human genetics* through simple 'brain development' by normal but slow 'evolutionary processes'. It was a quantum leap **precisely because a new force and power was required for humans to be humans**, completely distinct and very far removed from the animal primate. That is why the 98.4 percent of similar DNA in both *monkey and man* concerns the respective *physical bodies only*, and thus why **they both rot away at death**.

We are not our physical body!

We can conclude, therefore, that this inherently logical process that Ferrar Fenton reveals *is* exactly that which actually facilitated the entry of *Spiritual man* onto the Earth

It thus depicts the amazing event of the *incarnation*, the *entry*, of the **human/spiritual** from out of his former *non-conscious* state in the *non-material* Spiritual Realm, into the most highly developed **species of primate** then existing on Earth Only thereby could man *evolve* to become fully conscious of self.

'Spiritual' man – 'human' – now stands on Earth!

The reader who supports Bible Scripture literally and solely may now begin to see that there is no clash after all between the Creation account and Evolutionary development since both, in their co-joined natural perfection, could only have issued from the hand of The Creator Himself in any case. Employing Hegel's 'dialectic process' and Fenton's correct Bible translation, we have brought together the appropriate connecting threads from both the scientific and religious Disciplines to offer the reader definitive clarification of the Creation-process.

So there stands our **'Spiritual Origin'**; that of all humankind. From that stupendous happening, spiritual man, in his material home prepared over millions of years, began his new journey of development towards personal self-consciousness and knowledge. This journey, however, would span a certain, precisely ordained period of allotted time requiring accountability at the end of it. For with his request for conscious life came the responsibility of correct stewardship of his material home; the earth and all its creatures, as was once commanded!

The division and separating out into the races, peoples and languages of the earth still lay before him. History records that stewardship as one of mostly degradation, destruction, blood and war, with few intervals of true peace, grace and nobleness. Now, however, the time of accountability has arrived. We stand in the midst of the reciprocal effect of our bad stewardship as The Spiritual Laws set about the grim task of "balancing the books". That necessary "auditing process", which we now begin to observe with some considerable degree of alarm, is effected via the increasing outworking and activity of the unassailable power of the Elemental Forces of Nature!

The clarification herein of humankind's origin and entry into the material world of the earth as home should provide meaning and insight for many readers. With clarification should also come quiet confidence and peace of mind as to who and what one really is. Here, we outlined and explained the basic happening of the coming-into-being of Creation, and of man. We accompanied him on his journey downwards, from a *non-conscious* spirit seed in The Spiritual Realm to incarnation and *conscious* personal responsibility on the earth, and thence to the employment of his free will to determine his spiritual future under the outworking of The Eternal Laws.

Naturally, it could be expected that there is a lawful process by which he leaves this earth too. Whilst considerable detail is given to this process in later Chapters, it is appropriate to conclude here with a short paragraph to very sketchily outline the reverse process of his return journey, thus completing our cycle of *spiritual* life in this segment. [The reader should note, however, that this particular outline only explains the return ascent **if** The Spiritual Laws have been heeded. The process for a human spirit who **chooses** a path *opposed* to those Laws is, unfortunately for that human spirit, a very different one.]

Upon earthly death and *release from the physical shell*, **and providing he has earned the right to do so**, he begins his *return journey upwards* to his spiritual home. As he passes *into each correspondingly lighter sphere* – **the same that he traversed on his journey downwards** – *the heavier covering of the previous lower one is automatically discarded in accordance with its corresponding weight and that particular level's corresponding density.* In this manner his ascent continues until, finally, he stands at the threshold of The Spiritual Realm from whence he came.

This time, however, not as a non-conscious, unknowing spirit-seed, but as a fully conscious, purified, spiritual being – Spiritual Man. Here, he sheds the last cloak and is drawn across that boundary into his Eternal home, radiant in his spiritual purity having **earned** "...the crown of Eternal life". Thus is fulfilled the invitation of Jesus who stated:

"In the home of my Father there are many abodes. If it were not so, I would have told you: because I am going to prepare a place for you."

(John 14:2)

In order to earn this right, however, the next Scriptural quote [Matthew 5:26] should also be accepted:

"I tell you indeed, that you will not depart until you have repaid the very last farthing."

Therefore, to this end under "The Rules" i.e., Spiritual/Foundational-Science, we read;

"You, however, should be perfect, as your Father in heaven is perfect."

(Matthew 5:48, Fenton all.)

Given the possibly contentious yet potentially mind-extending implications of this Chapter, detailing the main points of the Biblical sequence of Creation here at the conclusion may provide simplified clarification via a greatly condensed overview.

2.4   Chronology of the Creation Process

2.4.1   The Key Points

The Utterance of the stupendous Creation-Words – "**LET THERE BE LIGHT!**" – thus resulting in: **The First Creation – (The Spiritual Realms.)**

1. The Creation of the Heavens and the Earth of **The First Creation** – "By **Periods** God created *that which produced* the Solar Systems: then that which produced the Earth."

   (Genesis 1:1, Fenton. Emphasis mine.)

2. The **Creation** of day and night (in the Heavens.)

3. The division of the waters which were **under** the expanse (firmament) from the waters which were **above** the firmament (expanse.) The firmament/expanse then named the Heavens.

4. The commanding of the waters **below** the Heavens to be collected in one place, and for dry land to appear.

5. The **Creation** of flora.

6. The Creator sets two great lights which divide day and night for Earth

7. The **Creation** of fish and bird life.

8. The **Creation** of animal life.

9. Then, the great **Creation** of man **in His Image** – both male and female – and the Blessing to rule over all flora and fauna.

10. The **completion** of the Creations at the end of the **sixth Age**. The Creator rests at the **seventh Age** and blesses and hallows the seventh **day**. [For earthly humanity's spiritual recognition and acknowledgement – and thus Worship.]

Note Scripture, Genesis 2:1, (Fenton.) "Thus the whole Host of the Heavens (as well as the Earth were completed)." This is the completion of The First Creation (i.e. Spiritual Realms).

   (Parentheses mine.)

And only then:

   The Creation of The Worlds of Matter, including our universes, solar systems and earth – **as planned by its Creator.**

11. After the completion of **The First Creation: The Spiritual Realms** – including all that was then **Created** (as revealed in Genesis 1:1-3) – the Creation of The Worlds of Matter through a long process of evolution leading to the forming by God of earth-man from out of **the dust of the ground,** who following a suitable time of evolution became the first human being, **the man with the Living Soul**. (As revealed in Genesis 2:19. All emphases mine.)

12. Earth-man gives name to every creature – **formed** from out of the **dust of the ground also**.

13. Even though God had **already Created** "man" in His Own Image (both male and female) in **The First Creation**, and had subsequently **formed earth-man** from out of **the dust of the ground**, there was still no earth-woman. (Biblical tradition states that she was constructed from a rib of the man.)

Now, whether this sequence is viewed absolutely literally, whether it is viewed symbolically, pseudo-scientifically or any other way, there are clear pointers illustrating a number of very different and very distinct happenings that occurred. This is clearly contrary to the one single sequence that the main Churches generally believe and teach as having ostensibly **created** man/earth-man. And, moreover, him only. Fenton unequivocally delineates these separate, stupendous events in clear sub-titles.

1. **The First Creation of the Universe by God = Elohim.**

2. **Creation of Man under the Shadow of God.**

3. **The formation of Man from the Dust of the Ground by the Ever-living God.**

Therefore, if we take careful note of points 3, 4, 9, 11 and 13, and similarly note the above sub-titles 1, 2 and 3 from Fenton's translation, a vastly different and more stupendous picture arises than the present, general belief of an aspiritual humanity somehow being in close proximity to a Power that we cannot even begin to comprehend. Points 3 and 4 *on their own* here strongly indicate two different places very far apart: one above the Heavens and one below the Heavens. The Creator of All the Worlds is clearly far further from us than we might want to believe. (In any case recognition of that fact arrives to all not too long after earthly death.)

The sequence we have outlined here (from The Bible) concurs with many of the scientific findings of Anthropology and Astronomy. Taken in concert, both views actually trace a path of evolutionary development that is consistent with rational logic and, moreover, encompasses and co-joins both the religious and scientific points of view. More importantly, however, this more logical sequence places man (us) in his correct place very far from a Creative Force that inherently possesses the Power to Create all that we know – and all that we do not – simply by an Act of Will. In short, by the Power of Creative thought. That is a power and an ability utterly incomprehensible to us. Such stupendous Power, moreover, will forever be beyond our extremely limited comprehension.

However, instead of that particular recognition being somehow problematical for us, we should be grateful for the fact that the incomprehensible immensity of the Creations graciously provides all that we will ever need for life here – **and life Eternal**. Such a marvellous and stupendous expansion for mind and spirit should thus actually offer the largest possible measure of inner peace and spiritual security possible. That is provided, of course, that we voluntarily choose to – **obey the Rules!**

Therewith are the long-contested arguments of Creation versus Evolution – Christian fundamentalism versus intellectual science:

– perfectly reconciled and harmonised.

3

THE SPIRITUAL LAWS! THE CRUCIAL KNOWLEDGE

"Oh the Ancient Truth! Ages upon ages past it was found.
And it bound together **a Noble Brotherhood.**
The Ancient Truth! <u>Hold fast to it</u>!"

(Goethe.)

"Without Revelation a Nation fades. *But it prospers* **by knowing the Law**."

(Proverbs 29:18)

"I come not to overthrow the Law **but to fulfil it!**"

(Matthew 5:17-18 Fenton.
Emphases mine.)

Three different quotes, but all relevant to the notion we inherently possess that "law" is both necessary and desirable for any society to function well. But what was or is this Law that Jesus as The Son of God stated He had come "not to overthrow", but "to fulfil"? If He came to fulfil The Law, and not to overthrow it, it must surely mean that *that* Law of which He spoke could not be overthrown, not even by Him as the Son (or Part) of God. That would further translate to the clear fact that just as He had to obey that Law so, too, are *we* necessarily subject in the same way to the same Law. More than the "Law of Moses" – and not that interpreted by the religious authorities of the day in sterile rigidity – but that same Law *given spiritual life and significantly added to* in Divine Power and greater Knowledge!

This Chapter precisely defines **Crucial Imperative No 6**:

That there are certain and precise *Inviolable Laws* which govern *all life* and to which *all* human decisions and processes *are subject*. In their inherent Perfection these Laws are, in their perfect outworking, **Absolute**. And are therefore **Immutable**; and thus **Unchangeable**!

It should thus be regarded as the key link to all the others, as the understanding of The Spiritual Laws is imperative for the complete understanding of the aim and purpose of this Work. And that is *to know The Law*.

As stated above: —
"*Without Revelation a Nation fades*. **But it prospers <u>by knowing The Law</u>**."

The notion that Universal Laws or Laws of Life govern what takes place "out there" in the cosmos is probably an easily accepted idea for most. The constancy of the motion of the stars testify to the existence of a powerful force operating to hold star systems in relative stability. The great scientist and astronomer, Sir Isaac Newton, noted that "...only a few fundamental laws..." governed the Universe. He also believed the same laws applied on Earth. So the concept of Universal Law is a well-established idea in the psyche of humankind. Most religions, too, accept and teach that certain sacrosanct laws exist and are necessary for societal stability and harmony.

Basic and fundamental "rules" such as are found in the three great monotheistic religions vis-à-vis, **"The Ten Commandments"** of the Christian faith, for example, can be clearly seen as inherently possessing the highest standards for living spiritually-correctly. Most religions and spiritual teachings similarly possess such guidelines. The further out we extend this theme, however, the more contentious the whole paradigm becomes. When we examine the laws of different cultures and ethnic groups we find ideas that differ markedly from the standard accepted by the great religions of the world – not that those followers necessarily practise what they ostensibly believe. Thus huge differences reveal themselves in human interpretations of this enigmatic concept called "The Law".

In terms of the Christian Faith, it is probably fair to say that many Christians would believe that The Ten Commandments *are* The Law. The Book of Leviticus also offers specific detail of precise law covering all aspects of human relationships. Often thought to relate to Jewish life, culture and religion solely, the Laws outlined in Leviticus reveal specific "Spiritual aspects" that are relevant for *all* peoples, simply by virtue of the fact that we all possess, and are affected by, precise natural processes centred on the human body. Whilst these aspects of Law are clearly that, is this The Law that Jesus referred to as that which He came "not to overthrow"? Or is there more?

The Spiritual Laws of which we speak can be stated to be that force or power which drives to its relevant, appropriate and commensurate end, a justified outworking resulting from the decisions we make. Whether made as individuals or globally-collectively, The Spiritual Laws return to us the inevitable consequences deriving from such decisions. In concert with that reality, the many parables of Jesus exactly illustrate the operation of The Spiritual Laws of Creation in the affairs of men. The outworking of the power inherent in them also brought into being the actual Creations, and the same power sustains and maintains it all. It is thus the primary factor in ensuring that we have an earthly home in which to exercise our free-will attribute, and thereby receive our appropriate "return/s".

The key Law in this particular case is called **The Law of Reciprocal Action**. We know it more generally in its religious guise as: "What a man sows, that shall he reap." Science broadly notates the same process as: "For every action there is an equal and opposite reaction."

Relatively few in number, these very exacting Laws, by virtue of their unchangeable and thus inviolable nature, *precisely determine and dispense appropriate and perfect justice specifically commensurate with the nature of the deed deriving from the particular decision taken.*

Completely automatic in operation, The Spiritual Laws take no account of religious, cultural, scientific or even political determinations and proclamations. Neither do they take into account whether or not humankind is even aware of them.

They simply are!

Only with the knowledge of them, and thus how they work in their individual and collective outworking, can earthly humanity ever hope to understand not just *why* the world is in crisis, but why concerted international efforts by so many well-meaning groups are not able, for the long term, to effect fundamental and sweeping change for the better.

Thus, global societies continue to unravel despite such efforts.

Since The Spiritual Laws provide the only sure mechanism whereby positive change can be wrought across the globe, rapid adjustment to them is imperative. However, given the diverse and fractious divisions permeating world societies, such a vision is simply not possible. That being the case in the collective sense, we can at least *individually* awaken to the recognition of them and thereby gift to ourselves the exact mechanism whereby we can perhaps attain a small measure of peace of mind at this time, for many, of frightening and uncertain change.

In the context of modern societies, then, the notion of prosperity goes hand in hand with the associated idea that science and scientific research are indispensable to developing prosperity. However, to prosper by "knowing The Law" is *not* about earthly science. It is about the ***recognition and application*** of the overarching Spiritual Laws of Creation which govern, maintain and drive all things, including science and scientific research and endeavour.

The Spiritual Laws are therefore the only means by which we can know why the mainly dark and bloodthirsty actions of humankind over millennia have produced a global society wracked by religious, cultural, political and ethnic divisions so polarised that even civil dialogue between groups and factions is not always possible now. Transgressions of the key Laws of Life for all on Earth *automatically bring forth the reciprocal effect upon all who so transgress.* It is a lawful effect, however, perfectly **just** in its outworking, for it will be exactly commensurate with the degree of good or evil that the various groups and races within humanity have visited upon each other over time. The reader should therefore *really* strive to understand the explanations that *interlink* the different Laws.

In the context of religious thinking and cultural tradition the word "Spiritual" may mean any number of things. In its distilled essence and form, however, *it should mean only one thing.* By **Spiritual**, we should mean "of the spirit" i.e., that which is **not** of the material but which occupies the *higher level.* We should not use this word to attempt to describe things that are concerned solely with the mundane and earthly, including some aspects of traditional cultures. And we certainly should not debase the inherent noble power of the word by attempting to ascribe to it practices or beliefs such as those pertaining to occult or psychic activity, for example.

If we, however, describe this word as being more uplifting, more noble in its origin, and therefore in its application more able to offer those higher virtues capable of producing the best kind of society – and if it *is* that which originates from out of the Highest Spheres – are we not then talking of absolutes? Are we speaking, then, of possibly needing to apply "rules" to achieve that desired state? And are we, in the final analysis, stating that such a thing can only be possible under clear, uniform, strict and **unchangeable Laws**?

The clear answer to all of the above is an unequivocal yes! We can, moreover, state such "guidelines" to be that perfection which is naturally inherent within **The Spiritual Laws**. It is thus important to clarify this amorphous thing called "The Law" in order to give better understanding of some of the many *incorrect* interpretations of this vitally important word – **Spiritual**. And therewith strive to illustrate its true meaning, thereby separating the beneficial from the clearly unhelpful, and certainly from the dangerous.

Irrespective of the basic tenets of the many and varied religions on Earth, The Law is invariably *perceived to have*, as its underlying foundation, a higher being or beings who are the guardians of that "Law", with those same beings watching over the people to whom they will have given it! Throughout history many races have striven to base their societies upon the ideal of The Law, with the Jewish people perhaps possessing the strongest application of it in their long history. If the Old Testament is read as an historical document rather than as a religious one, it is very clear that the ancient Israelites *only* prospered when they *obeyed* The Law. When they rejected it outright or even simply adopted the laws of the peoples around them, they invariably suffered invasion, enslavement and sometimes great slaughter.

By definition, the *customary law* of any race of people can *only* derive from the beliefs, customs and traditions that *that* particular group will have believed was correct for them at a particular time in their development. Unfortunately, however, the historical record for many ethnic groups and tribal societies reveal their particular law/lore as being also strongly derived from their *fears and superstitions*. So whilst that "customary law" may have served well for a given time of development, if a race proceeds normally and naturally through the various stages of "spiritual" growth and development, certain factors of that law should clearly *change* as greater insights hopefully lead *away* from the fear and/or superstitious aspects perhaps previously present within that group.

For the scientist, Higher Laws designated as being Spiritual might not seem to be of either great benefit or great consequence to science as a whole. However, the very opposite of that view stands as the truth of it all here; for it is exactly *that truth* which the colossus of science, Sir Isaac Newton, understood very clearly. Moreover, his recognition of certain inviolable and immutable and thus unchangeable Laws governing all things precisely accords with the very reason and purpose of this Work – for scientists and philosophers alike.

Therefore science and scientists should not think that the great, so-called "Bible Mysteries" which Theologians and Bible scholars endlessly debate over should not concern them as well. Because those debates are exactly about Forces and Laws that scientists are meant to understand more than others, it is precisely in their interests to resolve them. Far greater knowledge would be acquired as a result, thereby leading to greater discoveries.

> That is the primary purpose of science here in the material world; *to recognise, learn and understand The Laws of Creation* and then use that knowledge *to explain the outworking of Spiritual Law on earthly processes.*

So the general, overall tenor of this Work, which is about examining and explaining subjects usually regarded as the preserve of religion or perhaps philosophy, is nonetheless directed to the scientific establishment too – for the reasons previously stated. Science and Spiritual Law are not mutually exclusive. We will go so far as to say scientists need to seriously understand that Spiritual Law, the foundation for all processes, does not *need* earth-science in any shape or form. It is, and forever will be, the ultimate authority in and for all scientific processes undertaken – *irrespective of the views of science and scientists*. Science, therefore, inherently needing to function under precise **Creation-Law**, cannot exist *except* under the aegis and authority of that most ultimate of Law.

The nature of The Spiritual Laws or Principles therefore decree that they are the only model on which to base any society today because, *by their very constitution*, they are absolutely inviolable and unchangeable. Since these absolute parameters logically further decree that such Laws unequivocally transcend humankind's generally narrow views; in their clear perfection they are thus the ideal foundation for all societies and ethnic groups. Whilst we should certainly examine all laws which contribute to the sum total of all legislation that a given country or people might possess, only those aspects which accord with The Spiritual Laws should be retained. That which does not do so should be discarded once 'more correct laws' are formulated to replace them.

This Chapter explains those Laws!

The English empiricist philosopher, John Locke, (1632-1704) notable for his "Two Treatises of Government" which justified the English Revolution of 1688 opposing the notion of the "divine right of Kings", held the view that the idea of God was a "potential" of human reason. And that it was likely for human reason to know that God exists. Most of the Enlightenment philosophers also believed in the "reality" of a God, for the world was far too rational for that not to be the case, in their general view.

At times of human suffering, and given this seemingly inherent belief in God on the part of humankind, it is therefore not surprising to hear the anguished cries of: "If there is a God of Love, how can He let this happen?"; "How can there be a God of Love when there is so much misery and suffering in the world?"; "How can it be?", "Why him, her, them?"; "Why did they have to be taken?"; "I don't understand it!" etc., etc..

Very great puzzlement is also evinced at the seemingly unfair and untimely death of "good" people or young children, or in the birth of the disabled. Yet whilst there may not generally be clear understanding of the reasons for such seemingly "hard fate", the very fact that many people ask why "God should allow it" appears to bear out the Enlightenment philosophers belief of a probable knowing within man of the existence of a great and **All-Mighty "Creator"**.

Yet therein lies our conundrum, our non-understanding! We feel great pain and anguish during times of deep sorrow because the ultimate reason **why** is often difficult to understand. Words of solace and condolence are offered but, whilst they are comforting, they may not provide answers. What is then left? An experience that *can* serve to bring people together, but also an event – if deeply traumatic – with the potential to shatter lives and split families apart. And, moreover, can unfortunately also reduce the quality of life of those affected because the nature of the event itself and the ongoing memory of it may not *appear* to offer any *logical* reasons as to why. The resultant legacy may well be the inability to *ever* find reasons or answers, thus resulting in ongoing and unresolved heartache. Yet to be faced with seemingly unfair "blows of fate" should act as the *strongest* impetus to ask the key question: **Why**?

The Enlightenment philosophers encouraged rational enquiry about God by rejecting any mysterious doctrines and maintaining that the existence of God could be arrived at by introspection and human experience. However, it would be unhelpful if we became so absorbed in our enquiry or search that much else that is worthwhile and valuable in life is excluded. Therefore, in the continuation of one's life, one should adjust one's thinking and perhaps one's lifestyle to support the aim of finding that reason why. In order to find such answers, however, there must logically be some rational mechanism whereby this can be achieved.

The premise postulated here is that only *with* the knowledge of The Spiritual Laws of Creation can sense ever be made of our existence and our reason for being. Only a thorough knowledge of those Laws can provide a logical *thought-process mechanism* through which the question of apparently unfair and/or "hard blows of fate" *can* be answered, and thereby offer the potential for a more benign and enlightened global society than is currently the case.

A brief introduction to just two points of "The Law" should suffice to illustrate why there is such an entrenched general refusal by humankind to acknowledge the existence of Spiritual Law – let alone the inviolability of it. The same two points will further demonstrate how beliefs that do not acknowledge The Spiritual Laws effectively prevent basic understanding of the *why* of life's tragedies anyway.

Firstly, it is probably reasonable to assume that most people accept the notion that we possess "free will" i.e., we can, and do, make decisions for ourselves virtually every minute of each day. And that personal decisions via this mechanism should allow us full command over our individual destinies. If this were not so, we would be forced to assume that what happens in our lives is determined by factors outside our control. If such an "arbitrary force" did actually exist, it might perhaps be regarded as a mischievous or even rogue one given that some people seem to suffer more setbacks than might reasonably be expected to occur in a *normal* life.

Secondly, the simple act of making a decision about anything must presuppose an outcome of some kind. Most students of religion, philosophy, or even homespun logic will probably accept the concept that:

"...what one sows one must, or shall, reap".

Certainly for the general Christian community, this Biblical directive is sacrosanct in its perceived truth. If that is so, there must logically be a just and lawful mechanism that produces the outcome or the reaction to every decision made. If it is reasonable to assume the first part of the equation – that there will be an outcome from a decision made – then it is surely equally reasonable to assume the second; that there **will be a return** – without fail! The premise is thus; ultimately it is our own personal decisions that therefore determine all outcomes which subsequently affect us.
Science, in essence, states this process thus:

"For every action there is an equal and opposite reaction."

What happens, however, when these two cornerstones, i.e., the notion of *free will* and *we reap what we sow*, are brought together to try to make sense of tragedy and misfortune? For if each notion is true, and this work unequivocally accepts that truth, then any misfortune – and it is usually only misfortunes and tragedies that produce any kind of soul-searching for answers anyway – must have been set in place somewhere, sometime, **by the reaper**. Therefore, if we consider the heart of the two particular tenets to be absolute, then the **first absolute** would naturally presuppose that the **second one** is also – in terms of a logical and meaningful **connection and outcome**.

However, because the *reasons* for misfortunes are not always *immediately* apparent – whereby the concept and logic of "free will" and its equally logical *connection* of "reaping the effects" is clearly *visible* and thus understandable – *different* kinds of mechanisms are invariably proposed as explanations, or we despair of ever knowing why. The clear contention stated in *this* particular equation is that if both tenets are absolute and sacrosanct as an inviolable Law, then we cannot possibly postulate other reasons which exclude or alter either one to simply fabricate any such connection between our *free-will decision-making ability*, and *reaping what we sow*. And we certainly should not try to make it conveniently fit a religious doctrine or dogma or, indeed, any personal faith/belief mode.

Whilst we therefore possess the inherent freedom to make any kind of decision we may wish to, we must clearly recognise that we are absolutely *not free* to choose to *either accept or reject* the returning consequences! Under the inviolability of this absolute *equation of life*, **consequences must always derive from decisions**! That is the clear and unequivocal reality.

Now, if the two tenets are *not* accepted as being absolute and thus lawfully connected, then searching outside these two sacrosanct positions to try to find an answer might perhaps *seemingly* provide "other" alternatives. However if such an *answer* **denies** the inherently logical and thus lawful connection between a "free-will decision" and "...reaping what one has sown" – i.e., accepting that there must naturally be a consequence from making a decision in the first place – then that particular position naturally refutes the inherent inviolability of any "lawful connection" to begin with. Yet the two inviolable "cornerstones" of this *equation of life* unequivocally state that they clearly *must be absolute*, both in essence and reality.

The inviolability of "inherent justice" naturally contained within The Spiritual Laws ensures that they will *always* provide correct answers. It is an infallible mechanism that 'not only' does **not** compromise the absolute nature of the two "cornerstones" or "pillars"of our illustration, but *positively strengthens* the interlinking of all The Spiritual Laws to provide genuine solutions! Therefore, since the two "cornerstones" **are** absolute and lawfully connected, the clear contention here is that another Law – equally as valid and sacrosanct – must be taken into account if one wishes to understand **all** connections. It is that **other** Law, not generally recognised and accepted, which provides the key. Unfortunately, it is the refusal to accept this factual Law that gives rise to so much confusion and anguish when needing to find answers – for major problems, particularly.

> That crucial "other Law" – **The Law of Rebirth** – is explained later in this Chapter under its own sub-heading: **Rebirth! – Fact or Fiction?**

The concept of reincarnation, whilst not generally accepted by most Western religions or the scientific community, is an absolute belief for hundreds of millions worldwide. Multi-earth lives provide the only truly viable mechanism whereby the two "spiritually-lawful" cornerstones of *free will* and *reaping what one sows* can be **logically** explained – more particularly where an Earth-life does not offer sufficient time for certain categories of "reaping" to occur. It is not for nothing that Jesus stated quite emphatically [Matthew 7:7]: — **"Seek, and You Shall Find."**

He, by virtue of **His Divine Origin**, spoke always from the knowledge of **The Spiritual Laws of Creation**, for they inherently resided within **Him** as a *living part* of **His Divinity**! He was thus clearly able to survey all happenings, both the small and the large, in their complete cycles from cause to effect. Therefore, if any so-called 'answers' are truly so in terms of the true and definitive explanation, *they must inherently-encompass the* 'spiritual aspect' *firstly*.

In contrast to the Spiritual point of view taught by Jesus, a purely medical, scientific, religious, political or sociological explanation for a particular problem can only take in the material effect. Though the end *effect* may be seen or felt in the material, it is, nevertheless, the *result* of a "spiritually-willed" decision made somewhere, sometime by someone individually, or some group collectively. By virtue of a purely material application, earthly Disciplines are therefore **not able** to give a complete overview for, invariably, they are unable to see the actual starting point of such outcomes, irrespective of views to the contrary from within the individual Disciplines. This is not to decry the very great help that we can obviously obtain from Disciplines concerned with empirical paradigms. However, where it is a question of finding the actual source of many of our problems or the answers to life itself, earth-orientated practices are not able to supply this. Only in Spiritual Law and Its Source can we find these ultimate answers!

Despite the superiority of the Spiritual viewpoint over the materialistic one, the whole thrust of our much-vaunted, modern education system virtually denies the existence of anything other than what can be materially seen, heard, felt, or measured. Currently, the scientific and rationalist point of view reigns supreme, but there are other voices questioning the narrow strictures of such points of view. These voices are slowly swelling in volume and some are coming from within the scientific Disciplines too. In essence, the realisation may be slowly dawning that all we have been taught to blindly accept through the education and religious systems may prove to be very different from the actual reality.

We should ask the question: "What is the genesis of this irrational attitude and widespread denial that seeks to withhold from man the knowledge of his true Spiritual self, and therewith his actual origin?" Should this not be the ultimate goal of the various Disciplines rather than the present one of attempting to steer all away from this so-called "irrational and unscientific" view? Is there fear, then, of this unscientific, perhaps politically and even culturally incorrect word – **SPIRITUAL**?

The obvious problem encountered when discussing **The Spiritual** is that the very word itself is generally lumped with whatever ideas humankind may determine it to encompass. Things that originate from, or are connected to, the actual Spiritual Realm, can be deemed to be genuinely Spiritual. And because *only* the *truly* spiritual can *actually* be of **The Spiritual**, what is of that Realm is therefore sacred.

However, because the Realm of the so-called "beyond" is generally deemed as being "all spiritual", anything that is connected with or derived from it is also viewed similarly by some religions and cultures. Far too much is made of purely man-made icons being designated sacred and therefore regarded as spiritual in humankind's estimation. There thus exists the *farcical idea* that everything that man *decides* is sacred must therefore be so and, by extension, also Spiritual and thus Holy.

Nothing could be further from The Truth.

In fact some aspects of various cultures, such as the meanings ascribed to grotesque carved images and certain ancient practices, are so *aspiritual* in both form and connection that it is difficult to even begin to understand how the cultural adherents of those kinds of beliefs could ever declare them to be sacred or spiritual. The Spiritual Laws of Creation offer clear, objective solutions as to how a more open and correct mind-set can free both *cultural emotionalism* and *scientific rigidity* from self-imposed and inculcated beliefs that stubbornly cling to a wrong understanding of this vitally important *life-word* – **SPIRITUAL!**

The greatest teacher humankind has ever had is history, and within its pages may be found the struggle of individuals who have been lone and lonely "voices in the wilderness". Boat-rockers they were, all of them. Possessing the courage to raise their voices in protest against blindness and sometimes sheer stupidity they, the "champions of truth", possessed the clarity of vision or perception to *know* that certain "official" teachings and views were gravely in error. Those same lone, courageous voices were often stilled, silenced, to protect the ego and power base of those in authority who fought to maintain, *at all costs*, the "official version".

In some cases the 'lone voices' were able to convince the "authorities" of the correctness of their beliefs, though often after years of protest. Then, in an absolute farce, the "new knowledge" became the accepted norm; a norm or standard not only *accepted* by the ruling authority, but also *promoted* by it as being correct and therefore suitable for the masses. Do we think that it is any different today? No, we certainly do not, for mankind's collective ego has not yet humbled itself sufficiently to voluntarily recognise the very truth of what we must assert once more; that, historically, the essence of truth has never lain with the masses – only with the few!

A classic example is that of the view of Ptolemy (*ca*.AD 90-168), a Graeco-Egyptian mathematician and geographer who believed that the Earth was the centre of the universe and that the sun and planets revolved around it. In stating this view, he set in place a theory that remained unchallenged for about 1600 years. The probable main reason for such a long acceptance of a wrong belief was that it must have perfectly suited the egocentric interpretation of the Church. No voice was raised against it until 1543 when Copernicus, (1473-1543) a Polish astronomer, found that only with the sun at the centre of the universe could the planetary system work. From that point on the Ptolemaic belief was rejected – at least by the newly emerging sciences.

Unfortunately, this was not a belief shared by the Church and is graphically illustrated in the persecution of Galileo (1564-1642). Galileo, an Italian astronomer and mathematician, agreed with the claim of Copernicus that the sun was the centre of our universe. This "unacceptable view", however, led to his persecution by the Inquisition in 1633. He recanted, but is said to have muttered under his breath: "But it [the Earth] does move."

Another stark example was the debate between Flat-Earth theorists, led by the European Church, and the opposite belief that the Earth was spherical; accepted by scholars in some monasteries. Accepted also by Columbus and other navigators as being the *probable* truth, the latter purely by logical observations of the curved and disappearing horizon. History records that the journey of Columbus forced an immediate change of view within "the establishment". Long before then, however, Greek mathematicians already understood the truth of a spherical Earth.

Teaching "authorities" should learn to accept that the very nature of Truth guarantees that it cannot be muted or suppressed forever. It would be far better for them to keep a completely open mind to *all voices*. The one constant that will determine the *validity* of any definition of **The Spiritual** will be whether or not it accords with the *actual* **Spiritual Laws**, thereby separating the "superficial voices" from the "true ones". The lawful mechanism contained within the Living Laws thus determine which "voices" will ultimately fail and which will stand the test of time. This is the only true measure as these Laws are, themselves, Eternal. And within the life-path parameters given for humankind it is we who must finally acknowledge and accept this fact, since our life, being and sustenance are given only via these Laws.

So to glibly state that mankind is "not meant to understand the ways of The Creator" presupposes the requirement to submit to and accept all suffering in fatalistic ignorance. The Spiritual Laws decree that we actually **are** "masters of our own destiny", even if present events seem to suggest otherwise. It is our refusal to accept the Truth of The Law, *as it actually is,* that is the problem. The above historic examples together with the previously postulated premise that we are masters of our own destiny indicate that no one should be afraid to abandon dogma when it becomes apparent that it is clearly not true. We should especially beware of leaders who knowingly still maintain the old errors out of fear of a collapse of their authority and organisation.

On the relationship between science and religion, the scientific giant, Albert Einstein, observed:

> "Intelligence makes clear to us the interrelation of means and ends. But mere thinking cannot give us a sense of the ultimate and fundamental ends. To make clear these fundamental ends and valuations, and to set them fast in the emotional life of the individual, seems to me precisely the most important function which religion has to perform in the social life of man. And if one asks whence derives the authority of such fundamental ends, since they cannot be stated and justified merely by reason, one can only answer: they come into being *not through demonstration* **but through revelation**, *through the medium of powerful personalities.* One must not attempt to justify them, but rather to sense their nature simply and clearly."

As we state unequivocally throughout this Work, there should be no contradiction between science and religious/spiritual truth, and that science cannot supersede any such truths. Though noting the demarcation between science and religion, Einstein also understood the strong reciprocal relationships and dependencies between the two. He added:

> "Though religion may be that which determines the goal, it has, nevertheless learned from science, in the broadest sense, what means will contribute to the attainment of the goals it has set up. *But science can only be created by those who are thoroughly imbued with the aspiration toward truth and understanding."*

Einstein *summarises* his view of the science/religion relationship thus:

> *"Science without religion is lame, religion without science is blind."*

(Ideas and Opinions, p 42-3. All emphases mine.)

3.1   The Nature of the Spiritual Principles

"The Laws of Creation derive their eternal validity from the fact of God's Perfection.
On account of God's Perfection, His Will is therefore perfect. Consequently, The
Laws manifesting This Will are also necessarily perfect. They cannot be improved
upon, and they remain absolutely unchangeable."

(Building Future Societies, p.23.
Stephen Lampe.)

This inviolable premise logically stipulates that God cannot act in an arbitrary manner and
"do anything He wants". It may certainly be convenient to offer that kind of explanation to a
difficult religious question thereby seeming to temporarily get rid of the problem, but it still,
nonetheless, awaits a *correct* answer.

For if God is able to do "anything He wants" by virtue of the fact that He Is God, ***where
then lies His Perfection***? Since it **must** logically follow that if He Is Perfect and His Laws
are Perfect and therefore *unchangeable*, then any belief that states otherwise *automatically* casts
doubt on this accepted belief in **"A Perfect God"**. Quite simply, any attempt to *change* a
Perfect Law naturally *implies* that The Law *could not have been* perfect in the first instance –
if it then *needed* to be changed.

It is thus impossible to impute imperfection to A Perfect God!

Therefore the recognition of The Laws of Creation, *as they actually are in their inviolability*,
will finally return to **God** the **Perfection** that **Is His**.

Two thousand years ago Jesus, arguably the greatest, most wonderful "boat rocker" of all,
gave stern warning to the, then, leaders of the Church. The fact that He did not support
their practices is clearly apparent by virtue of His condemnation of them. The same lawful
condemnation applies today to all teachings and Disciplines which attempt to suppress the
Truth. From Matthew, 23:13. Fenton:

"Woe to you, play-acting professors and Pharisees! because you lock up the Kingdom of Heaven in the face of mankind; while you yourselves neither enter, nor allow
those arriving to go in."

In accordance with that clear message, The Spiritual Laws or principles that guide and
determine the course of everything throughout Creation must logically include the destiny of
man on Earth. These Laws are Eternal. Everything in Creation, including humankind, came
into being through the operation of them, and our continued existence here depends on them
also. The originator of these Laws is **"God, The Creator"**. Only what is inherent in His Laws
of Creation can ever come to full bloom and be sustained in Creation. By extension, all else i.e.,
activities not supported by those Laws, ***must inevitably fail***.

Even though The Spiritual Laws allowed us the gift of conscious life, they have not always
been clearly recognised. Throughout man's long and convoluted history, great and wise spiritual
teachers arose at varying intervals to call attention to them, Teachers such as Krishna, Zoroaster,
Lao-Tse, Moses and the Prophets, Buddha, Mohammed – and Jesus. At best, their Teachings
were sometimes not understood or sometimes misinterpreted. At worst, they were *knowingly*
distorted.

Because The Laws *were* insufficiently understood, misinterpreted, taken out of context or
knowingly distorted, it was not possible to consistently apply them beneficially. The origin of
the present dangerous rise of religious fundamentalism can probably be traced to this problem

of narrow, non-understanding. This unfortunate development, among many other increasing problems now facing us, may be seen as a direct correlation between *the immutability of The Spiritual Laws* and *our refusal to heed them*. The solutions to *all* our problems lie *solely* in a voluntary adjustment to them in a conscious, correct and consistent way.

Simply put, we have no choice but to understand and apply The Spiritual Laws to every facet of human life and not believe we can formulate better principles that are as effective. For it would be foolish to imagine that human beings can improve on The Will of The Creator, as we ourselves are only products of His Laws. Chaos and confusion will always be the result of attempting to deviate from them. No one can evade or change them, and The Laws apply equally to all in the same measure. To rich and poor, the powerful and the weak, the clever and the stupid, to kings and slaves. The effects are the same on those who know The Law as on those who do not, and ignorance of them does not keep their effects at bay!

If man's laws are compared with Spiritual Law we find that earthly laws differ from society to society whereas The Laws of Creation remain the same everywhere and are Eternal. Our laws are constantly in a state of review and can even be changed by public opinion or dictatorial decree. So what may have been perfectly legal yesterday may not be so today. By contrast, Spiritual Law is immutable and unchangeable, and will forever remain so.

The cost, complexity and duration of trials in earthly law courts indicate quite conclusively that our laws are not simple to understand and require lawyers who have needed to spend years of study to become conversant with them. Even then, however, there can be much disagreement over individual points of law. By comparison, The Laws of Creation are clear, concise and simple. Moreover, they are few in number, easily understandable, and do not require years of laborious study. They are alluded to in all the major religions and philosophies of the world's peoples. The chambers of Lawyers and Judges will contain row upon row of books of laws and statutes. The Eternal Laws, however, can be contained in just *one publication*.

The Eternal Laws have, as their infallible foundation, Justice, Love and Purity, and are therefore perfect in the dispensation of justice. By virtue of our present level of spiritual *immaturity* we, on the other hand, do not have such a benchmark. Despite the fact that we have many laws, we do not always see justice done. So-called "legal technicalities" permit clever lawyers to exploit the present "justice system" to set free people who have *actually* committed crimes. By contrast no one escapes The Spiritual Laws. Their infallible, automatic outworking ensures that Justice and Love are meted out in perfect balance at all times, even though not always immediately, or even apparently so. But meted out they always are!

The incorruptible nature of The Eternal Laws ensures that they will reign supreme. This means that in the determination of innocence or guilt in an earthly court of law, man's laws do not always offer protection or absolution should an innocent person be wrongly condemned and sentenced. The responsibility for that miscarriage of justice, however, will fall back on all those who contributed to it – as it must in all things. Attempting to shelter behind a veil of "fulfilling one's duty" in the ostensible application of justice via the Nation's laws matters not at all. We are all irrevocably tied to the consequences of our decisions, and a wrong conviction will eventually bring the inevitable reciprocal effect.

Judges and juries, then, have a particularly difficult task given the spiritually unhealthy state of our secular laws. Passing judgement according to such laws may satisfy the dictates of earthly society but, if the judgement is a transgression against The Laws of Creation, the judges are bound to reap the reciprocal effect of *their* spiritually-wrong decisions. For that reason, it should be in the interests of the judiciary to actively concern themselves with the knowledge of the only true Laws.

What should be seriously understood is the fact that the material worlds are *presently* in transition between one phase and another. Literally everything is in transition and upheaval, man and nature. Consequently man is being strongly compelled to heed these Laws under the increasing spiritual pressure currently being applied to all things. The effect of this pressure can be seen in the accelerating breakdown of societies and the increasing problems globally. In short, man's time of formulating his own policies is at an end. We will now be forced to adjust to The Laws of Creation, or perish. This increasing pressure, moreover, strengthens both the good and the bad.

Thus **the good** – *that which adjusts itself to The Laws* – **will prosper**. And **the bad or wrong** – *that which opposes The Laws* – **will collapse**. In this simple equation resides an infallible standard by which to measure events around us and to choose accordingly.

The Spiritual Laws of Creation, therefore, are relatively few in number. They are:

- **The Law of Movement**
- **The Law of Reciprocal Action**
- **The Law of Attraction of Similar Species**
- **The Law of Spiritual Gravity**
- **The Law of Balance**
- **The Law of Rebirth**
- **Grace: – A Gift of Divine Love**

We have softened their impact somewhat – in word form only, however – by also stating them in more recognised terms:

- **Movement: = Life**
- **Decisions Produce consequences**
- **Like Attracts Like**
- **Gravity: – Its "Spiritual" Dynamic**
- **Balance in Life: – A Vital Necessity**
- **Rebirth! – Fact or Fiction?**

The living dynamic of the above principles is such that their *inviolable effects* are *felt* as Laws whenever we oppose them. They *cease* to be Laws, and therefore become *helps*, when we abide by them. So by examining each of The Laws named, it will be shown that everything in Creation is interlinked and interdependent.

Note:

A brief explanation is also offered on the vital feature of **Grace**. It is an aspect lawfully linked with the perfect intermeshing of **The Eternal Laws**, commensurate with those decisions which *strive for*, or are *directed toward*, spiritual ascent.

How, then, should **The Spiritual Laws** be described? By examining philosophical, scientific, religious and spiritual works, clear and consistent reference to them can be found. Therefore they could be termed "Universal". Everyday observations of the natural world show this universality of The Laws in their working reality.

The philosopher Heraclitus (c.540-480 BC) of Ephesus in Asia Minor believed that this "universal reason" or "universal law" is something common to all and which guides not only every person but also everything that happens in nature. Yet he observed that instead of following this "higher guidance", most people lived by their individual beliefs. This "something", which was the source of everything, he called God or *logos* – meaning reason.

3.2   The Law of Movement!

"Movement = Life."

Heraclitus also postulated a new concept; that of 'flux' or 'continuous change'. He observed that everything 'flowed'; everything is in continual movement and that nothing stands still. He expressed this concept of constant change by saying that "...you cannot step twice into the same river". The river changes because "...fresh waters are ever [streaming] in upon you". Heraclitus thought that this concept of 'continuous change' "...must apply not only to rivers but to all things, including the soul of man". Rivers and men exhibit the fascinating fact of becoming different "...and yet remaining the same". We return to the 'same' river although fresh waters have [entered it], "...and the man is still the same person as the boy". (Philosophy History and Problems. Third Edition p 12-13.) Therefore, when we step into a river for the second time, neither we nor the river are the same.

Everything, literally everything, is in constant motion. Movement is the one activity that ensures the maintenance of life in all things. Without movement everything would become sluggish and eventually come to a complete standstill, a situation akin to death and disintegration. Therefore motion can be stated to be a most necessary principle throughout Creation. The higher and lighter the Plane of Creation, the faster the motion. Conversely, therefore, the further away from The Source of Life, as for example in the Material Planes, the more sluggish the motion. As "movement" is thus a vital principle, all other laws can be said to operate within the parameters of this most important Law. However, the movement must be of the *right* kind and in harmony with all else if it is to bring benefit.

Could we ever imagine life in the Universe and on Earth without the *elemental* activity of the Forces of Nature bringing *movement*? We observe the daily rotation of the Earth to give the very necessary 'contrast' of day and night for both diurnal and nocturnal activities of all plants and creatures in the circadian rhythm of 24 hour periodicity required for those processes. The Earth rotates around the sun to provide the four seasons. These in turn produce the different weather patterns needed for planting and harvesting. The motion of the winds ensures freshness and change where there might otherwise be staleness.

Consider the moon's rotation around the Earth, offering its different phases and bringing the rise and fall of the tides. Consider, also, the great ocean currents that constantly mix the waters of our "blue planet", and the movement of the continents over the liquid core of the Earth in plate tectonics, instrumental in the formation of new lands. Constant movement equals constant renewal. Further out into the incomprehensible vastness of the observable universe, galaxies of immense size wheel and rotate billions of suns to the same primordial rhythm.

Science has long discovered that individual cells, molecules and atoms are "alive" with the constant movement of sub-particles, with each fitting perfectly into its ordained place to become part of the whole. And even in the microscopic sub-atomic world where the behaviour of quarks and neutrinos appear to circumvent all the known *scientific* laws they still, nevertheless, follow the dictates of Universal Law. It is our non-understanding of those laws that force us to declare our lack of knowledge at such behaviour. The rocks of the Earth, even though appearing to be solid, dense and lifeless, are also awhirl with active movement. A crystal-clear glass of clean water gives no hint of the motion of electrons, protons and neutrons in the structure and composition of either the glass or the water. Animal and human bodies have the same basic activity in their molecular structure also, whether living and breathing, or dead and decomposing.

The physical body, with which we are all familiar, signals to us the need for constant movement in order to remain healthy. In breathing we quite automatically accept the rise and fall of the chest as the lungs inhale and exhale. The heart pumps blood in necessary circulation throughout the body. Exercise keeps the body healthy and strong, inactivity weakens it. The demands of the toilet call us to the process of the elimination of body wastes at various times during the day. Even in supposedly restful sleep there is still the need for the body to change its position more often than we might be aware of during the sleep state. Everything must obey The Law of Movement if it is to remain healthy and not stagnate.

Rivers and streams remain fresh and oxygenated through movement. The world's great river systems yearly transport millions of tons of silt to form large, fertile deltas at their mouths. In man-made lakes where dams block rivers to the point where the amount of draw-off prevents natural spillage, the horizontal layers of the impounded bodies of water can still have displacing-movement between them, even to the point of complete inversion of whole lakes.

In the world of birds and fishes, lack of the right kind of necessary movement has resulted in the loss of certain abilities that some once possessed. For example, there are fish that are no longer able to withstand the currents and must remain near the bottom. Certain birds in various parts of the world have lost the ability to 'become airborne' through not having used their wings over a long period of time. These examples showing the principle of adaptation, with which biological scientists are familiar, are a consequence of The Law of Movement.

Up to this point we have only examined the physical effect of this Law. In the first instance, however, it is a Spiritual Law. Therefore, in the case of the physical body, each individual movement must first be "willed" by the spirit, because the spirit is the *animating* force, "the power pack", within each of us. This *signal* between spirit and body happens so quickly as to be virtually simultaneous and thus mostly imperceptible in its time-lapse aspect.

The activity of the natural world demands that every creature and plant must strive to maintain its place or perish. Spiritual activity must produce the same, and more, if there is to be growth and ascent. Therefore, effort must be expended if we wish to achieve anything of lasting value. We cannot sit back and expect wonderful things to just happen. Whether applied to the physical, mental or spiritual, laziness in any one area is a transgression against this Eternal Law. Moreover, the different kinds of activities – *spiritual, intellectual* and *physical* – must always be kept in proper balance. Without spiritual activity as a necessary counterpoise, physical and intellectual expenditure of effort will ultimately be worthless. We can extrapolate from this that a genuinely spiritual goal will always have furthering values that will never change and, by definition, be far-reaching and beneficial.

Present trends allow people to eagerly anticipate retirement after a lifetime of work. The thought of the remaining years of life spent in blissful inactivity appeals to many. Yet this offends against The Law too. Of course the elderly could not be expected to maintain the same level of activity that a much younger person might. Nevertheless, for the older body to maintain reasonable health, movement of the right kind is still necessary. Fortunately, current directions now see more and more of the elderly pursuing this beneficial course. The "acceptance of change" that time and development naturally bring under The Law of Movement permits one phase of life to lead into the next, for movement is designed to bring about *further* development.

Conversely, "workaholics", some professional sports people, along with others engaged in constant frenetic activity, actually transgress this Law and will thus eventually harm themselves. A sense of balance should be maintained in all that we do by adjusting our pace to a natural rhythm which is connected to The Law of Movement. Perhaps the latter day phrase: "Everything in moderation", is a subconscious reaction to the increasingly unnatural pace of modern society.

In heeding The Law of Movement, we also need to obey The Law of Balance as well, for this Law is also a consequence of motion.

History's testament to the rise and fall of some of the great civilisations provides excellent examples of what occurs if the correct "Spiritual" movement is not maintained. The rise to greatness can show the right kind of movement, whilst the disintegration process invariably indicates the opposite. The Law of Movement decrees that no one person, group or Nation can simply stop and rest on past or even present glories. What has been achieved, if spiritually worthwhile, must be maintained, or stagnation, retrogression and disintegration will quickly follow. In the same way, persons who have been publicly honoured by society should be required to maintain that position of honour.

The propensity of many to attempt to live in the past offends against The Law of Movement also. The current strong cultural trend in some ethnic communities to promote tribal links and/or a return to tribalism clearly transgresses The Law of Movement in both the spiritual and material sense. The spiritual power and pressure inherent in this Law decrees that the tribal phase for any race is exactly that – just a phase. Consequently, any beneficial outworking contained within the power of The Law of Movement for a people will be greatest when and where *correct movement* is undertaken. For certain ethnic groups, that would translate into leaving tribalism behind and moving toward becoming one Nation, one people.

This does not mean that we should not assess history, or try to correct past wrongs. The Laws, however, require us, indeed command us, to *live* in the *present*. They further command us to strongly heed The Law of Movement – in the Spiritual sense particularly – if there is not to be stagnation and retrogression.

Thus, The Law of Movement decrees that absolutely nothing can ever stand still. Should a point of stagnation be reached, a new impetus must be developed to prevent the possibility of retrogression. Any new idea, though, should have, as its foundation, the application of Spiritual Law so that only upward movement is generated. For this Law will drive either upwards or downwards equally powerfully, but exactly in accordance with the kind of decision taken.

3.3   The Law of Reciprocal Action!

"Decisions Produce Consequences"

"Do not err; God cannot be deluded: for what a man *sows*, **that** he will also **reap**."
"If he sows for his *sensuality*, he will reap **perdition**; but sowing for *the Spirit*, from *the Spirit*, he will reap **eternal life**."

(Galatians 6:7-8, Fenton.)

The key word in the above Scriptures is **will**. It is not a word such as *perhaps*, for example, or *might*, or *maybe*, or *possibly*. No, the texts are quite unequivocal. They clearly state that we **will** reap what we sow! Other Bibles use the word "shall" in this context, but the meaning is obviously still the same.

In eastern religions the word "karma" is generally used to describe the very same effect/outcome. This particular word, however, unfortunately produces negative reactions in many Christians. Yet the very word perfectly represents the exact Law that Its Bringer, Jesus, taught. Thus:

"*A knowledge of the* **iron law of karma** *encourages the earnest seeker to find the way of final escape from its bonds.*"

(Autobiography of a Yogi. p563, Paramahansa Yogananda.
Emphases mine.)

3.3.1   Faith Versus Works

The theological argument of *faith* versus *works* can best be clarified using this "iron Law" as a guide. Faith is the primary aspect of a belief which strongly accepts that a particular thing is so and which therefore stems from a confident belief in the truth, value or trustworthiness of it. It is a belief, moreover, which does not rest on logical proof or material evidence. Faith, therefore, can perhaps be stated to be an implicit belief and trust in God and in the doctrines expressed in the Scriptures or other sacred works. Faith, however, even though a noble virtue, is nevertheless amorphous in its nature for its *actual* essence cannot be seen or touched. The New Testament documents many cases where faith, alone, produced miraculous outcomes around the presence of Jesus. The woman who believed that all she had to do was touch His robes to be healed, and the ones who stated that He had only to "...say the Word" and those for whom they sought healing *would* be healed. His acknowledgement: "Your faith has saved/healed you."

The story of the Captain who implored Jesus to heal his son whom he had left sick and dying at his home demonstrates **both** the faith paradigm **and** sure conviction. Believing implicitly that just The Word of The Son of God would heal his son brought forth a "surprised response" from Jesus. Matthew [8:10-11] records that He said to His followers:

> "Indeed, I tell you, I have never found such faith as this in Israel."

Faith in its sum and substance can therefore provide, and be, a powerful anchorage for one's religious beliefs, but it probably cannot be said to *be,* or *hold,* absolute conviction in the thing believed in. Faith, however, *should precede* **conviction**; that element of *sure and certain knowing* commonly derived from, but no longer *constrained by*, the faith paradigm itself.

Historically, great and wonderful works have been produced from and by faith, and the outworking of the great Law of **Sowing and Reaping** will automatically bring the appropriate "return effect" to the instigators and builders of those works. So remarkable blessings can derive from good works produced by faith alone.

If works are undertaken from **conviction**, however, – clearly accepting that that very word presupposes an *absoluteness of knowing about that which has wrought the conviction in the first place* – then the volition, the instigation and the building of the work/s proceeds with the concomitant sureness of knowing *exactly why* such a project is undertaken. Therefore such labour undertaken by either an individual or a group works *consciously* within the actual parameters of The Laws and their reciprocal outworking. Works produced through conviction, therefore, inherently carry within them a much stronger connection to the source of that particular certainty. Works produced by faith cannot inherently do so.

Faith possesses the *lesser value* of simply *believing it knows.*

Conviction, however, possesses *the sureness of knowing.*

In terms of the outworking of The Law of Reciprocal Action, then, the absolute perfection of The Spiritual Laws will return the exact reciprocal effect to both kinds of "builders" – whether through *faith* or *conviction.* In the final analysis, though, the faith/belief paradigm, which many in the Christian world promote as the only standard necessary for spiritual ascent, clashes diametrically with that which Jesus clearly stated:

> **"By their *works* you shall know them."**

When told by His Disciples – whilst preaching in a synagogue – that His Mother and brothers were waiting outside for Him [emphases mine], Jesus declared:

"Who is My mother, who is My brother? They are those who *carry out the Will of the Father*!"

The lament of Jesus over the little faith expressed by those of the race who were called to **support and follow Him** ring down through the centuries as an indictment on many today i.e., **"O ye of little faith."** Such paucity of faith during his life contrasted hugely with His great joy upon finding firm and unshakeable faith in He and His Mission from people not of that chosen race, such as the Roman Centurion.

How, then, should one carry out such **works**; through **faith**, or through **conviction**? Whose teachings should the well-meaning Christian follow? Present-day mainstream Church and Bible interpretation of Paul's ministry and philosophy has evidently and rather strangely concluded that Paul the Apostle taught that *faith, alone*, was sufficient. Jesus, on the other hand, *demanded* works. His admonition to "Take up the cross and follow Me" simply means that any believer in Him must *live The Laws*, and not simply pay lip service to them; thus *work*.

> **"I come not to overthrow the laws but to fulfil them."** – and – **"Go thou and do likewise."** – – (i.e., 'By My [**His**] example'.)

Did Paul live by 'faith, alone', or did he live by conviction? His amazing ministry bears unequivocal testimony to the fact that his **works** far transcended simple faith, for they were clearly imbued with the absolute **conviction** that can only derive from truly **knowing**.

The 'Christianised' 'Pauline philosophy' of 'faith, alone' – *which terribly distorts and denigrates Paul's great work* – now permeates a very large part of Christendom. It has unfortunately bequeathed to millions of Christians worldwide a spiritually dangerous mind-set that offers 'believers' little more than the 'broad easy path' Jesus warned against. To simply opt for faith, alone, without genuine works – even if only works to at least back up the faith aspect – fatally inculcates an acceptance that there is 'no need to do more'. Unfortunately, such an attitude basically derives from the unsound belief of many Christians that "He died for us", "for *our* sins". In our view this particular mind-set is an extrapolative excrescence basically formulated by Christian distortion of its so-called 'Pauline philosophy'.

There is obviously no doubt that Jesus died *because* of us! But the unshakeable belief of many that He died "for us" being sufficient to secure "a place in heaven" for 'them', logically ensures that the perfect and inviolable outworking of The Law of Sowing and Reaping cannot possibly extend its Grace and Blessings to such believers – **if** – it *is* **works that are demanded by Jesus, and thus by The Divine Laws!**
Consequently it would seem to be a very intelligent thing to choose to heed the *admonitions* of Jesus over Christendom's distorted 'Pauline philosophy'.

The necessary transition from **Faith to Conviction** – from **Faith to Works** – can only thus derive from, firstly; the *recognition* of **The Spiritual Laws of Creation** and, secondly; their *serious application* in one's life.

Now, since all of The Spiritual Laws are designated as Natural Laws – which outworking and fulfilment we observe and experience in the totality of our lives each day – it is vital to understand that the *infallible mechanism* for that outworking is actually the *inviolable perfection of **The Laws** themselves*. They are Laws of which the validity, authority, perfection, and therefore absolute inviolability, derive from The Divine Perfection of The Creator Himself. And are thus Laws that, without imperfection or deviation, return to us every nuance of every decision we make.

And because we sought conscious life and petitioned The Creator for it, The Spiritual Laws of Life, woven into the fabric of His Creation, are thus the Rules *by which we must live*.

Through petitioning for conscious life, we are forever *irrevocably bound* to the *living reality* that the gift of free will *automatically* imbued us with the *personal responsibility* to exercise that gift correctly by heeding **His Laws**, *and living accordingly*. A key Law by which the effect of our free-will inheritance is most clearly revealed and experienced is **The Law of Reciprocal Action**.

A prime example of the damage that can be wrought through transgressing this particular Law can be clearly noted in the relatively recent episode of "mad cow disease" in Britain. Short-cut economic practices in British agriculture resulted in the concomitant emergence of a human equivalent of the disease through the consumption of contaminated meat and meat products from infected animals. This resulted in the terrible slaughter of many thousands of infected beasts.

The Laws of Creation ordain that herbivores such as cows and beef cattle should not consume food derived from their own kind. Meat and meat products are the ordained natural food of carnivores, and the farming industry cannot arbitrarily *force* such a radical change in the diet of captive animals without expecting severe consequences. That shameful event produced a hard, "lawful" lesson for agricultural "science".

In the first decade of the 21st century, alarm bells sounded over the collapse of millions of bee hives globally. To the year 2011, hive losses in America had reached 50 percent, and Europe 40 percent. Quite obviously, this disastrous trend threatens a large and vital part of global food production. Many theories and reasons have been put forward for such a drastic collapse. One culprit is certainly the so-called 'modern' corporate farming method of single-crop plantings covering literally thousands of acres and the associated pesticide/herbicide use/overuse on those areas.

Pollination of such large areas of single-crop cultivation, particularly in the U.S., mean that there is not sufficient food there for the bees themselves. So, not only are the weakened bees more susceptible to poisoning by spray residue, but the current method of trucking thousands of hives thousands of miles every year to pollinate crops stresses the colonies, thus threatening more hive collapses. Recommendations from *real* bee experts for these *solely* profit-driven companies to plough up small pockets of ground in those *monoculture deserts* and plant wildflowers to feed those very necessary 'workers' have thus far largely fallen on deaf ears. The corporate ethos reigns supreme here too – so far!

The chemical companies claim their products are safe, of course. China, however, has openly acknowledged that in one fruit-growing *region*, continual pesticide use killed *all* the bees in that area. Consequently, pollination of the whole fruit crop must now be done by hand, a method which is acknowledged to be unsustainable in the long term.

Another foolish corporate idea – artificial insemination of queen bees in the lab using sperm from a *single* drone contributor – means that the necessary and natural *diversity* that would ordinarily occur when queen bees are mated by many drones during the nuptial flight, is denied those "corporate lab queens". The predatory 'viroa' mite currently infecting hives globally is proving difficult to eradicate. In many cases now, the mite has actually become resistant to the pesticides designed to kill them.

When will we finally learn the most valuable life-lesson necessary for our *physical* well-being here on Earth? That irrespective of all so-called 'advances' in science, Mother Nature's way is, and always will be, the best way!

Perhaps the 'hard lesson' in 'herbivore cannibalism' will manifest in a globally devastating way with the discovery and great concern about 'prions', that strange and potentially lethal 'protein agent' now perhaps implicated in the "brain-eating" diseases, CJD, BSE, sheep scrapie and 'kuru' (from New Guinea). Over the past few decades, American and Australian scientists observing and researching these diseases have noted the striking similarities between them.

At the same time, they have also noted the increasing incidences of variants of the disease, particularly among the young. It may be that 'prions' are similarly implicated in the E. coli bacterial illness responsible for large outbreaks of deadly food-poisoning overseas.

And the 'hard lesson' over bee colony collapse? If it continues, then the outcome is obvious – global starvation. Science notates the essence of **The Law of Reciprocal Action** thus: The book of Job (34:11), in succinct truth about this particular Law, perfectly states the consequential reality of such foolish "science" in just six gloriously blunt words.

"But man's actions return on himself."

Science, we know, notates the essence of this very Law thus:

"For every action, there is an equal and opposite reaction."

However, what is probably not accepted or even known is that there is not just simply an "*equal,* opposite reaction", but a reaction that is always "lawfully imbued" with *greater power **in the "return"***. It is thus very much more than might be expected to result from the originating decision.

In the case of our primary example of the moment, the possibility that "mad cow disease" may have crossed the species barrier to infect humans, should be regarded as unequivocal proof that **The Spiritual Laws**, which ultimately manifest as *physical* Laws, cannot be transgressed without **serious** consequences. The full potential horror of "mad cow disease" may still be a little way off as the great uncertainty is whether or not there may be a large pool of infected people quietly moving through an unknown incubation period.

According to research published in the British Medical Journal around September 20th 2002, more than 7000 Britons could face an increased risk of contracting the human form of mad cow disease. In this example alone we can clearly note that The Law of Reciprocal Action, as with all these Laws, necessarily supports every other Law as a part of all processes and outcomes.

But even with such obvious warning signs now clearly present, science, in its dangerously-incorrect mind-set that it can change the lawful processes of natural development against the Ordination of The Creator, are slowly taking this aberrant experimentation to what must be recognised and understood as being levels of actual insanity.

The position adopted by this particular branch of science states that by inserting human genes into cows, milk will be produced that will ostensibly heal various kinds of diseases in human beings. Such a misguided view, however, fails to even *begin to understand* that if we desire better outcomes in *all areas* of life – *including health* – then we must heed the very Laws of Life. That is how we gift to ourselves optimum health.

Perhaps the greater danger, however, lies in the insidious nature of the seductive, emotional propaganda that is used to sell the whole idea. That emotionalism ultimately feeds on the fear of millions of the sick globally whom GE science claims could be saved from so-called premature death if these "life-saving" techniques were permitted. The other beguiling aspect lies in the fact that not only are many political "leaders" hell-bent on supporting this branch of "science", but even within indigenous communities of the world there are those who have been seduced by this new and dangerous direction.

An interesting paradox arises here. The sophisticated technology of this particular branch of western scientific thinking – which regards the cow as solely a factory unit for the production of by-products to pamper people who, for the most part, have refused to live *correctly-healthily* anyway – have absolutely no idea of *either* The Laws which govern all science, which *ultimately constrains all wrong science* anyway, or of the *life-force* present in all animals. In striking contrast to that position, many millions in India view cows in a totally different light. Even though wrongly revering them as sacred, they nevertheless understand that their value lies in the animal just as it is *in its natural state* – as a giver of milk as food unadulterated by defective science. At least, that is the general position at this time.

The one note of sanity in the West thankfully lies in the swelling volume of people and groups utterly and implacably opposed to any such aberrant deviation away from the complete naturalness of the Perfection of The Laws of GOD, the earthly expression of which we may note in The Laws of Nature. Or, to use a better understood term, the "Natural Laws"! And no earthly science can ever oppose them with arrogant impunity. Of course, there is always a period of time for such experimentation to run its particular course, for 'free will' is never taken from us.

If the world's humanity were to truly spiritually awaken, then implacable opposition to all GE technology would be understood to be spiritually, and thus *scientifically*, correct. It would not be regarded as some kind of aberrant "green-fringe fanaticism" as it presently is. For we already have, among other disturbing incidents, the lessons of lower yields for GE crops, and the increasing spread of GE contamination away from original release points.

Gary Goldberg, when CEO of the American Corn Growers Association (ACGA), spoke about the harm GE technology has caused US farmers:

> **"This is a case of if we knew then what we know now, American farmers would not have been so easily convinced that GE crops were the way to go.** Our land has become contaminated with GE pollution that we cannot control or remove from our environment. Conventional farms are being contaminated, and we have no choice of GE or non-GE crops. **None of the promises have come true and it is time for farmers to understand that the promises that have been made and will continue to be made will not come true either.** We are losing export markets... Those markets can be filled by [other] farmers..."

> (Physicians and Scientists for Responsible Genetics.
> Parentheses and emphases mine.)

But even facts such as those outlined here are still not yet sufficient to convince the proponents of this dangerously-wrong foolishness – the scientists, the politicians and all others who subscribe to it – that any kind of experimentation with the actual genome of humans and animals to try to bring about a genetic modification or mutation will be far more devastating than just simple plant modification.

For whilst each species of the plant kingdom has its own specific genetic code, which gives it its particular perfection of function and form, the plants themselves do not possess the same *kind of life force* that humans and animals have. And it is that *specific kind of inner animation* that has driven the development of humans and given the many and varied species of animals their unique place in the world. Without any input from human "science", the evolution and development of all life forms has proceeded in accordance with a plan that permits the absolute perfection of each. It is a plan that GE earth-sciences could not even *begin* to emulate, yet arrogantly believes it can improve upon.

Such a serious transgression is not at all difficult to even prophesy against, for that will forever and always be the outcome of working against The Laws of Life in any case. The final outcome will therefore reveal itself in the reciprocal effect/s that each group – the supporters and the opposers – will one day subsequently receive. That, we can be sure, will be a "devastating return" for one side; that of its supporters.

The same scenario will very probably apply to the proponents of the 21st century's scientific 'darling' – **nano-technology**. Touted to improve the lot of humankind in many diverse areas, it holds the potential to make billions of dollars for certain global Corporations and their shareholders. Without any consultation from global consumers – and seemingly no opposition from Governments anywhere – nano-particles are now well-established in many products in some Western countries, even in their baby foods.

Even though ostensibly promoting better human health from oral hygiene to more effective medicines to prolonging life, and even to producing better and safer fuels etc.; very little thought was given to the detrimental effects that any new technology will inherently possess, by the scientists who developed the technology. Not just the development of course, but also the means to deliver it to we of the global masses. **Why not?** Because, through their research scientists, *nano-technology* is going to make a lot of money for some global Corporates and their financial backers.

Since the god-Corporate and money still reign supreme in the world at this time, concerns raised by opposing scientists about the long-term effects that *nano-particles* may have on the wider natural environment are ignored. The very fact that the inclusion of many varied kinds of 'particles' will rapidly increase in the food and drink industry, in clothing manufacturing, in the hair care and beauty products industries etc.; means that in their *uncountable billions*, they will be defecated from humans obviously – and probably from pet and farm animals too – rinsed out of hair, washed out of clothing, and all of it ending up in the soils, rivers and oceans of the world. And, quite logically, almost certainly taken up by the plants, animals and fishes of the total food chain.

Nano-technology: One more human technology that arrogantly believes it can *improve* upon the most effective developmental-process system ever devised – that of "**Mother Nature**". And one that surely believes [otherwise they would not do it] that there could not *possibly* be any detrimental effects from such *clever thinking*. The **"Error of Scientism!"** **"What we sow, we reap!"**

At a more 'everyday' level in the operation of this Law, its effect in the natural world will clearly show even the youngest gardener that if he wishes to *harvest* corn, he must *plant* corn, and if he wants to grow beans, he must plant beans. What would be the result if the "rules" were inconsistent and we were always uncertain as to what the sown seed would produce? Total confusion. And there is no confusion in The Spiritual Laws of Creation. Therefore, as it reveals its absolute certainty in the garden, so can the same certainty be observed in all other kinds of "sowing".

Closely connected with this fact should be the realisation that we therefore do not necessarily *"reap in the same season that we sow"*. Thus, whilst the time difference between sowing and reaping, or cause and effect, usually has set periods between the sowing and harvesting of seed for earthly food crops, no such set time-period can be determined for the sowing and harvesting of "Spiritual" seed. The Spiritual Laws alone determine the precise time of such "returns".

Within the various races and religions of the world, moreover, these natural Laws take no account of an individual's colour or belief. Rice sown by a white, brown or black man will produce exactly the same as for a yellow man. In the same way, wheat sown by a Jew, a Christian, a Buddhist, a Moslem, a Hindu, a Pagan, or an Atheist, will return only wheat at harvest time. As previously stated, this earthly effect well-reveals the fact that this Law, along with all the other Spiritual Laws, grants no special bias or favour to any particular race or religion. Neither should they be expected to do so.

The perfection of such Laws absolutely guarantees that they cannot possibly do anything other than dispense Perfect Justice to all men. Thus, if an Atheist or a Pagan sows goodness, they are lawfully bound to receive goodness; as will a Christian Bishop, a Hindu Monk, a Moslem Imam, or a Native Shaman. Therefore, it is not necessarily a man's belief or religion that determines whether he will *ascend* or not, it is *how he is in his inner being*. It is the

"Spiritual volition" of his inner nature toward all that surrounds him, both the seen and unseen, that greatly determines the outcome.

Spiritually, then, it would be wrong to think that membership of a particular religion or sect would guarantee "good returns" or *reaping* – or even salvation. The purpose of all religion should be to help to correctly interpret The Will of God as expressed in The Laws of Creation, thus showing us how we are to carry out His Will. If it can do that, then it fulfils its place, for religions should be recognised as means to an end and not ends in their own right. As previously noted, the dangerous rise of religious fundamentalism illustrates too narrow an interpretation of just "earthly religious law".

Now, since the current premise under the particular Law being discussed here is exactly that of "reaping what one has sown", but from the spiritual viewpoint overall, it is necessary to have a mechanism whereby this "Spiritual" aspect also produces "physical reaping". Anecdotal evidence from American medical research has shown that concentrated thoughts directed to a sick patient can directly impact upon the healing process of that patient. Thus what spiritual and even philosophical thinking has proclaimed for a very long time now, actually happens. In simple terms, good thoughts directed to a patient can hasten the healing process whilst bad thoughts can lengthen it.

The best-seller, "Sophie's World", offers a light-hearted insight regarding this quandary. From page 193:

> A Russian astronaut and a Russian brain surgeon were once discussing religion. The brain surgeon was a Christian but the astronaut was not. The astronaut said: "I've been out in space many times but I've never seen God or angels." And the brain surgeon said: "And I've operated on many clever brains but I've never seen a single thought."

Of course, neither view can conclusively prove that one or the other exists materially. And that is as it should be for neither are material in form. Nevertheless, in accordance with Spiritual Law, exist they do! Therefore, what might the above two anecdotes suggest to us?

They strongly indicate that thoughts, *despite* their invisible nature, *do* have the power to 'sway' our lives and produce visible effects. Our thoughts must thus have to be much more than empty vaporous things. To be able to 'pressure' in such a way, they must necessarily be imbued with some kind of inherent power. All the great Spiritual Teachings, even from ancient times, strongly advise to constantly strive to think good and pure thoughts. The emotive words of love, beauty, compassion and kindness automatically arouse in us vastly different feelings from words such as hate, selfishness, envy and bitterness. This small example, where the outworking of Spiritual Law is concerned, should serve to show that language alone is not the deciding factor here. The actual *volition* of the *producer* of the spoken word very strongly determines what is ultimately released *from* him "into the world".

Thus every thought we think, every word we speak produces a "form" that actually lives. The thought or word produces the actual form of it i.e., thoughts or words of hate or bitterness will produce those forms, *irrespective of whatever language is used as the medium of production*. Forms of love and harmony etc., are produced by the same mechanism. Because such forms cannot always be seen, that does not mean that they do not exist, for they can certainly often be felt. Neither can they simply and conveniently disappear. No, the forms that we produce, that we have given birth to, live on until such time as they return to us under this iron Law of Reciprocal Action.[1]

We, as the individual originators, are the *owners* of them. They are ours. Moreover, our thoughts naturally affect our immediate environment, family and friends. We may note how

---

[1]What happens to them whilst on their "journey" will be explained later on in this Chapter under the effects of "The Law of Attraction..."

refreshing it feels to enter the dwelling of a family who live a happy, balanced, harmonious life. Contrast that with a household racked by jealousy, hate and bitterness. A thoroughly unpleasant atmosphere, which is immediately perceived, pervades the place. The constant production of the corresponding *forms* "fills" the house.

It becomes their home too.

This process, then, can be viewed as *Spiritual sowing.* We "sow" through thoughts, words, volition, deeds and actions. It is precisely through this simple mechanism that humankind *forms and forms and forms.* Indeed, through the inherent free will of our spiritual nature, we are **unable** to stop forming. Therefore, if our thoughts are always good, we must naturally receive good returns. If they are constantly evil, that is what will be eventually received. If our thoughts and actions change between good and evil, we will receive mixed fortunes incorporating both those aspects. In this infallible mechanism lies perfect justice! We should therefore live by the admonition:

"As you wish men to do to you, do the same to them."

(Luke 6:31, Fenton.)

Such wisdom was given for our benefit under the knowledge of The Law of Reciprocal Action. Therefore, the greater strength and benefit will always lie in doing good deeds. The key to solving the many problems that beset us rests in the operation and understanding of this Law. For The Law of Reciprocal Action decrees that we cannot do anything other than continually *produce* our personal *works.* Yet because we cannot "physically" see them, it is difficult to accept that such a process might be possible.

Since thoughts have the power to alter perceptions, in cases where people act differently to their actual intentions i.e., as a "wolf in sheep's clothing" etc., The Law of Sowing and Reaping absolutely ensures that the "true" actions, including related thoughts and volition, are still all exactly weighed. The same unbending process takes place with people who make donations to organisations for some kind of personal gain or publicity, but do not accept or share their aims and ideals. This attitude is actually one of hypocrisy and is judged accordingly because of its base level of calculative premeditation.

A common Biblical quote clarifies the process perfectly:

Judge not, lest ye be judged!

A problem arises here because so few people have the ability to clearly assess the *true* intentions of others. So it is often difficult to know whether intuitive "gut feelings" are correct, simply because a person's appearance or actions may belie his true volition. And even whilst seeing his actions and hearing his words, we may still not know his real motives.

However, if the term "judge" *means* to "weigh" or "consider", then the points for and against any particular issue should *not* be seen as a transgression of the above Scripture. Clearly we are meant to employ our reason, intelligence and intuition to consider whether a particular thing is good or not. Therefore judging the actions of a person or an issue is vastly different from **passing judgement** on the person or issue.

In that light, the same Scripture from Fenton's translation of The Bible offers a clearer and better interpretation. From Matthew 7:1:

"Condemn not, so that you may not be condemned."

Now, whilst we have examined the mechanism that "produces our reaping", it is necessary to clarify the very important *reciprocal extension* of the process. The ostensibly enigmatic Scripture from The Book of Hosea actually offers perfect clarification.

" *And as they have sown only Wind,* **the Whirlwind alone shall they reap**."

(Hosea 8:7, Fenton. All emphases mine.)

Thus in the world of nature each seed planted produces a huge multiple of the same at maturation or harvest time. In some cases in the millions. Some crops require only a few months between sowing and harvesting. In the forest industry tree crops take many years to mature before felling and, depending on when planting took place, they may not be ready in a given lifetime. Even different varieties of the same kind of crop may mature at different intervals.

How should this be related to the great Spiritual Law of Sowing and Reaping? Quite simply, our spiritual sowing of either good or bad thoughts and deeds also returns a multiple of the same, in close association with another Eternal Law – The Law of Attraction of Similar Species – hence the truth of "reaping the whirlwind" in the previous Biblical quote. The differences in the time frame of crop maturation also have their equivalent in the Spiritual too, and apply equally to the thoughts, words, deeds, volition, and even prayers of people.

The outworking of all these factors provide the answer as to why sudden misfortune can visit itself on a "good person", or good fortune arrive to a well known "waster". That is also the reason why someone who is totally debased may not receive his personal "whirlwind" until very much later in life, or even after earthly death. Rest assured, though, it will come to him. Not, however, in the same measure as he meted out to others, but under the additional severity of the *whirlwind constant.*

If this were not the case i.e., without any form of ultimate justice, there would be little point in bothering with the good. In the jungle that would develop, it would be easier to simply "take whatever one wanted".

In this regard the following Scripture is more easily understood:

"PUNISHMENT IS MINE, I [THE LAW] WILL REPAY."

(Hebrews 10:30, Fenton.
Parenthetic addition mine.)

Thus, The Eternal Laws automatically keep track of all transgressors and, at the ordained time for that person, dispense the appropriate justice.

This does not mean, however, that we should not punish wrongdoers through our earthly justice system, otherwise there surely would be chaos. It simply means that nothing is missed in Creation, nothing can be hidden, and no individual can "get away" with any crime against The Spiritual Laws. The reciprocal effect, moreover, will always be greater than the strength of the original volition or deed under the outworking of the *whirlwind constant.* This process should offer some comfort as we observe more horrifying events and crimes that would have been unthinkable even a short while back, and which greatly increase in number and degree of brutality. Therefore the rule of law must be upheld at all times, as it should mirror our recognition of the "Higher Laws" along with a desire to build the right kind of society. Humankind's societal/religious "guidelines", however, need to fully accord with, and be adjusted to, those "Higher Laws".

It should also be a simple matter to deduce that we can only reap what we have *personally* sown. We cannot simply "sow" for others, or "reap" for them either, not even for a loved one. So a person constantly striving to do good and who receives bad experiences *apparently unfairly,* should understand that *he will have given cause for it at some point in the past.* As difficult a concept as this may be to accept, it ***is*** the causal reality of our problems. There is then nothing to be gained by bemoaning one's fate for this only increases the sense of burden and hardship. Recognition and acceptance of this lawful process, however, then connects us to the outworking of **Divine Grace.**[2]

In the global sense both our earthly home and the creatures upon it were given to humankind to nurture and protect, and to take only what was required. Look at the Earth today, however. The story is glaringly obvious. Poisoned and pillaged in a mind-set of rapacious, selfish greed under the name of progress and *good economic strategy.* Unfortunately, because such practices ultimately impact on all eco-systems, it is now time for global humanity to "pay the ferryman". Yet the price may prove to be well beyond our ability to pay. Learning the "Rules" and living by them may perhaps go some way toward lessening the cost. It will still be very high, however, as that cannot be changed now – though it can perhaps be reduced.

There must, however, be a truly genuine desire to want to change, to seek something better. Superficiality in this case will simply ensure not just more of the same, but increasingly severe "reaping". For, as with all of The Spiritual Laws, this particular Law operates from the smallest, even apparently insignificant individual happenings, to far-reaching global decisions and events made collectively, and thus subsequently "reaped".

And because the impact of "returning fate" may offer no apparent reason why, it is easy to rail against misfortune or bad luck, or to curse the fates and demand an end to hardship. Then, in times of deep pain with seemingly no way out, to desperately seek help in prayer. In the anecdotal experience of many, when danger threatens, *"when the chips are down"*, virtually *everyone* calls out to some Power Above! There are few who will not seek help at such times. This inner recognition, most often brought about by painful experiences, should help us to understand that the reaping of bitter fruits once sown should be seen as the best possible *spiritual* reminder that *we have strayed from the path ordained by The Creator.*

If our understanding of The Eternal Laws and how we stand in relation to them is then examined honestly and in genuine humility, such an assessment can only help us to grow spiritually. Through this process the lessons needing to be learned can be more readily identified. Consequently, as the necessary adjustments are made whereby only good seeds are sown, The Law of Sowing and Reaping will ensure a good return at the ordained time. Thus there should be less thought of hard, cruel, or undeserved fate. Yet neither should we be totally fatalistic about our lot in life. ***It is in our power to change it – at any time.***

Of course, change may not come overnight, but stubbornly refusing to change for the better will absolutely guarantee that *nothing* will change or, indeed, *can* change. The Laws of Creation actually ***do*** provide the means for happiness or misery. What is "Willed" from above for all human spirits is exactly peace and happiness through the understanding of Spiritual Law. What one *receives*, however, depends solely upon ***individual choice.***

The question or problem of the "evil within man" and/or how evil arose in the world – so long a point of debate – has its primary explanation within this Law. **It is simply the end-result of free-will choices**, which we all inherently make in any case very many times each day. And irrespective of whether the particular choice is made consciously and intentionally or in total ignorance of this law, The Law of Sowing and Reaping ***will***, nevertheless, ***always deliver the consequences***.

The Greek philosopher, Cicero, offers a simple and logically-correct explanation about this exact 'quandary'. In this particular discourse about the opposing views of Christianity and Stoicism, Thomas Godless asks Lactantius four questions on the subject.

> "My first difficulty", he said, "is that you do not seem to have been any better able than the Stoics to solve the problem of evil. How is the existence of pain and evil in

---

[2]The ramifications of this particular principle are examined later in this Chapter.

the world compatible with your view that the world is under the care of an infinitely powerful and infinitely loving God?"

To which Lactantius replied, "Thomas, I give you two answers. First, if Christianity offers men reconciliation with God, it is not required to solve every intellectual difficulty. But secondly, Christianity does provide a better answer to this age-old problem than Stoicism, because Stoicism is in principle deterministic, whereas the Christian God has given *freedom of choice to man...* He wants all things to serve him, not as automata but by free choice; but this gift of freedom involves the risk that man will *choose evil rather than good.* If God refrains from punishing the wicked in this world, that is a sign not of his powerlessness, but of his magnanimity. Epicurus insisted on human freedom, but at the expense of the gods' reality; the Stoics insisted on divine omnipotence, but at the expense of human freedom. Christianity allows for both."

(The Nature of the Gods. Cicero.
Italics mine.)

Despite the *intellectual* brilliance with which the Greek and Roman philosophers were able to debate the pros and cons of major issues such as life and death and good and evil; without the knowledge of The Spiritual Laws of Creation to ultimately define the lawful processes under which all events have their beginning, life and end, all their philosophic analyses and musings had to remain exactly that. For the final key to the puzzle was not available to them at that time. That fact notwithstanding, the long line of philosophic thought in many ways did provide the necessary step for the later entry and recognition – at least for some – of the **All** of Spiritual Truth and Law.

Thus, in this particular Law is fulfilled the fate or karma of humankind, and offers the solutions to the terrible tragedies which we witness today. Through the increasing spiritual power now entering the Material Part of Creation, all the deeds of thousands of years past are pressured to a quicker, final release, thereby also accelerating the **natural catastrophes.**

This *relentless pressure* and its attendant global events will not cease until all past cycles have closed, the deeds returned to their owners to face, and all opposition to The Eternal Laws has been removed. Then a new era will be ushered in. It will be a time of genuine peace and happiness, but only for those of the world's people, however, who have genuinely striven for the good.

Decisions Produce Consequences.

That is the subsequent but perfectly lawful effect of: **The Law of Reciprocal Action!**

3.3.2   Attitude to the Suffering

Given the obvious ramifications of this "Iron Law", it might be thought that we advocate total disregard for the plight of those in desperate straits. If, as is stated, people do bring suffering on themselves through non-observance of The Laws and that they are solely responsible for their plight, should compassion be shown for them? Are they not simply reaping what they have sown in this Earth-life, or perhaps an earlier one? And do they therefore deserve to be helped? The simple answer to virtually all aspects of the overall question is yes! Compassion and kindness are virtues that, if given without guile, can only bring a good return to the giver, for The Law of Sowing and Reaping should clearly show the need to do good at all times.

"Do unto others..." should be one of the key factors governing our way of life. It is difficult to imagine that anyone would actually want others to visit harm or evil upon them, yet there

are so many who seem to have little compunction in wishing that on others. That is the way of the coward, but unfortunately clearly the way of much of today's world too. It is not the path of nobleness, which is synonymous with true and genuine spirituality. Neither is it the way, therefore, of **the genuine warrior**, for a true warrior will live, and thus radiate, those higher qualities and virtues. Employing genuine spirituality from out of the **true** knowledge as both his *primary* weapon and shield, he will fight for, and protect and defend, the weak, the helpless and the downtrodden.

Any good works we do, we do solely for ourselves since the fruits of our deeds return to us as multiples of our original sowing under the aegis of the *whirlwind constant*. The possibility of helping sufferers should therefore be regarded as an opportunity to do good, to "sow good seeds". The cause of the person's suffering should not be our concern. In short, we should not "pass judgement". Given the general nature of human beings, most judgements are based on externals anyway. And a superficial assessment may belie the true situation. However, help given *should not be one-sided*, for that will not help the sufferer in the long term.

In any case the Perfection of The Laws automatically ensures that should a sufferer *not* deserve help, or should he need such experiencing to change his ways, then no one will cross that person's path who might be in a position to give help. Conversely, any necessary "crossing of paths" could mean that a connective origin might lie somewhere in the past e.g., as a "debt owed". In such a situation two opportunities are given for two different souls to expiate a possible past karmaic connection, sever it, and thus become free. If such an opportunity is not recognised, then, quite obviously, *the debt and connection remain*.

The inviolability of Spiritual Law means that all human beings will necessarily have ties to many people, and some will be to other races. Yet all will need to be resolved, even if the individual has no knowledge of such connections, or proffers cynical disbelief at such an idea. For the justness of The Laws will ensure that individual paths will cross at the appropriate time for any such bonds to be severed. Given the increasing spiritual pressure being relentlessly applied to the Earth and all the affairs of men in this time of final accounting, a superficial or cynical outlook or lifestyle will not be conducive to correct or timely recognition. Just as our past free-will decisions irrevocably bind us to the origin of all "returning karma" today so, too, are we offered the free choice to unbind ourselves from them when the opportunity arises. Conversely we are equally free to remain shackled.

Free-will permits us the choice of what we will sow in thought, word or deed. The outworking of The Law of Sowing and Reaping then returns to us a multiple harvest, in just accordance with the *whirlwind constant*. The explanations about free-will and thus the connected reciprocity deriving from it are precisely that of:

Crucial Imperative No 8:

> That we, the human Beings of planet Earth, *inherently possess* the ordained attribute of "**free-will**". That *not understanding* the so-called inequities or injustices of life has its *genesis* in human *non-recognition* and thus *non-understanding* of this most "**Crucial Imperative**".

Given the inordinate amount of suffering on Earth, the strange and inexplicable notion that we somehow do not possess the inherent human attribute of free-will is, on the surface, certainly perfectly logical and understandable to accept. Nonetheless, it is **precisely** that *perfection in logic* in this **Iron Law of Reciprocity** that is the *driving mechanism* behind **all** suffering. It is suffering, however, **reaped solely through our own decisions and actions**, and not through the operation of some mindless and unpredictable arbitrary force as many foolishly believe. Therefore, the authors of the very many books questioning the so-called injustices of life need only familiarise themselves with The Laws, particularly **The Law of Reciprocal Action**, to understand how and why free-will *is* the human reality!

Certain kinds of books, such as "The God Delusion" by Professor Richard Dawkins, basically reject any notion of free-will. Precisely that rejection, however, ultimately reveals the fatuity of human thinking. In the final analysis the *actual delusion* is centred around the inane belief that "human knowledge", alone, can determine the how and why of *every single facet of life*. That, of course, is plain and simple nonsense deriving solely from "human arrogance".

3.4   "Ten Men Will Take Counsel And It Will Come To Nought."

Isaiah 8:10. Thus spake the Great Prophet thousands of years ago in *one* of his warnings to humankind of just **one** of the sure signs of the *end-time demise* of human institutions. A time when it would become glaringly-obvious that *unworkable* human law, ideas, opinions, national self-interest, greed – and fear – would finally herald the impending complete collapse of human societies right across the globe.

The spectacle of riots and protests outside the venue of the UN "Climate Change Summit" in Copenhagen, December, 2009, gave clear voice to Isaiah's sure prophecy. And that was only *outside* the venue. Inside – where key discussions took place amongst numerous international officials – the *human* temperature was just as heated; where genuine consensus for *nurturing* the planet which *nurtures us* collapsed into recrimination, blame and self-interest. Headlines: 'Confusion and anger at Climate Change Summit'.

The largest ever gathering of international leaders [192 Nations] "...failed to reach a binding agreement". While some larger 'economies', particularly the US, pushed for consensus in some areas, many smaller Nations felt 'disappointed', and 'excluded from deal'. Denounced by smaller countries and amid warnings that "...it does not go far enough"; one US official stated: "Deal not enough to fight climate change." "No country is really satisfied with [the] deal."

Why should anyone be surprised at that outcome? Our very human condition at this juncture in our evolutionary journey simply *precludes* any hope of a genuinely equitable agreement to fairly share what are now dwindling resources amongst an ever burgeoning human population. For what the richer first-world countries *currently* possess, all others now demand as a matter of right.

The most necessary attribute of **wisdom** seems not to exist in the mentality of negotiators such as those at the Copenhagen conference representing the various countries and peoples of the world. Not any kind of far-seeing spiritual wisdom encompassing the very life-essence of **Creation-Law**; but, as in the past, always the short-term 'consensual-fix' ostensibly designed to overcome any and all objections. In the case of the "Copenhagen Summit", 2009, however, [universally accepted as a 'failure'], serious polarising rifts clearly emphasised the *power* of Isaiah's Calling to *warn* humanity — even from the long-distant past!

> The "Earth" also is *defiled* under the *inhabitants* thereof; because they have
> **transgressed** the "Laws",
> **changed** the decrees,
> **broken** the everlasting covenant.

(Isaiah 24:5, Emphases mine.)

In 1854 Chief Seattle of the Duwamish addressed Governor Isaac Stevens and gave what is probably *inadequately described* as; "...the most beautiful and profound statement on the environment ever made". Now preserved for posterity; his *full* address should *especially* be prominent in the homes and work places of all politicians, bankers, 'money-men', CEO's, Boards of Directors, and all who aspire to so-called 'leadership'. In truth, if we *really* wish to have any kind of planet worth living on, Chief Seattle's great wisdom should be made mandatory reading from an early age for **all** peoples of **all** races!

Taken from a more comprehensive analysis of his statement in the next Chapter, the following few lines appropriately encapsulate the foolishness displayed by national and perhaps even ethnic self-interest at 'Copenhagen, 2009'.

> "Whatever befalls the earth, befalls the sons of the earth. If men spit upon the ground they spit upon themselves.
>
> This we know, the earth does not belong to man, man belongs to earth. Man did not weave the web of life, he is merely a strand in it. Whatever he does to the web, he does to himself.
>
> One thing we know, which the White Man may one day discover – our God is the same God. You may think now that you own Him as you wish to own our land, but you cannot.
>
> The earth is precious to Him and to harm the earth is to heap contempt on it's Creator.
>
> ***Continue to contaminate your bed and one night you will suffocate in your own waste.***"

(Emphasis mine.)

At this present time in humankind's evolutionary journey; in ecological terms we stand on the edge of an abyss. Unless we change our thinking and attitude towards the single, great interconnected-organism that permits us life *down here* – **Planet Earth** – the majority of humankind will shortly topple into that widening chasm. The corporate 'gurus' call it scare-mongering or similar. They will also say we can solve all the problems that 'global warming' is wreaking on human societies now, never mind the exponential effect already evident. The equation is quite simple.

> **Planet Earth can only give as much of its *life-energy* as its own 'constantly-renewing ecology' will *actually allow*.**

Economies, societies and cultures of global humanity **must therefore respect and embrace Earth's 'natural program'**. The resources of the planet, though finite, can still be constantly sustainable if output, or *extraction*, equals input, or *correct conservation*. Earth's biosphere does *not* possess an 'endless-growth mechanism' for we 'lemming-like' humans now numbering in the **'too-many' billions**.

So, when extraction of resources *far exceeds* Earth's sustainable threshold just to fuel growth and consumerism for obscene profit – as has been the case with Western capitalism since the Industrial Revolution – degradation of the planet's 'life-system' is the inevitable result. Thus, Earth's 'supplies' are now in serious deficit. And that deficit is growing exponentially under impossible yet nonetheless precisely-related increasing human demands deriving from explosive population-growth. And therein lies the heart of the problem – *too many people*. To this writer's knowledge, only *one* internationally-syndicated commentator – Gwynne Dyer – has had the courage to state this clear fact.

Notwithstanding China's attempts to limit population growth there, for most governments, religions, cultures, ethnic groups etc., the idea of publicly promoting some kind of reduction mechanism for human population growth is, perversely, almost akin to 'suicide'. Yet that is *exactly* the outcome for our growing billions, *for we have had neither the courage nor the genuine inclination to institute real and necessary change.*

So now: More growth, more consumerism, more waste, more immigration into wealthy Western economies to fuel this insidious and fatally-compromised, never-ending, insane carousel called **Capitalism** degrades and finally destroys increasingly-fragile, global eco-systems. Concomitantly, also, destruction of *excessive* 'first-world' type lifestyles, and the *culling* of Earth's population.

Even a fool can understand that!

Should that sound warning bells for the political and economic 'movers and shakers'? Most definitely! However, as evidenced by more rapid degradation and destruction of more and more eco-systems, 'they', for this short time of 'pregnant pause' anyway, are obtusely blind and deaf to the glaring reality of the moment. The awakening, though, *will come soon* – hard and suddenly.

What drives this mad carousel? One word: **Capitalism** – *American brand capitalism.* And, of course, its twin partner in crime; the **share-market** – the shareholders of which 'continually demand' larger and larger 'profit-returns' no matter how derived or who or what suffers for 'their' dividend.

For there are more than enough well-documented cases where Western capitalism has destroyed living standards of whole groups of people by simple *abandonment* for a cheaper workforce and/or tax break elsewhere; after the initial foray to *raise* living standards by offering paid employment to produce the 'corporate goods' and its share-holder profits. And, too often, also, obscenely high earnings for such 'selfish-thinking' people – the C.E.O.'s and 'Boards of Directors'. Even the increasing involvement of 'Global Corporates' in the beneficially-growing 'Fair-Trade Movement' has only been seeded by consumers who are primarily *not* their share-holders.

Previously *seriously-exploiting* Third-world Nations for very large profits, it was never an altruistic decision for the *benefit* of the Third-world on the part of at least the greater majority of the larger 'Corporates', and also the I.M.F. Look at just Malawi's experience with this so-labelled "financial saviour", never mind the many other economies devastated by this rapacious and fundamentally evil organisation. No! The 'awakening and greening' of the Western consumer has forced the 'uncaring greedy' of the Corporate world to begin to change their ways, for 'large-profit economics' is the name of their game here too.

And what, in the final analysis, drives 'Corporate-capitalism', the real power that 'calls the shots' for Governments and global societies? One word – 'petrodollars'! Petroleum is the one single commodity and 'force' which has both permitted and driven capitalist expansion and its concomitant human demographic explosion from about one billion at the turn of the 20th century to numbers that can no longer be 'fed and watered' adequately in the first decade of the 21st century – over six and a half billion.

I hear cries of horror and *dismissive-derision* from all capitalists. Yet even the most rabid of them **cannot deny** that **by its very nature** capitalism **demands** growth and more growth to survive, thus generating the profits **needed** to fuel **more growth** for **still greater profits**. And only with *sufficient* petroleum supplies can *that kind of growth* be maintained. In a brutally-objective assessment of the impact of such an ethos and **associated monetary system** on human and natural life; in the final analysis it is quite simply insane – because *in its present form and application **it is completely unsustainable.***

And so, in the 21st century, more financial institutions, national and worldwide, have "...bitten the dust". **Many more will follow, until all that refuse to abandon their present 'aspiritual practices' collapse completely.**

As we strongly assert in this very Chapter: The *increasing Spiritual pressure* – or *spiritual-stranglehold* – now being *exponentially-applied* to all the affairs of men actually strengthens both the good and the bad. Thus *the good* – or that which adjusts itself to **The Law** – *will prosper*. And *the bad or wrong* – that which **opposes** Creation-Law – *will collapse*.

In that truism we have an infallible standard by which to measure events around us and to choose accordingly.

The greater insanity here is that the economic 'growth-engine model' based on 'oil', 'black gold', has finally run its course. In terms of human history, 'petroleum-power' represents just a short steep spike on the graph of human habitation on Planet Earth. Yet in that brief historical period now spiking downwards exponentially were fought the most destructive wars in our history. Global wars *only* made possible because of oil to drive the war machines and the industries which conceived and built them in their vast numbers, and which grew the societies that brought forth the men to man them.

"A Crude Awakening": Exactly the right Documentary – which should be mandatory viewing for all – for the latter half of the first decade of the 21st century, where, despite denials by certain Western Governments and petro-chemical industry 'gurus', oil output from virtually all of the major suppliers has already peaked. Soon, the battle will begin for what is still left. The strong will simply take from the weak in what will be a destructive and desperate struggle by the major economic and Military powers of the Northern hemisphere to control oil to maintain their growth and/or superpower status.

The 2011 uprisings in the Middle East known as the 'Arab Spring' pose an interesting question about the West's hell-bent determination to *enforce* democracy throughout *that* region and certain other parts of the world. Political analysts have noted that the countries which have received *special* attention from the U.S., particularly, are those who either possess large reserves of oil, and/or are not aligned with the West's international monetary system and its "enforcers" – the World Bank and the I.M.F. – and/or have actively lobbied to change global oil trade from the U.S. dollar to a gold standard. Such a move is untenable to both the U.S. and the E.U., for it would mean a virtual collapse of their economies.

It would also mean the end of the U.S. as a 'superpower', a notion that *really* frightens Americans. So how do you ensure that *that* does not happen? Simple. You use your superpower abilities to roam the world's oceans with large naval Task Forces, and you acquire and permanently man large military bases in strategic 'oil' locations. You also promote 'regime-change' where such regimes threaten 'your interests', and/or paranoia.

For without oil, modern societies simply cannot be sustained. Technologically advanced societies and economies must and will suffer irretrievable collapse. In its train, all the attendant anarchical horrors *automatically deriving from* major and widespread collapse of *once-stable* societal support systems and infrastructure.

The perfect example of the **Iron Law: The Law of Reciprocal Action.**

"What global humanity sows, global humanity shall reap!"

The 13-19th November, 2009, issue of "The Guardian Weekly" headlines:
Crucial data 'distorted' as global oil runs dry.

"The world is much closer to running out of oil than official estimates admit, according to a whistleblower at the International Energy Agency who claims it has been deliberately underplaying a looming shortage for fear of triggering panic buying.
The senior official claims the US has played [a significant] role in encouraging the watchdog to underplay the rate of decline while overplaying the chances of finding new reserves.
The allegations raise serious questions about the accuracy of the organisation's latest World Energy Outlook on oil demand and supply to be published this week – which is used by governments around the world to help guide their wider energy and climate change policies."

They go on to say that '...the World Economic Outlook will repeat its previous stance that oil production can be raised from its current level of 83m barrels a day to 105m. However, critics have argued that this cannot be substantiated by firm evidence and say the world has already passed its peak in oil production. Now the 'peak-oil' theory is gaining support at the heart of the global energy establishment. Despite the IEA in 2005 predicting that oil supplies could rise as high as 120m barrels a day by 2030, it was forced to gradually reduce this figure to 116m and then 105m last year, according to the IEA source, who was unwilling to be identified.' He added:

"The 120m figure always was nonsense but even today's number is much higher than can be justified and the IEA knows this. Many inside the organisation believe that maintaining oil supplies at even 90m to 95m a day would be impossible but there are fears that panic could spread on the financial markets if the figures were brought down further. And the Americans fear the end of oil supremacy because it would threaten their power over access to oil resources."

'A second senior IEA source, who has now left but was also unwilling to give his name, said a key rule at the organisation was that it was "imperative not to anger the Americans" though the fact was that there was not as much oil in the world as had been admitted.' He added: "We have [already] entered the 'peak-oil' zone. I think the situation is really bad."

America also uses vast amounts of another fossil-based commodity to power her industries and economy – coal; once called 'king coal'. Producing around 40 percent of US power generation, coal-fired power stations there produce about 37 percent of carbon emissions. [Source: BBC programme of alternative fuels; January, 2010.]

Who controls and promotes the coal industry in the US? Very large wealthy and powerful Corporates and their equally large numbers of investors who know there is still much money to made from coal generation; never mind the fact that it's contribution to global warming and/or carbon emissions is disproportionate in the extreme.

"**The West**. *Take the money and run. Do as thou wilt shall be the whole of the Law.* And the drugs internationals and the gambling internationals; *environmental destruction in the name of progress*; the sexual morality of the mole-rat with attendant plagues; the weapons of mass murder. *And only a few men and women had paused to consider* **that certain behaviour patterns might be wrong.**"

(The Helmet and the Cross. W. H. Canaway.
Emphases mine.)

American-style Capitalism, solidly entrenched as the economic model of *choice* for global humanity, now counts among its active adherents former communist foes. Also embracing this now rather 'shaky ideal' are races once under the yoke of colonialism. Two ethnic groups that have benefited financially from various kinds of Treaty or otherwise negotiated 'settlements' are Native Americans; of which some tribes hold considerable wealth from legalised casino operations, and the Maori tribes of New Zealand – also gaining considerable wealth from various 'settlements'.

Given Chief Seattle's clear statement – obviously stemming from the Native American peoples' long association with their environment; the deep spiritual wisdom he elucidates in his address could possibly cause one to wonder whether such peoples would think differently about their new-found tribal wealth. And thus perhaps lead away from the *now-failing* American-style 'Corporate-ethos' into a truly 'spiritualised' economic model which will not go the way of the collapsing *'capitalist money-go-round' carousel*.

Despite the fact that tribal peoples inherently possess an outlook on most issues probably different to their original European colonisers, Dr Elizabeth Rata, a Maori academic at Auckland University [N.Z.], identifies a key aspect of the impact of Capitalism on at least the thinking of current Maori leaders who 'control' this new wealth.

In her perceptive essay: "Retribalisation is all about money", Dr. Rata very succinctly notes:

> "...that the tribes have become capitalist corporations through the brokerage of their resources into the national and international economic system. Indeed, corporate groups, such as the new "classed tribe", suit the global order far better than those organisations of individuals who claim economic rights based on democratic principles."

> "Tribal-capitalism, along with both western and eastern forms of corporate capitalism, have profound implications for the future of democracy. The essentially pre-democratic nature of corporate capitalism urgently requires exposure and debate."

3.4.1 The Interlinked Global Monetary System: Reaping the Whirlwind! 'A Brief History Lesson.'

The perfect illustration of how **The Law of Reciprocal Action** has impacted on 'human arrogance' can be seen in the almost unbelievable 2008 collapse of once-proud financial institutions right across the globe. There stands perhaps the best 'reality example' of the inviolable nature of this *immutable* Law. It has clearly shown *how* the exercise of human free-will by individuals and groups in the vital 'global financial industry' has wrought carnage for tens of millions. Literally a case of 'sowing the wind' through, quite obviously, free-will greed. Unfortunately for the hundreds of millions who put their faith and finances in the hands of greedy and incompetent 'financial managers'; under the inviolable outworking of the great **Law of Reciprocal Action**, all "reaped the whirlwind". In this case, a Category 5 hurricane.

Note:

This brief history lesson in *this* sub-Chapter was originally written for a separate, now-published, Work well before that economic crash in America sent its viral-laden tentacles out to infect the rest of the world. In our increasingly uncertain times, knowledge of **The Laws of Creation** readily permits us to 'see' what will come next – *for this is precisely the period of global collapse.*

So: Corporate Capitalism – American style; will we continue to be seduced by you and embrace you more tightly in the belief that your way is the only way? Yes, of course we will. For that is the economic model taught in probably most universities, from which 'Ph.D. toting' economic 'gurus' spew forth to man failing banks and financial houses that yet *still* pressure governments and social paradigms across the globe. Of course, it is not that the *genesis* of the present completely *interlocked system* is American, but was nonetheless perfected there by extremely wealthy men and families of primarily European origin, in concert with the then relatively small but super-wealthy group of home-grown [American] magnates.

> **Note:** The following excerpts and quotes are taken from an early seventies-era book: "**NONE DARE CALL IT CONSPIRACY**". The author, Gary Allen – along with Larry Abraham – had difficulty finding a publisher willing to 'take it on'. (Concord Press. Rossmoor, California.) Once published, however, it became a runaway best-seller in very short order.

- First printing. February, 1972. 350,000

- Second printing. March, 1972. 1,250,000

- Third printing. April, 1972. 4,000,000

United States Congressman, **John G. Schmitz**, wrote this **Introduction**. (Emphases mine.)

> "The story you are about to read is true. The names have not been changed **to protect the guilty**. After reading this book, you will never look at national and world events in the same way again. ...
>
> At first it will receive little publicity and those whose plans are exposed in it will try to kill it by the silent treatment. For reasons that become obvious as you read this book, it will not be reviewed in all the "proper" places or be available on your local bookstand. ...
>
> Having been a college instructor, a State Senator and now a Congressman, I have had experience with real professionals at putting up smokescreens to cover up their own actions **by trying to destroy the accuser**. I hope that you will read this book carefully and draw your own opinions and not accept the opinions of those who of necessity must attempt to discredit the book. **Your future may depend upon it**."
> October 25th, 1971.

The many years since 1971 may well have provided data for opponents of the book to offer a different, even recent-historical, perspective. Notwithstanding that 'possibility', what absolutely cannot be refuted in any way whatsoever is the final sentence in John G. Schmitz's **Introduction** to **None Dare Call It Conspiracy**.
i.e. *"Your future may depend upon it."*

Look, now, at what that 'Back to the Future' prediction has wrought for millions of American families alone. Not only have many lost jobs and homes, but whole life-savings have been literally 'wiped out' as well. And from the fall-out, globally, tens of millions jobless.
Gary Allen notes that American President **F.D.R.** once said:

"In politics, nothing happens by accident. If it happens, you can bet it was planned that way."

The whole of human history clearly attests to the fact that through exercising our inherent, free-will attribute, we *humans* engineer human events and outcomes. Decisions must *always* produce consequences – or 'outcomes'! Thus the unseen yet nonetheless immutable 'driving power' of **"The Law Of Reciprocal Action"**.

Gary Allen tells us that decades ago Professor Carroll Quigley, who taught at the Foreign Service School in Georgetown University and also at Princeton and Harvard, produced a 1300 page, 8 pound tome – *Tragedy and Hope* – detailing exactly the process by which the world became economically interlocked, *and who engineered it*. Thus the **How** and the **Why**! The **Why** is simple enough: Professor Quigley states it as:

> "...nothing less than to create a world system of financial control in private hands able to dominate the political system of each country and the economy of the world as a whole."

The **How**, however, is the stuff of conspiracy; of which we all must disbelieve and mock or be labelled silly conspiracy-theorists. Yet Montagu Norman, a former head of the Bank of England, stated:

> "...that the Hegemony of World Finance should reign supreme over everyone, everywhere, as one whole *supernational control mechanism*."

To that conspiratorial end, the author, on page 9, very early on asks a key question.

> "Why is it that virtually all 'reputable' scholars and mass media columnists and commentators reject the cause and effect or conspiratorial theory of history? Primarily, most scholars *follow the crowd* in the academic world just as most women follow fashions. To buck the tide means social and professional ostracism. The same is true of the mass media." (Emphasis mine.)

So despite the fact that 'lone voices' are often labelled 'conspiracy theorists', the history that Professor Quigley details is exactly that – the *history* of *how* the *world* financial system became *interlocked*.

Perhaps the most interesting aspect of the 2008 financial crunch which began in the U.S.A. is the fact that the American Constitution – a defining humanitarian document by any standard – espouses certain freedoms and inalienable rights written into it by America's Founding Fathers. Yet despite the sacrosanct nature of that document, certain of those 'rights' have nonetheless been *subverted* by 'modern legal machinations' in the U.S. The same kind of 'activity' can now be clearly seen to have occurred in the subversion of the financial system by powerful and greedy individuals and self-interest groups.

Gary Allen noted that: 'The architects of The American Constitution revolted against the near-total government of the English Monarchy. Knowing that having no government at all would lead to chaos, they set up a Constitutional Republic with a very limited government.' Thomas Jefferson said:

> "In questions of power then let no more be heard of confidence in man, but bind him down from mischief by the chains of the Constitution."

Allen writes that Jefferson knew that if the government were not enslaved, people soon would be, so the Constitution *fractionalised* and *subdivided* governmental power in every way possible. Under such a system no segment of government could amass enough [political] power to form a dictatorship.

Financial power – and thus control – is far more potent, however, and America's Founding Fathers certainly understood that reality. Wealthy European bankers had long perfected the technique of bank/wealth consolidation, and through key men of those banking houses migrated the same ideas to the "New World". The Bank of England, Bank of France and Bank of Germany were not owned by their respective governments, but were privately owned monopolies granted by the heads of state, usually in return for loans. Under this system, Reginald Mckenna, President of the Midlands Bank of England, observed:

> "Those that issue the money and credit direct the policies of government and hold
> in their hands the destiny of the people."

From the earliest days, the Founding Fathers had been conscious of attempts to control America through money manipulation, and they carried on a running battle with the international bankers. Thomas Jefferson wrote to John Adams:

> "...I sincerely believe, with you, that banking establishments are more dangerous
> than standing armies..."

From a very early time in American history, banks were primarily independent entities and often individually-owned, set up to serve a need: e.g.; as brokers in the early fur trade. So in the 'cow-towns' and mining towns of a rapidly-growing 19th century America, these independently-owned banks sprang up to service the increasingly sophisticated, permanent towns 'across the frontier'.

However, individually-owned banks did not suit the aims and goals of the European bankers then becoming firmly established in the key cities of the east. Plans were formulated to bring all banks under a single controlling umbrella. But how to achieve it and make it stick? Create artificial panic. Senator Robert Owen, a co-author of the Federal Reserve Act, (who later deeply regretted his role), testified before a Congressional Committee that the bank he owned received from the National Bankers Association what came to be known as the "Panic Circular of 1893". It stated:

> "You will retire one-third of your circulation and call in one-half of your loans..."

The next 'panic', in the autumn of 1907, was precipitated by the American banking tycoon, J.P. Morgan. Historian Frederick Lewis Allen tells in *Life* magazine of April 25th, 1949, of Morgan's role in spreading rumours of insolvency of the Knickerbocker bank and The Trust Company of America, which rumours triggered the 1907 panic.

> "Oakleigh Thorne, the president of that particular trust company, testified later
> before a congressional committee that his bank had been subjected to only moderate
> withdrawals ...[and that Morgan's machinations] ... had caused the run on his bank.
> From this testimony, plus the disciplinary measures taken by the Clearing House
> against the Heinze, Morse and Thomas banks, plus other fragments of supposedly
> pertinent evidence, certain chroniclers have arrived at the ingenious conclusion that
> the Morgan interests took advantage of the unsettled conditions during the autumn
> of 1907 to precipitate the panic, guiding it shrewdly as it progressed so that it would
> kill off rival banks and consolidate the pre-eminence of the banks within the Morgan
> orbit."

Frederick Lewis went on to explain that the "panic" which Morgan had created, he proceeded to end almost single-handedly. He had made his point.

> "The lesson of the panic of 1907 was clear, though not for some six years was it destined to be embodied in legislation: the United States gravely needed a central banking system..."

After the Panic of 1907, Senator Aldrich, even though having no technical knowledge of banking, was appointed to head the National Monetary Commission by fellow Senators. A tour to Europe, courtesy of American taxpayers, quickly followed. There, wined and dined by the owners of Europe's central banks, they 'studied' central banking. No meetings were held and no reports were made for two years. Aldrich, along with Paul Warburg and other international bankers, staged one of the most important secret meetings in the history of the United States. Rockefeller agent Frank Vanderlip admitted many years later in his memoirs:

> "Despite my views about the value to society of greater publicity for the affairs of corporations, there was an occasion, near the close of 1910, when I was as secretive – indeed as furtive – as any conspirator .... I do not feel it as any exaggeration to speak of our secret expedition to Jekyl Island as the occasion of the actual conception of what eventually became the Federal Reserve System." (p.46)

Gary Allen writes that the secrecy was well warranted, for at stake was control over the entire economy. 'At Jekyl Island, B.C. Forbes in his *Men Who Are Making America*, notes':

> "After a general discussion it was decided to draw up certain broad principles on which all could agree. Every member of the group voted for a central bank as being the ideal cornerstone for any banking system." (Page 399)

It is interesting to also note here the following points:

- Warburg stressed that the name "central bank" be avoided at all costs. Instead, it was decided to promote the scheme as a "regional reserve" system with four (later twelve) branches in different sections of the country.

- Out of the Jekyl Island meeting came the completion of the Monetary Commission Report and the Aldrich Bill.

- Warburg proposed that the bill be designated the "Federal Reserve System" but Aldrich insisted his own name was already associated in the public's mind with banking reform and that it would arouse suspicion if a bill were introduced which did *not* bear his name.

- So strong was public opposition to such reform that Aldrich's name attached to the bill proved to be the kiss of death, since any law bearing his name was so obviously a project of the international bankers.

- Because the Aldrich Bill could not be pushed through, a new strategy was devised.

The Federal Reserve Act was passed on December 22nd, 1913, by a large majority in the House, but a narrower margin in the Senate. There *was* genuine opposition to the Act, but it could not match the power of the bill's advocates. Conservative Henry Cabot Lodge Sr. proclaimed with great foresight:

"The bill as it stands seems to me to open the way to a vast inflation of currency ... I do not like to think that any law can be passed which will make it possible to submerge the gold standard in *a flood of irredeemable paper currency*." (*Congressional Record*, June 10th, 1932. [Italics mine.])

After the vote, Congressman Charles A. Lindbergh Sr., father of the famous aviator, told Congress:

"This act establishes the most gigantic trust on earth. ...When the President signs this act the invisible government by the money power, proven to exist by the Money Trust investigation, will be legalized. ... ...
The new law will create inflation whenever the trusts want inflation. ..."

How powerful is the "central bank" of America? The Federal Reserve controls [our] money supply and interest rates, and thereby manipulates the entire economy – creating inflation or deflation, recession or boom, and sending the stock markets up or down at whim. The Federal Reserve is so powerful that Congressman Wright Patterson, chairman of the House Banking Committee, [maintains]:

"In the United States today we have in effect two governments. ... We have the duly constituted Government. ... Then we have an independent, uncontrolled and uncoordinated government in the Federal Reserve System, operating the money powers **which are reserved to Congress by the Constitution**." (Emphasis mine.)

Allen notes that 'neither Presidents, Congressmen nor Secretaries of the Treasury direct the Federal Reserve! In the matters of money, the Federal Reserve directs them. The uncontrolled power of the "Fed" was admitted by Secretary of the Treasury David M. Kennedy in an interview back in 1969 for the May issue of *U.S. News and World Report*'.[3]

Q. "Do you approve of the latest credit-tightening moves?"
A. "It's not my job to approve or disapprove. It is the action of the Federal Reserve."

Allen writes that 'the members of the Federal Reserve Board [are] appointed by the President for fourteen year terms. Since these positions control the entire economy of the country they are far more important than cabinet positions...' (p.56)
Prior to the actual day of the crash of 1929, Paul Warburg, one of the architects of the Federal Reserve Act, provided the warning to sell. That signal came on March 9 of that year when the Financial Chronicle quoted Warburg as giving this sound advice:

"If orgies of unrestricted speculation are permitted to spread too far ... the ultimate collapse is certain ... to bring about a general depression involving the whole country."
The author says: 'To think that the scientifically engineered Crash of '29 was an accident or the result of stupidity defies all logic. The international bankers who promoted the inflationary policies and pushed the propaganda which pumped up the stock market represented too many generations of accumulated expertise to have blundered into "the great depression".'

[3]The history of the 'Fed' may be viewed online at www.docu-view.com ["History of the Federal Reserve (money wasters.)]

Can we state "the collapse of 2008" to have been a depression? Not according to the 'experts'. It tended only *towards* a recession they say, never mind the fact that factory closures were the result, along with millions out of work globally. It is said that 'when America coughs, the world sneezes'. Since the "Great Depression" there have been regular recessions, along with hardship for many; but not all.

Gary Allen notes that: 'Each of these has followed a period in which the Federal Reserve tromped down hard on the money accelerator and then slammed on the brakes. Since 1929 the following recessions have been created by such manipulation.'

- 1936–1937   Stock Prices fell fifty percent:

- 1948   Stock prices dropped sixteen percent:

- 1953   Stock declined thirteen percent:

- 1956–1957   The market dipped thirteen percent:

- 1957   Late in the year, the market plunged nineteen percent:

- 1960   The market was off seventeen percent:

- 1966   Stock prices plummeted twenty-five percent:

- 1970   The market plunged over twenty-five percent.

Since then we have had the "oil-shock" crisis of 1973, and regular downturns in the 80's, 90's and the first decade of the new century to the definitive "crash" of 2008. So either it is all manipulated by very wealthy 'insiders' to increase their wealth markedly, or the so-called economic gurus are not expert at all – despite their much-lauded university qualifications. We should not forget that in the West at least, the media outlets of newspapers and TV etc., are primarily controlled by just a few super-wealthy tycoons and their families. So any suggestion of conspiratorial financial or share-market manipulation by the same 'super-wealthy' can easily be shut down through public ridicule and/or disinformation.

Despite the latest 'crash' bringing about the free-fall of global stocks and swallowing up banks and billions of dollars to simply disappear into an 'invisible vortex' somewhere, governments and the larger international banks were still able to find the mind-boggling tens of billions to prop up the tottering, inter-connected edifice from total global collapse. Now, in 2011, the *country* of America is in debt to the tune of around *14 trillion* dollars. So much of America is not owned by Americans at all but by foreign guarantors of multi-billion dollar loans to help keep all things American at least 'above water'.

The 'private' Federal Reserve Bank, the International Monetary Fund and the World Bank. Three powerful financial entities with massive and *historically-unprecedented* global control. Akin to The Three Musketeers mantra: **"All for One – One for All!"** – *all* felt the crunch together.

That is not the end of it by any means, however. No! When the *final* collapse does arrive, it will not be **The Three Musketeers** then who might rescue each other. For the managerial practices of obscenely rewarded 'financial experts' – like those who ran the ridiculously, but *appropriately*, named "Freddy Mac" and "Fanny Mae" entities – will finally be understood to have been similar to the antics of **"The Three Stooges"**. Unfortunately, however, without the humour; just the suffering – for millions!

Yet the buzz-word of the 'big three' at this time is still Globalisation; the concerted target of angry, alienated and galvanised peoples from all nationalities and all walks of life. Money is power in this rotten, insidiously-evil, inequitable world *we humans have created*. Latter-day

Chinese economic 'pressure' in the guise of aid in Africa and the Pacific have seen countries subvert part of *their* control and perhaps sovereignty to the controlling-power of money. China is the new emerging economic superpower, to which most countries kow-tow for free-trade deals. At least that was the position before the 2008 global collapse closed factories and sent Chinese workers scurrying back to the hinterland.

Do we think that this small history lesson is necessary? Or should we continue on as before? Perhaps we should take serious note of Einstein's marvellous definition of senility:

"To keep on doing the *same* things and expect *different* results."

By virtue of Einstein's wonderfully-logical insight here, along with certain historical realities, it would be foolish to believe that the current kinds of 'rescue packages' that have been applied to the global financial crisis by various governments will *once and for all* finally cure a 'very sick system'. Quite clearly, the 'same-old' will simply repeat the 'same-old'. We should therefore take serious note of this short history lesson, for 'what has gone before' **will replay again**; and probably sooner rather than later, **if** – as **George Soros** has long-tried to warn – there is **no change in the system itself.**

From science: **"For every action, there is an equal and opposite reaction!"**

From the more decisive power inherent in **Spiritual Law**: **"What Global Humanity Sows, Global Humanity Shall Reap."**

In this case, however, precisely because of the tightly-linked global monetary system – to which the Nations of the world have *voluntarily surrendered* their financial sovereignty – the associated "reaping" was seeded by a relatively few. Therefore:

"What 'financial experts' *sowed*, the 'whole world' *reaped*."

Conceived in Wall Street, the mantra, **"Greed is good"**, became the ethos of 'financial gurus' worldwide before the global bonfire turned to ash what effectively was a massive pile of 'irredeemable paper currency'. Greed: Certainly not one of the spiritual virtues humankind is seriously enjoined to live by. Glaringly-obviously, an opposite kind of ethos *would not* have brought the spectacular financial meltdown that occurred. In 2009 the currency speculators were trading again. No curbs have been placed on such practices by the *new regulators*, yet these *manipulators* produce *nothing* of value. All seek personal wealth only.

As we all now dramatically understand from the hard lesson of 2008, the **'reaction'**; the **'reaping'**, is far more dire than any *standard* prediction could possibly have foreseen. Thus can we observe the Truth of **Creation-Law**:

That the 'reaction/reaping/outcome' from every/all originating decision/s *must always be greater in the 'return'*. If we were to state that fact ten million times, and say it *yet again*; it could *never change* in its *immutable* and *inviolable* outworking.

Director Michael Moore, much maligned by some but nonetheless possessing the requisite courage to document shocking realities about life and Law in "the land of the free"; in his movie, **"Capitalism. A Love Story"**, exposes the hypocritical and callous greed of America's 'money-men'. Deriving from that very 'mind-set'; the subsequent collapse of industries and the social disruption and dislocation of a huge segment of American society.

Perhaps to add "insult to injury"; Gerald Celente, CEO of Trends Research Institute who predicted the 1987 stock market crash and the fall of the Soviet Union, says that by 2012 'America will become an undeveloped Nation'. "Food riots, squatter rebellions [documented by Michael Moore], tax revolts and job marches..." will characterise the 'revolution'.

> "We're going to start seeing huge areas of vacant real estate and squatters living in
> them .... Its going to be a picture the likes of which Americans are not ... used to.

Its going to come as a shock and with it, ... a lot of crime. [That] is going to be a lot worse than it was before because in the last 1929 Depression, people's minds weren't wrecked on all these modern drugs – over-the-counter drugs, or crystal meth or whatever it might be. So, you have a huge underclass of very desperate people with their minds chemically blown beyond anybody's comprehension."

The predictive accuracy of Gerald Celente and Trends Research Institute is vouched for by prestigious American institutions such as CNN, USA Today, CNBC, The Atlanta Journal-Constitution, The New York Times, 48 Hours/CBS News, The Detroit News, The Los Angeles Times and The New York Post. And, in perhaps a truly mad twist, *The Wall Street Journal*.

The city of Detroit would surely be a perfect example of what Celente is saying. Once the great *car-city* offering wealth for successive generations of millions, a bulwark of industrial might during the Second World War – and from where the great harmonies of black soul music from the Motown record label were gifted to the world – that once proud metropolis is now a shadow of its former self. Documented in **"Requiem for Detroit"**, the city of the present is revealed as a model for the very real nightmare of 'post-industrialisation collapse' in other cities globally. The near-death of Detroit's once vibrant car industry has seen its population reduce from just under four million to around eight hundred thousand in only a few years.

The inevitable end-result of such a drastic population collapse is urban decay on an unprecedented scale where very large parts of the city are now wastelands. Crime and arson, where empty homes and offices are torched by bored and disaffected jobless youth, are rampant. Paradoxically, there is one positive emerging from the urban ruin of Detroit. Groups of residents who have chosen to stay have adopted a 'village-mode' mentality, becoming increasingly self-sufficient by growing their own food and building localised urban economies based on that growing trend. That will surely be, of necessity, the way of the future for large urban-centre populations facing similar collapse.

There is no doubt that America *will* collapse. For despite the strong ethos of Calvinism *and* **"Manifest Destiny"** that defined early settlement, that 'pairing' failed to *permanently anchor* the *right* governmental and societal moral and ethical foundation in the country. So what we now witness for America and its people is nothing more than the inevitable 'reaping' from the 'sowing' of two *solidly-entrenched* aspects of the *American ethos*.

One is the disturbing, sometimes terrible, at times evil, decision-making on the part of certain branches of successive American Administrations, particularly since the late 1950's. For no country can promote itself as a God-fearing and obedient Nation *ostensibly* embracing the associated Higher Laws that must come with such a stance and then hypocritically continually transgress those very Laws without there being serious repercussions for *all* in the land. For *all* have taken part in the democratic processes that have brought forth the politicians who enact *human* laws which *always oppose* the **Higher Immutable**, thus **Inviolable**, **Creation-Law**.

The second is the almost *rabid* promotion across the globe of American-style Capitalism, which has revealed itself to be a two-edged sword – *as it would*. Even though very much a Communist State, China's enthusiastic embracing of so-called *clever* American business 'know-how' has not only threatened industry in America, but in many other countries globally. Now that China has recovered from the 2008 'collapse' and is once again in a high-growth mind-set, there is the very real possibility that if the trend continues *without interruption*, China will soon wrest from America the dubious and totally *aspiritual* title as 'the world's only superpower'.

In *human* history, the **legacy** of the rise and **fall** of **all** the 'great' empires has resulted in the world we know today. If we follow, *chronologically*, the time-line of the emergence, life and collapse of all previous 'empires', we can observe a most interesting *broad-sweep aspect* therein. It is one which basically notes that the **closer** to our present time particular 'empires' flourished, the **shorter** their **life-span** – particularly from the 19th century.

Now the *last* two 'empires' that will ever exist on earth overlap in tandem. Though both regimes would 'diplomatically' deny it, both are nonetheless vying for global supremacy, militarily and economically. Militarily the most powerful country to have ever existed, the U.S.A. is nonetheless on the wane. The rapid rise of the U.S. – primarily in the 20th century – and China's spectacular and escalating ascendency in the first decade of the 21st century coincides in real time to vastly increasing ***spiritual power and pressure*** driving literally *everything* to its final point of either *upliftment* – or *total collapse.*

Our "waning empire", the U.S.A., ostensibly holds **The Creator** and **His Laws** as its core ethos, yet lives a sham life. Our "ascending empire", China, on the other hand views its past and its future destiny as being inextricably intertwined with "the ancestors" – thus holding to the "spiritually-dead" ethos of "ancestor worship". So both must, and will, fall!

As we stressed early on in this Chapter: "*Without Revelation a Nation fades.* **But it prospers** <u>**by knowing The Law**</u>."

Thus **the good** – *that which <u>adjusts</u> itself to The Laws* – **will prosper.** And **the bad or wrong** – *that which <u>opposes</u> The Laws* – **will collapse.** In this simple equation resides an infallible standard by which to measure events around us and to choose accordingly.

The nightly news images of "**Global Societal Collapse**" bear immutable witness to this *unstoppable* force.

Greed is good! Therefore consumption must be good, for consumption means greater profits for Corporations and their shareholders – and China. By extension, Capitalism must also be good, for that is the mechanism which brought it all into being and allows it to continue. Even though it can surely be seen that it is unsustainable in its present form, the mad carousel of Capitalism – which no one person or organisation [apart from George Soros apparently] has the courage to call for an end to and institute a different mechanism for trade etc., – continues to steadily and inexorably fail.

The world runs on hypocrisy! Whether it be in economics, politics, religion, or focussed on cultural, ethnic and racial 'priorities'; all say one thing – but do another. And all would deny doing such a thing. Such is the way of the shrewdly-calculating human intellect; totally devoid of ***truly genuine*** spiritual aspirations.

An example; the great ecological disaster of 2010 – the Gulf of Mexico oil leak. Finger-pointing and blame – at weak Government legislation, at Corporate oil-giant greed and shoddy operational short-cut practices etc., – cannot mask the reality that irrespective of who or what was to blame, the resultant outcome shows the *immutable outworking* of the great and inviolable **Law of Reciprocal Action: What we sow we [MUST] reap!** An overly-affluent society that based the greater part of its economy and wealth on oil; that has long-consumed far more than it had a moral right to, now struggles to understand how such a disaster could have occurred.

An alternative view states that allowing millions of litres of crude to spill for months, thereby destroying part of the fishing industry, would help the U.S. Govt. to open more of the Gulf to more oil exploration. The standard chemical used to sink and disperse the crude oil is known to be ten times more toxic than crude itself, thus devastating marine life. Since 'home-grown' oil lessens dependency on foreign oil, the U.S. Govt. has now opened virtually all of the Gulf to exploration.

In the aftermath of the financial bonfire of 2008, President Obama issued new directives to change the 'system' so as to prevent any future repeat of the meltdown. He blamed the financial crisis on "a culture of irresponsibility". Commenting on the billions of dollars lost through 'a record [number] of mortgage foreclosures ... on mortgage loans and securities backed by subprime mortgages', he said: — "It was easy money. But these schemes were built on a pile of sand."

The Obama plan gave new powers to the Federal Reserve to oversee the entire financial system. It is hoped that the central bank will be able to deal with the kinds of problems that were allowed to build to such an extent that they finally overwhelmed America's financial system in the spectacular "Bonfire of the Billionaires".

It was a 'bonfire' so life-changing that a few of the world's super-rich, because of their losses, amazingly even committed suicide; never mind the fact that those particular individuals still had billions left to play with. Surely the perfect illustration of the great Spiritual Truth: *"What does it profit a man if he gains the whole world, but loses his soul."* And from Luke; a warning from the past for today. [Fenton, 21:34-36]

> "But take care of yourselves, for fear your hearts should be loaded with debauchery, and drunkenness, *and business cares*, and that day come swiftly upon you like a snare; for thus it will come upon all dwelling upon the face of the earth. Watch, therefore, at every season, offering prayer; so that you may be prepared to escape *all the coming calamities...*"

Surely here is the greatest warning yet to the corporate world and its financiers, exchange-rate manipulators, share-market fanatics and all of similar ilk who elevate the *god-corporate* and the *god-financial* before all else.

Will President Obama's plan work? Only time will tell, of course. However, two years after the great crash, 2010 saw European governments struggling to cope with *new* levels of high debt. And 2011 not only sees that trend worsening, but also the curious fact that none of the *real* Wall St. villains have yet been called to account.

One sure way in which the capitalist greed generated from Wall St. would be eliminated forever would be for 'Mother Nature' to bring forth for the U.S. two possible nightmarish scenarios, both already primed and waiting. "She", after all – *with her truly wondrous power* – is the best "lawful" destroyer of man's works and societal infrastructure, and Governments *know* they could never really cope with a real *super* natural disaster. For it **is** given over to the **"Forces of Nature"** to finally bring to an end humankind's so-long-standing – and still ongoing – foolish and totally intransigent opposition to the very Laws and Rules set into Creation which we were to obey, that we might know *genuine* peace and harmony.

The great eighth century Prophet, Isaiah [24:4-6], succinctly encapsulated in just **one sentence** *exactly* what it was that we *should* have obeyed – *but did not*. That single sentence/prophecy – *which we must reinforce often* – provides the very **why** for the societal horrors now upon us, never mind the *far greater* global angst awaiting its time of *full impact*.

> 'The "Earth" also is defiled under the inhabitants thereof; because they have
> *transgressed* the "Laws",
> *changed* the decrees,
> *broken* the everlasting covenant.'
> 'Therefore has the curse devoured the "Earth", and those that dwell therein are desolate:...'

How many times do we have to be warned? The outcome for our unbelievable arrogance...? The great Prophet does not mince words.
"Therefore has the curse devoured the "Earth", *and those that dwell therein are desolate*:..."

Reported in *The Economist* in January 2005 – **UN Warns of Apocalypse Now** – UN emergency relief director Jan Egeland painted an apocalyptic picture.

'Earthquakes, floods and other natural disasters could kill millions in the world's mega-cities and time is running out to prevent such catastrophes, the United Nations warns. Mega-cities have 10 million or more people, many concentrated in slums.'

"Perhaps the most frightening prospect would be to have a truly mega-disaster in a mega-city," Egeland told the World Disaster Prevention Conference. "Then we could have not only a tsunami-style casualty rate as we saw on Boxing Day, but one that's one hundred times that." He said "time is running out" to prevent such a catastrophe.

The greater Tokyo area, with a population of more than 35 million, tops the list of mega-cities, followed by Mexico City at 19 million, greater New York at 18.5 million and Bombay at 18.3 million.

One apocalyptic scenario for the U.S. is the supervolcano in Yellowstone, *'due'* to blow again. The Yellowstone caldera would discharge so much material that American society would be reduced to Third-world status in very short order. The impact from the same material would also be disastrous globally. From Matthew 24:19-22, Fenton:

> "...Pray, however, that your flight may not come during the winter, nor upon a Rest-day; for there shall **then** be wide-spread affliction, such as has **not been known since the beginning of the world until now**, no, nor will *ever* be known again...."

The second *destroyer* for the U.S. could well be the *active* Mt. Cumbrevieja volcano in the Canary Islands. If it were to erupt and fulfil the absolute *worst-case* scenario, the result would be a true *mega-tsunami* impacting the Eastern seaboard of the Americas' from Newfoundland to Central America, with the major hit on the U.S. Travelling at a speed of 720 km per hour, it would take just 8 hours to cross the Atlantic and destroy all cities and infrastructure along that coastline. [Question: Could the Yellowstone supervolcano eruption in its turn also trigger a Mt. Cumbrevieja eruption? A frightening scenario for the U.S.]

Some scientists estimate that the wave *could* reach as high as ***500 metres at impact***. Such a wave would easily destroy not only the cities along the East Coast, but would reach many miles inland via the large rivers that flow into the Atlantic. Devastation would virtually be complete, and financial and infrastructural recovery might well be impossible. Mt. Cumbrevieja, too, could reduce the U.S. to Third-world status. Wall St., however, would be effaced from the earth.

> "And there will be signs in the sun, and moon, and stars; and upon the earth nations in despair, as when in terror of ***the roaring and raging sea***; men expiring from fear, and apprehension of what is coming upon the world:..."

> (Luke 21:25-26, Fenton.)

So: If we take the one stark and irrefutable fact that emerges from the 2008 financial 'experience'; it is:

> "That the 2008 virtual collapse of the global money markets clearly reveal that its *foundation* was wrong. For it was founded just on human ideas and greed, ***not*** on the knowledge of **CREATION-LAW**. So to continue with policies that have proven time and time again to not only be problematic but to cause suffering and social distress to the many whilst insulating the *super-wealthy*, eventually guarantees a completely-irretrievable, total and utter collapse. Only then, however, can a new and ***spiritually-equitable*** financial and trade foundation finally be established."

So is The Law written! So shall it one day be!

<u>America</u>: How far your <u>spiritual fall</u> since your moral high point and great blood-sacrifice in The Second World War, and your noble generosity toward others immediately following that terrible era! How much must you <u>yet reap</u> through the Immutable outworking of "<u>CREATION-LAW</u>"; let alone your appalling 'legal' distortions of just the 1st and 2nd Amendments – on their own – of your <u>once-ennobled</u> Founding Constitution?

3.5   The Law of Attraction of Similar Species!

"Like Attracts Like."

The outworking of this Law is aptly expressed in sayings such as "Birds of a feather..." etc.. How strongly mankind even unconsciously relate to this particular Law is illustrated in another saying: "You can tell a man by the company he keeps." In essence, we constantly live this Law at the everyday social and work level even though we may not be aware of it or its far-reaching implications. Yet its effects can be readily observed around us every single day. Like-minded people gravitate toward certain occupations and professions. In our recreational time the same factors apply. A more striking example, however, may be found at large social gatherings where small groups will form themselves based on what they have in common. It may be their religion or spiritual beliefs, political leanings, profession, musical tastes, sports, language or race, a particular love of something, or even a shared hatred. It can be any number of things or varying combinations, but it will always signal "The Law of Attraction..." in operation.

Some ancient peoples were aware of the effect of this important Law and more or less followed it subconsciously in that they separated out into occupational and educational classes, crafts and Guilds. Within that spiritually-correct system, every member of society had the opportunity to live and develop to his fullest potential within each particular "level" attained. Unfortunately, societies gradually changed into divisions of upper, middle and lower classes. This development eventually embraced the full social spectrum of envy and hatred on the one hand, and conceit and arrogance on the other, until finally ending in class tension.

What is infinitely more beneficial, and clearly desirable, is that the various occupations and socio-economic groups in societies develop in such a way that they stand "side by side", thus offering the greatest possibility for "working together" harmoniously. Genuine self-esteem for every group could develop to its fullest potential then. And because the different sectors will possess abilities that the others might not have, each becomes a necessary link to every other, thus producing a sound whole. Anti-social problems should then gradually disappear as a better society develops under the correct recognition of this Law. The key consideration here, however, is *"Working Together, Side by Side!"*

In a completely different kind of example, gardening can show the extent of this Law quite graphically. In the practice of "companion-planting", one type of plant or group of plants assists the growth and development of others. An "inappropriate" plant, however, can actually prevent the "companion" from reaching full maturity or producing fruit. In the wild communities of plants this "Law of Attraction..." guarantees a natural balance of the various groupings. With the exception of a few species, the animal world operates under the same principle, as do the birds and fishes. The advantages of groupings are quite obvious, a greater protective umbrella and care of the offspring probably being the primary consideration. In working together, food supplies may be more secure and the group entity is better able to develop a higher social structure, which lone individuals cannot achieve.

"The Law of Attraction..." also guarantees that if a particular species is split, the split parts will seek to re-unite when given the opportunity. In terms of the attracting quality, whole species that are similar will attract, and split parts of the same species will also strive to re-unite. This Law is a fundamental necessity for everything seeking union in Creation.

What does this mean for us, the human species? And where do we place this powerful force of attraction between men and women? Because of its nature and place in Creation, the human being also carries, as an inherent quality within it, the desire for union. The human creature as such is a species in Creation that is split. The two split parts, male and female, under the immutable driving power of The Law of Attraction of Similar Species, will therefore seek to re-unite. Sexual instinct aside, this basically explains the *natural* attraction between man and woman.

As previously noted we possess, by virtue of our spiritual nature, the ability to produce the forms of our thoughts, words and deeds. What has not been stated, however, is the fact that these forms, which are our *works*, are *whole species*. Therefore, under the outworking of this particular Law, they, in turn, attract *similar species*. Since man is unable to *stop forming*, what, then, do we have? What we thereby produce are extremely large groupings of correspondingly *similar* forms to the *particular kinds of thoughts generated*. These homogeneous groupings can be designated as "power centres".

This is an apt description as they *do* possess power. By utilising the power inherent in our everyday thought-processes, we not only produced them in the first place, but automatically sustain – and thus maintain – all the many and varied "centres" now in existence. The dark, dangerous and evil; and the light, good and beneficial. And depending on our personal nature and volition, we therewith automatically connect to those with which we will have a respective affinity. We can, moreover, greatly increase the size and power of these "centres" by "feeding" them *greatly intensified* thoughts, particularly those of hate, envy and anger etc.. So, where do these "power centres" reside, and what is their function?

They exist in their non-material state [in fine matter] alongside our heavier physical environment. The subtle but nonetheless very real pressure generated by the various "power centres" is sufficient to affect the affairs and even destiny of men – *if* we of humankind **choose** to *attach ourselves to*, and therefore *extract substance from*, the particular "power centre/s" of our choice; i.e., the one/s exactly corresponding to the nature of our thought/s at any given time. For each "centre" corresponds with, and attracts to itself, the *same kind/s* of forms. Thus there are "power centres" of all the virtues and vices from the "works" of humankind. Our imagination, on its own, will readily offer an indication of how some might look. Those of hate, jealousy and bitterness must be ugly to witness, whilst those of love and kindness would be havens of happiness and peace.

A small illustration of how The Spiritual Laws intermesh and how the effect of these "power centres" on human beings can be so terribly devastating – *even if the recipient has absolutely no knowledge whatsoever of them* – can reveal how insidiously-powerful they are.

We now know that ignorance of The Laws cannot *prevent* the dispensing of true Spiritual justice. Marriage and the family unit, by virtue of the closeness of the relationships, is invariably a place where much emotion – both beneficial and unhelpful – is generated. Should a situation develop where what might once have been a relatively happy unit degenerates into a difficult and perhaps bitter experience for one or both partners, the emotional pain will produce forms associated with that turmoil.

The whole unfortunate episode will be compounded by third-party involvement and/or children to the marriage. If there can be no reconciliation or resolution and a breakdown is inevitable, the emotional pressures generated might be such that the normal strength of one of the partners is temporarily rendered far weaker than would otherwise be the case. With the ebbing of "Spiritual strength" – this "strength" being at the same time also "Spiritual protection" – in the belief that one's hopes and dreams are about to be dashed, there may arise in the mind of *the one most likely to suffer the greatest loss*, the wish to "do something about it".

More particularly with the possible estrangement from everyday contact with perhaps much loved children.

This potential chain of events may only begin as just the emotion of hurt and then perhaps anger. If it stays at that level and is resolved relatively peacefully, nothing untoward should occur to bring about a dangerous situation. However, should it develop further to the point of one partner "wanting to get even", the forms generated by the powerful emotions of such a situation – i.e., those of hate and revenge – begin the process of attracting around that individual correspondingly similar forms from the relevant "power centre/s".

His developing volition for revenge is thus *strengthened* to a considerable degree under this "Law of Attraction of Similar Species". If the individual cannot then generate sufficient spiritual strength to *resist* a rapidly weakening *former good volition*, and thus *change the forms around him*, it could well be that at the moment of greatest weakness, the pressure from the "attacking" similar forms "forces" the carrying out of a tragic deed.

How often do we hear comments evinced with great puzzlement: "How could he/she have done that?" "It is so totally out of character!" "I would never have believed that he/she could ever be capable of doing that!" In times of normalcy, it might never have happened. However, with the *base volition* at such a time vastly amplified by *other* attracted forms, the receiver is rendered *temporarily* incapable of clear and logical reasoning. Other "forces" have "taken over". That lawful process offers a good explanation of the Biblical Scripture of Ephesians 6:12:

> "Because our fight is **not** against blood and flesh; but against **the sovereignties**, against **the powers**, against **the commanders** of the **darkness of this world**..."

Unfortunately, however, it is a darkness we have created. With the exception of true insanity – and/or in cases where the personal free-will volition of a person is temporarily rendered impotent by a stronger *occupying entity* – the individual perpetrator is spiritually responsible for his actions. Therefore, irrespective of the circumstances – or even possible provocation – it still rests with the individual whether or not he chooses a good volition or a dark one. It should never be forgotten that we are always subject to *the whirlwind constant.*

We may *believe* we are only *sowing the wind* but, under Spiritual Law, we **will** *reap the whirlwind.* The harvesting must always be greater than the sowing and this is equally true in good or bad. Neither can we escape the effects of our works at earthly death. The following Bible Scripture (Revelation 14:13) states it succinctly:

> "...and **their works** accompany them."

Consequently, no one can escape Spiritual Justice purely because one conveniently dies an earthly death. No, the "works" spoken of here are composed of **all the forms** produced by our thoughts, our words, and our actions or deeds. Because we are the producers, the originators, of them, they are tied to us until such time as we finally undertake to expiate them, either upon their return to us as possible hard lessons or experiences, or we bring about a change in the nature of them by a corresponding change in our own personal attitude and spiritual volition. Thus, in strict accordance with The Laws of Justice, *what has not been dealt with and completely expiated on the Earth* waits to be faced in the planes of what we loosely refer to as "the beyond".

For we **cannot** escape "our works". *They follow us purely and simply because they must –* **because they are ours**.

As we have previously noted, the birth of Jesus into the Jewish race provides an excellent example of how "The Law of Attraction..." operates in its inviolable way. As a people with strong religious conviction, the Israelites through their prophets divined the existence of The One

Invisible God, thus anchoring a channel of *knowing acceptance* of, and for, messages and events from that Highest Source. The strength of this exalted belief, even in times of hard persecution, was such that it reached upward to The Godhead Itself thus permitting the strongest possible *Spiritual awareness* of It at that time. The Jewish people, therefore, were able to provide that vitally-necessary "connection" for the birth of Jesus to take place. Hence the reason why Jesus, The Son of The Invisible God **could**, and **did**, incarnate into that particular race.

For only with such a sure conviction from the Jewish people could the appropriate connections be established for such an event to take place. Without this inner divining of the "Highest Heights", a necessary attracting quality for this happening was impossible. An incarnation by Jesus into any race other than one with the requisite Spiritual belief of the Highest Spheres would mean a huge gulf of non-understanding, so is not possible under The Laws of Creation. Quite logically, therefore, an incarnation into a savage tribe of idol worshippers would have been a rather pointless exercise for the entry of The Son of God onto the Earth.

3.5.1   Spiritual Qualities as the First Consideration

Because we are inherently imbued with the nature and quality of The Spiritual, the potential to develop the correspondingly more ennobled characteristics of that attribute *should* be the primary factor that determines to whom or to what we will be naturally attracted. Most people will have probably felt strongly drawn to certain persons for no *apparent* reason other than a feeling of an especially strong bond. Sometimes to our great surprise – though it should not be so under the effect of "The Law of Attraction..." – we may even discover that certain meetings quickly produce bonds that are far stronger than those we experience with some members of our own immediate family.

As previously alluded to earlier in this Chapter, a particular story in the life of Jesus illustrates this fact perfectly. From Matthew 12:48-50, Fenton:

When told that His mother and brothers were waiting to see Him, replied:

"Who is My mother? and who are My brothers?" Then extending His hand in the direction of His disciples, He said, "Why, *those* are My mother and My brothers! For whosoever does *the will of* **My Father** *Who is in Heaven,* **he** is My brother, and sister, and mother!

Spiritual qualities, therefore, should be recognised as the correct thing to strive for in the first instance, even if it means breaking free from the sometimes cloying and selfishly-emotional demands – and even *odious control* – that some *within* family groups *thereby* generate. The present generally low level of spiritual maturity exhibited by human societies today is clearly demonstrated by the fact that, for many people, only race and ethnicity are the main considerations in their relationships with others. This lack of understanding for the deeper and finer qualities ensures that this superficiality places outward appearances such as skin colour, race, physical looks, fashion and religion etc., foremost.

Spiritual knowledge, particularly the right knowledge of The Law of Rebirth, will show the relative unimportance of such things as a person's race or nationality. The basis for assessing the worth of a human being can then be made on character alone. The following Biblical quotation probably best encapsulates this. From Matthew 7:18-20, Fenton. [Emphases mine.]

"A useful tree *cannot produce* bad fruit; nor can a *worthless tree* produce *good fruit.* Every tree *not producing* good fruit will be *felled* and used *as firewood.* Reject their produce; for by this you can **recognise** them."

3.5.2   Families and Children

The ramifications posed by the question of how and why particular souls incarnate into certain family groupings under "The Law of Attraction..." are so far reaching that if humanity were to *truly know* and **live** this knowledge, much of society's ugly side could be made non-existent – in perhaps just a few generations. Whilst that may seem a very broad statement, an examination of the serious importance of it and the equally grave responsibility attached to it should become evident to the open-minded reader, more especially if one is a parent, or wishes to become one. Since procreation is very much the norm rather than the exception, the significance of our opening sentence should be of primary interest to this group particularly.

Who has not heard the statement at some time, often given as an emotional outburst: "I didn't ask to be born!" – or: "I didn't choose my parents!" Unfortunately, **not so**! Notwithstanding that reality, it is nevertheless not an uncommon utterance, particularly from the young who may be subject to spiritually-wrong family constraints at the time that natural development calls them to enter the phase of adulthood and independence. Random selection does not operate here, but under the determination of one's 'free will', The Laws of **"Attraction..."**, **"Reciprocal Action..."** and **"Spiritual Gravity..."** most certainly do. These Laws basically determine the geographical location, the particular family of "lawful choice" and all other circumstances into which one is born, for an act of procreation simply provides *an opportunity* for *individual souls in the "beyond" to incarnate on Earth.*

Since there are many souls awaiting such an opportunity, certain precise factors will finally bring the "correct one" to the prospective mother. The kind of soul that eventually incarnates, crucially governed by Spiritual Law, is largely, though not solely, determined by the *family environment* and *connections* to the *pregnant mother* particularly. Strong similarities between the incoming soul and the mother or other members of the family may also have a bearing on *who* finally arrives. Or perhaps the prospective soul may have ties to a particular person or group of people that the prospective mother has close connections with. That potential can act as a powerful force of attraction for the souls surrounding her who are awaiting an opportunity to incarnate. Thus women, who are the providers of the "Spiritual bridge" and are the **primary link** by which incoming souls are able to enter the Earth plane, have a very great responsibility here.

Past life connections to various members of the family can be a strong determinant as well, and one which may later provide either harmonious relationships, or severely strained ones, depending on the circumstances of the past association. In all cases, however, the particular soul that finally inhabits the growing foetus will have been strictly determined according to Spiritual Law. It will thus possess all the necessary characteristics to fulfil its particular role and purpose within the family grouping, and in its own *personal* life-path as well.

The entry of the soul into the growing foetus, also determined by Law, takes place about the middle of pregnancy.[4] The seal of attraction is then complete and the soul takes full possession of its new home – the growing body in the mother's womb. She might well have mixed feelings, which may range from bliss to unease. This will depend on the nature of this *new stranger* she is *compelled to accept*.

The emotionally-charged issue of abortion takes on an entirely different hue when viewed

---

[4]This entry time has been corroborated, **unknowingly**, by Dr. Robert Winston (of "The Human Body" fame). His statement to this effect was made in Part 1 of his *second series* of Human Development. That series traces the birth, life and development of a group of newborn babies to adulthood. His observations of major changes around the time of mid-pregnancy – which his narration outlined – indicated that much more happens in, and to, a growing foetus at precisely this time than just a continuation of normal physical development within the womb. Thus what Spiritual Law inviolably states, medical science has now noted – albeit unwittingly at this time.

from the perspective of Spiritual Law. According to The Eternal Laws by which we are granted life and sustenance, abortion is not the automatic right of any mother at any time during pregnancy. Of course, there will always occur certain life-threatening situations that may necessitate the need for difficult decisions in this respect. But the strident cry of: "My body, my right!", does not remove the Spiritual consequences wrought through unnecessary abortions by all involved – for there *is* "freedom of choice" here too. However, in both freedom of choice and the so-called *right* to "abortion on demand", those Spiritual consequences nevertheless remain.

Even a purely foetal abortion – in the early stages of pregnancy before the entry of the soul – does not absolve the participants of the spiritual repercussions of such an act. From the waiting soul's point of view, all its hopes and aspirations for that particular Earth life with its chosen parents, and the mutual opportunities of spiritual growth for both parties, is effectively lost. Whether or not a second opportunity for incarnation might present itself for the *same players* via another pregnancy could only be determined under the outworking of Spiritual Law.

> So regardless of what the medical profession, women's groups, or lawmakers have determined **for themselves**, abortion *after* the entry of a soul into the growing foetus **is similar to physical murder** under those *very exacting* and **immutable** Laws of Creation.

It is a foolish delusion to believe that the act of ending the life of a human being as a purely "convenient solution" would not carry *serious spiritual consequences* for the perpetrators. Consequences, moreover, that impact upon *all* who *support* such practices.[5]

The birth of disabled children is therefore not without purpose either, whether for the mother, the family or, not least, for the disabled one. Because these events are strictly governed by Spiritual Law, it is only through the knowledge of them that full understanding can be gained as to why such an event will visit itself upon a family group. It is surely certain, however, that in the caring of the disabled one, the nature of the handicap will allow both family partners the necessary spiritual experiencing for which the birth was perhaps ordained. Permitted, moreover, through the *free-will decision of the parents for sexual union* thus leading to the ensuing procreative event. In this case, it is important to understand that it is only the *physical body* that is disabled, thus one *physically constrained for life* **on Earth**. The inner, animating core of the spirit, the *real* child and adult, is never so!

The infertility of certain couples is also not an arbitrary act. The inability to naturally produce offspring is similarly governed by "Spiritual Law". In other words, there will be a very good reason for this, even if not readily apparent. It may well have its origin in the long distant past, with its reciprocal effect translating in a deep desire to want children in the present, but not easily being able to, or possibly not at all, even with modern medical procedures. Infertile couples should thus determine whether or not it is within their ordained life-path to pursue parenthood. It could mean that having no children might allow them to fulfil a particular purpose more completely, whereas having children may make it much more difficult, or even impossible.

A more enlightened attitude would see couples planning for children solely from the *Spiritual point of view*. Where no children are desired, conception would simply be avoided. The very nature of physical desire between couples – which should be viewed as both a natural and

---

[5]It is interesting to objectively observe the plight of certain peoples today whose *primary method* of birth control is abortion. The acceptance of this kind of birth-control regime, in the case of very populous countries, translates to hundreds of thousands, possibly millions, of destroyed lives over many years. The now more rapid reciprocal effect of all *spiritual* transgressions accelerates the consequences of this particular practice in such societies. The subsequent accelerating deterioration of the *material* and *social* environment of such Nations is hardly surprising because the whole land becomes a vast, "reciprocal-reaping collective" for the particular peoples concerned.

especial gift to permit complete consummation of the love felt for each other – means that the possibility of pregnancy is ever-present. With an understanding of the processes that determine the kind of new family addition that could arrive, however, future prospective parents will be better able to plan for the reception of children who will be more aware and enlightened then might otherwise be the case without this new knowledge.

Just as the new soul will provide certain experiences and lessons for the family group into which it has incarnated, its new family and circumstances will offer similar provision for what it will need for its spiritual growth too. Viewed in this light, the wish to want a child should be more seriously considered because such a desire should be tempered by the acceptance of the responsibility to provide the correct upbringing for any offspring. Children are not ours to *own* and neither should we see them as arriving to us as a completely clean slate upon which we can write our own *personal program* for them.

With each act of procreation, the opportunity is offered for a soul to reside with us until such time as its ordained path or personal choices calls it to travel *its own* individual journey. If we have attracted spiritually and guided well, "offspring" should naturally develop the inner urge to make good decisions for themselves whenever crossroads are reached. Hopefully, the decision made then will be in accordance with The Eternal Laws, thus ensuring a good return for those we have nurtured and set free.

Under the outworking of this "attracting-process" a family of noble people will generally attract noble souls. The arrival of a so-called "black sheep" might indicate that the pregnant woman may have allowed a less-than-honourable person into her immediate sphere *around the time of the entry of that particular soul.*

> Under the ***immutability*** of The Eternal Laws, a *dark soul* seeking to incarnate on Earth ***will always drive back a lighter, more noble soul seeking the same opportunity.***

This simple yet profound process is purely the *lawful* and *inviolable* outworking of **The Law of Spiritual Gravity**.

Perhaps earlier generations intuitively understood this process in part, in determining pregnancy as a time, or term, "of confinement". Thus as a period of "protective separation" from detrimental effects of society. This custom would offer natural spiritual protection, more especially up to the entry of the soul into the foetus. It is unlikely, however, that "modern feminist views" would accept such ideas. Nevertheless, these strict and lawful "spiritual" processes cannot be circumvented by so-called "modern attitudes" – social or medical![6]

The effect of "The Law of Attraction..." around families and crime has produced some interesting statistics. Police records in many countries have recorded whole families – even generations of families – where crime in its myriad forms is regarded as the norm by such groups of wrong-thinking people. Sometimes, however, even in that kind of situation and against all the odds, a member of such a "family" may choose to follow a different path. Thus the more noble and truly Spiritual characteristics of compassion, courage, inherent respect for justice and inner grace, for example, are ***not*** biologically inherited. Similarly, the uglier traits of humankind are not inherited that way either.

Nevertheless, it is still The Law of Attraction of Similar Species that *primarily* determines the make-up of families. Therefore, it should not be presumed that a soul with an innate propensity to live a less than noble existence on the Earth must necessarily do so. Our inherent

---

[6]We may note this spiritually-cleansing preparation-time around the incarnation of Jesus. There, the Annunciation by the Messenger to Mary helped her to *prepare* her spirit and body for the reception of His Divine Core during the pregnancy.

free-will factor gives such a person the opportunity to break free from any base propensities, no matter how strong, *if it so chooses or wills for itself.*

Genetic processes, which are by no means accidental, are what give rise to the physical characteristics of parental offspring. The Law of Reciprocal Action ensures that in such situations only those who have "sown the appropriate seeds" are incarnated into families and places where they are bound to enjoy genetic advantage or, conversely, suffer from hereditary disability. By way of example, as a given disease is conquered in a particular part of the world, those souls whose karma *might* need the living experience of that disease will only be able to incarnate in a country where it still exists.

In the light of this knowledge, we should re-examine our current thinking as to who or what actually constitutes a "victim". The present day tyranny of the "poor victim of circumstance" syndrome virtually allows some people of this mind-set to commit even crimes of shocking violence under the umbrella of this excuse. In truth, such terribly wrong attitudes debilitate and spiritually degrade society. We should recognise this for the wrong attitude, the "emotional disease", that it actually is and set up re-education programmes to smartly correct such incorrect, aspiritual thinking.

That is not to say, however, that help should not be offered to those in need. On the contrary, with this correct knowledge, *exactly the right kind of help* or education can be given, thus allowing for the possibility of the complete elimination of this societal "illness". That would provide the necessary foundation for nobleness and *individual responsibility* to become the norm instead of the present practice of socially or culturally entrenching the totally wrong idea of "non-responsibility" into the very people who desperately need a complete change of thinking.

Consider, also, if the Earth could be rid of all diseases and the causes of human suffering, any souls that needed to experience such suffering would not have the opportunity to be able to incarnate here. Consequently, we can further extrapolate that if we – all humanity – really strove to be truly noble in all our thoughts, words, aspirations and activities etc., it would become impossible for any unworthy spirits to incarnate on Earth simply because *the connecting bridge of attraction* would not be there. Through this recognition and process, a more enlightened humankind could make the Earth what it was originally ordained to be – *a paradise*. More to the point, that is what could and should have happened. Our choice, our responsibility, solely, however.

To this end it is important to understand that the present thrust of globally entrenching the concept of "my rights", transgresses virtually *every aspect* of **Creation-Law**. Almost nowhere now do we hear of responsibilities, duties, or obligations. We hear only the increasingly strident and selfish cry of: **"My rights!"** In the case of the relationship between parents and children, this translates into a mad tyranny where children's *rights* have become more important than their *responsibilities*. Just as parents have responsibilities to their offspring, so, too, should children be taught to fulfil this aspect of Spiritual Law.

By first putting in place the attitude of responsibilities and duties to each other, we automatically create an environment where rights can become synonymous with duties, for under Spiritual Law fulfilment of *duty and responsibility* must *precede* any claim to *rights*.

Therefore: *Children can only claim **rights** if they loyally perform their **duties**.*

3.5.3 Why there is so much Violence and Evil on Earth: The "Divine Warning" to Mothers

The ultimate reason for the huge levels of violence committed by evil men upon their fellow men today is not necessarily because of religious, political or geo-political considerations; or ethnic or racial tension; or wealth versus poverty or any other *excuse*. Those are simply the societal or religious parameters that offer the framework under which such people can carry out their evil works. The *true* answer lies in the knowledge and outworking of The Spiritual Laws/Principles. The problem today – which has nevertheless been with us for a long time now – is precisely about; —

— the kinds of human souls permitted entry onto the Earth from darker regions in the beyond to whom fellow humans on Earth should <u>never</u> have stretched a hand.

Quite simply, through the justly lawful process of procreation and incarnation under the aegis and outworking of "The Law of Attraction...", particularly, **doors have long been opened to the lower regions of the beyond.** The huge numbers of the more evil-minded human souls forced to be there under the *immutable outworking* of "The Law of Spiritual Gravity" (explained further on in this Chapter) are offered a *bridge* by which they can return to Earth. These bridges of attraction, in the very first instance, **are the mothers of the various global communities into which such souls incarnate.**

We speak of responsibility as being one of the key factors for creating a better society, *but ignorantly refuse to accept, or even believe in, the very kind of ultimate responsibility that would prevent such dark humans from arriving on Earth to wreak murderous havoc in their later years.*

The main contributing factors here are the **terrible distortions** of the original religious teachings given to mankind over millennia. Such twisting of the clear original sets the parameters whereby **whole societies today now live their respective delusions about the absolute rightness of their particular religion, solely.** Within those societies the children, *especially*, are naturally significantly-exposed from birth to every nuance of societal or cultural interpretation of the particular **religion** into which they are born.

If we examine revelatory prophecy very objectively, we may note that in —

Crucial Imperative No. 8:

> That we, the human Beings of planet Earth, *inherently possess* the ordained *attribute* of "**free-will**". That *not understanding* the so-called inequities or injustices of life has its *genesis* in human *non-recognition* and thus *non-understanding* of this most "**Crucial Imperative**".

— we discover a very compelling reason [**freedom of choice**] why a comprehensive and terrible *"cleansing"* is virtually the only solution left to prevent wrong religious and cultural teachings from permitting the entry of evil-minded souls onto the Earth in the future. Such a final end will bring to a juddering halt any further opportunity for the evil-minded to incarnate here. For, quite obviously, *many* of the women of the world – from birth inculcated with the particular "mind-set" of the various races, cultures and religions **into which they had <u>chosen</u> to incarnate** and who therefore **primarily** provide *the bridge of attraction* to waiting souls – **will not be here either.**

The reader should seriously **dwell awhile here** and strive to understand **why Jesus, The Son of God**, should so strongly warn His Disciples in the **way** that He did, when *they* asked Him to tell *them* what would come upon the Earth and humankind at the closing of the age – these times now!

A specific, <u>Divine</u> and very blunt warning goes out to the <u>women</u> who will be <u>mothers</u> at the time.

> "But **alas for those <u>with child</u> and those <u>who nurse</u> in those days**! Pray, however, that your flight may not come during the winter, nor upon a Rest-day;

for there shall **then** be wide-spread affliction, such as has <u>**not been known**</u> since **the beginning of the world until now**, no, nor will **ever** be known again. And if those times were not cut short, *not a man would be saved*; but for the sake of the chosen ones, those times will be cut short.

(Matthew 24:19-22, Fenton.
Emphases mine.)

The Book of Mark states the warning equally strongly.

"But **alas for those <u>with child</u>, and for the <u>nursing women</u> in those days!** And pray especially that your flight may not take place during the winter. For in those days there will be affliction, such as has <u>**never been known**</u> **since the beginning of the creation which God created until now, and such as shall** <u>**never be again**</u>. And unless the Lord had cut short those times, *none could be saved*;...

(Mark 13:17-20, Fenton.
Emphases mine.)

Even on His grievous, agonising walk to His execution at Golgotha, more warnings to women:

And a large crowd of the people followed Him, including women, who were beating their breasts, and lamenting Him. Jesus, however, turning towards them, said, "Daughters of Jerusalem, weep not for me; but weep for yourselves and for your children. For now the days are coming, during which they shall say, Happy are the barren, happy the childless, and happy those who have never nursed."

(Luke 23:26-31, Fenton.)

The *clear warning* to the women at "the end of the times" also strongly hints that the destructive period will come upon the world suddenly and unexpectedly, but last only for a relatively short time. Hence his further warning that the period of destruction would therefore need to be on a scale "...not seen before, nor will be seen again", in order to *complete the job*. Thus the need to cut the times short or *no one* would be left.

Whilst the measure for interpreting Bible Scripture – particularly the words of Jesus as recorded in the Gospels – is often a very broad one with many offering their personal ideas on meaning, no interpretation of the *primary sentence directed towards women in the above quote* has thus far crossed the path of this writer. Since we have stated what will surely produce outcries of horror from women's groups and civil and human rights advocates as well, let us now analyse what that specific warning to the world's women – from the knowledge of the Highest of Law – *actually relates to.*

And given by One in Whom inherently resided exactly that Living Law.

[The whole thrust of this writing is to *enlighten* and *point the way* to that very **All-Truth** from which we derive the spiritual knowledge of **Creation-Law**, so written herein!]

Therefore, in terms of a soul incarnating to a mother *anywhere* in the world, to *any* culture, race or religion; the **primary aspect** of the event is that the **new-born** is **not** the **personal property** of the mother, the associated family, or the particular group into which it is born. In the very first instance, it is its *own individual person*. It is a *singularly individual spirit* which has journeyed through this part of Creation *primarily for its spiritual purpose*. The various families *into which* it had previously and successively *incarnated* under the absolute immutability of the key Laws of "Attraction..." and "Rebirth", **unequivocally reveal** that it is **not** the property of anyone else.

New-born babies are very much welcomed, nurtured and protected by most mothers of the world, and strong bonding is a natural and desirable feature of the mother/baby relationship. That we certainly agree is absolutely the right thing. However, since we are assessing **the actual meaning of Christ's warning to mothers at this end-time**, then other, more powerful considerations must come into play here if there is to be any kind of logical meaning according to the outworking of "The Spiritual Laws of Life": — **CREATION-LAW!.**

The deaths of babies and children invariably strike a painful chord in most people. That is because the vast majority of adult human beings only see the *physical* happening; the death of a small, vulnerable and often helpless little person. What we do not see is that which is *released* from that small body; the *actual person* – the *spirit* who would have grown to adulthood – now *free* of the body, but at a tender age, however. Sometimes the loss is so great for the nurturing mother who carried and delivered the soul into the world that her emotional grief may be inconsolable. Therein, however, **rests the substantive meaning of the warning to women.**

Thus, the gift of a child is exactly that – a gift. Inviolable Spiritual Law unequivocally states that children may arrive *when least expected or planned for* and, as is painfully obvious to all, **can be taken at any time <u>without</u> the parent's permission being sought.**

So the loss of any child should be *spiritually understood* to have been a gift for whatever time *was ordained for it*; particularly for the mother, but also for the wider family. Oftentimes at the moment of greatest grief – unfortunately too often – blame is sought for the loss. Regrettably, therefore, if that blame should be directed towards The One Who gave Life to all anyway, *including* the grieving mother, then the outworking of The Law of Reciprocal Action must, and *will*, run its eventual course.

In the case of catastrophe-related destruction of global societies and their human populations – and also because the demographics of the Earth's population show a large proportion now quite young – any destructive effects may impact on this group perhaps disproportionately. One can readily understand the prophecy where, at that time, "great wailing and gnashing of teeth" will occur. The Indian Ocean tsunami tragedy is a case in point; so much outpouring of aid globally, but so many children dead and so much inconsolable grief and anguish. The same was experienced by Chinese mothers as a result of China's 2008 earthquake. There, however, a harder dimension because of that country's "one-child" policy.

The one element in what we are stating that *could* serve to *help* mothers, particularly, over the loss of children is the lawful fact that babies and young children, because they have **not** reached the age of spiritual responsibility, are **not so subject** to the outworking of The Law of Reciprocal Action – the **'Iron Law' of Karma**. Therefore, unlike adults who *are* so subject to that *full* outworking – and who thus are lawfully propelled to that Plane which *they* had prepared *for themselves* – babies and children, precisely in accordance with the Perfect Justice of The Spiritual Laws, will find themselves in one of the 'Lighter Planes'. There to be cared for and undergo growth and development alongside *other* human spirits *also residing there*.

The clear connotation here, in concert with the warning of Jesus to mothers, is **to seek out and strive to understand the knowledge of The Eternal Laws**. So that, should the situation arise where a mother must *let go* one she has brought into the world, she will do so *with **understanding gratitude** to He Who granted her the ability to **bear** the child in the first place*, and gratitude **for the time** *she was permitted to be with that soul*. As previously stated, for those who would curse in hate or anger, The Law must, and will, bring the reciprocal effect! Such inviolable, Lawful, outworking simply cannot be altered!

That is precisely why it is stated that the millennial phase will be one of peace *for the few who are left.* In the first instance, it will be forced upon those who survive through the discipline of *adjusting* to The Laws as they actually are; as we should have done long ago. Secondly, those *who would have* refused to bend or bow will simply *not be here.* Given the increasing levels of evil and bloodshed that men are visiting upon each other now, it is unlikely that such dark practices will be permitted to continue for very much longer. Only when the evil-minded, *through their personal choices*, have self-destructed, will there then be peace and harmony for the few left on Earth.

That is why it is also stated that the Earth will be cleansed so comprehensively; and cleansed through the outworking of Perfect and Just Laws! After that period, human offspring will be born healthier and more spiritually-aware, because there will not be any dark souls incarnating onto the Earth again. For human mothers, the births of the new-born will no longer carry with it the pain of childbirth that has long been the case. In concert with the subject matter of this particular sub-Chapter, this key related question arises.

Question: Why have human mothers suffered so much during a process that should really be a defining moment of blissful joy — without pain?

3.5.4   The Universal Pain of Childbirth.
The Enlarging Baby Cranium: A "Medical" Mystery.

Whilst touching on the phenomenon of **the enlarging baby cranium**, this sub-Section mainly assesses the aspects of, and reasons for, the **universal pain of childbirth** for birthing mothers. So whilst primarily concerned with the *pain* of childbirth, we also necessarily connect to a corresponding and *linking* segment in Chapter 8: **The Emergence of Language.** Specifically the sub-Chapter; **The Biblical "Fall of Man": A Disastrous Legacy for Global Humanity**; sub-Section, **The Enlarging Baby Cranium: The "Lawful" Reason**.

In the final analysis, even though these two aspects are intrinsically connected by virtue of the origin of firstly the universal pain of childbirth and secondly the enlarging baby cranium, it does not at all mean that birthing pain is **caused** by the phenomenon of enlarging craniums – though of course it can be. The seeming paradox here is that **despite** their inherently-close association with regard to the **genesis** of **both** aspects, they **could** nonetheless be **construed** as stemming from **different** beginnings – i.e., in terms of what we will reveal as the **actual** reason/s for **both**.

With the pain of childbirth now universally accepted as being very normal, women individually, women's groups, and all of the medical profession dealing in obstetrics especially, should *really* consider *why* that is so. Or perhaps even why that *need* be so.

As a writer who occupies the male end of the gender spectrum, I am sure that many women will be amazed at the sheer effrontery of my comments. For what would a mere man know of a woman's feelings and emotions in childbirth? Of course that is absolutely correct *insofar* as the physical and emotional experience is concerned, and I am sure that no man would ever *presume* to know. However, what we can never push away is the clear fact that the 'mechanics' of the process which occurs from conception to birth takes place under the aegis of precise, non-negotiable, *non-emotional*, **Creation-Law parameters**. So irrespective of what we may wish to place on childbirth, women's notions and feelings, father's notions and feelings, philosophical, cultural or social beliefs and commentary, etc., the fact will forever remain that the path from conception to birth – even if generated by in-vitro fertilisation – is, *unarguably*, absolutely subject to **Immutable Creation-Law**.

On the question of 'birthing pain', therefore: It is well known that the contractions necessary to propel the baby toward birth are painful for all women, never mind an enlarging baby cranium to complicate matters further for some. And even though the *pain-threshold* for birthing mothers would obviously vary, the 'normal' human birthing process associated with 'labour' and 'delivery' nonetheless produces pain for all, so epidurals are common. Therefore, especially centred on that reality, what we state explanatorily in the *two linking sub-Sections* to *be* the *actual reason/s* for the high pain levels *and* enlarging baby cranium will most certainly be branded ridiculous, trite, foolish, uninformed and/or uneducated to the point of being ignorant, totally unscientific — and perhaps even dangerously religious. And thus will surely offend many!

The opposite, however, stands as The Truth here!

For no matter how many times in this Work we *necessarily repeat* the following clear and unarguable fact, it will not *yet* find easy accommodation with the educational establishment, *particularly*. So therefore once more for all educationalists and their political masters:
The present, deplorable state of global societies *unequivocally testifies* to the *sure reality* that we human beings not only ***do not*** live according to the true and *absolutely inviolable* **Creation Laws of Life**, but each generation born travels further and further ***from them***. The responsibility for that resultant non-recognition can be laid squarely at the feet of *aspiritual* education parameters leading to a crucially-dangerous lack of ***genuine*** *life-knowledge*. That reality has been instrumental in the commission of increasingly darker deeds by the many millions born year by year. Now, finally, we are brought face to face with our foolish arrogance. The previous sub-section explained the **HOW**.

Now we will explain the **WHY**. Firstly, however, let us *seriously* stress the fact that the actual answer to both our key questions — and I can hear many disbelieving cries of; "Oh no, not more religious rubbish' — really is in that especial;
"Primary Book of Foundational-Science": **The Bible!**

In the previous Chapter we explained, necessarily in a very basic way, the step-by-stupendous-step of the complete Creation-process beginning with the *immediate creation* of male and female in **The First Creation**. Then very much later in **Subsequent Creation**, the "coming into being", the *forming*, of animal-man "from out of the dust of the ground". Finally, the *entry* of the human-spiritual aspect *into* those prepared primate vessels which *thereby* permitted and facilitated *our human* growth and development to this present, 21st-century evolutionary point.
Human reproductive ability subsequently burdened an Earth groaning at the seams with a population at the 7 billion mark and rapidly increasing. With it, however, a cranial *abberation* in foetal development. The clues to the resolution of both the problems we address in this sub-Section may be found in specific texts in **The Book of Genesis** under the sub-heading: **The Temptation Of Eve**.

The story of Adam and Eve, whilst taken *literally* by many millions, should really be understood as being *more symbolic* of the *entry* of sin into the world. In other words; *a free-will choice producing a specific outcome under the inviolable outworking of* **The Law of Reciprocal Action**.
In the context of the two questions we address here – the universally-tolerated 'birthing pains' and the enlarging baby cranium which medical science is currently puzzling over – certain

key Scriptures unequivocally answer the question of pain. They also, paradoxically, offer *the clues* that *link* to Chapter 8; which *there* provides the *complete reason* for the growing problem of the enlarging cranium in human babies.

So: The **singular reason** for Eve being commanded *not to eat* [ingest] of *just one* particular tree in the Garden of Eden lies in the *effect* that *that particular fruit* had upon her and Adam once they had *tasted* [ingested] it. The tempting serpent asks Eve:[7]

> "Is it true that GOD has said, you may not eat of every tree of the Garden?"
> And the woman replied to the serpent, "We may eat of the fruit of the trees of the garden; but of the fruit of the tree which is in the middle of the garden, GOD has said, 'do not eat of it, and do not even touch it, *lest you die*'."
> But the serpent answered the woman: "You will not die; but GOD knows that at the time you eat of it, your eyes will then be opened, and you will be like GOD, acquainted with both good *and evil*."
> So the woman *perceiving* that the tree was *good for food*, [tasty] and *beautiful to the eyes* [alluring], and a tree **stimulating** to the **intellect**, she took some of its fruit and ate it, and gave some to her husband with her; and he also ate it.
> Then the eyes of both of them *were opened*...

> (Genesis 3:1-7, Fenton. Emphases
> and parenthetic additions mine.)

The key point here centres on the well-known fact that for we humans, *forbidden fruit* is invariably perceived as *tasty*, *alluring*, and *stimulating* to certain senses in an *inappropriate* way, or *stimulating* for the *wrong reason/s*. Therefore, the notion that an *actual reptile* tempted Eve does not at all hold up to just plain and simple logic. And **Creation-Law** cannot be anything other than logical; either in its "Form" and "Essence", or in its *inviolable outworking*. The 'serpent' that enticingly tempts humankind is the quiet, insidious, ever-so-seductive voice which our *inner 'spiritual' conscience* strives to warn against. Unfortunately, however, the *outer and worldly 'intellectual'* part of us invariably ignores such warnings therewith leading to our embracing of the *wrong* aspect, and thus to our **spiritual fall**. So to taste of *fruit* that will bring **spiritual** death is simply to choose a path that *opposes* **The Spiritual Laws of Creation**; thus one that *no longer* adheres to a *spiritual* way, but is the chosen [by humankind] *intellectual* way. [The way of the 'shrewdly-calculating' intellect.]

To repeat: Eve [humankind] rejected the [correct] *spiritual way* and chose, instead, the alluring *intellectual way* – **solely**. Now it is "the way of the world" with all its attendant aspiritual garbage and increasing problems. We therefore *sowed the wind* in the [female] *decision*, but now *reap the whirlwind* – primarily for women in this case – in the [female] *outcome*. For in Genesis 3:16, Fenton (emphases mine), we read:

> But to the woman He said, "I will increase your sorrows and your joys. *You will give birth to children* **with pain**;..."

Of all creatures on Earth human woman, certainly, is burdened with painful birth of offspring. Whilst other life-forms *can* have difficult births, for the most part they go about their birthing-business with relative ease and few complications. Rather than being a *relatively* uncomplicated, *natural* event, human birthing has virtually become a 'medical' procedure with, at times, a whole team of medical staff actively involved. Of course that is exactly right if there are complications,

---

[7]Eve: *Khavah*, or *life-container*.

but the development and necessity for there to be specialist wards in modern hospitals as the accepted norm now seems to be a 'reversal' of what should be more a 'natural order'.

In the case of serious birthing difficulties, both the affected mother and attending obstetrics professionals really need to take into account the knowledge and outworking of **The Spiritual Laws of Creation**. For within certain specific and connecting Laws therein will often be found the *actual* reason for such traumatic births. In other words, irrespective of what the physical/medical considerations might indicate for the particular problem or for the mother, certain connecting links between her and the newly emerging soul may hold the deeper reason. In such cases, the *medical* situation will simply *parallel* the final *outworking* of the more decisive *spiritual* aspect.

The question of the enlarging baby cranium is one that Western obstetrics' specialists and researchers, particularly, are currently striving to answer. The equation is quite simple, though of course problematic: An *enlarging* baby cranium needing to exit the womb through a pelvic girdle that is *not* enlarging. The natural accompaniment is the potential for increased pain and a longer time in labour. Now why should that be? What factor or factors prevent such a logical accommodation? Why will Mother Nature not provide the obvious solution; hold the cranium to a size that is exactly right for natural, uncomplicated and *relatively* painless childbirth for human mothers?

For that is the case with millions of herd animals that must give birth quickly and easily for simple survival of their offspring which must be ready to run with the herd just hours after birth. Natural predators 'sort out' any problematic births. Certainly in the wild with mammals that produce multiple births [a 'litter' of wolf pups for example], the females usually give birth easily, lick the litter clean and suckle them immediately. And without any requirement for 'extra care'.

Where human interference in the form of specific breeding occurs, however, there we may see birthing problems – as in the case of the English bulldog. Bred for bull-baiting, the now too-large-head is so problematic for the birthing bitch that 95% of births are cesarean. Free whelping is not recommended.

> **Note:** Given the very contentious nature of this subject, the *female* reader, ***most especially***, must understand that we are *not comparing* the birthing experience of human mothers with that of other mammals. What we are explaining here is an *outcome* for our *human* species that animals — by virtue of the fact that they inherently possess the attribute of *instinct* only and **not** *free will* — could *never ever* set in train. So it is crucially important to withhold judgement here until one has *read through* the full, *explanatory*, texts.

At first glance, therefore, a connection between a newly-recognised medical problem [perhaps more relevant with Western birth-mothers] and human **Language** may seem tenuous at best and perhaps even rather silly at worst. However, as we state throughout this Work, it is *not possible* for there **not** to be answers to the questions that affect we humans *on Earth*. In this particular case, the *actual* reason/s will certainly *not fit* with accepted medical-science protocols [or even beliefs] in *either* research *or* "best practice parameters" in modern-day, first-world obstetrics.

Nonetheless, there *is* an answer. Moreover, not only *is* there an answer to both the subjects under consideration here, it *is* **in** The Bible! And it is an answer/reason in exact concert with the great and inviolable **Law of Reciprocal Action** — *The Iron Law of Sowing and Reaping.* [We of the human species will yet learn that we simply *cannot* transgress **Creation-Law** with impunity and still believe there are no *consequences* from doing so. The *greater* the degree of transgressing, the *more severe* the consequential outcome – as has *resulted* from these two problems.] Precisely because the enlarging baby cranium aspect centres on the skeletal frame of the human being, the *actual answer* in the final analysis *automatically* incorporates **scientific** realities.

So why should a completely natural process become so problematic for humans that more and more 'C sections' are performed for all sorts of reasons? An increasing number are, of course, elective; but that is not the main consideration.

Here is the primary issue once again: In more or less 'evolutionary' terms, why has the brain case of the human baby enlarged to such a degree that the head size in relation to body size is now so disproportionately big at birth that it can pose serious problems for delivery? Recent calculations of the cranium-size of *new-born babies* – in Western births – on average run to over **12%** of total body mass, while in *adults* the same represents just over **2%**.

The *actual* and thus *ultimate cause* of this 'medical' quandary in humans centres precisely on our wonderful *gift* and *inherent* attribute of *free-will*. Therein lies the paradox. Animals etc., by virtue of having no such attribute, cannot possibly ever be similarly burdened. We of global humanity, however, having *long-chosen* our path, are now *reaping* the consequential outcomes in the present.

There is the *primary* answer for the *spiritually-perceptive* reader; but probably not for the *non* spiritually-*receptive* intellectual. The intellect of man, whilst absolutely necessary for tasks on Earth, has no *perceptive* spiritual capacity *whatsoever*, so has no affinity with higher *Spiritual knowledge*. That is why many noted and lauded 'intellectuals', in commentary and/or in their writings, rail against the reality or even *notion* of 'inviolable absolutes' such as **Creation-Law** and **Spiritual Truth**. The terrible but nonetheless *self-wrought* tragedy *resulting* from this non-recognition and non-acceptance – and thus rejection of *immutable* **Creation-Law Truth** by the very people who, educationally, sway hundreds of millions to *their* non-recognition – is a world blind to the very knowledge that could 'turn things around'.

Isaiah, the great 'Old Testament Prophet' from the eighth century B.C., warned that humankind *would reach* this very point we are now *fruitlessly* struggling with. **WHY?** Specifically for scientists, educationalists, theologians, noted intellectuals – and also for birthing mothers today – from 24:5-6, [Fenton, emphases mine], once again **Isaiah speaks**:

> "The 'Earth' also is **defiled** under the **inhabitants** thereof; because **they** have **transgressed** the Laws,
> **changed** the decrees,
> **broken** the everlasting covenant.
> Therefore has the **curse** devoured the 'Earth', and those that dwell therein **are desolate**:..."

[The whole picture of the enlarging baby cranium cannot be fully elucidated here in this Chapter, for, as earlier stated, this particular question has precise resonance with, and to, human language. So the concomitant and *complete* reason for this abberation can be read in Chapter 8: **The Emergence of Language**.

Specifically the sub-Chapter; **The Biblical "Fall of Man!": A Disastrous Legacy for Global Humanity**;

sub-Section, **The Enlarging Baby Cranium: The "Lawful" Reason!**]

3.5.5 Sexual Orientation and Creation-Law

Sexual orientation: Personal choice – or other? Homosexuality and lesbianism: Natural – or an aberration? Do these attitudes and practices contribute to imminent **"Global Societal Collapse"**; or do they not? What does **The Law** say?

As a general rule among probably *most peoples* historically, anything outside the man/woman union within societies was, for the most part, regarded as unacceptable. Thus running the gamut from undesirable, to offensive, to anathema. In some societies even to this day, punishable by death. Moreover, many cultures regarded – and still regard – the fertile woman as a blessing. When high infant mortality rates were once the norm in all societies, *producing-unions* maintained the numbers necessary for a society to be sufficiently viable for just simple survival to begin with; and for expansion and self-protection as a necessary adjunct.

So what has changed today? Whilst there have always been cultures where non-heterosexual preferences were tolerated/accepted/embraced, the attitude and rulings of the Christian Church, in this area, primarily shaped the overall ethos of Western Nations. Notwithstanding changing societal attitudes and government-enacted legislation to legalise 'civil unions' for 'other kinds of relationships', the prevailing sentiment is still more one of non-acceptance to anything outside the man/woman paradigm.

In a truly strange and curious twist, however, the Teachings of Jesus are often used to justify *both sides* of the debate/clash, even from the pulpits of *opposing* ministers. Perhaps this *aberration* of *irreconcilable-divergence* stems from two *very different* interpretations of the so-called Christian-love ethos.

The *incorrect belief* that Jesus died to cleanse all human beings of their evil dispositions [i.e., *everyone's sins*] in His 'great act of Love' is seemingly the basis for an 'all-forgiving' attitude among some Christians towards virtually everything. For it *ostensibly* seeks to 'emulate' that 'loving sacrifice' in the Churches' interpretation of so-called 'Christian love' and forgive even serious transgressions, sometimes against the very Law Itself. Whilst there should ultimately be forgiveness – tempered by compassion of course – *true justice* must still nevertheless prevail.

In the final analysis, however, what is mooted as love is anything but, because it invariably fails to take into account **Justice**. **Creation-Law** *absolutely decrees* that **Love** and **Justice** cannot be separated. **They are one!** So where one is used without the other, **The Law of Balance** [explained further on] is then seriously transgressed.

Love: A small word, but one that has inadvertently caused so many problems due to the wrongful application of it in the unfortunate belief that it was always correctly applied. Because of its spiritually weak, earthly interpretation, we might designate the overall concept inherent in it as being almost a 'religion of earthly love'. For it is one thing to reverentially proclaim a belief in this power of love, but another to then apply it so wrongly that its distorted application produces the worst kinds of injustices. We need to therefore understand that **The Love of The Divine**, which produced the incomprehensible vastness of the physical universes – thus permitting us our material home – is actually severe, objective and impartial in its outworking. And therefore cannot possibly be equated with the weak, emotional, earthly caricature that we have produced in the *human* rendition of the word *love*.

For the moment putting aside non-heterosexual considerations: Perhaps the best kind of example to illustrate this premise is in the area of personal relationships, particularly in the search for a marriage partner. The emotional damage wrought largely by Hollywood's image-makers, coupled with the belief that pre-marital sex is necessary to determine whether two people will be 'suited' to a life together, has generated the ludicrous and almost farcical situation where 'shopping around to sample the goods' is believed to hold the key to a 'perfect marriage of true love'. Basically, in such situations, the concept of love is therewith reduced to the idea that it must surely be present in the intense feelings and emotions experienced with the 'best sexual partner'. Whilst such an encounter may certainly provide very powerful feelings of intense emotion, acceptance, and feeling good about oneself and that partner, it is not likely to be *true love*.[8]

---

[8]Interestingly, evidence suggests that in more simple and basic societies where "arranged marriages" are the norm, there appears to be a higher level of marriage fidelity, faithfulness and loyalty than that

In any case, if all such experimentation actually produced true love, we would surely not have the current, high divorce rate of the West.[9] Moreover, one would never know whether the *next* potential partner would be 'better' than the 'present *true* love'. This current societal attitude promotes views such as that recommended by Kathleen Quinlivan, a Canterbury University [New Zealand] sexual researcher who proposed that students:

> "...regardless of their sexual orientation...", should be allowed "...to explore a range of sexual identities and their implications."

One would have thought that any individual would have the free-will right to do so in any case. One does not need a University graduate to state a fundamental personal right to experiment and make a particular choice.
In her view it was important to recognise:

> "...the diversity and differences which existed within communities..." which would benefit "...gay, lesbian, bisexual and heterosexual youth alike."

What is interesting in this case is that such views pressurise youth into possibly believing that the average boy/girl relationship – which, by the way, is the only kind that will **naturally** produce offspring – might somehow be unsound. And that the impressionable young must therefore be able to 'chop and change' to suit prevailing 'liberating expectations'. The ultimate horror in the present climate of inane 'political correctness' is, of course, to be labelled homophobic or something similar.
Reverend Gerald Hadlow, an Anglican minister, [New Zealand] on precisely this subject succinctly stated a necessary hope:
"Perhaps one day our youth will rediscover love, commitment."

From the standpoint of **Creation-Law**, we are not *the least bit interested* with any individual's personal choice – **in anything**! What we state throughout the pages of this book is that the inviolable outworking of **The Spiritual Laws** is absolute – *for every decision made*.

For the *purposes* of *this* particular discussion, then: **If** The Laws contained in The Bible, for example, *are* absolute, then the *kinds of advice* promoted by Kathleen Quinlivan for young people to 'liberate' themselves *from* the *so-called* 'debilitating constraints of homophobic views' are, in reality, nothing more than an advocacy of unnecessary and potentially dangerous experimentation. It is a view driven by the foolish emotionalism contained in the current global 'my rights' mindset. Why?

> Because under the *ultimate and non-negotiable* parameters of **Creation-Law**, any actual *'debilitating constraint'* is, *by extension*, then **actually present** in all so-called 'liberating sexual practices'. And therefore also in sexual orientation preferences **different** to that which **The Eternal Laws** decree as being *spiritually correct*.

So the actual *'debilitating constraint'* here is brought about simply by shackling oneself *to completely incorrect beliefs*.

present in our so-called sophisticated, western cultures. Perhaps the key word here is responsibility, with duty as a close adjunct. We do not, however, advocate the 'arranged marriage' as the perfect solution, for personal *free will* should *always* determine the choice of a partner.

[9]Notwithstanding the societal stability that long-term marriages offer, we should nevertheless understand that some unions are meant for a particular time only. When such a union has run its ordained course, there is little to be gained in 'forcing' a continuation of it.

In any case what social scientists determine for themselves and Western societies is rendered totally *irrelevant* by the sacrosanct nature of **Creation-Law**! For whatever choices we make *will bring* the reciprocal return; *without fail*. That is the inviolable outworking of **The Law of Reciprocal Action** operating in the lives of each of us. Therefore, the belief that one can somehow become *spiritually-liberated* by choosing a sexual preference which *does not* encompass the man/woman union is, in a word, ***wrong***! Whilst our explanations may not fit at all with present societal mores, it is nevertheless especially important for young people to know that the age-old boy/girl relationship which brings more boys and girls onto the earth, is not only *perfectly okay*, but unequivocally derives from **The Eternal Laws**!

For any human being to *deny* the very obvious fact that the physical form of woman ***perfectly complements*** the physical form of man in a ***natural union of intimacy*** is laughable. For the two forms provide the ***only*** natural connection possible. Therefore, *despite* what the very loud global minority promote as being *natural*, any and every other intimate union of human beings in their physical forms is, by definition, naturally **unnatural**. That is not to say that such unions may be deemed politically and socially *acceptable* in the various cultures and societies of the world, but that is an entirely different matter.

The purpose of this Work is to elucidate **Creation-Law**; which ***decrees/commands*** only ***naturalness*** throughout Creation – especially and including **The World of Matter** and its *inhabitants*. All else – which can only come into existence via the free-will volition of we human beings in any case – ***must***, and ***will***, be finally driven by the **Pressure** and **Power** of that very **Law** to its *demise*; a polite word in this case.

Liberal ideas such as we have examined in this overall segment, anchored primarily in the intellectually-derived 'Human Rights' mentality now solidly entrenched in mainstream Western thinking, have thus found their final end-excrescence enacted in the earthly legislative law of many countries. In 'earthly law' where 'voiced opposition' to such laws can, in certain circumstances, be *perversely deemed* an actual 'criminal' offence.

Dr Alan Duggan, an Australian researcher into "Male Health", stated to an Auckland Unitec seminar that anecdotal evidence from studies carried out in Canada and Australia suggest that young male suicide statistics may lean as much as *30 per cent* to more suicides 'among homosexual men than straight men'. From that line of research alone, one can see that the higher suicide rate amongst this group does not indicate any kind of 'liberation' at all – rather the opposite. Dr Duggan opined that the research results pointed to a *'sexual orientation/identity crisis'* in this group.

Once again, and purely for the purposes of this discussion, *if* "The Spiritual Laws of Creation" are not believed to be absolute or not believed to exist at all, then *disbelievers* should simply continue to live on in their *disbelief*, particularly of the effects of **The Law of Reciprocal Action** visiting any hard suffering upon them. In all cases under the aegis and increased power inherent in the "whirlwind constant".

> **Do not then, however, apportion blame elsewhere if personal decisions and desires should visit return effects *vastly different* to what one might have wished for – before the fact.**

In any case, it must eventually 'all come out in the wash' one way or the other. As stressed a number of times in this Work, The Spiritual Laws cannot be transgressed with impunity – either by any one person or any so-called *'liberated group'*.

From ***our*** free-will viewpoint, we really ***are*** all free to choose our particular likes, but we nonetheless affirm that those same decisions are most certainly *not* free of *the spiritual consequences*. Thus, whilst it is everyone's personal right to so choose, have the ***courage*** to then *accept* the reciprocal effect of those decisions and do not expect that all others must agree with, or even approve of, any particular choice of sexual orientation. Despite possible disapproval or even revulsion toward certain choices and/or practices, however, such choices nevertheless ultimately remain the preserve of the 'choosers' and should at least be *respected* as that by all others.

The Book of Leviticus provides interesting reading in this regard. One's personal views – or perhaps sexual orientation choice – would probably engender one of two reactions when examining this particular Book of The Bible; a strong or angry emotional one, or perhaps more relaxed acceptance. Regardless of individual views, however, and even though perhaps more addressing the Priesthood from the Tribe of Levi, 'Leviticus' nevertheless provides a valuable insight and guide for more correct *spiritual living* than current so-called 'liberating' views are probably prepared to accept.

For example, Verses 6-29 of Chapter 18 of **'Leviticus'** are sub-headed:

The Laws of Affinity, and Marriages and Sex.

The most interesting aspect of those twenty three Scriptural Verses [also Chapter 20:1-21] is the fact that they embody much of the cultural/social and moral foundation of *most* societies, cultures and religions globally. Why should that be so? Historically, why have non-Christian societies also regarded these kinds of 'Rules for Life' as fundamental for their social stability too? Alluded to or written about in other religious works, the detailed substance of the Sexual Laws in the face-book of the Christian religion – The Bible – quite simply supplies the spiritual and moral parameters for *correct* human living.

Copulation in the *manner* of a man and woman where it is actually *not so*, is therein labelled an **abomination.** In the present climate of 'anything goes", such *words* are mostly regarded as just irksome *religious irrelevance.* However, under the *inviolable* outworking of **The Creation Laws of Life**, *absolutely relevant* and ultimately **death-dealing** in the *second* sense.[10]

> The *natural* human/societal *repugnance* toward sexual involvement in practices such as paedophilia, incest and bestiality etc., clearly reveal that *abhorrence to activities which encompass the immoral and unnatural* is therefore *fundamentally inherent* in the psyche or spirit of human beings. Thus, to stand *outside* that 'inherent compass' means exactly that.

With regard to current views, we can perhaps describe modern man's general interpretation of love as little more than 'emotional self-indulgence' which, when ostensibly expressing love toward another, too often means: **'I want *you* to love me!'**

However, if the foundation for a union is a *genuine* spiritual bond in the first instance, then we may more safely say that *true love* is probably present. Within such a partnership, moreover, all other factors – including that of sexual intimacy – will invariably be emotionally and physically fulfilling also. And because the correct foundation of **The Spiritual** was striven for first as the most important part of the union, it will naturally have the greatest *potential* to be an harmonious one too.

Therefore genuine love will always be concerned with what **spiritually benefits** the other, and not necessarily with what might be personally gratifying or agreeable to him. Thus, the latter-day concept of 'tough love' for wayward teenagers owes its relative success to the fact that its 'genesis' is anchored in the Justice of **Spiritual Law.**

Because the application of the word, love, mirrors a lack of *true* understanding of the meaning of it as contained within The Spiritual Laws, the admonition to "Love thy neighbour" and "Love

---

[10]Fully explained in the Chapter: "The Second Death".

your enemies" does not mean *giving them what they want* or what pleases them. It means only doing for them that which will benefit them *spiritually*. If it means possible hardship from *their* personal point of view, then that may actually be the correct kind of *love*. Otherwise how else can they learn, or grow?

> **To that end the spiritual explanations contained in this Work elucidates and expresses that 'new concept' in its necessary severity, thus offering Love and Justice in Spiritual Knowledge!**

We of global humanity must therefore find the strength to apply the concept of *love* in the right way – if we wish to live spiritually-correctly. This means that even *family* members should not demand what others may have worked hard for under an emotional-blackmail mode in a totally wrong and selfish use of the word. Misplaced indulgence would mean the continuation of the same faults in the *generations* and, by subsequent extension, holding them within the various races. The end result is that *everyone* continues to slide *further* on the *downward* path. That would not be displaying love. On the contrary, by acting thus one would place oneself in the position of not acting spiritually-correctly toward a fellow human being, even if of the *same race or family*. This different and radical view contrasts greatly with what we have too readily accepted thus far as 'true love'.

So where does this kind of 'love' fit in societies seeking respite from constantly deteriorating standards and morals – let alone just the increasing struggles of everyday life in the glaringly-obvious reality of **"Global Societal Collapse"** *across the board.*

For some Christians and Christian groups, their particular brand of 'Jesus-love' sanctifies homosexuality and lesbianism because – according to this belief – all practices where 'love' is present must be natural and thus in concert with 'genuine' Christian principles. With regard to the weak, Christian application of the word, love, we should note that Jesus, Himself, as a manual worker under Joseph the carpenter, would have been *physically strong* in the first instance. The fact that He was also obviously Spiritually-Powerful and not weak and vacillating, is clearly illustrated in the New Testament in His very severe admonitions to many people, *particularly to men of intellect.* His admonition to:

> **"Go and do thou likewise!"**

– is clear testimony to His 'Loving severity' toward humankind. We should therefore regard 'love' as a very real and consistent 'power' in which there will be found no weakness, or illogical or emotional indulgence. We must learn to emulate Jesus, the personification of Divine Love in all its 'Loving severity'!

Thus: Love is a <u>Power</u>, not an emotion!

Wherever it is applied, every application of the word, *love*, must carry the same connotation if we wish to at least ameliorate some aspects of the nonetheless *now unstoppable* **"Global Societal Collapse"**. A self-inflicted 'collapse' under the aegis of the inviolable and immutable outworking of **The Law of Reciprocal Action.**

3.6 The Law of Spiritual Gravity!

"Gravity: – Its *Spiritual* Dynamic."

In accordance with *Newton's* "Law on Universal Gravitation", the idea of a force of gravity is readily understandable in the physical sense of the word. Quite logically, heavy objects fall to the ground whilst very light substances e.g., vapour, may rise. So the effect we see *materially* is the form by which this Law, **The Law of Spiritual Gravity**, manifests on Earth.

The everyday outworking of the effect of The Law of Gravity is revealed in a non-conscious way in earthly sayings that underpin this concept in society as a whole. However, whilst the effect of this particular Law clearly displays obvious *physical* characteristics, it is first and foremost a *Spiritual* one. For instance, we often speak of "heavy thoughts" and "light thoughts", or the effect that a "heavy person" may have upon us as opposed to the much more enjoyable company of a "light person". Evil thoughts and practices are rightly recognised as being "heavy". On the other hand, noble thoughts and deeds are accepted as occupying a far higher level.

Thus the same gravitational effect that takes place in a physical setting also occurs in a non-physical environment. It is one, moreover, which impacts very decisively on the fate of man *after* his earthly demise! That is because the actual person or individual is more than just a heavy physical body. Our true self, or actual conscious personality, is that of our inner animating core – our spirit.

That is who and what we actually are.

At earthly death, therefore, we simply discard, or step out of, the physical form that all human beings are obliged to take upon entry onto the Earth plane. This shell, our overcoat, is then subject to the natural processes of decay and disintegration in accordance with The Laws of Nature – which are the *earthly outworking* of The Spiritual Laws of Creation. This completely natural process thus allows the soul body, which consists of a number of non-physical bodies enveloping the spirit, to become free of its previously heavy "garment". However, it is not then able to go wherever it wishes, for this process is determined by The Law of Spiritual Gravity acting upon all the "works" connected to each individual. (Thus the Biblical warning: "*Their works shall follow them.*")

Base propensities and activities whilst in the physical body on Earth weigh the *coverings* of the spirit down causing it to *sink*, to fall away in a direction *opposite* to its true origin in The Spiritual Realm. Thus the entity regresses. The depth/s to which it sinks is strictly determined by the extent to which it indulged in wrongdoing that, in turn, gives it its corresponding "Spiritual weight" or heaviness. The particular level to which it sinks will be *peopled* by those with similar base propensities or weaknesses, in accordance with the *inviolable* and thus *non-negotiable outworking* of The Law of Attraction of Similar Species.

It is important to understand that under The Eternal Laws, **only here on the Earth can good and evil live side by side**. Every other Plane of Creation is formed according to its comparative "weight" – lightest and purest at the top, and heaviest and darkest at the bottom. In this lies the most wonderful justice because each individual spirit automatically ends up in the Realm corresponding to its *personal volition*, thereby automatically receiving **what it strove for most**.

If a recently departed spirit has lived a life of, say, lust and greed for example – a very good illustration given the deplorable state of humankind today – it will be drawn to the same level as others similar to it. In such an environment similar souls will give full vent to their propensity for lust and greed upon each other continuously. This same happening will be repeated in other places at other levels where the propensities for violence, drunkenness, nicotine and drug addiction, gluttony, laziness, and anger etc., hold sway. There, in situations as depraved and potentially as hopeless as that described, is the place we call "hell".

Yes! Hell is what <u>we</u> have created but need not, and <u>should not</u>, ever have done so!

Yet even there The Eternal Laws, which also automatically incorporate Divine Love, are ever watchful for souls who, through inner recognition, finally become disgusted with themselves and their tormented environment and petition for their release from it. With this *personal* awakening to the truth of their situation and the longing to be *free* of it, a way is automatically opened for such souls to *begin* their ascent to the next higher level.

Through that awakening to personal recognition and concomitant desire for change, they become different in *nature* to their particular environment, thereby ensuring *an automatic separation from it* in accordance with the justice inherently contained within **The Spiritual Laws** – notably:

"The Law of Attraction of Similar Species" and **"The Law of Spiritual Gravity"** under the outworking of **"The Law of Movement"**.

[We should note that **"The Law of Attraction..."** is, inherently, also a *"law of repulsion"*.]

Thus *any* soul can ascend, even out of such grievous circumstances, if its *desire* to do so is sufficiently *strong.*

Contrast that situation with one where a soul has striven to do noble deeds all its earth life; where it had sought to find Spiritual Truth; where it had offered compassion and kindness; where its thoughts and aspirations had sought elevation. Such a life makes a spirit light and buoyant. Upon shedding its physical shell at earthly death, its spiritual lightness draws it upwards toward Planes of Light. There it will find spirits who exhibit the same kinds of noble traits it had developed. Whereas the inhabitants of the lower regions are surrounded by their own base volition, those in the higher Planes of Light experience the living reality of the greater contentment and happiness synonymous with striving for more noble aspirations. Thus, Perfect Justice!

For those who *choose to believe* that spiritual ascent lies **solely** in a belief of faith in Jesus, consider His severe words from Matthew 5:26:

> *"I tell you indeed, that you will not depart until **you have repaid the very last farthing.**"*

And again in part from Matthew 5:18, Fenton, [All emphases mine.]:

> *"...that until the heavens and the Earth shall pass away, a single dot or hairstroke shall not disappear from the law, until **all has been completed**".*

The Law of Spiritual Gravity has existed since time immemorial, yet it is interesting to note that Newton's theories and discoveries in the *earthly* environment paved the way for a rapid increase in knowledge of astronomy which thus allowed for further interstellar discoveries. Moreover, the simplicity of The Laws that hold the moon in stable orbit around the Earth without it either crashing into it through Earth's stronger gravitational pull or simply heading off into space convinced Newton, as previously noted, that only *"...a few natural laws apply to the whole universe"*.

He demonstrated that The Laws which govern the planets of our solar system's elliptical paths around the sun are the same Laws that also govern all moving bodies, and therefore apply everywhere in the entire universe. Notwithstanding the Hermetic adage of "as in heaven, so on Earth", his radical view of the time generally put to rest a divergent belief that there is "...one set of laws for heaven and another here on Earth". Because Newton believed that the same natural laws applied everywhere in the universe, this would clearly have posed a potential "crisis of faith" for any Orthodox Church view of God. Newton's own faith, however, was never shaken.

On the contrary, he regarded the natural laws **as *proof* of the *existence* of a great and All-Mighty God!**

3.7   The Law of Balance!

"Balance in Life: — A Vital Necessity."

"Virtue, then, is a disposition involving choice. It consists of a mean, relative to us, defined by reason and as the reasonable man would define it. It is a mean between two vices – one of excess, the other of deficiency."

(Aristotle, 384-322 BC, from
Nichomachaen Ethics, Bk. 2)

Had Aristotle lived today he would probably be horrified at the excesses relating to such things as extremes of wealth, and in personal body-development. In his view these kinds of activities and practices were just as unbalanced as someone who only uses his head. He considered such extremes to be an expression of a warped way of life. Aristotle also applied the "Golden Mean" to human relationships. He believed that we must be neither cowardly nor rash, but courageous (too little courage is cowardice, too much is rashness), neither miserly nor extravagant but liberal (not liberal enough is miserly, too liberal is extravagant). The same applied to eating. He thought it was dangerous to eat too little, but also dangerous to eat too much. The ethics of both Plato and Aristotle contain echoes of Greek medicine. **The Law of Balance**, in its perfect outworking, encompasses Aristotle's "Golden Mean".

Aristotle believed that for some acts there is no "mean" at all. Their very nature, such as spite, envy, adultery, theft and murder, already implies "badness". These are bad in themselves and not in their excesses and deficiencies. One is always wrong in doing them. (Philosophy History & Problems, Samuel Enoch Stumpf, p 99) Achieving a happy or "harmonious" life, therefore, can only be attained by exercising balance in temperament.

Generally regarded as probably the first philosopher/scientist, Aristotle divided everything in the natural world into two main categories. In one corner he placed what he termed the non-living things such as rocks, clumps of soil and drops of water etc., and in the other the classification of "living things". He further divided this latter group into two other categories; "plants" and the "other creatures". This last was finally divided into two sub-categories; animals and humans.

Aristotle further reasoned that the "form" of man comprised three parts; a plant-like part, an animal part and a rational part (the soul or "divine reason"). In his view, man could only live a good life and achieve happiness by using all his abilities and capabilities. In the three forms of happiness that he identified, the first was a life of pleasure and enjoyment, the second as a free and responsible citizen, and the third as a thinker and philosopher. All three needed to be present at the same time for happiness to be attained within the individual, for he rejected all forms of *imbalance*. Thus, The Law of Balance was well understood in those earlier years.

In Spiritual terms this Law, in its effect and outworking, should anchor the necessary *balance* between "giving" and "receiving". In everyday tasks, many even mundane things automatically obey this law, like a baby taking its first faltering steps, or a young child learning to stay upright on a bicycle, waiters balancing plates of food in cafes, or even the simple act of walking. On construction sites we observe large cranes with enormous working booms counter-balanced by opposing shorter boom lengths appropriately counter-weighted to achieve safe working balances. The activities of trade and monetary transaction may require the use of scales for various purposes. In many judicial systems, justice is depicted by a set of scales held by a blindfolded woman, traditionally meaning: "Justice is blind". Perhaps, however, echoing the wish that a correct weighing and examining in the Courts might be the outcome. For if there is no balance, where lies justice? Justice should not be blind, therefore, but **all-seeing and spiritually-discerning**.

The simplest and most quietly obvious example of The Law of Balance is in breathing. We must naturally balance exhaling with inhaling. Correct breathing is vital for optimum health, but shallow breathing into the top of the lungs only does not provide this. The solution in this case is to regard the "outbreath" as the key. Exhaling properly and emptying the lungs will automatically ensure that a full breath will next be inhaled. Many a respiratory disorder can be at least relieved with consistent and correctly-balanced breathing.

In the home and in the Nation, the need to balance the budget is important in order to live within our means. The daily intake of food generally indicates a basic understanding of the need to try to achieve a "balanced diet" for optimum health i.e., different kinds of foods in appropriate proportions. Quite obviously, too much of just one type of food is not only inappropriate and tiresome, but is also not beneficial for the normal digestive system. Balancing the necessary intake of food is the need to eliminate body wastes as a natural result of this process. Any imbalance resulting from poor digestion or constipation makes us feel unwell.

Workaholic burnout as a result of "all work and no play" is also a transgression against The Law of Balance . Conversely, a life characterised by no work is equally harmful, even after retirement. The right kind of work for each individual should be a feature of the retirement years to help maintain the health of the body until death. Where the elderly happily engage in appropriate activity, higher levels of health are achieved. And where job opportunities are not readily available for someone wishing to work, low self-esteem may be the outcome, thereby resulting in a decline in the emotional and physical health of that individual.

The Laws of Creation show us that they inherently possess Divine Love. Love is thus the greatest Power. Also inherent in this as a part of Divine Love is Perfect Justice. The two cannot be separated. The Law of Balance, under the aegis of the power of Love and Spiritual Justice, ensures that *everlasting rest* is not at all the reality of the after-death situation. No one *rests in peace*! That particular concept/belief must surely rate as one of the *strangest* of human *inventions*. We are **compelled** to accept the responsibility of our life's decisions and **live them out**, so to speak, even after our physical demise. Then, our "personal books" are audited to determine where there is imbalance, after which we must spiritually address it, i.e., put it right!

If more people recognised this stark reality – which cannot be circumvented in any case – there might arise a better attitude to many things, since earthly death is the "great leveller" for all. A knowledge of The Law of Balance would therefore certainly benefit the elderly and those consciously approaching death through illness or accident etc.. Perhaps a greater effort might then be placed on "balancing one's spiritual account" long before being *overtaken* by earthly death.
Unfortunately, however, our present way of thinking clearly shows a general propensity for two things:

1. To seek as much wealth in the shortest possible time.

2. For a life of ease ever-after *on Earth*.

Great wealth can achieve wonderful goals and is not, in itself, a bad thing. However, if it is used for base, superficial or selfish ends, it loses its great potential and value and spiritually degrades the holder/s of it. It is a sad indictment on today's society that goals or earthly activities with a *spiritual content* are not regarded or valued highly as befits their *true* worth. The scales of global society are well and truly tipped toward overindulgence, base passions and immorality, to our spiritual *and* physical detriment.

Benjamin Franklin (1706-90) observed that if there were no limiting factors in nature, one species of plant or animal could engulf the entire globe. The balance is maintained because many species hold each other in check. Man is the only "spanner in the works" here, as his activities invariably create imbalance.

In what is arguably the most difficult yet necessary part of the everyday life of the human spirit i.e., that of personal relationships, the correct application of The Law of Balance between "giving and taking" offers the key to harmony and progress in all situations. Whether in marriage between partners, in a family situation between parents and children, between employer and employee, or between groups or Nations; in each particular case the concept of giving and taking needs to be correctly understood.

Parents desiring to have children must be aware of the need to balance this with the duty to care for the child in the right way.[11] Where parents offer spiritually-correct protection and nurturing to their children, this must be balanced by the obligation of the offspring to then respect their parents, but only where parents or care-givers have *earned the right* to be respected, of course. For why should parents be *automatically honoured* by offspring if they are not *deserving* of honour?

The ostensibly sacrosanct Commandment, "Honour Thy Father and Mother", should be very carefully thought about as to its **correct** meaning. Societal statistics clearly reveal the fact that many parents are not worthy to be honoured in any way at all by their children. Violence, drunkenness, drug-taking and abuse etc., can never be raised as the kinds of examples and behaviour for children to be exposed to, and certainly not to aspire to. Even though individual souls are brought together in family groups under the precise and lawful outworking of Spiritual Law, it still behoves parents to live – and thus teach by example – the correct Spiritual principles of life.

We should understand, therefore, that this **Commandment** was given **first and foremost for parents**. It was, in the very first instance, for parents to **honour** the concept and duty of **Fatherhood and Motherhood** so that they *would* become such parents as *could* be honoured by their children. For it was surely not the children born to their union who made the decision for their parents. In the light of Perfect Love and Perfect Justice, it is *absolutely inconceivable* that the Perfection of The Creator would *Command* children to honour parents who had no right to be honoured.

> That is the *true meaning* of this **Commandment**: That parents live *correctly* **according** to **The Law**, and **thereby** imbue the *status* of *parenthood* **with honour**.

Yet, for one or two Churches, the "letter of the law" here is so strictly enforced that some family groups within them live not in love and harmony, but in fear. We may therefore wonder how many children, raised by strictly religious parents who, themselves, did not obey the Commandments or live correctly, yet nevertheless still hypocritically demanded that they be honoured. We can be sure that many a child or young adult has suffered greatly under this kind of arrogant and hypocritical, *religious* injustice.

Once the child has reached an age where it is physically able to assist in the home, it should be required to do so in order to balance the parental care it receives. Its form of assistance would be commensurate with its age and abilities. A child brought up *without* the application of this Law in its life may not develop any kind of purposeful work ethic, nor garner the correct social skills and attitude necessary to interact in a naturally balanced way with others. An attitude of personal selfishness is often the outcome that, unfortunately, may become ingrained for life. The spiritually-correct concept of "tough love" for wayward children today might not have been needed for many had The Law of Balance been applied from the outset.

---

[11]The huge rise in child abuse and paedophilia, even in family groups, clearly attests to terribly imbalanced and sick societies.

It should not be assumed, however, that the overall application of The Law of Balance necessarily requires a *similar* kind of return contribution or payment to that received. Personal circumstances may decree otherwise. In such cases the recipient will fulfil the requirements of this Law if he evinces deep and genuine gratitude for the help given. Or perhaps he may be in a position to tender good advice to his benefactor who can then put it to good use for himself. So, regardless of personal situations, everyone is able to fulfil the demands of The Law of Balance in some way. The fact that many do not unequivocally reveals our *actual* level of spiritual immaturity where the unhelpful human traits of selfishness, thoughtlessness, or just plain bad habits have become more the norm.

Thus, in respecting this Law, we should not unnecessarily worry about what should be given in return. It behoves us to simply give the best of what we have and what we can, *relative* to what was received and what we are *able* to give. If this should mean genuine thanks only, without guile or deceit, then the demands of The Law are fulfilled. Legal contracts are not included here, for that is a different matter. Everybody, rich or poor, is therefore able to *live* this most necessary Law. Even the poorest can give out of themselves gratitude, a heartfelt prayer, or even a kind look to the giver. So long as the heart is pure and the intention genuine, the essential considerations from the standpoint of The Spiritual Laws will have been fulfilled.

The outworking of The Law of Balance in the present time can be powerfully observed in a specific problem area now coming to acute prominence. Mankind's questing nature and technological drive guaranteed that he would journey to and explore lands far from his birthplace. And, of course, colonise and settle some of them. Major wars have also been a driving force for people to escape to safer areas and perhaps settle there permanently. Prior to the Age of Exploration such "refugee movements" were generally confined to the continent of Europe. Because the population numbers were not high, the "resettling" impact could be absorbed much more easily than is the case today.

During the Industrial Revolution, however, the situation changed dramatically. The industrialised Nations – of which many were the main Maritime ones also – shipped into their burgeoning economies thousands and thousands of workers from other places around the globe. Some went voluntarily, others were enslaved. Whilst it made some Nations and individuals very wealthy, the balance of the world's peoples was, from then on, more drastically altered than at any time before. The huge dislocation caused by The Second World War compounded the problem considerably.

With a global population now at seven billion and increasing rapidly, and with more people seeking a so-called "better life" in lands sometimes at an opposite end of the globe, the huge and fundamental imbalance in the ethnic mix of peoples in the different countries of the world that began in earnest just a few centuries ago has now become like a "sword of Damocles" hanging over many countries of the more wealthy West. That unfortunate legacy has produced desperate acts of violence, political instability, social unrest and urban terrorism on a frightening scale previously unknown. The whole process has now resulted in demands for stronger measures to curb immigration in the refugee crisis of the present day.

The ostensibly compassionate practice of Western Nations accepting refugees from parts of the world where unstable, corrupt or oppressive regimes hold sway does not *ultimately* solve the problem for the people of the country concerned. *They, themselves, should strive to bring about correct change within.* Unfortunately, however, external pressures often undermine well-intentioned efforts to bring about necessary change. Dubious foreign policy objectives of some Western Governments, big business dealings, UN mandated operations and badly monitored aid programs have all contributed to abuse, corruption and incredible suffering for millions.

It is precisely this kind of aspiritual, greedy and ignoble behaviour that has *driven* much of the refugee problem. It is not our purpose to analyse the global situation of *'the why'* of refugees to any depth here. The world's news and refugee agencies do an admirable job in highlighting these problems through supplying a surfeit of visual images.

What we unequivocally state, however, is that these kinds of problems, *as with all others*, have their origin in mankind ignoring the very Laws that drive and govern all outcomes from every decision made. Thus we note the clear and unequivocal fact that the world, its peoples, its systems, its religions etc., are in serious and dangerous imbalance. For not one thing, not one decision, stands alone in the world. All are ultimately connected.

Crucial Imperative No 9:

That **all** is ***interconnected***; that nothing stands ***in isolation***!

Because they *are* all in some way connected, a decision in one part of the world produces a ripple effect in every other – even if not perceived immediately or at all. This lawful effect can thus be seen developing *more and more strongly* in the international and religious tensions now surfacing over refugees and immigration.

Thus we have desperation and riots, people smuggling, religious and ethnic tensions and hatred. Whilst such situations are traumatic for the people involved, the often unfortunate outcomes deriving from these events nonetheless simply reveal the emerging end-effect of this particular outworking under the aegis of The Law of Balance. It places increasingly stronger spiritual pressure on all of humanity to recognise and understand why there is so much discord in a practice that "seemingly" seeks to *help* the downtrodden. That in itself is a noble and correct ideal, of course, and forever will remain so. If not applied and effected spiritually-correctly, however, then disaster will be the end-result. That is the path we currently tread. There may well be a place for refugee assistance into other countries, **but the reason must be a spiritually correct one in the first instance.**

Governments that accept the entry of a particular group to their country should fully understand the import of such a decision, for The Law of Balance will *ultimately redress imbalance* wherever it occurs, irrespective of the reasons for the original decision. In the case of latter-day pressures to accept refugee quotas, the same Law does not mean *equal* balance in ethnic numbers, it is more about the *balance of harmony* – for that country and that society and culture. Refugee groups that refuse to integrate in an harmonious way should perhaps consider whether they should have remained in the country of their ethnic origin after all.

The various peoples and cultures of the world **are meant to be different and diverse.** Those essential differences, however, are obviously most powerfully-reproduced and *harmonised for the benefit of all peoples of the world* in and through the "beauty of the peoples and cultures" *within the borders of the lands that represent and actually are of that people.* Of course we all understand that movement and settlement into other lands to seek a better life or freedom from oppression or persecution is a natural aspect of humanity. And without those sorts of motivational considerations, many millions of the world's peoples would not now be generationally-settled into countries far removed from ancestral homelands.

The increasing and strident racist vitriol we now hear from so many quarters may not be so much racist but more a sub-conscious knowing that *so much* ethnic resettlement over such a relatively *short period* has not permitted sufficient time for *normal and natural assimilation* as perhaps occurred in times past. In any case, there are no solutions or answers in the same old arguments that each "side" continues to push – those *for*, and those *against*. Because the problem now virtually feeds on itself, the only alternative insight that *might* have *once* brought order out of increasing chaos is probably no longer viable. Therefore, in accordance with the mandated purpose of this work, we unequivocally state that the posturing and bluster of politicians and concerned individuals and groups worldwide for increasing refugee quotas into so-called "better" countries *will fail* without the *correct* "Spiritual" insight.

Equally for those individuals and groups who stand in opposition; they, too, must take into account the essential knowledge of Spiritual Law if they are to correctly understand the true nature of what is currently fermenting to its final conclusion. Spiritual knowledge and concomitant application of it by both groups – the authorities on the one hand and the supplicants on the other – would have provided the only solution. It is unlikely that *that* will be the outcome anywhere now.

The Law of Balance has been transgressed very seriously for a long time now. Therefore, *balance will be restored equally seriously,* **but in a much shorter time period**.

3.7.1   To Give, or to Take?

"It is more blessed to give than to receive!"

(Acts 20:35, Fenton.)

These words of Jesus, like many of them, have been so misunderstood or so grossly misinterpreted that even with the very best of intentions it has become difficult to fulfil His words of The Law in the way He originally taught them. Yet the question of whether one should give or take is readily answered in the understanding that in The Law of Balance between giving and taking, *giving* always ranks first. Unfortunately, through the well-intentioned but misplaced "generosity" of some social groups and churches, "taking" as a "social right" has become a way of life for some people and families who have no idea they should also *give something* in return.

Whether intentional or not, this transgression of The Law of Balance has a detrimental effect on the one who is a constant receiver, not least to the individual's self-esteem and self-respect. Moreover, children raised in this environment may become unwitting transgressors of this Law later in their life, also to their detriment. Thus, through a lack of understanding of an Eternal Law, well-meaning people can actually perpetuate and enlarge a social problem. Notwithstanding their good intent, in certain cases it does not always translate to giving the correct and necessary kind of "Spiritual" and material help actually needed.

A thorough knowledge of The Spiritual Laws is the only way that humanity can address its increasing social problems. In determining the best way that we might offer help, we should always be cognisant of the ancient Asian saying:

> *"Give a man a fish, and you feed him for a day. Teach him to fish, and you feed him for life!"*

At the beginning of this Chapter we stated that each Law examined would intermesh with all the other Eternal Laws to produce a perfectly balanced whole, and that the reader should be able to perceive the connections between them all. In this case, and as a simple example, one can easily deduce that *giving* in the correct way is better because it is connected to "The Law of Sowing and Reaping". The act of giving is identical with the practice of sowing. For each seed will, at its appropriate time, provide multiples of the same kinds of seeds for the *giver*.

Conversely, that which one extends the hand for – the seed taken or received – is like a harvest. Once consumed, it ceases to exist. With each receiving, a cycle is closed. Whenever we give, however, we start a new cycle. Through this process, therefore, it is always better to give than to receive. Of course, any giving should not be coloured solely by the selfish desire for a large return, thus losing sight of the correct Spiritual reason to want to give in the first place. When viewed in this light, the words of Jesus take on a far deeper and richer meaning than might previously have been understood.

As we noted in the earlier sub-heading, **"Families and Children"**, the current social propensity to demand one's rights, whether individual, children's, youth, ethnic, cultural, social, legal, religious, or any other; in the first instance lives the aspect of "taking"! In the sense of The Spiritual Laws, it is a negative and selfish attitude, for rights are *only* obtained by the fulfilment of responsibilities or duties. Therefore, ***the fulfilment of duty and responsibility must come before any claim to rights***. This vitally necessary attitude should be inculcated into every individual through education in the home, in the schools, in the collective workplaces, and perhaps more especially in gaols.

Consider the effect on society if, instead of demanding more and more "rights", we all immediately and radically changed our way of thinking to encompass a new, more tolerant and giving attitude which saw us all become concerned with *responsibilities, duties and obligations* **toward each other**. Between parents and children, teachers and students, employer and employee, between religions and ethnic groups, even between individuals within those ethnic groups, from the criminal to his victim, and the individual to society.

In one single stroke of "attitude", our present kind of oftentimes selfish society could be instantly transformed into one that actually lived the completely beneficial aspects of Spiritual Law, particularly that of "The Law of Sowing and Reaping". Virtually overnight, all manner of social problems and crime *could* disappear, and confrontation could also quickly become a distant memory; a memory of pointless, debilitating argument, anger and violence. Whilst this may seem an unworkable utopian ideal, nothing more than a pipe dream, it is *exactly possible*. In any case, without such a change the misguided "Human Rights first" ethos will continue to ensure that the current "my rights mantra" will simply further entrench a particular and insidious selfishness in society.

Thus one should give out of a genuine desire to help, and in the manner most *spiritually* beneficial to the recipient. The Eternal Laws therefore urge everyone to give, and no one should practice or indulge in one-sided taking. As previously stated, however, it would be wrong to expect any kind of *particular* return from the person to whom one has given, as the act of giving is then denigrated to an unspoken, selfish, strings-attached, silent demand – for something in return. In the strict lawfulness of this process, what should be recognised is that what might be received in return for what one has given does not necessarily depend upon the recipient. This may initially be a difficult concept to adjust to. Yet whether or not it is believed the recipient deserves it, whether or not he is grateful or ungrateful, and even whether or not he is actually aware that he has been helped, all such considerations are ultimately irrelevant. In any case ingratitude for any kindness shown will bring its own "reward" to the "ungrateful one".

It is a very human trait to seek recognition for any kind of help offered, yet the outworking of The Law of Reciprocal Action applies here equally as much as our attitude toward the suffering. What comes to us as our exact due – our reward as it were – arrives in the manner and at the time so ordained under The Spiritual Laws. Since we do not necessarily harvest in the same season that we sow, the time of its return may not be immediate.[12]

The same principles should apply whether the giver or receiver is an individual, a group, or a Nation. Here, also, it is more blessed to give than to receive. Many developed Nations give aid and technical assistance to others, and this serves to promote some measure of peace, harmony and goodwill in the world. If every recipient Nation were to give something in return, a wonderful system of dynamic exchange and interaction would emerge, thus advancing global development in the right way. Every recipient Nation *can* give something in return, be it cultural

---

[12]The immediacy of financial transactions are a different matter, concerned solely with business expectations and practices, unless perhaps fraud or deceit is planned.

exchanges, or only genuine gratitude and appreciation.

At this point it is timely to reiterate that under the increased spiritual pressure now pouring onto the Earth and its inhabitants, all past imbalances will be forcibly, and therefore severely, corrected. In future, deviation from The Law of Balance will not be able to be sustained for as long as has been possible thus far. The present structural problems that can be observed in the national and global economies, in particular through failing banks and financial institutions, are a direct result of mankind's total disregard for, and lack of understanding of, The Law of Balance. The disruption inherent in the economic and social stress of major restructuring programmes world-wide is the result of the effect of this increased pressure now culminating in urgent attempts to restore balance where, previously, there was imbalance; even if it appeared *not* to be the case.

Therefore the first task of the restructuring agencies should be to ensure that the process is carried out for the right reasons and under the knowledge of this "Law of Balance", with due regard for the respect and integrity of those duly affected. Restructuring purely for the sake of doing so, without clear reasons and goals, will only ensure unnecessary upheaval. So it behoves the architects of necessary change to become thoroughly conversant with The Eternal Laws, especially The Law of Balance, if they wish to succeed. Quite obviously, only those areas that actually *need* restructuring should be worked upon. Any area that is already in balance should be left alone, whether in international trade, in the financial system including setting exchange rates, in the determination of prices for goods and services and in industrial relations.

Since most Company restructuring involves the down-sizing of work-forces and their pay rates, with the generally greedy practice of those who institute the changes greatly increasing their own salary levels, it would be timely for such people to become cognisant of this Law, if only for their own spiritual growth. Otherwise their "greed", or their "works", will one day *pursue them*, for The Law takes no account of supposedly "sharp" business practices.

In terms of the attitude of such "Boards of Directors" or "C.E.O.'s" to the workers who help produce the business profits for them, the correct application of this Law is well illustrated in the admonition; Luke 10:7, Fenton:

> "...for the workman is entitled to his wages".

In the international arena, the practice of advancing huge loans to poorer, under-developed Nations, and then expecting outrageously exorbitant interest charges from them, has been rightly likened to a blood transfusion – "...from a **sick** patient to a **healthy** one". Where is the fairness and balance in such cases? To cite global monetary vagaries as the reason why cheap loans cannot be advanced from rich Nations to poor, quite clearly shows that we should quickly set about bringing it into balance. Thankfully, a new idea is fermenting among some lenders to institute more equitable payment methods. Systems that permit the electronic transfer of large currency amounts to reap huge profits simply because of a small shift in an exchange rate somewhere in the world are clearly obscene and strongly offend against monetary balance. Such practices should serve as a warning that this completely out-of-balance, globally-interconnected monetary system cannot be sustained, simply because the Spiritual pressure of The Law of Balance will one day bring about its collapse.

Over a decade ago the December, 1996, Edition of Time Magazine noted a subtle but growing shift in the attitude of *some* of the richest Americans. In the opinion of billionaire Ted Turner, the wish of the majority of those Americans to make *Forbes* magazine's listing of the 400 wealthiest, "...is destroying our country", claiming that 'the richest' are so afraid of slipping down the *Forbes* list "...that they hoard, rather than share, their wealth".

Turner issued a challenge: change the *system* and rank the biggest 'givers' instead of the biggest 'getters' (takers). Microsoft's online magazine *Slate* took up that challenge and launched the *Slate* 60. Gathered from publicly available sources, it lists, by families or individuals, the largest charitable donations in the United States.

If this list becomes as important to the rich as the *Forbes* list has thus far been, it may well open up a veritable torrent of financial help where it is needed most – in assisting the unemployed back to work and to self-esteem. For under Spiritual Law, the wealthy have a duty to provide; not hand-outs, but means, schemes and employment, whereby the less fortunate can contribute meaningfully toward their respective societies and to their own self-worth. Some of the super-wealthy are now doing more than that; by targeting the sick and disadvantaged.

A welcome new ethos among some of the super-wealthy has now seen many millions of dollars channelled toward projects such as medical aid to Africa. The work of the "Gates Foundation" founded, of course, by Bill and Melinda Gates, seems to have pricked the conscience of other wealthy individuals who are also now offering financial help to the needy.

Notwithstanding such generosity we should, nonetheless, not leave this particular segment without offering this most wonderfully appropriate Biblical quote from Mark 8:36, Fenton. [Parenthetic addition mine.]:

"For what will it profit a man if he should gain the whole world and forfeit his life? "(lose his soul?)

A quote from "Building Future Societies. Spiritual Principles of Nation Building" by Stephen Lampe, page 39, offers a further thought-provoking note:

> More than 150 years ago, a French economist, Pierre Boisguilbert came to the recognition of the utmost importance of balance. He wrote:
> "Only equilibrium (balance) can save everyone; and nature alone, to repeat, can achieve this. On our part, we should give and give, and nature will restore balance."

The right balance must be struck in all aspects of our lives and not just economic re-structuring. The rapid increase in one-parent families shows the urgent need to restore balance in personal relationships, in social interaction with others, and in all human activities. The breakdown of large Nations to smaller ethnic States is little more than the restoration of balance to peoples once forced to become, for them, part of a larger and often alien system.

The British Commonwealth is one example of this ongoing process. Once an Empire of disparate countries and peoples ruled by the force of arms of the "Mother Country", it has now developed into a *relatively* easy voluntary association of most of those former colonies, bonded by more or less common goals, aspirations and ideals. Such links, moreover, have allowed the many varied races in the Commonwealth to develop a generally greater degree of knowledge and tolerance toward each other, particularly in the areas of race and religion, than might otherwise have been the case under continued British Military dominance. And that is as it should be.

In its current format, the British Commonwealth, *thus far*, stands as a reasonably good example of what can be achieved through voluntary goodwill, with the concomitant ability to play a beneficial role in international affairs. However, if the common binding force were the knowledge and application of The Spiritual Laws of Creation, the Commonwealth example and its resultant international effect would be much more powerful.

The Law of Balance between Giving and Taking may, if there is sufficient time left, one day play a fundamental part in true international understanding when peoples and races finally stand **SIDE BY SIDE**, helping and furthering one another in mutual respect. The ideal time for such a process to begin is always in the present, of course. The vital recognition that every people, every race, possesses earthly and spiritual values which are indispensable for humanity as a whole will, hopefully, one day arrive. And because other peoples and races may not inherently possess exactly the same attributes, a vital exchange of those values should then become the norm. But such exchanges that occur must underpin the right balance between Giving and Taking; in precise accordance with the *immutable outworking* of this Law.

Whilst the inherent characteristics of The Law of Balance can obviously be applied to most situations, the most critical should be to urgently seek the correct balance between the **material and spiritual** in our individual lives. In the intellectual sense, man presently stands astride the apex of his technological pyramid. Spiritually, though, he grovels in the dust at its base, stunted and blind. If any kind of reminders were needed to induce us to begin to redress the balance of the scales toward The Spiritual, one need only look at everyday world events.

In that clear revelation *humankind unequivocally reveals the level* **it has chosen!**

3.8   The Law of Rebirth!
"Rebirth!" – Fact or Fiction?

The one absolute we all accept without question, irrespective of race, religious beliefs or political leanings etc., is the factual reality of birth, life and death. These three facets, at least in their *physical* happening, also represent the only belief or reality for many. The processes of all three, moreover, are absolutely identical for all individuals insofar as the *mechanics* are concerned. Only the individual life paths will be different due to the factors of race, geographical location, education, wealth and status etc., but both the *spiritual and physical* **processes** *for each remain the same.*

The term "miracle of birth" echoes our amazement and wonder at this event. The Spiritual Laws that govern the development of the growing individual and determines the final characteristics of it are constant and unchangeable. Thus the many billions of human births have followed the same lawful process. Inherent in The Laws is certainly the provision for development, but not for wrong experimentation, deviation or transgression, however. So even when using the procedure of in-vitro fertilisation, doctors are not able to operate outside the parameters dictated by this Universal Law.

It is the same with the 'death process'. Without exception we are forced to accept the absolute inevitability of it at some point in life. Universal Laws operate here in their immovable perfection too. For the step from a living, breathing, animated physical body to a cold, lifeless shell is exactly the same everywhere in the world. The manner of dying may be vastly different, i.e., disease, war, illness, accident – in peaceful sleep even – but the process is nevertheless identical. Indeed, it could not be otherwise. Yet whilst we are able to observe the *physical* processes of the steps of birth and death, and can clearly see the after-effects of birth, we do not necessarily accept that there may be after-effects of earthly death too.

Why not, however? If the evidence of our own eyes with regard to the irrefutable processes of birth and death governed by strict, consistent laws in the *physical* happening can be readily accepted, why should it not be a simple step to know *intuitively* that the outworking of The Spiritual Laws do not simply come to a convenient halt at that point simply because we may *believe* or *wish* otherwise?

By virtue of the inviolability of those Laws, humankind can do little else but submit to them, for there is no other choice. Even in cases of suicide or murder, the physical processes must still inevitably be the same. However, even though The Laws are *physical* in their visible effect, they are, nevertheless, still *Spiritual* in origin. It is worth deep consideration that even The Son of God, Jesus, had to be born of a woman on Earth. The Creator could not just simply place Him on the Earth as a fully-grown man – notwithstanding the strong religious belief among many that: "God can do anything He pleases".

From this standpoint consider, again, the later words of Jesus:

> "Do not imagine that I have come to *abolish the law* and the prophets; I have not come to abolish, *but to complete them.* For I tell you indeed, that until the heavens and the earth shall pass away, a single dot or hairstroke *shall not disappear from the law*, until **all** has been **completed**."

(Matthew 5:17-18, Fenton.)

Thus, the "Natural Laws" could not be circumvented then, not even by Jesus Himself, nor can they be today – or ever. Not by force of arms, wealth, political power, scientific/intellectual disbelief, rationalist theories, the "Sceptic Societies" of the West and, not least, by religious dogma. Ultimately there is no choice for humankind but to submit to the processes outlined, since it is Spiritual Law that drives everything in Creation. By virtue of our free will we *can* choose to *oppose* those Laws. However, the outworking of them will eventually guarantee the appropriate kind of hard and bitter reaping for such opposition.

What we cannot change at all is the *actual*, and thus *Lawful*, outworking of the death process itself. Since every incident or event that occurs must have some kind of starting point or origin, it should be a simple matter to deduce that the sudden, unexpected arrival of painful experiences in our lives can only be the result of a *previous* decision made elsewhere.

We constantly stand, therefore, in the **centre** *of all our* **returns**, *both good and bad, exactly in accordance with all the free-will decisions responsible for* **every returning reciprocal effect**.

However, because there may not be any recollection of the actual originating decision or event in the present lifetime of an affected individual, or in the lives of others closely associated with that person which could have brought about such a consequence, any *end-effect event* must clearly presuppose *another* possibility, i.e., the concept of more than one Earth life from where such an outcome *could* originate. As previously stated, this is not a view readily accepted in Western thinking, though it is a basic tenet of billions of the World's peoples. So just as we can reduce the question of whether there is life after death to either there is, or there is not – for it surely cannot be both – we can also ask the same of *one life versus many*.

Within the restrictive parameters of "the one-life concept" of current Western thought in the scientific and intellectual Disciplines and/or in religious doctrines, genuine solutions to society's increasing problems simply cannot be offered. Very unfortunately for disbelievers, therefore, ignorance and/or rejection of The Law of Rebirth cannot, in any way whatsoever, alter The Truth of its actual reality and outworking. This general and widespread "unbelief of the West" *can* be accepted if there is nothing more than just a *physical* body to contend with. Conversely, if the body *is* no more than just the physical shell – i.e., the 'cloak' housing the *actual* you and me – then, just as the processes of **Creation-Law** allow for **one** birth, why could it not allow for **others** where, at each incarnation, *another*, but *different*, 'outer cloak' is taken on in precise accordance with that Immutable Law?

This particular insight provides the *actual meaning* about the promise of "...the *resurrection of the Flesh*", stated by Jesus. This particular "resurrection" does **not** mean that bodies long dead will suddenly rise from their graves at some point soon and become clothed in the 'physical form' of the original owner. This strange and totally illogical belief *seemingly* derives from the Scripture that *ostensibly* states: "All *the* dead shall awaken."

In light of the rapidly increasing degeneration of all aspects of global human activity; if we exercise logic and reason to strive to determine what it might truly mean, then we will intuitively recognise that *that* Scripture is actually a *warning*. It is a warning, moreover, that lives the essence of **The Law of Reciprocal Action**, and is thus a **severe admonition** to humankind to **spiritually awaken**.

For the particular Scripture *as promoted by global Christendom* is not even the correct wording. The true meaning is:

> "All <u>that</u> is dead shall be awakened." Thus it is the awakening of *all*, **everything**, that is **spiritually** *dead*.

The *alarming increase* in our problems globally can be more readily understood with that vital revelation. It means that *all* belief systems, *all* Disciplines of human endeavour, *everything* that *we humans* have held sacrosanct or sacred, *everything* that *we* might thus far have stated to be inviolable; *all* must now be forced to show where it *truly stands* in relation to The Spiritual Laws of Creation. Thus the spiritual pressure that is now being exerted more powerfully with each passing day upon *all* our beliefs and activities, *forces the awakening* of those belief systems and activities. It does not matter whether they *ostensibly* hold scientific, philosophical, religious or political 'truths'. Without exception, *everything* will be subject to this severe and relentless clarifying and cleansing process.

All that does not stand true – thereby suffering collapse in the awakening – thus *reveals* that it **was** dead and *needed* to be **awakened** i.e., *that it did not have as its foundation and guiding principle,* **the knowledge of Creation-Law**. This "awakening process", this *resurrection*, applied in accordance with the inviolability of The Law of Rebirth, thus permits each one the opportunity to "put right" past wrongs. Through this mechanism of Divine Grace, man is gifted the means whereby he may *earn* his ascent [return] to his Spiritual origins, his true home. "Resurrection of the *Flesh*" is thus a Divine Grace providing the means whereby we are given numerous opportunities to return to the Earth to *atone* for past transgressions *committed* in the earthly.

Yet, despite inherently possessing clear and ultimately irrefutable logic, reincarnation as a concept has fuelled debate for centuries. Even though a very large proportion of the world's peoples accept it as a factual part of man's *total* existence, the Judaeo-Christian religions generally do not. The basic belief of reincarnation in some form or another has been accepted by most in the Indian sub-continent for the past 2,500 odd years, and in other parts of the world for a long time too. It is interesting to note, however, that the so decisively important doctrine of reincarnation – of rebirth as a human being – was only expunged from Christian creeds by a very small majority decision at the Council of Constantinople in 553 AD. What was effectively lost through that decision of appalling ignorance and ego was the greater understanding of the *seeming* inequality of the world and, indeed, the Love and Justice contained in The Creative Will of God.

Consider, if at that fateful Council meeting only a few men had decided differently, *reincarnation would now be a matter of course for Western "religions" also*. Had that happened, there would not exist the present fortress of doubt and prejudice against the whole notion of "rebirth". In its place would be greater freedom of thinking, rather than this terribly unfortunate constraint into which our current thought-processes have fallen, and solely because of that unfortunate decision taken by a few powerful men centuries ago. In general, it has succeeded in removing any possible larger outlook to the greater connections of our existence, and to the incredible vastness of Creation as a whole.

Because of that decision, we have created the unhealthy situation of not readily accepting death as a natural part of life, or as an ongoing transitional step in our complete existence.[13]

The great difficulty with trying to meaningfully grapple with the rapidly increasing problems in society as a whole, is that there often *appears* to be no logical cause for it all. Is it any wonder that suicides are on the increase, particularly among the more impressionable young who are often too emotionally immature to cope with the *seemingly* insurmountable. They seek answers but no one will give them the only *correct* one. Our so-called "educators" reject the very thing that *would* provide the necessary enlightenment. Yet even *they* continue to ask: – **'Why'?** Australian Children's Advocate and "National Treasure", Professor Fiona Stanley, on the subject of increasing youth suicide there, soberly observed:

> "Despite all that we now know, and all the research that's been done, ***nothing is getting any better***."

The concept of reincarnation will need to be accepted as fact if society wishes to find answers to its problems, for the deliberate rejection of it only pushes away the day of reckoning. It must be understood, however, that reincarnation is governed by the strictness of The Spiritual Laws too. Contrary to some beliefs and misconceptions, therefore, one **cannot** return as a tree, an insect, or an animal.

So, in direct contrast to the cultural or ethnic beliefs of various peoples, our ancestors cannot be such things as those. Inanimate objects have no connection with human Spiritual origins, and neither do psychically produced forms that some indigenous groups revere. Therefore, living, animate creatures such as eagles, tigers and whales etc., must forever remain their own kind. Humankind's collective Spiritual ancestry can *only* centre around being human.

Simply and logically put: The Laws of Nature absolutely decree that we **cannot change our species**. They thus further decree that under The Law of Rebirth we can only return as human beings. Carrying with us, moreover, all that we have **previously sown**. Some experiences we are forced to live through may well have their origin in previous Earth-lives. And how we live our life now will determine what will come our way in the future, perhaps even in a later Earth-life. Whole Nations and races must collectively reap what they have sown as well.

The destruction of the Axis Powers during The Second World War is a particularly good example of whole peoples and races suffering collectively through the outworking of decisive Spiritual Laws in concert with their *free-will decision* to embark upon global war and conquest. And in the maelstrom of that devastation may be seen horrific outcomes for certain races; outcomes possibly derived from decisions made in the long-distant past, but which required resolution in another place and time among other peoples. Under the aegis of The Laws of **"Reciprocal Action"**, **"Attraction..."** and **"Rebirth"**, mainly, the perfection of those **Spiritual Laws** decree that **events** which produce "mass victims of tyranny" do not *necessarily* have their **actual genesis** in the historical circumstances **immediately preceding** the particular incident or event.

The extent and degree of suffering that might be *Spiritually-lawfully* required to enable a group or even a whole people **to awaken to the reason for their plight** may need a long period of time from causal decision to end-effect to bring about the correct and exact circumstances for final resolution and expiation. Ordinarily, the group or race imposing the suffering would then set in train the reciprocal consequences of its actions which it must expect to receive one day too. The difference now, however, is that the time of return is considerably

---

[13]The details of that meeting are examined more specifically further on in the Chapter that outlines the actual death process.

shortened whereby all past events strive for resolution under the pressure of The Spiritual Laws as they drive the release of all reciprocity.

The Western medical profession's general refusal to accept this quite logical view of a multi-life concept and become locked, instead, into a single-life one unfortunately translates into the practice of often attempting to go beyond reasonable limits in order to preserve "life". At all costs seems to be the view, rather than simply accepting the dignified inevitably and reality of a "natural transition" to, and through, earthly death. Of course life should be extended for as long as it is reasonably possible to do so, but not at the expense of unnecessarily prolonging what should be regarded as the completely normal process of exiting Earth-life. Neither should death be *desperately fought against* when medical reality clearly indicates an imminent demise. The dying one is not actually helped thereby.

Reincarnation offers the only viable mechanism for mankind to make rational sense of the misery, suffering and tragedies that beset the world today in such a relentless manner. Whilst it also brings good fortune and happiness for some, it is the tragedies deriving from past incarnations that need more urgent clarification.[14] However, as the actuality of reincarnation is a "Living Law of God" – which no one can change – it behoves us all to learn what we can about the actual mechanism and process which, in its concept and outworking, actually provides the greatest measure of certainty about Earth-life and life thereafter.

The Indian sage, Paramahansa Yogananda, wrote much about how to live correctly. Perfectly correct living, however, is really only possible with the knowledge of all The Laws of Creation. Even though actively seeking what he intuitively perceived was that complete knowledge existing somewhere on Earth during his lifetime, certain pre-conceptions he harboured effectively prevented his taking the final step to personal recognition when given the crucial opportunity which would have led him to it. Notwithstanding that missed vital moment, his inherent wisdom nevertheless offers a good blueprint for basically correct living.

His knowledge of reincarnation offers a brief insight into his particular wisdom.

From the sub-heading: **"How We Live This Life Determines What We Are in the Next."**

> "We have been given the power to reason out where we go and whence we have come. But we don't take enough pains to analyse ourselves and our lives. Otherwise our common sense would tell us that whatever our character is today it will continue to be after death – perhaps a little better or a little worse, depending on how much effort we are making to improve ourselves. You go along 365 days a year, year after year, and perhaps you have made some progress, but your nature will be the same after death as it was before death. You will not become an angel just because you die! Only the body changes. Death makes no difference, otherwise. Death is like a gate you will pass through. Your body will be gone but you will be in every other respect the same. If you have a violent temper, you will not leave it behind, at death, with your physical body. Your violent temper will remain with you until you conquer it. If in your present life you have observed the laws of healthful living, in your next incarnation you will possess a healthy body. The last portion of life is more important than the first, because what you are at the end of this life is what you will be at the beginning of the next.

---

[14]We will not examine this subject to any great degree here for it is clarified further on in another contentious religious issue; that of **"The Second Death"**.

The first part of life is usually stupidly misspent, in a sort of bewildered state. Then romance comes, and finally disease and old age; the struggle with the body starts... The body is a trouble most of the time:... Always trouble, trouble! *That is why it is so necessary to your happiness that you realize you are not the body...*"[15]

(Man's Eternal Quest. p.219, Italics mine.)

As a final notation on this subject, reincarnation, as an inviolable Spiritual Law, must live the fullness of that fact **without deviation.** This Law also naturally exists within The Laws of Nature, which are themselves a mirror of The Eternal Laws. All dovetail into each other in perfect outworking. As previously stated, perhaps the refusal of many Westerners to accept reincarnation may be due in part to the promoted belief of some Eastern religions that one may be required to return to the Earth – for various purposes of atonement – as an animal, a bird or an insect even.

Atonement is a most necessary requirement in the outworking of our inherent free-will decision-making ability under The Law of Reciprocal Action – a Law which unequivocally states in Galatians 6:7:

"What a man sows, that he will also reap."

Reincarnation therefore provides the only "earthly" *long-term mechanism* under which transgressions against The Law **can** be atoned for and expiated. As it is also a Law of Nature or a natural Law, we strongly reiterate that such Laws unequivocally state that it is not possible to change one's species, **irrespective of any belief to the contrary**.

Crucial Imperative No 3:

That being more than just a physical body means we naturally and *inherently* possess a *separable entity* **within** the material form. And that *that* is the *actual* life-force, the *animating* core, that is *actually each individual!*

So as previously stated: The inner animating core of man – his actual life-force – is **spirit**, whilst that of the animal is **soul**. They are two very different species of *animating* power from two different *levels* in Creation. Therefore, in this context, the human spirit must always remain a human spirit, with absolutely *no possibility* that it could somehow transmigrate across *immovable spiritual boundaries* to become a life-form **different** to that ordained for it by the *unalterable* Laws of Creation. In reinforcing-reiteration: Humans remain humans. **We cannot become animals**.
And, just as surely:

Animals cannot "develop" into humans!

In summary the process of reincarnation, whereby a human spirit is ordained by Law to accept rebirth on Earth, is subject to, and affected by, the collective outworking of all The Spiritual Laws of Creation. The free-will decisions of his previous life, or lives, will determine who he will be in the next one, what his spiritual lessons will be, and what he can also spiritually offer that group of souls into which he will be incarnated – to those who will be his earthly family. That, in turn, will determine such factors as to whether he will be born disabled or complete, whether his new circumstances will be one of wealth or struggle, whether of the same race, geographical location or religion as his last incarnation, or one completely different.

---

[15]An apt description from The Bible refers to the body as "the deadly carcass".

Irrespective of those considerations, however, the circumstances of his next incarnation will precisely offer the necessary conditions he will need for **his** further spiritual maturing in the first instance. The key point in all of this is the fact that he is still master of his own destiny. In that sense his inherent spiritual free-will provides the mechanism whereby he can always and at any time set in place new decisions for himself. The new direction, called forth by those decisions, will of course change or modify his present life-path originally ordained for him by Law through the outworking of all his previous decisions. Certain *"experiences of the spirit"*, however, will be part of his necessary path and may perhaps even provide a lifetime of hard struggle.

Whether or not that is the case may well depend upon the lawful outcomes of previous personal decisions acting upon him as he lives out his present life. Even if he should live spiritually-correctly, yet still experience a lifetime of struggle, The Spiritual Laws will nonetheless set in train *beneficial* returns for a *future* time. For the more *powerful experiences* will be impressed upon his spirit *in any case*, be it through *great joy* **or** *tragedy*.

Thus, The Laws of Creation intermesh to bring about precisely lawful outcomes. Yet it always remains with the individual as to what those personal outcomes will be. As stated regularly throughout this Work, only the **decision** is **free**, the **consequences** are **not**! So in cases where two options are presented, whilst we will always have a **50%** option or **choice**, there is always only a **100% outcome** *after* the decision has been taken.

Of course there is nothing to prevent one from modifying or radically changing the original decision with a second, or even third one. Those decisional changes will ultimately then be signalled in its corresponding outcome at some future point.

3.9   Grace! A Gift of Divine Love.

Even though not perhaps a Law in the strictest sense, the inclusion of the key aspect of Grace in this Chapter about The Spiritual Laws is vital because the concept and outworking of the Spiritual attribute of Grace impacts decisively and beneficially on the fate of anyone who recognises the error of their ways and subsequently seeks a more enlightened path. The entry of Grace into one's life, therefore, will manifest through the outworking of Spiritual Law in reciprocity deriving from spiritually-correct decision-making – even if the particular decision required needed to be a material one.

Grace is an inherent quality of Divine Love. Also inherent in Divine Love is Justice. However, the Love that is defined here has no affinity whatever with humankind's emotionally-distorted idea of this most noble Power. Thus, under the outworking of Grace – which *originates* from The Divine – help and guidance are given to humankind with each passing moment. In order to reap the benefits, however, the guidance needs first to be *recognised* as such, and then *lived* accordingly.

Since The Spiritual Laws contain both the cornerstones of Love and Justice, they return only what is *spiritually* beneficial. By heeding Spiritual Law, we give no cause for any "unwanted returns". In its distilled essence, therefore, "Spiritual Love" is pure, even *severe* if necessary. In certain cases it *needs* to be *severe* in order to bring about the necessary *awakening* to force the question: **"Why?"** Yet we must ever be mindful of the fact that we ourselves will have given cause for that event or trial somewhere, sometime, in accordance with the inviolable outworking of The Spiritual Laws.

The kind of Love outlined here is thus not the caricature spawned and given form by collective humankind. That "aberration" has become so distorted that it is now used to encompass virtually every kind of debased activity under "modern", liberal thinking. This kind of human distortion carries no justice or spirituality within it. In keeping with current, prevalent attitudes, attempts are continually made to separate that which cannot be separated – genuine **Spiritual Love** from true **Spiritual Justice**.

In the most wonderful of ironies, the twin forces of Spiritual Love and Justice will eventually teach humankind that they are, indeed, inseparable. We have produced a weak form we call love but which, in reality, is more often than not a mask and poor excuse for overly liberal, over-emotional and vacillating *self-indulgence*. In short, we have substituted the pure Power of Love with earthly emotionalism. In its pure form genuine Love stands far above such incorrect ideas. Compassion should not be confused with what is described here either, for compassion is an attribute of unconditional Love. When one has accepted, understood and finally worked through all that must be personally expiated, The Spiritual Laws or Rules then become strong and furthering helps for one's spiritual growth, thus expressing the Power of the genuine Love. The **"Gift of Grace"** lives in the essence of that inviolable Truth!

The **"Gift of Grace"** therefore permits even the worst transgressions to be completely expiated, if one *genuinely* seeks to put right his wrongs. Despite the fact that The Spiritual Laws operate strictly here, too, the overriding attribute contained within the outworking of The Laws in this case is that of Grace and forgiveness. If being "pursued by one's works" presupposes a "return" of even severe difficulty and hardship, it is important to understand that by simply *changing* our spiritual volition for the better, we automatically begin the process of *altering* the forms – both their intensity and severity – of "our wrong works" previously produced. For they will, at some future point, surely and certainly return to us.

Therefore, under the process of reciprocity in "awaiting our works", someone who has lived a life of dark, horrific deeds is absolutely condemned to fully reap his "personal whirlwind" either here on the Earth or when passed from it, *so long as there is no effort or attempt to change his ways*. Total ignorance of this cause, or even disbelief of it, cannot alter the returning effects either. As we need to restate, this lawful path mirrors Divine Justice that, at the same time, is also Divine Love.

The returning reciprocal effect to a hardened soul should thus provide the necessary experiences and potential for a spiritual awakening, a re-appraisal of one's personal situation, and some deep "soul-searching". Should that individual stubbornly fight against this process, ***more of the same is assured.*** Yet this should not be seen as some kind of retributive punishment from some arbitrary God or Power. It is simply the *personal* "reaping" from the *personal* "sowing", ***irrespective of when sown or why***.

What of one with many years of living a depraved or evil lifestyle, and with total and selfish disregard for the welfare of his victims, however? What happens when such a one suddenly finds himself faced with the unnerving reality that his attitude and conduct were "all wrong"? What then? Ordinarily, we would probably say he still deserves to pay for everything he meted out to others. According to societal Law, that would probably be the case and society would no doubt be well pleased with such an outcome. Indeed, it is appropriate that correct punishment be meted out, for society has a right to protection from such individuals. In any case, our earthly laws should indicate the clear recognition that we cannot function without order.

Therefore, even if a 'criminal' has been *dealt with* through justice handed down by earthly Courts, this does not mean that all is necessarily "paid for". The more crucial debt, **the spiritual**, may still await resolution. However, if our miscreant – through the honest recognition that his previous ways were wrong – then genuinely seeks to mend them and make atonement, he sets in place for himself the mechanism whereby the *impact* of the *returning* retroactive *consequences* of his previously dark volition can be greatly *lessened*. Of course the desire to *want* to change must be an absolutely genuine one, for The Spiritual Laws are not fooled by the subterfuge and deviousness that human beings often engage in. Genuine humility, moreover, must be an accompanying factor in such a change.

What, then, is that process? Since we inherently-possess the attribute of "free will", and because there is only *one* *neutral power* streaming through and animating all of Creation – including the material worlds – our "free-will" endowment ensures that this *neutral power* is *refracted through us* to good or evil purpose. Precisely, however, **according to how we <u>choose</u> to use it**. Under the outworking of The Law of Attraction of Similar Species, if our volition is dark, we automatically make connections to, and attract in and surround ourselves with, similar species. If the opposite is the case, via the same process of connection and attraction, we lock ourselves into a vastly different kind of "power stream". It is one, moreover, which will bring beneficial effects at the time that the outworking of The Laws decree.

Thus, in the *voluntary spiritual change* that the felon of our example has undertaken, he has changed his "nature of attraction" from one originally leaning toward darker things to those much lighter. Since this change is subject to The Law of Spiritual Gravity also, there occurs within and around him a *lightening effect* as a result of his decision to change his ways for the *good*. Now he attracts to himself *beneficial forms* corresponding to his *new* volition. But where does this place him with regard to the returning effects of perhaps a long life of degrading deeds? The Law of Sowing and Reaping must still hold sway. That cannot change.

Now, however, through his newly-activated, lighter connections corresponding to the *new* volition with which he now surrounds himself – quite automatically – a lighter and stronger force envelops him. This acts like a cocoon against which some of the retroactive effects of his past volition and deeds can be *nullified*. Some may still penetrate to him. In which case they will be of such a nature as he *still requires* for growth and ascent and, moreover, may therefore need to be *fully experienced materially* for complete expiation under Spiritual Law.

The experiences from it, however, will enable him to further develop spiritually. Some returning effects may only need to be redeemed symbolically, perhaps something even as innocuous as a kind word to a complete stranger. Each case will be different for every individual. But nonetheless in strict and unyielding accordance with Spiritual Law operating in concert with the Gift of Grace, so demonstrating both Perfect Justice and Perfect Love, two important cornerstones of:

The Spiritual Laws of Creation: <u>Creation-Law!</u>

Therefore, if we do not wish to be pursued by any former "unpleasant works", it is essential that the knowledge of The Eternal Laws be regarded as a serious spur to help nullify the reciprocal effects of them. Thus, via the perfection of **Creation-Law** and Its inherent **Gift of Grace**, we are enjoined to strive only for what is good. Such striving will ensure the reciprocal effect of greater peace and happiness.

3.10   Conclusion

"Power comes out of the barrel of a gun!"

(Mao Tse Tung.)

"Physical strength will never permanently withstand the impact of spiritual force."

(Franklin D. Roosevelt.)

"The pen is mightier than the sword!"

(Original, "Arms give way to Persuasion!"
Cicero.)

Here we have three vastly different quotes occupying opposite ends of the "spiritual spectrum". Each one, however, generating its own specific kind of "return" under the aegis of The Spiritual Laws. The first concerned solely with earthly results, but ultimately returning spiritually-driven corresponding ramifications of no small import, and the other two having connections to both. In the first quote are sown the seeds of its own destruction because its inferior "form" is correspondingly attached to weaker and therefore lower and baser levels.

The latter, however, if writing *Spiritual Truth*, is equal to the second because of its powerful connection to The Source of all Life. By virtue of that fact, any such writings connected to that Source produce "forms of spiritual power", as opposed to the "baser forms" produced by the gun *if* the use of it is for strictly totalitarian purposes with the aim being control and/or enslavement.

Whilst The Spiritual Laws are the infallible and unalterable *driving mechanism* which produce the consequence or outcome for every decision made, it is vital to understand that any spiritual transgression incurred will be made more against the "rules for correct living". They are those that all the great religions and spiritual and philosophic teachings have recognised and espoused over millennia. Thus one *can* transgress The Law of Balance. In the true sense of the word, however, one cannot actually *transgress* The Laws of **"Rebirth"**, **"Attraction..."** or **"Spiritual Gravity"** etc.. However, transgressions against the "rules of life" such as are stated in **The Ten Commandments**, for example, even if done in complete ignorance of them, nevertheless unequivocally sets in motion the driving *return-mechanism* that is inherent in the *power* of **Spiritual Law**. In this case, more specifically in **The Law of Reciprocal Action** (*Sowing and Reaping.*)

The reader should thus understand that **The Ten Commandments** – which the Law-Giver Moses received for **all** of humankind – are the necessary accompaniment of **The Spiritual Laws of Creation**. Both issue from **The Creator** for the harmonious order of **His Creation**. However, whilst they are "The Rules", so to speak, The Laws that drive and sustain everything are vitally important to know so that we may understand *why* **The Ten Commandments** must be regarded as very necessary "Rules for correct living".

It is equally important to recognise, also, that it is *Spiritual Power* that we actually use in all decision-making. Even our thought processes use the same power. It permeates every part of Creation, for it is **the life-force of the whole**. However, it *does not at all mean* that our utilisation of that power necessarily produces genuinely spiritual outcomes. Unfortunately, and as global societies clearly reveal, the volition of humankind has produced mainly *aspiritual* ones. Clearly evidenced by the global situation, the mechanism inherent in The Spiritual Laws drives everything to its particular outcome.

3.10.1   Recognition of The Law! The "Crucial Imperative" for All of Humanity.

The inviolable outworking of The Law of Attraction of Similar Species coupled with the severe admonition:

> "...by their works ye shall know them..."

– can now be seen very, very clearly in the worsening state of virtually all global societies and in our rapidly degrading environment.

Thousands upon thousands of years of "producing works" absolutely opposed to The Laws of Life have brought us to a point of *final crisis*. If we have learned little else in our long tenure on Earth on which we humans were tasked to be the guardians and nurturers of Truth and Law and protector of the bounty which the Earth provided, we will certainly now learn that The Law is absolute, and Inviolable. We will therefore experience more and more severely the foolishness of our collective transgressions.

The **"Crucial Imperative"** for the diverse groups that comprise global humanity is to recognise The Truth that **The One Law** is **The Only Law** for *all* of humankind. The many long centuries where religion and not Truth held sway to produce so much evil bloodshed and slaughter, has "heaped-up" an invisible yet very menacing "tsunami of reciprocity" which will break with *greater devastating force* over mankind *than is already occurring at present*.

Earth-science and earth-business, co-instigators and co-producers of products and processes that have fashioned virtually all the poisons which contaminate land, water, people and animals alike; you, too, have added your terrible share. It will not be enough to say:

> *"But we produced good things too."*

The few good things produced and/or undertaken have never been sufficient to offset the development and growth of "power centres" exactly commensurate with the free-will production of "goods and services" that have no affinity with the True Laws of Creation, but were nevertheless produced by religious and scientific ignorance, ego and arrogance.

The aeons-long transgressions against Divine Law have, under the aegis of "The Law of Attraction of Similar Species", primarily produced our vast, dark "power centres". Undetectable to the earthly senses, and still less to *disbelieving scientific empiricism*, the greater mass of each one quietly waits for the moment when precise outworking of **The Law** decrees its time of *full reciprocal release upon global humanity*.

Explanations of **The Spiritual Laws of Creation** have been outlined in this earlier Chapter as a most vital adjunct to the correct understanding of our "reason for being" and overall purpose in life. The degree to which these Laws have been explored should be sufficient for at least a *basic* understanding of them. For only with the help of that crucial knowledge could this book, which offers the necessary help to surmount what is rapidly approaching, be written.

Therefore, in order to explain *how* and *why* every aspect of the rest of the Work interlinks with and connects to all the threads within the whole, regular reference will, *very necessarily*, be made to:

THE LAW!

4

ELEMENTAL LORE OF NATURE

"Blow, blow, thou winter wind. Thou art not so unkind, *as Man's ingratitude* [**to Man**!"]

(Shakespeare, "As You Like It", Act II)

"Look deep into nature and you will understand everything better."

(Albert Einstein.)

Crucial Imperative No 4:

That we, the human beings of planet Earth, must ***fully understand*** *the true nature* of **The Forces of Nature!**

Therefore understanding the **true nature** of "The Forces of Nature" provides the clearest ***foundation*** for a more *correct understanding* of **The World!**

(Author. All emphases mine.)

4.1   The Circle of Life

"Man has a poor understanding of Life.
He mistakes knowledge for wisdom.
He tries to unveil the Holy secrets of our Father,
the Great Spirit.
He attempts to impose his Laws and ways on Mother Earth.
Even though he, himself, is part of Nature,
he chooses to disregard and ignore it
for the sake of his own immediate gain.
But the Laws of Nature are far stronger than those of Mankind.
Man must awaken at last, and learn to understand

how little time remains
before he will become the cause of his own downfall.
And he has so much to learn. To learn to see with the heart.
He must learn to respect Mother Earth –
She who has given life to everything;
to our Brothers and Sisters, the Animals and the Plants;
to the Rivers, the Lakes, the Oceans and the Winds.
He must realise that the Planet does not belong to him,
but that he has to care for and maintain the delicate balance of Nature
for the sake of the wellbeing of our children and of all future generations.
It is the duty of man to preserve the Earth
and the Creation of the Great Spirit.
Mankind being but a grain of sand in the Holy Circle
which encloses All Life."

(Attributed to White Cloud, a principal chief of the Iowa tribe.
More probably stated by "Wa-cha-mon-ya";
regarded as the tribe's greatest orator.)

The clear wisdom of the Native Americans is beautifully and powerfully encompassed in the above statement. The advent of satellites and manned space stations has, for the first time in humankind's history, shown us all how incredibly beautiful, fragile and "lonely" the Earth – our "blue planet home" – actually is. The sure knowledge inherent in those words from a technologically-illiterate Native American people from the 19th century reveals the spiritual emptiness of much of Western "culture". Paradoxically, however, it is really only since those first space photographs appeared some years ago whereby the realisation has gradually dawned that we are not separate groups, races or Nations with our own closed eco-systems divorced from every other.

4.2   Earth-science and Elemental Lore.

Such pictures have reinforced the unequivocal fact that every action on Earth will ultimately impact globally somewhere, somehow, some way – just like ripples radiating outward from the impact of a stone thrown into a pond. At least that is the realisation among those who are sufficiently awakened to understand the truth of this glaring reality. Unfortunately, however, too many of Earth's inhabitants still regard their own personal space and aspirations as being the most important thing. Nevertheless, those who are too obtuse or too ignorant to care will one day experience the Iowa tribe's sage, intuitive observation that "Man must awaken ... and learn to understand how little time ... remains before he will become the cause of his own downfall." This Chapter will offer explanations as to why – and how – "White Cloud's prophecy" **will be fulfilled!**

Interestingly, in our time, the world of science which we look to for answers has also offered a sobering prediction. One, moreover, that reinforces White Cloud's *vision* for the Earth. The 1992 Earth Summit in Rio, attended by one of the largest gatherings of Heads of State in history, was heralded as a singularly-definitive eco-event. It was one designed to produce a lasting international accord for protecting the world environment. Yet, on 18 November, 1992, just five months after that ostensible environmental milestone, more than sixteen hundred senior scientists from seventy one countries, including over half of all Nobel Prize winners, released a signed document titled, "World Scientists Warning to Humanity". The document began:

> "Human beings and the natural world are on a collision course. Human activities inflict harsh and often irreversible damage on the environment and on critical resources. If not checked, many of our current practices put at serious risk the future that we wish for human society and the plant and animal kingdoms, and may so alter the living world that it will be unable to sustain life in the manner that we know. Fundamental changes are urgent if we are to avoid the collision our present course will bring about."

The warning went on to list the crises in the atmosphere, water resources, the oceans, the soil, the forests, bio-diversity and human over-population. Here the words become more urgent:

> "No more than *one or a few decades remain* before the chance to avert *the threats* we now confront *will be lost* and the prospects for humanity ***immeasurably diminished.*** We, the undersigned, senior members of the world's scientific community, ***hereby warn all humanity of what lies ahead.*** A great *change* in our stewardship of the Earth and life on it *is required*, if vast human misery *is to be avoided* and our global home on this planet ***is not to be irretrievably mutilated.***"

Surely a sobering view in any sense of the word.

> "Nevertheless, when the 'World Scientists Warning to Humanity' was released to the press, Canada's national newspaper and television network ignored it, while in the United States, the *Washington Post* and the *New York Times* rejected it as 'not newsworthy'."

> (*The Sacred Balance*, David Suzuki, p.4-5
> Emphases mine.)

Whilst this eminent group of clearly learned men have rightly identified the gravest crisis humanity has yet faced, the scientific field in which they operate is, however, still not able to offer exact and definitive answers and solutions to most of their concerns. Dr David Suzuki's recent work notes this paradox inherent in all science. That is precisely because earth-sciences are constrained by the very parameters it imposes upon itself, i.e. its narrow world of empiricism. We once more restate a key point of this work: that this unfortunate "scientific" viewpoint fails to take into account or even acknowledge – let alone understand – that all scientific endeavour must embrace Creation-Law first if it is ever to offer complete and meaningful answers to the never-ending questions it continually finds itself faced with.

Thus David Suzuki points out on page 19 that:

> "Scientism, the aura of authority carried by scientists, has made us believe that knowledge obtained by scientists is the ultimate authority, that as we accumulate information, our capacity to understand, control and manage our surroundings will grow correspondingly. But the basic principle of scientific exploration contradicts this faith: knowledge comes from empirical observations, which are "made sense of" by hypotheses, which in turn can be experimentally tested. All information is open to being disproved. As Jonathan Marks has pointed out":
> "...the vast majority of ideas that most scientists have ever had have been wrong. They have been refuted; they have been disposed of. Further, at any point in time, most ideas proposed by most scientists will ultimately be refuted and disposed of... Science, in other words, undermines scientism."

The more recent "Johannesburg Summit on Sustainable Development" revealed that few of the recommendations from the Rio Summit were fully implemented. For whilst the Johannesburg conference *itself* was notable for all the right ecological speech-making, the aftermath inevitably suffered the same fate as the previous Summit – namely all talk and little action. 'Concerned scientists will once again continue to try to bring about a change of direction in the thinking of the political leaders and industrial power-brokers of the world "before it is too late".' Unfortunately, we have very clearly already reached the "too late".

White Cloud's appropriate introduction for this current Chapter and the inherent truth of it harmonises with those eminent scientists, for it is essential that we embrace the vitally important aspect of the wisdom stated there and add it to the sum total of knowledge that is our rightful inheritance. But it must be well understood if it is to bear the very best "fruit".

Prince Charles, once ridiculed quite savagely for his ideas on the environment and modern architecture – but perhaps more for what were once considered fringe ideas on sustainable growing and farming practices – has, in the new brutal reality of a poisoned and polluted planet, been completely vindicated. Yet it was quite clear to anyone with even the smallest amount of common sense that the comments of Prince Charles even many years ago rang true.

The sustainable farming and gardening methods he has introduced and developed at his Highgrove estate has captured the attention of farmers and agriculturalists.

Poundbury, a new village architecturally designed with environmentally sustainable principles for people first and cars a very distant second, set on 400 acres of the Prince's Duchy of Cornwall, has also attracted serious attention. The British Government has embraced the Poundbury principles, and city planners and high officials from numerous countries as far afield as the United States and even Saudi Arabia have visited the village. Others are planned. Will there be an ongoing and expanding legacy from Prince Charles' vision?

The relevant National Geographic article notes:

Two decades ago when he began this crusade, many British farmers felt his experiments were a rebuke to their efficient modern methods. "He was publicly ridiculed. It was withering," recalled Patrick Holden, director of the Soil Association, the main organic growers body. But since then, the area in Britain farmed organically has increased more than a hundredfold. How much of that can be put down to Prince Charles and Highgrove?

> "I don't think it can be overestimated," Holden said. "He has emerged as the clear global leader of the sustainable agriculture movement, **and rightly so**."

(Emphasis mine.)

Another high-profile global leader of environmental note is Al Gore. A similar crusader over decades, and similarly ridiculed in the beginning, he has emerged as the "voice of clear reason" highlighting global warming.

His crucially important documentary, "An Inconvenient Truth", in one sense also concurs with White Cloud's visionary statement and prophecy. But in another, Al Gore's seminal work hugely extends that ancient wisdom via the aid of exceptionally good science. The documentary should perhaps now be understood as almost the final evolvement of the work that a few insightful scientists began in earnest just a few decades ago and who had the courage to speak out about their concerns, and the ongoing work by more and more concerned scientists since. The disturbing trend of human activity and its impact on the planet and its resources is incontrovertibly clear in the documentary.

Al Gore's almost "tongue-in-cheek" comment at one point in his documentary actually reconciles the science/religion divide, at least on this crucial issue, for global humanity. Scenes of devastation of human "works" and desolation of natural landscapes in the documentary brought forth the wry yet fundamentally truthful comment:

"It's like taking a major hike through The Revelation."

As we explained in the Preface, whilst the scientific discoveries and concomitant analyses of his documentary are, in a word, brilliant, the ultimate knowledge that inherently underpins all earth-sciences must be taken into account too – exactly that which Pope Benedict XVI has correctly challenged empirical science to "recognise". The ancient wisdom of White Cloud and the modern knowledge of science can then harmonise perfectly. So if we are to have a more greatly clarified and harmonious existence in our material world, then the knowledge of the "true nature" of the "Elemental Forces of Nature", perhaps more than any other, precisely offers that mechanism whereby scientific ideas need not be "refuted and disposed of" in the future.

Instead, via the knowledge of Creation-Law, science can finally become "genuinely knowing" through recognising and understanding the connection with those forces which govern the immediacy of our earthly environment. Forces, moreover, that also operate in *direct correlation* with our attitude and behaviour, thus our *collective* decision-making process. Unfortunately, it is a human behavioural-attitude which, for the most part, is based on ignorance of the Natural Laws which, however, then impact detrimentally on both the natural world and the societies we create.

Therefore, as we observe the increasingly unpredictable and sometimes disturbing "weather-havoc" globally, the explanations of the "Elemental Forces" will hopefully offer greater understanding as to "why". Whilst the foundation for the process we outline is still that of The Spiritual Laws of Creation, in the context of the subject matter of this Chapter, the *outworking* of the *reciprocal return* of our free-will decisions is placed in the hands of those "elementals" whose activities we loosely refer to *as* the "Forces of Nature". Thus the "**Lore** of Nature" that we refer to in the Chapter heading is also the "**Law** of Nature!"

Under the mantle of that duality it is important to understand what The Laws of Nature refer to and actually mean. Let us state quite unequivocally that whilst these Laws are Spiritual in origin, their *main* effects can be clearly observed and felt as *"weather"* and *"earth-movements"* – in all their various forms. Alternately soft and gentle at times and raging and destructive at others, the destiny of mankind is irrevocably intertwined with the "elemental" activity contained within the weather patterns, and earth-movements in Plate Tectonics. This is clearly a concept vastly different to what meteorology teaches us.

It will probably therefore require a leap of quantum proportions for most to even *deign* to consider such an idea. Yet the strange and unpredictable weather patterns and the uncanny rapid rise in natural catastrophes world-wide must surely be cause for concern and, no doubt, some speculation as to the *actual* cause. Even the more spectacular weather effects which trigger catastrophic natural disasters are not divorced from humankind's collective earthly activity.

Since all things are interconnected and intermeshed in some way, humankind, even though a very small component part of the whole, nonetheless exert a disproportionately large measure of decisive impact *in our part of Creation* through the constant exercising of its collective free-will endowment. The consequences which spring from that decision-making process under The Law of Reciprocal Action ensure that we do, indeed, *"reap what we sow"*.

A large and increasing measure of that "reaping" is returned to us by way of *natural disasters*. We need to constantly remind ourselves that only our *decisions* are free, the *consequences* are not! In that single reality lies humankind's immense responsibility through being granted the gift of "free will". Understanding the *true nature* of the **Forces of Nature** therewith offers meaningful answers to many of our collectively-induced problems, **and to the reason for all natural disasters**.

Let us therefore once more reinforce a key aspect of The Law, from which this particular Chapter derives its mandate. The fundamental truth that:

The 'Laws of Nature' embody the <u>material</u> expression of "The WILL Of GOD" on Earth!

We began this Chapter with a decisive but possibly enigmatic statement regarding the necessity to understand the *actual nature* of the Forces of Nature, thus perhaps presupposing a very radical view of the natural forces around us. Perhaps radical in the sense that it may not accord with current scientific thought, but certainly not radical in its spiritual reality. What do we mean by this? Sage wisdom from a 'medicine-man' of the Native American Sioux Nation may provide science and the more suburbanised man of today a glimpse of what we are revealing here. Lone Man, a late 19th century Teton Sioux brave, shares that wisdom.

> 'When I was a young man I went to a medicine-man for advice concerning my future. He said':
>
> "I have not much to tell you except to help you understand this earth on which you live. If a man is to succeed on the hunt, he must not be governed by his inclination, but by an understanding of the ways of the animals and of his natural surroundings, gained through close observation. The earth is large, and on it live many animals.
>
> The earth is under the ***protection*** of something which ***<u>at times</u> becomes <u>visible</u> to the eye***."
>
> ('Warm Earth' Magazine. Emphases mine.)

Most assuredly, humankind stands in stunned awe when the Elemental Forces of Nature spectacularly destroy his works, whether by earth, wind, fire or water. As we are all aware, the forces that can produce gentle lapping waves and soft summer breezes can also spawn winds and waves of immense power capable of unbelievable destruction. So, too, the healing warmth of fire in winter can be quickly transformed to raging firestorms in forest and city. (In 1998 the BBC produced a four-part series on global weather from the "Our World" programme. The narrator quite regularly used the interesting term, *"species of weather"*, to describe some of the different kinds of more severe weather events we are subjected to.) It is an interesting and unusual description to emerge from out of a purely scientific documentary. If not exactly "species of weather", our clear contention is that we *are* talking about actual *forces* of nature – forces that can bring either gentleness or raging destruction.

The history of early man provides testimony to his belief of the "supernatural" nature of these forces. He feared the lightning and thunder, and could no more control the elements in his time than can modern man today, despite his technological sophistication. Herein lies the paradox! Ancient man accepted the elements as living entities which gave him the forest for building materials and food, the sea for other foods, and good weather for the ripening and harvesting of his crops.

Those same "beings" could also visit great desolation upon him and his works with destructive weather formations. His naturally close connection to the "Elemental Forces" enabled him to give name to each 'being' associated with a particular elemental activity. Through his developing knowledge, he identified male and female 'beings' with clearly demarcated tasks, with each occupying a precisely defined place in their hierarchy.

Because early man had no control over "elemental" activity and believed he was at the mercy of these powerful 'entities', appeasement and worship of them became a living reality for that particular stage of his development. It is significant to note that, virtually without exception, *every developing race* has recorded the presence and existence of these "nature beings" – from the tiniest to the gigantic – depending on their particular role and activity. In his observations of the "gods", as he came to regard them, he ascribed to them human traits. The vagaries of the weather at times, as though he were being played with, gave rise to a mischievous entity – a joker. Kings and queens ruled over this huge and powerful "elemental" domain and over all the lesser "gods" who inhabited it. We should note that **every race** acknowledged their existence, gave them appropriate names out of their language, and incorporated that "knowledge" into their respective cultures.

Conversely, traditional science has determined that weather is *caused* by a combination of precisely configured and measurable scientific formulae involving all aspects of meteorology. Insofar as the visual and material effect of weather is concerned, that is obviously the case. We observe approaching storm fronts and feel their immediate effects, and we also enjoy clear skies and bask in the warmth of high pressure systems. From the cosiness of the lounge in winter, we can be entertained by well-groomed, witty and knowledgeable weather presenters who offer a dazzling presentation of the next few days' weather assisted by a world-wide network of sophisticated satellite detection and measuring equipment, all assessed by banks of powerful computers.

Yet even with this vast array of modern wizardry, there are still reasonably regular, embarrassing glitches in weather forecasting, with sometimes even glaringly opposite outcomes to particular forecasts. As we move from there into the arena of volcanic and earthquake activity projections, it becomes much more difficult to be absolutely precise in predicting either the various levels of projected activity relating to them, or the time of the disturbance. Or whether such activity might be waxing or waning if it is not clearly obvious. So even though undeniable advances have been made in the better detection of impending geological incidents utilising modern sensing instruments and analytical techniques, we are still a long way from any scientifically-acknowledged breakthrough-mechanism to accurately predict such potentially devastating events.

In quite recent times, however, we have a precisely recorded event where the population of a major Chinese city [Haicheng] was evacuated before being struck by a powerful earthquake. That precaution resulted in literally tens of thousands of lives being saved. Moreover, this was achieved not so much by technological means but by careful observations of the behaviour of animals and birds, and via the monitoring of ground-water levels.[1] Thus we have two vastly differing mechanisms for the prediction of this kind of *elemental-force* activity.

We can therefore offer explanations as to which method will produce the greatest benefit and protection for modern man, provided he does not cling to his solely intellectual pursuit of technological sophistry to the exclusion of all other possibilities. A key requirement is that he is open enough to allow his spirit to lead him to a greater understanding of the 'true nature' of these awesome forces. Then, rather than believing he might one day be able to "control" this power – **which he cannot in any case** – he will be able to work "consciously" with it, for his obvious benefit.

4.3 Philosophic and Religious Connections to Elemental Lore

When the development of man's spiritual or religious leanings from his earliest beginnings is examined, the various stages that he had to travel through can be readily observed. Since he did not possess the sophistication for total discernment that we today are able to have – by virtue of having travelled along this developmental path for a far longer period – the brave new world of early man mostly offered a bewildering array of powerful forces that had to be fought, appeased, or worshipped. In the beginning, therefore, Animism as a belief and religion held powerful sway over his everyday world for a long period of time.

---

[1]China currently has an earthquake monitoring force of 10,000 scientists and observers.

Thus he observed and learned the ways of not only the animal and plant worlds, but also those of the "elemental forms" that inhabited every part of his "natural" world too. He gave name to them and to a large degree regulated his life around the activity of what he "knew" to be fellow inhabitants of planet Earth. Different from him both in form and activity, but nevertheless as much a part of the world as was he, and who could offer the greatest help to him. So from them he learned the properties of healing herbs, how to grow his food and what to harvest from the wild. He also learned the ways of the weather and heeded their warnings of impending natural catastrophes. This knowledge is the vitally necessary connection we have long since lost.

During that phase of animistic worship, early man sometimes incorrectly ascribed elemental entities to the natural fixed forms such as trees, rocks and mountains. He was not able to discern that these particular aspects of the natural world did not possess the same kind of life-force such as animals or humans have – as is still believed by some of the world's peoples today. Those "fixed forms" of Nature have a different "life-force" and they provide *habitations* for the *elemental beings* that he observed in and around them.[2]

As man's understanding of his developing world expanded so, also, did his understanding of the "elemental world" around him. From observing the simple activity of the Nature Beings close to his immediate environment, his inner sight began to reveal the higher levels of their Realm where far larger 'Beings' of greater power exerted their authority on everything in the World of Matter. Thus certain races whose development proceeded according to the ordained path that man was to take, recognised the Higher Realm of the Elemental Beings; the "gods of legend". Early cultures attempted to emulate their activity and borrowed from them ideas they could incorporate into everyday life.

Arguably, the peak of this particular path of development probably culminated in the classical Greek period known as Hellenism, which blossomed from near the end of the fourth century B.C. to approximately 50 B.C. The Greeks refined advanced mathematical principles and constructed magnificent buildings of great beauty in symmetry of form. In the classical perfection of their architecture and sculptures we can readily note the purity of form, thus suggesting the application of the **Spiritual Law of Balance** and the concomitant usage of pure mathematics under the aegis of **The Law of Numbers**.

Great strides were made in medicine, too, not least aided by the great philosophical debates and treatises of men like Plato and Aristotle. They sought to define and understand the nature and place of man in the known Universe and, moreover, the relationship and possible reality of a dualistic concept of man in being both a material form and a spiritual or "soul" entity as well. This highly accentuated preoccupation with the form and inner aspect of man may well have resulted in the perfection of form evidenced by Greek sculptures of the human body.

Paradoxically, the *philosophical ideas* of Plato and others, essentially being only a step toward the *sureness* of *spiritual knowledge*, might not have been necessary had man's original spiritual connections been retained. Rather than philosophy and theory by Plato, we might have had more "Spiritual Truth" by him and others. Of course, elements of the truth may certainly be contained within those essays, but they cannot be stated to be definitive works of *absolute* Truth.

The Greeks nonetheless achieved a profound level of knowledge through their greater recognition of the Elemental Beings even though, similar to most other peoples, they also wrongly

---

[2]In terms of the justice of **The Law** that permeates *every* part of Creation, it would be totally against every idea of 'perfect justice' whereby *immobile* life forms such as trees, plants and rocks, would have an inner animating core such as that which animals and humans possess. Only in beings or life forms who are **able to escape**, or otherwise **offer resistance when danger threatens**, is this particular kind of inner life-force present. Were this not the case, the harvesting of trees for housing and warmth, or the taking of rock for road construction etc., would take on vastly different "spiritual" overtones than purely one of general beneficence for man.

regarded them as gods in their polytheistic beliefs. Nevertheless, they were the first to *more completely* understand the relationship between themselves and the Animistic Realm which their particular level of development permitted them to "see". Thus, because they were able to "perceive" the activity above and around them, all the benefits of that Realm were available to them. That insight allowed them to "borrow" themes and ideas from those higher levels, and the Greeks built much of their society accordingly. Thus their history, culture, medicine (the Hippocratic Oath) architecture and language, expressed their correct recognition of the place of these *forces* probably more vitally than most other races did.

The attitude and thinking of the Greek philosophers toward the ruling deities in their pantheon of gods (the Animistic Beings) is well illustrated in Cicero's "The Nature of the Gods". In the form of a dialogue, their 'nature' is debated by representatives of the Greek schools of philosophy. A condensed, brief thread of thought provides that easily understood insight.

"My belief is that the universe and everything in it has been created by the providence of the gods and is governed by that providence through all eternity. — If you grant their existence, you must admit that the world is governed by their providence. — So you must either deny that the gods exist at all ... or else, if you admit their existence, you must also admit that they are active in the higher sense. What could be better then that their activity should be the government of the world? Therefore the world is governed by the wisdom of the gods.

If it were otherwise, it would follow that there must be some power better and stronger than that of the gods, whatever this might be, inanimate matter or the great blind forces of necessity, which have created all these wonderful works that we see around us. In that event the nature of the gods would not be supreme in excellence. It would be subject to that other nature or necessity which ruled the earth and sky and sea. *But nothing is more excellent than the divine [The Divine] and to divinity must belong the government of the world.* God is not subject to obey The Laws of nature. It is nature that is subject to The Laws of God.

If we admit that there exist beings of divine wisdom, then we cannot exclude the working of their providence in the great design of the universe. Or are they unaware of what is of importance and of how such matters should be ordered? Or too weak perhaps to undertake and sustain such great responsibilities? But such ignorance would be contrary to the nature of the gods and it is not in accordance with their majesty and power that they should be too weak to sustain without effort the burden of their office. From which it follows, as we seek to prove, that the world is governed by the wisdom and foresight of the gods.

If gods exist (and they do exist) then to be gods they must be living beings. But not only living beings. They must also be rational beings, joined one with another in a sort of peaceful and harmonious commonwealth, ruling the world as though it were a single state or city. There must be found among them the virtues which men recognize in truth and reason. The same law too which seeks to foster justice and expel evil. From this we can see that it is from the gods that wisdom and good sense are given to men. In recognition of this it was the custom of our ancestors to pay divine honours to Reason, Faith, Virtue and Concord. - - If Reason, Faith, Virtue and Concord are to be found among men, whence can they have come down to Earth but from the gods? Since we have some measure of sense, rationality and wisdom, the gods must have them in far greater measure. They must not only have them but use them too in the greatest and most admirable works. Now there is nothing greater or more wonderful than the universe as a whole. Therefore it must be governed by the wisdom and the foresight of the gods.

(Book 11, p.155-157)

Whilst that particular discourse is an indication of the Greek perspective of philosophic thought with regard to perhaps a more elevated concept of the role of their gods as rulers of the universe, there was also the recognition and acceptance of the other helps that assisted mankind. Cicero noted that whilst there were other philosophers who held it true that the entire world is kept in order and ruled by divine insight and reason, at the same time they believed the gods also looked after the life of men in a counselling and helping way.

> *In their opinion fruits and other products of the soil, changes in the weather, the seasons and the planet generally, by which everything the earth produces is made to grow and ripen, are gifts of the same gods – for mankind.* And since this belief in gods was not the result of education, old custom or law, and since universal agreement among the philosophic community was well established, there was therefore the firm conviction that the gods existed. Such a conviction could only stem from an inherent, implanted or, as he avers, *"an inborn conception of them"*.
>
> As this point is almost invariably given unlimited recognition, not only by all philosophers but also by the uneducated, we must certainly admit that there is in us the pre-comprehension of the gods, as I have called it before; or should I call it pre-knowledge.

Therefore, Cicero believed, the existence of the gods must be admitted.[3]

The Greeks' correct spiritual development to that particular point permitted them the insight to "know" that much more existed in Creation than just the material world, simply by virtue of their recognition of the Elemental Beings (their gods). Unfortunately, however, they basically concluded that the "Gods on Mount Olympus" – as they perceived them to be – were the absolute height of Creation. Yet the Apostle Paul, in his first address to the men of Athens, noted that the Greeks had divined the probable existence of the One invisible God when he stated to them:

> "Men of Athens, I perceive beyond everything how deeply religious you are, for, going about and studying your objects of worship, I even found an altar upon which had been inscribed:
>
> TO AN UNKNOWN GOD
>
> What therefore you unknowingly worship, I proclaim to you. The God. Who made the Universe and all in it."
>
> (Acts 17:22-24, Fenton.)

Without sure conviction of a "Divine Realm" or a "Higher Creation", any further spiritual development for the Greeks was stunted by that uncertainty. The one race that did conclusively divine the Highest Spheres – in fact all the way to the seat of The Godhead – was the Jewish race. As previously noted, their recognition of The Source of All Life paved the way for an eventual connection that would allow Jesus, The Son of God, to incarnate among them. Their prior recognition of the "Elemental Forces of Nature" can be clearly noted by the help accorded to the Israelites by these "Nature Beings" – sometimes spectacularly so – on many different occasions during their exodus from out of Egyptian bondage under the leadership of Moses.[4]

---

[3]The mechanism by which we inherently possess such pre-knowledge has already been explained in Chapter 2. We will revisit the process further on in this one.

[4]We may note the same interaction between man and the "elementals" in other places within The Bible, examples of which will be used later in this Chapter to illustrate the spiritual and physical validity of this "Elemental-force premise".

From the Greek homeland the same knowledge was used to create a new Empire – that of Rome. However, because the transportation of this belief and culture was effected by a relatively small number of Greeks, the native Roman people who had not developed to the same "level of seeing" *as a complete race*, did not have the natural recognition of this Higher Realm that the Greeks possessed. So whilst the Roman Empire prospered and grew very powerful, the connections to, and worship of, their "gods" were far more tenuous than those which the Greek Empire enjoyed.

Certainly, history records that the Romans feared their differently named deities and proffered many gifts and sacrifices to them over millennia, but this was probably based more on dogma and doctrine than actual conviction. The end result was that the Roman Emperors eventually became convinced of their own direct lineage from their "stone gods". Corruption of the "founding-belief" eventually brought about the demise of Rome and allowed for the subsequent new emerging force of Christianity to supersede both Greek and Roman thought.

Christianity has been the main religion of the Western world since its dissemination thereto via the Roman Empire. From out of The Bible, Christians have striven to supplant the "stone and wooden gods" of those races to whom they introduced their new, more enlightened, teaching. Yet even though we live in an increasingly sophisticated world, a surprising number within *certain* races today still retain ties to, and revere, some of their gods of old.

Such intransigence surely reveals why humankind is burdened with so much distress. For it shows that we do not really advance spiritually, but in many ways remain stagnant and locked into defective and unworkable concepts.

By way of example, Jeremiah's letter to those taken captive to Babylon by King Nebuchadnezzar that long time ago illustrates that even amongst the Jewish people of the time – despite their long history of worship directed *away* from "stone idols" – fear of Babylonian "gods" was present. Jeremiah explained why they should not be feared. For exactly the same reasons, carved effigies today should not be acknowledged, revered or, worse, worshipped. Jeremiah's almost "tongue-in-cheek" advice amazes by its stunningly-clarifying analysis of the *stupidity* of such fear-ridden worship.

> "Now in Babylon you will see gods made of gold and silver and wood, which are carried on men's shoulders and inspire fear in the heathen. So take care not to become at all like the foreigners or to let fear for these gods possess you. Their tongues are smoothed by the craftsmen - - but - - cannot speak. When - - dressed in purple robes, their faces are wiped because of the dust from the temple, which is thick upon them. "...the god holds a scepter, though unable to destroy anyone who offends it. It has a dagger in its right hand, and has an axe, but it cannot save itself from war and robbers. Therefore they evidently are not gods, so do not fear them."

Jeremiah continues with the observation that when they [the gods] are set up in the temple, the attendant priests and the believers do not seem to notice the fact that they are actually lifeless, yet still attend them and worship them.

> "Their eyes are full of the dust raised by the feet of those who enter. They do not notice when their faces have been blackened by the smoke of the temple. Bats, swallows and birds light on their bodies and heads; and so do cats. From this - - they are not gods, so do not fear them."

A key point of Jeremiah's letter about the foolishness of such practices is wonderfully stated in the next few passages.

"Having no feet, they are carried on men's shoulders, revealing to mankind *their worthlessness*. And those who serve them are [a]shamed because through them these gods are made to stand, lest they fall to the ground. If any one sets one of them upright, it cannot move of itself; and if it is tipped over, it cannot straighten itself; yet gifts are placed before them *just as before the dead.*"

"These things that are made of wood and overlaid with gold and silver are like stones from the mountain, *and those who serve them will be put to shame. Why then must anyone think they are gods, or call them gods?"

(The Apocrypha, *The Letter Of Jeremiah*.
Extracts from pages 178 and 179, Emphases mine.)

Today there are probably more gods than ever before, for we have technological ones, scientific ones and monetary ones now. These, too, are worshipped, revered or feared by those who serve them in their different associations and ways. So it is extremely vital that the explanation of the "gods of legend" are offered, because the timely recognition of their true nature as Elemental Beings will offer to those who do so recognise, huge protection when the time of humanity's trials burst in full strength upon us. Then all false gods, whether stone, technological, scientific, monetary or whatever, will have had their time too.

Like the Greeks and Romans, other races such as the Nordic and Germanic peoples also reached the level necessary to recognise the Nature Beings and thus also the knowledge of the Elemental "gods", with the Norse naming their high fastness, Valhalla. During their depredations in other lands, the Norsemen came into contact with Christianity and they, too, eventually embraced the new religion. This acceptance of a completely new idea ensured that the original, once-sure beliefs would eventually die away. Notwithstanding that unfortunate demise, certain aspects of the old beliefs were still retained in the fables, myths and legends of those groups.

The active retention of this kind of knowledge was held more strongly in the less-developed tribal groups in the different parts of the world still untouched by this new thought of Christianity. Unfortunately, the generally superstitious minds of most of these tribal groups allowed major distortions to enter into their view of the Animistic world, and they did not reach the degree of actual knowledge necessary to recognise the higher levels of that Realm. Moreover, their particular views generally produced fear and wrong worship which effectively kept the door to greater knowledge firmly closed. So whilst a natural and necessary connection to "other-world realities" was retained, to all intents and purposes the vitally necessary working knowledge of, and connection to, the Realm of the Elementals and Nature Beings above us was effectively lost here also.

And whereas some of the "indigenous peoples" have at least retained a strong belief in the validity of their legends as possible truth, other more "intellectual races" – including those of European origin in the new worlds of America, Canada, Australia and New Zealand – have virtually severed this *connection* completely, not even bothering to retain them as fables. With the embarkation of millions from old Europe to the new lands in a relatively short space of time, the severing of strong family and cultural traditions developed over centuries was considered more or less necessary in order to face the challenges of a new way of life freed from the constraints of a dogmatic and blinkered Europe. This dogmatism was epitomised either by the superstitions of the rural peasantry, the bigotry of the controlling political and religious authorities, or the arrogance of the ruling aristocracy.

"Freedom from restraint" from old Europe paradoxically seeded a strange "new idea", especially in America. Historically, we are able to note the curious emergence of the concept of "Manifest Destiny", itself just as bigoted and probably more arrogant as that which was ostensibly left behind. In essence it decreed that the new lands were more fit for the new people than for the indigenous inhabitants. In place of a benign, caring and conservation-minded approach, with a mutual merging of cultures offering benefits for both peoples, the goal was to exploit and *tame nature* in the frontier land, and subjugate and civilise the "primitive natives" in the process. The "new Americans" and the actual land of America itself would have been far spiritually richer today had the concept of "Manifest Destiny" espoused humility and the biblical admonition to "...do unto others..."

This "new way" of the New-world peoples clearly and unequivocally illustrates our assertion that the necessary connection to the "Elemental forces" was no longer a part of their life. This loss, in the same way and for the same reasons that the Greeks eventually lost it – rapidly developing and generally crass intellectualism almost completely supplanting the intuitive-spiritual insight – guaranteed the seeds for the material degradation of planet Earth. For without *genuine* veneration and gratitude for the earthly home, we sow the seeds for our eventual demise, drowned in our own poison. It may be that we will one day look back and recognise the technical revolution itself as a perilous path opposing all that was natural and spiritually lawful in the world.

Unfortunately for "Western Nations", generally, their god of science has determined that such notions as "Elemental Beings" cannot possibly be entertained as belonging to a "rational, logical and intelligent" society, even though the "face-book" of their religions, The Bible, speaks of them clearly enough. Moreover, missionaries who ventured forth out of Europe into the new "heathen lands" generally condemned this natural and necessary connection ordained by The Creative Will, and applied various labels such as superstition, blasphemy and even demonism to it. Thus the relegation of what was once accepted as factual knowledge, even if not fully understood, to the realm of myth and legend by man's new "intellectual sophistication", is to our grave detriment. For the more correct place of the intellect was to assist man in the fulfilment of his earthly duties, which is why it is vital for scientific and other earthly endeavours. In this, its proper and ordained place, it rightly produces technological marvels and great feats of construction.

> So **Spiritual-man**, with the *potential* for achieving *true greatness* in *both* the Material and non-Material Worlds of Creation, sadly became merely ***intellectual man*** more concerned with *earthly analysis and theory*. Greater ***spiritual*** activity, as was ordained *from the beginning*, could have ensured corresponding outcomes; which thereby *would have produced* an harmonious earthly home for *all* human societies.

Instead, man's rejection of the twin-realities of the knowledge and outworking of Spiritual Law and the existence of the "Elemental Forces" has now wrought a degraded and poisoned planet Earth we nonetheless still call 'home'.

Two key events in the history of man had a major bearing on the acceptance, or otherwise, of "Elemental aspects". One was the religious madness of the Dark Ages, and the other was the later, perhaps more enlightened, Age of Reason. During the course of the Dark Ages and the accompanying Inquisition, the Christian religious authorities, who were at the height of temporal power, decreed that anything remotely connected with "Nature Beings" be branded as heresy and "demonism". Consequently, even the simple and innocent act of picking herbs or fungus in the forest for food or medicine resulted in the torture and death of perhaps thousands of harvesters, mostly women, who were invariably accused of being witches and in league with the devil.

During the exploration and colonisation period when the "white cultures" of Europe exported religion and criminals to the lands of indigenous tribal peoples beginning about the 1700s, the Christian Church once more came up against strong conviction about the existence of "Nature Beings". However, if it was totally unacceptable in their own societies where innocents were killed in the name of their God for this "heresy", it would certainly not be tolerated in the new lands. Consequently, it was quickly opposed and/or suppressed there as well. Thankfully, the madness of "torture by religious numbers" finally relinquished its hold on the psyche of the European Church with the beginnings of the more scientific "Age of Enlightenment" in the 18th century.

What did those budding scientists make of the previously unseen world around them then, however? With the greater surge of intellectualism to scientifically rationalise the natural world, the catchwords, "prove it", became the rationale of empiricism that everyone and everything had to bow to. What could not be physically seen, touched or heard was relegated to the realm of nonsense until such time as the new religious god of science decreed otherwise. Of course, as more powerful instruments were developed, what was very recently dismissed as impossible was revealed as living reality. It is curious that the scientific community, even in our present age of so-called great enlightenment, still tenaciously clings to that same view of "not possible" until proven *scientifically*.

Yet the reality for *all time* will be, that regardless of the adulation they may heap upon themselves with each new "discovery", scientists seem not to understand – or at least publicly acknowledge – that what might be lauded as a major discovery has, quite naturally, *always existed*. Even with the production of a new element which science might suddenly produce, it was never a question of an actual *creation* of a new substance, because the necessary building blocks for that fusion were *always available*.

Therefore, if we apply the same criteria to both science and religion – each generally vehemently opposed to any such notion of "Nature Beings" – to that exact same subject, we have the factual reality that **either** Elemental Beings exist, or they do not! Only *one* reality is possible here, not two. If, in fact, they really were a figment of emerging man's fertile and fearfully superstitious imagination, then the problem resolves itself and we need no longer bother with it. However, if the *opposite* is true and they actually *do* exist and *are* a living part of the total activity in Creation and thus also here on Earth – even if outside of our physical senses – then that clearly poses a huge problem for both science and religion. For an accommodation would have to be made somewhere in both Disciplines, and one that *actually fits*.

Everything that is in the World can only exist under the aegis of Creation-Law. Precisely because of that immutable fact, it naturally follows that any actual existence of "Nature Beings" will have been *ordained* by The Creative Will. It is the same Will, moreover, under which *both* the Disciplines of science and religion are *freely permitted* to disseminate their 'doctrines'. Quite logically, then, if "Nature Beings" *do* exist and ancient man *did* understand their place and *actually observed them*, then the obvious reality for latter-day man is that **we** have lost the ability to see them. What, then, might that imply?

Since modern science has relegated "Nature Beings" to the realm of superstitious myth and legend, and because their existence probably cannot ever be proved by scientific means, it follows that the scientific community will probably never accept even the possibility of such 'beings'. Notwithstanding this attitude from that particular direction, Dr Lyall Watson, an eminent Biologist, [perhaps one of the very few "knowing voices in the scientific community"] produced a remarkable series of books exploring the intellectually-perceived "no-go zone" between empirical science and the "other-world reality". In that series he has documented some stunningly remarkable and totally unexpected insights.

In particular, his books, "Supernature" and "Gifts of Unknown Things" reveal amazing incidents inexplicable according to man's accepted scientific criteria but naturally factual under the higher knowledge of Elemental and Spiritual Law. As a scientist, he was able to bridge the *humanly-created* "impossible zone" between the Discipline of science and the less clearly defined area of religiosity, and logically marry many aspects of the two-world beliefs. His research has greatly helped to dispel the myth that such a "no-go area" actually exists in the first place.

In reality it cannot, for all things between the *tangible* and the equally-real *intangible* are, in various ways, precisely and *lawfully* connected anyway. As in:

Crucial Imperative No 2:

> That we, the human beings of planet Earth, are not solely a physical entity, but also necessarily possess a *non-material* inner animating core: *For the physical **cannot** – and therefore **does not** – animate the physical!*

And what of the Christian Church? Is there anything in their 'doctrines of faith' that even *faintly allude* to the existence of such 'beings'? They are certainly accepted in many races, religions and teachings other than orthodox Christianity. We have already mentioned the assistance afforded Moses. Two instances of particular note were the parting of the Red Sea and the "pillar of fire" which guided his vast caravan. The others being "manna" from heaven for bread, birds for meat, and water under the surface of the ground accessed by Moses who knew where it lay hidden.

The Bible contains examples of even supposedly savage animals not offering harm to particular individuals where, in the situations described, they perhaps normally would. Daniel in the lion's den stands as a prime example. But perhaps a very brief examination of one especially celebrated event from The Bible may offer the greatest relevant insight into this question of "Elemental Beings" and their ordained activity alongside humankind.

Most people with even a rudimentary grasp of The Bible, even from "Sunday School" level, are probably aware of the story of the "miracle" of Jesus calming the wind and waves during a storm on the Sea of Galilee. In this particular instance the Disciples, alarmed at the increasing strength of the storm, were fearful for their lives.

From The Book of Mark we read:

> And a very heavy gale began to blow and the waves rushed into the boat, so that it was rapidly filling. And He Himself was at the stern asleep on a cushion. They accordingly aroused Him, exclaiming, "Teacher! Do you not care if we perish?" Upon awakening, He restrained the wind, and said to the sea, "Silence! be still!" The wind then lulled and there was perfect calm.
> "Why", He asked them, "do you doubt in this way? How is it that you cannot yet have faith?"
> But they became terrified; and said to one another, "What can He be? for even the wind and the sea obey Him?"

> (4:37-41, Fenton.)

This event is accepted by Christians as one that actually occurred but are probably inclined to label it a miracle. However, what may not be generally comprehended was what **actually** took place in this most interesting happening. To understand it fully, we must apply The Spiritual Laws of Creation to it, since absolutely nothing can take place in any part of Creation except under the aegis of them. And since Jesus Himself declared that He had "...not come to abolish The Laws but to complete them", the calming of the wind and the waves could only be possible under those Eternal Laws. Now, by virtue of His Origin from out of The Divine, He would clearly have known of the existence of the "Elemental Beings of Nature".

Moreover, not only would He have been aware of them but, because of His High Origins and associated Power over all else below that level, all "Nature Beings" and their activities would have been **naturally subordinate to His Command**. For it would be foolish to believe that He was rebuking the ***actual substance*** of water and wind. No, the clear illustration here is that He was admonishing a *force* or *energy* that has its *field of activity* in what we loosely call the *natural world* and *weather*. A 'force' which gave rise to the increased agitation of the wind and water that instilled fear in the Disciples, thus the "Forces", or "Beings", of Nature!

Acceptance of this event as being one of unequivocal truth presupposes the clear inference that the only viable mechanism under which the "calming of the wind and waves" could have occurred in the manner illustrated – in particular being **commanded to cease their activities** – is via the activity of "Nature Beings". Therewith do they fulfil their ordained purpose under the umbrella of inviolable Spiritual Law, of which Jesus would have perfectly understood every single ramification.

Through this clearly recorded incident, we are able to offer one more illustration to show that "Elemental Forces of Nature" *produce* the *effects* of the varying levels of interrelated weather outcomes in storms, natural disasters and catastrophes which so effectively destroy man and his works. This occurs through the direct correlation between spiritually-wrong *personal and collective decisions* produced by *our spiritual volition,* and the subsequent outcomes returned to humankind under The Law of Sowing and Reaping – as we must continually reinforce.

Such a radical view will no doubt produce smiles of incredulity, perhaps more so on the part of weather scientists and forecasters. Yet, as stated previously, it does not take all that much imagination to wonder at the increasing frequency and intensity of storms world-wide. Or of extreme weather patterns producing intense and prolonged droughts virtually alongside areas of devastating inundations. What we are also observing is the more frequent use of superlatives needed to *attempt* to describe the continuing catalogue of Mother Nature's "handiwork".

Words such as the heaviest, longest, driest, severest, worst in living memory, and worst ever recorded, etc., clearly reveal an emerging pattern that is not solely the product of journalistic jingoism. Something very different is now taking place on Earth the like of which we have not experienced before, something that is producing a feeling of uncertainty and unease in the minds of more and more people. And something that cannot be completely explained by the felling of the rain forests, the enlargement of the hole in the ozone layer, nuclear proliferation, global warming, or a burgeoning global population. Even the feared "El Nino" phenomenon, which is clearly capable of producing great devastation, is simply only the activity of these Elemental forces.

It is interesting to note that the U.S. Geological Survey, the body responsible for monitoring earth-movements in the United States and elsewhere, has observed a large increase in world-wide earthquake activity over 7 on the Richter scale in the decades *from* the 1930,s and 40's. Up until the point when records were first kept, numbers of earthquakes of that magnitude were relatively infrequent. The most interesting aspect of these findings is that various people who have studied this data do not know *why* such a huge increase has occurred. However, since nothing can occur without a reason, and as everything must take place under the umbrella of The Eternal Laws, the answers can be found within *those parameters*, even if "scientifically unacceptable" *at this point in time.*

For the purposes of clarification, let us suspend any disbelief in such a *seemingly* preposterous notion, greatly extend *our personal parameters of possibilities*, and allow vastly different perceptions to hold sway for the moment. Let us assume the correctness of the assertion that "Elemental" activity is the mechanism by which weather patterns and related geological activity are generated. And, moreover, that the increasing extremes of natural phenomena via this mechanism have a definite cause and purpose. What, then, might be the trigger? To understand the cause, we need to revisit the structure of Creation so that we may understand the "whence, whither and why" of the "Elemental Beings" also.

In Chapter 2, we offered explanations as to **how** and **why** Creation came into being. The reader may wish to return to that particular segment to familiarise himself with the complete process. At this point we will quickly skim over the main happenings in a brief memory refresher.

So, in answer to the petition of many varied creatures who could not come to conscious life in the immediate vicinity of the immense power of The Creator, lower Planes of habitable worlds at necessarily vast distances from His "Proximity" were permitted to come into being under The Creation-Words: **"Let There Be Light!"**

As each Realm coalesced out at its ordained level of Creation, the inhabitants for each of those Planes were able to take on form and begin their *conscious existence*. The final outcome of this "fractional distillation process" was the forming of the Material Worlds encompassing the Earth and the vast physical Universes. But because the denser, physical Realm of mankind must naturally occupy that lower part of Creation which is *not eternal*, it was not able to generate its 'own warmth' to produce the requisite parameters for conscious life there.

By "warmth" we do not mean the interstellar mechanisms of thermonuclear energy etc., that gave rise to the formation of the billions of suns and star systems in the physical Universes. We refer to the "warmth" of the *life-force* of Creation Itself – which is separate from the immense heat generated during the formative processes of all celestial globes – but which nevertheless allow those formations to come into being also. This particular "life-warmth" is naturally present in both The Eternal Realm of The Spiritual and also in the Elemental Realm.

The Material Worlds, which did not inherently possess this necessary "warmth" or "animating life-power", received it from what we might term the "Elemental Realm". All the "Beings" of the Elemental Forces – the powerful and the small – have their origin there, but carry out their activities throughout all the Planes of Creation. Thus, it was the "energy" of The Spiritual, utilised by the "Nature Beings" involved with the formation of the vast Universes, that gave life-warmth to our material home. Perhaps as a clearer description, we may liken the "nature beings" to the "maintenance workers" in the hive holding everything together.

> There we have the "whence, whither, and why" of the "Elemental forces" too. Not "scientifically rational", of course, but nonetheless spiritually, and therefore *Lawfully*, correct in its *basic* overview.

The reason why man must know of the existence of "Elemental Beings" is quite simple. As explained in Chapter 2, as human spirits journey downward from The Realm of The Spiritual to seek incarnation in the Material Planes in order to develop "personal self-consciousness", they necessarily traverse other Realms, including that of the Animistic. As they travel through the lower Planes, each of which is of a naturally-heavier *consistency* than the previous higher one, the "journeying spirit" is compelled, quite logically, to accept a covering, or "body", of the same substance and consistency of the particular Plane transited through. Consequently, one of our "cloaks" corresponds precisely to that of the Animistic Realm. It is this particular covering or "body" that allows us to connect to, and understand, the "Elemental Beings" of the "Forces of Nature", and their activity.

This necessary connection offers us the means whereby we *can* work consciously with them as once the early races did. Such a working on Earth could produce a wonderful imitation of the beauty and harmony of the higher Spiritual Spheres, for our material benefit also. However, because we voluntarily cut off this vital connection, we have produced a mainly intellectual world devoid of any real Spiritual-Truth aspirations. Thus we struggle to make sense of an increasingly poisoned and degraded planet, for which we seem unable to put into place meaningful, long-term answers. If we do not now strive to re-establish that vitally important connection and begin to seek out the necessary knowledge and understanding of them, there will be nothing to look forward to except more problems wrought by more people crowding into reducing areas of increasing degradation! A thoroughly unpleasant and rather frightening outcome.

That will be the ultimate end-result anyway, simply because of our stubborn refusal to accept this reality. Paradoxically, because we of humankind desperately need this vital connection for our very survival, it is critically important to offer the very knowledge that may turn the tide for those who hold the desire to learn about them. Those who genuinely embrace this desire would gain a greater level of insight into the inner and outer workings of the natural world. Whilst intimately involved in the formative processes of, and activity in, all the Spheres of Creation, the Elemental Forces, by way of a precise and lawfully ordained process, are also concerned with all human activities.

To explain the further *why* of this connection, we need to **fully** understand that, of all creatures in Creation, only the human spirit inherently possesses the gift of free-will.

Crucial Imperative No 8:

> That we, the human Beings of planet Earth, *inherently possess* the ordained attribute of "**free-will**". That *not understanding* the so-called inequities or injustices of life has its *genesis* in human *non-recognition* and thus *non-understanding* of this most "**Crucial Imperative**".

Every other inhabitant within Creation carries out their life and activity in strict accordance with The Creative Will, including the Elemental Beings. From free-will, however, derives the ultimate spiritual responsibility of **accountability**. Accountability for all our thoughts, words and actions.

Now, at this time in the spiritual and evolutionary development of mankind, our collective "karma" over millennia – which for the most part consists of dark, debased and degraded activities – is being returned to us with increasing strength and frequency under the lawful outworking of the interlinked and inviolable Laws of Creation. This lawful process marks the closing of all cycles – again activated by our free-will – for *global humanity*. It is the unenviable task of the "Elemental Beings", through the generation of increasingly severe effects of the world's weather patterns and catastrophic natural disasters, that "returns" a large part of this "payment" to us. It is thus in exact accordance with both the *individual* and *collective* spiritual volition of all humankind under the outworking of The Law of Reciprocal Action in the first instance.

> For present-day mankind, then, **individual outcomes** are, even now in the earlier stages of the "cleansing", **simultaneously** being resolved within the parameters of the **collective happening**.

We reiterate the key point of a previous paragraph; the reinforcement of our assertion that "The Laws of Nature" are inherent in "The Will of God". In other words, the "Elemental Forces of Nature", in their ordained purpose and activity, carry out The Eternal Will. Under the inviolable Law of Sowing and Reaping, the "Elemental Beings", both the large and the small, *produce* the *reciprocal effect* of mankind's decisions.

So, what is the actual mechanism that will ultimately bring about our "collective fate", and how will the "Forces of Nature" achieve this? We should be perfectly clear from the above explanations, therefore, that the "Forces of Nature" **will** bring about the "renewal" of the Earth under the outworking of the Natural Laws which are, at the same time, The Spiritual Laws. We should thus strongly note a key point; that these events will occur at the precisely ordained time, *"irrespective of the condition of the inhabitants"*.

The term condition in this case means the *spiritual condition*, or level of *spiritual maturity* of the inhabitants. Therefore, as we continually reinforce, since most of man's decisions for all his time on Earth have leaned far more toward war, strife and degradation of his material home, we can expect that the collective reciprocal return of that volition will be severe and destructive, returning *tenfold* our original "choices", albeit in perfect justice, however. Thus for humankind, that *tenfold-factor* is "delivered" under the lawful aegis of the "whirlwind constant".

It is important to understand two major happenings in the overall and ultimate fate of man here. Firstly, as already explained, it is given over to the Elemental Forces of Nature to visit upon humankind the end-result of our transgressions – our refusal – to live according to The Spiritual Laws of Creation! Disbelief or ignorance of those Laws will not stay the effects at the appointed times for the events alluded to, simply because it was our primary responsibility to seek out those very Laws, and then live accordingly. And because we have collectively chosen to embrace beliefs and practices totally opposed to those Adamantine and Inviolable Laws, the *reciprocal outcomes* of *severe* destruction cannot now be stayed.

The complete process is therefore two-fold. The first is the initial cleansing of the Earth itself. By cleansing, in this instance, we mean by *catastrophic events* that will not only destroy, but *sweep away* all mankind's practices and processes not in harmony with **The Laws of Creation**. Those *same* events will naturally account for very many of the Earth's people who *also* had not *submitted*. Post-catastrophe/cleansing will then see the regeneration of all eco-systems and natural processes that had suffered degradation, poisoning and destruction at our foolish hands. Human practices and processes that *are* in accord will *not* suffer destruction.

As you, the reader, are now very cognisant of, much of the information in this book is derived from The Bible, a Work we have designated as **"A Primary Book of Foundational-Science!"** Along with the logical processes therein – with which we have examined *some* of our "Bible Mysteries" thus far – might we also find within that Work clear revelations whereby we can understand the *actual Why* of our poisoned and degraded Earth? And thereby *further reinforce* our unequivocal premise that **The Bible** really is *"scientific"*.

4.3.1   The Prophet Isaiah's "Reeling Earth"

To that end and from that especial Book, the Great Prophet, Isaiah, in brutal visionary-prophecy, describes the **what**, **how** and **why** of the complete cleansing of Earth of the very many humans who refuse to heed The Eternal Laws **as they actually are**.

> 'The "Earth" is utterly broken down, the "Earth" is clean dissolved, the "Earth" is *moved exceedingly*.
>
> The "Earth" shall reel *to and fro* like a drunkard, and shall be *removed from her place*.'

> (Isaiah 24: 19-20. Emphases mine.)

How much of that chilling potential can we attribute to human decisions, societal attitudes and concomitant global activity? Isaiah certainly pulled no punches in identifying *why*. Bad human decisions will obviously produce bad outcomes, not only for human societies but for the planet as a whole. And that is surely our present legacy and reality. —
Decisions = consequences!

> 'The "Earth" mourns and fades away, the "World" languishes and fades away, the haughty people of the "Earth" do languish.
>
> The "Earth" also is defiled under the inhabitants thereof; because they have *trans-gressed* the "Laws", *changed* the decrees, *broken* the everlasting covenant.

Therefore has the curse devoured the "Earth", and those that dwell therein are desolate: therefore the inhabitants of the "Earth" are burned,[5] and few men left.'

(Isaiah 24: 4-6, Italics mine.)

Fenton's translation is more stark and will therefore more closely approximate the frightening power of the event in terms of what we should expect and thus seriously heed.

> "For windows from on high are opened,
> And the earth's foundations shake!
> And the land with crashing crashes,
> And the land with breaches breaks!
> Tottering land meets ground that totters,
> Staggering earth like drunkard staggers,
> And flapping, quivers like a tent;
> And her crimes are heavy on her,
> She will fall, nor rise again!"

(Isaiah 24:20, Fenton.)

What might modern-day scientists and 'empirical science' make of the above statements? Except for the relatively few who have broken out of the strait-jacket of 'empirical intellectualism' [or intellectual empiricism], most would probably dismiss the whole idea of Bible prophecy – accurate enough to pinpoint future events of such catastrophic power sufficient to produce a "reeling Earth" – as religious nonsense. Ferrar Fenton's translation of just one line of Isaiah's vision [24:20] —

"And the Earth's foundations shake!"

— should strike a chord of serious warning for all scientists whose field of 'expertise' lies in anything even *remotely* connected with the Earth.

So: What does this *really mean* for the earth-scientist? More to the point, perhaps, should scientists take note of such prophecies, or be derisively dismissive of them? As we have already stated, what Isaiah was gifted to 'see' and give warning for future humanity was the ***vastly amplified activity*** of 'Plate Tectonics'.

When first mooted early last century, it was, of course, dismissed by the "scientific establishment" as impossible nonsense. Now we all know **Plate Tectonics** to be "scientific" fact. Surely a perfect example of **"The Error of Scientism"**. A "reeling Earth" which "shakes its very foundation"? Is this impossible nonsense too? Not now! For this we also now know to be "scientifically feasible". How?

Earth-science and global humanity have the quite recent experience of knowing that *the whole Earth* can actually shake from just one, albeit very large but nevertheless **single**, earth-movement. The devastating and catastrophic experience of the Indian Ocean tsunami, Boxing Day, 2004, has surely shaken any scientific scepticism that such a thing was not possible. In any case, what has *already occurred* a number of times in the past with obviously catastrophic consequences for the Earth could well happen again — a truly cataclysmic 'pole shift'. Such an event would *absolutely* fulfil Isaiah's vision.

A "reeling Earth" with mountains and islands 'moved out of their places' would certainly result from a 'pole shift'; with, of course, unimaginable and horrendous death and destruction.

---

[5]The *true* meaning of 'the burning of Earth's inhabitants' is explained in Chapter 12; sub, Destruction by "Fire".

A similar, though perhaps *less destructive* outcome could also occur with multiple, simultaneous earth-movements, or as a very rapid 'sundering' ripple-effect. The destruction and devastation wrought by earth-movements on that scale would produce tens, if not hundreds, of millions of lives lost. So the precedent for Isaiah's "shaking Earth" has now been experienced by 'science' and present-day humanity!

Should we hope that the Great Prophet's *harder vision* will not eventuate? Or has human behaviour and activity already proceeded too far past what is acceptable to *immutable* **Creation-Law**? If so, it is simply because; "...they [*we*] have **transgressed** the "Laws", *changed* the decrees, **broken** the everlasting covenant."

The damage we have wrought is easy enough to see and simple to understand in terms of what that means for global humanity. For within the parameters of the upheavals that will accompany the "earth-cleansing process" will also be the reciprocal outcomes for all human beings too. That will take effect for each individual, for families, for the various races, for Nations and, not least of course, for the numerous *aspiritual* religions and belief-systems humankind have spawned. The extent to which individuals and/or collectives will be affected will depend on the degree of *compliance* or *non-compliance* with The Laws of Creation. We should probably more correctly say – in place of compliance/non-compliance – **acceptance or rejection**!

Those who 'make it through' will "spiritually awaken" to a renewed and rejuvenated Earth. Isaiah's further prophecy of a greater promise fulfilled will reveal itself after the 'removal' of all that did not live in "The Law".

"When New Skies I create and New Earth,
Nor the Old be remembered, or brought up to mind."

(Isaiah 65:17, Fenton.)

The more decisive event – though the time ordained for it cannot at all be stated – must and will take place at its appointed time much further in the future for those humans *then* on Earth. That **event** is the natural process of disintegration that all celestial globes must undergo when its point of dissolution for the further process of renewal arrives – thus also for planet Earth. However, it is **separate from** humankind's present and near-future reaping, but will nonetheless arrive at its ordained *far-future* time.

The "mechanics and process" of that upheaval is more the subject of the later Chapter, "The Second Death", which is the outcome for *that* human spirit who utterly *rejects* the very knowledge that would spare him the worst possible fate. A fate, however, ultimately brought about by personal free-will decisions. The following "Crucial Imperatives" provide precise keys to understanding how such an outcome is lawfully possible.

Crucial Imperative No 2:

That we, the human beings of planet Earth, are not solely a physical entity, but also necessarily possess a *non-material* inner animating core: *For the physical* **cannot** *– and therefore* **does not** *– animate the physical!*

Crucial Imperative No 3:

That being more than just a physical body means we naturally and *inherently* possess a *separable entity* **within** the material form. And that *that* is the *actual* life-force, the *animating* core, that is *actually each individual*!

Now, if we *truly are* near the point where the *"cleansing" or "tribulation"* is due to set in, then we should be able to detect at least the *beginnings* of that process via *increased Elemental-force activity*.

This effect should thus clearly reveal itself in more and more disruptive and destructive weather patterns affecting societies and countries detrimentally. Quite obviously, there *is* such increased activity, the like of which even weather scientists now view with alarm. This new "weather development" therefore clearly heralds this impending cleansing process. Even once obtuse governments and their politicians have now realised the potential for greater disasters seen thus far through human-induced "global warming".

As our fate is tightly bound to the spiritually-lawful activity of the "elementals" who are tasked with returning the reciprocal effects of all our deeds; in the same way that we must reap "our bad", it is equally true – and certainly more desirable – that we will also reap any "good" that may be ours at this time. Therefore, if we wish to survive this impending cleansing now "waiting in the wings", we need to do what this Work has constantly enjoined thus far and will constantly stress throughout. We need to become voluntarily accepting of, and conversant with, The Spiritual Laws. By changing our attitude and volition to one of conscious recognition and acceptance instead of perversely maintaining one of cynical, disbelieving rejection we would reap, instead, the benefits that ensue from working with and alongside the "Elemental Forces of Nature" under the inviolable outworking of those Perfect Laws!

This knowledge being so vital to our very existence, we once more restate them. They are:

1. **The Law of Movement**

2. **The Law of Reciprocal Action (Sowing and Reaping)**

3. **The Law of Attraction of Similar Species**

4. **The Law of Spiritual Gravity**

5. **The Law of Balance**

6. **The Law of Rebirth**

7. **(The "Divine Gift" of Grace)**

The first step is to re-establish connections to the "Elemental Beings" by first recognising that they are a very real and necessary part of life in the material worlds. By this change we fulfil our ordained purpose in consciously working with them. With their guidance and help we *could* have created a paradise on Earth, and thereby have been true "stewards of the Earth" as was once commanded for humankind. Now, however, under the *serious need of their protection*, we *may perhaps* survive the "cleansing" of our poisoned home when that ordained time shortly arrives. The sure guarantee of not accepting this "life belt of hope" is that of destruction in any case, exactly in accordance with our collective, aspiritual *volition*.

Such a "doomsday scenario" will invariably produce different responses from within the various sections of any society of course, and there have been *imminent* doomsday predictions for centuries. Yet whilst there are many believers in an approaching "end-time" today, there will surely be disbelievers too, both from within and without the various religious groups. Intellectual science, also, by virtue of its basically *aspiritual* nature, will be generally unreceptive to such ideas. Nevertheless, the outcomes alluded to will conform to "scientific laws" because they, in turn, can only derive from the higher Spiritual Laws, as we continually reiterate. What we have not previously had before are the necessary *Spiritual explanations* whereby *greater* sense can be made of the increasingly severe weather patterns and geological activity globally.

The views of disbelievers are ultimately **completely irrelevant** anyway. Irrespective of what they may espouse, and from whatever Discipline or source they may derive their beliefs, what is outlined and explained here *are* the connective-processes that will bring those events which humankind must soon experience, for they are set in motion by the very Laws of Life. In a truly wonderful paradox, it is the *same* "mechanism of Law" that gave rise and life to all disbelievers and to all science in the first instance.

Therefore, all we need do is *quietly watch and wait* as the verification of what has been stated, and why, becomes the living reality for all. Since we contend that that is the inescapable reality, let us continue on with our analysis of "Elemental Lore" and offer other insights into this "brave new world" for those who may yet still awaken spiritually. We will, however, still offer respect for all other beliefs, in accordance with humankind's ordained free-will right to choose individual paths.

Western societies – and perhaps more particularly America with its greater technological bent and promotion of the corporate, capitalist ethos – will generally have scant regard for "Elemental" beliefs. It is interesting to note, however, that Japan, that dynamo of corporate wealth and global trend-setting, actually retains extremely strong links to "Elemental beliefs" behind the corporate facade the country presents to the rest of the world. Not only are there many shrines and temples to "Elemental Beings" in the strong Animistic religion of Shintoism, the language itself actually incorporates the sounds and sound effects of "Elemental" activity. Yet, in a perversely-selfish paradox, this same culture has no qualms about stripping much of the world of all that it materially needs to feed its own personal wants in apparent direct contravention of a strong religion that ostensibly venerates all that the natural world offers.

The Fairy Tales from old Europe that many fondly remember from childhood directly trace their origins to Elemental activity. The early Teutons and other similar European groups un-equivocally accepted "Nature Beings" as factual reality. And in many rural areas of Europe today, such acceptance is still strong.

Paradoxically, had we retained an unbroken connection to the Animistic Realm, the world could have been much more than classical Greece once was. For such clear insight would have guaranteed greater help and advancement from precisely those Elemental Beings placed in Creation to assist us in what would have been our natural, step-by-step, *spiritual* development. The proliferation of chemical poisons and the development of some of the world's current energy systems which offer only nightmarish end-scenarios, would not have arisen. In their place would have been **given** natural, sustainable energy and natural sowing and harvesting methods.

Instead, much of what we have produced on the planet without that vitally necessary connection are areas of poisoned, denuded and degraded "chemical deserts". The mega or super-cities of even the so-called "first world" harbour areas that are little more than ugly, decaying hell-holes holding the wreckage of thousands of diseased, drug-ridden or malnourished humans housed in filthy slum areas – or not housed at all. The third world's starving equivalent are camped out in refugee hovels, often in unproductive desert lands. Because of the bounty of the Earth overall, we should *never* have reached this point.

Yet that point has finally been reached for millions simply because we severed the connection to our greatest help in the foolish belief that man could do it better. In the most "bitter-of-pills" scenario, it will probably only be the *continuing reality* of such nightmarish situations that **may perhaps** finally induce **some** of humankind to awaken to the only true knowledge with which to alleviate the suffering of hundreds of millions of our fellow travellers.

However, it is imperative to seriously understand that *that* "true knowledge" is all about the singular source of the "Life-power" which maintains and sustains literally everything in Creation. It is completely "**neutral**", neither good nor bad. Therefore, there are *not* two

Powers operating in Creation as so many believe. Precisely because of our Spiritual Origins and inherent *free-will* attribute, we humans act like refracting lenses and are thus able to *direct* this "power" to whatever purpose we *choose*. Moreover, we cannot stand divorced from or even **stop** the process as it is completely automatic. Therein lies the "accountability" that we must accept for the stewardship of planet Earth – our material home. The consequences derived from this free-will "refractive-mechanism", whereby the "Elemental Forces" return to us the reciprocal effects of all our deeds, must logically correspond precisely to the kind of stewardship *chosen*.

So if we compare the reality of man's history against the command to live according to The Spiritual Laws, it is not difficult to understand that an incredible amount of reciprocal effect is heaping against us like a huge tsunami about to break. We are in the vanguard of it at this present time as we observe how more and more strange and virulent diseases appear and mutate, the increasingly changeable and unpredictable weather patterns, the natural catastrophes of greater and greater frequency and intensity, and the insurmountable problems of all kinds.

However, all that "angst" is still nothing more than just the "beginnings" of the "complete reaping" yet to occur – as the Great Prophet, **Isaiah**, foresaw and prophesied millennia ago.

4.4   Native American Spirituality: A European View

Let us digress from our present thread for a moment and, in a brief outline, examine the attitude of the North American Indians to their environment, particularly the beliefs of those of the Great Plains and the forest-fringe dwellers.

Jostein Gaarder, author of Sophie's World, notes that in this present time of great concern for our poisoned "home", a new thought of "ecophilosophy" has emerged. Arne Naess, a Norwegian philosopher and one of the founders of this "idea", coined the word, "ecosophy". He and others – mainly in the West – believe that "...western civilisation as a whole is on a fundamentally wrong track, racing toward a head-on collision with the limits of what our planet can take". Moreover, the idea that man is "...master of nature ... could prove to be fatal for the whole living planet".

Prophetic words indeed! Many years after they were stated, the reality is plain for all global citizens to see and be concerned about.

Consequently, these particular philosophers "...have looked to the thinking and ideas of other cultures ... and have also studied the thoughts and customs of so-called primitive peoples – or 'native peoples' such as the **Native Americans** – *in order to discover what we have lost*".

(*Sophie's World*, p 384-5. Emphases mine.)

The ancient life of the Native Americans of the Northern United States revolved very much around the sharply delineated seasonal changes that characterise the Continental United States. The mountain range of the Rockies running in a north/south direction rather than across the land means that sudden unseasonable Arctic blasts can occur unpredictably, reaching as far south as Florida at times. By striving to understand their "feeling" for the environment, we may deduce whether or not there existed genuine knowledge of the Elemental Forces of Nature and not simply a fear-ridden, superstitious attitude of resigned acceptance to the natural forces surrounding them. Either in the movement of life-sustaining animals, or in the vagaries of the weather.

The Plains Indian, utilising mainly the bison to provide virtually all of his shelter and clothing needs, was *acutely attuned* to the minutest changes in the natural environment surrounding him, and therefore to the weather too. Whereas certain Indigenous peoples fearfully saw dark and dangerous entities at every turn – forms that had to be *appeased* or countered in some way –

the Plains Indian, in stark contrast, generally saw only *the greatness of the "Elemental forces" serving, nurturing, and protecting his world.*

In his veneration of those "forces", he not only gave thanks for all he was given, but sought to emulate their goodness in the way he related to those animals and birds whose lives he necessarily took for food, clothing and shelter. The ethos of the Native American Indians before the arrival of the European inherently encompassed that elevated outlook, where gratitude to the "Great Spirit" was invariably the first consideration. It was not fear of their environment but rather respect for life and veneration of its "Giver"! That recognition is well exemplified in one short sentence taken from a lengthy address by: "One of the most important figures among Native American leaders of the eighteenth century..." That "most important figure" was a Seneca leader popularly known as "Red Jacket" because of a British Officer's jacket he wore. His actual name was Sogoyewapha.

From "Red Jacket's commentary on the spiritual beliefs of the Native Americans (1805)", we read:

"For all these favours we thank the Great Spirit, and Him only."

(North American Indian Chiefs, p.18
Karl Nagelfell. Emphasis mine.)

One can note powerful, intuitive insights here that closely approximate the essence of The First Commandment. In the case of the Native Americans, however, it is clearly a voluntary reverence stemming from a quite natural recognition of the beneficence of the natural world which, in turn, draws its offerings from the Great Spirit – their term for The Creator! Contrast that stance with the fear element promoted by some churches toward the same Commandment from the time of the Dark Ages even to the present.

Red Jacket addressed the European colonists attitude to land and religion too. In the following observations, (p.19, emphasis mine) he sagely notes:

"You have got our country, but are not satisfied... You want to force your religion upon us... We understand that your religion is written in a Book... Brother, you say there is but one way to worship the Great Spirit. If there is but one religion, why do you white people differ so much about it? ... Why not all agreed, as you can all read the Book? ... We are told that your religion was given to your forefathers... We also have a religion which was given to our forefathers and has been handed down to us... It teaches us to be thankful for all the favors we receive, to love each other, and to be united. *We never quarrel about religion.*"

In this exceptionally noble outlook lived the strongest connections to the Elemental Forces, and equally powerful veneration of "The Giver of Life". Even though sometimes needing to take the lives of his own at times, it was not generally in complete disregard for that life; again in stark contrast to that which other peoples savagely displayed. Whilst the Indian "brave" was most certainly a fearless warrior, it is unlikely that this aspect of him ever degenerated to the more and regular blood-thirsty practices of some races. Generally it remained as noble as it was possible to be in the circumstances of his existence, in both the pre and post-European phases of his life.

For even under extreme provocation and duress at the encroachment of European settlement, and the more brutal behaviour of the "Frontier Army" at times, the demeanour of this people generally remained far more noble than should have been expected of any race. Their veneration for the natural world that was inherently carried within, instilled in them the strength they closely identified with in the power of the 'elements', and in the power and natural nobleness of the bison and the eagle.[6]

Thus, what we have lost is exactly that for which we offer explanations here, and is exactly that which the Plains Indians once had to an ennobled degree. Even though these latter-day philosophers are endeavouring to find that lost knowledge, which they obviously believe exists, will they be able to accept the notion of **non-material** "Elemental Beings"? And despite being "invisible" to virtually all of humankind, they are nevertheless capable of exerting huge, weather-induced, physical effects on the environment. They are effects that, in a clearly **material** way, have the power to devastate man and his works.

With regard to the Plains Indians' culture and our assertion that it was most likely the vast openness of the land that produced such an ennobled outlook in the inhabitants, Colin F. Taylor, in his book: "Native American Myths and Legends", notes the powerful effect the Great Plains exerted. The following notation strongly reinforces our premise about it.

> "There seems to be something within the unique environment of the Great Plains which causes a people to live with such vivid intensity and an awareness and understanding of the things around them. The Plains Indian was so much in daily association with his environment and so dependent upon it, that not only animals but plant life and even some inanimate objects were believed to have a spiritual existence. There was an awareness of a great power – the energy or moving force of the great universe – which, in the sacred language of the Lakota shamans, was called Skan or To and the blue of the sky symbolised its presence."

From the same publication, a senior Cavalry Officer whose Military Service encompassed this part of America, had this to say about the initial effect the Plains could have on people.

> "The first experience of the Plains, like the first sail with a cap full of wind, is apt to be sickening. This once overcome, the nerves stiffen, the senses expand and man begins to realize the magnificence of being."

> (Col. Richard Dodge, 1877. p.41 both.)

If a European could experience and realize "the magnificence of being" without possessing an inherent veneration for the environment of the Great Plains, consider how deep that respect had become for its inhabitants – a respect nurtured for obviously far longer than Europeans. A more striking example of the deep, innate understanding that the "Red Man" had for his environment, however, is now preserved for posterity in what is probably *inadequately described* as; "...the most beautiful and profound statement on the environment ever made".

Like "White Cloud's statement" of great wisdom at the beginning of this Chapter, there does not appear to be anything else in existence to even remotely approach the pure nobleness of the address given by the Great Chief Seattle, Chief of the Duwamish, upon "surrendering" his land to Governor Isaac Stevens in 1854. After the "Great White Chief" in Washington made an "offer" for a large area of Indian Land and promised a "reservation" for the Indian people, Chief Seattle "offered" *his* wisdom! Surely, the most noble address on the environment ever, and from which we will offer a few quotes. Such a wonderfully powerful document should grace every home!

---

[6]In our view, if one even cursorily examines the attitudes of most races to the "natural world", it is patently clear that this lost knowledge-connection sought by Arne Naess, could only be found – in its deepest reverential and natural expression – in some of the Native American peoples. Perhaps more particularly before the arrival of, and corruption by, the "new Americans". Their way of being and interaction with their environment, even around that genocidal time-period, provide that particular essence of reverence and veneration for the natural world that the philosophic-seeking would more readily understand.

4.4.1   Excerpts from Chief Seattle's Address

"The Great Chief Washington sends word that he wishes to buy our land.

For we know that if we do not sell, the White Man may come with guns and take our land. The idea is strange to us. If we do not own the freshness of the air and the sparkle of the water, how can we buy them?

We know that the White Man does not understand our ways. One portion of land is the same to him as the next, for he is a stranger who comes in the night and takes from the land what he needs.

The earth is not his brother, but his enemy and when he has conquered it, he moves on.

His appetite will devour the earth and leave behind only a desert. The sight of your cities pains the eyes of the Red Man.

There is no quiet place in the White Man's cities. No place to hear the unfurling of leaves in spring or the rustle of an insect's wings. The clatter only seems to insult the ears.

The air is precious to the Red Man for all things share the same breath – the beast, the tree, the man, they all share the same breath.

The White Man does not seem to notice the air he breathes. Like a dying man for many days he is numb to the stench.

I have seen a thousand rotting buffaloes on the prairie, left by the White Man who shot them from a passing train.

I am savage and do not understand how the smoking iron horse can be more important than the buffalo that we kill only to stay alive. For whatever happens to the beasts soon happens to man. ***All things are connected.*** [**Crucial Imperative No 9**: *That all is interconnected; that nothing stands in isolation!*]

Whatever befalls the earth, befalls the sons of the earth. If men spit upon the ground they spit upon themselves. This we know, the earth does not belong to man, man belongs to earth. Man did not weave the web of life he is merely a strand in it. Whatever he does to the web, he does to himself.

Our warriors have felt shame and after defeat they turn their days in idleness and contaminate their bodies with sweet food and strong drink. It matters little where we spend the rest of our days. There are not many.

But why should I mourn the passing of my people? Tribes are made of men, nothing more. Men come and go like the waves of the sea. Even the White Man, whose God walks and talks with him as friend to friend, cannot be exempt from common destiny.

One thing we know, which the White Man may one day discover – our God is the same God. You may think now that you own Him as you wish to own our land, but you cannot. The earth is precious to Him and to harm the earth is to heap contempt on it's Creator.

The whites too shall pass; perhaps sooner than all other tribes. Continue to contaminate your bed and one night you will suffocate in your own waste.

But in your perishing you will shine brightly, fired by the strength of the God who brought you to this land for some special purpose... That destiny is a mystery to us for we do not understand when the Buffalo are all slaughtered, the wild horses tamed, the secret corners of the forest heavy with the scent of many men and the view of the ripe hills blotted by talking wires. Where is the thicket? Gone. The end of living and the beginning of survival.

So if we sell you our land, love it as we have loved it, care for it as we have cared for it... And with all your strength, with all your mind, with all your heart, preserve it for your children and **love it** – as God loves us all.

One thing we know. Our God is the same God. The earth is precious to Him. Even the white man cannot be exempt from the common destiny. We may be brothers after all."

(Chief Seattle, 1854. With kind permission of
"Friends of the Earth." Emphasis mine.)

We have woven a particular thread from out of Chief Seattle's complete and extremely powerful, painful address. Contained within his statement is much of the living essence of The Spiritual Laws of Creation which we can easily recognise. If used as a guide, the exquisitely noble words of great wisdom by an equally great and noble Native American Chief can help all peoples to understand the difference between that which they may *believe* to be spiritual, and that which the substance of Chief Seattle's wisdom points to in its actual *reality*.

It is thus vitally important to accurately discern *between* psychic, elemental, and genuine *spiritual* activity. Only man's wrong volition is responsible for the production of aspiritual *psychic forms* and *their* associated activity. It is **never** produced by *Elemental* or truly *Spiritual* forces, for both serve only The Creative Will! By this measure, we may understand *how* to differentiate between genuine *Elemental messages* of warning that might be given for our safety, and unreliable *personal feelings*, perhaps generated by the emotions or by fear. Most importantly, though, we need to learn to recognise clear **'Spiritual Guidance'**. For such guidance will *always* be beneficial. That will be the measure of its validity.

The history of man certainly does record numerous incidents where warnings received from strictly Elemental activity, or "signs", resulted in the prevention of accident or death in some way. That is not to say, of course, that every single natural event involving all the elements of nature, and every animal, insect and bird that we see, or that might otherwise catch our attention, means that something is "absolutely going to happen". To believe that is to nurture foolish superstition and generate uncertainty and perhaps fear at every turn. More often than not such things will be the normal and natural activity of all the other natural life-forms around us.

Warnings, nevertheless, *are* sometimes given for our protection and, if recognised as such, should be acted on immediately. Discernment is the key in knowing what to listen for and what to ignore. It naturally follows, therefore, that superstition cannot provide that appropriate level of discernment. The only sure way to *absolutely know* is to be thoroughly conversant with the workings of "Elemental Lore", for it is the "Elemental Forces" that will sound any such warning. Our continued existence is interlinked with their ordained activity. To achieve *that* level of discernment, however, the requisite understanding of the higher Spiritual Laws is the "First Imperative" here. It is unfortunate that we have become so obtuse that the warnings *constantly* being given to us now are rarely heard. To our serious detriment, we have virtually lost the ability to correctly perceive **"protective discernment"**!

4.5   The Elemental Connection to the Animal Kingdom

To illustrate how we can learn and benefit from animals, some examples of their natural ability to sense impending changes in the activity of the Earth offer a serious guide. Because earthquake lore invariably records the fact that many animals become agitated before any major earth-movement, in the context of this particular Chapter it is therefore necessary to also examine this phenomenon. Earthquakes can trigger other crustal changes or movements such as in volcanic activity, and can also set in motion hugely destructive tsunami. Since many of the world's great cities are clustered around natural harbours for purposes of Maritime trade, and the frequency of larger earthquakes is increasing, perhaps more attention should be paid to the activity of animals in these areas, particularly.

For many years the scientific-intellectual mind-set of seismologists tended to dismiss stories of precursory animal behaviour as scientifically useless or as something akin to greatly exaggerated folk-tales. However, quite recent large quakes in China produced thousands of reports of strange animal behaviour so compelling that earthquake scientists from other countries are now reconsidering such phenomena. We restate our previous contention that this has *always* been the natural pattern because earth movements *are* an *Elemental activity*, to which all animals are closely attuned. "Elemental Lore" therefore takes no account whatsoever of what earth-sciences may so decree. It is therefore extremely heartening to note that on 19 July 2002, Discovery Channel screened a programme from its "Natural Mystery" series precisely about the precursory behaviour of animals, birds and fishes. On that programme, Jim Weir, a retired American geologist, stated:

"Mother Nature is far more reliable [than science]."

Modern seismic instruments are capable of detecting even the most minute changes in the Earth's electrical and magnetic fields, even patterns of sub-audible sound. Yet whilst these changes may be subsequently shown to *precede* seismic activity, they do not always. However, in the long history of recorded phenomena of this nature, animals, birds and fishes, far more sensitive to such tiny stimuli, react immediately in the sureness of *knowing* that an earth movement is imminent. Therefore, we can surely state that we have a "constant" in this behaviour pattern, even if a non-scientific one. Clearly, however, far more reliable than much of our "modern" detection equipment.

So what might we deduce from this? Marine scientists marvel at the sonar abilities that mammals of the order Cetacea (whales and dolphins etc.,) possess, but are unable to definitively explain it apart from using scientific terms that perhaps closely approximate their theories. Similarly, animal reactions of the kind we outline cannot simply be slotted into a solely scientific pigeon-hole either. Whilst the *physical* event can certainly be recorded as electrical activity or something similar, nevertheless, it is an *elemental happening in the first instance* – and one driven by *spiritual* power. This is the mysterious factor that science cannot measure with its instruments, and to which the animal world, itself strongly connected to the Elemental world to the strongest possible degree, reacts.

A few examples recorded in "The Handbook of Unusual Natural Phenomena" (Eyewitness Accounts of Nature's Greatest Mysteries) by William R Corliss, Arlington House Crown Publishers, New York, may offer clearer illustration.

In the sub-Chapter, "The Curious Supersensitivity of Animals to Impending Quakes", Corliss records how the consternation of dogs, horses, cattle and other domestic animals are referred to in the records of most great earthquakes. Fish are also frequently affected. In the London earthquake of 1749 roach and other fish in a canal showed evident signs of confusion and fright. During the Tokyo earthquake of 1880 cats inside a house ran about trying to escape, foxes barked, and horses tried to kick down the boards confining them to their stables.

Whilst we may not be overly surprised with such frightened behaviour of animals *during* a tremor, it is an entirely different matter when animals clearly sense something *about* to happen when contraindications appear to suggest otherwise. As if aware of an earthquake's imminent arrival, Corliss recorded that:

> "...ponies have been known to prance about their stalls, pheasants to scream, and frogs to cease croaking a little time before a shock..."

(p.291)

Interestingly, geese, pigs and dogs appear more sensitive in this respect than other animals. Calabrian folklore, after the great earthquake there, recorded that the neighing of a horse, the braying of a donkey, or the cackle of a goose was sufficient to cause the inhabitants to run from their houses "...in expectation of a shock". (p 291)

At the time of this quake, sand-eels, which usually bury themselves in sand, came to the surface. Many birds are believed to show their uneasiness before an earthquake by hiding their heads under their wings and behaving in an unusual manner. Some South American peoples believe that certain quadrupeds such as dogs, cats and jerboa rats give warning of coming danger by their restlessness. And sometimes immense numbers of seabirds head inland before an earthquake, as if alarmed by the commencement of some sub-oceanic disturbance.

In Chile, before the shock of 1835, all the dogs are said to have escaped from the city of Talcahuano. One scientific explanation for such behaviour has been advanced by Professor Milne who believes that some animals are sensitive to the small tremors that precede almost all earthquakes. He suggests, moreover, that animal intelligence, as the result of their own experiences which will have taught them that small earth tremors may be precursors to a large shake, would then register alarm at any future indications of major earth movements.

Interestingly, Corliss states that signs of alarm days before an earthquake are probably accidental. This statement is clearly contradictory for, quite obviously, any signs of alarm even days before an earthquake *actually occurring* must logically be cognitive prescience on the part of the animals concerned, purely by virtue of the *arrival* of the quake, so can hardly be deemed accidental.

But what do other publications report about this interesting phenomena. Corliss records the "American Review of Reviews" as itemising the following:

> "In connection with the fearful catastrophes of recent date in Italy, California, and elsewhere, which, like so many others of like nature will long retain a hold on human memory, attention has **again** been called to the fact that many animals give intimations of such great disturbances in advance by certain particular and often unusual conduct. It is particularly such animals as have their abode underground that often indicate, days before the event, that something unusual in nature is about to occur, by coming out of their hiding places underground into the open.
>
> Aelian mentions that, in the year 373 before Christ, five days before the destruction of Helike, all the mice, weasels, snakes and other like creatures, were observed going in great masses along the roads leading from that place. Something similar was noticed also, later, though not to so marked an extent as in the case mentioned by Aelian. This leaving of their subterranean abodes by underground creatures on such occasions might possibly be explained by the emission of various malodorous and noxious gases during these disturbances of the earth."

(Emphasis mine.)

However, not only do animals living underground furnish indications that something out of the ordinary is about to happen, larger animals do so as well. Cows, horses, asses, sheep, and many birds, even, seem to get premonitions of particular natural phenomena and events. Corliss records that in 1805, during an earthquake:

> "...the cattle at Naples and its neighbourhood set up a continuous bellowing some time *before* the event, at the same time trying to support themselves more firmly by planting the forefeet widely apart; the sheep kept up a continuous bleating, and hens and other fowl expressed their restlessness by making a terrible racket. Even the dogs gave many indications of uneasiness at the time. The actions of animals

observed during the great earthquake of 1783 seem to have been most remarkable. Thus the howling of the dogs at Messina became so unendurable that men were sent out with cudgels to kill them".

Corliss further notes that their noise was most marked during the progress of the earthquake, while it was difficult to pacify the animals in the vicinity for some time, even after the cessation of the shocks. Dogs and horses ran about meanwhile with hanging heads, or stood with outstretched legs "...as if aware of the need of planting themselves firmly". Horses that were ridden at the time stopped and stood still without orders "...trembling so at the same time that no rider could remain in the saddle".

Corliss catalogues Scophus as telling the story of a cat during an earthquake at Locris "...which set up a most dismal caterwauling at the approach of each new shock, meanwhile constantly jumping from one point to another. The roosters kept up a continual crowing, both before and during the earthquake". In the fields Scophus also observed hares so in fear of "...the terrestrial disturbance that they made no attempt to escape and seemed in no way disturbed by his presence. ...sheep could not be kept on the right road, notwithstanding the efforts of shepherd and dogs...", but scattered "...in affrightened haste to the mountains".

Birds, also, seem to have premonitions of the coming of such catastrophes. During the earthquake of Quintero, in Chile, in November 1822 "...the gulls uttered all sorts of unusual cries during the whole of the preceding night and were in constant restless motion during the quake". And on February 20, 1835, the day before the earthquake at Concepcion, also in Chile, at ten in the morning great numbers of seabirds, mostly gulls, "...were seen to pass over the city landward, a phenomenon not to be explained by any stormy condition of the weather. It was fully an hour and a half after their passage, at 11:40 of the forenoon, before the earthquake came, one so disastrous that nearly the entire city was reduced to ruins". Even the fish in the sea seem to be disturbed at the approach of an earthquake. Alexander von Humboldt, the famous traveller and naturalist, tells of having observed "...the crocodiles of the Orinoco leaving the water..." and escaping to the forest during an earthquake.

During the 1930's some scientists wondered whether the growing mountain of anecdotal evidence on pre-quake animal behaviour might be sufficient to help predict impending earthquakes. Corliss cites the publication, Nature, as reporting that the Japanese undertook the first experiments – perhaps not surprising given the huge amount of tremors Japan experiences.

Corliss notes that "...two Japanese seismologists, Dr. Shinkishi Hatai and Dr. Noboru Abe, observed that catfish (Siluroidea) in natural conditions showed signs of restlessness about six hours before earthquake disturbances were registered on their recording apparatus". Since catfish are ordinarily placid, unresponsive creatures, experiments were made to test that seeming precursive responsiveness. Catfish placed in an aquarium were tested three times a day by tapping on the supporting table. When no earthquake was impending "...the fish moved lazily or not at all". But about six hours before a shock "...the fish jumped when the table was tapped and sometimes swam about agitatedly for a time before settling down upon the bottom again". Several months of testing showed that in a period when 178 earthquakes of all degrees of severity had been recorded "...the fish had correctly predicted 80 per cent of the shocks". They showed no discrimination in their movements between slight local shocks and more serious distant shocks. The experimenters think that the catfish "...are made sensitive through electrical changes in the earth, since it was only when the aquarium was electrically earthed, through the drainpipe, that they responded to a coming earthquake". (*Nature*, 132: 817, 1933.)[7]

The Chinese have always believed that the Earth provided all the messages required to predict earthquakes. Sometimes the messages are so clear that precise predictions can be made.

---

[7]In terms of "Elemental Lore", it is quite logical that catfish would respond when conditions of what would be their more natural environment were re-created, whereas any form of shielding *might not necessarily* provide that same response.

Such was the case in the Haicheng earthquake of 1975 where dozens of abnormalities pointed to an impending quake. Apart from solely animal behaviour, sudden changes and unusual variations in groundwater levels were also catalogued. Two days before the quake struck, 90,000 residents were evacuated. At 1030hrs on the precise day predicted, the final warning was given and the rest of the city emptied. Nine hours later the quake struck. Measuring 7.3 on the Richter scale, it destroyed or damaged ninety per cent of the city's buildings but few deaths resulted from it. (Source: Encarta, BBC and "Our World" programme – "The Savage Earth")

The world's greatest recorded natural disaster occurred in China in 1556 in Shensi province where a single earthquake killed 800,000 people. Such devastating earth movements have prompted Chinese officials to collate testimony concerning premonitory signs from the rural populace, particularly farmers. China currently possesses the world's largest computer network for collating earthquake data. With hundreds of millions of people tied closely to the Earth, and who are perhaps more attuned to subtle changes in their environment than people resident in cities, the authorities have achieved some success in earthquake prediction.

Unlike Haicheng, however, the "messages" from the Tangshan quake, whilst very numerous, were not as clear. After the Tangshan earthquake the following report was filed by Shen Linghuang, a Chinese writer:

> "A stock-breeder in Northern China got up to feed his animals before dawn on July 28, 1976. He is a member of the Kaokechuang People's Commune which lies only 40 kilometres away from the city of Tangshan. When he went into the stable, he found that instead of eating, his two horses and two mules were jumping and kicking until they finally broke loose and dashed outside. At that moment, a dazzling white flash illuminated the sky and huge rumbling noises were heard. The Tangshan earthquake (magnitude 7.8) had struck.
>
> This occurrence was reported to Chinese scientists during a survey of the earthquake-affected areas around Tangshan. Their mission was to find out about the feasibility of an earthquake prediction programme that made use of observations of animal behaviour. This survey, covering Tangshan and 400 communes in 48 counties around it, was conducted by Chinese biophysicists, biologists, geophysicists, chemists, and meteorologists shortly after the earthquake.
>
> Through interviews and discussions with local people, the scientists collected information on 2,093 cases of unusual animal behaviour in the time shortly before the earthquake. Nearly all of the anecdotes were passed on to the scientists by survivors of the earthquake themselves; the majority of the reports involved domestic animals. Some examples included goats that refused to go into pens, cats and dogs that picked up their offspring and carried them outdoors, pigs that squealed strangely, startled chickens that dashed out of coops in the middle of the night, rats that left their nests, and fish that dashed about aimlessly."

(*Earthquake Information Bulletin*, 10: 231-33, 1978, Corliss, 291-94)

In the case of the Haicheng earthquake, the authorities, armed with similar kinds of information – and completely accepting of its validity – took the precaution of being "wise before the event" and ordered the evacuation of the city before the quake struck. Compare this example with the people of Messina who went out to kill the howling dogs. Humans cannot match the sensitivity of animals to earthquake precursors, so the subtle signs that set dogs to howling invariably pass by humans undetected. This unfortunate state of affairs is solely the result of humankind closing a necessary connection to the same forces and signs that animals immediately react to, and which is a potential lifesaver. For we also possess a similar ability. All we need do is recognise those 'Forces' and then utilise that ability to heed any warnings received; for our protection too.

The observation of animal behaviour predating the occurrence of earthquakes goes back centuries. Even as far back as 100 AD, Pliny, the Roman writer, advocated then that such behaviour be used for predicting earthquakes.

Volume II of "Earthquakes and the Urban Environment", G. Lennis Berlin, CRC Press, records interesting observations of animal behaviour.

> "Zoo animals refuse to go into their shelters at night; snakes, lizards, and small mammals evacuate their underground burrows; hyperactive insects congregate in huge swarms near seashores; cattle seek high ground; wild fowl leave their usual habitats; domestic animals become agitated."

The earliest published accounts of unusual animal behaviour in the United States were for the 1906 San Francisco earthquake where a Miss Finette Locke kept detailed notes of this phenomenon from cases reported to her. In a summary of her notes published in the 1908 report of the State Earthquake Investigation Commission, several of her observations were:

> "Horses whinnied before the shock... Several instances were reported where cows stampeded before the shock was felt by the observer. In other cases cows about to be milked are said to have been restless before the shock... Lowing of cattle at the time of the shock was very commonly reported, and in some cases this is said to have occurred a little before the shock. The most common report regarding the behaviour of dogs was their howling during the night preceding the earthquake."

The lowing of cattle at the *time* of the shock should surely be a natural expectation. So it appears surprising that such behaviour be considered unusual, in contrast to that *preceding* a tremor. Vol. II of "Earthquakes and the Urban Environment" offers an interesting insight into the changes in attitude that are obviously occurring within some of the scientific Disciplines. The following quote echoes this new awareness.

> "Until quite recently, accounts like these were usually met with skepticism (scepticism). However, this view is changing, largely due to the apparent successes the Chinese have had in using erratic animal behaviour as an earthquake precursor ... farmers are instructed to watch for unusual activity in their animals, and observers are even stationed in the Peking Zoo to watch for any unusual animal activity. Erratic behaviour is reported to a local seismological brigade."

A booklet issued by the Seismological Office of Tientsin offers observers hints on how to use unusual animal behaviour for predicting earthquakes. A translated summary states:

> "It is easy and simple to use animals to predict earthquakes. Certain organs of animals may acutely detect various underground changes before earthquakes. Both historical and recent surveys of large earthquakes prove that animals have precursory reactions."

And an earthquake prediction verse from the same translated publication notes that:

> "Animals are aware of precursors before earthquakes: Let us summarise their anomalous behaviour for prediction. Cattle, sheep, mules and horses do not enter corrals. Rats move their homes and flee. Hibernating snakes leave their burrows early. Frightened pigeons continuously fly and do not return to nests. Rabbits raise their ears, jump aimlessly and bump things. Fish are frightened, jump above water surface."

Upon being rescued from her damaged apartment building after the Taiwan earthquake of 1999, a Mrs Chu reported that the fish in her tanks became agitated the night before. She noted that they kept swimming into the sides of their tanks so forcefully as to cause bleeding. (Discovery Channel documentary.) And in the more recent devastating earthquake and tsunami aftermath affecting the countries bordering the Indian Ocean, CNN reported many deaths in the destruction of a Tourist Hotel located in a National Park. Officials feared the worst for the wild animals resident in the protected area – which was why the Hotel was built there. Expecting to discover large numbers of dead animals, they found, to their amazement, that they had left the area and moved further inland, above the farthest reach of the waves that *subsequently* washed inland. Using senses that we have no comprehension of, they simply moved out of harm's way – before the event.

The high geological activity of the San Andreas fault in California offers ideal monitoring conditions for American geologists. This very visible fault is generated by the Pacific Plate moving past the North American Plate. However, even though both plates are moving in the same northwestwards direction, the Pacific is moving faster than the North American. That "speed differential" effectively means that the "relative movement" of the two Plates is in opposite directions.[8]

Increasing "Western" scientific interest in the possibility of utilising animal behaviour for earthquake predictions is illustrated by a perhaps belated admittance from U.S. scientists at a 2 day conference sponsored by the USGS (US Geological Survey) in October 1976 in noting that: "...there may be some truth in the belief that animals can sense some environmental change that precedes an earthquake".

The Conference heard that:

> "...the activity of captive pocket mice and kangaroo rats is being monitored at sites near the Palmdale bulge, and the motor activity of cockroaches is being monitored at sites near Hollister, Twin Lakes, and Anza – sites close to active faults. Preliminary results from the second study indicate that before the occurrence of small earthquakes, there is a marked increase in their motor activity".

(Conference Notes, p.38-39)

4.6   The Elemental Connection to the Human World

Having examined a few examples of connected elemental and animal activity for our purposes, and apart from the previous reference to Jesus and the storm on the Sea of Galilee and the help given to Moses, are we able to cull a little more from The Bible to illustrate our assertions that other "ordained beings" such as "nature elementals" are a reality. One of the Psalms of David offers a curiously worded Scripture. But perhaps not so curious when the knowledge of Elemental Beings is taken into account.

> "Thou Who maketh Thine angels into winds and Thy servants into 'Flames of Fire'."

(Psalms of David. Capitals mine.)

---

[8]It is generally accepted that the San Andreas fault will one day produce one of the largest earthquakes ever experienced by man.

An interesting passage in The Book of Isaiah also sheds further light on this "reality" in terms of a definitive, relative place within Creation for such "entities" – at least as indicated in The Bible. The prophet, Isaiah, sometimes referred to as the Great Prophet, is generally held in high regard in possessing greater clarity of spiritual perceptive depth than perhaps some of the others.

In concert with **Crucial Imperative No 5:**

> That because the physical Universe is a *material* expanse, it is therefore *not* without end. **It is finite!**

Isaiah 18, Verse 3, states:

> "All ye **inhabitants** *of the world*, **AND** dwellers *on the earth*, see ye, when He lifteth up an ensign on the mountains; and when He bloweth a trumpet, hear ye"

(Emphases mine.)

In that Scripture we can readily note a clear delineation of **two** distinctly separate groups having their sphere of activity in **two** different places **not** closely connected. It seems perfectly clear that the "**inhabitants** *of the world*" are *not* the same "beings" as the "**dwellers** *on the earth*". This clear separation is further accentuated by the wording of "inhabitants *of*" and "dwellers *on*", and in the use of the conjunction, *and*, in the sentence. From our explanations of the various Planes of Creation, we could well conclude that Isaiah might actually have possessed the spiritual insight to *see* some of the other inhabitants of Creation aside from just the "dwellers on the earth". Whether this was so or not does not alter the obvious fact of his seemingly sure statement here.

Throughout history, what humankind term the instinct of animals has provided wonderful tales of near misses and lives saved from disaster when unusual behaviour of domestic pets such as cats and dogs have alerted their owners to imminent danger. Anecdotal evidence also reveals that domesticated animals such as horses have refused to continue along a path for no apparent reason, even with the strongest urging. Then, onto the very area that the animal refused to enter, a slip comes crashing down.

In such cases it is *not* any inherent instinct of the animal that causes it to shy away from certain areas at those precise moments, even if it had taken the same path regularly for many years. It simply heeds a warning given to it that danger is imminent, because it is able to see *where* the warning comes from. Today only a few people possess that similar faculty. This inherent ability in animals can be explained by the fact that their animating core (the inner life-force) originates in the Animistic Sphere. That is also the plane of origin of those Beings that have their field of activity in what we usually call Nature, i.e. air, fire, earth and water, about which, among others, Isaiah the Great Prophet seeks to enlighten us. Therefore the similarity of their origins naturally provides the clear possibility for each to recognise the other.

Despite the fact that our Origin lies in the higher Spiritual Sphere and we are "spiritual beings" in essence, we nevertheless also possess an "animistic body" as well as other "coverings" as explained in Chapter 2. We are therefore perfectly equipped to recognise the Elemental Beings, by virtue of that inherent "animistic attribute". Yet humanity as a whole generally derides such "childish" or fanciful notions. Unlike the animals whose origins stand closer to them, and who thus live consciously in this "Creation-reality", we supposedly more "aware" human beings have allowed the *same* and *necessary* connection to virtually die within us.

However, a clear case of a strong 'human' connection to The Forces of Nature involved a small 'primitive' tribe on the Andaman Islands during the 2004 Indian Ocean tsunami catastrophe.

Living there in virtual isolation, the Onge people hold to very strong beliefs about the 'spirits' of the sea and land that are in constant battle over control of their respective domains. In broad terms, their 'world-view' states that 'bad spirits' are constantly trying to upset the balance of the Earth, whilst 'good spirits' strive to maintain it.

As a people, they constantly 'monitor' the 'struggle' between the two forces. Consequently, they are 'in tune' with what is happening to the land and sea of their homeland. Despite being relatively close to the epicenter of the 'quake' in an open stretch of sea, all survived the tsunami through observing, 'listening', to what those 'forces' were indicating.

Contrast that with the behaviour of first-world European tourists in the seaside resorts of Thailand on that fateful day. Well educated with University degrees and high salaries and equipped with all the digital devices of the West, 'family films' shot that day revealed an amazing lack of appreciation of what was about to happen. Not only by tourists, but by most of the Thai people there. After watching the tide recede a long way very suddenly and quickly – and knowing that it was clearly a very unusual event – most simply watched the receding tide with curiosity/fascination and stayed on the beach.

Perhaps the most telling aspect of how far most human beings are removed from the 'forces' of the natural world now, was when the tsunami-wave was in sight and approaching quickly. Even when the roar of the wave could be clearly heard, that was still not sufficient to galvanise people into action. The commentary by some on the size and speed of the wave while actually filming its fast approach simply boggles the mind. Questioning what was "really going on" and "what is it" minutes before it hit beggars belief.

As we have stated strongly elsewhere in this Work, intellectual man of the 21st century has not only completely *lost* his once strong and beneficial connection to The Forces of Nature, he no longer even *believes* in such beneficial aids. He has become too clever for his own good. Of course, a catastrophe of such magnitude could be expected to produce very many deaths. However, it is clear from the documentary evidence that many lives need *not* have been lost.

In terms of a religious or spiritual view of the event, Father Raj, who lives on the South Indian coast affected by the tsunami, was asked his view of why. He opined that "...we should all understand that God is Justice". "He is also Mercy and Compassion but Justice too". "And we must all realise that when great catastrophes occur". Father Raj stated that [God] "...is not happy with some of the things we are doing." His Justice, therefore, "...had to be experienced". Indian Buddhists accepted the view that Karma was at work over that awful time. [The outworking of **The Law of Reciprocal Action** may be seen in these two views.]

Paradoxically, because it *is* precisely the "Elementals" who are tasked with the preparation and bringing about of those happenings we call natural disasters and catastrophes, we will yet re-learn and fully experience the foolishness of our attitude towards this vital, God-Willed activity. For it is they who know exactly **when and where** sudden changes in Nature are about to take place.

Therefore all events in this category, such as landslides, sudden water eruptions, the bursting of a dam, tidal waves and inundations, volcanic eruptions, rocks dislodged from mountains, trees falling, the caving-in of land undermined by water, and virtually everything connected with *natural events*, are all the ordained activity of the "Nature Beings".

If, then, such an event is imminent, the possibility exists for an animal or person approaching the spot to be warned by these "elementals". Their presence and warnings, even though generally unseen by human beings, may produce feelings of distinct apprehension or unease such as a "cold feeling" or "hair standing on end", and may be sufficient to induce an individual not to want to proceed further. The behaviour of the animal may be markedly different, however. It is invariably startled, its hair bristles, and it may simply *refuse* to go any further.

Without this knowledge, such an experience of distinct unease or apprehension would probably imbue one with fear, particularly if one's cultural frame of reference encompassed the belief of forest or mountain entities, or psychic or phantom forms, or even the fear of earth-bound souls. We may wonder how many such warnings from out of the compassion of The Light have been given to humankind over millennia, and how much of it was treated with fearful apprehension, or totally ignored, or obtusely not perceived at all?

> Given the increasing frequency and intensity of storms world-wide, we should be careful that any such "help" given is not *pushed away* out of *fear* or *derision*. We should, instead, learn to gratefully accept such beneficial aid!

Now, if we recall the earlier explanations in this Chapter regarding the connections between our free-will ability and the return of all our "sowing" via the activity of the "nature beings", we may begin to discern the reasons why man very often finds himself in dangerous situations with the potential for death or serious injury. For this reason we should emulate and refine the Chinese example and pay more attention to animals and thus learn from them.

Therefore, if we coolly and *objectively* observe the increasing "elemental activity" world-wide in natural disasters and catastrophes of greater and greater intensity and frequency, it is very clear that man does, indeed, **stand blind to the true nature of the happening**. These explanations may offer the reader the possible connecting reasons why some intensely hot Eastern Australian or Californian bushfire-storms, which can completely destroy a brick dwelling and melt metal and glass, will sometimes leave a next-door *wooden* dwelling virtually untouched. Ordinarily, such intense heat would generally "explode" the wooden structure even before the fire will have reached it. Scientists puzzled by this phenomenon need only to think *outside* earth sciences' empiricist tunnel-vision and embrace the far wider knowledge explained in this Work to gain a *more correct* overview.

Insights will thereby be gained as to perhaps why, during the Ash Wednesday firestorms around Melbourne in the early 1980's, some of the houses that were left relatively intact, even though directly in the fire-path in some cases, were then reported destroyed or severely damaged by a major deluge a few months later. For under the outworking of The Spiritual Laws, much that we are **forced to experience**, and the **timing** of that experience – even in natural disasters and catastrophes – is **not** necessarily an arbitrary happening.

What we term catastrophes and disasters are often just simply "changes" in the natural world around us. The fact that many may die during such upheavals is due to the obvious reality that wherever such increasingly-more-frequent changes occur, there will invariably be people in the way. Sometimes relatively sparsely populated, at other times in areas where millions reside. That is humankind's blunt reality!

What should again be recognised here is that the "Elementals" are active in every sphere of Creation, and not solely on the Earth. Just as we have small "Nature Beings" whose area of activity is concerned with the smaller plants of the world, and larger ones concerned with seas and mountains etc, so are there also beings of immense size and power whose field of activity reaches out into the forming of galaxies, suns and planets. And all active under the aegis of The Creative Will![9]

A *conscious knowledge* of the *workings* of the "Elemental Forces of Nature" should offer the clear realisation that no race or people can lay claim to "ownership" of land, rivers or the air. We are enjoined to be stewards and nurturers of the land over which we must pass. And further enjoined to leave it in at least a good a state as, or preferably better than, that which we might

---

[9]Perhaps we may now understand that it was the activity of the "Elemental Beings" whose "ordained work" brought into being our own planet Earth and raised the various lands out of the sea. Thus we may view the "Creation-legends" of different Indigenous peoples as "Elemental events" brought about by the larger and more powerful "Nature Beings" of the Earth.

have inherited. Therewith to produce beauty and harmony for the time we are permitted to be on it.

Such powerful statements of truth regarding "ownership of land" should be marked well because, at any moment, the incalculable power of the "Elemental Forces of Nature" can quickly devastate any tract of land, or destroy any works on it. *It is a process, moreover, that occurs somewhere on Earth every hour of the day* – and it is increasing. This fact alone should sound a cautionary warning to develop more humility toward the inherent "Elemental power" within the land, and therefore caution also in foolish demands to "own" or "control" it.

Therefore, in terms of establishing the strongest possible connection to the "Elemental Forces" in our overall relationship with them and their ordained activity, we should learn *never to curse the weather*, regardless of the reasons we may wish to do so. For in doing so we curse the actual *ordained activity* of those "Elemental Beings" of the "Forces of Nature" and, by extension, that Perfection which is The Creative Will! Far too often we use human-emotional terms in describing the weather as being, for example, bad, ugly, lousy, rotten or shocking. Since weather cannot intrinsically be such as that, to hear this more or less constant litany of many expletives, even, unequivocally reveals how far we are from any real understanding of the "true nature" of the "Forces of Nature".

Weather is weather – that's all!

Elemental activity may *produce* very stormy conditions which, in turn, may also *generate* violent winds and destructive waves. Or the same kind of activity may *produce* searing heat or bone-chilling cold which may even result in deaths. Such *productions* are **not arbitrary**, however. That is the "imperative of weather" which humankind need to learn quickly if they are to understand the reasons for the unusual weather patterns which will yet bring far greater destruction than at present! Quite clearly, then, all of humankind is subject to every nuance of weather change and activity, and not solely in terms of food production.

At the Meteorological Society's Weatherwatch conference held in Auckland in November 1996, the CEO of the Insurance Council of New Zealand, Mr David Sargeant, stated then that extreme weather is a growing threat to New Zealand's economy. He also noted that: "...catastrophic weather events, such as damage from the severe winds and flooding brought by hurricanes, represented the greatest threat to the survival of the world's insurance industry".

"And that the rise in natural catastrophes should not be ignored."

(Emphasis mine.)

We are certainly now more aware that such prophetic words from over a decade ago were not alarmist in any way. Moreover, our assertions that "Elemental activity" will yet bring far more destruction through natural disasters more quickly, thus seriously affecting every aspect of all economies, was well illustrated in the graph which accompanied the report on the conference. An analysis of the years from 1960 to 1984 showed that costs to the Insurance industry world-wide from such events remained more or less manageable, varying between a few hundred million U.S. dollars to a high point of about 24 billion, equating to an average annual cost of approximately 5 to 7 billion. Yet the decade from 1985-1995 demonstrated an almost year by year increase depicted by a steeply-rising exponential curve, culminating in a 110 billion dollar cost in 1995.

In the years since that conference took place, the world has reeled in almost disbelief at the scale, frequency and intensity of all manner of catastrophes that have occurred. Now, of course, governments and global businesses are scrambling to try to solve or avert the looming crisis. It is now far too late for remedial action, for the "tipping-point" has well and truly passed. Those who cried "wolf" for so long *are now vindicated*. It is unlikely, however, that the majority of politicians (and some scientists) will have the courage to *publicly admit* that their years of disbelief and/or dithering have *seriously exacerbated the chances of any kind of meaningful reversal.*

Mr Sargeant attributed the increase in weather damage of recent years to a combination of factors that generally all scientific agencies subscribe to. Factors noted were: "Population density, increased living standards, industrialisation in high-risk areas and vulnerability of technologies, along with changing climate conditions." However, whilst these factors are constantly put forward as the reasons for severe weather increases, the same conference was told that even with global warming still on the rise:

"Scientists still could not attribute the observed effects to a specific cause."

(Emphases mine.)

Professor K.U. Sirinanda of the University of Brunei said:

> "People are not attuned to climate change. We need to have environmental education on a democratic scale or whatever you call it ... to convince policy makers of the importance of these issues."

Such clearly correct views are, paradoxically, probably just a pipe dream, and that conference just another in a long line of them which will bring no real change at all – simply because most of all preceding similar ones have not. A very appropriate Biblical quote from Isaiah 8:10 for this present time has resonance for most conferences now.

"Take counsel together, and it will come to nought."

So whilst the "Weatherwatch" conference produced the standard reasons for the increasing concerns about the severity of global weather patterns and noted the end results of these changes, it was unable to "*...attribute the observed effects to a specific cause*". In other words, the conference delegates did not *understand* or *know* the **actual causal reason** for them. As we have explained in this Work, the reason lies in the Spiritual connection *between* our inherent free-will decision-making ability and the *returns* we must experience through *wrongly using* that "spiritual gift" *to continually 'break the rules'.*

As we must reinforce often, the "reaping from our sowing" is returned to us via the ordained activity of the Elemental Forces of Nature acting under The Creative Will. That is the precise reason why such conferences achieve no real change, and will not do so in the future either. That is simply because most of society – *including and especially those in authority or power who could institute the greatest change* – generally regard such ideas as religious or "fringe-garbage".

However, since an exponential factor can be readily observed in all events now, all we need do is sit quietly – and watch and wait. In the meantime, perhaps we should be – for scientific/intellectual empiricism – crassly religious here and **restate** the answer of Jesus to His disciples when asked what the end-time would be like. His reply is chronicled thus:

> "...for there shall then be wide-spread affliction, such as has not been known since the beginning of the world until now, no, nor will ever be known again. And if those times were not cut short, *not a man would be saved*".

(Matthew 24:21-22, Fenton. Emphasis mine.)

That is one "Bible Mystery" now given greater explanation. To this end, we should once more carefully note Chief Seattle's beautiful words of powerful truth and understanding. "If men spit upon the ground they spit upon themselves ... to harm the earth is to heap contempt on its Creator."

In probably the saddest of prophetic and paradoxical ironies, and simply because he *voluntarily allowed the knowledge of the "Elemental Forces" to die within him*, man will surely *curse* the power of the weather *as brought by them*, when it *finally destroys him and all his **wrong** works*. Thus at the very time when he would **need their protection to the greatest possible degree**.

In what will obviously be a stupendously-powerful happening on a truly grand scale will be revealed the inviolable Truth alluded to in Chief Seattle's address. For mankind on Earth, that humanly-wrought destructive phase – which we unequivocally state must and will occur – shall be experienced as **the ultimate justice and outworking of Spiritual Law in the collective reaping of our collective whirlwind**!

As this is the prophesied happening for humankind – thus no longer a "Bible Mystery" – that will visit itself upon us, it behoves every person with even the faintest hint of "intuitive unease" today, to begin the process of setting within him the knowledge that will offer understanding and protection at that time. All peoples, therefore, irrespective of whatever their particular societies or belief systems might deem correct or valid, must first begin with a thorough grounding of "Elemental knowledge" and all its interrelated connections to the activity of man.

However, this clear need may require far more inner-seeking, value-change and discipline from certain races who *currently* demonstrate that they are incapable of *collectively* generating this most necessary requirement at present. This reluctance, or plain outright disbelief, runs the gamut of all peoples within the cultural spectrum globally. From the fearfully superstitious to the sophisticated scientific and technologically superior –

> – most of the world's peoples will aver that they *already* know it all and will thus be *derisively-dismissive* of the kind of vitally essential knowledge *as is explained here*.

In very broad terms, therefore, the basic cultural parameters of Indigenous and Western races overall may well determine where each group stands in relation to any recognition of the Elemental Beings of the Forces of Nature. Indigenous peoples *should generally* be more easily able to develop the greater recognition and a more correct attitude toward "Elementals" than perhaps the Europeans can – **as a complete group**. In reality, of course, there should be no difference whatsoever between the two groups, for The Law states quite unequivocally:

All can see – if they are really willing to see!

Further to that, however, must be the realisation that **it is the individual, alone**, who must ultimately accept full and personal responsibility for all his beliefs and decisions under the outworking of Spiritual Law – even ones concerning Elemental Beings.

Becoming more accepting of the other-world reality of Nature Beings thus offers all of humankind the means whereby – *if he so chooses* – he can establish the correct and necessary foundation for his physical and spiritual protection against the greatly accelerating "Elemental activity" that we already observe in the almost daily news items world-wide. This powerful, unstoppable activity that even scientists are now beginning to refer to as "weather disasters" and "weather havoc", will soon completely engulf our rapidly deteriorating and degraded planet Earth. For we have **not** been true stewards of our earthly home, and it is now time to pay! Recognition of Spiritual Truth *as it actually is* automatically provides the strongest, natural connection to the "Elemental Forces".

Therein lies the Divine promise that: *"The Meek Shall Inherit the Earth!"* But the meek in this case are not the weak, the earthly subservient, or the servile. They are the *humble* who, by their *humility and modesty*, have become *spiritually strong* through genuine and grateful acceptance of **Spiritual Truth**. Thus: **Divine Truth!**

4.6.1 "Avatar": The 'Too-Late Lesson' for Global Humanity

"A picture is worth a thousand words."

"Avatar": The international Blockbuster movie that gave the world a new perspective on 'life' and 'life-forms'. What *worth* can we apportion to that quite amazing visual experience? As of this writing: Is the unprecedented interest in this 'internationally acclaimed' movie simply one of entertainment, 3D style? Or might its popularity *perhaps* stem from a long-buried intuitive knowing in the very psyche of we humans that the connection to the life-force which the **Navi'** have to **Eywa**, their 'Earth Mother', we also once consciously possessed – and lived? Or will this valuable *educational tool* now be looked upon as nothing more than 'the next genre' to come out of Hollywood movie-making?

Just perhaps, however, James Cameron's spectacular production might *re-seed* a glimmer of that 'once-knowledge' to hopefully produce in the 'inner spirit' of viewing millions a sense of *unease* – or better still **fear** – about what we have done and are still doing to our "home-planet" Earth; like the Navi's "Home-tree". An ongoing example is the destruction of the Amazon rainforest. Backed by powerful Corporations – the equivalent of the 'superpower' depicted in **Avatar** – the same kinds of destructive-processes displaces peoples living in harmony with nature in that jungle environment.

In this Chapter we have sought to awaken, re-awaken, demonstrate and elucidate the fact of that once-known but now long-lost association with the connective-fabric of life, *still today* woven into every facet of the 'Natural World'; the **'Gaia'** hypothesis. If we summarise just some of the key points of that Elemental-force paradigm – and thus **reality** – present throughout this whole Work, we will also see the very same kinds of threads so brilliantly depicted in James Cameron's movie.

1. What IS life, exactly?" ***"Is it chemical, spiritual, or a combination of both?"***

2. **Crucial Imperative No 9:** "The Interconnectedness of All Events..."

   That **all** is *interconnected*; that nothing stands *in isolation*!

3. Latter-day philosopher Arne Naess's recognition that man took a fundamentally wrong turn into an *over-reliance* on technology which, *for spiritual growth and ascent*, we of Planet Earth did not need to do. Naess rightly determined that, perhaps paradoxically, the indigenous people who still maintained a strong natural/spiritual connection to Earth were the Native Americans. For Example, points 4, 5 and 6:

4. White Cloud's **"Circle of Life"**.

5. Lone Man's recognition that: "The earth is under the ***protection*** of something which ***at times* becomes *visible* to the eye.**"

6. Chief Seattle's **"Address on the Environment"**.

7. The primarily European settling of the New World of America with the arrogant ethos of **"Manifest Destiny"**; the exact attitudinal-trait of the 'superpower' portrayed in **"Avatar"**.

8. The consequential effect that *that* particular ethos has unfortunately *bequeathed* to global humanity.

9. Now displayed in The Prophet Isaiah's succinct encapsulation [24:4-6] of **Why** we have now reached such a dire point.
    Isaiah's sage warning for *this* – **our** – time:

    'The "Earth" also is defiled under the inhabitants thereof; because they have
    transgressed the "Laws",
    changed the decrees,
    broken the everlasting covenant.'

    'Therefore has the curse devoured the "Earth", and those that dwell therein are desolate: therefore the inhabitants of the "Earth" are burned, and few men left.'

The *spiritually-aware* reader will understand the linkages in the itemised enumerated points. Probably not so the intellectual-empiricist, however – many of today's scientists. Yet the very first point – which the scientific community cannot agree on – in its obvious reality **actually manifests biologically and thus materially** to clothe Planet Earth in millions of **fixed** plant forms, thereby providing habitation for similar numbers of **mobile** species – *including we humans*. This fundamental and most crucial difference between *crass empiricist-intellectualism* and *spiritually-intuitive discernment* derived from the recognition of the actual **Life-force** present in Nature, was graphically portrayed by the two opposing 'factions' in **Avatar**.

Echoing the final battle of the movie, the Military ethos of the very destructive Vietnam War [personally experienced by this writer], produced one of the most famous quotes to come out of that debacle. A U.S. Army Officer tasked with rooting out Viet Cong entrenched in a 'friendly' village; after the battle stated:
"We had to *destroy* the village in order to *save* it."

Avatar: Inadvertent wisdom? Perhaps a subtly-guided warning to at least a few on earth 'to wake up and change'. Or is there a subliminal message in that movie that reveals to us our swansong, *before* the **Elemental Forces of Nature** really begin their ordained work in earnest? Not just the odd earthquake and tsunami here and there, but the *final venting* of their *justified fury* – prophesied millennia ago for this very time – for what **we** have done to this once-pristine world.

A relatively recent example – and similarly echoing the rough-shod attitude and arrogance of the 'superpower' depicted in **Avatar** – was the '**Manifest Destiny**' ethos of the 'new Americans' who emigrated there primarily from Europe to settle the 'New World'. [Point 7]

Two species endemic to North America had resided there for a very long time before the arrival of the new unthinking, ignorant, *predator*. The Bison, numbering in the millions; and the other – the Passenger Pigeon – in the billions. Yet within virtually a few generations, the Bison were slaughtered almost to extinction, and the Passenger Pigeon completely so. The last one, "Martha", is 'stuffed' and displayed in a glass case in the Smithsonian.

In the long and sorry human history of blood and killing for all the wrong reasons, these two examples may perhaps be viewed by some as 'not so bad'. However, under the outworking of every aspect of **Creation-Law**, all activities that have transgressed that inviolable **Law** must produce the commensurate 'payment' by we lemming-like humans.

Along with the inevitable and appropriate *cleansing* to completely rid Planet Earth of such humans, is the very necessary requirement for us to really understand the **'Why'** of disasters and catastrophes. Clearly on the increase, they are not at all arbitrary for the peoples affected but are the end-outcome of, primarily, the great and Immutable: **Law of Reciprocal Action!**

So in the ultimate choice of whether to believe or disbelieve in the existence of especially the more powerful **Elemental Beings of Nature** – irrespective of whether we label that *reality* Elemental, Spiritual, or even of The Divine – in the final analysis it is a 50% pick. That individual choice, however, unequivocally equates to a personal and final **100% outcome**. This blunt fact we should all mark well.

For the Indigenous peoples of the world and for the more technological Western races there is, in the final analysis, **no other choice but to awaken to the truth of their existence.** That awakening **will arrive** in one of two ways in any case; either *voluntarily*, or through *very hard experiencing*. From Luke 21:25-26, Fenton:

"And there will be signs in the sun, and moon, and stars; and *upon the earth* **nations in despair**, as when *in terror of the roaring and raging sea*; men *expiring from fear*, *and appre-hension of what is coming upon the world...*"

5

JESUS: HIS BIRTH, DEATH AND RESURRECTION

"Do not imagine that I have come to abolish the law and the prophets; *I have not come to abolish but to complete them.*"

(Matthew 5:17, Fenton.)

"I come to throw **fire** upon the earth; *and how I wish it were **already kindled**!*"

"Do you imagine that I have come to give **peace** to the earth? Not at all; I tell you, *on the contrary, **contention**.*"

(Luke 12:49-51, Fenton.
All emphases mine)

For the roughly two billion Christians who comprise the "Global Church", a revisionist analysis of key and sacrosanct tenets of the Faith might be seen as a possible blasphemous challenge to the very cornerstone of the Christian "reason for being". This Chapter purposefully offers the revisionist view simply because there are clear and very disturbing discrepancies between the "official theological standpoint" surrounding the life and death of Jesus, and that which The Bible *actually states*.

Given the fact that the "global Church" comprises so many staunch, unquestioning believers, why should we believe that our analysis of events surrounding the time of Jesus has merit or relevance? After all, literally thousands of books about Jesus, mostly written by very eminent intellectual Church scholars and Theologians over many hundreds of years, have been produced. How can what we say even dare to stand alongside the heavyweights of the academic/religious world?

Should we view the stated "Church position" as a question of "might being right", and is it therefore also a question of; "the greater number must be correct"? Notwithstanding what is probably the view of the major Churches anyway, the words from the Very One Whom the "global Church" rightfully and correctly reveres offers a very sobering insight into the exact reason for this Chapter, and thus for its challenging stance.

If we therefore state that we accept the words of Jesus as recorded in The Bible, should we blithely gloss over His statements therein, or should we give them serious credence? Most believers will say they accept His words. That being the case, where does that place the two billion Christians currently alive and well on Earth with regard to what we state about His birth, death and resurrection?

Only one answer has credence here! Ultimately it is all about acceptance or non-acceptance of what *actually is* the Truth about everything connected with, and surrounding the life of, Jesus.

When it is warningly stated that **"God is not mocked"**, it bluntly means that every nuance of every happening concerned with **His Will** is also not to be mocked. That fact must therefore be unequivocally applied to all events surrounding the life and times of Jesus too. The blind acceptance of teachings that defy rational logic and which therefore transgress what are clearly natural processes – **The Creator in His Divine Perfection being the Absolute of all that is natural** – means that such beliefs deny the very **Perfection** inherent in **Him** and **His Will**, of which Jesus was and is Part!

And because Jesus stated that He came "not to overthrow The Law, but to fulfil it", an associated question must logically be: "What Law; Whose Law"? It certainly cannot be human law. It must therefore be **The Law** – from out of **The Divine** – purely and logically because that was and is the **Origin** of **Jesus, The Son of God**! Since such Perfection of Law cannot possibly be open to human interpretation or opinion, why is it that within the "global Church", diverse and differing opinions and interpretations abound, and all taken from the "same book": **The Bible**?

Red Jacket's sage observation about "white man's religion" from the previous Chapter finds perfect resonance here too.

> "We understand that your religion is written in a Book... Brother, you say there is but one way to worship the Great Spirit. If there is but one religion, why do you white people differ so much about it? ... Why not all agreed, as you can all read the Book? ... We are told that your religion was given to your forefathers... We also have a religion which was given to our forefathers and has been handed down to us... It teaches us to be thankful for all the favors we receive, to love each other, and to be united. *We never quarrel about religion*."

> (Emphasis mine.)

It might be said that we, too, are attempting to do the same, and that this Chapter and Book are no different – just another interpretation. However, there, in that assumption, the difference ends. For what we are unequivocally postulating is *completely at variance* with the "cornerstone tenets" of *all* the Christian Church communities. Moreover, the explanations herein follow brutally-logical paths. Since The Creator's Will and Law cannot possibly be anything *but* logical, only a *logical* analysis will come closest to divining the true picture, in necessary accordance with **The Law**!

The subject matter and explanations about Jesus in this Chapter, and indeed in this complete Work, therefore unequivocally stands aside and apart from all *'expert' religious and academic* opinion.

May the reader find within this particular segment the clear truth of our assertions!

*   *   *   *   *

5.1   JESUS: Bible Scripture versus "Church Distortions".

"Do not imagine that I have come to abolish the law and the prophets; *I have not come to abolish but to complete them.*"

(Matthew 5:17, Fenton.
Emphases mine.)

In the Preface we broadly yet decisively explained the path humankind should have taken to bring about a spiritual and harmonious "paradise on Earth". That path was to have been through the great Truths given to humankind through those Called for the purpose. Clearly, that did not happen. Even the powerful and sublime intervention of The Son of God Himself – *the true sacrifice on the part of The Light* – still did not induce humankind to genuinely recognise the actual nature of the Perfect Truth He brought. In its place and founded upon it we have, instead, just religions – thousands of them. And within all, distortions of that Truth to varying degrees, and all claiming to have the correct interpretation.

Therefore, since we state that we unequivocally accept the Perfection of The Laws of God for all things, by virtue of such a sure conviction within the very broad parameters that Bible *interpretation* currently encompasses [i.e., the broad, easy path]; a critical assessment of two *seemingly* contentious issues in the life of Jesus – two "Bible mysteries" that this particular Chapter addresses – is imperative.

Laws: Perfect in their inception, conception and fulfilment. Perfect? Unequivocally yes. And perfect in accordance with the very Laws that Jesus came to fulfil. Any "imperfection" or contention, therefore, will only be "formed", and therefore given life and credence, by human opinions and beliefs.

In order to ensure that we do, indeed, possess a clear mandate for what we now state herein, let us formulate for ourselves a series of questions to show exactly that. In any case, irrespective of whatever one may choose to believe about the birth, life and death of Jesus, the particular questions posed here must be faced honestly. If not faced thus, then he who still doubts *automatically denies* the inviolable Perfection of The Creator.

1. Question. Can the **"Perfection of God"** be called into question?

   Answer. No!

2. Question. Can a Perfect God produce imperfect Laws?

   Answer. No!

3. Question. If we accept the premise that The Almighty is, and must therefore be, Perfect – by virtue of His Nature – must His Laws of Creation similarly also be Perfect?

   Answer. Yes!

4. Question. If His Laws are Eternal, Inviolable in their Perfection, and therefore Unchangeable, can any event then take place *outside* the parameters of that stated *Inviolable* Perfection?

   Answer. No.

5. Question. Would such an absolute and illogical impossibility reveal believers of any such event to thus be gravely in error?

   Answer. Yes!

6. Question. Would any such beliefs therefore pit themselves *against* the very Laws that The Almighty Himself has ordained for all of Creation?

   Answer. Yes!

7. Question. If the answers to all our previous questions unequivocally deny **any imperfection** in The Almighty and His Laws, can we still continue to believe that He can change His Perfect Laws at will in order to bring about a particular event?

   Answer. No!

8. Question. If we, nevertheless, still persist in incorrectly believing that He can somehow transgress His Own Perfect Laws to "do as He pleases", would that suggest earthly religious doctrine as being the *fostering agent/s* for such views in order to thereby suit a said dogma?

   Answer. Yes!

9. Question. By virtue of such an inherently unsound concept, can we thus therewith illogically and very incorrectly impute to The Creator – Who must forever innately be **"The Perfect God"** – the *earthly failing* of imperfection?

   Answer. Clearly and unequivocally: **No!**

Thus, only with such Perfection in The Godhead and The Eternal Laws that have issued from It, could there be a Creation for Jesus to enter in the first place. And, also, by extension within those Creation-parameters, precisely these peculiarly human debates about His so-called "virgin birth", Crucifixion, Resurrection and Ascension. By virtue of the only correct answers that could possibly be given to our series of questions, we have gifted ourselves a clear and honest mandate to continue.

5.2   'Virgin' Birth and 'Immaculate' Conception?

Just as the *physical* death of Jesus at the end of His life marked His exit from earthly life, so did His birth as a baby herald His *physical* arrival onto the Earth and into earthly existence. For in accordance with the inviolability of The Divine Laws *He came to fulfil*, **The Son of God could not circumvent The Law that to be born of woman on Earth, the seed must first be placed within the womb by a natural procreative event**. Subsequent to impregnation, a lawful gestation period of nine months in that *especially-chosen* and thus **especial** womb.

Here, however, a singularly contentious question arises with the inescapable truth that in the twin realities of *physical* birth and *physical* death, one must obviously always follow the other. Yet for a large number of people, that reality is conveniently discarded in the case of Jesus. Since the purpose of this essay is to boldly question certain strongly entrenched sacrosanct beliefs in Christian Theology, the key one now is the truth or otherwise of the so-called "virgin-birth" of Christ.

Since we cannot deny the fact of Mary's earthly pregnancy or the earthly birth of Jesus as a baby, should we dare to believe that those *earthly* processes might just have been *preceded* by an *earthly* conception too? Or is that going too far? Or is it simply a matter of religious fear masquerading as "the ostensible guardian of religious righteousness" standing ready to condemn any attempt to delve logically into what was clearly *a completely natural event*? For Jesus issued, and was thus delivered, from Mary's womb. Even though a perfectly natural birth, it was, nonetheless, one of stupendous import; an incarnation ordained and sanctified by **Divinity Itself**.

Now, because every human spirit incarnating on Earth requires a physical vessel in which to dwell and through which to work, Jesus, too, needed a *physical body* to carry out **His** Work. However, all such bodies must enter the Earth plane in baby form from a birth-mother. This is only possible with an earthly conception to begin with.

Does the idea of an earthly conception, then, denigrate the greatness or purity of the person of Jesus or His inherent Divinity? No, of course not. What about the purity of Mary herself, or her especial Calling? Would we regard her as being somehow soiled or impure if a conception was necessary before Jesus could be born onto the Earth? Here, again, of course not. If we did, it would be very difficult, indeed, to reconcile the birth of The Son of God from out of a woman of the Earth whose necessary purity for that purpose was somehow *compromised* through a *natural* act of copulation **Divinely-sanctified** for **The very One *from* The Divine**.

So, would a possible father for the purposes of a necessary conception debase the body of Mary who would carry to full term the earthly vessel that Jesus, *in His Divine reality*, **would inhabit and work through**? For such a high and purely ordained purpose, moreover, might not such a man/father be similarly **chosen from Above**? And would such a union for that highest possible purpose not therefore constitute an **"immaculate conception"** in the truest sense? If not, why not? If not, would it be because The Bible *appears* to state otherwise?

The birth of Jesus out of Mary must be very correctly regarded as being of the most sublime purity. That correct recognition, however, should not automatically condemn every other mother before or since as being unclean or impure simply because a normal conception was obviously naturally required before a subsequent birth could be realised. If the resultant viewpoint from *some* religious quarters is of that mind-set for all births *other* than that for Jesus, then it is one which is dangerously distorted. For any such misconstrued stance would foolishly denigrate the very ordination of The Almighty in the outworking of His *Perfect Laws* which state that if a man and woman wish to produce offspring in the ordained *natural manner*, they must firstly become **"one"**. Surely no argument there. Even animals have to *obey* that reality.

In any case, the state of marriage should not necessarily be regarded as the *only* institution under which a child should be conceived. If we fully understand that the inherent key attribute of The Almighty must be Love in its Divine Purity, then the very notion of a *completely pure yet natural process* of conception to birth, as in the case of Jesus, offers the same *potential* for purity for every other human mother too.

A clue to the reason for the wide Christian acceptance of the "virgin birth" as truth may lie in the interpretation by Matthew of the title, the "Holy Spirit". For he reports:

> "...the origin of Jesus the Messiah was thus: Mary, His mother, was promised in marriage to Joseph; but before their union, she was found to have conceived *from* the Holy Spirit. Her husband Joseph, however, was a righteous man; and not wishing to degrade her, felt inclined to divorce her privately. But while reflecting about it, he saw a messenger from the Lord appear to him during a vision, saying":
> "Joseph, son of David, you need not be afraid to accept your wife Mary; for what is conceived in her was *__produced by__* the Holy Spirit:..."

> (Matthew 1:20, Fenton. Emphases mine.)

Because it was so stated by one of the Disciples, it is now forever regarded as sacrosanct in its *apparent* meaning. That is; that the egg – from which the ***physical foetus*** would grow to become the ***physical vessel***, the ***body***, ***of Jesus*** inside the womb of Mary – was somehow literally impregnated by "The Holy Spirit" simply to produce ***just the mortal or physical cloak***.

What needs to be fully understood here once more is that the *mortal cloak* of Jesus **was not Him** solely and completely. It was simply **the body** that **housed** His **Divine Core**. We should further understand that the ordained path of *every* physical cloak is to return to the Earth out of which it is ultimately constituted.

> "And man goes to the *earth that he was*,
> And **his Soul** will *return* to the GOD **Who gave it**!"

> > (Ecclesiastes 12:6-7, Fenton.
> > Emphases mine.)

It was **His Divine Core** – which at the same time **was He personally** – which **returned to become One With the Father**. The forming of His physical body did **not** require the Power of The Holy Spirit to produce it. Physical bodies by the score are produced every day of the week on Earth.

> However, the *entry* of **Jesus** *down into* the depths of the World of Matter *from out of* the **Highest Heights** of **The Divine Realm**, *to subsequently incarnate* **into a human foetus on Earth**, clearly **did** need **The Holy Spirit** to effect it.

So, one of the keys to a final understanding of this whole question must take into account the true meaning of the Title, **Holy Spirit**, in strict concert with the way that Matthew refers to it for the conception of Jesus. (We will *conclude* this segment with that essential knowledge.)

For the moment, however, two points must be considered if the question of the "virgin-birth" of Jesus is to be finally answered satisfactorily-correctly. One is the inviolability and absolute Perfection of the Living Laws of The Almighty, of which we have already made a clear determination. The other is the *true* meaning of the word *conceive*, and of the word, *virgin*. The Christian Church's imposition of a narrow, intellectual constraint upon the meanings and usage of the words in this particular case fails to understand that:

> *...word meanings relating to activities and ordinations from The Living Light* **must inherently be fundamentally more comprehensive and far-reaching in scope than any earth-orientated faith/belief dogma or doctrine.**

In human thinking the word, *conceive*, is invariably and immediately associated with pregnancy;

1. 1 a. 'To become pregnant with'. Or:

2. b. 'To begin or induce the conception of'.

   However, if we apply other meanings to the word:

3. 2 a, 'To form in the mind, to become possessed by'; or

4. b, 'to *formulate*; *devise*: *conceive a plan*' –

   – then a far more comprehensive picture is revealed.

If we now revisit Matthew's narration, we have the phrase, "**conceived from** The Holy Spirit"; and a second, "**produced by** The Holy Spirit". Yes, it could be seen to be "playing with words". But what actually **was** *conceived from* and *produced by* The Holy Spirit here? Other Bibles use slightly different phrasing, but all must *ultimately* **mean the same thing**, simply because Jesus was born to Mary – under the aegis of the Grace of The Almighty and His Inviolable Laws!

Matthew's narration in The Jerusalem Bible states:

"...she was found to be with child through the Holy Spirit". The angel of the Lord then says: "...because she has conceived what is in her by the Holy Spirit".

From the King James Bible the same passages respectively read:

"...she was found with child of the Holy Ghost". And from the angel: "...for that which is conceived in her is of the Holy Ghost".

With such *apparent* clarity, it is eminently clear why so many well-meaning Christians will not even begin to question the so-called "virgin-birth". Unquestioning loyalty to a high ideal carries a certain measure of greatness. Where it is a matter of The Truth or otherwise of a particular event, "set in motion" by The Living Laws of God, however, then any *presumed* absolute sureness of the given belief must inherently conform to, and comply with, those very Laws. Any position that does not do so – irrespective of how strong or self-sanctified the belief may be from a human/religious viewpoint – must therefore *set itself against* the **very sanctity** and **Inviolability** of the Perfection of The Laws of God. And therefore **against** The Almighty Himself.

If, however, we accept the idea of a *physical* 'resurrection' and 'ascension' for Jesus, then the current, accepted belief of a *'virgin-birth' according to Christian Theology* **might** make sense. Nonetheless, such an idea would need to somehow accommodate the possibility of a Divine Being from the Realm of The Almighty Himself in some way becoming physical in a kind of **Divine totality** on **Earth** through *an actual conception from* that High Source.

Using the more logical, more rational meaning of the word, *conceive*, here, inherently encompasses a far greater reality that transcends and transforms narrow earthly parameters.

Thus, to *form in the mind*, to *formulate*, to *devise*, to *conceive* – a **plan**, whereby Jesus, The Son of God, would incarnate on Earth in a human body. **That** was what was **conceived from**, and **produced by**, The Holy Spirit.

It was an **Immaculate Conception**, *conceived* in **Plan and Ordination**, and thus *produced by* **The Holy Spirit!**

We should recognise that the term, **Holy Spirit**, is a **Divine Title** relating to a **specific Being** of **Divine Origin**. It is not some kind of amorphous, super-endowed force or power that can perform any act arbitrarily, against the very Laws that are in Him and which He fulfils without compromise or deviation. For that is the meaning of **Perfection** – exact, faultless, complete! Therefore, the whole and special production **does not** refer to the simple, earthly matter of the impregnation of a human woman, of which there are probably millions at any given *moment* – but certainly many thousands.

That being the case, it should not be at all difficult to understand that whilst the earthly foetus was formed according to natural processes, **the entry of The Divine Core of Jesus into that earthly vessel** was, indeed, carried out **in accordance with The Divine Will through Divine Activity!**

In other words, **The Living, Divine Essence of Jesus, as a Part of God, was brought down to Earth from out of the Highest Heights to then enter the vessel prepared for Him** – – i.e., the growing *foetus* in Mary's womb.[1] Simple to understand, but truly stupendous as a living happening! And perfectly natural according to The Law He came to fulfil.

---

[1] Upon His death, He had then to return to His Origins and become "One with the Father", as He Himself stated.

In its *earthly* aspect, the historical narrative from the time indicates that in Mary's village the man with whom she *necessarily* **'became one'** – *precisely to facilitate the 'ordained' pregnancy which would bring forth the **body** for the **Divine Jesus*** – was known to *many*, thus the inclusion of and reference to him in anecdotal records of the period. Indeed, Mary was vilified *because* of her very brief but *necessary* association with the man *when out of wedlock*, hence Joseph's disquiet. As a devout Jew, Joseph would surely have had no hesitation at all in accepting as his wife a woman who was "with child from the Holy Spirit". What an incredible honour.

The historical reality, however, simply serves to show the complete naturalness of the whole event in the first place; as it must clearly be if it is to accord with the Perfection of Creation-Law. Thus, the *actual father* was also one *especially chosen*, to thereby *absolutely* ensure an *immaculate* conception for the *pregnancy* which would house **The Divine Core** of **Jesus**.

If we now analyse the meaning of the word, *virgin*, you, the reader, may perhaps *intuitively-recognise* a plain and simple truth in interpretative-logic here too. For even though we believe our previous analyses have offered a clear enough picture of the 'forces' and 'processes' that brought Jesus onto the Earth, we should still nevertheless go through this last little exercise in word-meaning.

Thus the accepted meaning in current doctrine regarding Mary, interprets virginity and/or the "virgin birth" as stating that **she had not ever had sexual intercourse with a man.** We must therefore conclude that Mary became pregnant through a method that somehow precluded all the natural processes that The Living Laws of God unequivocally state to be *inviolable*. Such a notion, of course, would have to go against the very Laws that Jesus Himself stated He had come to fulfil – as we must continually reinforce.

However, if we apply broader parameters to the *concept* of 'virginity' in the context of the *complete organic process of childbirth*, then we may begin to discern a far deeper and more natural meaning for the word than is currently applied in the case of Mary. Moreover, if we extend the very essence of the word, "virgin", and apply it to a *process* that had *not ever come into activity before*, then we can correctly state that *prior to* the particular activity, the key aspects associated with it must have been *virginal*. Within Mary, therefore, the organs of procreation and reproduction were **virginal** for the birth of Christ. That is:

They had not come into activity in this manner prior to that exalted birth.

So a "Virgin Birth" – *in its true meaning* – *was* the reality for Jesus.

Thus did He fulfil every last nuance of The Law by which, and for which, He came **down** to the Earth! If we are able to grasp the fact that **The Holy Spirit**, both in **Term** and **Title**, is exactly synonymous *with* **The Holy Will**, then we will see that the *true* Title here is **The Will of GOD!**

Therefore: The whole process of the entry of **The Son of GOD** onto the Earth centres on the nigh incomprehensible nature of **The Love** of **THE ALMIGHTY** Gifting **Jesus** to a falling humankind, so that from **Him** we might learn **The Truth** and not fall 'completely'.

That Divine outworking, however, was **conceived from**, and **produced by**, **The Holy Spirit**. Thus through **He** Who was then, and Who is today, and Who forever will be – **The WILL of GOD: The Son Of Man!** [Exactly as clarified in Chapter 2: **The Origins of Man...**, and in Chapter 12: **The Two Sons Of GOD.**]

If the truth of it all was such that God could change His Perfect, Inviolable and thus Un-changeable Laws at will – and therefore somehow permit "imperfection" to arise to suit human religious opinion and interpretation – we should ask ourselves this simple yet brutally-obvious question: 'Why did He not place Jesus on Earth **as a fully grown man?'**

Such a *simple* solution would have completely obviated the need for His babyhood and childhood phase. And why could The Almighty not do that? Because the Perfection of His Laws do not, and could not ever, permit such arbitrary happenings.

For the Laws governing earthly procreation just as naturally also mirror the inviolability of their unchangeable Perfection. This fact offers the absolute premise once again that even here, *in the conception of the earthly vessel for Jesus*, The Laws *could "not be overthrown"*, as He Himself clearly stated.

An earthly procreation can *only* occur when the natural Laws governing this process are fulfilled, and this was so with Jesus. In the same way that *that* natural act of procreation was spiritually-elevated to especially produce His earthly body, every *normal* sexual act similarly carries the same *potential* for a pure conception too. Unfortunately, however, many conceptions occur as a result of drunkenness, drug use and/or general social debasement, and cannot be considered even remotely pure.

An Especial Note:

If we are *ever* to *truly understand* what this incredibly powerful *sexual-force* is *really for* and how we should *use it correctly*, we need to have *precise knowledge* of the connection, process and outcome. And that is: **The Spiritual Knowledge!**

For the world reels under the insidious pressure of a multi-billion dollar global industry that promotes sex and more sex in all its forms, both natural and deviant. In 2011 of the high-tech 21st century, the darling of digital-entertainment – high-resolution **3D** – offers what is probably the ultimate *viewing* medium for *digital voyeurism*, pornography in **3D**. Given the irreversible trend to 3D laptops etc., a veritable flood of 'new porn' is surely guaranteed. The drug companies add their billion-dollar earnings contribution as well. What hope for the *average* human to be just *normal*?

The question should thus be asked:

"Why do humans constantly seek greater and greater pleasure in an act that is inherently and naturally extremely pleasurable in the first place?"

Very clearly, global humanity is foolishly-compromised here, for **The Law of Balance** is seriously transgressed; never mind **The Iron Law of Karma** – [**The Law of Reciprocal Action.**]

In terms of the 'ennobled-aspect' of sexual intimacy, then: From the Highest **Knowledge-source** ever brought *down* to the Earth, we herewith itemise what should be the *primary* considerations. It is *precisely* that **Knowledge-source**, moreover, from which the explanations herein are derived and to which *this whole Work points*.

1. Just as the needs of the physical body of food, rest, sleep, exercise and bodily elimination in their turn etc., must be satisfied, so should the natural desire for sexual intimacy. To struggle *against* the *natural* instincts is unhealthy.

2. Fulfilling the natural desire of the body can only *further*, not hinder, the *development* of the *spirit* in the inner [man/woman]; otherwise The Creator would not have placed this desire within us.

3. As with all activities, excesses are harmful. **The Law of Spiritual Balance** must therefore be heeded here too.

4. The *human/physical aspect* decrees that the act be undertaken with a fully matured and healthy body; not one *artificially* stimulated or very weakened.

5. The *spiritual aspect*, in necessary concert, decrees thus: That it should only occur; '*...when perfect spiritual harmony has existed between both sexes. And in its consummation, therefore, sometimes strives towards physical union as well'*.

6. So, in clarifying encapsulation: **'*Physical union not only serves to procreate, but from it is furthered the equally valuable and necessary process of an intimate fusion [an inner blending] and a mutual exchange of vibrations, thus producing higher spiritual power.'***

Therein lies the power, purpose, beauty, love and pleasure in the sexual intimacy between man and woman! And therein, also, will be found the great and necessary: **Spiritual Virtue of Trust!**

Notwithstanding the obvious fact that a *natural* level of sensuality will always accompany consensual sex, adhering to the ennobled considerations notated above will *greatly help* any conception to be "immaculate".

In the context of the *reason* for Jesus's birth, however, let us take this argument of the perfection or non-perfection of The Laws to the next obvious step and "allow" God to make us all sinless and perfect, but of course *without* free-will and *personal spiritual responsibility*. There would then have been *no need* for Jesus to come *all the way down* to Earth at all. He would have thus been spared His life of struggle against an intransigent people who, even though awaiting **His** Coming, nevertheless *still murdered Him*.

Thus the words of Jesus in declaring that He had come to "...fulfil The Law", must surely mean exactly that. Without exception, we are all born under **The Law**, we produce "our works" under **The Law**, and we die under **The Law**. Throughout our complete existence, for however long that may be, we receive the "returns of our works", good or bad, under the aegis of **The Law!**

Let us once more in reinforcement strongly reiterate the fact that since the physical body is *not* the "animating power" of any individual, the "inner animating power" that actually *was* Jesus, was therefore *not that* of His physical body. That was of material substance – 'dust to dust'; thus of the Earth. His "inner self" revealed **Itself** *through* the powerful radiations *emanating from* the physical shell He was obliged to take upon entering the World of Matter; in strict accordance with The Eternal Laws. **The 'Radiating-Power' within Him was of Divine Origin.**

These facts naturally call into question the notion of a *physical* 'resurrection' of Christ. We believe there are sufficient pointers in the previous explanations for the spiritually-perceptive reader to deduce the Truth of what actually occurred here as well. Further on in this Chapter we offer more pointers to a greater clarification of not only *the actual* Resurrection, but *the* Ascension also.

5.3   Mission of the 'Three Wise Men' [The 3 Kings]

An interesting theme emerges with the whole issue surrounding the birth of Jesus, His subsequent and difficult Mission, and His death as a supposed, necessary, propitiatory sacrifice to cleanse the world and humanity of sin. (That is actually quite a strange and illogical view when looked at brutally-objectively.) Nevertheless, if that *were* the case, what role did the Three Kings or "three wise men" play in the overall picture, in terms of what *they* achieved? More to the point, perhaps, what might have been their *actual* role and mission?

We have their names and, according to recent research, we have a clearer picture of who they were and where they came from – probably Parthian from the Persian Empire. We also know they travelled for a long time to finally arrive at the birth-place of Jesus. Was this just guesswork? Highly improbable. For how could they know where to go by simply guessing? History informs us that they were wise in the art of astrology – the forerunner of astronomy – and thereby divined the Holy Event. After so much preparation and "guidance" – never mind the long camel/horse journey itself – why, then, just bring expensive gifts to the Child ... and simply ride away?

If, however, we are prepared to consider another and more spiritually-meaningful reason – in terms of so much preparation to locate one Child, albeit a very special One – then we should consider their status to begin with. In the first place they were kings in their own right and so possessed great wealth. Secondly, they were evidently highly regarded as wise men and rulers. And *all three* were carefully and *collectively* guided to find **Him**.

A logical extrapolation of those three points would suggest they were "Called" for that task. History well records the fact that the Mission of Jesus was constantly opposed by the religious authorities of the day who saw in him a danger to *their* authority and who subsequently *succeeded* in their plot to kill Him. That being the case, might it not be possible that the *primary* purpose of those three powerful men was to take Him into their care and protection so that He might carry out His Work relatively unhindered?

Consider how different His Life and Work would have been had they accomplished *their* mission. In the first place, Jesus's life would not have been cut short so tragically. Under the protection of the Magi, His sublime Commission would have unfolded to its utmost point, which was *not* death by crucifixion. Given that the Three Kings recognised Him as The One sent from Above, we would further expect that royal scribes would probably have been appointed to record His every Word; all His Teachings. How different the "Christian world", particularly, would be today. However, because the Three Monarchs failed to recognise their *true Calling* and task, what we subsequently have as a result of that unfortunate error is a more fractured, divided and divisive "Christian religion" than perhaps would otherwise have been the case had Jesus received that crucial protection.

It may not ultimately have prevented a violent death at some point in His life, but a strong blanket of royal protection from the "Three Kings" might well have induced certain religious authorities to tread more carefully with regard to His Person. At the very least we might have had historical access to a far longer Ministry by Him, with perhaps His Teachings eventually recorded by Him personally. Of course, in terms of what actually occurred, it is all supposition. Interestingly, many who are religiously-inclined subscribe to a rather strange view which states that *if* a particular thing takes place, it does so because it *must automatically be* **The Will of God**. That particular notion completely fails to understand that human beings have *free will* in *all* matters. Therefore, the path of a prophet, or even of a Son of God, can either be helped or hindered by those who might cross that path – including and especially The Three Kings.

The Magi, by not placing Jesus under their care and protection – even though clearly guided to find and acknowledge him as The Awaited One – nonetheless ultimately hindered His Mission. Not purposely or from dark intent, but rather through not fully recognising their primary purpose. The fact that Herod – fearing the prophecy about the "King" that would be born in his time – in ordering the slaying of all male children up to the age of two years, surely reveals that the true purpose of the "Three Kings" in their ordained journey *was* to find and protect the Child.

The warning from the Messenger of God to Mary and Joseph to immediately journey to Egypt to escape Herod's wrath therewith reinforces the fact of our sure statement. A human failing of severe proportions necessitated direct and rapid intervention from The Light to ensure that The Son of God's Mission would not be cut short by a vengeful despot, with obviously severe ramifications for future humanity. Had Herod succeeded in killing Him as a baby, the world today would be completely bereft of the essential knowledge He bequeathed to humankind. Even though His Teachings have suffered appalling distortions, they nonetheless have, at least in part, still shown the way forward for many. Without such life-knowledge, an ongoing, more or less permanent, "Dark Age of horror" would probably have been the resultant legacy.

Failure rather than fulfilment is the unfortunate legacy of humankind in its unbreakable bind to The Creative Will. Unbreakable, because It granted us conscious life; and unbreakable because it was The Creative Will we were meant to serve as our primary "Crucial Imperative"! The error of the Three Kings unfortunately bequeathed to future Christians and the world the ongoing contention about His life and Mission. And thus even the very issues we address in this Chapter.[2]

5.4   Resurrection and Ascension

The Resurrection and Ascension of Jesus must surely rank as one of the most religiously contentious issues ever. Science, by virtue of its empiricist base, would *quite rightly* reject notions of the *physical resurrection* of a very dead body. Science would probably also reject the whole idea of *Ascension*, physical or otherwise. In bygone days, any opposition to the once all-powerful Church position that Jesus was resurrected physically, would certainly have bought an immediate death sentence and execution. Yet the very Scripture we use as the introduction to this particular Chapter clearly states that precise rules hold unequivocal sway for all, including The Son of God Himself Whose words we accept they are.

Physical resurrection and ascension! What should reason and objective logic tell us about it? We are surely enjoined by the Living Law Itself to employ what all humans are gifted with, the attribute to think and weigh with intelligence, logic and reason. If forcibly locked into either an earthly-empirical or a fundamentalist-religious framework, the issue under discussion here might appear to be satisfactorily validated for some, perhaps even for many.

In the final analysis, however, an event such as a *physical* resurrection and ascension, which radically departs from "natural" processes, cannot be held up as being logical in any way whatsoever. Correct clarification, therefore, must inherently rely on the truth and outworking of the very Laws that Jesus Himself stated could not be overthrown. And which He, according to the lawful parameters thus contained within them, also had to submit to at **His** death.

Because our mandate derives from the Perfection of The Spiritual Laws, we can also now seriously question and challenge the second crucial part of this particular essay i.e., the strong, entrenched belief within probably most Christian communities that a *physical* resurrection and ascension is *somehow* valid. To this end a key question needs to be asked with regard to the "resurrection" of Jesus. Can a man, any man, in a flesh and blood *physical body* weighing somewhere around 70 to 80 kilograms and very surely pronounced dead, realistically rise from that dead state to then live some kind of ***physical*** reality, **eternally**?

Whilst we certainly accept that Jesus was able to call the dead to life, it was done so under the strictest aegis of the Living Law, of Which He Himself Was and Is a Living Part. [The full explanation of the processes surrounding earthly death may be read in later Chapters.]

If we therefore employ the knowledge of Spiritual Law to apply the processes of death to the fate of Jesus, we are left with His irrefutable statement – that we must often reiterate – that He had *not* come "to overthrow The Law, but to fulfil it". Not just to fulfil it to a somehow

---

[2]The *apparent* final resting place of those men – or at least their skulls (revered and crowned in gold and precious stones) – is the Cathedral of Cologne. According to the historical narrative, it was especially constructed to house those very relics.

convenient earthly-belief level, but to fulfil it *completely*. He, therefore, was also subject to all the natural and lawful processes that mark earthly death. As it must be in every single case, those processes for Him, too, called for **the normal exit of His "inner animating core" from the mortal cloak He was obliged to take upon being born of a woman on Earth**.

So if we now track to the end of Jesus' life, the extremely tenuous rationale offered to ostensibly support a "physical resurrection" has always been that He *had* to have risen in a physical body **simply because His own was not in the tomb in which He was placed**. In its supposed "reasoning" such a one-dimensional view is akin to **medieval superstition**. Quite clearly, Jesus *had no choice but to vacate* His tortured, bleeding and dying body on that "Cross of Death" when His time of exit thereupon arrived. Jesus died a physical death, as all who are born onto the Earth must.

The Perfection of The Laws of God simply cannot allow for anything other than complete naturalness in all things, so a death-process for Jesus different from the norm is simply out of the question. Perfect Laws represent the *ultimate level* of naturalness, so aberrant scenarios are impossible. Therefore, whereas the inner core of human beings is that of Spirit, corresponding to the point or Realm of our Origin, the inner core of Power *that actually was Jesus*, was then, and is forever, **Divine** – precisely corresponding to His Origins from out of The Godhead.[3]

We know that after His death Jesus was taken down from the Cross and buried in a tomb owned by Joseph of Arimathea. What do we read post-Crucifixion, however? That even those closest to Him *did not recognise Him when He appeared before them*. Mary *did not recognise Him to begin with*. Mary Magdalene, too, *did not recognise Him immediately*. Even two of His Disciples on their way to Emmaus *did not recognise Him for hours* even though *He walked and spoke with them for that length of time*. How could it be possible that after a short interval of *just days*, those closest to Him *did not recognise Him immediately*? What does this clearly infer?

> It unequivocally infers that had He been in His **physical** body, **recognition would have been immediate.** Therefore, and in concert with the lawful outworking of the earthly death process, it is obvious that it must have been **another and different body they saw**.

The theological idea that it was His "transmuted physical body" they saw does not hold water, for The Laws of Creation do not permit the "transmutation" of a physical body for anyone; not even in a "one-off" situation for The Son of God. "The Laws" are quite clear on this. The exit of the "inner being" from the "physical-body part" means that *that* part is then irrevocably subject to the normal and natural disintegrating process.[4]

Spiritual Law informs us that a less dense envelope or body is able to penetrate denser objects. His sudden appearances inside locked rooms in which the Disciples regularly gathered thus testifies to the fact that He could *not* have been in a *physical body*. It is not lawfully possible

---

[3]The explanations on the inviolability and Perfection of The Laws of Creation about the "calling of the dead to life" by Jesus in Chapter 9 offer a fuller, clearer understanding of the issue under discussion here. The reader can therefore use those same explanations as the foundation for understanding the standpoint upon which we base "the what and the why" of our explanations surrounding His "Resurrection and Ascension". That particular Chapter about the "death process" provides sufficient information to thus understand the portent of this particular segment. The earlier Chapter, "The Origins of Man – Genesis and Science Agree", similarly offers clarifying explanations about the nature of the complete entity, man.

[4]The "substitution-premise" that some writers and theologians hold dear, seemingly answers this particular question as far as they are concerned. For them, the answer to most of the issues surrounding the Crucifixion and Resurrection seem only to make sense if there was a *substitute* for Jesus on the Cross. Some researchers point to Simon of Cyrenaica as that substitute. Jesus was even supposed to have watched His own "death walk" hidden from sight. Or that He survived the actual Crucifixion, then later on left the Holy Land with His "wife" to live elsewhere on the planet – France or Britain.

to "rarefy" a physical body. Physical bodies cannot penetrate material doors or walls. Not His physical body, therefore, but one that we all possess too.

A non-physical **Ethereal body** of the **consistency** of *that Realm **through which we journeyed*** to incarnate on Earth. And, unless through our own *aspiritual* deeds we remain *trapped* in "the world", the *same* Realm through which we *all* must journey again – *'if we wish to return home'*. It is a body, moreover, **that can exist on the Earth** – hence the millions of Earth-bound souls.[5]

This "other-body" reality thus answers the question of *how* Thomas could *feel* the wounds of Jesus. It is simply a matter of **the same _kind_ of body _within_ Thomas** i.e., of the **same consistency**, bearing witness to the world of this lawful event. Thomas was *invited* to "touch" and "feel" surely because he was "Thomas the doubter".[6]

An obvious question begs an answer here. 'What really did happen to the physical body of Jesus?' We know that guards were posted outside the tomb to prevent the theft of it. Therefore, the story goes, it could not possibly have been stolen, for thieves would have been seen. So the only possibility left is that **we all meekly submit to the belief that Jesus did rise from the dead in His physical body.** And that apparently seems to satisfy the majority of Christians in their various Churches.

Of course, the other logical possibility must not ever be entertained **lest the whole, carefully nurtured structure totters and comes crashing down.** For the reality is that soldiers on sentry duty *do fall asleep*, or they can be bribed to turn a blind eye. Or perhaps the sentries, in strict concert with The Law under The Will of The Almighty, were rendered unconscious for a time to thereby graciously permit a few especially chosen ones to quietly remove the earthly body of Jesus so that it might be placed where it would **never ever fall into unbelieving hands**.

Thankfully a small but steadily growing body of religious scholars now subscribe to this "probability", and that His Resurrection and Ascension was thus a "spiritual" event, not a physical one. Deriving their ideas from historical narrative and ancient texts quite recently discovered but ignored by mainstream Christian Churches, this newly-emerging and **correct view** is exactly that which we state in the previous paragraph – that Jesus was moved from His temporary burial chamber and placed in a secret, permanent vault.[7]

For if that particular scenario is regarded as impossible, as blasphemy or heresy even, then we have a **major and insurmountable problem** with the fact that Jesus had to subsequently **return** to The Father. To thus levitate and ascend in that same supposedly **physical body** to a **Realm** that is obviously **non-physical**. To a level, therefore, immeasurably Higher and thus far beyond the incomprehensible reaches of the farthest universes even. Such an idea simply beggars description, for it is implausible in the extreme. In fact, **it is patently impossible!**

As He stated to his Disciples, He would one day leave the Earth and become, again, **One with The Father**. In the light of His sure statement, the question that must be put to the whole issue of **The Ascension** is: "**What is the natural reality of God?**" Human beings,

---

[5]These are the departed who are ignorant of the path they should take and who therefore, of course, are *not* meant to be Earth-bound.

[6]Interestingly, Thomas's fulfilment of his amazing mission to India after that must surely be seen to be one of *transformed conviction* from a previously doubting nature.

[7]The *ostensible* discovery of the ossuary of Jesus in a tomb which also *ostensibly* housed the ossuaries of most of his immediate family members has brought forth the notion that His bones were later recovered from the second chamber to be placed in the "family tomb" as per Jewish tradition. Israeli archeological authorities, very tightly controlling this "discovery", have not allowed any public examination of the bones. For if they were actually those of Jesus, then precise and particular aspects about certain of His bones *would rock Christianity to the core*. That particular and crucial knowledge about the body of Jesus *is revealed further on in this Chapter*.

of course, cannot *ever* answer that particular question. We cannot possibly know, in any kind of "experiential-way", anything *above* our particular origins. By asking that question, however, *we are not seeking an actual answer to it.* We are simply, yet graphically, illustrating the fact that a huge and fundamental problem exists with any belief that Jesus ascended to become One with The Father *in His physical body.*

Do we therefore also believe that The Almighty sits down to a meal? Or that He must subsequently use a toilet, as we must in the physical world? Of course not. It is an utterly ludicrous thought, and one certainly tending towards the blasphemous.

> *However, that kind of physical reality must be accepted as inescapable for anyone who persists in the patently absurd notion that Jesus ascended in His physical body.*

He said often enough:

"My Kingdom is *not* of this world." "I come into the world and I leave the world." What is so difficult to understand here? His Kingdom was not of the physical world that we presently occupy. It was of a non-material reality – above the heavens even. For **His Origin** and thus **"Home"** is **The Divine Realm!**

If such a simple certainty cannot yet be grasped, and one still persists in the belief of a physical-body ascent, then the next question is:

> "At what point or level in the ascent did the necessary transition from a *physical* form to a *non-physical* one take place, **in order for The Son of God to become One with God The Father**?" And: "How much food did Jesus take for the return journey?"

Staunch Christians may regard such questions as a mockery or a defilement of an ostensibly sacred or holy belief. If so, then it is clearly a closed-spirit viewpoint, for the questions posed here are extremely valid and must be honestly answered if any actively-promoted, conceptual belief of a physical-body resurrection **and** ascension is to hold any kind of credibility whatsoever. The impossibility of a *physical-body ascension* must therefore somehow follow a similarly impossible *physical-body resurrection* in terms of any credible physical-mode answer here.

This particular distortion of The Truth may possibly derive, wholly or in part, from an incorrect, primarily Christian, interpretation about the fate of the dead at the end-time. This belief *ostensibly* states that then:

"All the dead shall be awakened".

The sentence as it stands conjures up horror-filled images of all the dead emerging from their graves and somehow being *reconfigured* to the physical specifications conforming to their original bodily appearance. And presumably to the same level of knowledge and belief they possessed when they died. How they could ever possibly understand the why of the very different world they will supposedly enter after emerging from their earthly graves, no one seems to have answered.

What about Christians who have been cremated, and whose ashes – at the deceased's wish – have been scattered in more than one location, or even at sea? Fish food. Surely problematic is the question of the hundreds of thousands of believers – including Church martyrs – burnt to ash by marauding armies over centuries. Problematic, also; the very many *true believers* burnt at the stake by the twisted "Dark Ages religious madness" of the very Church that should have protected them. Ash given to the earth becomes just dirt. That reality is **The Law —** **CREATION-LAW!** No chance of reassembly there.

The whole idea in its continued belief to the present is nothing more than just latter-day religious madness stemming from Christian fundamentalism's fear and ignorance. Fear of *their interpretation* of **'Judgement-Day'**, and ignorance of the *true* meaning of that particular Scripture. In this case, therefore, what has been so terribly distorted over centuries by such wrong thinking is **not** the meaning of the prophecy in the first place.

It is not even the correct wording.

It is not that "*all **the** dead*" shall be awakened, but that:

"All <u>that is dead</u> shall be awakened!"

A huge and fundamental difference emerges with the removal of just one word and the inclusion of two others. Those two simple words are crucially-decisive; for the **now correct** Scripture immediately conjures up a more **accurate** picture. ***All that is spiritually dead shall be forced to awaken.*** This does not at all refer to, or mean, those who have long since died, it means literally **everything** that has not adjusted itself to the correctness of **CREATION-LAW**. As we have already explained and reiterate once more, everything that has not voluntarily adjusted itself to **The Law** will thus be *forcibly awakened* to thereby reveal its true nature.

Social structures, concepts, attitudes, religions, families, Nations etc., will be affected according to the level of compliance or non-compliance of The Law by individuals and organisations prior to this crucial point. At this present time we can observe this "awakening and revelatory process" in such diverse activities as are practised within the corporate world and in Churches and religions. By extension, the previously hidden activities of leaders and senior persons within them will also be subject to this relentless spiritual-sifting process.

Nothing will escape this now quite necessary and long-ordained and eagerly awaited "Spiritual cleansing". Not one thing, organisation or activity is, or will be, exempt. The perceptive reader should now readily understand the great gulf between a belief that *incorrectly says*: "All **the** dead", and one that *correctly states*, "all **that is** dead"!

We have presented what is a logical explanation of events pertaining to the birth and death of Jesus, and clarified His Origins. What we will now examine is the interesting exercise by the many who attempt to deny **His Divinity**; to somehow prove that He was just an ordinary Earth-man. Should we once more tiresomely reiterate the absolute fact that all born onto the Earth must use the form ordained for that purpose, the physical form of either man or woman? There, we did!

The sole purpose the body serves is simply that of a vessel. It is the cloak or overcoat that the life-force in each and every one on Earth needs as an habitation for physical life. It is so simple a concept, and so perfect. Yet it provides such fertile ground for scenarios that are so ridiculously impossible that one wonders how the authors could have possibly thought them up. The truly amazing thing about "other-body" realities is that the time eventually arrives for each of us to be forcibly thrust into exactly that separating-out process we call earthly death. So was it for Jesus too.

Then, yes then, through the experience dawns the realisation for most that they had wasted their lives on things that really did not matter, but would now cause them major problems in their non-earthly body. In any case, the academic world's seeming preoccupation with Jesus and his earthly physicality *completely misses the point* of the whole quite stupendous event – His entry onto the Earth as a very necessary act of "Truth-bringing". "Heed the Word, not the Bringer" should be the primary consideration. In the very first instance it is **what** He brought,

His Teaching, The Truth inherent in His Divine Core, which should always have been *the first* and *principal thing* to be understood. It was precisely His Word, and not Him *personally* as a "man among men", that was, and is, **decisive for all on Earth.**

What we have today, however, is a virtual cult based on the "personality of Jesus". Evangelical Christians promote the rather strange idea of the necessity for a "personal relationship" with a Power that human beings could not even approach. After His earthly death He warned Mary Magdalene not to touch Him. Having exited His physical body the **Divine Power** that was inherent **in Him** *was no longer constrained by the recently-vacated, heavier material cloak.* His Power therefore *radiated much more strongly from Him* then. Even as a "man among men", the Power was still sufficient to effect healing from the radiations emanating from Him *through* just His "physical" covering.

Unfortunately for the Christian Church mainly, but for all of humanity ultimately, the true meaning and purpose of His coming from the Highest point in the *non-material*, Eternal part of Creation all the way down to the lowest point of the *non-eternal*, material Earth has not ever been understood correctly. And to teach that a *physical body* can somehow rise to the **Highest part of the non-material, Eternal Divine Realm** is surely the ultimate blasphemy.

Blasphemy: It is the word that Christians are often wont to use against those whom they believe denigrate their ostensibly sacrosanct interpretations of Bible Scripture.

I am sure we all accept that The Laws of God are sacrosanct. We would probably further accept that their outworking must be so too. Therefore, in concert with Jesus's serious admonition that He had come to "fulfil The Law" – the reciprocal outworking of which we have clearly explained – what fate must await the Christian Church and its followers for continuing to promote a belief that is *completely illogical*, and thus *absolutely wrong*? The very Law Itself *will bring without fail* the commensurate reciprocal consequences to all who would dare to denigrate: **The Perfection of The Law!**

So here, in concert with that Perfect Law, we both ask and answer the key question:

"What really did happen to the body of Jesus?"

Well, should humankind ever be *permitted to find* the *actual location* of His earthly cloak, the many who have written about Jesus and The Holy Grail and have propounded final resting places in locations as diverse as India, Pakistan and even the South of France – and most assuredly all Christians who believe He ascended to His *non-material Eternal Home* in some kind of transfigured *earthly body* – will then know that they were *all very, very wrong.* (The approaching and inevitable appearance in the sky of the **Sign** of **The Son of Man** will produce the same recognition; and very much more besides.)

So, what, exactly, will be revealed to the world should humankind ever be *permitted* the discovery of the especial earthly body of Jesus, and how will we know that it truly is He? More importantly in the context of such a claim, **how and why can we so conclusively state such a radical and defining proclamation**? The answer is simple.

NOTE:

This Book, along with other writings and publications from **"Crystal Publishing"**, is *ordained to enter the academic world of both science and religion* for serious debate about – and thus dissemination therein of – the knowledge of **The Law** from out of **The Divine Will.** These Works, therefore, are *key bridges* which *can* lead 'seeking humankind' to that very **Source.** The explanations contained within these writings are therefore derived from that **Highest of Knowledge!**

Only with such a *singular mandate* can we thus offer the keys which will provide the clearest revelation that, *prior* to any such discovery, it will be *"proof positive"* that *that* particular body *is* the *earthly cloak* of Jesus. For notwithstanding the recent, *ostensible*, "discoveries" of supposedly the ossuaries of Jesus and His extended family and examined by Israeli archeologists, any sure conclusion that it might be Him must take into account *certain absolute facts about particular bones of any skeleton stated to be His.*

Therefore, in revelatory clarification: The body that served The Son Of God on Earth rests in a sealed cavern under Jerusalem. At the entrance to the cave three crosses are engraved over the right hand arch. The body inside will show evidence of crucifixion, *but the bones in the legs* are <u>not</u> broken. In the row of upper teeth in the skull, *an eye-tooth is missing.* And on the gravestone which covers His body is engraved a specific mark or sign: **His Sign!**
The missing eye-tooth or canine is obviously singularly significant. But why have we emphasised the fact that the legs on this especial body are not broken?

The particular agony associated with crucifixion centres around the fact that being suspended from nailed palms or wrists means; that to ease compression of the lungs and possible asphyxiation, the naturally-sagging body must be held erect. However, as one can readily note when gymnasts perform the "crucifix position" on "the Rings", only the strongest and fittest men in their prime can hold such a position for any length of time. Therefore, the very position of the arms affixed in that "crucifix position" in an *actual crucifixion* means that it is virtually impossible for crucified, invariably tortured, men to do so.

What they could and did use, however, was the leverage point that the *nailed feet* offer. It is the only means whereby the crucified one can relieve the crushing effect of a sagging body – in effect to push up, to stand, *in excruciating agony*, on that driven-through spike. The burial Laws at the time meant that crucified Jews could not remain on the cross on the Sabbath so had to be taken down and buried before sunset. Breaking the legs of Jesus would have ensured a quicker end on that particular **"Cross of Torture"**.

The Book of John provides a clear account of that part of the process.

> "The Judeans, therefore, since it was preparation-day – for that day was the Great Day of the Week of Rest – so that the bodies might not remain on the cross on the Sabbath, requested Pilate that they might be removed after their legs were broken. The soldiers, therefore, came and broke the legs of the first, as well as of the other one crucified with him; but when they came to Jesus, and seeing that He was already dead, *they did not break His legs*. One of the soldiers, however, with a spear pierced His side; when blood and water issued from it.
>
> "And the eye-witness gives this evidence, and his evidence is truthful; and he himself knows that he speaks true, so that you may believe. For these events happened, in order that the Scripture might be verified: A BONE OF HIM SHALL NOT BE BROKEN."[8]

> (John 19:31-37, Fenton. Emphasis mine.)

In that last capitalised sentence [by Fenton] lies the key to any so-called "discovery" of the body of Jesus, *for it must show signs of crucifixion.* At the very least, therefore, there will be damaged foot bones from the driven spikes – *but the legs will not be broken.* So far, the Israeli Archaeological Authority has not agreed to any close examination of the bones in question and, indeed, is unlikely to ever do so.

---

[8]Fenton obviously understood the great importance of the last sentence in John's Scripture for it is Capitalised. [That is not the case with some Bibles.]

5.5   Jewish Condemnation of The Son Of God

Now, what of that group of human beings who first hailed Him as The Messiah with Hosannas and then later reviled Him? "Crucify him" was then their hate-filled mantra. They, the Jewish people, called to receive The Son of God in their midst. Where do they fit in the outworking of Creation-Law which ordains that all transgressions against The Divine Will must be expiated to their final point of resolution? The historical record clearly shows that the Jewish authorities continually sought the death of Jesus, to the degree of fabricating lies about Him. The legal term today is "entrapment".

The failure of the Three Kings to recognise that their mission was to protect Jesus set in motion the train of events that would finally bring about His murder. Herod ascertained from the Magi the exact time the star made its appearance and instructed them to learn all they could about the child and report back to him. However, having been instructed by a dream not to return to Herod, they returned to their own lands by another road. Furious at being tricked and fearing the prophecy that a King had been born there, Herod ordered the killing of all new-born male children around the time of Jesus' birth up to the age of two years.

Upon the instructions of a "messenger of the Lord", Joseph and Mary immediately journeyed to Egypt to escape the reach of Herod. Upon Herod's death years later, Joseph was then directed "...to go into the land of Israel." Unfortunately, surely due to his long absence in Egypt, the powerful events of the exalted night of the Divine birth in Bethlehem slipped from Joseph. Along with Joseph and Mary, all who experienced those events then were meant to have borne *stronger witness to it for the world* during their lives. As previously explained, the Three Kings, *called* to be the primary witnesses for all time, would have changed the course of history then and forever had they fulfilled their primary task of protecting the child.

The non-recognition of Jesus as the prophesied Messiah by the Jews – **who waited for Him then and are still waiting for a Messiah today** – seems to hinge on the fact that the prophecy about Him correctly named Bethlehem as the town in which the Messiah was to be born. Jesus, however, became known as "the Nazarene", for that is where Joseph lived – in Nazareth. Could the Jewish people claim that such an error was a simple and legitimate mistake, and therefore not expect any repercussions from the whole, terrible series of events at some future time? Ordinarily, that might possibly possess some saving grace – it was all just a mistake.

The Book of John, however, in recording the arrest of Jesus, reveals what was surely the murderous attitude of many within the Sanhedrin toward "the troublemaker".

> "The troops, then, headed by their colonel, and the Judean officers, arrested Jesus, and having bound Him, they conducted Him in the first instance to Annas; because he was the father-in-law of Caiaphas, who was high priest for that one year. Now it was Caiaphas who advised the Judeans that *"It is profitable for one man to die on behalf of the people."*
>
> (John 18:13-14, Fenton. Emphasis mine.)

In this case, therefore, the stakes are crucially higher. What might be now dismissed as a "simple mistake" was, in truth, a hypocritical calculation to get rid of Jesus. That action resulted *in the torture and murder of an innocent man* in the first instance. That in itself is wrong. Secondly and crucially, that particular *murder* was against The One Who, gifted in Love and Grace from The Creator, *came to help humankind out of the mess it had mired itself in.* But Who, then, however, was *rejected* by the very people 'called' from the time of Moses to prepare for His Coming. Is that not incredibly arrogant and foolish?

If there was, or is yet still to be, severe reciprocity from that repulsive act of blind hatred against The Light Itself, what form might it take? *Or might it just perhaps have already occurred?* We should note here the discourse of Pilate to the baying crowd, and their replies to him.

> "What then," asked Pilate, "shall I do with Jesus, Whom they call the Messiah?" "Let Him be crucified!" was their unanimous reply.

> "Why?" he asked; "what crime has He committed?" In reply, they yelled out more savagely than before, "Let Him be crucified!"

> Pilate ... took water and washed his hands in the presence of the mob, saying, "See, I am innocent of the blood of this just Man; look to it yourselves!"

> Then in reply to him, the whole mass shouted out, **"Let His blood be upon us and upon our children!"**

> (Matthew 27:22-25, Fenton. Emphases mine.)

And so Pilate handed Jesus over to be crucified.

In that last terrible and hate-filled imprecation, the inviolable outworking of the very **Commandments** given to that race by their great Patriarch, **Moses the Law-Giver**, began their silent and long-reaching work. It was the Jewish race that was Called to lead the way for humankind with the greater knowledge of **Creation-Law** brought to them by The Son Of God. Through the elucidation of them by Jesus in their very midst and thus under His initial guidance, they could have succeeded. Burdened with religious ritual that held them fast to the 'letter' of Jewish law, they failed in their task, for they did not want it. Because of *that* murder, the ancient prophecy that foresaw the death of Jesus was fulfilled. Not, however, because it was the Will of God that it be fulfilled, but because it could be prophetically seen that *the Jewish people would go against the very laws and prophecies they were meant to obey*.

Thus: That failure was prophesied long before Jesus came onto the Earth!

So, what can we deduce from the events of 2,000 years ago for those who shouted:

"Crucify Him!"

The Book of Luke records the Admonition of Jesus to "The Daughters of Jerusalem" as he was led to Golgotha. From Luke 23:26-31, Fenton:

> And a large crowd of the people followed Him, including women, who were beating their breasts, and lamenting Him. Jesus, However, turning towards them, said, "Daughters of Jerusalem, weep not for me; but weep for yourselves and for your children. For now the days are coming, during which they shall say, 'Happy are the barren, happy the childless, and happy those who have never nursed.'[9] Then they will begin to SAY TO THE MOUNTAINS, 'FALL UPON US'; AND TO THE HILLS, 'BURY US'; because if they do this with the green tree, what must happen to the rotten one?"

---

[9]His warning to the women who lamented Him at that specific time has been interpreted by some Bible "scholars" as a warning about the impending wholesale slaughter of Jerusalem's inhabitants under the Roman Commander, Titus. However, what we should read here is *a larger warning* from The Son of God that The Law of Reciprocal Action would reach down through the centuries *to all the women and mothers of the world who reject The Living Word*; The Law that we must all, in the final and absolute analysis, embrace in gratitude and therefore live by. For we can clearly see, if we wish to, the ramifications of His severe warning to women at the end-time; *'Woe to the woman who is with child and nursing women'*. See full explanation in sub-heading, "Why there is so much Violence and Evil on Earth: The "Divine Warning" to Mothers", Chapter 3 – **The Spiritual Laws** *The Crucial Knowledge*.

The Spiritual Laws of Creation offer clear explanations of *all* The Laws and their outworking. They provide the keys for greater understanding of reciprocity for the murder of Jesus which we examine at this point in our story.[10]

Bible prophecy and Scripture thus speak of the fact that "...generations will not pass until all has been fulfilled". And we further know that our works or deeds follow us into the beyond after earthly death and, under the aegis of The Law of Rebirth, may wait many centuries before exactly the right time and circumstances converge for possible expiation. Therefore, the notion that "crimes of enormity" committed against certain races throughout history are *always* committed against *innocent people* does not necessarily correspond with the perfect and inviolable outworking of The Laws of Creation.

The concept or claim of innocence for dark deeds committed can be used for at least two reasons:

1. Ignorance and/or disbelief of any inviolable and thus constraining Laws to begin with.

2. The recognition that inviolable Laws may or do exist, that the consequences of dark actions are inevitable, but that any potential for a "possible guilt aspect" may hold at bay, even subconsciously, acknowledgement and thus *acceptance* of the long-committed deed.

The obvious ramifications that such *inviolable* Laws presuppose for the individual or group in the necessary expiation of particularly heinous deeds, such as the murder of One from out of The Godhead, means that The Law will, without fail, one day "visit the appropriate reaping" on such a group.

"Ignorance is bliss!" But is it really? In terms of expiating past transgressions, ignorance of The Laws does not stop their sure outworking. Ignorance or disbelief, therefore, **cannot stay** the reciprocal return. The same applies to the second point. Knowledge of, but refusal to accept, the lawful reciprocity of dark deeds may add **more suffering** to the **inevitable reaping** for the **deed perpetrated** than otherwise might have been the case. The darker and more savage the act, the stronger will be the "lawful return". In the case of serious transgressions by whole peoples, it naturally follows that the group as a whole *may*, at a future time, **"yet reap together"**.

However, due to the lawful outworking of The Laws of "Rebirth...", "Attraction..." and "Reciprocal Action...", it does not necessarily follow that the group present at a particular event in history that must require expiation – such as the murder of Jesus – will all incarnate together at a given future point for that expiation to occur. **Yet they may.** In any case, unless the individuals present at the event who *did* contribute in even the *smallest* way to the deed **had not come to recognition of their part in it since that time**, then the long reach of the Justice of The Law would require them to be back on the Earth around the time it was ordained that **all karmaic cycles must close.**

In the case of the murder of **Jesus**, then; it is not only those who shouted "Crucify Him" who will "reap the appropriate return", but all human beings who have rejected **Him** and **The Living Truth He** brought to humankind. In the case of those directly and indirectly involved in the actual, incomprehensible event – who thus took part in **His** murder – and those who were willing servants of the plotters and planners; all would need to be on Earth when **The Son of Man** proclaimed **His** presence. And therewith to recognise **Him** through the **All-Truth He** would bring which would clarify **The Truth** surrounding the life and **True Mission** of **Jesus**: **The Son of God**. Recognition of that crucial **Truth** by the perpetrators and supporters *could thereby* bring expiation for them.[11]

---

[10]Especially note "The Law of Reciprocal Action" in Chapter 3.

[11]The Christian reader, particularly, should very seriously strive to spiritually absorb the contents of Chapter 12: The Two Sons of God. **In truth, however, the crucial knowledge about "The Two Sons of God" is for every human being on Earth and in the beyond. In short, for all!**

Since all karmaic cycles have been closing rapidly for some time now but more exponentially in the present – hence the "increasing reaping" everywhere on Earth today – we should yet note how history records countless events where various races perpetrated horrific acts against others. In those kinds of unfortunate episodes in human history, we may thereby better understand the inviolable aspects of The Law.

World War II saw perhaps the greatest ever concentration of dark deeds perpetrated against many races in many different parts of the globe. The world also witnessed the curious phenomenon of mass non-responsibility from the citizens of the main perpetrating groups. They gave as their excuse or reason; they were just "following orders", or had no choice – particularly where they were led by a megalomanic/charismatic leader. In any Nation or race, however, the inviolable outworking of The Law does not absolve any person – who simply "follows a leader into mad savagery" – of personal responsibility.

The "one-life-only" school of thought, which does not take into account the lawful outworking of precise and inviolable Laws, will naturally describe those on the receiving end of "crimes of enormity" as *innocent victims*. The reality is, however, that under those very Laws, what has taken place is simple reciprocity under the aegis of The Laws of Rebirth, Attraction... and Reciprocal Action – "What we sow, that shall we reap" – in the first instance. So races and peoples who continually lament that they are the *victims* need to recognise, understand and accept that The Laws do not deliver injustice. That is impossible. At this rapidly-closing time of humankind's odyssey, people and races receive or "reap", **simply because they once "sowed the seed"**.

The horrific experience of the Jewish people at the hands of the Nazi Regime during the Holocaust brought forth strong statements from some survivors about whether or not there could be a God. Anecdotal reports from 'camp-survivors', particularly from Auschwitz immediate post-liberation, noted liberated Jews proclaiming: "There is no God." Some survivors interviewed even quite recently *still* held to that belief

On the surface, such a view may be perfectly understandable given the years of traumatic suffering some survivors underwent at that particular "death-camp". However, if analysed logically, such comments are really silly in the extreme for they seek to **blame God** for **all** human misfortune. Moreover, the same comments ultimately incorporate, and thus focus on, a too-strong emotive/cultural overtone centred on a people with a strong religious history of being regarded – in their own eyes – as "chosen by God".

So in terms of that nonetheless horrific episode in Jewish history, do we seriously believe that it was The Creator Who formed the Nazi Regime and subsequently built the 'death-camps'? Of course not. Human beings perpetrated that suffering – on other human beings. And even where the great and Immutable **Law of Reciprocal Action** must 'return' the 'consequence' of a previous and perhaps long-forgotten dark deed upon a people, it is still the human being/s who set reciprocal events in motion to begin with.

That does not at all mean, however, that the "perpetrators of the deed" possess the "right" to so deliver retribution. That belongs to the Justice of The Light.

"Vengeance is mine, I will repay", states The Law.

Therefore, the only sure way to not suffer severe and traumatic "reaping" is to recognise, understand, and live **The Truth** of **The Law**. That process offers the sure mechanism whereby "hard reaping" can be lessened or nullified to begin with, and ultimately expiated completely.

> **Reader:** Observe the *increasing suffering* of the *Earth's peoples*; of those *around you*, and **understand the processes** that have *brought it about*. For the **reaping** from the **sowing** will surely and inexorably *increase exponentially* anyway. So: **Learn The Rules** and *lessen*, for yourself, at least *some* of humankind's *future reaping*.

5.6   The Book Of Revelation and The Holy Grail

As we are presently discussing the life and earthly death of Jesus and how His death, particularly, has created a virtual industry around it, we should examine a singular feature that many writers have connected him to. It is a connection that, for millennia, has imbued many individuals and diverse groups with the unquenchable longing to embark on, ostensibly, the greatest spiritual quest of all – the search for The Holy Grail. The numerous stories that history holds about this worthy task are steeped in the highest and noblest aspirations that human beings could possibly bring to bear on any endeavour.

The key element in the search for The Holy Grail is the seemingly inherent "knowing" that it is an object so holy and sublime that its very existence seems supra-earthly in nature. To seek so assiduously for something so apparently unattainable over such a long period of time carries with it a certain kind of nobleness-of-spirit almost worthy of the object itself. For all that, however, no one researcher has actually produced what can be definitively stated to be The Holy Grail.

It is believed by some to be the cup which Jesus used at the Last Supper, by others the cup which was used to catch His blood. A number of claimants around the world hold different kinds of cups or vessels, but the very fact that there *are* numerous claimants obviously calls into question the authenticity of any to lay claim to possessing *the* actual icon – *in terms of what the object is believed to be and the power it is felt to hold.* This "search", like so many "other-world" research efforts, suffers from the common human condition of only seeing the subject matter from the earthly point of view; solely from the physical/material.

It is therefore puzzling that the many authors who have written about The Holy Grail, even though professing a strong belief that it is something so high and sublime that only the purest of human spirits are permitted to behold it, **can still publish reams of paper trying to conclusively prove that it somehow exists in material form on Earth.** Even the many documentary and film makers who have looked at it seem not to be able to leave the material/Earth paradigm.

So an object ostensibly worthy of the highest veneration, and which only the purest can serve, in the human mind ultimately comes down to something so mundane as an ordinary, everyday clay or wooden cup – notwithstanding the iconic status of the vessels concerned.

Certain authors and claimants, however, have even tried to link The Holy Grail to an Earth-based, Jesus-connection by hypothesising a substitute at the Crucifixion, and a subsequent marriage to Mary Magdalene, thus producing some kind of genus different to the rest of humanity by virtue of a postulated Divine, royal bloodline. And thereby bequeathing to humanity an earthly genealogy carried by certain, mainly European, families living today. That hypothesised "sacred bloodline", at least for them, apparently seems to be, or hold, the secret of The Holy Grail.

How insidiously impressionable such damagingly-incorrect ideas can become is evident from unprecedented interest in runaway book sales of one publication on exactly this subject. The motion picture about it was a blockbuster, thus further swaying many millions more globally and taking them all away from the actual truth of it – *a Truth crucially vital for all human beings to know.* So now, for increasing numbers it would seem, The Holy Grail was, or perhaps still is, a woman.

Clearly, a woman's body *is* a vessel in living form. It receives, and it delivers. Unfortunately for such believers, however, it is not, or ever was, or ever could be, the pure Vessel, the Pure Chalice, that is the *true* Holy Grail!

In any case, who dares ask the obvious question: "Where are the pure human spirits *down here* who would be worthy enough to hold or guard it?" None! Why? Quite simply:

Because the true and <u>only</u> HOLY GRAIL is <u>not</u> of the Earth!

How could it possibly be? That is **why** it **is** so **Holy**! We, therefore, cannot **ever** actually see it in its "living reality" – let alone get anywhere near it.

The **form** that is associated with The Holy Grail – that of a Chalice – is known simply by virtue of the fact that especially blessed ones long ago received a "radiated picture" of it from out of the Highest Realms of the Eternal Part of Creation. From them, through their writings, it entered the consciousness of a particular group of humanity whose "collective spirit" was thereby awakened to a longing to seek it out. The process should be seen as something akin to a "subconscious seeding" of a vital, indeed crucial, piece of knowledge for global humanity. Even in recent times, others have received "pictures" about it as well.

"Music Forms", a book by Geoffrey Hodson, offers a tantalising glimpse into what Wagner may have seen – or at the very least perceived – when writing his great work, Parsifal. Dr Gordon Kingsley, Music Director of Beverley Hills Church in Hollywood, California, worked with Geoffrey Hodson on this project. Hodson was renowned for his amazing "second-sight" abilities, and employed it to analyse the forms of some of the noted classics from the great composers. Wagner's "Parsifal" was one chosen. Parsifal is the primary figure in the "legend" of The Holy Grail.

In "The Overture From Parsifal", [bars 45-47, pages 32-33], Dr Kingsley offers his comments on what he believes the music represents and symbolises. A few short extracts indicate the sense of majesty he perceived in it.

5.6.1   The Eucharistic Motif

"In his music drama "Parsifal" Richard Wagner reached a height of sublimity which even he had not previously attained ... there is added another element – sacredness. We are on holy ground. The first sounds of the prelude convey a sanctity not of this world, a peace, indeed, which passeth all understanding. It is the motive of the Eucharist. - - - '...it is the old, old story of man's ascent to God. It is only natural that the composer should represent this conception in a musical motive which in itself seeks to carry the listener to higher realms'."

5.6.2   The Grail Motif

"The Grail is the chalice which contained the 'life-blood' whose ruby radiance streaming forth in blessing, enveloped everything within the sphere of its mighty influence. The very structure of the music suggests this all-embracing benediction..."

Geoffrey Hodson described what he observed in each of the two Motif compositions. More importantly in this case, he also produced colour-prints of what he *saw*; a Chalice clearly not of the Earth. As with the other great compositions chosen for the project, the pictures really are "worth a thousand words". For Kingsley and Hodson to, respectively, bring forth such sublime words and pictures from the great work, Parsifal, Wagner must surely have perceived that the Grail Chalice – **The Holy Grail** – *was* supra-earthly in nature.

That being the case, why the continual attempts by so many Grail researchers, historically, to tie it to Jesus on Earth? For once the tidings of it reached all the way down to Earth through the few gifted to perceive its existence, the answer **was always available to any earnest seeker dedicated to unearthing the mystery of it.**

Since many researchers *have* connected The Holy Grail with Jesus and His earthly Mission, this is the appropriate point in the Work to **reveal what it really is**. Despite the fact that those same researchers have vainly attempted to make it some kind of earthly object imbued with supra-earthly power, *in the strangest paradox* the very nature of their research *clearly indicates something not of the Earth.*

A clue lies in the words Jesus spoke to Pilate on the day of their fateful meeting: "*My kingdom is not of this world.*" His words clearly indicate something *vastly different* to the ongoing notion of any kind of *earthly* association. The words reveal that in the final analysis *direct* connections to Jesus not only *do not* lie in the earthly, they ultimately *cannot*.

By virtue of its supra-earthly nature, The Holy Grail can truly be stated to be a "Sacred and Holy Vessel". Over centuries and even to this day men have racked their brains to try to solve what is ultimately a Divine Mystery. It is most certainly a mystery in the sense that we can never ever behold it or know anything of it in its living reality. It is not, however, a mystery about *what it is* or, indeed, that it *really does exist*.

From Fenton's Bible, the "Revelation of John" in 19:6 tells us what The Holy Grail *actually is*. Dr Kingsley's comments about the "life-blood" streaming forth in blessing are surprisingly insightful. [Emphases mine.]

> Then He said to me, "**It has come! I, the Alpha and the Omega, the beginning and the end. I will freely give to the thirsty from the <u>fountain</u> of the water of life!**"

Through just those few stupendous words we can more readily understand parts of the legend of The Holy Grail where, if the power, "the water of life" that streams forth from The Chalice, is withdrawn, *everything* decays and dies including, of course, *unbelieving humanity*. The *actual* Holy Grail, therefore, is what we are all meant to recognise and know as literally the "*fountain of the water of life*" dispensing Divine Power for all of Creation, and thus for all here on Earth too.

*   *   *   *   *

From GOD, through HIS WILL: — IMANUEL — The Alpha and Omega!

The Holy Grail is thus The Highest Creation of GOD!

*   *   *   *   *

Grail researchers need only adjust their thinking to this inviolable Truth and very much that was hitherto regarded as once unknowable would quickly fall into place. Determined but ultimately fruitless efforts to prove some kind of "Jesus/Holy Grail/Earth-connection" deny **Him His Very Origin** from out of **The Divine**. The Lawful and humanly-unbridgeable gulf naturally existing between such **Divine Sublimity** and our *far lower level* of earthly humanity in just **Subsequent Creation** automatically precludes, as a matter of course, any such connection.

Jesus came to Earth to lead humanity back to **THE LIGHT** through the knowledge of **THE ONE LAW**. He therefore gifted all on Earth the opportunity to return from whence we originally came – our *true home* in a Higher Realm. [We all surely know His words of Divine Love which reveal that fact: 'In my Father's House are many mansions. I go to prepare a place for you.'] However, any possible 'return home' is absolutely predicated on living that **ONE LAW – CREATION-LAW** – *inherent* in **HIS Divine Essence**.

He did not come to found a Divine bloodline; by any standard a *nonsense-notion* focusing *solely* on human ego. Yet the extreme foolishness of such an idea nevertheless continues to be promoted. Men had became so entangled in wrong ideas and teachings that **the way home was effectively lost.** Had The Love of The Almighty not inclined towards an erring and spiritually-sinking humankind to send a Part of Himself to Earth in Jesus, mankind would have sunk irretrievably. He was not sent to die, therefore, **but to rescue mankind.**

Despite all the trials and indignities He suffered, He did not shun physical death when it drew near but remained resolute, deliberately facing it for the sake of **The Truth** He brought into **The World of Matter.** By shedding **His blood** on that terrible **"Cross of Crucifixion"**, He placed **His** very "Seal of Conviction" on *all* that **He** had *said* and *lived.* With His death, the way to **The Light** was now open. He had won the victory for **The Love of The Father**, for the **Love of Truth** and the *Love of Man.* For He had subjugated the powers and forces that had striven to destroy **His Message** and **His Work**! And therewith, as the incontrovertible historical record unequivocally reveals, man's *faith* in **The Truth** of **His Word** was *strengthened* by **His Victory.** *So Jesus died* for – *thus* **because of** – *the sins of men.*

If He had given up His Work in fear of His many enemies, doubt would have assailed the faithful. The seeds of Truth He sowed in the spirits and consciousness of men then would not have taken root to subsequently spread to all corners of the Earth.

> Had it not been for *the sin* of *turning away* from **The Creator and His Perfect Laws** and thus *introducing* dark and evil forms onto the Earth in the first place, ***Jesus would have been spared His Coming, His suffering and His death on the Cross.***

> *It is correct, therefore, to say that for the sake of 'the sin' which led to mankind's 'fall',* *Jesus came, suffered and was crucified*, but that irrefutable fact is not a blessing for Christians or mankind in any shape or form. Those who had the chance to save Him from a terrible end – the once-chosen and blessed Jewish race – agitated for Barabbas over The Son of God. To Pilate, they shouted: 'Crucify Him'. Standing as an *indictment* against all of mankind from that singularly-dark moment of far-reaching portent, it was and still is an especially damning indictment against the Jewish race. For even today, they still refuse to recognise that **The One** sent to them *at their petition*, really was their **Awaited One** at that time.

His Crucifixion was not, and could never ever be, an act of "necessary sacrifice" to take away the sins of a weak and spiritually-lazy, earthly humanity. The millions upon millions of Crucifixes that have *inundated* the Earth for millennia should thus be looked upon *far differently* to what has been the case thus far.

> Yes, the Crucifix *should* be approached with awe and reverence, **but see it for what it really is, and therefore what it truly means!**

5.7   Crucifixion of The Son Of God: Medical Forensics Speak

Up to this point we have examined a number of issues of contentious moment centred on the life, death and its aftermath for Jesus, The Son of God. Irrespective of the many differing viewpoints about these events, however, a clear and absolutely unequivocal Truth is nonetheless sacrosanct here. And that is:

That the actual happenings in the Life and death of Jesus could only have occurred according to firmly established, inviolable Laws. As we have already explained, it is impossible for anything to take place except under precise and lawful processes, irrespective of what human/Christian opinion – either from lay persons or academics – might wish to state or believe.

Since that *is* an inviolable Truth in itself, let us put aside all selfish notions of how wonderful it all was that The Son of God Himself was sent down to this Earth in an act of Noble Love on the part of The Almighty to save **us** from **our** sins. Instead, and from a scientific/medical perspective, let us *really and closely* examine the whole process of the Crucifixion of Jesus in a probing, 'blow-by-blow', assessment of His 'journey of terrible suffering'.

While doing so, we should very seriously understand that the incredible pain He suffered throughout *never let up*. It was *constant*. It was not at any time relieved by 'first-aid' or convenient pain-killers such as we would immediately grasp for at the onset of even very mild, 'inconvenient', pain.

From childhood, Christians are conditioned with a mindset which *superficially* and ***incomprehensibly*** says that Jesus suffered and died on The Cross to save *them* from **their** sins. Nothing, however, about what that suffering *really meant* **for Him**. Not, however, for the 'believing Christian' who will *never ever* experience such a thing, but who nonetheless preens himself with sickening false piety in the truly strange belief that he is 'absolved' from all **his** sins and 'thereby saved'.

That being the perverse and pervading belief in Christendom, let us all journey with Jesus to His agonising death. Whilst on that grievous walk to His place of execution, we should put aside every shred of 'religious' thought, and – ***objectively*** and ***logically*** – try to fathom *how* and *why* around two billion otherwise well-meaning humans on Earth can *accept* and even *strongly promote* a belief whereby the excruciatingly-painful torture that **The Son Of God** was cruelly subjected to can *somehow* be the ***'right thing'***. Even in an earthly Court of Law, such an idea would be 'thrown out' as unjust. Yet so many believe that **'The Power of All Creation'** would nonetheless *sanctify* such an *appalling injustice*.

[Perhaps we should ***all*** have long-understood that just as **The Creator** is **Perfect Love**: **He** is *also* **Perfect Justice**!]

Firstly, then, we should watch the terrible 'scourging' by Roman soldiers. Secondly; the mocking and the placing of a 'crown of thorns' upon His head. Next; accompany Him every step of His cruelly-agonising 'death-walk' laden under the crushing weight of a heavy wooden beam. And thence finally arrive with Him at Golgotha: His place of execution.

Are there any hand-clapping, 'praise the Lord' Hallelujahs there? No! Of course not. It is too cruel, too painful, ***too unbelievable***. Yet every Easter on so-called 'Good Friday', hundreds of millions of Christians in their thousands of Churches across the world perversely 'celebrate' this ***worst*** of ***all*** murders.

"BLACK FRIDAY!" That is the reality for all time.

Note: The medical and forensic analyses of the Crucifixion of Jesus we now outline is sourced from the History Channel Documentary called **"Crucifixion"**; screened on **'Black Friday'**, 2009. It is a harrowing Documentary that *all* Christians should view, for it is to date the most graphic depiction of Jesus's painful suffering. [In this writer's view, far more so than Mel Gibson's, "The Passion of The Christ"; itself regarded as a very graphic depiction of The Crucifixion.]

The primary contributors for our elucidation about the *Biblical/historical narrative* of the medical forensics associated with the **Crucifixion of Jesus** are:

- **Dr. David Ball, M.D.**   ER Chief, Ret., Tri-Lakes Medical Center.

- **Dr. Robert M. Norris, M.D.**   ER Chief, Stanford Medical Center.

- **Jonathan Reed, Ph.D.**   Professor, University of La Verne.

- **Richard J. Hoffman, Ph.D.**   Professor, San Francisco State University.

- **Sarah Stroud, Ph.D.**   Professor, University of Washington.

- **Dr. Mark Benecke.**   Forensic Biologist.

- **Daniel Smith-Christopher, Ph.D.**   Professor, Loyola Marymount University.

This particular segment of our overall journey of *logical* enlightenment is offered as a help primarily to those Christians who are 'content with their faith'. However, the 'blind-faith' attitude that many Christians seemingly display is really no faith at all, for it simply demands that *the faithful* 'accept without question' all they are told. Specifically and especially on the question of whether or not Jesus came to Earth 'to take on the sins of men' and 'die on The Cross to save them'; without keen examination of this subject from either the 'Christian teacher' or the 'Christian follower' to ensure an absolutely correct answer – i.e., according to **The Will Of God Whom** all Christians will state they want to serve – the warning of a very well known key Bible Scripture should be the primary driver to "get it right"!

"When the blind lead the blind, all will fall into the ditch." [abyss]

Since there are a number of quite different interpretations and beliefs around this question, it is patently obvious that many Christian 'congregations' have thus 'not got it right' at all. Yet every one of them will *swear* that *they* are *saved* by *their* belief, and/or their *group interpretation*. Unfortunately, as we all surely and logically understand, the *correct answers* that must *inherently* *reside* in the events and meaning surrounding Jesus's death *cannot possibly* allow for an *infinite number* of 'saviour-scenarios' here.
The knowledgable analyses of the above contributors will help the average or 'seeking' Christian make more sense of a momentous and portentous event that ultimately affects *all* of humankind.

Crucifixion: A slow death of maximum suffering, used as a method of Capital Punishment for over 3,000 years. It was practised in various forms long before Roman Legions occupied the land of Judea at the time of Jesus. From the more simple but excruciatingly-painful practice of 'staking' a body to hang suspended from an upright stake, true crucifixion – the body affixed in the 'crucifix position' on a wooden 'cross' – was perhaps a 'torturous refinement' of 'staking'.
Death by crucifixion was essentially designed to discipline the many peoples conquered by Rome. Her vast Empire required policing methods designed to ensure that the "Pax Romana" – 'The Peace of Rome' – was kept. Crucifying criminals, dissidents and revolutionaries alike who threatened that 'peace' set a severe example to others contemplating the same. Instilling fear of a terrible and agonisingly-painful death in Roman subjects probably did help hold the 'Pax Romana'; for crucified victims were often left to decompose on the cross for all to see. A further unsettling dimension for both the crucified and the travelling public was the fact that crows often sat on the heads of victims to peck at the eyes. Perhaps the most notable crucifixion *event* was the execution of 6,000 gladiators taken from the slave Army of Spartacus after his defeat. They stretched 125 miles along the Appian Way from Capua to Rome.
By the time Jesus walked the Earth, the Romans had well-perfected the 'art' of crucifixion as we know it today. Two forms of 'the cross of crucifixion' were used by the Legions. The **Tau**

– in the shape of a **Capital T**; and the **Latin** – in the shape of a **lower-case t**. Both consisted of two parts: The **Stipe**, the *upright beam*; and the **Patibulum**, the *cross-member*.

Since the Roman Army crucified countless thousands, their no-nonsense approach to all they undertook would have ensured a practical, efficient method for the purpose. The **Tau**, being simpler, was therefore probably more commonly used because the top of the **Stipe** is in the reach of soldiers.

A new look at the whole question of Roman-style crucifixion offers greater insights into the death of Jesus. Notwithstanding the obvious fact that Roman soldiers were well practised in the *mechanics* of crucifixion, considerable effort in time and manpower would nonetheless have been required to nail and/or affix the many tens of thousands crucified over the term of the Roman Empire; if the Latin Cross was the preferred option.

The simpler and thus more likely method was to first set the upright beam – the **Stipe** – in the ground. The wooden cross-member – the *mortised* **Patibulum** weighing about 100 pounds to which the victim was affixed – was then lifted up by soldiers and fitted onto a matching tenon on the **Stipe**.

5.7.1 The Roman 'Flagrum': The 'Scourging' of "The Son Of God"

scourge *n.* **1.** A whip used to inflict punishment.

2. Any means of inflicting severe suffering, vengeance, or punishment

scourging *tr.v.* **1.** to flog.

'Scourging' commonly preceded crucifixion. It was carried out by soldiers wielding the Flagrum, a Roman whip designed to flay skin, tissue and muscle, and thus produce excruciating pain and terrible wounds. It consisted of several strips of leather into which were tied pieces of metal, nails, glass, bone and lead weights; basically anything that would cut into flesh.

> "To be crucified was to say that you were no better than a slave. You are worthy of death. And part of the crucifixion process – you might say the drama of crucifixion – was to scourge you."

> (Richard J. Hoffman, Ph.D.)

The victim was stripped of all clothing save perhaps for loin coverings, and tied by the hands to a wooden post. Two Roman soldiers would stand either side of the victim and alternate whip strokes. The severity of the flogging was largely determined by the viciousness of the soldiers. Long-practised in war and killing, soldiers of the super-efficient, well-disciplined and ruthless Roman Army were very far removed from the more squeamish nature of modern Western peoples who often require counselling as a way of coping with what are often just the simple realities of life on Earth. Since crucifixion as a punishment was common, soldiers would often experiment on the hapless victims. Dr. David Ball explains:

> "What you would expect from a Roman Flagrum would be complete tearing away of the skin down to the ribs. And this results in bruising to the inter-costal muscles, which impairs respiration ... and actually causes bruising to the lungs... And that leads to a very serious medical problem called 'pulmonary contusion'. That will lead to 'pulmonary oedema' and impaired respiration. It is a very serious injury."

In this medical-trauma analysis of 'scourging' and crucifixion, we reiterate that it is an analysis of *the suffering of Jesus*, primarily as recorded in The Bible.

Dr Ball notes that scourging a human being with the Roman Flagrum produced wounds that [are] "...so severe that it has been compared to a shotgun blast at close range."

Robert M. Norris, M.D. explains:

> "The muscles would have been torn, hanging; basically ribbons of flesh that were bleeding profusely ... deep tissues of larger vessels that can't clamp down so easily. Profuse bleeding decreases blood supply leading to hypo-bulimic shock ... not enough blood circulating around heart to profuse vital tissues; the muscles and the organs."

A prime purpose of 'scourging' was to:

> "Create a mutilated body up on the cross ... [for] ... a mutilated, visceral experience on the part of the viewers who were attending the crucifixion. ... We don't really know how Jesus was scourged. The Gospels don't give us much detail. But it's quite possible that it was fairly severe because Jesus dies within a day. And He dies before nightfall."

> (Jonathan Reed, Ph.D.)

> "He was beaten nearly to death. He was macerated. He was bruised. He had massive damage to the backside, and massive damage to the inter-costal muscles, and massive damage to the lungs and the kidneys themselves through the bruising process."

> (David Ball, M.D.)

Narration: 'When the scourging is finished, Jesus's back is an unrecognisable mass of torn and bleeding tissue. This brutal beating will dramatically affect the final hours of Jesus's life.'

5.7.2   The 'Burden' of the Cross

The present, widely accepted, notion in Christendom is that Jesus was made to carry or drag a complete **Latin Cross** weighing several hundred pounds roughly a mile to Golgotha, then nailed onto it whilst it was on the ground, both raised up together, and the Cross then positioned in a pre-prepared hole. If that *were* the true scenario, it would have taken a superhuman effort to carry or drag such a weight that distance with a body severely-weakened and already near death as a result of the torture and mutilation at the hands of the Roman soldiers ordered to 'scourge' Him.

The Bible narrative reports that 'Simon of Cyrene' was seconded to carry Jesus's Cross after His strength finally gave out.

> "I do not think it is either practical – from a Roman perspective – to have individuals carry entire crosses. Nor do I think it is likely possible as a physical feat."

> (Sarah Stroud, Ph.D.)

Experts generally agree it is more likely that Jesus would have carried only the Patibulum, which nonetheless weighed around 100 pounds – a huge weight for a badly tortured man to carry any distance.

> "For this point the victim would already be in some degree of shock due to blood loss from the scourging. So now we've put a 100 pound beam on the person's back; strapped their hands to it. And now the heart is tasked to pump even harder and harder to supply the leg muscles to get him to the execution site."
>
> (Robert M. Norris, M.D.)

Whipped up by Caiaphas and key members of The Sanhedrin, the emotional turmoil connected with the trial and sentence of Jesus would surely have wrought tumultuous agitation among those who watched Him walk His last pain-wracked mile – to Golgotha. The Bible tells us that Jesus fell under the weight of the Patibulum. Dr. Norris explains the 'medical' ramifications of such a fall.

> "The full force of His body and that 100 pound weight on the backs of His shoulders would have been centred on His chest. That slammed the heart against His breastbone, the sternum, inside. That could bruise the heart."

> "A bruised heart is a very serious injury. The muscle has been damaged, and so it tends to stretch. And as the heart is pumping, that stretch increases and you have a balloon we call an 'aneurysm'. That 'balloon' becomes thin-walled and can rupture."
>
> (David Ball, M.D.)

This type of injury is similar to chest trauma sustained in a car accident when an unrestrained driver impacts onto the steering wheel. Now bearing the added pain and trauma of a bruised heart from His fall, Jesus is forced to continue His grievous walk to his place of execution.

5.8 The 'Murder' at Golgotha

5.8.1 The 'Nailing'

> "The bio-mechanics of a crucifixion is quite interesting. It all depends very much on the angle in which you secure the limbs and all the body parts because this will determine how much physical stress will either be on the bones or connective tissue. ... The maximum stress that you can have on the tissue, on the bones, is between 40 and 60 pounds. This may cause the tissue to rip or the bones to break so that the whole system of crucifixion won't work..."
>
> (Dr. Mark Benecke.)

It was found that in tests with arms set at an angle in a crucifixion:

> "...*each* hand bears the whole weight of the body, and not *half* the body-weight for each as we might ['logically'] expect. Therefore, an average weight man will tear away from the cross if nailed through the hands."
>
> (Dr. Mark Benecke.)

Dr. Norris explains that if the nails were placed instead into the wrist, i.e., into the small bones of the wrist where there are [dense] fibrous sheaths around these bones:

> "...they would have held. The pain, however, would be excruciating because the large median nerve which provides sensation to the forearm and hand passes right through this area of the wrist."

Commenting on the 'pain factor' when the wrists are 'nailed, Dr. Ball states that:

> "The median nerve, whether it's lacerated, or whether it's impinged upon as the nail pushes against it ... it's going to be like *burning, severe pain.*"

The Gospels imply that Jesus is nailed through the hand. In the ancient Greek language, in which The Bible was originally written, the word for hand describes both the hand and the wrist. So the bony area described is where most experts believe the Romans drove the nail into Jesus's hand. They would probably not have relied on the nails alone, so also tied the arms to support the weight of the body. Dr. Norris notes:

> "The ultimate outcome in terms of how long the person survived probably was dependent in some particular way in how the feet were attached."

The feet were most likely attached in the 'stacked' position – one foot on top of the other as commonly depicted. This position, whilst encouraging a quicker death, produced excruciating pain.

> "If you place the soles of the feet flat against the upright, the individual cannot lock their knees. They have to support their weight with the thigh muscles. Or hang completely from the [hand] nails."
>
> (David Ball, M.D.)

This fiendishly torturous position made it far more challenging for the victim to breathe. Scholars of crucifixions generally do not believe that artistic portrayals in paintings and Hollywood movies depicting a wooden block under the feet of Jesus are correct. For why, after such prolonged torture, would the Romans then offer *any* victim even the smallest measure of 'comfort'?

> "There are a series of nerves that pass through the feet in that area that would cause tremendous stimulation of those sensory nerves and just [exquisite] pain from that. And every time the victim would try to rise to exhale, that would stimulate those nerves."
>
> (Robert M. Norris, M.D.)

Dr. Ball says:

> "A person nailed to the cross is going to be searching for a comfortable position. He may relieve the pain on the medial nerve and lift himself up, but he creates muscle pain. When he drops himself down he relieves the muscles but he finds the pain has recurred in the medial nerve and the shoulders."

In excruciating agony Jesus tries to find relief from the intense pain wracking every part of His body. He strives to breathe freely by pushing up on the spike driven through His feet. In doing so the exposed nerves on His cruelly-mutilated back rub on the rough-hewn post. Robert M. Norris, M.D. concurs:

"Every time He would lift Himself up on the Cross, that would drag these torn shredded tissues of the back across the rough wood of the Cross, reopening the wounds, re-stimulating the nerves in the back causing further bleeding and, again, causing tremendous pain."

Dr. Ball notes that:

"There is no comfortable position on the Cross. There is no position where He is even relatively pain-free."

Narration: 'Jesus hangs in agony. The end is near. He's beaten, dehydrated, exhausted. He's suffering from external trauma and internal injuries; all life-threatening conditions. But what ultimately kills Jesus? Today, science may have the technology to decode the ancient evidence and discover the exact cause of Jesus's death on the Cross. ... Since His arrest nine hours earlier He's been beaten and abused. His crucified body is wracked with pain as He struggles to breathe. The cruelty is clearly taking its toll. But what is the ultimate cause of Jesus's death?'

"There were so many things that were going on at the same time. Any one of them at a certain point could cause someone's death; the dehydration, the blood loss, just the severe trauma to the muscles."

(Robert M. Norris, M.D.)

Medical experts believe that Jesus's physical deterioration begins with exhaustion, for He has not slept for over twenty four hours. Moreover, since His arrest He has had nothing to eat or drink.

5.8.2   His Final Moments

"The death-process is definitely underway. ... the scourging started the process with the contused lungs, bruising to the muscles, damaged kidneys."
"I don't think that it's fair to say there is one cause of death on the cross. I think it is multi-factorial, and all of these things are taking place in a typical crucifixion."

(David Ball, M.D.)

Narration: 'His blood-loss is made worse by the constant tearing of the wounds on His back as He moves up and down on the Cross in order to breathe deeply. The loss of bodily fluids means He's probably suffering from hypo-bulimic shock; a condition in which the heart is unable to pump adequate blood to the organs, muscles and vital tissues. On top of that, decreased respiratory volume means carbon dioxide is building up in the lungs and reducing oxygen in the blood; a condition known as hypoxia. Ultimately, this could lead to suffocation.'

"He's probably becoming somewhat hypoxic at this point, Again, from the increased work of breathing, and inadequate blood volume circulating around. He is near death."

(Robert M. Norris, M.D.)

Deriving from His fall with the weight of a 100 pound Patibulum on His back, it is very probable that Jesus is suffering from 'blunt chest trauma'. 'The ensuing internal damage could easily include a bruised heart.'

"When an individual has sustained a bruise to his heart, this bruise creates a soft spot in the muscle. Every time the heart pumps, there's pressure on that soft spot that has the tendency to cause a ballooning out. Or, as we call it, an aneurysm."

(David Ball, M.D.)

Narration: 'Jesus's cardiovascular system is under enormous stress. His heart is pumping upwards of 170 beats per minute. An aneurysm puts Him at even greater risk. If left untreated it can rupture. And there's another factor that can contribute to the death of any victim on the cross.'

"The pain of crucifixion is unimaginable. ... the pain over time is so excruciating that the bodily functions give out. You die simply of pain."

(Jonathan Reed, Ph.D.)

Narration: 'Any one of these [conditions] can be fatal. But Jesus has not yet given up. According to The Bible He is able to speak despite His weakened condition.'

"He was carrying on conversations that were lucid and clear. So we know that His brain was being adequately supplied at this point with enough [oxygenated] blood."

(David Ball, M.D.)

Narration: 'After several hours, Jesus seems to know that the end has come. The Bible says that he called out His final words – and then dies.'
His final words: **"Father. Into your hands I commit my spirit."**

Dr. Ball states factually that:

"If He had died of hypo-bulimic shock – as some people say – He would have fainted. He would not have been able to holler out with a loud voice and then suddenly die."

Whilst some see asphyxiation as the cause of death, Dr Ball explains why that is very unlikely. He sagely observes that if a crucified man has: "...enough air in [his] lungs to holler out, [he] will not be in any danger of dying of asphyxiation. That cannot happen."

"That He had enough strength and enough mental clarity to cry out very effectively means to me that something catastrophic was happening. And He knew that it was happening."

(Robert M. Norris, M.D.)

Given the searching medical analysis of the final moments of Jesus's life, experts believe that the most likely cause of death is from His bruised and damaged heart. Dr. Norris explains the process: "Gradually His heart is failing. The fluids would begin to back up in the lungs, around the lungs, and actually around the outside of the heart; inside the heart sac – the pericardium."

The pericardium is a sac of fibrous tissue filled with a water-like solution that surrounds and protects the heart. Dr. Ball explains:

"With His pulse rate going to 180 or even more, He is under an enormous cardio-vascular stress load."

Dr. Ball opines that under such extreme stress, the bruised heart of Jesus ultimately ruptures. It would feel like a heart attack, and Jesus would know His death is imminent. The ruptured heart continues to beat. With each pulse, however, it pushes blood into the pericardial sac until the heart finally stops.

That is the one, single, blessing for The Son Of God in His whole unbelievable journey of horrific, agonising torture to His execution on the 'death cross' at Golgotha:

For His terrible ordeal at the hands of men is finally over.

> "You've got a heart that is ruptured. It's not functioning any more, it's not pump-ing. But you've got a pericardial sac that is under pressure. Taut."

(David Ball, M.D.)

The spear of a Roman soldier reveals the proof of Dr. Ball's medical analysis of the actual death of Jesus.

> "According to the Gospel of John, a Roman soldier takes a spear and sticks it inside Jesus to make sure that He's dead."

(Jonathan Reed, Ph.D.)

The Gospel narrative states that blood and water 'come out' from the wound. Dr. Ball explains what has taken place:

> "What you have to understand is they've gone through this pericardial sac to get to the heart. The pericardial sac is under pressure. The blood has settled. So immediately you've got this flow of blood followed by clear fluid, which is described as water in The Bible."

Narration: 'After about six hours on the Cross, Jesus Christ is dead. It's a relatively short time for crucifixion [by Roman standards], which can last for several excruciating days. Arrested on the Thursday night of the Passover holiday; by Friday morning soldiers are preparing to nail Him to the Cross. By that afternoon He will be dead.'

The final act played out both on Golgotha and for those in the Sanhedrin who actively plotted to bring about His death, was wrought by a powerful earthquake. Sufficiently strong to shatter the floor of the Temple of Jerusalem, the convulsive transfer of energy from the Earth to the great building tore asunder the heavy curtain that protected **The Holy of Holies**.

The odds of *that* particular earth-tremor occurring with such precise convergence to, *osten-sibly*, *'coincide'* with the exact moment Jesus died, would surely be in the order of millions to one. That natural event should be *proof enough* of how terribly wrong His execution was, for even the **Forces of Nature** vented their anger and fury at the *murder* of **The Son Of God**: **He Who** once Commanded *the same* to cease their 'storm-work' activity on the Sea of Galilee with the admonition: **"Peace. Be still!"**

For the Jewish race, what was once the Holiest Treasure on Earth – the *sanctuary* of which even **Moses the Law-Giver** *could not enter* on the decades-long journey to the 'promised land' – *was no longer so*. The curtain that formerly 'spiritually-symbolically' protected it, rent in two by the power of the tremor at the murder of **The Son Of God**, signified the *separation* of man from **The Almighty** – *not the opposite*. It was not a *reconciliation*, as many from 'Christian academia' will argue. The Jewish Priesthood, once Called to serve and protect that

Holy Treasure; by *their* dark deed were made *redundant*. For, shortly after, the Jewish race lost possession of The Holy of Holies and it *disappeared from history*; a *further* indication of the **singular enormity** of that particular crime.

The historical aftermath of the execution of Jesus saw develop among Christians and their Church a radical but nonetheless strange change in perception concerning the 'Latin Cross of Crucifixion'. Initially His death only reinforces the perception of the cross as an horrific tool of oppression. Yet, over time, the symbolism of crucifixion underwent an ironic transformation. Very interestingly, the documentary, **Crucifixion**, asks the most pertinent question of all in this regard.

> *"How does this implement of torture and execution become an iconic symbol of hope and salvation despite the fact that it continues on into the 20th and 21st centuries?"*

The answer is brutally logical.

A Teaching, a Church or a Movement that has **Truth** *at its core and as its* **practice** *would not, indeed* **could not**, *possibly accord such an instrument of torture the perversely altered state of reverence and even worship that the Latin Cross/Crucifix now holds for around one third of global humanity. Only a* **religion** *could bring such a thing about, for religions hold very little of* **The Pure Truth**. *Hence the unbelievable state of hate and violence between religions in the present.*

The path to that detrimental point of 'altered perceptions' probably began when the Roman Emperor Constantine became Christian after 'seeing' a vision in the sky prior to a battle. It is said that an accompanying voice told him: "In this sign you will be victorious." Believed by Christians to be the 'Latin Cross', Constantine's victory on the battlefield thenceforth set 'that' cross as 'the form of salvation' for the Church and its followers.

> "It's under Constantine's rule that the cross becomes a positive symbol for the first time. And it's a symbol of Christianity. And because of that, you can no longer use it as a tool for shameful death."
>
> (Jonathan Reed, Ph.D.)

So in the strangest of 'turnarounds', the cross, once identified with the most fearful kind of death, and an object to inspire terror in the hearts of men, is now a symbol of piety and faith which Christians now use in the shape of their churches, for their rituals, and in their art.

Christianity becomes the dominant world religion. Despite the long history of cruel torture inherent in the practice, crucifixion is almost exclusively associated with Jesus. Even though documented crucifixions are rare after the Romans, this brutal punishment nonetheless persists throughout the centuries. The crucial event of The Second World War saw Hitler's Nazi regime use this method of torture. Sarah Stroud Ph.D, notes:

> "It was a display of power. It's always a spectacle, and it's always sadistic. ...it was often used against individuals who actually posed some sort of threat or had committed a wrong against the State. [However] The use of it against individuals who were already victims or already captives and completely powerless seems especially perverse."

Even today in the Sudan/Darfur region where genocide is rampant, crucifixion is sanctioned as a method of execution. In 2002 Amnesty reported that 88 people, including two children, were sentenced to death by crucifixion. Perversely, then, it would seem; the image of Jesus's agonising death on the Cross remains one of our most powerful icons. Jonathan Reed emphasises the fact that:

> "When Christianity adopts the Cross as its key symbol, it also defines itself as a *religion* that focusses itself on suffering, and a *religion* that focusses on atonement. And so the Cross itself, maybe more so than any book written, has had a profound impact on how Christians think about their religion, and their religious experience."

Narration: 'Yet the cross and the roots of crucifixion reach back long before Jesus. He was just one of the many [countless] victims of this brutal death sentence. From ancient civilisations to modern regimes, crucifixion carries the same meaning. It's not just about killing. Crucifixion is about torture, fear and control.'

> "Crucifixion should be a *warning*. Crucifixion should make us *ask questions* about *unjust* and *horrific treatment* of other people. The cross should be a symbol that says: **Never treat someone like this!**"

> (Daniel Smith-Christopher, Ph.D.
> All emphases mine.)

The murder of The Son Of God stands as the most heinous crime in the history of the world, for He came to lift humanity out of the depths to which it had *voluntarily* sunk. Human ego and religious power had subverted Spiritual Truth and Law. Proclaimed by the Old Testament Prophets, the subversion of It resulted in a rigid dogma that wrought suffering for many, and meant that Jesus had to come to Earth to Light the Way back to **The Truth**.

The later Messengers of His Truth encountered the same blind perversity. The explanations of The Truth which they were called to Teach to the peoples among whom they were incarnated, became – in short order after their deaths – just religions.

Historically, have we human beings ever really revered **Envoys** from **The Light** or, indeed, **Its** Prophets? Almost all suffered from human perversity and mockery, *when* they proclaimed *on Earth*. If stripped down to 'bare bones', it is the *adulation of human beings by human beings* that has long-reigned supreme in the world. Today, the rock stars, sports stars, movie stars and the fashion models etc., are the *things* of adulation, even reverence.

That being the case; apart from the regular 'Easter Shopping Guide', what do we invariably see advertised as a *primary enticement* for the 'Easter holiday period' the Christian West celebrates? Yes, there are the Church services. And there are re-enactments of His Crucifixion which, *in no way whatsoever for the 'participants'*, could possibly give *any* degree of understanding of the terrible pain and suffering that The Son Of God had to endure at the hands of blind, religious fools. In truth, it is a *perverse mockery* to re-enact His torturous suffering.[12]

So: On every anniversary of His hideous execution, the one thing that probably most Western Christian children look forward to are chocolate eggs, laid – in the strangest, impossible concept – by a rabbit; the wealth-producing 'Easter Bunny'. Is that surely not the most perverse distortion of a crucial date that all Christians should *fully understand* in its *true* meaning? For in its *yet-to-be* rapidly-closing spiritual reciprocity, the long-reaching outworking is one of menacing and *growing* portent for global Christendom.

---

[12]It is something akin to the 'annual fast' that overfed Western children in communal 'rah-rah, jolly-jolly' groups take part in for *just* 40 hours to *somehow* gain *understanding* of the plight of children so starved that, for many, **death** is **their** outcome. Unlike the 'empathists' who receive a hearty meal and congratulations at the end of their 40 hour 'famine ordeal'.

Of course, it's all just fun for the children, isn't it? That is what Western society has determined as being suitable for Easter. Well, the end-cleansing – *already upon us and increasing in scope and scale* – will sweep that and every other kind of appalling distortion aside and away for all time; along with all those who cling to aberrant ideas which distort **The Truth**.

A dangerous aberration stemming from the Crucifixion of Jesus centres on the so-called 'Christian Cross of Salvation'. The *shape* of the Latin Cross produces the *form* of a "sword". As a 'belief-token' or symbol *ostensibly* declaring that by His death on the Cross **The Son of God** took away their sins and that of the world; this terrible and appalling *Christian distortion* of the execution of Christ means that the wrongly-revered Crucifix 'spiritually forms' a **"Sword of Judgement"** for all who wear, revere or display it!

If Christians, particularly, do not believe thus, yet still say they follow the Teachings of Jesus; then how do the two thousand million that make up global Christendom reconcile His warning to the world? In the truly strangest of ironies, He – **A Part of The Godhead** – was perversely accused of *blasphemy* by Caiaphas and others of the ruling Sanhedrin for *being* What He *actually* Was and Is: **The Son Of God**. Yet He was nonetheless executed.

Since an exponential factor can be readily observed in all events now, let us *restate* the answer of Jesus to His Disciples when asked what the end-time would be like. His reply is chilling. From Matthew 24:21-22:

> "...for there shall then be *wide-spread affliction*, such as has *not been known* since the beginning of the world *until now*, no, nor will *ever* be known again. And if those times were *not* cut short, *not a man would be saved*".

Centuries before Jesus came to Earth to admonish humankind to obey **The Law** if they wished to *live and return home*; Isaiah, 24:5-6, 'the great Prophet and Servant', had long warned so.

(Fenton both. All emphases mine.)

> "The 'Earth' also is defiled under the inhabitants thereof; because they have
> <u>transgressed</u> the Laws,
> <u>changed</u> the decrees,
> <u>broken</u> the everlasting covenant.
> Therefore has the curse devoured the 'Earth', and those that dwell therein *are desolate*:
> therefore the inhabitants of the 'Earth' are *burned*[13] and *few men left*."

Now you, Christian believer, and perhaps even you, "Bible scholar"; but certainly all who live tremulously in piety in the belief that The Son of God, sent down to Earth by The Creator of all that is good to bring The Living Word to a base and evil humanity: Now that you *better-understand* the **true** horror and suffering of He Whom *you* profess to follow; where in His admonition or that of the great Prophet, Isaiah, do you find the sure salvation of two billion Christians? It is *arrant nonsense*. It is, in truth, *a dangerous death-delusion*.

Do you honestly believe that The Son of God went willingly to an horrific death to save *you* from *your* personal sins? Do you really believe that the Perfect Justice of God is displayed there; that an innocent man should be put to death for *the wrongdoing and evil of others*?

---

[13]The term, 'burned' – describing a recurring theme of End-time destruction that numerous Bible 'scholars' have puzzled over for many centuries – *in this case* does not refer to fire in the ordinary sense. The Scripture pointedly states that only the 'inhabitants' of the Earth are 'burned', *not* the Earth itself. A full and detailed explanation can be read in Chapter 12: **The Two Sons Of God**: Sub; **Destruction by "Fire"**.

As we have often stressed, such an injustice is not even accepted in earthly courts of law. If it were, imagine the outcry – from all of you especially. So why and how can human beings who proudly call themselves Christians [i.e., *followers of, and believers in, Christ*] accept a notion that such a thing would be acceptable to **The Creator Himself: He Who is Perfect Love — but also Perfect Justice?**

If you truly believe that such an *aberrant* tenet would be acceptable to **The Almighty**, then you must also logically accept the notion that the group of Roman soldiers who actually carried out His Crucifixion *were blessed for all time*, and would *follow Jesus into Paradise upon their death*. And what about Judas? Why has sainthood not been conferred upon him? Surely he, too, must be included among the especially blessed – even before that particular group of Roman soldiers – *for is he not the key player in this ridiculous and infantile scenario*?

> If the death of Jesus was a necessary sacrifice blessed by God, then that is the *only* logical conclusion for you to draw. For if you do *not* believe that either Judas or the soldiers *were* so blessed in that way, **then your whole absurd Christian ethos centred round "His necessary sacrifice" fails utterly.**

Notwithstanding the pure truth of that statement, if you yet *still seriously believe such a thing*, **then do not hide behind 2,000 years of Earth-time to shield you from *that* most insidiously-evil event.** Instead, have the inner courage to put yourselves in the place of the small group of executioners at His Crucifixion and *actively take part* in the murder of The One Whom you profess to believe in. Be part of that Roman squad on that terrible day that you nauseously commemorate so wrongly: **Black Friday.**

Help to lay the cruelly-tortured and bleeding body of **The Son of God** on that rough and splintered "cross of death". Feel **His** blood spattering on *your* skin – for there are no niceties such as rubber gloves to protect *your delicate hands*. Next, take up the hammer. And with it, drive the nails through **His hands** into the wood of the crossbeam. Ensure, however, that you do it *correctly* so that the weight of **His** especial body will not tear *His once-healing hands* away from those terrible spikes when that dark, death-cross is raised.

And as you 'drive those nails home', remember to look into His dying, pain-wracked eyes and say to Him:

> *"I nail you to this cross because in my deed I prove my great Christian love for you because you came to die for me and my sins. Even though you have already suffered so much, I offer you yet more pain and torture. I know you will understand and will one day welcome me into your Kingdom because I have now proved my faith to you by helping you to die on this cross."*

How foolish a belief. How utterly absurd.

Such a belief is tantamount to idolatry of the worst kind, but self-idolatry – of human beings – and not of reverence and worship of **The Most High** or of He Who was and is a Part out of **Him**.

JESUS: The SON OF GOD; designated as both **The Word Of God** and **The Love Of God**; that is who you symbolically murder each time you tremulously "...thank 'Him' for dying for *your* sins".

Even the words of **The Bible** – that *especial* Work which you hold up to the world as **The Living Word Of God** – condemns that terrible act in no uncertain terms. Peter, the Apostle designated by Jesus as "the rock" upon which His Teachings could be built, "tells it like it is". After receiving "Power from On High" at Pentecost and speaking in the various dialects of the region, the crowd that had gathered accused the Apostles of being drunk. Peter countered with the following:

> "Men of Israel! Listen to these statements: Jesus the Nazarene, a Man pointed out as from God by powers, and wonders, and signs, which God did through Him amongst you, as you yourselves know; *having betrayed*, you *murdered Him by crucifixion* through *lawless hands*..."

> (Acts 2:22-23, Fenton.
> All emphases mine.)

What happened next? The words are certainly clear enough; *betrayed, murdered*, through *lawless* hands! Was there great cheering that they were *saved* by His "death on the Cross"? That is the certainly the *seemingly* unbreakable belief amongst latter-day Christians. Yet, what do we later read as "The Effect of the Discourse" of Peter? In Acts 2:37, the exchange between him and the gathered crowd shows that at least some there had recognised the wrong in *that* Crucifixion.

> Now on hearing it, they were *stung to the heart*, and said to Peter and the rest of the apostles, "Men, brothers, *what shall we do*?"
> But Peter said to them: "*Change your minds*..."

Quite clearly, if they *had* been pleased and *at peace* with 'the Crucifixion', they would not have replied in that way. The recognition for at least *some* there had finally hit home, for they were "...stung to the heart...", did not know what to do, and were now *afraid*.

As it once did to that fearful crowd then: When the horrific realisation finally dawns on latter-day Christendom that such beliefs are so *illogical and wrong* that they border on a kind of *religious insanity*; it will be among you Christians, primarily, that a very large measure of the "great wailing and gnashing of teeth" will occur. What will you say or do then?

In conclusion: Let us, in quiet contemplation, *seriously think upon* a singularly-poignant "poem" about the life of *this* Son, **Jesus**; perhaps the greatest radical to have ever set physical foot on Earth. As we unequivocally state, however, *will not do so again*, for **He** is **The One** Who *returned* to **The Father**. Yet Whose very Words – from out of **Divinity** Itself – many were "called" to disseminate amongst the world's people. Illustrated in the following poem is an unknown author's salute and great love for Jesus and His Highest and most Noble form of **Radicalism – Perfect Love!**

Radically noble in the sense that He was **prepared to accept death on the Cross if that was the only way by which He could anchor the Truth of His Teaching in the consciousness of humankind for all time. Jesus – The Word and Love of God** and surely the most innocent of all – even though suffering the grossest indignities until finally succumbing to the brutal act of murder perpetrated against Him, *yet still offered up the greatest prayer of intercession ever for the senseless blind who committed that atrocity.*

His noble prayer thus stands as an indictment against those who murdered Him then, *and against those today* who still very wrongly believe that His painful and brutal death on *that* Cross could somehow be sanctified and Divinely Blessed by An Almighty God as some kind of loving act of propitiatory sacrifice to cleanse the evil and sin of an *undeserving* humanity.

The very words of the prayer itself stand in rightful accusation against such an evil distortion of the great and incomprehensible Love of The Creator.

"Father forgive them, for they <u>know not what they do</u>!"

Thus: ***They did the <u>wrong</u> thing***.

Through an anonymous yet spiritually-insightful poet, the pure and ennobled form of the Christ's Mission rings down through the centuries and is **baptised in its own unequivocal message of sublime radiance and great Spiritual Power!**

5.9   One Solitary Life

Here is a man
who was born of Jewish parents
the child of a peasant woman...
He never wrote a book.
He never held an office.
He never owned a home.
He never had a family.
He never went to college.
He never put foot
inside a big city.
He never travelled two hundred
miles from the place
where He was born.

He never did one of the things
that usually accompany greatness.
He had no credentials but Himself...
While still a young man
the tide of popular opinion
turned against Him.
His friends ran away.
One of them denied Him...
He was nailed to a cross
between two thieves.

His executioners gambled for
the only piece of property
he had on earth... His coat.
When He was dead
He was taken down;
and laid in a borrowed grave
through the pity of a friend.

Nineteen wide centuries
have come and gone
and He is the centrepiece
of the human race and the leader of
the column of progress.
I am far within the mark
when I say that all the armies
that ever marched,
and all the navies
that were ever built...
have not affected the life of man
upon earth as powerfully as has that

One Solitary Life!

6
STIGMATA

Crucial Imperative No 6:

That there are certain and precise *Inviolable Laws* which govern *all life* and to which *all* human decisions and processes *are subject*. In their inherent Perfection these Laws are, in their perfect outworking, **Absolute**. And are therefore **Immutable**; and thus **Unchangeable**!

(Author.)

The bulk of this Chapter is sourced from the Booklet: "Stigmatised, A Necessary Clarification of the Phenomenon of Stigmata" by Mr. R. M. Duraisamy who wrote it to explain Stigmata and related aspects of Christ's life and death for Indian Christians, primarily. The ***singular and crucially-vital point about Stigmata revealed in his essay*** – to our knowledge not thus far recognised and/or written about – is given "life" here too. This profound insight is so simple and revealing in its "conceptual-truth reality" that it is difficult to understand why it seems not to have found its "voice" a very long time before now.

Whilst this very telling revelation should bring forth exclamations of joy and a sense of spiritual freedom from Christians, particularly, the opposite is probably more true. Its *explosive nature* would surely be regarded by religious authorities as being especially dangerous to their controlling dogma. In other words ***the actual reason why Stigmata does occur*** is as stupendous as it is severely indictful against all of global humanity, not just Christians.

This edited version of the complete text revisits subjects examined earlier in the book, in particular the previous Chapter. However, because the phenomenon of Stigmata requires serious attention, we deem it necessary and prudent to include, where relevant, previous analyses around the life and death of Jesus, especially.

In addition; included in *this* particular Chapter/text are crucial scientific analyses sourced from Ian Wilson's book, "The Turin Shroud". The contentious debate surrounding the "image" on "The Shroud" requires scientific input to balance the singular faith/belief aspect of global Christendom. For *that* "Image" has precise resonance to the perhaps equally-contentious phenomenon of Stigmata.

So, why the marks of Stigmata? Why should such marks appear on anyone? Why, historically, on the relatively few? Why not on everyone? Why, on particular individuals, were they so accentuated over a long and painful period of time? And why was one such Stigmatic, in perhaps the most celebrated and documented case of all, eventually shut off from the world by the Catholic Church?

A favoured method of execution by the Romans, crucifixion accounted for the deaths of many hundreds of thousands of prisoners, dissidents, mutineers, slaves, criminals and others over the long time-period that the Roman Empire ruled. Yet the signs of Stigmata are exclusively associated with just **one crucified individual**, not the uncounted numbers who died that way. That must surely be regarded as a mystery. Or is it? Stigmata, whilst not a "Bible Mystery", certainly fits into the category of a "post-Bible mystery". Therefore, can light be shed on this most unusual and scientifically-problematic phenomenon? Indeed, it can!

The occurrence of Stigmata is a phenomenon that is rather rare, yet is of immense portent for all mankind. Stigmata traces its genesis to an event two thousand years ago when a lone Preacher came to Earth with His Message of Divine Love, Justice and Salvation – for whomever was willing to accept It.

That event was the Crucifixion of Jesus!

For His trouble He was unjustly crucified. He was made to suffer a most excruciatingly-painful death on a wooden cross; at that time, as we know, a common method of execution!

Those who have since been reported as bearing the marks of the Crucifixion are said to have been "stigmatised". The marks of Stigmata, of course, are the wound-marks that Christ Himself bore at the time of His murder. They are the wounds arising from the crown of thorns on His head, the nail-piercings in His hands and feet, and the spear-wound in His side. This is aside from all the whip-lashes on His body, for before He was crucified He was mercilessly whipped by Roman soldiers. They had no idea Who they were torturing!

The reasons for His execution were purely political, thus very far from any *spiritual* considerations. The leaders of the "churches" of that time – or rather the Jewish scholars and priestly dignitaries – recognised that their power over the people was waning. Already for a long time they had had to withstand the erosion of their political control through the domination of Rome. Now they saw how their spiritual control was also being taken away, but through the power of one man who was able to suffuse the masses with a true longing for God; something that the priests themselves had been unable to do. The religious control they had formerly exerted was shown for what it was – a tradition-based system of religious dogma that was essentially lifeless and provided no genuine understanding of Spiritual Truth; of Creation-Law!

> **That is why Jesus came to Earth.** It was to set humanity *free* from narrow *religious* interpretations that could not possibly *permit the ascent* of we human beings back to our true home of **Spiritual Origin**.

The Romans on the other hand did not seem to be overly concerned about the agitation attributed to Jesus. When confronted by a question as to whether one should pay one's taxes to Rome – a question deliberately intended to trick Him into saying something seditious against Rome; Matthew (22:21, Fenton) recounts Jesus's simple answer:

"Return," He then told them, "Caesar's own to Caesar; and God's dues to God!"

Such stern reprimands did not sit well with the Jewish Sanhedrin, but they could not use any of His statements against Him at that time. As long as Jesus did not oppose the paying of taxes to Caesar and did not stir up any revolt against Rome, there could be no grounds for taking Him before the Roman Governor to be tried.

Only when they learned that His followers believed Him to be "The Son of God" could they then distort this fact to their advantage. Consequently, lies were fabricated that He deliberately intended to overthrow Roman rule there and proclaim Himself "King of the Jews". This was the spur the Sanhedrin needed to insist that the Roman Governor, Pontius Pilate, place Jesus on trial. However, Pilate found there were no charges to answer. John, in his Gospel, (18:38, Fenton) intimates that Pilate's soul was so moved that he asked of Jesus the age-old question:

"What is Truth?"

According to the Biblical narrative, Pilate bluntly told the crowd that in his opinion Jesus was innocent. The Jewish leaders, however, wanted Him out of the way. In certain situations – in this case, the Passover – a protocol existed between Rome and the Jewish authority that allowed for the release of a prisoner in exchange for another condemned to death. Jewish religious leaders demanded that right and chose the release of Barabbas. Jesus was to be crucified. The Roman Governor had no choice but to acquiesce. He, however, washed his hands in front of the crowd to signify that he considered Jesus innocent.

Thus, one of the most singularly-cruel punishments that could ever befall a human being, let alone a *true Messenger of God*, was perpetrated. Christ therefore being *The Son of God*, how much greater would the *reciprocal effect* of the very Laws of Creation be for all those responsible for that evil crime?

Unfortunately, the same principle applies today in the general reaction of nearly all churches and religious organisations to any genuine Truth-bringer. Afraid they will lose their power over their followers should someone enter their congregation with true enlightenment, they strive to do everything they can, either overtly or covertly, to discredit the new knowledge or destroy the person's reputation. And in the past, to even eliminate the "troublemaker" altogether if possible!

The evil happening two thousand years ago was a most unfortunate outcome for all of mankind. Christ was killed because of the jealousy, fear and hatred of the *priests of that time*. Most Christians, however, would like to see in this a higher guiding Hand driving those events in order to provide for mankind a propitiatory sacrifice for the forgiveness of all sins. However, such beliefs contradict the natural Law of Sowing and Reaping, of Karma, which is also the Law of Love and strictest Justice. Therefore it is illogical and foolish to believe such a thing.

As we have previously explained in Chapter 3, that Law is one of the most supreme in Creation. It returns to each person exactly what he deserves, without any deviation, and contains the *ultimate* reason as to why there is so much suffering in the world today. The Creator, in His Eternal Perfection, does not intervene in the operation of this Law, because The Law is Perfect in its inviolable and *automatic* outworking!

In this regard, we state "The Supreme Premise". It is the ultimate standard for questioning any aspect of faith. This Premise is beautifully summarised in one single, simple sentence:

God Exists and He is Perfect in Every Way!

This very Perfection, on its own *precludes* the possibility of such a propitiatory sacrifice for mankind. For it would mean that many would be afforded a place in Heaven at absolutely no cost, with no *personal* effort at development. There would thus be the potential for "double standards" and therefore also imperfections, which are absolutely out of the question in anything instituted by The Almighty.

For those who would still like to maintain the Christian doctrine, we refer to a Parable given by Jesus Himself:

> There was a householder who planted a vineyard, and set a hedge around it, and dug a wine press in it, and built a tower, and let it out to tenants, and went into another country. When the season of fruit drew near, he sent his servants to the tenants, to get his fruit; and the tenants took his servants and beat one, killed another, and stoned another. Again he sent other servants, more than the first; and they did the same to them. Afterward he sent his son to them, saying, "They will respect my son." But when the tenants saw the son, they said to themselves, "This is the heir; come, let us kill him and have his inheritance." And they took him and cast him out of the vineyard, and killed him.
>
> (Matthew 21:33-39)

It is very clear from this parable that the landlord *did **not** send his son to be killed*! He sent his son in the hope that the tenants would treat him better than they had treated the servants he had sent out beforehand to collect the rent. It was an expectation on the landlord's part, a hope that they would **heed his son** instead. But this hope was not fulfilled because of fear on the part of the tenants.

In this parable, Jesus unveiled the entire happening of His own Earth-life, as well as that of The Son of Man, Who He promised would come at the end-time for the Judgment! God the Father sent Jesus to "collect the rent" from humanity, essentially demanding from humanity stern adherence to The Laws that God had instituted in the whole of Creation. For this purpose He had to teach how to live according to these Laws. His Commandments to love God and love one's neighbour clearly give us everything we need to live according to The Laws, provided that we understand His words correctly!

Out of His Infinite Love, God thus sent Jesus as the Messiah of Salvation, hoping He would be listened to, so that "...whosoever believeth in Him shall not perish, but have everlasting life." (John 3:16) To believe *in* Christ, however, simply means *to believe Him*, to absorb the Word of Truth that He offers us and transform it into deed so that, gradually, we may purify ourselves. Or, rather, so that we may wash ourselves clean of all our former guilt! But God's wish for mankind was *not* fulfilled because ***instead of accepting His Son, we crucified Him***!

Thus the symbol of Christendom has become a wooden cross to which a murdered Saviour, depicted as wearing little more than a loincloth and a crown of the sharpest thorns, is crucified. His head drooping to one side, blood streaming down His lifeless countenance from the crown of thorns, and out of His hands, feet and side. But this is no cross of salvation; rather is it *a cross of suffering*, a cross of death, which, in an accusing way, symbolises: **A sword of Judgment!**

It is very important to understand that, historically, the Crucifixion of Christ is perhaps the most unique ever recorded. No other is known to have followed such a sequence of events. For instance, the uncountable thousands crucified over centuries did not generally have crowns of thorns placed on their heads. And in most cases, those sentenced to crucifixion took such a long time to die that soldiers broke their legs in order to hasten the death process. But in the case of Christ, it is recorded that they did not need to do so, because He had already departed the physical body. In addition, a soldier had to pierce His side with a spear in order to verify that Christ really had died!

Two thieves were crucified along with Jesus. Classical and contemporary paintings often depict them on smaller crosses, one on either side of Jesus. Below these three wooden crosses stood a howling mob who were mocking the crucified Christ. "If thou be the Son of God, come down from the Cross", they jeered, not realising the spiritual karmaic processes that were already underway – processes which would eventually return to them the fruit of all their evil tenfold, as per the "whirlwind constant". One of the thieves, despite the excruciating pain of his own crucifixion, also challenged Christ: "If thou be the Son of God, save thyself and us!"

The other thief, however, rebuked the first, acknowledging that *they* were crucified because they had actually *committed* a crime, whereas Christ was *innocent* and thus *wrongly* condemned. On the cross, despite his pain, this second thief *acknowledged* the terrible injustice and besought Jesus to remember him in His Father's Kingdom. That transforming confession and the recognition of all his personal guilt, coupled with the intense suffering of the crucifixion-process became, for that second thief, the instant purification of *all* his former wrong-doing. In that single moment all his past transgressions were *completely atoned for and expiated* and, moreover, *without* the slightest deviation in the immutable and inviolable operation of **The Law of Reciprocal Action**.

For him, and *him alone in that moment*, therefore, Luke [23:43] records that Christ spoke the following words:

"Truly, I say to you, today you will be with me in Paradise."

The thief who mocked Christ, however, spiritually bound himself much more decisively in the returning reciprocal karma, for he did not take the opportunity to completely redeem himself like the second thief.[1]
Because they took a long time to die, the legs of both thieves were broken to hasten their death. *Jesus, however, exited His body quickly.* Thus there was no need to break *His* legs.

In our discussions on the "Death Process" in a later Chapter, we note the fact that a spirit that has striven after only material things is more tightly bound to the Earth after death. Binding oneself to matter makes the death process much more difficult than it need be. One who is not so bound to matter, however, will not have to experience such a death struggle. Thus an incarnated Part out of God, and even a truly enlightened spirit, will not be bound to the Earth at the moment of death. It is because of this fact that Christ exited His physical body far more quickly than was expected by His executioners!

When the time came to hasten their deaths, the Roman soldiers could not believe He had died. To ensure that such was the case, one thrust his spear into Christ's side whereupon blood and water gushed out from His side.

But John, the Disciple of Jesus, [John 19:36], in his account of Christ's Death, recorded that:

For these things took place that the scripture might be fulfilled, "Not a bone of him shall be broken."

From these explanations, it should be clear to all that The Crucifixion of Jesus was, indeed, historically *singularly-unique*. It was one, moreover, that seems not to have been repeated since that time!
Contrary to the assertions circulated in many quarters, the record clearly shows that the physical body of Christ could *not* possibly have survived such a Crucifixion. The fact that He exited His physical body quickly means that the connecting cord between Him and the body would have been severed instantly, thereby totally precluding the possibility that He could have

---

[1]The reader should take careful note of the events that took place around and between those three crucified men. For the phenomenon of Stigmata had its genesis there that day.

returned to His body to re-activate it – as He had done for the dead whom He called back to life.[2]

We now know that once the connecting cord between the soul and body is completely severed, there is no possibility of a so-called *physical* resurrection in that way. This is totally impossible because it would mean that God's Perfect Laws of Nature would have to be called into question. And we know from "The Supreme Premise" that it cannot be thus. Because Jesus was not an "ordinary being", He would have exited the body far more quickly than any human, thus completely severing the connection between His inner core and the material body. So here, once again, we face the irrefutable fact that:

Jesus Christ did not rise from the tomb – in His earthly body!

That which The Bible records as His Resurrection was a *spiritual event*, like much else depicted in that especial Book. As we have explained in the Chapter about His life and death, it was His *ethereal* body – different from the gross material body He previously bore – in which He later appeared to the Disciples. This was why they did not initially recognise Him, as is written in The Bible. Had it been Christ *resurrected physically* – in his original body – they would have recognised Him immediately!

Naturally, His ethereal body also bore the wound-marks, i.e. the Stigmata. For mankind's crime against Him also had *ethereal ramifications*. It was because of this that one of His Disciples, Thomas, was able to thus *ethereally feel* the wounds in Christ's ethereal body, and thereby convince himself that it was indeed *the resurrected Christ!*

6.1   The Turin Shroud

The most recent scientific findings concerning the Turin Shroud – the Shroud in which Jesus was stated to have been later wrapped in – actually confirm everything that has been written and said on the subject of Christ's death. It was originally thought that this Shroud was a complete hoax, especially since the scientific world had ostensibly dated the fabric of the Shroud to the middle of the second millennium. However, in early 2005, one of the scientists from that panel – just a few weeks before his death – testified that the part of the fabric they had dated was actually patchwork that had been cleverly added to fix worn-out parts of the Shroud, and that the Shroud itself could be anywhere between 1500 and 3000 years old!

The scientific world has essentially concluded that the Shroud was indeed once used to cover a body that *had* been crucified in *exactly the same manner* that Christ Himself had been. However, scientists cannot verify that *this* Shroud was in fact the one used to wrap Jesus's body shortly after His death. This is quite understandably the natural limit of science, which relies far too heavily on empirical evidence without at the same time exercising the power of the *spiritual intuition*. Nevertheless, we should not ascribe any blame to the "Shroud scientists" who have done the world a great service by presenting the results of their analyses.

The "Stigmata-wounds" are clearly distinguishable on the Turin Shroud, along with the "spiritually-serene" face equally-clearly imprinted like a photograph on the fabric. Even though marking this Shroud as a sacred memento of Christ's Life, it is more especially one of His death. Since only Christ is recorded as having had a death that exactly matches the scientific analyses of the Turin Shroud, it can be concluded that the Shroud of Turin is most likely the very Shroud in which the body of Jesus *was* wrapped!

Moreover, the mystery surrounding the *seemingly* strange but defining imprint of His physical features on the Shroud need not be deemed a mystery at all. The physical body, having served

---

[2]See full explanations in relevant Chapters about the "Death Process" and the "Silver Cord" of The Bible.

Christ as the 'cloak' He wore for His lifetime on Earth, would have been so suffused with His radiant power that, even after His Death, it could have "burned" into the Shroud in which His body was wrapped. In this case, the residual radiation emanating from the body would have suffused the fabric of the Shroud with the body's features! Thus it is a question here of a "residual radiation-process", which resulted in the imprint of His physical features on the Shroud. And that is precisely why science cannot yet come to any final conclusion as to exactly *how* the Shroud was imprinted, because the process was an *ethereal* one, **generated and driven by the Divine Power that had come to Earth in Christ**!

> "The obvious question is how a genuine dead body, cold in the tomb, could produce some kind of burning or radiance sufficient to scorch cloth, acting in so controlled a manner that it dissolved and fused blood-flows onto the cloth, yet created at the same time the perfect impression of a human body. ...something along those lines appears to be the only explanation."

> (The Turin Shroud, Ian Wilson.
> Pages 279-80)

The effect that the Hiroshima bomb produced at the moment of detonation, e.g., the 'prints of shadows that had been cast by its light', and a few vague 'human silhouettes', gave credence to a radiative-process being responsible for the image on the Shroud. On pages 280-1, Ian Wilson writes:

> "The Shroud was ... seemingly scorched from within rather than from without, and by a process of necessity far more controlled than the blast from an atomic bomb. ...the impression is inescapable that rather than a substance, some kind of force seems to be responsible for the image. ... Whatever formed the image was powerful enough to project it onto the linen from a distance of up to four centimetres (according to Jumper and Jackson), yet gentle enough not to cause distortion in areas where there would have been direct contact.
> The idea, then, of some form of thermonuclear flash being the force in question is obviously more than idle speculation.
> ...whatever caused the image must have been some extremely high intensity, short duration burst, acting evenly upward and downward. Thermal chemist Ray Rogers of the Los Alamos Scientific Laboratory [actively involved in the testing of the Shroud], [used the words], 'flash photolysis' [in] a mere millisecond of time."

We know that The Gospels explicitly describe Jesus as 'a man with a power', a power specifically recorded as being drawn from Him; and a man who worked miracles. From pages 282-3: The Turin Shroud. [Parenthetic addition mine.]

> "It was perhaps a manifestation of this power which took place at the Transfiguration – the extraordinary incident described by three Gospel writers when, on a high mountain, the aspect of Jesus's face changed and He appeared in brilliant light, his clothing 'dazzlingly white' and 'as lightning'." ...

> "Even from the limited available information, a hypothetical glimpse of the power operating at the moment of creation of the Shroud's image may be ventured. In the darkness of the Jerusalem tomb the dead body of Jesus lay, unwashed, covered in blood, on a stone slab. Suddenly, there is a burst of mysterious power from it. In that instant, the blood dematerializes, dissolved perhaps by the flash, while its image and that of the body becomes indelibly fused onto the cloth, preserving for posterity a literal 'snapshot' of the [spiritual] Resurrection."

We would aver that the Transfiguration of Jesus described by His Disciples points not to any element of ecstatic religious fervour on their part, but to a Creation-Law event given only to human beings sufficiently worthy to receive such an experience. Science really needs to open itself to 'forces' and 'processes' that will *never* be found in earthly universities and laboratories. Pope Benedict XVI's Address early in the book correctly challenges empirical science to "wake up" to a lawful truth. It is one that would benefit science most of all. Perhaps very especially in this case.

> "Modern scientific reason quite simply has to accept the rational structure of matter and the correspondence between *our spirit and the prevailing rational structures of nature as a given*, on which its methodology has to be based. Yet the question why this has to be so, is a *real* question, and one which has to be remanded by the natural sciences *to other modes and planes of thought* – to philosophy and theology."

A human spirit, even the most enlightened one, would not be able to leave behind such features on a cloth on exiting from the physical body in the death process, because spiritual power does not possess that requisite level of radiation. We must understand that the spiritual is a quite different species from **The Divine**, which latter is **Of God Alone**. For this very reason, therefore, no human being is Divine or bears a part of The Divine within.

Given that empirical technology will probably never advance sufficiently to pronounce conclusive proclamations on these kinds of non-material events and processes, perhaps it is time for science to 'intuitively-conclude' that the "**Being**" around Whom this Shroud was wrapped, was not a mere 'human-spiritual', *but came from "The Divine"*.

Numerous Prophets, Called ones, Messengers and Truth-bringers have been sent by GOD for many thousands of years. The *singularly-unique phenomenon* of the "Turin Shroud", however, has direct resonance with just **one particular Bringer of The Truth**. We should therefore ask ourselves the deeper questions as to why this is so, and not hold solely to just scientifically observable facts. It is the purpose of science to *assist* in this, but we cannot use scientific answers as the only basis for any judgment here. As Pope Benedict XVI has publicly stated, empirical science must open itself to a very different and ultimately greater reality. The *sole* basis for the search for true and final answers, however, can only lie in the knowledge of **Creation-Law**.

From the four Gospels in The Bible we have the accounts or testimonies of Christ's followers, and in the Turin Shroud *we have visible proof of Christ's identity and the wounds He bore*. How, then, do we account for the phenomenon of *people becoming stigmatised*, and who therefore have to bear the wounds of Christ?

This is a question which both Christians and non-Christians need to seriously think about, for it is surely not without especial reason that this phenomenon actually *does* take place among certain individuals. In permitting such an event, Nature is clearly trying to tell us something of crucial significance. The very fact that Stigmata does occur, even if only occasionally, means that such an event does *not* overstep *inviolable* Laws of Nature!

6.2   Stigmatics

The occurrence of Stigmata itself cannot be disputed for there are, documented quite clearly, scientific accounts of the phenomenon. Hundreds of "stigmatised" individuals have been studied over centuries, and in more recent times documentaries have been made about them. The actual phenomenon is something that especially makes non-believers in Christ rather uncomfortable, for they then have to reckon with the possibility of something extremely special about

Christ Himself. Precisely because particular human beings are compelled to bear His crucifixion wounds, it is vitally important to delve deeply into it. In order to therefore recognise and understand that there really is very much more to it all than religious hysteria and fanaticism, a deeper, more intuitive probe should long since have been undertaken.

We are, of course, only referring to true Stigmata, not those other documented cases of hypnotically-induced Stigmata, or Stigmata produced as a consequence of over-zealous fervour. Genuine Stigmata occurs where the person involved suddenly develops the crucifixion wounds, without any prompting from auto-suggestion or similar stimulation. Although these wounds have been known to be inconsistent at times, e.g. in slightly different places for different people, these diverse manifestations are all immediately representative of one common happening: **The Crucifixion!**

History has recorded their names for all to know. Individuals like St. Francis of Assisi (1186-1226), St. Catherine de Ricci (1522-1589) in former times right up to relatively more recent persons like Padre Pio (1887-1968) and Therese Neumann (1898-1962), as well as persons still alive today like Giorgio Bongiovanni (1963).[3] For the purpose of this discussion, however, we will focus on one particular Stigmatic. Her life on Earth was linked – in the strangest and subtlest way – with the fate of India in the first instance, and that of the rest of the world in the second!

That person was *Therese Neumann* of Konnersreuth, Germany! The key person with whom her spiritual path was linked was the spiritual teacher from India, Sri Paramahansa Yogananda! [The reader should really strive to absorb the following explanations concerning Therese Neumann, particularly, for the events surrounding the meeting between her and Sri Paramahansa Yogananda *are unprecedented in terms of what <u>should</u> have developed* for a very large portion of global humanity then, and subsequently for humankind's *collective* future.]

In 1935, Sri Yogananda perceived that his spiritual master, Sri Yukteswar, was calling him back home to India. At that time, Sri Yogananda was in California, having established the "Self-Realization Fellowship". Whilst enroute to India, he felt "to make a pilgrimage to Bavaria" to see Therese Neumann. In his autobiography he cited some fairly well-known facts about her.

She was born on Good Friday 1898, and when twenty years old was injured in an accident and became blind and paralysed. In 1923 her sight was restored, ostensibly as a result of prayer to St. Therese of Lisieux, and later her paralysis also disappeared. In 1926 she received the Stigmata on her head, breast, hands and feet. Every Friday she experienced the Passion of Christ and suffered all of His own agony in her body. After World War II, however, she no longer experienced the Passion every Friday,[4] but only on some specific sacred days of the year. Although she only spoke German, she would go into a trance on the days of her passion and utter words that have since been identified as ancient Aramaic, the language of Christ's time, and would even speak Hebrew or Greek at times.

Sri Yogananda's meeting with her was a most fascinating event, and quotes from a small segment of his autobiography give a very interesting account:

> The saint told me something of her weekly trances. "As a helpless onlooker, I observe the whole Passion of Christ." Each week, from Thursday midnight until

---

[3]Anyone who wishes to delve further should study specific events surrounding these persons. Many books have been published about them and various articles are available on the Internet.

[4]Why such a dramatic change after the Second World War? What had taken place **prior** to the marked change in her condition to bring about such a reduction in the frequency of her stigmatic suffering? Clearly something of very great import did occur. Unfortunately for Therese Neumann, however, it was not to her ultimate benefit, even though she suffered *less stigmatisation* as a result. The key event that took place actually occurred during that war, but it did not impact solely on Therese Neumann. Ultimately, it impacted on all of global humanity.

Friday afternoon at one o'clock, her wounds open and bleed; she loses ten pounds of her ordinary 121-pound weight. Suffering intensely in her sympathetic love, Therese yet looks forward joyously to these weekly visions of her Lord.

I realized at once that her strange life is intended by God to reassure all Christians of the historical authenticity of Jesus' life and crucifixion as recorded in the New Testament, and to display dramatically the ever living bond between the Galilean Master and his devotees.

("Autobiography of a Yogi", Paramahansa Yogananda.)

Here, then, is a clear admission of *one* of the purposes of the Stigmata!

The phenomenon unequivocally testifies to the historical authenticity of Christ's existence and His death!

Not only, as Sri Yogananda surmised, just "to reassure all Christians", **but more decisively to testify before the entire world that Christ did live and that He did die!** To the believers and non-believers, to Christians, Muslims, Sikhs, Hindus, Jews, agnostics and atheists, *this fact will therefore stand for all eternity*!

No archaeological evidence found today can corroborate to a much greater extent the truth of the fact that Christ did indeed live and was crucified! And this fact alone should serve to counter certain assertions that Christ went to India (after His Resurrection) and subsequently died there, supposedly somewhere in Kashmir. Or He went to the south of France with His "family". For if He had *survived* the Crucifixion – and it is clear from the nature of His death as recorded in The Bible and the unspoken testimony of the Turin Shroud that He could *not* have —

— *then there would be **no logical reason** for the Stigmata.* And, therefore: **The Crucifixion of Jesus would have had no real significance for humanity!**

The simple logic of it all calls into question the Islamic belief that it was not Christ who died on the cross, but someone resembling Him. If that were the case, as Islam teaches, *then the occurrence of Stigmata would be completely pointless and would serve no spiritually-useful purpose whatsoever.* It then becomes a random-chance occurrence which, however, cannot exist according to The Laws of Creation. Ultimately issuing from **GOD HIMSELF** they are therefore Perfect, and thus *cannot be imperfect in any way to thereby permit arbitrary deviation from that inherent **Divine Perfection**.*

In bearing the wounds of Christ and having to suffer in the same way as He, but for years on end, Therese Neumann *openly testifies to the fact that Christ did exist, that He was crucified and that He died in the process.*

Sri Yogananda goes on to describe in his autobiography a test he carried out during his pilgrimage to Konnersreuth. He put himself into a trance and established "telepathic and televisional rapport" with Therese Neumann. At this time she had already begun to bleed, and the cloth around her head was already drenched in blood, for she also bore the head wounds symbolising the crown of thorns placed on Christ's head. Her garment was also red with blood, due to the wound on her side, corresponding to the thrust of the Roman soldier's spear into Christ's side.

Sri Yogananda's description:

"As I was in attunement with her, I began to see the scenes of her vision. She was watching Jesus as he carried the timbers of the Cross amid the jeering multitude. Suddenly she lifted her head in consternation: the Lord had fallen under the cruel weight. The vision disappeared. In the exhaustion of fervid pity, Therese sank heavily against her pillow."

It is important to note that Sri Yogananda had developed a powerful psychic ability, which is clearly evident from his autobiography. He had gifts of clairvoyance, and the ability to see previous incarnations. Consequently we should not be surprised, therefore, that he could see the past incarnation of Therese Neumann as it really was.

In truth, this is precisely what should have taken place!

We know from the story of Therese Neumann's life that she had many visions of the last hours of Christ's life. Why would that *not* be the case if, according to The Law of Rebirth, she actually was physically present there witnessing these events *two thousand years ago?* We would presume, having personally seen the events of the Crucifixion of Christ, they would have been burned into her soul for all eternity so that, even in successive incarnations, the experience would be sufficiently powerful to manifest as visions and trances. This is a perfectly logical explanation, and one that would explain part of why Therese Neumann had these experiences. But what about the *Stigmata*, the wounds she bore, and the immense amount of suffering that she had to experience in her lifetime; *every week for many years?*

The Law of Reciprocal Action provides the answer, for it is the Law of Perfection and Justice, while at the same time a Law of Love and Forgiveness! Residing in that Law, therefore, is both Justice and Love, Severity and Forgiveness. There is never any imbalance or imperfection, and all explanations of such phenomena have to accord with The Law, and therewith according to the Supreme Premise:

"God Exists and is Perfect in Every Way!"

The answer to the 'riddle' of Stigmata is therefore *not* what the Catholic Church has propounded for centuries! That church has *wrongly exalted* the person of Therese Neumann and other Stigmatics and beatified them, thus attempting to place them at the level of those *who truly fulfilled* The Will of God in former times!

Through the unique Knowledge of the "All-Truth" now on Earth – from which we source the very explanations herein and to which we point – we can now understand a process that has thus far been veiled from humanity. As stated earlier on, the answer to this "mystery", even though profound, is nonetheless *simple* to grasp. We therefore ask the obvious: 'Why was it not recognised and understood long before now – by Christian Church leaders, particularly?'
Here is the reason **WHY**:

> *Those who bear the **genuine** marks of **stigmatisation** were persons that, at the time of the **Crucifixion** of **Jesus Christ**, mocked or tortured **Him**; thus directly contributing to His immense suffering on that Cross!*

That reality would have produced the immediate karmaic effect of stigmatisation on those persons, first in the *ethereal* world – because *fine matter* is far more "responsive" to "spiritual thought and deed" than gross matter; and only later, under the *immutable* outworking of **The Spiritual Law of Rebirth**, in *subsequent* incarnations as *gross material manifestations*. Thus the *souls* of those individuals were immediately struck in the reciprocal action, which thereby brought about the same wounds upon them in fine matter, exactly corresponding to those that

Christ, as a result of His torture, was forced to bear. In all successive incarnations on Earth, those wounds also manifested gross-materially, either partially or wholly, whilst at the same time the stigmatised persons had visions of the last hours of Christ's suffering, for which *they* themselves were *directly responsible*!

In this very unique and clear process and outcome may we understand the warning to human beings to obey The Law or:

"Their works shall follow them!"

Every wound that Christ was forced to bear as a result of being tortured thus became ethereally imprinted *on* the torturers. Those wounds could only manifest materially according to precise earthly circumstances, however, and therefore it is quite likely that not all Stigmata manifested in the same manner for all Stigmatics. But that is only due to the "coarse nature of gross matter" and its reduced level of "mobility". It is also interesting to note that in the various cases of stigmatisation, as in that of Therese Neumann, **the wounds could not be healed or treated in any way**, and were at times **even worsened through treatment**.

Hence to be stigmatised is no blessing as the Church contends, but is instead only a curse! There does lie in the suffering, however, a blessing for the person concerned *if and only if* he comes to recognition of his former wrong-doing. When that recognition is made, the karmaic bonds are loosened. If the person then lives *correctly*, according to The Laws of Creation, then the karma can be expiated and the person freed from it. Thus, that dark two-thousand year old deed, though severe enough to be *life-threatening* to the very *spirit*, can nonetheless certainly be forgiven the transgressors. However, if the *correct* recognition is *not* made, there can be no expiation of the deed. Instead, karmaic reciprocity for the long-committed deed will ensure *continual suffering* for the Stigmatic both on Earth and in the 'beyond'.

All those souls who mocked Jesus have thus had to bear the wounds produced by Stigmata. So that outcome should tell us something else. We should again question *why*, as a *result* of the Crucifixion of Jesus *only*, has such a strange phenomenon taken place? Why is something similar not observed through the martyrdom of many other prophets and Truth-bringers? Is there something special here that distinguishes Jesus from any of the other Truth-bringers?

> Unequivocally, yes. And that is because Jesus was *not* an ordinary human being. He was, and still is – **in Title** – **"The Son Of God"**. Thus "**A Part Of God**" from out of **"The Divine"**.

Why else would a crime as loathsome as **HIS** Crucifixion result in such phenomena even two thousand years later, for many Truth-bringers have been killed in the past? Since their Message was always in stark contrast to the teachings of the priests of the churches or temples of their time, they were oppressed and persecuted too. Yet there is no record of people being born hundreds or thousands of years later and mysteriously developing wounds corresponding to the nature of the martyrdom or torture of the original prophets, not to mention the added gifts of receiving visions and messages!

A crime committed against **a Son of God** is a very different matter, however. It means *that it can and should be expected that* **the persons responsible** *would be* **branded accordingly** *in their* **subsequent incarnations**, *and that mysterious signs and phenomena* **would accompany such a happening**.

And that is precisely the case in the stigmatisation at Konnersreuth, and in all similar cases!

The reader must, of course, judge for himself and make up his own mind on the subject. He should not superficially examine facts and simply acknowledge "possibilities" here. The nonchalant response of most seekers to what is clearly and unarguably *an earthly visible proof about Jesus* is testimony to superficiality and spiritual indolence. As Jesus Himself taught, even if an angel were to appear before mankind, they would not believe!

All the evidence lies there before us, and the Knowledge of The Eternal Laws provides the answers! In acknowledging and accepting with conviction the clear and irrefutable evidence here, we arrive at one absolute conclusion:

"Stigmata" testifies to The Truth of The Divinity of Jesus!

The timing of the appearance of stigmatised people is also rather compelling. Apparently there are *no known records* of stigmatised individuals appearing until the Thirteenth Century or thereabouts. This seems to indicate two things; either there were no stigmatised persons before that time, or there were and for some inscrutable reason these kinds of occurrences were never documented or mentioned. The second alternative is rather difficult to accept, given that so much had already been meticulously documented even in those days, and that the occurrence of Stigmata would have certainly raised much uproar in the church. Thus we are left with the first possibility as being far more likely.

In terms of karmaic events, the appearance of Stigmata a relatively long time after Christ's death makes perfect sense. On passing over into the ethereal world, the souls who had mocked Christ would have initially been bound to a very low Ethereal Plane where they would have experienced the Stigmata *for the first time*. Reincarnations or rebirths do *not* take place instantly, and in the normal cycle of karmaic events there is often a period of hundreds, or even thousands, of years between successive incarnations. Only when these souls have reached some degree of maturity and realise they need to close a cycle *on Earth* would they be granted, by Law, a further incarnation here. Thus, within the first few hundred years or so of Christ's death, it is highly unlikely that there were any stigmatised persons on the planet! Two thousand years later, however, there have been a greater number of Stigmatics as the souls personally responsible for His murder awaken in the beyond and strive towards a new incarnation, and *perhaps* expiation; subject, however, to the individual's free-will choices.

The source of this knowledge gives far deeper explanations about this process and also gives the identity of the tortured soul, Therese Neumann, at the time of Christ. That is an explanation which borders on the personal, so each one should strive to recognise this for himself.

That the Catholic Church has beatified stigmatised persons in the past without applying the immutable and inviolable **Law of Sowing and Reaping** that Jesus Himself taught, shows how human beings would much rather elevate themselves – even in the midst of acute suffering – instead of looking within for the source of that suffering. As stated earlier, the Churches could have very easily determined this fact themselves had they earnestly sought for the answer. God does not will suffering among the creatures of His Creation. As we have strongly refuted, that is a positively silly notion lacking even the *smallest measure* of logic and intelligence. Such views literally scream of crass *intellectualism*, and thus *aspiritual* insight. Man should not experience suffering at what *should be* the *height* [this present time] of his spiritual development on Earth. Suffering is thus a clear pointer to personal and collective transgressions *against* **Immutable Laws of Creation**!

It is therefore quite astonishing that even the highly gifted Sri Yogananda could not see beyond the vision of the Passion of Christ and clarify from it the *true reason* for the stigmatisation of Therese Neumann! It is our sure conviction that *he* was meant to have shown *her* what she herself had done to *receive* the Stigmata. Had he done so, the testimony he would have given through his clairvoyant abilities would have confirmed for her what The Living Truth *had already made known many years before that time!* And had *that* been the case, Sri Yogananda would not have returned empty-handed to India, for he would have absorbed deeper explanations about The Law of Reciprocal Action [*Sowing and Reaping*], the *primary driver* that wrought Therese Neumann's *reciprocal* suffering.

Deeper enlightenment for him would have ensured that, upon his return to India, his encounters with many prominent personalities – especially Mahatma Gandhi *only a few months after his visit to Konnersreuth* – would have given to India a much greater Spiritual Knowledge of Creation! More crucially for a very large number of human beings of that time, Gandhi would have surely embraced the new knowledge that Sri Yogananda was tasked to return to India with, and thereby the distinct possibility of recognising the essence of the Truth *he*, also, was searching for then.

The world is a far poorer place because of the failure of Sri Yogananda, for Gandhi would surely have left an ongoing legacy which might perhaps have eventually led many of the millions of his followers to a better understanding of the interconnectedness of Creation-Law:

Crucial Imperative No 6:

That there are certain and precise *Inviolable Laws* which govern *all life* and to which *all* human decisions and processes *are subject*. In their inherent Perfection these Laws are, in their perfect outworking, **Absolute**. And are therefore **Immutable**; and thus **Unchangeable**!

Crucial Imperative No 8:

That we, the human Beings of planet Earth, *inherently possess* the ordained attribute of "**free-will**". That *not understanding* the so-called inequities or injustices of life has its *genesis* in human *non-recognition* and thus *non-understanding* of this most "**Crucial Imperative**".

Crucial Imperative No 9:

That **all** is *interconnected*; that nothing stands *in isolation*!

Unfortunately in his case; from preconceived notions and ideas he himself admitted in his autobiography, Sri Yogananda went to Konnersreuth in the hope of meeting a "Catholic saint". He had thus *already* wrongly enthroned her as such. Preconceptions can be a significant hindrance to *pure clairvoyance*, in itself a great aid for humanity. The crucial emphasis here, however, being *pure* clairvoyance.

Clairvoyance, in the sense of being able to see and hear ethereal things, is simply a gift. But it is left to the bearer of the gift as to how he uses it. If a clairvoyant or telepathic person bears impurity within, then he can only connect to low Ethereal Planes. On the other hand, if he is spiritually pure and enlightened, he *can* connect to Higher Realms. Thus messages and visions of clairvoyants cannot always be readily trusted. To seek help or information via clairvoyance means that the supplicant must be absolutely sure where the clairvoyant's message comes from!

In Sri Yogananda's case, while he was already enlightened about many things, he went to Konnersreuth in the *highly mistaken belief and assumption* that Therese Neumann was a blessed Catholic saint. This terribly wrong assumption formed an ethereal barrier to his receiving any more information than just that. His mind was already made up on the subject, and this opinion ethereally took on a form, a barrier, that prevented him from seeing the complete happening. Had he gone to Konnersreuth seeking the uncontestable Truth about Therese Neumann, a totally different outcome would have resulted from his visit to her!

He could thereby have perhaps subsequently 'swayed' many world events, especially those pertaining to the true recognition of Christ in India through Gandhi!

A deep and objective analysis of this entire process should be carried out in accordance with The Laws of Creation. Much would then become clear for all. And instead of glorifying certain individuals, the Catholic Church hierarchy, particularly, should recognise the actual truth surrounding Stigmatics and put right this terrible distortion.

However, this should not occur with cases of stigmatisation only, but also with certain visions and prophecies, such as *the Third Fatima prophecy*. Whilst it does not belong to the main topic here, it does nevertheless warrant a few brief points. Though not a "Bible Mystery" either, the Fatima prophecies have piqued the curiousity of millions globally.

6.3   The Third Fatima Prophecy

> Interpreted by the Catholic Church as a prophecy about an attack on a Pope, in truth *it did not at all refer to the attempted assassination of the late Pope John Paul II* as the Church proclaimed. It was actually a much greater warning *for all humanity.*

The Third Fatima prophecy categorically makes reference to a "Holy Father" robed in white, climbing a mountain, and being struck from all sides by soldiers who fired bullets and arrows at him, while all the other bishops and priests around him died one by one. According to this prophecy, this particular bishop or pope was killed before a Cross on that mountain, and two angels, one on either side of the Cross, collected the blood of the martyrs and sprinkled it on those souls who were to later make it to God.

Where and what is the connection between this prophecy and the attempted assassination of the Pope John Paul II, where the only commonality is the date on which the vision was received and of the attempted assassination? There is none whatsoever! In fact, the attempted assassination was not by a group of soldiers, but by a single gunman who later claimed he was acting in conjunction with the Third Fatima prophecy – which had not, then, been revealed. While this has led to the rather strange conclusion that the gunman was inspired by The Holy Spirit to commit such an act against the Pope, a strict understanding of The Laws of Creation tells us that *that* interpretation is ridiculous. The gunman was not *inspired* by The Light at all. He clearly had his own agenda. Perhaps that was the key motive of certain "forces" in all of this; to obscure the Truth of what the Third Fatima Prophecy was referring to.[5] For, apart from these facts, there is absolutely no correlation between the events of the vision and the attempted assassination.

On the other hand there is a surprisingly far greater similarity between the events described in the prophecy, and those concerning One Who, along with two special helpers, lived on the Austrian mountain of Vomperberg. After His death, which to some degree resulted from persecution by the Nazi Regime, His work was continued by others.[6]

---

[5] "Because our fight is not against blood and flesh; but against sovereignties, against the powers, against the commanders of the darkness of this world..." (Ephesians 6:12, Fenton.)

[6] Any further discussion on this particular subject would be going too far at this stage, and is reserved for a later time and/or those human beings who have become far more enlightened in recognition of The Truth!

6.4 Christendom's Bondage to 'Distortions' of Bible Truths

The numerous misinterpretations and appalling distortions around the life and death of Jesus unfortunately hold millions of so-called "believers in Christ" in serious bondage to many wrong beliefs. Should well-meaning Christians be overly concerned, and does it really matter? Most certainly it does. Whilst virtually all Christian Denominations will forcefully argue that *their* Bible interpretation is correct, the very fact that so many *are* so bound by *different notions*, shows that very few really think about the death and legacy of Jesus seriously at all. Superficiality, spiritual weakness and just plain laziness will one day soon wreak its terrible havoc amongst the so-called "faithful".

Through distortions that are made of Christ's life and Teachings, a second *symbolic* crime is committed against Him. Those who claim that He came to die for all sinners so that all who believe in Him can be easily forgiven and granted a place in Heaven should be aware that there is *no record that Christ ever taught such a thing!*

And even if there were such a record, it could *not* be The Truth but instead an insidious forgery, for The Truth is synonymous with Perfection. As we have already strongly stated, Perfection implies both Love and Justice, mercy and severity. No man can be forgiven his sins without the compulsion to atone for them *karmaically*. This necessitates *multiple Earth-lives*. Once he has recognised his former errors and atoned for them, his "slate is wiped clean" and he is forgiven. That is the *real secret* behind the "Blood of Jesus taking away our sins". It was **through recognising The Word of Jesus and living according to It**. Brought at the cost of His shed Blood on the Cross of Suffering, that is the only way whereby our transgressions **can** be "washed away".

Even the thief on the cross who begged Jesus to remember him in His Kingdom had to personally atone for his wrong-doings. He, however, was *already* atoning for it on the cross, and, through his *complete recognition* of Jesus borne in the experience of the most *severe* suffering, was *completely* purified! Here, again, we note the immutable outworking of Divine Justice, which is synonymous with Divine Love. The other thief who reviled Jesus and who was subsequently 'earthbound' for centuries; through the inviolable outworking of **Reciprocal Law** necessarily experienced several incarnations 'on Earth'. Each time, however, bearing the wounds characterised by Stigmata!

In India there is ongoing belief that before Jesus began His Mission He journeyed to the subcontinent to study the Vedic knowledge there, which He then took back to Israel. Although there are many similarities between His Teachings and those of the Vedas, such a thing *did not happen*. The Vedas *do* contain many grains of Truth. And Christ, being The Word of Truth Incarnate, would have taught only that which accords *with* the Truths in the Vedas. But Christ did not need to learn anything from the ancient Hindu philosophy of that time, *because He already bore all Knowledge of The Truth, Living, within Him!* In His comprehensive explanations of the impending World Judgment when The Son of Man would come, He went far beyond what the Vedas teach. This knowledge is *not* available in such fullness in the Vedas!

Those who spread such terribly-incorrect rumours about Christ have no idea of the very unfortunate reciprocal effect their deeds will ultimately return them! In this case, it is an attempt to belittle the personality of Christ, making Him personally subservient to the Vedic knowledge, thereby also demonstrating that Indian spirituality is *supposedly* supreme in the world! In accordance with The [Iron] Law of Karma, what must be the outcome for the many swamis and gurus who teach this wrong concept? It is a fate probably far worse than mere stigmatisation, for they symbolically murder not only His Word but His very Identity!

Every seeker of The Truth who is unsure about Christ and His Mission should *seriously study* the explanations presented herein. In all such endeavours, however, we must remember that it avails us little if we only recognise Christ's personality **but choose not to call His Teachings to life within us** and thus not live accordingly. We would then be worse off than those who know nothing of Him – **Who He really Is!**

Christ gave the essence of Truth simply and plainly. It is brilliantly summarised in two short Commandments He bequeathed to all mankind:

> "Thou shalt love the Lord thy God with all thy heart, with all thy soul, and with all thy mind!"

> "Thou shalt love thy neighbour as thyself!"

(Matthew 22:36-29)

Unfortunately, we have not really understood His simple Message of Love at all. In its stead, we have distorted that very concept; hence the unbelievable degree of hatred and intolerance permeating human societies right across the globe. Rarely do we show any real love and compassion to our neighbour *in the sense* in which The Son Of God *demanded* of humanity. Still less, therefore, do we offer genuine Love to **God Himself.**

Wrong interpretations, false doctrines and erroneous philosophies perpetuated over thousands of years have conditioned societies, through their religions and cultures, into a mind-set that actually places love of self and family first. And, by natural association, love secondarily for only that which touches the society or culture – like 'ripples in a pond' weakening in strength as they travel further away from the nucleus.

Those insidious *conditioning* practices, perhaps not even *recognised* as such, have nonetheless brought the present-day problems global humanity now faces. Nightmarish outcomes, *already* experienced by some societies, have thereby necessitated the *crucial need* for humanity of this present time to at least have an *understandable* explanation of the Creation in which we live, and **The LAWS Of GOD — — CREATION-LAW — —** operating therein.

That knowledge, and **only** that knowledge, offers the way *forward* and *out of* the unbelievable mess *we* have mired *ourselves* in – already long-signalled by "Societal Collapse" across the globe.

7
RIGHT BIBLE/WRONG BIBLE

Crucial Imperative No 1:

That "**The Bible**" should not be regarded as simply a religious work. The Bible should be *recognised* as a ***scientific Work*** for all of humanity, for it is a ***Book of Spiritual and scientific Truth and Law!***

(Author.)

The above Chapter heading could ordinarily seed volumes of research and commentary on the vast literary and scholarly field related to and encompassing The Bible in its myriad forms, guises and translations. The Chapter itself, however, is relatively short. Our aim here, therefore, is not historical research in any form. It is *primarily* to show how *one lone translator* and his *especial* Bible – out of very many has succeeded in *correctly identifying* the processes that permitted the human race conscious life on Earth. For only with the ***correct knowledge*** of our origins can we ***completely fulfil*** the purpose for which we exactly sought that conscious existence. Correct knowledge in this case should mean clear recognition, and therefore no need for further debate or contention. [We also examine and clarify one other "Bible Mystery"; the enigmatic Number 666 of "The Revelation".]

In the case of our origins, however, a cessation of debate there will not occur for a little while yet, for the religious and scientific minefield centred on "human origins" fills volume upon volume of *ostensibly sacrosanct* written text in the very many diverse "halls of learning" around the world. If we hold to just one side of the divide, then we may readily note that the one constant in the world of human religious beliefs is the incredible proliferation of so many. From the reasonably logical, the lyrically beautiful, the oppressively unhealthy, the illogical, the ludicrous, the tyrannical, the superstitious and the evil. So many, and all generally self-serving.

Under the outworking of The Law of Attraction..., beautiful words *should* attract people of altruistic or ennobled mind. They can also imprint very strongly on the impressionable and the superficial, however. To attract even millions of followers or adherents, therefore, the simplest thing to do is write beautiful words. Pretty words, unfortunately, can often only be just that, words without real substance. So, unless such "beautiful" teachings actually translate to a logical statement showing *how and why* it all came into being and how it thus holds together

– complete with Perfect Law and "no gaps" – then following such a teaching will not lead a *genuine* seeker to something Complete and Perfect.

Nowhere is there to be seen or heard what should be stated as the obvious conclusion. That we, the people of the Earth, groan under our own self-imposed, massive burden of religious machinations, lies, deceit and fraudulent hypocrisy. The Old Testament, if read either as a religious work or as an historical document, reveals this clearly.

The New Testament on the other hand, whilst certainly strongly restating the Justice of the Laws of God, is, however, also imbued with the message of the Love of God – Jesus – as Its [The Law's] necessary accompaniment. Because we have derived much of the content herein from The Bible – and not simply from "beautiful words" found elsewhere – the question will no doubt arise as to the validity of the one chosen as our benchmark: The **Fenton Bible**.

If asked why, in our view it reveals a far greater level of "spiritual insight" than other Bibles and thus provides a more correct interpretation overall. However, whilst we primarily accept Fenton's Bible for this work, it does not mean we condemn outright every other. Free-will is the benchmark here too. In any case near-future events will highlight all false writings and interpretations and the beliefs spawned by them, and similarly reveal the followers of those beliefs.

Despite favouring Fenton's Bible as our major benchmark among English-language Bibles, the linguistic work of Martin Luther in his translation should be recognised as a particular watershed in Bible translation and interpretation too. His challenge to the, then, Pope's one-world view was a singular act of very great courage. It was one, moreover, that brought him the threat of death from the very seat of "all-power" in the Western world at the time. His stand paved the way for others to similarly question the status quo, and subsequently seeded the Protestant Reformation.

7.1   The Number 666 of 'The Revelation'

The enigmatic number 666 of The Revelation has greatly puzzled Bible-readers, Bible students and Theologians alike. Regarded as a real "Bible Mystery", the main Documentary Channels of "Discovery", "National Geographic" and "History" have all produced a number of Documentaries around this subject of very great interest to so many, interviewing many Theologians and Bible Scholars from numerous Universities and Bible Colleges in the process. The most striking aspect of the many diverse interpretations, ideas and theories from the "experts" is the *division of opinion* over what it is *supposed* to mean. And whether the number applies to a person, who that person was or might be, and whether it, the number – or he, the person – applies to the Roman era, or is specifically about today. That marked divergence of opinion translates to a rather large 2,000 odd years of time-difference, so represents an extremely broad sweep in which to theorise about the "mysterious" number 666!

The *correct* interpretation of the number 666, however, adds immeasurably to the sum total of our understanding of The Revelation, particularly. In terms of its significance to outcomes which are decisive for humanity, therefore, it is similar in that respect to what we revealed as the *true* Holy Grail.

On the subject matter here, however, Luther's translation of the particular Scripture centred on the number 666 offers an incrementally more correct interpretation of the 'mystery' than does Fenton's Bible. The relevant passage from Revelation 13:18 (Fenton) reads:

> "Here is wisdom. Let whoever has intelligence adjudge the number of the beast;
> the number is a human one; and **his** number is six hundred and sixty six."

(Italics mine.)

While being correct with regard to the single italicised word, *his* – for *that* is what the number 666 **actually refers to** – it is not *exactly* correct overall. However, by emphasising that the number 666 **identifies the one particular man to whom it refers**, Fenton may have perceived more about the deeper meaning of that number than he indicates in his full-text interpretation. For the use of the lower-case, *h*, in the word *"his"* [number] reveals that he understood it to be the number of a *man* who was *not* **Divine** in **Origin**. Fenton would have capitalised the **H** had that been the case.

Notwithstanding that probability, Luther correctly translated the relevant Scripture as being the *"number of a* **man**", not a *"human"* number as Fenton did. The King James Version also translates it basically-correctly. By virtue of his powerfully-guided work in shaping the German Language, what Luther gave to the "666 mystery" was the *key* to *solving* it. The number 666 is thus connected with the "beast with two horns":

"I also saw another beast come up out of the earth; who possessed two horns like a lamb, but spoke like a dragon."

(Revelation 13:11, Fenton.)

Various interpretations have thought the beast to be individuals, or religious or earthly powers of different centuries. However, through the *special* knowledge and insight of one man who derived his wisdom from the same Source from which this book also derives its knowledge and mandate, we herewith include the answer to the "666 Bible Mystery". The great knowledge inherent in **The Law of Numbers** provides the solution.

"For the beast with two horns (= 2 words) stands for the *world-embracing* concept *The Sin!* But the name of the man who has the same number as the beast called *The Sin* is *John the Baptist!* The number 666 is explicitly given as the key to it.

Like any other number, the number 666 also bears within it the sharpest contrasts. Thus with the number 666 there is on the one hand the sin in the service of the darkness, the cause of all evil, the adversary of God; it is the sin which rules the world, entices to evil, and ever again persuades to the worship of the first beast (13, 1) which embodies the absolute dominion of the earthbound intellect.

On the other side stands John the Baptist, the high and pure spirit, the faithful and humble servant of the Light, the blessed mediator of Divine Revelation; as a powerful warrior against the sin, his name swings in the same number."

(*A Gate Opens*, p 349, Herbert Vollmann.)

Simple, but profound. The free-will aspect inherent in human beings permits each of us to also choose which *form* of the number 666 we might wish to gravitate towards or embrace – the darker aspect, or the lighter and higher side.

Thus the number 666 of popular interpretation, as a man of exceptional power who will soon arise to dominate the Earth and somehow enslave global humanity to do his bidding, is a myth. It is one more terrible distortion of the revelatory Truths in The Bible, but more particularly in this case of The Book of Revelation! The millions of wasted words in numerous books on the subject, along with the so-called 'expert analyses' in various Documentaries, will soon be revealed for the *foolish notion* and thus non-understanding that *that* particular and serious error really represents!

7.2 Fenton's Crucial Insight to The Book of Genesis

Notwithstanding Luther's seminal Work, the bulk of key Biblical references *herein* still primarily derives from Ferrar Fenton's re-translation of The Bible. Because Fenton's Work is unfortunately not all that well known and thus not readily accepted to the degree it really should be, it is therefore not 'mainstream'. Despite that, however, we firmly believe that what it contains is vital to a better and more logical understanding of Creation, Scripture and related theological issues. To that end, we further believe it important for the reader to know that key people in a number of Christian Denominations and in the Linguistic and Theological fields supported not only the progress of his singularly amazing effort, but endorsed the finished product too. [See end of Chapter.]

For such a line-up of distinguished luminaries to support and approve a *single* individual's translation of The Bible – at a time when the King James Version was regarded as probably the definitive holy work – must surely mean that Fenton's "translation" struck a powerful chord within the spirit of those eminent men. In our view, one lone individual, genuinely and intuitively guided by the Living Light through the spirit, will achieve a far greater degree of "spiritual accuracy" in translation than will a committee or working group engaged in the same activity. One is more strongly guided by the spirit, whereas the many will be shackled too strongly by the collective, *debating* intellect. In the most curious of paradoxes, it is exactly that 666 aspect embodying the "absolute dominion of the earthbound intellect" which *prevents* the spiritual intuition from *perceiving* spiritually-correctly!

A perfect example of this can be found in The Jerusalem Bible, Reader's Edition. A short introductory note from the Publishers, Darton, Longman & Todd Ltd., adds weight to our assertion.

> "The English text, though translated from the ancient texts, owes a large debt to the **many scholars** who collaborated to produce *La Bible de Jerusalem*, which the publishers of this English Bible gratefully acknowledge."

> (Bold emphasis mine.)

In the critical example we have chosen – [Chapters 1 and 2 of **The Book of Genesis**] – to show the difference in translation between one who is guided from Above and a committee appointed by earthly peers, two vastly and fundamentally *different* interpretations of the 'Creation account' can be clearly read. On the surface such a distinction might be seen to be 'splitting hairs'. The opposite view, however, is inherently far more spiritually-correct: That only in a true and logically-correct interpretation of our origins, and therewith the recognition of our ultimate purpose, can humanity ever hope to move forward in global knowledge and harmony. For it is *'precisely' religious disharmony and intolerance* that has been one of the root causes, and still is today, of so many of our problems for so long.[1]

In our example of the moment – our origins – we will use *'two' very different* Bible interpretations from just *one* religion. Notwithstanding the far too many appalling distortions of "Bible-Truth" that global Christendom perversely clings to, Christianity is nonetheless the *singular religion* which, *primarily* through the Teachings of The Son of God in that especial Work, *automatically incorporates* the deeper life-knowledge of **Creation-Law** and **Truth**. The *religion* itself, however, unfortunately has too many offshoots. Yet despite the fact that the

---

[1]According to an estimate in 1950, in 3,875 years of Earth history there have only been 323 years of peace, but 8,250 peace treaties. In the 60 odd years since, there has not only *not* been one single year of peace, but humanity has engaged in more disputes in more places with many more peace treaties than at any other time in history.

face-book for *all* Christians is the same – namely The Bible – almost all these many and varied groups accept a Bible interpretation virtually individualised for those self-same, diverse assemblies. If we extrapolate that small fact to encompass all the religious writings in the world, what do we then have? It is a truly ludicrous situation where The Truth simply does not emerge clearly anywhere. It is virtually all "lost truth", little more than just religion. The fact that The Bible sells so well and is apparently the "best-seller" of all time, translates perfectly into a "global business" of ever new *incorrect* Bible translations.

Thus, in re-translating Genesis, Fenton *intuitively understood* that there are actually **two different Creations** of man – **one closest to God** in the Higher Spiritual Realms and **the other of man of Earth** much further down in the "Material Worlds".

The translators of the much more recent "Jerusalem Bible" fail to recognise this key point. Their interpretation of Genesis gives **two separate accounts** of what they *believe to be* **the same Creation**.

The Jerusalem Bible reads thus:

> **GENESIS**
>
> 1. **THE ORIGIN OF THE WORLD AND OF MANKIND**
>
> 2. **THE CREATION AND THE FALL**
>
> **"The first account of the creation"** – which is Chapter 1. **"The second account of the creation. Paradise"** – which is Chapter 2.

Fenton's Bible on the other hand *delineates the two Creations*:

> **GENESIS**
>
> 1. **THE FIRST CREATION OF THE UNIVERSE BY GOD = ELOHIM**
>
> 2. **THE CREATION OF MAN UNDER THE SHADOW OF GOD**
>
> 3. **THE FORMATION OF MAN FROM THE DUST OF THE GROUND BY THE EVER-LIVING GOD.**
>
> (All emphases mine.)

In reiteration, in our view such a vital and fundamentally *far-reaching* difference *between* the two Bibles can be better understood if we recognise that Fenton's monumental task was essentially guided by his inner spirit – from Above. Thus *deeper* insights were available to him to *more correctly* explain the stupendous nature of the Creation process.

Conversely, the translators of The Jerusalem Bible [and most other Bibles] are not similarly blessed. For their translations of the key points in Chapters 1 and 2 of The Book of Genesis quite clearly reveals that by *not* recognising a necessary demarcation line between the far higher Spiritual Worlds and the much lower Material Planes consisting of both *fine and coarse matter*, respectively, they thereby automatically place **The Creator of all the Worlds** on a level *far lower than can actually be the case*. [And thus man of Earth far higher than is *possible*.]

> In other words, what is thereby produced through *non-recognition* of just the *mechanics* of the actual **Creation-process** is a totally jumbled, *illogical* and *unworkable* **Creation-structure**.

A simple comparison between the *"many scholars"* interpretation of the Creation phase of Genesis in The Jerusalem Bible and that of the lone interpretation of Fenton therefore reveals a singularly and thus vastly different outcome. As formerly stated, it is an extremely *disturbing* difference. For one: The Jerusalem Bible and others similar, clearly show that it is much more **an intellectual exercise of interpretation**, for it views the Creation-process *from the Earth upwards*. Fenton's, on the other hand most certainly guided from Above, lifts the receptive reader *off* the Earth into a spiritually-correct awareness of an incomprehensible Creation-process that must inherently originate from *out of* **The Divine Realm**, and which then *proceeds downwards* towards the Material Worlds.

Interestingly, with the large amount of "Old Testament era discoveries" derived from modern science and archaeology, such a recent analysis of The Book of Genesis in The Jerusalem Bible, seemingly offering a more Earth-orientated interpretation of the Creation process, paradoxically appears very similar to the Middle Ages Church position whereby everything revolved around, and/or centred on, the Earth. That "apparent" viewpoint, moreover, does nothing to reconcile the long-standing debate between science and religion on this subject. Yet, as we have strongly stated, Fenton's correct interpretation **does** bring reconciliation and closure to it, as a correct analysis and interpretation should.

The proponents of the respective Disciplines and viewpoints need to leave behind, discard, *expunge* out of their consciousness this tired and incorrect teaching that really does smack of an egocentric "Earth-human religion". And, instead, adopt a far more expansive and recognitive attitude and mind-set toward all that emanates from Above. For we human beings surely did not create ourselves.

Fenton's intuitive awareness of that far greater reality, especially powerfully narrated in his marvellously guided work in "Genesis", paints a picture that *should naturally awaken the spirit within every reader*, and particularly *every scientist and theologian*. If not to the same degree of knowing as he, then at the very least to the *realisation* that something really has been *amiss* for a very long time now in the *standard* Church position regarding the Creation process.

Unlike the lone Fenton who employed the intuitive faculty of his spirit for his translation, the *'many scholars'* who contributed their particular level of 'expertise' to The Jerusalem Bible clearly mainly utilised the inherently-aspiritual and thus *intellectual* thought-processes for *their* assessment and interpretation. Especially so with The Book of Genesis. Were this *not* the case, they would *not* have *persisted* with the use of the word **day** – 'the first day', 'the second day' etc., – to attempt to *rationalise* and thus *fit* such a stupendous Event as the Creation of all that we can see, *and the far greater part of The Whole that we cannot*, into the "7 Earth-day time-frame" that is now the completely-wrong but nonetheless accepted norm by billions world-wide. Only spiritually-correct insight, such as Fenton possessed, *permits divination* of the *true nature* of the otherwise *humanly-incomprehensible* Creation-process.

7.3   Intellectual Volition versus Spiritual Volition

7.3.1   Intellectual Volition

Whilst we may perhaps believe that both *spirit* and *intellect* might be identical in nature – or at least quite similar and thus ostensibly able to perform the same tasks and fulfil the same roles – that is not the case. Even though being an essential aid which we absolutely need to effectively carry out earthly work, the *intellect* is completely unsuited for higher tasks such as the divining of Spiritual Truths. Being an ordained tool for things of the material world, *intellectual* work is necessarily and strongly tied to just everyday *brain activity*.

Precisely because it is a very necessary aid, the *intellect* can and should be used to offer explanations of spiritual or non-material subjects and matters once the *spirit* has intuitively recognised the validity of such connections. The rightful place of *intellectual activity*, therefore, is that of transforming Spiritual guidance *for* earthly activity into the *corresponding deed* on Earth, such as in science, architecture, technology and societal infrastructure etc..

Since *intellectual activity* relates to the earthly deed, **Intellectual Volition** – whilst obviously closely connected to the carrying out of the physical task – should be more an "inner force" wanting or desiring ennoblement of all that the *intellect* is capable of achieving on Earth and in earthly life. Despite the fact that both terms might appear to mean the same thing, a high and ennobled **Intellectual Volition** does not at all mean that any associated task will *automatically* translate to a correspondingly ennobled or pure form *at completion*. Though of course *it should*.

Unfortunately, the **Intellectual Volition** that permeates much of global humanity today may well be the *least ennobled form* it has *ever* been in the long and sorry history of mankind. For the most part it is very powerfully driven by *crass materialism* and the associated desire to acquire great wealth for its own sake, and therefore not necessarily for any kind of altruistic purpose or goal. This kind of **Intellectual Volition** thus *automatically* sows the seeds of its own destruction. This we see in collapses in the corporate world, in the main religions and in the once-stable ethos of earth-science as it now grapples with the rapidly-changing dynamics of global warming. Perhaps the *kind* of *intellectualism* we allude to may be found more in the formulation of societal laws driven by political considerations and/or control, that, in certain societies, causes greater problems and suffering than need be for those peoples.

7.3.2 Spiritual Volition

Spiritual Volition, by contrast, is that power which, when energised by the Spirit – the inner, animating core of all human beings – effectively determines its own life path and thereby its subsequent fate. By virtue of its nature as the *power-pack* and *animating force* within each of us, it possesses the free-will attribute to connect to ennobled activities, or to base, ignoble ones. It thus sets in train the appropriate "reciprocal returns" for itself. If used spiritually-correctly, our **Spiritual Volition** will strive, in the first instance, to seek connection with, and guidance from, **The Origin of All Life**! It will further strive to hold to *all the Virtues* whilst we are on Earth thereby anchoring *personal* **spiritual** *threads* to Higher and Lighter Realms *above* the Earth, to which we *can* thus be drawn *after* earthly death. **Spiritual Volition** will thus provide the perfect foundation for *all* scientific and medical research, and the aegis for *all* philosophical and spiritual work and education.

With *both* **Intellectual Volition** *and* **Spiritual Volition**, the key word **Volition** – in its *motive-desire feature* – can either ennoble, or debase. One, the *Intellectual aspect*, when concerned with earthly activity only, *will* weigh down the spirit if used for debased or dishonest activity, thereby *preventing* the spirit from fulfilling its ordained role.

Through the very *life-power* inherent *in it*, the *Spiritual aspect* is able to *drive* the entity to paradise or to perdition; depending on what the *owner* chooses. So it is crucially-necessary that balance *between* the *Spiritual* and the *Intellectual* aspects *within* us be striven for, exactly as The Law of Balance ordains. Through ignoring the inner guidance of our Spirit and concomitantly strengthening the use of our *intellect*, however, *we* have seriously transgressed that vital Ordination. The subsequential global result is clear for all to see.

Thus the huge and fundamental difference between the two respective aspects of the word, "**Volition**", is perfectly stated in the following Scripture from Matthew 6:19-20, Fenton.

> "Do not hoard up for yourselves treasure upon the earth, where moth and canker destroy, and where thieves may burrow through and steal; but store up your treasure in heaven, where neither moth nor rust destroy, and where thieves cannot dig through nor steal: for where your treasure is, there your heart will also be.

7.4   Summary of Key Points of the 'Creation' Process

To emphasise Fenton's more correct and crucial analysis of The Book of Genesis, we reproduce from Chapter 2 the main points of the Biblical sequence of Creation.

The Utterance of the stupendous Creation-Words – **"LET THERE BE LIGHT!"** – thus resulting in: **The First Creation – (The Spiritual Realms.)**

1. The Creation of the Heavens and the Earth of **The First Creation** – "By **Periods** God created *that which produced* the Solar Systems: then that which produced the Earth."

    (Genesis 1:1, Fenton. Emphasis mine.)

2. The **Creation** of day and night (in the Heavens.)

3. The division of the waters which were **under** the expanse (firmament) from the waters which were **above** the firmament (expanse.) The firmament/expanse then named the Heavens.

4. The commanding of the waters **below** the Heavens to be collected in one place, and for dry land to appear.

5. The **Creation** of flora.

6. The Creator sets two great lights which divide day and night for Earth.

7. The **Creation** of fish and bird life.

8. The **Creation** of animal life.

9. Then, the great **Creation** of man **in His Image** – both male and female – and the Blessing to rule over all flora and fauna.

10. The **completion** of the Creations at the end of the **sixth Age**. The Creator rests at the **seventh Age** and blesses and hallows the seventh **day**.   [Parentheses mine.]

    Note Scripture Genesis 2:1 (Fenton.) "Thus the whole Host of the Heavens (as well as the Earth were completed)." This is the completion of The First Creation (i.e. Spiritual Realms).

And only then:

> **The Creation of The Worlds of Matter,** including our universes, Solar Systems and Earth – **as planned by its Creator.**

11. After the completion of **The First Creation : The Spiritual Realms** – including all that was then **created** (as described in Genesis 1:1-3) – the Creation of The Worlds of Matter through a long process of evolution leading to the forming by God of Earth-man from out of **the dust of the ground,** who following a suitable time of evolution became the first human being, **the man with the Living Soul.**

    (Genesis 2:19. All emphases mine.)

12. Earth-man gives name to every creature – **formed** from out of the **dust of the ground also**.

13. Even though God had **already created** "man" in His Own Image (both male and female) in **The First Creation**, and had subsequently **formed Earth-man** from out of **the dust of the ground**, there was still no Earth-woman. (Biblical tradition states that she was constructed from a rib of the man.)

As previously stated, whether this sequence is viewed absolutely literally, whether it is viewed symbolically, pseudo-scientifically or any other way, there are clear pointers illustrating a number of very different and very distinct happenings that occurred. It is not the one single sequence that the main Churches generally believe and teach as having ostensibly **created** man/Earth-man. Fenton unequivocally delineates these separate, stupendous events in clear sub-titles.

1. **The First Creation of the Universe by God = Elohim.**

2. **Creation of Man under the Shadow of God.**

3. **The formation of Man from the Dust of the Ground by the Ever-living God.**

Points 3, 4, 9, 11 and 13, and the above sub-titles 1, 2 and 3 from Fenton's translation, reveals a vastly different and more stupendous picture. Points 3 and 4 *on their own* strongly indicate two different places very far apart: one above the Heavens and one below the Heavens.

The sequence thus outlined concurs with many of the scientific findings of Anthropology and Astronomy. Taken in concert, both views actually trace a path of evolutionary development that is consistent with rational logic and, moreover, encompasses and co-joins both the religious and scientific points of view. More importantly, however, this more logical sequence places man (us) in his correct place.

Therewith are the long-contested arguments of Creation versus Evolution – Christian fundamentalism versus intellectual science – **perfectly reconciled and harmonised**.

So the effectiveness or otherwise of any Bible translation must ultimately be predicated on whether or not it actually achieves its goal. With regard to The Book of Genesis, specifically, that goal should be an interpretation that unequivocally reveals it to be *as it actually happened*, actually *was* and therefore as it *really is* and *must be*. All other contentious notions that the many Bibles of the Christian world interpret differently, even if only in the most subtle differences, must yet still therefore be according to Divine Ordination consistent with the Perfection of The Laws that derive solely from The Divine Will. Translation by a group [any group] that fails to achieve this *necessary* degree of *spiritual correctness* inherently lives the sage observation about one of the signs of the "end-time".

"Ten men will take counsel, and it will come to nought."

The same can perhaps also be applied to the "collective counsel" exhibited by devout followers of the religious leaders of so many self-styled cults and groups of recent times. In the glare of global media exposure, many have come to nought in often tragic ways. Many more will eventually follow the same path into oblivion at this time of full accountability.

7.5 Fenton's Translation of The Bible

Complete and genuinely clarifying insights can therefore only derive from the ultimate knowledge contained within The Laws of Spiritual Truth – Creation-Law! Fenton's wonderful insights, though not derived from the "complete knowledge" of **The Law** – *not available to him at the time* – nevertheless must have been especially strongly guided by, and assisted from, that Perfect Source.

Logically, however, guidance of such strength and clarity cannot simply be just "force-fed" to an individual. The monumental undertaking that Fenton embarked on and completed so powerfully had to have, from his side, the commensurate measure of *spiritually-intuitive insight* for such a task – thus a completely *open* and *trusting* spirit. Genuine humility, therefore, had to have been strongly and naturally anchored *within him*. For only in *true* humility could he have received such clear guidance from Higher Sources.

Such was the clarity of the guidance given and subsequently received, that not only did he *clarify* Creation and Evolution in his translation of **The Book of Genesis**, but his spiritually-intuitive insight *correctly translated* a crucial, opening sentence from **The Book of Revelation** too. He has therewith provided *the golden key* to the actual *fulfilment* of Bible Prophecy for this very time. That, also, is given light; here in the following Scripture!

> "Blessing and peace to you from **the One** Who Is, Who Was and **Who comes**; and from the seven Spirits which are before **His throne**; **and** from Jesus Christ."

> (Revelation 1:4-5, Fenton. Emphases mine.)

The strongly emphasised portions of the above Biblical quote should be *more than sufficient* for you, the reader, to recognise the full import of. If not, then Chapter 12 explains the complete *fulfilment* of Fenton's decisively-guided and fundamental insight *into* that singularly-defining Scripture.

Fenton's key task for humankind and the Christian community, particularly, obviously struck a chord with the many eminent Theologians and Scholars who supported and endorsed his great Work. For they clearly agreed with what he undertook and what was subsequently *gifted* to the world.

Where are the same today – the *truly* spiritually-perceptive Theologians and Bible-Scholars of 21st century academia?

A very broad spectrum of key Academics, Christian and otherwise, to whom Fenton was indebted were Drs. Westcott and Hort, the Finnish Professor Tischendorf, Professor Alford, and Bishops Wordsworth and Bloomfield. During its progress the work was approved by Professor J. S. Blackie of Edinburgh University; Dr.Tait, Archbishop of Canterbury; Dr. Benson, Archbishop of Canterbury; Prof. Oliver Wendell Holmes, of Boston U.S.A.; Prof. C.A.L. Totten, of Yale University, U.S.A.; The Very Rev. E. Plumptre, D.D., Dean of Wells; The Rev. H.S. Champneys, Rector of Epperstone; The Rev. J. Bowen, B.D., Rector of St. Lawrence, Pembroke; Keshub Chunder Sen., Calcutta, India; The Rev. H. Stretton, Vicar of Eastville, Lincs.; The Rev. Charles Garrett, Ex-President of the Wesleyan Conference; The Rev. J. Davis, D.D., Ontario, Canada; and *numerous* others.

8

THE EMERGENCE OF LANGUAGE

"Reason manifests itself **above all** in language. And a language is something *we are born into*. It is thus not *the <u>individual</u>* who *forms* the language, **it is the language which <u>forms</u> the individual**."

(Hegel. Emphases mine.)

"From the tip of our tongues, sacredness begins."

(Ancient Navaho wisdom. 'Code-talkers', World War II.)

Spirit and language are *inherently inseparable*!

8.1 The Development and Spiritual Ramifications of: The "Forming" Word!

In the closing segment of Chapter 7 [Key Points] we reiterated the stupendous step-by-step processes that brought Creation and Evolution into being – explained more fully in Chapter 2 [**The Origins of Man, Genesis and Science Agree**]. The requirement for every person to recognise the primary events of the Creation-process whereby we arrived to live a state of conscious life on Earth is crucial for understanding why we are here at all. Irrespective of the creation-stories of all the various races, religions and cultures, our beginnings must logically have been the same. However, notwithstanding our common origin and journey of our spirit-core down to the material worlds to incarnate in the vessel long-prepared in its evolution for that ordained role, we need to also recognise the struggles of the very first Spirit-men aeons ago at our beginnings on Earth.

Picture, therefore, *Spiritual-Man* at these very first beginnings. Into the environment of the physical world he takes his first faltering steps. The Earth thus far has only known the activity of the animal kingdom where countless millions of different species interact in perfectly balanced cycles of life. Each has its own particular call according to its design. Some are loud, raucous and dangerous. Others mellow and sweet, but all contributing to the symphony of the Earth's natural sounds for that time. The voice and languages of man would be a new sound, an intrusion perhaps? Yet one that held the potential for noble enhancement, or vulgar coarseness.

The rich diversity of man's languages was still far in the future. Before that could happen, this new addition to the world's creatures would need to develop into a fully-matured human being. For it was not *fully developed* human spirits that incarnated into the most highly developed anthropoids that were prepared for this event, but *spirit-seeds* from The Spiritual Realm, the actual "home" of Spiritual man.[1]

Early man had first, therefore, to develop into individual personalities in the World of Matter. As formerly stated, the physical body of man is, indeed, derived from the animal, but his *inner animating core* is from the higher Spiritual Realm. Thus the "receptacle-body", prepared over aeons to one day receive the *human-spiritual*, necessarily underwent a fundamental and far-reaching change with the *entry into* those bodies of *exactly* that human-spiritual aspect. In place of the previously-existing *animistic souls* inside the especially developed "primate forms", the *new* inner animating "life-force" for humans – *the spirit* – now became established through incarnation into the prepared vessels i.e., the most highly developed anthropoid forms. So, in accordance with that requirement, male *spirit-seeds* incarnated in animal bodies of the male sex, and female *spirit-seeds* in those of the female sex.

Leading on from these very first incarnations, *continuing* incarnations of human spirits could now take place through the natural procreative process under The Law of Attraction of Similar Species. This process resulted in the demise and extinction of those groups of anthropoid apes that did not develop to a level *sufficient* to *attract* the human-spiritual aspect then preparing for entry into the material world. Anthropologists have discovered that in the early history of man, a number of branches of the "anthropoid family tree" terminated for no *apparent* reason.

We have already stated the clear and logical fact that:
The *physical body* does not **animate** the *physical body*.

Crucial Imperative No 2:

That we, the human beings of planet Earth, are not solely a physical entity, but also necessarily possess a *non-material* inner animating core: *For the physical* **cannot** *– and therefore* **does not** *– animate the physical!*

The science of genetics may determine that to be the case, but it is not possible for the purely material nature of genes *to animate and provide the actual "life-force"* for the human entity. The processes within, however, will certainly be impacted by their connective 'authority', but genetic perfection or otherwise in humans is *not* determined by genes; *by themselves, alone.* The combined interconnectedness of all the natural Laws and their processes – inherent in the overarching umbrella of **Creation-Law** – determines the final make-up of each individual, **thus its personal genetic configuration too.** But it is the **animating power of the spiritual core** – which is forever separate from the material body with its genetic properties – **that drives the very life of humans.**

For that species of anthropoid ape which successfully developed to the required stage, therefore, the ensuing entry of human spirits naturally permitted the next phase of development for

---

[1]Consider the parable: "A sower went forth to sow..." (Matthew 13:3)

it. This great evolutionary change *from* animal-man *to* Spiritual-man thereby allowed for the development of that originally-prepared, select anthropoid form, to our more refined, present-day physical form. With the arrival of 'The Spiritual' into the animal bodies, a critical event occurred for this new race called man.

This was the concomitant development of human language.

It was a singularly evolutionary event of huge proportions with obviously far-reaching implications. The inherent urge of the human spirit to seek communication with others gave vocal expression to his thinking, volition and intuitive perceiving, and allowed the formation of the organs necessary for this. To this end an important and closely-linked change took place in his physical form, clearly demonstrating the difference between man and animal, a difference only discovered relatively recently.

That vitally important distinction was *the gradual sinking downwards of the larynx.*

In the world of the animal, but more especially that of the apes, there was no change in the position of the larynx. Only through this *sinking of the larynx*, this re-positioning of that organ of communication, could the *simultaneous forming of the human shape of mouth and nose* occur. That crucial event made possible the complete voice and vowel reproduction that is probably the defining and characteristic feature of humankind.

At this point in our analysis we can combine the two aspects of *non-material spirit* and *very earthly genes* to confirm the processes outlined in the Chapter on our Origins that ultimately produced "the talking human".

Time Magazine science writers Michael D. Lemonick and Andrea Dorfman report that:

"A team led by molecular geneticist Svante Paabo of the Max Planck Institute for Evolutionary Anthropology announced that *the human version* of a gene called FOXP2, which plays a role *in our ability to develop speech and language*, evolved within the past 200,000 years – *after anatomically modern humans appeared.* By *comparing* the protein coded in the *human FOXP2 gene* with the *same protein* in various *great apes* and in mice, they discovered that the amino-acid sequence *that makes up the human variant* differs *from that of the chimp* in just <u>*two*</u> locations out of a total of 715 – an extraordinarily small change that may nevertheless explain the emergence of all aspects of human speech, from a baby's first words to a Robin Williams monologue."

(Critical emphases mine.)

1. Question: Why should the *human version* of the *same gene* permit the development of speech and language in humans and *not in apes*?

2. Question: What [different] factor or factors are necessarily present [or not present] in the 'evolutionary-developing' human that allows for such change *if the gene is basically the same* – even to *the code*?

3. Question: What has taken place in humans that has obviously *not similarly occurred* in apes?

The answer is brutally obvious – or should be – even to the most hard-nosed geneticist. A more powerful feature must obviously and logically be present *in the human* if both *share the same* "speech gene", even accepting the fact that the human variant differs from the chimp "in just <u>*two*</u> locations out of a total of 715". Yet one develops *the major and fundamental ability* to speak eloquently, and the other remains animal – with absolutely no chance that the "twain shall ever meet".

That fundamental difference, gentlemen of science, is our "inner, <u>animating</u>, *spiritual* core"!

That crucial knowledge of our **Spirit** — which we have clearly explained and will continue to reinforce — **is not the preserve of any other creature!**

It was thus the development of the organs of speech, powered by our ***spiritual*** nature, that permitted communication between members of the budding human race. The projection of only the most basic sounds in the beginning, to eloquent oratory and abstract intellectual theorising in the later millennia of his grand march forward, was not an instant happening, however. This process of development necessarily required a long period of time as humankind formulated new words to "frame" ever new discoveries and new and evolving concepts to add to his continually developing vocabulary.

For it should not be supposed that spiritual man arrived on the Earth with the innate and automatic ability to instantly converse with great skill and eloquence from an inherent vocabulary of already known words and some form of pre-programmed meanings. If we accept the literal interpretation of the forming of man from out of the "dust of the ground", then we *may possibly* accept that scenario. However, that is *not* the reality. In our part of Creation, evolution and *development* are the *norm* rather than the exception – in both the great and the small.

Therefore, the development of sufficient skill and ability to enhance the medium of speech as an effective means of communication from simple interchange to more complex discussion – to the area of discord-resolution even – could not possibly be attained in a short time-period. The process was necessarily long and exacting, and probably in concert with the parallel development of larger and larger social groupings.

Interestingly, however, this process of speech development and vocabulary acquisition, which for man took hundreds of thousands of years, can be seen *in one single lifetime* anywhere in the world in the natural growth of children from babyhood to the teen years. Therefore, today, when a new-born begins its Earth-life with a cry, and through the process of imitation learns to speak within the first few years, *it undergoes all the stages of development which humankind necessarily underwent over that long period of time*. This is achieved by the sinking of the larynx and is repeated ***with each new birth***. Research since about 1905 has allowed embryologists to establish that this "descent of the larynx" begins at the end of the first year of life and lasts up to the eighth or ninth year.

Lieberman and Crelin, in their essay, "On the Speech of Neanderthal Man", state this same process in rather more technical terms:

> "Of all the living primates only man has an extensive supralaryngeal pharyngeal region that allows all of the intrinsic and extrinsic pharyngeal musculature to function at a maximum for speech production by changing the shape of the supralaryngeal vocal tract."

> (Negus 1949, p.216)

Lieberman's study of the anthropoid apes and of the other apes, including macaques, has shown that "...they are denied the true, correct vocalisation: simply because they do not experience the descent of the larynx".

Consequently this "...descent of the larynx to its lower position in adult man" ... would thus confer "...advantages in communication".

Interestingly, Lieberman and Crelin [p.218, emphases mine], also state:

> "The adult human laryngeal position is not advantageous for either swallowing or respiration. The shift of the larynx from its position in New-born and Neanderthal

is advantageous for acquiring *articulate speech* but has the disadvantage of greatly increasing the chances of choking to death when a swallowed object gets lodged in the pharynx... The **only function** for which the **adult vocal human tract** is better suited is **speech**."

Thus, via this "shift-mechanism", a space is formed at the back of the throat, one which the anthropoid apes (and all other apes) do not have. It is a space necessary for the utilisation of our freely moveable tongue to make the very fine movements required for vowel vocalisation. In essence, it is a true vowel space. It can therefore be clearly seen that the formation of our own human language, especially of the different vowels, is only possible with this "vowel space".

In the opinion of researchers, Lieberman and Crelin, Neanderthals possessed an essentially non-human vocal tract, but probably made maximum use of his large brain to establish vocal communication. That utilisation, in their view, would perhaps "...provide the basis for mutations that lowered the larynx and expanded the range of vocal communication in modern Man's ancestral forms". (p 218) With regard to the time-frame required to perfect vocalisation skills, Lieberman and Crelin observe that with this stage of man's evolutionary development, particularly, his speech probably meant that:

> "...limited phonetic ability was probably utilised and that some form of language existed. Neanderthal man thus represents an intermediate stage in the evolution of language. This indicates that **the evolution of language was gradual**, that **it was not an abrupt phenomenon**".

They also say:

> "The reason that human linguistic ability appears to be so *distinct and unique* is that the *intermediate stages* in its evolution are represented by *extinct species*."

> (p.221, All emphases mine.)

They further state:

> "Fully developed 'articulate' human speech and language appear to have been comparatively recent developments in Man's evolution."

From our particular perspective we note their view that:

> "They may be the primary factors in the accelerated pace of cultural change."

Their research into Neanderthal's linguistic ability coupled with this observation is, in their opinion:

> "...consistent with the inferences that have been drawn from the rapid development of culture in the last 30,000 years in contrast to the slow rate of change before that period".

> (Dart 1959, p 220)

Time writers' Lemonick and Dorfman quote Eddy Rubin, director of the Department of Energy's Joint Genome Institute in Walnut Creek, California, as noting that Neanderthals weren't nearly as primitive as many assume.

"They had fire, burial ceremonies, [and] the rudiments of what we would call art. They were advanced – but nothing like what humans have done in the last 10,000 to 15,000 years."

Lemonick and Dorfman go on to state what is probably the standard view of evolutionary geneticists that:

"...we eventually outcompeted them, and the key to how we did it may well lie in our genes".

And that specific "genetic blueprints" plus the:

"...genomes of gorillas and other primates, which are already well on the way to being completely sequenced – will begin to explain precisely what makes us human..."

The conclusion can therefore be reached that man's ancestral form, quite clearly evolving from some basic shape close to that of the apes, was similar in configuration to the vast majority of mammals in that the epiglottis reached right up to the palate. Thus why the *animating power* of the **Spirit** was necessary to begin the process of language development, which parents can observe in the first few years of their own offspring's development. The simple yet unequivocal logic contained in this process should offer greater certainty as to the How and the Why of our early development, and further strengthen our assertions on humankind's origins in Chapter 2.

Despite the clear conclusions reached by Lieberman and Crelin, science still foolishly persists in trying to establish a language-potential in primates. Dr Tecumseh Fitch, writing for the journal, *Science*, noted that the key principle common to all human languages is beyond monkeys. They could not encompass complex rules called "phrase structure grammar" that underpin every human language, he said. These findings clearly show a sharp limit to the ability of animals to engage in open-ended communication. Because studies had shown monkeys to have a rudimentary grasp of grammar, scientists had hoped they could master more complex language. Research by Dr Fitch and Professor Marc Hauser from Harvard University suggests this was wishful thinking. Working with cotton-top tamarins, a New World monkey species, the scientists found that the tamarins were able to perceive the breaking of simple grammar rules, but were oblivious to more complex violations.

Clearly Tamarins cannot master language. It is simply impossible for primates, both apes and monkeys, to reach any evolutionary point whereby speech could naturally develop. As reported in the "Independent", Dr. Nancy Minugh-Purvis, an anthropological scientist from the University of Pennsylvania, has discovered a gene responsible for the heavy jaw muscles in primates to have been "switched off" 2.4 million years ago, thus permitting a lighter jaw and concomitant enlargement of the brain case in the probable branch of our human ancestors. Despite such "scientific" findings, they in no way change the absolute parameters required for speech. That specific requirement is inviolable. The ability to speak requires the animating power of the "Spirit", an attribute which only human beings can, and do, inherently possess.

Therefore, for science once more: – **A necessary proclamation!**

It is impossible for animals, *even monkeys and apes*, to possess – *now or ever* – **the innate ability to "speak"**. It is through **the power of the Spirit, *solely*** – the inner, **_animating_** core of man – that humans are granted *the ability* to form and speak complex language. Animals, *possessing the **inferior** animating core of soul*, **cannot ever**. Those are the Rules – from out of "The Laws of Creation!": **Creation-Law!**

Lieberman and Crelin have already scotched any such possibility. Does science really believe that "new scientific discoveries" can somehow circumvent or change **Immutable and Inviolable "Creation-Law"**?

So, now, back to our journey: In those far-off days of man's humble beginnings, how did the forming of the language proceed? Spiritual man was like a baby needing to formulate new sounds to be new words with distinct and clear meanings. In their evolutionary physical development, the posture of early man gradually changed from a bent ape-like one as they walked, to the upright stance we have today. As the larynx descended and the human mouth developed to its present shape, the initially hoarse and probably guttural sounds would have gradually become much more clear vocally. In the beginning, humankind probably communicated with familiar gestures and sounds gleaned from the natural world around them. Individual sounds would then become groups of sounds which became words. These words subsequently became sentences. The ability to produce whole sentences allowed for the extension of the language, with the eventual capacity for far greater expression.

As we explained in a previous Chapter, *words become the actual **forms*** of the particular ***sounds*** *produced*. They thus evoke a clear and concise ***picture*** as to their ***meaning***. This was man's great *responsibility* in being given the gift of speech – to use the *"forming power"* of the spoken and written word to *upbuild*. Unfortunately it has too often been employed for the opposite. Today, with many thousands of languages and dialects scattered throughout the world and its peoples, the Spiritual Power inherent in the "formed word" is no different now from what it was when man took his first, hesitant, vocal steps into what was his spiritual future.

What is important to realise is that language was intended *only* for the good. Yet our historical record clearly reveals thousands of years of *wrongful* application of it by humankind. Therefore, because *every* language has the same *relative* or *comparative* degree of *power*, all languages should be treated as a *spiritual gift*. Language thus offers the most wonderful means of expressing, in a precise and specific way, all that a race, culture, or Nation is capable of attaining. Thus the aspect of "spiritual power" inherent in all speech and language decrees that we not only *produce* all our *works*, we actually ***"form"*** our particular cultures.

A fine example of the power of correct use of language from a much earlier time can be noted in the great philosophic debates of the Greeks and, to a lesser extent perhaps, the Romans. This power they understood well.

> "Then there is the marvellous and godlike gift of speech. Do not you Academics call it 'the mistress of the world'? Through speech we are able to learn things of which we would otherwise be ignorant and to impart what we have learnt to others. Through speech we can encourage, persuade, console the sorrowful, dispel the fears of the terrified, restrain the headstrong, cool anger or lust. It is the power of speech which has bound us together in the bonds of justice, law and citizenship. It has raised us from a life of brutal savagery.
>
> It is almost incredible to those who have not studied the subject what pains nature has taken to confer on us this gift of speech."
>
> (*The Nature Of The Gods*, Cicero, Book 11, p 183)

It is shameful that we in the 21st century have allowed language to be divested of its inherent power for *Spiritual elevation* through uncaring attitudes towards it. In this electronic age the slovenly practice of shortening words in the new phenomenon of "txting" is a prime example. Whilst it clearly has certain advantages – convenient and cheap – texting sets in train an attitude of "short-cutting" that *actually degrades* the Spiritual Power inherent in all language. Irrespective of the actual language, texting now *infects* a very large proportion of at least the developed world, but this insidious "virus" is rapidly making inroads into the developing world too.

Should we be concerned? Or do we regard this new way of communicating as "progress", leaving behind "restrictive rules of grammar" in the drive toward greater and greater freedoms? Freedom! The cry of man from his earliest beginnings. True freedom, however, must incorporate the very essence of the actual concept and living form of the word: **RESPONSIBILITY!**

So, do we see any shred of the responsible use of language in the practice of "txting" in the direction it is obviously "developing"? Unfortunately, no. They who produce the electronic gadgets – along with their shareholders of course – welcome the huge financial returns on sales of "mobiles", so would not find cause for complaint there.

Nonetheless, "short-cutting" language will ultimately have a very detrimental effect on the society that sanctions it. It was to be expected, therefore, that standards in literacy among younger students would inevitably reduce. The State Examination Commission of Ireland has reported disturbing findings that the rising popularity of text messaging on mobile phones poses a threat to writing standards among Irish schoolchildren. Should we be surprised here? Of course not.

The problems resulting from this lazy and ill-disciplined practice are frequency in errors in grammar and punctuation, with the use of phonetic spelling producing little or no punctuation, and the practitioners reliant on short sentences, simple tenses and a limited vocabulary. Clearly, the whole unfortunate direction poses a real threat to traditional conventions in writing. Clear communication and direction is surely a must for any society if it wishes to maintain a reasonable level of business acumen, scientific and medical endeavour and research etc., let alone all things connected with the printed word.

For in its precise mathematical association with letters, combinations of letters, words and sentences etc., The Law of Numbers, under the aegis of The Law of Reciprocal Action, will "return" the appropriate consequences to all who misuse language. As we have stated at the very beginning of this Chapter, language is: **The "Forming" Word!**

Notwithstanding the previous example of the point we modern humans have reached in *our* attitude towards language, the momentous potential in the transitional effect of animal-man becoming spiritual-man would be that which the power of the spoken and, in turn, the written word would spiritually-exert on his world. Not just on the Earth, but in his part of Creation also.

However, man would need to tread many diverse paths, produce much offspring and people many lands before the full and generally unfortunate impact of this decisive "speaking ability" could be gauged and measured. Separating out and populating the different parts of the Earth guaranteed the formation of new languages with new words to give name to newly-discovered plants and animals, along with sights and sounds not seen or heard before. Via this vital and stupendous evolutionary happening, the way was now cleared for spiritual man to begin to record his exciting yet sometimes painful journey through "history". The establishment of "ground rules" whereby small bands of "new humans" could consolidate and begin to prosper, would be an obvious advantage.

In a very quick journey of compressed time, we can visualise the emerging family groups banding together to form larger, clannish organisations. This would serve the purpose of increasing their chances of success in hunting and for gathering food, provide protection for the group and allow for greater social development. Continually expanding groups would also prevent the possibility of inbreeding, which would be a consequence of maintaining a small group for an extended period.

The slow, gradual process of building groups of families into tribes, and tribes into confederations of tribes and so on, until whole Nations and races became fully established across the ancient "known world", would occupy a span of many, many thousands of years. The primary medium of communication, the language, would provide the pivotal role in this process. Language thus offered the means whereby practical, working rules to maintain cohesion and harmony in the growing organisations could be formulated – vital preparation for the very much later and more difficult task of governing Empires stretching across many lands. That was a long way into a very distant future, however.

Incidental to this procedure, therefore, was the requirement for expanding groups to seek new lands and territories – sometimes far from their origins – thus giving rise to the establishment, over time, of a language different to that of the old homeland. One perhaps similar, but perhaps not. Even with this diversification, however, certain elements in the languages of particular ethnic groups were retained as the basic root-foundation, thus indicating a common origin which we can trace today – particularly within the Indo-European group of people. Most Indian and Iranian languages belong to this Indo-European family of languages. Some Asian, South American, and Pacific Island languages share similarities also.

Humankind's territorial expansion did not result in an equal and uniform level of language development among the increasing numbers of different races and Nations, however. For example, races that were more concerned with merely the *basics* of life and with a *limited* view of the world naturally developed a *simple* language that mirrored *limited knowledge* about *fewer* things. That was not the case with people who were developing more technological societies.

Thus the different, emerging peoples subsequently developed their particular culture and characteristics in concert with their language. Some qualities would already have been inherent in most as a *core aspect*, but certain other traits would have developed as a consequence of various factors affecting their development, such as environmental ones for example. For each group, however, each developmental phase added to their respective store of knowledge and thus word-usage over-all.

Environmental considerations such as a warm or temperate climate with favourable food-producing conditions might allow an emerging race the luxury of food surpluses for trade and, therefore, the accumulation of wealth. A colder or harsher environment enforces the need for a more or less constant survival attitude with perhaps less scope for large-scale trade activity. It is not surprising therefore that, generally speaking, the earlier, more advanced civilisations first emerged in the warmer, more fertile regions of the Earth, notably around the Mediterranean, North Africa and the Middle East. Also in parts of China, India and South America. Of course, favourable climatic conditions were not the sole reasons for such an emergence. An inherent questing and technological bent were also required, since some societies in other warm climes remained basically simple and tribal.

With acquisition of food being a primary need for man, and shelter being a close companion, climatic factors would naturally be a key factor in determining his overall development.[2] If, then, the question of food and shelter in a "friendly climate" is resolved to the point where it does not present a problem and allows time away from the activities of food gathering – hunting, fishing or agriculture – "spare" or "leisure" time can then be channelled to other pursuits.

For example, dwellings which may have begun as rudimentary shelters could then be expanded to become much more comfortable and elaborate homes. From humble beginnings later gradually arose the great civilisations featuring large, planned, paved cities with public buildings, places of worship, and even piped water. In terms of language and vocabulary extension, this "expansion of the people" allowed the *intellectual* aspect of the race to evolve toward greater expression of abstract thought and philosophy.

Maslow's "hierarchy of needs", defines this process in latter-day "psycho-babble". Abraham Harold Maslow (1908-1970) developed a theory of "motivation" which describes the process by

---

[2]It is certainly a truism, that it is easy to be a conservationist until one is "cold, wet and hungry"!

which an individual progresses from basic needs such as food and sex to the highest needs of what he called "self-actualisation". In his opinion, "humanistic psychotherapy", usually in the form of group therapy, was the best way to help the individual through these stages. (We would opine that the better, simpler and more sure way to achieve that desirable state is to embrace the knowledge of Creation-Law and live by It. Self-realisation [or "self-actualisation"] derived from *genuine* spiritual knowledge and awareness would surely produce, from such a decision, a naturally-beneficial outcome.)

The overall drive, energy and population levels of the various emerging races might well determine who would emerge to become the great Nations and/or "Empire-builders" – as opposed to those who would simply be administered or absorbed by others. The establishment of larger groupings of peoples into complete Nations by the most energetic or magnanimous races might mean a correspondingly faster level of development of their administrative and building skills than perhaps those who were simply conquered or enslaved. History records the fact that some groups simply became slaves or servants of the strong.

Generally speaking, the languages of the "Empire-builders" developed rapidly as a result of continually evolving capabilities. This expansive attribute developing in those particular groups allowed for the subsequent emergence of a different way of thinking and speaking. Literature, religion, poetry, music composition and art gave impetus to a large degree of elevation in the language. Abstract or intuitive ideas and views became the science of philosophy which required the development of a whole new vocabulary to clarify such thinking. Notwithstanding the obvious fact that the nonetheless *inexorable* language-development *process* of early humankind quite naturally took some considerable time, did it *proceed*, however, in *accordance* with the design of The Creator Who, under the aegis of His Eternal Laws, granted we human beings the gift of conscious life? As this work is vitally concerned with that "reality", it is important to examine this question further.

Therefore: Early man still retained contact with the *non-physical* world from whence he came, thus holding an innate understanding of his connections to there. His "spirit", guided by that still-clear connection to those other Realms and to higher Spiritual Teachers, led his thinking and intuition. Consequently, the forming of words *initially proceeded* in accordance with the power inherent in The Laws of Creation. With clear guidance and strong intuitive perception, man was able to impart to *all* that he gave name, the *correct spiritual form* – remembering that The Spiritual is actually the *foundation* for all that exists in the Material. The non-material or abstract concepts also received their particular *word-coverings*. They, too, *resonated* with *their* correct spiritual meanings. So as men "built" their language *spiritually* in the early epoch of development – and as all forms of ennoblement are founded on the Eternal Principles and application of Creation-Law – they were bound to receive the "reciprocal returns" of peace, happiness and *harmonious* advancement.

8.2   The Biblical "Fall of Man": A Disastrous Legacy for Global Humanity

So, for a very long time, early humans lived in a period sometimes referred to as "**The Golden Age of Man**". In the course of his development, however, the purity of his previously strong *spiritual* intuition and volition unfortunately began to falter. This was brought about through man *strengthening his intellect* to a point where the *necessary balance between* the spiritual *and* intellectual aspects within him tipped more decisively **towards** the intellectual side. Consequently, his original, clear guidance suffered because a *barrier* was erected which *blocked* the formerly strong connections. This *barrier* was the too-strongly-earthbound *intellect*.

The language *subsequently formed* began to degenerate as a result of the *effect* and associated *application* of greater and denser *materialistic thinking*. Through this most unfortunate yet nonetheless *free-will decision*, over time man *severed* his connections with the Higher and lighter Spiritual Realms of his Origin and became, instead, enmeshed in darker thinking which was alien to his spirit. Increasingly *cut off* from the knowledge of its origins and walled-in by the *all-dominating intellect*, his **spirit** could no longer exert sufficient strength to alter his newly-chosen, aspiritual course, and so humankind *fell away* from the original and pure knowledge.

That 'process' constituted the "great fall of man"!

Therewith is that particular "Bible Mystery" explained! Spoken of in many legends and religious writings:

> The '**Fall of Man**' *was the result of 'man' finally placing his* **intellect** *in the* **leading position**, with the *subsequent relegation* of his '**guiding inner spirit**' to an *increasingly* **reduced** *role*, thereby bringing about his **fall**. It was thus a **turning away** from **The Creator** and **His Eternal Laws**.

This definitive happening in the evolutionary history of humankind is depicted in The Bible as the story of the building of the Tower of Babel which resulted in the great "confusion of tongues". [Genesis 11:1-9] The story of the Tower of Babel denoting the *scattering of the languages* should be viewed in the first instance, therefore, as a *spiritual event* describing a process that, in this case, was **not** primarily a *literal* building of a tower to heaven. It is vitally important to understand the *true spiritual meaning* of this happening. The edifice of Babel was a tower of *arrogance and presumption* fuelled by man's personal ego through his greater and greater disregard for Creation-Law; more especially in relation to language in this case. What should have been retained and *developed further* was *spiritually-appropriate employment* of correct word usage. By choosing an opposite path, a 'confusion of the language' gradually spread to all of the world's peoples.

This should not be interpreted to mean the development of many *different* languages, however, for *this would have been the natural situation in any case*. That was not the problem, and not the process. Neither does it mean that communication between the various peoples with their different languages would necessarily have been difficult. The "scattering" represented far more than just simple, physical differences in word-sounds, structure and meaning. In reality, it was an event of decisive *spiritual* proportions!

Men no longer *understood* each other because the *Spiritual* qualities of honesty, nobleness and purity that were the hallmark of the *early* development of the *form* of the language, underwent drastic change. Disregard for The Laws of God brought about a fundamental and far-reaching shift in the "kinds of forms" *created* by collective humankind. These new, *mutated forms* of pride, ego, selfishness, personal advantage and disregard for their fellow-men, became the normal produce of mankind. In that process is revealed the meaning of the *"scattering of the languages"*.

With that event, a wrong volition and attitude entered the earthly languages. Words appeared which had not until then existed and which were alien to the pure volition of the *first* human spirits. Words that were dark and evil; words formed from out of the evil deeds and thoughts of men. Like an insidious virus it spread throughout the languages of the peoples. Through this process, all the evil that can possibly occur in this world was produced by humankind over the thousands of years since. In accordance with the inviolable outworking of The Spiritual Laws of Creation, mankind had no choice but to give name to each evil, because the various *forms* produced arose, **living**, *within human beings* – exactly *corresponding* to the *free will* choices made.[3]

---

[3] "Tower of Babel" insights sourced from "A Gate Opens" by Herbert Vollmann.

Thus today we can readily see the culmination of all those past errors. The *spiritual* transgressions against the language which humankind thoughtlessly engage in clearly reveals how it is misused more and more through meaningless rubbish, empty talk and evil thinking. Ever more carelessly the meaning of words is distorted, particularly under the now socially accepted standard of "political" or "cultural correctness" and crass political power aspirations. This insidious process is just one of its many soiled shields. Thus debate in the various political chambers of many countries – the very place where one would expect such standards to be, at the very least, *upheld* – sometimes degenerates to foul-mouthed mud-slinging.

The high concepts of justice, love, purity, truth, humanity, freedom, peace and faith, whilst still bandied about, no longer hold the *elevated* position within society that even a few short years ago they would have. In accordance with man's present nature, he imputed to those ideals insidious meanings corresponding more to his increasingly selfish, material goals. Aims far removed from the pure application that these inherently noble concepts actually mean and represent – thus **HYPOCRISY!**

It should be perfectly clear to any keen observer, therefore, that the degradation of the language and its latter-day use conclusively reveals the *depths* to which *we* have *voluntarily* fallen. Once the "darker deeds" and the associated "growing evil" had given birth to the ***living form of the words*** connected with the ***deed*** and entered the ***language*** of the race, both these aspects became ***alive*** *within that particular race*. The whole then became a "dark well" into which all could dip and drink, with the "forms" even becoming "culturalised" and perhaps deemed to be "politically correct".

And the true magnitude of this "disaster" is not at all understood – or even recognised!

Thus, today, the language has, to a large degree, become befouled, evil and ugly with even the youngest children contaminated. Who, now, really cares? Unfortunately, very few; for *all* of global humanity have fallen away from the pure connection to Higher Spheres that were once enjoyed in former, more Spiritually-enlightened, times. Thus words used to describe dark and evil deeds within *any* language are *clear proof* that such things are an *inherent part* of that particular race, since those members, alone, have *spawned* the deed and its *associated* "living word-form".

Consequently, the objective examination of any language will quickly reveal the true "inner condition" of the "collective soul or spirit" of that particular race. Whilst all languages inherently encompass concepts and "forms" of enlightenment, the balance scales of all races are also clearly weighted toward baseness, and some more so than others.

Therefore, when speaking of the "fall" of man we should intuitively understand this to be his "spiritual fall", which we should clearly recognise as the loss of the once sacred, strong and necessary connection to The Source of Life. By supplanting the *spiritual* part within us – the *leader* – with the *intellectual* part – the *assistant* – we could do little else *but* fall away.

The difficulty in redressing that balance today is exacerbated by our *inability to recognise* that this adulation of the intellect ***actually constituted*** the **'fall of man' *to begin with***. That inability, in the strangest of ironies, is caused by our too-strong a reliance on ***that very intellect***, in the belief that it, and it alone, can provide all answers and solutions. Unfortunately, that is what is *directly responsible* for the *worsening problems* of humankind. As a further irony, the propensity of "modern man" to want to "intellectualise" everything – even *spiritual* matters – would *not have been possible* **without** the *means of the language* to express such incorrect and inherently unworkable concepts in the first place, the ***forms*** of which are now very self-evident.

A sharp differentiation should be made here between the more natural, *intuitive* beliefs associated with *genuine* knowledge and Truth, and the need for earth-sciences to utilise *intellectual* talent and ability to actually *construct* workable concepts for the benefit of humankind. Despite the obvious need for *intellectual input* into earthly existence, the fact that the intellect is *unable* to recognise Spiritual Truth because of its ordained purpose in fulfilling the earthly or material task means that:

> *Modern intellectual man* has now lost **the very means** by which he can **actually** and readily **recognise Spiritual Truth in the first place**, i.e. via his spirit. A spirit now, paradoxically, very much *suppressed* by the all-powerful and much-lauded *earthly intellect*.

In concert with exactly that now problematic "intellect of man", we will digress slightly to complete the explanations to the following question we first examined in Chapter 3.
So: For earth-science, specifically medical science and brain research: —

8.2.1   The Enlarging Baby Cranium: The "Lawful" Reason!

> This sub-Section connects back to a corresponding and *linking* segment in Chapter 3: **The Spiritual Laws: The Crucial Knowledge**.
> Specifically the sub-Chapter; **The Universal Pain of Childbirth. The Enlarging Baby Cranium: A "Medical" Mystery**. In *this* sub-Chapter we provide the *full linking knowledge* to *especially explain* the **why** of the enlarging baby cranium.

In concert with the discussion of the moment, the question of what exactly constitutes our human **life-force** needs to be brought into this analysis. As we have previously stated in a number of places, that dynamic is either an animating power *separate from* the human body – which is *our* absolute conviction – or it is a *non-separable*, **solely material**, 'life-force' inherently-fused into every cell nucleus throughout the whole human system. Thus for empirical science, a genomic lattice-work completely permeating every part of the entire body that, in a computer-like way, controls, regulates and maintains all bodily processes. Yet, in what would then be the most *illogical* association of all *if* such *really* were the case, to *also* possess the ability to somehow still make **free-will** decisions.

As stated in "**Author's Note**" and in Chapter 2; "**The Origins of Man: Genesis and Science Agree**", National Geographic Channel queried *exactly* this 'life-force' question in two separate Documentaries: "**Birth of Life**", and "**Human Ape**". The associated and most relevant point asked was:
"**How did *non-living* material come to life?**"

The History Channel, too, seeks the same kind of definitive answer. The series, "**How Life Began**", asks:
"**Where did [this] life come from? What <u>IS</u> life, exactly?**"

And in a *space* of perhaps *insightful prescience*, the Series further and *crucially* queries:
*"**Is it chemical, spiritual, <u>or a combination of both</u>?**"*   (All emphases mine.)

In 2009, Documentary Channels examined the phenomenon of the human baby's enlarging cranium. According to the various researchers interviewed, the baby's head will only fit through the pelvic girdle *one way*. So unless the baby receives a 'signal' to rotate its head to the right position as it approaches that point, the head – and therefore the rest of the body – will not get through the pelvic girdle to transit into the birth canal. In some cases, evidently increasing, even that is no longer *naturally* possible; thus requiring Cesarean deliveries for *every* baby born to those particular mothers.

The question for medical researchers presently studying this 'development' must surely be: **Why**? Ordinarily, evolutionary-type processes – such as appears to be the case here – will ensure that development or change in one area will be matched by the appropriate 'developmental-response' in the correspondingly-affected area; for this is not a 'mutation'. In the case of the human female pelvic-girdle configuration, *continuing enlargement* of the birth baby's 'head space' to keep pace with an enlarging baby cranium would only be viable if we reverted back to the stronger skeletal structure of Neanderthals. However, the heavier bone required for larger pelvic girdles, thus leading to correspondingly larger hips, means much slower bi-pedal locomotion. An enlarging pelvic girdle in the finer skeleton of the modern female form would probably eventually result in a weakened skeletal structure, so would not be a good outcome in terms of optimal 'evolutionary' or 'growth' development to accommodate enlarging baby craniums.

The 'head rotation manoeuvre' that babies perform in order to exit the womb has produced two divergent opinions among researchers. One view holds that *that* has *always* been the case, whilst the opposite notion tends towards it being a more or less 'evolutionary' development now necessary for the mother to deliver the baby safely – precisely *because* the brain case has been gradually enlarging over a very long time. So even allowing for the relatively soft bones in the skull of babies which offers some degree of 'flexing' at birth; increasingly, according to some opinions, that is evidently still not sufficient to permit birth without the necessary 'head rotation'. Essentially, then, we have a situation where one part of this equation – the pelvic girdle of birth mothers – cannot *safely* keep developmental pace with the enlarging heads of babies.

As we have stated in the corresponding, *linking*, segment in Chapter 3: **The Spiritual Laws**; sub – **The Universal Pain of Childbirth.**
The Enlarging Baby Cranium: A "Medical" Mystery – and restate once more in reinforcement:
"Why will Mother Nature not provide the obvious solution; hold the cranium to a size that is exactly right for natural, uncomplicated and *relatively* [though perhaps not completely] painless childbirth for human mothers?" Millions of herd animals must give birth quickly and easily for simple survival of the offspring which, in most cases, must be ready to run with the herd just hours after birth.

Why is this completely natural process becoming so problematic for humans that more and more 'C sections' are performed for all sorts of reasons? In *evolutionary* terms, why has the cranium of the human baby enlarged to such a degree that the head size in relation to body size is now so *disproportionately* big at birth that it can pose serious problems for delivery?

Echoing Einstein's deep understanding of where *real* knowledge *truly* comes from, the answer to the question we address in this segment can be *intuitively understood* from the explanations in *this* Chapter. Einstein's truly remarkable insights transcend by light-years the general lot of certainly the great bulk of global scientism to begin with.

> "The intuitive mind [*from the spirit*] is a sacred gift and the rational mind [*intellect*] is a faithful servant. We have created a society that honours the servant and has forgotten the gift."

> (Einstein. Parenthetic additions mine.)

And as we have necessarily quoted for scientists elsewhere in this Work, the great man stated that he never came upon any of his discoveries;

"...through *rational* thinking".

"And if one asks whence derives the authority of such fundamental ends, since they cannot be stated and justified merely by reason, one can only answer: they come into being *not through demonstration* **but through revelation**, *through the medium of powerful personalities.* One must not attempt to justify them, but rather to sense their nature simply and clearly."

"But science can only be created by those who are thoroughly imbued with the aspiration toward truth and understanding."

(Ideas and Opinions, p 42-3.
All emphases mine.)

The *reason* for the enlarging cranium in babies lies in the *seriously-aberrant* **development**, over millennia, of the human brain. The *present-day* configuration of the two primary parts – the cerebrum and the cerebellum – hold the key to **why** the brain case is enlarged beyond its original, *lawfully-ordained*, structure.
The cerebrum: The large rounded structure of the brain occupying most of the cranial cavity, divided into two cerebral hemispheres. Commonly called the '*large brain*'. Therein lies a clue. [For as we noted in the 'linking section', recent calculations of the cranium-size of *new-born babies* – in Western births – on average run to over **12%** of total body mass, while in *adults* the same represents just over **2%**.]
The cerebellum: [diminutive of cerebrum] Often referred to as the '*small brain*'. [There lies one other part to this "mystery".]
According to neurological research, the structure of the brain responsible for regulation and coordination of complex voluntary movement, lying below the occipital lobes of the cerebral hemispheres.

Empirical brain research, even though identifying and correlating individual areas of the brain to precise processes and functions within the human body, does not provide the *actual* answer to the enlarging cranium. Scientific literature notes that birthing by human mothers has always been more difficult than for other mammals due to narrow bi-pedal hips. These two seemingly-unrelated aspects nonetheless provide the connecting link to the question of the enlarging baby cranium. From all that we have explained thus far in this Work, the reason *should* be clear enough.
Question. The brain?: Insufficient use — or over-use? Centred on that very question, let us itemise a few points that will help to both focus and clarify the direction we must take to understand and resolve this problem for science.

- "Use it or lose it"; a well known but nonetheless apt truism.

- Under-development stunts growth and creates imbalance.

- Over-development will also create imbalance, but of a different kind.

- Both those aspects of brain *activity* are thus an *abberation* by virtue of the resulting *imbalance aspect*.

So, over-development of *anything* in *any* field can result in unexpected outcomes and/or ones not necessarily commensurate with the original projected/assumed parameters for the particular thing. [In this modern era obsessed with the 'body beautiful', body-builders can develop any part of the body relatively easily. It is therefore possible to 'bulk-up', for example, just one arm to produce an *aberrant* form emulating the large protective claw that certain crabs possess – which is *natural* for *them*.]

As an historical engineering example, original designs for bulk carriers [ships] and a particular type of bridge worked perfectly well and safely when kept within *original*, specification parameters. However, when **modified beyond that safe original**, some failed; with resultant loss of life. We may ask: '*What has engineering got to do with brain-development?*' Well, the *principle* is no different. Develop **anything** beyond its original, **ordained purpose**, and it must obviously **fail** that purpose.

So is it with the human brain! The *over-development* of the *intellect* has resulted in the present-day, *aberrant* phenomenon of a brain-case enlarging to accommodate that greater and greater – and unfortunately much lauded and desired – intellectual capacity of *modern*, though now *very aspiritual*, man. Language, or more precisely the misuse of it, has been a *major driver* in this process. Man had two choices: Maintain the *spiritual power* that he *originally* imbued language with; or fall away from that vital life-connection and *subvert* and coarsen it with the *increasingly-dominant* aspiritual, *earthly* – and thus **Earth-bound** – intellect.

An important and related question is: 'How has this *distortion* from the time of the *story* of Eve's transgression carried itself down through the generations to the present?' The step to that progression begins thus:

> But to the woman He said, "I will increase your sorrows and your joys. *You will give birth to children **with pain**;..."*

(Genesis 3:16, Fenton.
Emphases mine.)

The connecting answer to our associated query – which the non-Christian community will no doubt regard as religious claptrap – nonetheless *also* lies in The Bible. Notwithstanding the sure 'slings and arrows' of official academia, the *actual* reason for the present aberration yet resonates with very simple *scientific* principles. Once again, *over-development* is the key to understanding the secondary aspect of the overall 'enlarging-cranium' question. Now we get to the nub of the problem with regard to the primary subject matter of *this* Chapter.

The Bible speaks of, and strongly condemns, *the* 'Hereditary Sin' of mankind. The obvious pointer to **what** and **why** lies in the word 'hereditary', i.e., something 'passed on' – from one generation to the next. Equally obviously, that clearly cannot mean – again as so many otherwise well-intentioned Christians firmly believe – that we have *all inherited*, and are thus *all tainted*, by the so-called *original sin* of Adam and Eve. That *fundamentalist* tenet is so *completely* wrong that any argument to support it simply *cannot* be made. For if it *were* correct, it would logically mean that we do *not* possess the attribute of 'free-will', and are thus subject to consequences *not* of our own making.

That is as illogical as it is ridiculous. Such a *distorted* concept of Truth does not even *begin* to resonate with the **Perfection** of **Creation-Law**. For we are warned that we must "reap what we sow" [but solely, *individually*, through *personal* choice/s], which even Christian fundamentalists cannot logically argue against. And that is:

Decisions Produce Consequences!

As with so many strongly-defended, so-called, sacrosanct tenets and beliefs of global Christendom, the *terrible distortion* here lies in the *non-understanding* of *exactly* what was originally set in train by Eve's[4] [*humankind's*] serious act of disobedience: Thus what was passed on through the *generations* to the present-day to be now puzzled over by brain and obstetrics researchers. The *actual* transgression, as we once more explain, was *choosing* to *no longer follow*

---

[4]Eve: *Khavah*, or *life-container*.

the original *spiritual* path *ordained* for earthly humanity *for all time*. The ***sin*** is represented by the *tasting* of the *forbidden* fruit, i.e., the 'falling away' *from* the ordained spiritual path with the *inevitable* and thus subsequent *over-strengthening* of the *worldly* intellect. The *serpent* in the story represents the *insidious cunning* of the *Earth-bound*, therefore *aspiritual*, **intellect!**

What became – and actually *still is* – the **'hereditary aspect'**, **is** hereditary *solely because* the over-stimulation, the over-strengthening, of the intellect resulted in an *imbalance* of the once *equal-sized*, harmoniously-active *front and back brains*. Through millennia of *over-cultivation*, the consequently-developed far greater mass, the 'large brain' [**the intellectual brain**] now *almost completely fills* the brain case. The other *once-complementary* **spiritual** part – now referred to as the 'small brain' – is completely **stunted** through __non-use__. With each generation born, therefore, the *intellectual part* of the brain grew *disproportionately larger*.

Stimulated through more and more *aspiritual* ways and ideas, particularly in education, that continual development meant that the *size* and *power* of the *intellectual part* of the brain *had to increase*. The resultant and inevitable legacy is, quite logically, the enlarged brain case evident today! Perhaps, to coin a 'today' phrase: **"Enlarged to the max."**

We global participants of the aspiritual educational paradigm that has held sway for millennia – but now at its *greatest* strength – have *passed on* that aberration, **hereditarily**, to *all* successive generations in our individual genealogical lines. That very long process of *intellectual* 'over-stimulation' resulted in the need for *more* room in the cranium. Even though enlarging only minutely-incrementally over millennia, the resultant outcome is sufficient to force the question **why** from the scientific community. Thus all of humankind is now affected by wrong ideas and teachings, and our earthly home contaminated by that **aspiritual poison.**

So, until and unless there is an immediate and very massive fundamental shift in the educational ethos that the ruling university elite clings to, the most that can be expected from that quarter is *more questions* producing *more research* to try to answer the next lot of **questions**. Never the final answer! But it keeps those presently in control forever in control, doesn't it?

Just as we have offered logical explanations for a number of scientific/religious questions as yet without definitive answers from those two Disciplines, so, too, has the quandary of the enlarging baby cranium also found logical resolution here.

As we will very strongly state a number of times in this Work, only with the recognition and acceptance of the knowledge-aegis inherent in: —

Crucial Imperative No 2:

That we, the human beings of planet Earth, are not solely a physical entity, but also necessarily possess a *non-material* inner animating core: *For the physical **cannot** – and therefore **does not** – animate the physical!*

— — and — —

Crucial Imperative No 3:

That being more than just a physical body means we naturally and *inherently* possess a *separable entity* **within** the material form. And that *that* is the *actual* life-force, the *animating* core, that is *actually each individual!*

— will earth-science ever begin to finally complete their millions of text-books that, in the final analysis *without* the immutable and inviolable knowledge of **Creation-Law**, really only just ask more questions. The classic case of: **"The Error of Scientism!"**

Pope Benedict XVI has correctly called to science to think differently:

"Modern *scientific reason* quite simply has to accept the rational structure of matter and the correspondence *between our spirit* and the *prevailing* rational structures of nature *as a given*, on which its methodology *has to be based*. Yet the question why this has to be so, is a *real* question, and one which has to be remanded by the natural sciences *to other modes and planes of thought* – to **philosophy and theology**."

Notwithstanding that clear rationale from a greatly respected academic, the very *language* of the *dominating intellectual-educational authorities* of the many diverse countries, societies and cultures across the globe will surely *cry out* <u>**against**</u> the immutable **Creation-Law Truths** herein! So the final excision to bring to an end humankind's ongoing hereditary production of *aspiritual poison* will thankfully be forced upon us.

Isaiah, the Prophet, in **language** *powerfully-resonating* with **Spiritual Truth** and **Law**, warningly proclaims to humanity of this present era precisely what *we* are directed to explain in this Work. In this case – and thereby powerfully assisting *our* Mandate – we will, very thankfully, let the great Prophet and Servant of **The Creator** speak:

"The 'Earth' also is **defiled** under the **inhabitants** thereof; because **they** have ***transgressed*** the Laws, **changed** the decrees, <u>**broken**</u> the everlasting covenant. Therefore has the **curse** devoured the 'Earth', and those that dwell therein **are** **desolate**:..."

(Isaiah 24:5-6, Fenton.
Emphases mine.)

Very much later, the great Prophet's dire warning for humankind was more strongly stated by One Who possessed the Absolute Mandate to so Proclaim. Since an exponential factor can be readily observed in all events now, the answer of Jesus to His Disciples when asked what the future-time [our time] would be like, is chilling.

"...for there shall then be **wide-spread affliction**, such as has **not been known** since the beginning of the world **until now**, no, nor will **ever** be known again. And if those times were **not** cut short, **not a man would be saved**".

(Matthew 24:21-22, Fenton.
Emphases mine.)

8.3   The Two "Faces" of Language: Spiritual and Non-Spiritual "Examples"

As probably the best example of the power of language to initiate sweeping change down through the centuries, we need look no further than to the Ministry of Jesus. Sent to this Earth to guide mankind back to knowledge of The Truth – and as previously stated, in accordance with "The Law of Attraction..." – He could only incarnate into a race that had developed sufficient *Spiritual-insight* to intuitively accept the *reality* of The One Invisible Creator. So it was that Jesus was born, by Law, into the Jewish race; a people with the necessary level of Spiritual development for that connection to be made. A people, moreover, whose law and *language*, through the admonitions of their many prophets, clearly echoed that understanding.

Aside from being totally pointless, a birth into any other race could not have been possible, as we have already noted. Only a people with the requisite degree of even *symbolic* affinity or understanding could prepare the way for a Being Who stands far *above* The Spiritual even. The language and spiritual *form* of The Torah basically provided the necessary "bridge of attraction". The entry and purpose of Jesus on Earth gave mankind a far different perspective of the power of language through His use of it in the purest, Spiritual way. His whole ministry was remarkable for the fact that He taught the Truth via the medium of the *spoken word*, not that of the written. Thus the "living power of language" is best illustrated in the manner in which Jesus "spoke the Truth", and its resultant and *undeniably* powerful effect upon the world.

However, even this stupendous Event and help from Above still did not change man's basic intransigence toward the pure Truth given at that time. The distortions and errors caused by the "playing with the language of the Truth" have caused great confusion, particularly among the numerous Christian denominations.

Another distortion, ultimately no less important than that of the words of Truth handed down to humankind, was that associated with the many and varied "gods of legend". Through the unfortunate development of greater intellectual sophistry in the new peoples collectively, the original strong and natural connection to, and knowledge of, his Spiritual Origins became more and more clouded as the intellect grew *disproportionately stronger*. The inevitable result saw spiritual man's once secure ties to his Higher Origins virtually severed. And with it a particular and vital connection that was meant to be an ongoing and special help in his earthly activities for all the time of his earthly stay.

In the beginning, he lived his life completely aware and accepting of the other-world (ethereal) currents around him, and of his connections to what we term the "beyond". More importantly, he worked in concert with other Beings who have their origin in another Plane of Creation and who are active not only on the Earth but in every other Realm of Creation also. Indeed, without their essential activity, man would never have had an Earth to call "home" in the first place. Today, only a very few people scattered throughout the various races have the ability to still see these "helpers", even though we all see and feel the effects of their necessary activity every minute of the day. These are the "Nature Beings" and Elementals whose names are found, *virtually without exception*, in the languages of *all* races on Earth.[5]

The cutting away and eventual *rejection* of the *reality* of the "Elemental Forces of Nature" through the *elevation* of the intellect subsequently *guaranteed* that a huge gap of knowledge would develop in the historical narrative of the evolving journey of virtually all peoples. Some, though, would consciously retain this knowledge longer than others. In virtually every case, however, what was once sure and certain Truth, securely and knowingly embedded in the languages of the various peoples, eventually became relegated to the realm of uncertain myth and legend. Rather than being retained as clear knowledge, it was transposed into either "romanticised literature" of the culture of the particular race concerned, or became stories to be feared.

Some of the more intellectual races, notably those from Western cultures, have virtually severed this connection totally, not even bothering to retain them as fables. The so-called more primitive or not-so-advanced races have at least retained a strong belief in the validity of their legends as possible truth. Unfortunately for Western Nations generally, their *god of science* has determined that such "notions" cannot possibly be entertained as belonging to a "rational, logical and intelligent" society. Interestingly, however, the main book of their religion, The Bible, speaks of them clearly enough. Thus the relegation of what was once accepted as factual knowledge to the realm of myth and legend by "intellectual reasoning", is to our detriment. Notwithstanding this particular path, the many languages of the world's various peoples still bear testimony to a time when man accepted the evidence of his factual experiences, and thus gave name to all that he knew existed in the Elemental World of Nature.

As formerly noted, the rightful place of the intellect was to facilitate and assist man in the fulfilment of his *earthly* duties, which is why it is so vital for scientific endeavour and

---

[5]Previously explained in Chapter 4: **"Elemental Lore of Nature"**.

why it has produced technological marvels and great feats of construction. In those particular endeavours the language naturally provided the exact parameters by which this aspect of man also developed. As ordained from the very beginning, however, *the spirit was to lead and the intellect to assist*. Sadly, spiritual man, with the potential for achieving true greatness in the material world and in Creation, became *merely intellectual man more concerned with earthly analysis and theory*.

> Paradoxically, therefore, greater ***spiritual*** input and activity would have produced ***intellectual works*** which would have been of *correspondingly greater* benefit for humankind than is presently the case. e.g., our poisoned, degraded, earthly home.

Ironically for modern-day man, the purpose of science was always to explain – via the language of course – the workings of all Creation-Law and their effects in the physical world. By this process, man could re-discover his true place *in* Creation. Instead, he denies himself the very means by which to recognise the knowledge and connection that can bring about that re-discovery – that of **his Spirit**. Now, instead of a powerful, uplifting, Spiritual language at our command we have, in its place, only a *weak shadow* of what it should be, thus *contaminating* virtually all the "works" we currently "produce".

We should never forget, therefore, the powerful lessons that history constantly endeavours to teach us. For in that grand sweep can be seen how the power of language stirred men and Nations to great deeds. The welling-up of nationalistic fervour by the generation of powerful and emotional oratory has galvanised whole peoples to destroy even numerically superior forces bent on their conquest or destruction. The greatest war the world has ever experienced produced especially stirring words of power from Winston Churchill which greatly helped the British people withstand the onslaught of Hitler's Air Force during the "Battle of Britain". The American radio-journalist, Edward R. Murrow – living in London during that period – opined that Winston Churchill "*...mobilised the English language and sent it into battle to fight for democracy*".

The power of language to move people patriotically can be clearly and powerfully seen at events where National Anthems are played. The words are sung with great feeling and emotion and are an obvious pointer to the power inherent in *all* languages when used correctly. It is the "living form" *embodied in the words* which actually produces that effect, thus which holds and strengthens the corresponding connection for each race to their particular homeland.

The same effect can be felt when the hymns or *spiritual* songs of a given people are sung at times of great distress or during reverent worship. There the inner spirit perhaps senses its lost connection to a Higher, intangible 'Force' far removed from the problems of everyday living. A strong upwelling of emotion is invariably felt then. The particular *forms* of distress or loss – or even inner joy felt at that moment – strive to establish or re-establish a connection with an intuitively-perceived Higher, more powerful, protective presence Above; therewith to, respectively, find solace and comfort, or express gratitude. Hence the words *clothe* the *form* and *power* of the *spiritual* meaning and are thus *felt* emotionally. Of course, this is also true with opposite kinds of living word forms, but these bring forth ugliness and discord. *The potential for self-imposed distress, therefore, provides the very reason to use language only in an ennobling way.*

Jostein Gaarder, author of Sophie's World, in his analysis of the German philosopher Hegel, on page 307 writes of Hegel's philosophy with regard to language. As quoted at the beginning of this Chapter: "Reason manifests itself above all in language. And a language is something we are born into." He argues that a language can manage quite well without the personal involvement or input of an individual of that particular race, but the individual *cannot* manage without that language. [Emphasis mine.]

*"It is thus not the **individual** who forms the language, it is the **language** which forms the individual."*

A quite logical extrapolation from that truism thus accepts the premise that *whole races, also, are "formed" by their individual languages*. We recognise, or perhaps inherently associate, various characteristics of different races with their language. The fact that specific languages generally "belong" to particular races is usually sufficient to conjure up images that "fit" the people of those races. Conversely, our natural acceptance that other races will invariably be different from us automatically inculcates the belief that they will probably speak a language different from ours also.

What of the less developed races, the smaller groups and tribes around the globe, however? And what comparative level of language development did they achieve? In general their more restricted view of the world, governed by narrower perceptions signalling less knowledge of fewer things, and perhaps strongly laced with superstitious views, resulted in comparatively simpler languages. Thus, through the many diverse languages, we *see* the different, historical life-paths and subsequent fortunes of the world's various peoples quite clearly written on the pages of time. Recorded history has generally been written by dominant races with perhaps stronger, more assertive languages.

Certainly, the history of humankind clearly records many instances of suppression of the language, history and culture of minority groups within the sphere of totalitarian regimes. Yet, whilst such activities in other societies past and present are rightly condemned, the same kind of "official" language suppression and distortion through the pressure of vocal minorities today virtually enshrines the dangerously insidious practice of "political" or "cultural" correctness too. The inanity of it all is too clearly evident when it becomes a criminal or cultural offence to speak on certain issues – even with correct language usage – in case it offends someone, somewhere.

By hijacking a word for a particular labelling purpose, even words once simply understood have become so distorted that previously unacceptable practices have become "main-stream acceptable" in their associated word-usage. Racial issues involving change or distortion in language meaning also occupy this wrongly elevated place. Unfortunately, a spade cannot always be called a spade today. In ways that cannot be quantified empirically, this completely wrong development seriously impacts upon those societies which weakly bow to such tyranny. The insidious erosion of true "language-freedom" in the *spiritual* sense, especially pertaining to the actual Truths within the great religions, is an unfortunate and ultimately debilitating consequence of such appeasement by primarily weak politicians who first set in place and then fawningly-serve their politically-weak regimes.

Notwithstanding all that is wrong with our use of it, certain languages have developed to a point of convenience and value where they are now regarded as the world standard for particular activities. Thus, for example, we have Latin for scientific classification of 'flora and fauna' and the German language generally synonymous with precision and engineering excellence.[6] English is the preferred language of international business and aviation.

Nevertheless, for all its obvious necessity the language, in its general application formed by the power inherent in the human spirit, is now a sad, polluted and degraded shadow of what it could and should be. Whilst it will continue to evolve, of course, if it is to be of maximum benefit for humankind, it should do so only under the umbrella of The Eternal Laws.

This should not mean the relaxation of even basic rules of grammar and spelling under "modern and enlightened" educational curricula simply because it fits with some misguided

---

[6]The German language also holds a particularly elevated level of *spiritual* value. Primarily seeded by Martin Luther, the language developed and evolved over time to reach its zenith towards the end of the 19th century – Hohe Deutsch – High German. [Further on in the Work the reader will discover the precise and very important reason for this specific reference to the German Language.]

notion that it somehow provides a more "level playing field" for all students. No longer do we appear to strive for individual excellence as would befit the outworking of Spiritual Law. Far easier to adopt a "herd-mentality" and simply produce average "automatons" who won't be "emotionally disadvantaged" by not having the same "level of achievement" as the rest of the herd! That kind of neutering process offers nothing more than a lowering of standards within the particular society because it rejects the vital necessity of sound, healthy discipline which is ultimately voiced through language. To use a "modern" term, it is simply a "dumbing-down" process.

Despite the fact that languages are important to retain within individual cultures in any given land, a particular language may not necessarily be the best one for general, everyday use. Therefore, where there may be indigenous bi-culturalism associated with a more globally-accepted dominant language within the land – such as English for example – that will probably always be the main medium of language communication. Simply because, in terms of sheer logic, it is a commonsense position. Certainly, the less-dominant language should be retained, for all languages are a gift *through which the peoples' culture* **can** *be more nobly expressed.*

Its retention, however, must ultimately be the responsibility of the people concerned, for it is *their* language after all. It is not anyone else's. If, however, there is insufficient interest in retaining it *for themselves*, then that would simply show the lawful process of how and why the demise of part of the cultural heritage of a race occurs. It would thus reveal that particular race's *own unwillingness* to hold on to it. Latter-day renaissance interest for languages almost lost is clearly a correct and admirable thing. For the language of any people perhaps offers the greatest medium for the complete cultural expression of that group, and therefore should not be allowed to die out.

In summary, language, with its inherent "forming power" under the aegis of Creation-Law, can either uplift a people or drag them down. Upliftment or degradation will depend upon whether that medium is used to *spiritualise* the talents and abilities within the group, or is used to pervert or *coarsen* those gifts. For from the *thoughts* are produced the *words*, and from the *mouth* via the respective language, the *issue* of those words. The words then *frame* or *clothe* the **form** of the corresponding activity or *deed.*

The Book of Matthew offers a strong pointer to this spiritually-lawful and precise relationship between the use of words for good, or for the opposite. He recounts how Jesus rebuked the Pharisees intent on entrapping Him. In Chapter 12, verses 34-36, (Fenton) Matthew notes this reference to the power inherent in language.

> "...how can you preach purity, when you are yourselves depraved? The beneficent man draws from his treasury of purity, goodness; and the depraved man can only produce depravity, from his stores of depravity! I tell you, however, that every vile *idea* that men give expression to, they shall render a reason for it in the Day of Judgement".

And the King James Version (Matthew 12:37) completes it thus. [All emphases mine.]

> "For by thy *words* thou shalt be justified, and by thy *words* thou shalt be condemned."

A further powerful statement is made in Chapter 15, verse 11, where Jesus proclaims to a large crowd:

> "Listen and understand! What goes into the mouth does not corrupt the man; but what comes out of his mouth does corrupt him."

And in Matthew 15:16-20, in reply to His Disciples obviously puzzled by His explanations, He said to them:

> "Are you ignorant even yet? Do you not know that everything going into the mouth proceeds to the stomach, and is from there evacuated? But what come out *from the mouth* proceed *from the heart*, and *corrupt* the man. For there come *from the heart* wicked thoughts, murders, adulteries, fornications, thefts, perjuries, blasphemies. *These* are what corrupt the man..."

Thus all languages possess words that run the complete gamut of human volition. From soaring forms of spiritual upliftment, to ugly and befouled ones. The particular "word forms" chosen for general discourse or debate which issue from the mouth of speakers of any given language will produce the corresponding "living forms" of either upliftment or debasement, exactly as Jesus explained. Therefore *liberal beliefs* that Biblical pronouncements of the kind we have quoted have little relevance for modern man and equate to nothing more than "fire and brimstone" preaching, are *themselves* rendered *irrelevant* by the reality of rapidly degrading societies world-wide. For global societies are ultimately the **end excrescence** of all the "forms" produced by the many **aspiritual** deeds in the medium of all the diverse languages of **collective humanity**.

8.4   Language in American Culture and "Entertainment"

The development of the entertainment industry, particularly from the movie studios and in the medium of television, has spawned a particular brand of "language-ethos". Spewing forth from the big screen over the past 80 or so odd years and the small screen for about 50 years, movie and television studios worldwide have produced the spiritually-strange force of **'entertainment'** – more especially from Hollywood. Producing great wealth and power for the few, the American "entertainment industry" sways the lives of billions globally.

Under the aegis of the American Constitution, particularly the all-encompassing, all-embracing "Free Speech Amendment", very few curbs have been placed on what producers and directors can say or show there. And, of course, American **entertainment** is exported all over the globe. Since the visual aspect is almost invariably accompanied by "The Script", language, by inference, has followed the trend of the visual medium into the more extreme, the more crass and the more debased. Music lyrics have followed a similar trend. What price freedom – in the ultimate sense? True and genuine freedom must presuppose the requirement to exercise *responsibility*. Not simply responsibility as espoused and formulated by secular demands and law, but responsibility under the greatest aegis of all – that of **Creation-Law!**

Voices raised in protest today against rapidly-falling moral or social standards invariably die away under the too-greater-pressure exerted by the masses seeking *more entertainment* of more extreme, so-called, *entertainment value*. Aided, quite naturally, by the wealthy power-brokers who produce, supply and control it all.

Yet, on October 15th, 1958, in a keynote and now definitive speech to the Radio-Television News Directors Association and Foundation (RTNDA), Edward R. Murrow, the famous news presenter and journalist for CBS Corporation, questioned the direction that Radio and Television might take American society. His speech runs to six pages of type so we will regrettably only reproduce a few very pertinent points from a discourse in which every sentence is most pertinent.

More especially for that group of citizens who proudly call their Nation "the world's only true superpower" and, concomitantly, "leader of the free world". We would therefore recommend that every citizen of America – along with almost everyone else since all cultures are strongly impacted, if not entirely subsumed, by American "entertainment" – read or freely download Murrow's complete speech from the **"Keynote Speech"** page on the website dedicated to his life and work at: Edward R. Murrow.

The uplifting power inherent in language for the betterment of society, as he indeed employed it, rings out in that speech. It can now be seen as prophetic, and his *clarified intellect* permitted him to know that *at the time*. The high point of the American Nation, industry and people was The Second World War and its immediate aftermath. Forced to reject isolationism, America mobilised its great industrial might and millions of servicemen to fight and help defeat a monstrous evil. Without that monumental effort the world might well have entered a new dark age. Post-war America then nobly helped defeated and destroyed enemy to rebuild their war-ravaged countries and economies.

Freedom *without* spiritual responsibility post-war, however, seeded a sliding away from previously firm and relatively-ennobled values. American "culture" is, today, now riven with spiritually-aberrant ideas and practices – the so-called *Freedoms* guaranteed by *The Constitution*. Apart from certain strong European societies and other religions, the "culture" most "in demand" almost everywhere else globally is, unfortunately, that of the USA. American "culture" is successfully exported through the "swamping effect" of the American movie and television industry; *hence the grave importance of Murrow's speech*. Paradoxically it was exactly the movie industry – albeit as more an independent production – through which George Clooney very fortunately brought the life and speeches of Edward R. Murrow to the attention of the world.

Murrow's speech to the RTNDA began with opening remarks which quantified his need to broach, at the time, a contentious but necessary subject.

> "This just might do nobody any good. At the end of this discourse a few people may accuse this reporter of fouling his own comfortable nest, and your organisation may be accused of having given hospitality to heretical and even dangerous thoughts. But the elaborate structure of networks, advertising agencies and sponsors will not be shaken or altered. It is my desire, if not my duty, to try to talk to you journeyman with some candour about what is happening to radio and television.
>
> "Believing that potentially the commercial system of broadcasting as practised in this country is the best and freest yet devised, I have decided to express my concern about what I believe is happening to radio and television. These instruments have been good to me beyond my due. ... But I am seized with an abiding fear regarding what these two instruments are doing to our society, our culture and our heritage.
>
> "Our history will be what we make it. "And if there are any historians about fifty or a hundred years from now, and there should be preserved the kinescopes for one week of all three networks, they will there find recorded in black and white, or color, evidence of the escapism and insulation from the realities of the worlds in which we live."
>
> Murrow noted that in the television schedules of all networks between the hours of 8 and 11 p.m. one would find only brief and "...spasmodic reference to the fact that this nation is in mortal danger.
>
> "...during the daily peak viewing periods, television in the main insulates us from the realities of the world in which we live. If this state of affairs continues, we may alter an advertising slogan to read: LOOK NOW, PAY LATER.

"...If there were to be a competition in indifference, in insulation from reality, then Nero and his fiddle, Chamberlain and his umbrella could not find a place on an early afternoon sustaining show. ...some courageous soul with a small budget might be able to do a documentary telling what, in fact, we have done – and are still doing – to the Indians in this country. But that would be unpleasant ... *we must at all costs shield the sensitive citizens from anything that is unpleasant.*

"I am entirely persuaded that the American public is more reasonable, restrained and more mature than most of our industry's program partners believe. Their fear of controversy is not warranted by the evidence. I have reason to know ... that when evidence on a controversial subject is fairly and calmly presented, the public recognizes what it is – an effort to illuminate rather than to agitate."

On the emerging ethos and traditions of the developing television paradigm in America, Murrow noted:

"If they but knew it, they are building those traditions, creating those precedents everyday. Each time they yield to a voice from Washington or any other political pressure, each time they eliminate something that might offend some section of the community, they are creating their own body of precedent and tradition. They are, in fact, not content to be "half safe".

On the question of television Editorials:

"It is much easier, much less troublesome to use the money-making television and radio merely as a conduit through which to channel anything that is not libellous, obscene or defamatory. In that way one has the illusion of power *without responsibility.*

"What, then, is the answer? Do we merely stay in our comfortable nests, concluding that the obligation of these instruments has been discharged when we work at the job of informing the public for a minimum of time?

"I am frightened by the imbalance, the constant striving to reach the largest possible audience for everything; by the absence of a sustained study of the nation. Heywood Broun once said: "No body politic is healthy until it begins to itch." I would like television to produce some itching pills rather than this *endless outpouring of tranquilizers.* It can be done. Maybe it won't be, but it could. ...do not be deluded into believing that the titular heads of the networks control what appears on their networks. They all have better taste. All are responsible to stockholders... But they must schedule what they can sell in the public market. And this brings us to the nub of the question. ... The Corporate image."

Murrow was not sure what this phrase meant, but he thought that it might signal a desire on the part of the corporations who pay the advertising bills to have the public imagine or believe "...that they are not merely bodies with no souls panting in pursuit of elusive dollars. They would like us to believe that they can distinguish between the public good and the private or corporate gain. So the question is this: Are the big corporations who pay the freight for radio and television programs wise to use that time exclusively for the sale of goods and services?

"Is it in their interest and that of the stockholder to do so? The sponsor of an hour's television program is not buying merely the six minutes devoted to commercial message. He is determining, within broad limits, the sum total of the impact of the entire hour. If he, always, invariably reaches for the largest possible audience, then this process of insulation, of escape from reality, will continue to be massively financed, and its apologist will continue to make winsome speeches about giving the public what it wants, or "letting the public decide".

"I refuse to believe that the presidents and chairmen of the boards of these big corporations want their corporate image to consist exclusively of a solemn voice in an echo chamber, or a pretty girl opening the door of a refrigerator, or a horse that talks. They want something better, and on occasion some of them have demonstrated it.

"Why should not each of the big corporations which dominate radio and television decide that they will give up of their regularly scheduled programmes each year, turn the time over to the networks and say in effect: "This is a tiny tithe, just a little bit of our profits. On this particular night we aren't going to try to sell cigarettes or automobiles; this is merely a gesture to indicate our belief in the importance of ideas." The networks should, and I think would, pay for the cost of producing the program. The advertiser, the sponsor, would get name credit but would have nothing to do with the content of the program. Would this blemish the corporate image? Would the stockholders object? I think not.

"We are currently wealthy, fat, comfortable and complacent. Our mass media reflect this. But unless we get up off our fat surpluses *and recognize that television in the main is being used to distract, delude, amuse and insulate us*, then television and those who finance it, those who look at it and work at it, *may see a totally different picture too late*.

"Perhaps no one will do anything about it. ... I cannot believe that radio and television, or the corporation that finance the programs, are serving well or truly their viewers or listeners, or themselves.

"I began by saying that our history will be what we make it. If we go on as we are, then history will take its revenge, and retribution will not be limp in catching up with us. ...and here might ensue a most exciting adventure – exposure to ideas and the bringing of reality into the homes of the nation.

"To those who say people wouldn't look, they wouldn't be interested, they're too complacent, indifferent and insulated, I can only reply: There is, in one reporter's opinion, considerable evidence against that contention. But even if they are right, what have they got to lose?

"Because if they are right, *and this instrument is good for nothing but to entertain, amuse and insulate, then the tube is flickering now and we will see the whole struggle is lost*.

"This instrument can teach, it can illuminate; yes, and it can even inspire. But it can do so only to the extent that humans are determined to use it to those ends. Otherwise it is merely wires and lights in a box. *There is a great and perhaps decisive battle to be fought against ignorance, intolerance and indifference. This weapon of television could be useful*."

(All emphases mine.)

The interesting point about Murrow's life and his approach to the use of language in a spiritually-ennobled and thus upbuilding way is that his radio career emerged around roughly the same time-space that Hitler occupied, but essentially during World War II. History well records the fact that, unlike Murrow, Hitler used "the power of language" in a charismatic way to very effectively seduce and pressure *a whole people* to embrace an idea so dark and evil that it will forever stand as one of the worst examples of "man's inhumanity to man".

The prophetic insights of Edward R. Murrow, perhaps the most celebrated "lone voice" warning about the potential of radio and television for education and enlightenment to be subsumed by **entertainment**, have *already been borne out*. Television's particularly insidious nature has seduced generation after generation to the belief that the present situation of *hours of mindless drivel* is "very normal". And the financial power of "media capitalism" will ensure that the downwards trend will become "more normalised" in Western societies at least.

The most recent example of "escapism" is the extremely curious phenomenon of "Second Life". Set in cyber-space, it has exactly borne out Edward R. Murrow's prediction; "*...and recognize that television in the main is being used to distract, delude, amuse and insulate us*". Whilst not television in this case, it is nonetheless one of the more strange things to emerge from the electronic medium *to distract, delude, amuse and insulate.*

And Why? For what purpose? Is not the real world real enough? Do we really think we can escape what is readily recognisable in the parlous state of the planet *whilst still actually living on it*? Or is it ultimately about the spiritual paucity of our individual lives and existence? In blunt objectivity, the concept beggars logical and reasoned understanding. Escapism of this kind would not rear its unfortunate head if the correct knowledge of **Creation-Law** were the *foundation* of primary education for *all* societies. Since it is not, and not ever likely to be with present-day humanity, then *abberations* of this kind will be more the *norm* than not for the time we have left.

Notwithstanding the strangeness of the whole concept, however, might we discover a deeper meaning and reason for "Second Life" and its growing millions who "live" there? Perhaps it is a reaction by many people understandably appalled and even sickened by the worsening state of global societies, and who therefore seek a better, more peaceful, less violent world than is currently the case with our "real world". In truth, it may well be the cry of the "inner spiritual core" of *at least some* who engage with "Second Life" for there to be a world as they would desire it or wish it.

Thus, in the present, the much more intensified **entertainment paradigm** "across the board" is the driving energy of an industry of unprecedented financial power that has insidiously and completely embedded its seductive products into computers, mobile phones and ear devices etc.. The trend has resulted in the strange, *latter-days*, phenomenon of "the *mobile* **bent-head** *'txter' with mobile*". The overall trend has also affected walkers and joggers who, even on *people-free* forest trails, seem to prefer some kind of *ear entertainment* to the necessary peace for the spirit that a quiet environment can provide.

The great wisdom of Chief Seattle requires to be heard here again.

> **"There is no quiet place in the White Man's cities. No place to hear the unfurling of leaves in spring or the rustle of an insect's wings. The clatter only seems to insult the ears!"**

How should we combat such insidiously-powerful 'forces', or do we even want to? On the one hand they inexorably drive all global communities downwards away from *true* Spiritual elevation. And in a "hand in glove" association on the other, in the most subtle way cunningly *normalise* that dark process of *degradation.*

And few there are that raise voice in protest!

In the final analysis we cannot change others. We can only change ourselves. That is, and must forever remain, the final and unequivocal ramification of The Living Law for every individual! Perhaps, though, we can help to *change* perceptions in those around us, or those who cross our path. How, then, can we *achieve* that kind of ennobled aim?

We should never forget that *inherent in the human word* are vestiges of **The Living Word of God**, out of which Creation – and thus our life and being – arose. Whilst not possessing any *creative* power as such, the *human word **will still nevertheless*** automatically impress upon the wider human environment of Subsequent Creation – i.e., both the material and non-material worlds – a powerful, *formative*, impact.

This inherent "forming-pressure" characteristic of the human spirit therewith *produces* unseen forms and forces which, if wrongly applied over a long period of time, *sets in motion* devastating consequences.

So it is crucially important to always use earthly language in the *right* sense. We can achieve this by using a manner of speaking that is *controlled* by the *spirit*. Only in this way can man work constructively *through* the language, and thereby develop its inherent life and potential to the fullest and *highest* expression of human-spiritual *ennoblement*!

That is responsibility absolute: The ultimate responsibility through being granted the gift of conscious life!

9

THE FIRST DEATH

The Process? — The Same for __All__ of Humankind!

"And do not shrink in fear from those who kill the body, for they are not able to kill the soul."

(Matthew 10:28, Fenton.)

"Do not dread those killing the body, and who after that have nothing worse to do."

(Luke 12:4, Fenton.)

"The more *spiritually* one lives, the less *fear* there is of *death*."

(The Soul – Whence and Whither. p.186,
Hazrat Inayat Khan. Italics mine.)

"If we go to the root of the matter, it is our concept of death that decides our answers to all the questions which life poses."

(Dag Hammerskjold.
Secretary-General, United Nations, 1953-61)

The essence of the two *Biblical* quotes clearly indicates that physical death is not that which humankind should be morbidly fearful about. Of course, we should not be frivolous or superficial about any death, or whether it affects us personally or not. That is not the intended meaning behind the quotes anyway. By them we are meant to understand that death is not the end, and that earthly death is only a transitional phase or process. And one of many in the complete time-frame of our total existence.

Of all human experiences in its absolute inevitability, death probably ranks highest on the fear scale for certainly the greater majority of human beings. For we all must accept, and thus eventually undergo, this "journey to somewhere". Historically and to the present day, our many and varied cultures have grappled with this seemingly unknowable enigma, but without real knowledge of it. So for most human beings, in the background of everyday lives insidiously lurks the great question: "What really does happen at death?" If that question were put to ten individuals, we would probably hear ten different opinions. Even with fifty or a hundred people, we would note many more ideas about this "death process". Now if the sample group were to track into the thousands, then religious, cultural, ethnic and even medical and scientific notions would surface in clear divisions.

Those divisions could logically be extrapolated to reflect probably the totality of humankind's beliefs towards the concept of "death". Therein, however, lies what is really the illogical stupidity of it all. For irrespective of race, religion, culture, ethnicity, education level or any other variable, there can only be *one* single immutable, inviolable – and thus *unchangeable* – process for the earthly end of *every* human life. Any thought to the contrary is simply silly in the extreme. Since that is the reality, then we can safely and logically say that virtually all human ideas about the actual "death process" will be wrong. Ignorance most certainly rules this aspect of so-called human knowledge! Where, then, might we find the actual answer? Only in **Creation-Law** knowledge – to which the *whole* of this Work leads – may we find the *complete* and *exact* answers and explanations.

Therefore: Given the glaringly-obvious fact that there is not even a *basically-correct* "across-the-board" global consensus about earthly death, true knowledge about it can *only* come into *every* society and culture when the aeons-long perpetuated ignorance about it is literally smashed into oblivion forever. Why is it so important to know? Simply because knowing – before the fact – the Truth about the Laws that govern both the *mechanics* of the actual death process and the *phases* that we must *all* go through immediately thereafter, would absolutely ensure that we human beings would *never again* behave as we have done for the thousands of blood-letting years that is our foolish legacy.

So, if analysed from the standpoint of Creation-Law, the two Biblical Scriptures that head this Chapter should be readily accepted as a viable and logical outcome of being born onto the Earth in the first place. For there appears to be little point in living for one generally indeterminate length of time only to have it all end in a complete expunging of the conscious personality in "blackness" in a hole in the ground. The terrible circumstances and life-path that millions are born into must logically presuppose clear and precise reasons for such outcomes. To simply subscribe to a belief that fatalistically accepts that such dire situations are out of our control is to also accept that we are no different from animals which are driven by instinct alone.

Since humankind possesses the attribute of free will as an inherent part of his spiritual heritage, to accept "any station in life" in dumb resignation in the belief that it cannot be changed, or believe that we cannot institute change within the society or group we may find ourselves in, is to allow the perpetuation of that wrong belief to burgeon. And via this attitude or belief, bequeath to future offspring the same straitened circumstances and the same spiritual apathy. By exercising our free will in the conscious recognition that the outworking of The Spiritual Laws *do* offer inherent Justice, we automatically tap into the life-stream of that Universal Power and the outworking of the *Justice contained within it*.

We arrive, thereby, at the sure knowledge that physical death is nothing more than a transitory phase – a rebirth into the next world for our further experiencing. Of course, strict **rules** govern the process, as it does everything in Creation. By adjusting ourselves to The Laws or Rules, however – with the subsequent gaining of the spiritual knowledge that is a natural accompaniment of them – we can fully understand, and thus *consciously experience* one inevitable day, this ostensibly "fearful" thing called **Death**!

Crucial Imperative No 2:

That we, the human beings of planet Earth, are not solely a physical entity, but also necessarily possess a *non-material* inner animating core: *For the physical* **cannot** *– and therefore does not – animate the physical!*

A most crucial aspect of The Law which determines our individual "after-death" destination was revealed in the previous Chapter. Language, or the *forming* of it as it issues from each of us, will decisively impact on the "kind of place" that we must journey to under the driving power of The Living Law. As the Book Title states, this work is directed towards explaining "Bible Mysteries". Perhaps the greatest mystery for most humans is what happens at, and/or after, "death". This current Chapter, therefore – and the one following – offer the knowledge needed to understand the two key features of the *complete* death process and not simply just the procedure of exiting the physical body at the "first death", *earthly* death.[1]

Before we begin to explore "death", we need to firstly tie in the most important "language-aspect" of it to the "after-death" reality. The Bible really does supply enlightenment here. When it is said; "...their works shall follow them", it means that apart from the deeds and lifestyle one has lived, language will naturally have played a decisive role. Reproduced from the previous Chapter is the *reinforcement* of how critical language, or how we use it, is to **our post, Earth-life future**.

Crucial Imperative No 9:

That **all** is *interconnected*; that nothing stands *in isolation*! —

— is very clearly demonstrated in the following Scriptural quotes from The Book of Matthew. Perfectly resonant in the previous Chapter on the "Forming" Power of Language, it also finds its place equally relevantly in this Chapter too. To a far greater degree than most people would ever believe, the normal, everyday use of language largely determines the "after-death" outcome!

From the relevant paragraphs of the previous Chapter, we reproduce the main points of Matthew's narration on the subject.

"...how can you preach purity, when you are yourselves depraved? The beneficent man draws from his treasury of purity, goodness; and the depraved man can only produce depravity, from his stores of depravity! I tell you, however, that every vile idea that men give expression to, they shall render a reason for it in the Day of Judgement".

"For *by thy words* thou shalt be *justified*, and *by thy words* thou shalt be *condemned*."

(Matthew 12:37)

"Listen and understand! What goes into the mouth does not corrupt the man; but what comes out of his mouth does corrupt him."

And the reply of Jesus to His disciples:

---

[1]That statement is not, nor is it intended to be, a riddle, for The Bible clearly indicates the **two** key events that, for humans, comprise one or the other of two potential outcomes.

"Are you ignorant even yet? Do you not know that everything going into the mouth proceeds to the stomach, and is from there evacuated? But what come out *from the mouth* proceed *from the heart*, and *corrupt* the man. For there come *from the heart* wicked thoughts, murders, adulteries, fornications, thefts, perjuries, blasphemies. *These* are what **corrupt** the man..."

(Matthew 15:11 and 15:16-20, Fenton.
All emphases mine)

So language strongly determines *where we ultimately reside* after processing ourselves through **The First Death**, because language *is inextricably linked with our life and deeds.*

The great unknown that has surrounded the inevitability of earthly death has taxed the minds of the greatest thinkers, philosophers, scientists and theologians since man's earliest beginnings. However, even though much thought has been devoted to unravelling this "mystery", no clear and unified position has ever issued from the ranks of the "learned". Since the death process is exactly that – a process, *and the same for all* – it is thus eminently clear that the individual standpoints of the respective Disciplines on this issue differ greatly in interpretation or belief as to what exactly does take place. In other words, despite all the theorising and pontificating from lofty academic perches, *they simply do not know.*

Over centuries, various mediums, visionaries, clairvoyants and mystics have all sought to divine the actual happening too. Many have claimed to have made contact with people in the "beyond" and some have published their claims. Except for the few who keep at least a reasonably open mind on the subject, most of those kinds of stories are dismissed and ridiculed. Still, the fact remains that we *do* leave the Earth at death. The dead body we leave behind in our likeness is testament to that. We, as a living entity, are no longer in it. So, where have we gone?

The one constant that can be absolutely relied upon in life is the certainty of dying, sooner or later. Chapter 7, Verse 6, from the "Wisdom Of Solomon" (The Apocrypha) states it wonderfully succinctly:

"...there is for *all mankind* — one entrance into life — and a — common departure".

Therefore, since death comes to us all without fail, it would be logical to believe that we would occupy ourselves far more with the how and why of it than we actually do. Most, however, push it away. For very many, death is too fearful to even contemplate. Still, it should at least be thought about from time to time, but in a constructive and objective way. For if after earthly death *life* does continue on, is it not reasonable to assume that upon that discovery many people who *have* passed on would then want to contact those whom they had recently departed from – those whose lives would have been so intimately intertwined with theirs whilst on Earth? Cold logic would aver that *that* would probably be the case. However, because a major separation from the physical/material environment of the Earth has occurred, any kind of subsequent contact could only be, therefore, via a *non-physical* method.

Now, consider: What if a few mediumistic people *were* able to be the portal by which people in the "beyond" could pass on their experiences? Should we automatically reject all such stories? Or should we perhaps see in at least some such claims the possibility of a clear Grace from Above whereby we *can* be helped to a clearer understanding of the transition through the death process to "further life" in the next "Realm"? Since this Work unequivocally accepts that premise, let us note one such person's desire to offer us this very help.

In 1895 a Mr A. Farnese transcribed the experiences of a "Spirit Author" who gave his name as Franchezzo. The work, "**A Wanderer in the Spirit Lands**",[2] describes Franchezzo's journey after his earthly death. From the perspective of the major thrust of *this* book – namely the explanation of **The Spiritual Laws of Creation** – the dedication by him in *his* work is very interesting since it perfectly concurs with what *we* state is imperative for **all of humankind** to recognise! Key aspects are noted here.

Dedication by the Author:

"To those who toil still in the mists and darkness of uncertainty which veil the future of their earthly lives, I dedicate this record of the Wanderings of one who has passed from earth life into the hidden mysteries of the Life Beyond, in the hope that through my experiences now given to the world, some may be induced to pause in their downward career and think ere they pass from the mortal life, as I did, with all their unrepentant sins thick upon them.

It is to those of my brethren who are treading fast upon the downward path, that I would fain hope to speak, with the power which Truth ever has over those who do not blindly seek to shut it out; for if the after consequences of a life spent in dissipation and selfishness are often terrible even during the Earth-life, they are doubly so in the Spirit World, *where all disguise is stripped from the soul, and it stands forth in all the naked hideousness of its sins, with the scars of the spiritual disease contracted in its earthly life stamped upon its spirit form* – never to be effaced but by the healing powers of sincere repentance and the cleansing waters of its own sorrowful tears.

I now ask these dwellers on Earth to believe that if these weary travellers of the other life can return to warn their brothers yet on Earth, they are eager to do so. I would have them to understand that spirits who materialize have a higher mission to perform than even the solacing of those who mourn in deep affliction for the beloved they have lost. I would have them to look and see that even at the eleventh hour of man's pride and sin, these spirit wanderers *are* permitted by the Great Supreme to go back and tell them of the fate of all **who outrage the laws of God and man. - - - - -**

As a warrior who has fought and conquered I look back upon the scenes of those battles and the toils through which I have passed and I feel that all has been cheaply won – all has been gained for which I hoped and strove, and I seek now but to point out **the Better Way** to others who are yet in the storm and stress of battle, *that they may use the invaluable time given to them upon Earth to enter upon and follow with unfaltering step the Shining Path which shall lead them home...*"

(The Dedication of FRANCHEZZO.
"A Wanderer In The Spirit Lands".
Emphases mine.)

The "Better Way" that Franchezzo alludes to in his warning plea to humankind clearly means a "better way" than that which the world presently practices and which, as he so correctly terms it, is *"the downward path"* which *"outrages the laws of God and man"*. His clear recognition reveals that *only* by heeding The Spiritual Laws and living the "Better Way" might we thus then be able to step upon the "Shining Path" to return "home". That first step on the true path

---

[2]This book has recently been *re-published* by **Crystal Publishing** and is now available online through: **www.crystalbooks.org**

"home" – after living the "Better Way" however – is transiting through the process of earthly death.

What we all know to be true is that death is invariably accompanied by huge emotional struggle and anguish for those left behind. Yet that reality simply reveals the large degree of *non-understanding* of the actual process. If the *mechanism* of the death process were understood, that must surely help to ease the pain of those grieving. For there would not then be the *non-comprehension* that is the usual demeanour of those who gather at funerals. The emotional hurt at the loss of a loved one can generally be coped with, but the reasons why to other questions that often surround "death" invariably imposes a greater degree of angst on mourners.

9.1   Death, the Great Leveller

For the one shortly to travel that inevitable path, the first reaction is usually disbelief, then perhaps denial. Denial brought about by the fear of it, or the thought of how unfair it may seem to be, and possibly not wanting to leave family and friends. However, for those who have *knowledge* of the process of death – and thus of The Laws which govern it – that person is better able to accept its earthly inevitability. With calm confidence he can approach his time knowing that it is a necessary transitional step with the opportunity for greater enlightenment, – **"if The Laws have been lived correctly"**! Franchezzo's harder experiences suffered after departing the Earth offer the very reason to heed those very Laws.

The wide reluctance to accept death as a completely natural process, coupled with most people's fear of it driving an associated desire to "stay on the Earth forever", has given rise to the offering of substantial rewards from wealthy individuals for a formula to stop, or considerably slow down, the ageing process. This line of thinking has thus resulted in the insanity of not only freezing corpses for exorbitant fees, but also just heads for a lesser fee – to ostensibly await a "re-awakening" and cure from the expectations of future, "advanced medical knowledge".

However, as we have firmly stated in previous Chapters, it is the ***spirit*** that is the "animating power" within the physical shell. Once that severs itself from the material body, the natural Laws decree that the shell will decompose. Therefore, regardless of how far medical science may develop to, it will *never* be able to effect such an impossible 'miracle'. All that has been achieved here is the provision of a very expensive, refrigerated grave. And, of course, the inevitable decomposition of the corpse once thawing occurs, with absolutely no chance of a re-awakening.

Relatively recent Frankenstein-like scenarios which call for "head transplants" have also emerged. The cloning of humans and the growing of foetuses for replacement body parts has been widely discussed, and already experimented with. There was also, until quite recently, the belief that there would be an inexhaustible source of animal body parts – mainly from pigs – for xeno-transplantation into humans. And all these ideas spring from people who are, supposedly, 'highly educated and intelligent'. Medical science has since recognised that such operations could trigger a global pandemic of a deadly new disease. Experiments by the Natural Environment Research Council of Britain have revealed that pig hearts and kidneys carried potentially deadly animal retroviruses, "...dashing hopes that animals could one day supply spare parts for human surgery".

Notwithstanding such a clear *scientific* message, xeno-transplantation has once more reared its totally unnatural and ugly head whereby a new group of "so-called medical experts" from New Zealand are revisiting the "pig concept". It is interesting to consider what 'form' those who promote and support such aberrant ideas might take once free of their physical shell, and thereby in the guise of their new, non-earthly body under the aegis of Reciprocal Law. As Franchezzo warned:

"...where all *disguise* is *stripped from the soul*, and it stands forth in all **the naked hideousness of its sins**, with the *scars* of the *spiritual disease* contracted in its *earthly life* stamped upon its *spirit form* – **never** to be **effaced** but by the **healing powers of sincere repentance** and the **cleansing waters of its own sorrowful tears**".

Researchers have noted that cancer viruses *will* jump species, "...in the real world, not just in artificial laboratory settings". Virologist Robin Weiss, who first demonstrated that pig viruses could infect human cells, said: "Xeno-transplants do not *seem* to pose a big risk. But then BSE and HIV were not *thought* to pose big risks when they were first discovered." [Italics mine.] This particular recognition will *not* come as any great surprise to the spiritually aware, for any kind of cross-species tampering is a serious transgression against The Spiritual Laws of Creation, producing equally grave reciprocal returns.

In the case of "head transplants", there still appears to be "approval by association" from at least one Christian Church so far. Dr Robert White, Professor of Neurosurgery at the Case University in Cleveland, Ohio, has proposed exactly this idea – where a person who has a complete and healthy body but is brain-dead, could be "married" to one who is quadriplegic or similar, but who possesses a "good head". This "marriage" would ostensibly produce one good and whole "productive unit". The key question is – who would that person actually be? Which one of the two "part-units" inhabits and *animates* the "completed new body"? For only one can. That means the other one must die to facilitate the union – if the operation is successful to begin with. For both "spirits" cannot co-exist as "dual animators" in the "new unit".

Once again, the problem with all medical researchers who subscribe to this kind of "medical advancement regime" is that they seem not to even *begin* to understand that The Laws of Life decree that we are *very much more* than just a material body. We only have life during the time that the *inner animating core* – the spirit with its outer soul-coverings – is **present** in its individual "physical form". Earthly death is the *separating out* of the physical "overcoat" from the "soul-body" and "spirit-core". **It is that simple, that logical and that perfect!**

And that, exactly, once more, is:

Crucial Imperative No 2:

That we, the human beings of planet Earth, are not solely a physical entity, but also necessarily possess a *non-material* inner animating core: *For the physical **cannot** – and therefore does not – animate the physical!*

Dr White, who 'claims' to have already successfully transplanted the head of a monkey onto another more than twenty years ago, states himself to be a committed Catholic, is a frequent visitor to the Vatican, is a member of the Pontifical Academy of Sciences, and helped to set up the John Paul II committee on medical ethics. Why, we wonder, do we not hear of these kinds of medical "experts" proposing to set up committees on "spiritual reality"? In fact, it is precisely *because* they lack any *true* knowledge of the connections *between* the material body and the inner animating *spiritual* core, that they do not. For they, too, must also possess the exact same "configuration", otherwise they could not *live* to wax expert on such matters.

In truth, this "life connection" is the *very knowledge* that should be taught as the **key foundation for all healing and medicine in all Medical schools globally.**

Yet there is another insidious and evil practice that has arisen through this non-acceptance, or lack of knowledge, about death and life-after. And that is the reported growing trade in body organs. Given the oftentimes dark nature of man, there is probably no doubt that some unfortunate people are murdered for selected parts. Anecdotal evidence from investigative television journalists probing into such allegations strongly suggest that in parts of India – which is one source – children have already been sold for this trade. Chinese prison guards have been convicted and jailed for selling body parts of prisoners.

Unfortunately for all involved in this dark and **spiritually-repulsive** "body-parts-replacement business", it is not only the murderer who will reap the consequences of the deed in this case, but also the recipient, the surgeons who perform the operations, and finally all those who *harbour* similar thoughts of organ acquisition. All share *spiritual responsibility* for such a crime under the outworking of Creation-Law, even if they believe otherwise. In any case, all participants soon discover the huge error of their wrong belief when they, in turn, die. It is then that they must *fully experience* the consequences of their chosen belief and deed.

The final say on the practice of organ transplants may be delivered by "Mother Nature" herself in her incomparable and **inviolable** outworking. The medical profession is presently struggling with the problem of the increasing inefficacy of the current crop of antibiotics used to treat infections. Sarah Boseley, in the 'Guardian Weekly' of 20.08.10., writes:

> 'The era of antibiotics is coming to a close. In just a couple of generations, what once appeared to be miracle medicines have been beaten into ineffectiveness by the bacteria they were designed to knock out. **The post-antibiotic apocalypse is within sight.** Hyperbole? Unfortunately not.'

Evidently a gene called NDM 1 passes easily between types of bacteria called enterobacteriaceae [such as E coli and Klebsiella] and makes them resistant to almost all of the powerful, last-line group of antibiotics called carbapenems – "...the most powerful group of antibiotics we [once] had..." said Professor Tim Walsh who discovered the gene.

> "In many ways, this is it. This is potentially the end. There are no antibiotics in the pipeline that have activity against NDM 1-producing enterobacteriaceae."

'For a long time now, doctors have known they were in a race to stay a few steps ahead of the rapidly growing resistance of bacterial infections to antibiotics. Dr David Livermore, director of the antibiotic resistance monitoring and reference laboratory of the UK Health Protection Agency, in talking about transplant surgery where patients' immune systems have to be suppressed to stop them rejecting a new organ, leaving them prey to infections, and the use of immuno-suppressant cancer drugs', noted:

> "A lot of modern medicine **would become impossible** if we lost our ability to treat infections. ... The emergence of antibiotic resistance is the most eloquent example of Darwin's principle of evolution that there ever was. ... It is a war of attrition. **It is naive to think that we can win.**"

(Guardian Weekly: All emphases mine.)

However, radical 21st century science *may* now have the answer to organ transplantation in humans; at least for one internal organ at this time. Basically, in a process called 'printing', a newly developed laboratory technology using human kidney cells 'layers' more cells on top of each other to *form* the kidney. Complete and *fully functional* kidneys have already been transplanted into waiting patients in the United States.

Notwithstanding the huge, *seemingly-beneficial*, ramifications for present-day humanity right across the globe, as we stated earlier on; despite the fact that medical-science drives these kinds of breakthroughs, in the final analysis a great underlying fear lurks in the deepest recesses of *most* humans. **It is the fear of death!** In a world where virtually *everyone* – especially scientists – seem to *desperately* push away even the *idea* of dying, we all really need to accept that *earthly death is a completely natural part of true life.* In any case, we are all *forced* to accept it when our time of *transition* arrives.

Let us, then, keenly examine this "death thing". Knowledge empowers whilst ignorance clouds: Fact! The problem with attempting to understand the death process is that the incremental steps which do occur cannot be seen with the physical senses. It is thus for most; the unknown. What exactly does happen when we observe the last exhalation of breath from a body? At that particular point, what was formerly a living, breathing, talking entity has suddenly become a still and silent, rapidly-cooling shell. What has happened to the 'force', the 'energy', the 'power' that a few short moments before gave this now lifeless shell the ability to live, laugh and love during its tenure on Earth? Can such a thing as its "life" simply dissipate into "nothingness"?

It would seem to be inconceivable to believe that *that* would be the case. After all, it is an energy source that can enable human beings on the one hand to produce great architectural works, wonderful symphonies and technological marvels and on the other to stand incredible tests of privation and extreme cruelty of so many perverse kinds over long periods of time – and still survive. So could that "life" simply just "disappear" at earthly death? Well, that is certainly the belief of many.

The other possibility is that this "animating power" does not disappear into oblivion but is actually a *different kind* of living form from that of the physical body. And there are those who believe that. For those who subscribe to such a view, the general acceptance here is that the physical body is really the outer shell from which the person who previously occupied it has now departed. There is a large third group who do not know what to believe about this apparently uncertain process. For the purposes of this introductory phase, let us initially assume that we do not have any answers.

The question of whether there actually is such an "inner animating force" has already been resolved in Chapter 2. Yet those within the Medical profession, who work intimately with the living entity, invariably evince uncertainty about the true nature of it all. Moreover, these are the people who utilise their considerable talents to slice, cut, remove and sew. The beating heart in the chest could well induce one to arrive at the belief that we are, after all, just a physical body animated by a very efficient pump for the blood whilst also possessing an electrically-driven brain-computer programmed to control all other functions and life's decisions. If this is so, then the demise of the body at what we term death is simply a process of the pump stopping, a cessation of electrical activity in the computer of the brain – or vice versa – with a subsequent stilling of all bodily functions. This belief necessarily rejects the possibility of a separate animating entity which leaves the body at this time, so a black hole of nothingness *is* the only logical outcome here.

The obvious fact governing these differing ideas is that we have only **two choices** for arriving at a correct conclusion, and we have an equal **50%** chance of getting it right or wrong – in terms of **the choice**. Either there *is* an inner animating force, or there *is not*. There cannot be two positions here. However, that even-chance choice must necessarily translate to a **100% outcome**. To be wrong is to be *completely wrong* with either choice – and not just be **50%** in error.

For those who ostensibly claim no interest or concern, such an outcome might be considered to be a personal non-event. However the *actual* reality of the death process will quickly shake the foundations of that particular belief. For those who wish answers, however, it surely behoves one to choose correctly, for initial peace of mind at least. Malcolm Muggeridge, the famous British social commentator, was once asked if he believed in "life after death". He thought that the more intelligent thing to do was to "hedge one's bets", even if one found it difficult to conceive of such a possibility. In his words – "just in case"![3]

The question of personal responsibility for how one has lived one's life is a further factor which may have a bearing on one's attitude toward possible concern about death. If the "notion" of "life after death" is dismissed out of hand, we might perhaps assume that proponents of such thinking, even if conceding that *possibility*, might not necessarily equate the process with a concept of ultimate personal responsibility for the individual life lived – *if a less than noble lifestyle has been the case*.

Yet what of believers who **unequivocally** accept that the physical body is the material shell of the animating life-force – that of either a soul or spirit? The question which needs to be addressed here is whether or not there is **complete dissipation** of this "power source" at earthly death, or a **retention of it** in some form. In this particular situation we can once more reduce the outcome to only one of the two possibilities. Again, *it can only be one or the other*. One more **50% choice**, and one more **100% outcome**.

A firm conviction of absolute dissipation or dissolution of any such "innate energy-source" is, quite logically, completely incompatible with a concept of **personal responsibility** for how one has lived one's life. Quite logically, also, full acceptance of "personal responsibility" can only *naturally* apply where there **is** the retention and continuation of a "life-force" in the form of a *complete and* **conscious** *being*, otherwise there is no point or purpose to such a belief/concept.

> In the *final* analysis, ultimate **personal** responsibility *logically requires* some **form** to act **on** and **through** – for **itself** and its **outward expression**.

For our part, little more need be said for the completely wrong belief in a deep black hole of "nothingness". Within the context of this Work, therefore, let us examine the other possibility open to us. Here we have a concept of the acceptance of the physical body containing an animating "energy source" which, upon earthly death, retains its form and accepts *personal* responsibility for its "life lived". Religious leanings of many persuasions teach this very concept. At this point the issue becomes somewhat clouded with many varying ideas as to the final outcome.

Now, whilst some are decidedly similar in content, any difference in belief as to the *actual end result* nevertheless logically represents a point of disagreement regarding the *true* and un-equivocal nature of the happening. Quite simply, there cannot possibly be any differences since the *actual death process itself*, apart from the naturally differing events leading up to it, **must be exactly the same for all**. And, moreover, totally in accordance with The Spiritual Laws of Life itself.

That is our absolute premise and contention! Irrespective of one's race, colour, religion, belief, geographical location or any other factor, the process is exactly the same for all. Indeed, the idea that there may be differences because of the aspects mentioned is completely untenable, and really quite foolish. Unfortunately, not being able to physically see every individual step has produced an impossible maze of opinions and theories to cloud and confuse the issue. If, however, the premise that the "death process" is subject to absolute Law without deviation is correct, all that is required is to *recognise* the outworking of those Laws and apply them to this contentious subject for our complete edification.

At present there are many books on the subject of "near-death" or "out-of-body" experiences, and a number of researchers have compiled reports from the experiences of the dying. Dr Raymond Moody is perhaps the best known. Dr Moody's research noted that at times of severe

---

[3]In ultimate spiritual reality, the term death-process to denote *earthly death* is actually a misnomer, for it is really a "transitional-life process". Nevertheless, we will continue to use the more common term to simplify matters.

illness or injury resulting in such a "close encounter with death", all subjects recorded very similar experiences, with the *consistency* of the experiences being the common *constant*. The many differences in race and nationality, social and economic status and religious preference produced no differences in the experiences. Even suffering different diseases or illnesses and receiving different medical treatment, the basic event was remarkably similar. Yet, should this be a surprise? If it is a lawful process without deviation as we contend, we should expect to discover exactly this fact.

Therefore, if there can be such a thing as an out-of-body experience, then there must necessarily be another body perfectly capable of existing consciously outside of the physical one. This we have already outlined in Chapter 2 in the explanations of our Spiritual Origins. There, we identified our inner life-force as having its Origin, and therefore home, in The Spiritual Realm far above the material plane of the Earth. The "energy source" which is the animating force for our physical body, we know as the Spirit. It is the actual, and very real, you and me!

Plato, who accepted the belief that the soul leaves the physical body at earthly death, interpreted its particular realm as the "world of ideas". He also noted the fact that most people have a superficial attitude toward these ideas, being content with a life "among shadows". As a consequence of this they "paid no heed to the immortality of their own soul".

Plato perhaps also intuitively understood the idea of a proffered "attribute of grace" in the connection of the soul to its origin. In his philosophical comment he states:

> "...when perfect and fully winged she [the soul] soars upward".

> (*Philosophy History & Problems*, p 63)

Thus the soul yearns to return home to the world of ideas. It longs to be freed from the chains of the body. Yet even *after* Plato's enlightened teachings for the time, Epicurus, (341-270 BC) a Greek philosopher who accepted the teachings of Democritus and his "dispersal theory" of "soul atoms", believed that death should not concern us because as long as we exist death is not here. And when it does come, we no longer exist.

Unfortunately for Epicurus, his incorrect views would have been swiftly demolished at his death. It is important to therefore define and understand the nature of Spirit, which we possess as our actual inner being and by which we are drawn upward to our Origins in The Spiritual Realm after the completion of our "schooling" in the material world. Provided, of course, we have not placed a barrier between the two thus preventing our return. In any case, the many designations that people ascribe to this word, Spirit, should be clarified so as to more clearly understand its meaning.

People who are highly educated, witty, intelligent and widely-read, and able to converse well about all they have learned are often regarded as being "rich in spirit". Or perhaps they may be gifted with a talent for producing original ideas. But the designation "rich in spirit" is not strictly correct in either case. Neither can we call a person who is steeped in knowledge about their particular traditions and culture "rich in spirit". Unless there is a conscious and knowledgeable connection to the Higher Spheres, such knowledge is really only concerned with culture or tradition.

Therefore Spirit is something completely different. As previously explained, the true Spiritual Worlds lie far higher than the Earth Plane, and form the upper and lightest part of Creation. Spirit is thus more an *independent consistency* composed of *that substance* which *comprises* The Spiritual nature of those Higher Realms. Spirit can perhaps be best described as having, or expressing the quality of, *deep inner feeling*, but is not the same as being "highly intellectual".

Neither does Spirit refer solely to the emotions. They are given to enable us to fully *live* an experience – irrespective of whether it be joyful or painful – to the greatest depth possible. But being emotional is not the same as having "deep inner feelings" of a spiritual kind. The Spirit, being the producer of the language, is therefore able to express itself in writings and in activities of sublime beauty such as art and music. Possessing the inherent ability to "intuitively know" the emotions of love, hate, joy and sorrow, it also naturally possesses inherent longing for its original spiritual home, as Plato correctly perceived.[4]

As formerly explained in the Chapter on our Spiritual Origins, the journey of a human spirit from the Plane of The Spiritual to the Material necessitates the need to traverse all the intervening Realms. Each one is a different consistency, lightest toward the Higher Planes and heaviest towards the lower, exactly according to The Law of Spiritual Gravity. As we journey downwards, we are required to take on or wear a cloak or body of the consistency and material of the particular Plane being traversed, with each lower one more dense the nearer we come to the gross material Earth. Thus, by the time we reach the Earth, we will have enveloped our spirit, our inner core – the *actual* you and me – in a number of coverings, each one exactly corresponding to the consistency and material of the particular Plane descended through.

Now, we might well wonder where all these *coverings* are? Since each, in turn, envelops the previous coverings on the journey downwards, they are logically all inside us. By virtue of the different consistencies of each, however, they are prevented from *blending* with each other. We may view this as a kind of *uniting*, similar to the way a collapsible telescope is held together. The huge difference between that basic material example and the human process is the mechanism or force which *holds us together* as a complete and self-conscious entity. That power is "radiation". It is that which holds together everything in Creation – from the greatest thing to the smallest.

The science of physics has long recognised that everything radiates, and that the "apparent" solidity of all material substance is due to just this radiation. It is a specific radiation which, in a sense, "magnetically" connects the elementary particles.[5]

The physical body is obviously the immediate first part of "we/us" as the complete entity. It is that specific part which intimately interacts with our physical environment. With it we are able to utilise the senses of sight, smell, hearing and touch etc., to carry out earthly tasks and fulfil particular desires. In itemising the **three key components**, and working from the material body inwards, we find that the **outer mortal physical cloak** – that which can be seen in a mirror – in turn has a closely connected **astral body**, the *prototype* of the physical. Its consistency, though still composed of material matter, is obviously not anywhere near as dense, however.

These two "bodies", in their turn, envelop other still finer "cloaks" that correspond to their respective spheres of origin beyond the Earth. In the Ethereal World – that which we loosely call the beyond – the **ethereal body** covers the **soul**. Inside all these coverings resides our **spirit**. That is who and what we actually are! To reiterate once more – the **spirit** and its immediate coverings enveloped by the **ethereal body**, but *excluding* the **physical** and the **astral** can **basically** be *collectively designated* as the **soul body**. It is important that we clearly identify and understand the three main parts of the total entity, for we will need to remember them in order to follow the complete process of earthly death. [We will repeat these very relevant designations often.]

The phenomenon of "phantom-pain" that many amputees experience derives from the fact

---

[4]The cause of the seething restlessness, frustration, discontent and anger that seemingly pervades the peoples of the world like a terminal disease today, may possibly lie in the anguish of a collective humanity which has lost its true place in Creation and is **no longer able to find its way back to its Origins**.

[5]It is interesting to note that this radiation, which emanates from virtually everything, can be captured by Kirlian photography, either still-life or on video. The truly amazing aspect of the process, however, concerns the constant movement of the various colours being radiated. These appear to correspond to the different properties of the subject being photographed, particularly the relative strengths of the various parts of the energy-field. Whilst there is a school of opinion which deems this energy-field to be the actual aura of things, science states the radiation to be electro-magnetic. Still, radiation all the same. Perhaps the word aura is too unscientific, too new-age! Nevertheless, that is what it seems to be.

that we possess these different "bodies" of varying consistency within each of us. When an amputee loses a limb, the corresponding "limb" of his "astral" body remains complete within him because, obviously, it cannot be *physically* severed. However, the various non-material bodies that reside within his, now, less than whole "physical form", nevertheless still exert subtle 'pressure' upon him and his physical environment. He may, therefore, from time to time, "sense" or still "feel" the "lost limb". Anecdotal evidence would strongly suggest that those in the medical or psychiatric profession are highly sceptical or dismissive of such beliefs. However, as we will state often within these pages, either a thing is so, or it is not. Since we are dealing here with the fact of inviolable Creation-Law, this so-called "phenomenon" unequivocally resides in the *"is indeed so"* category!

Thus, within the material substance of our physical body resides our spirit, the actual animating power – the life-force – for the now *multi-layered* body. However, in order to *connect* the individual coverings so that the **volition** *of the spirit can act on the complete entity*, we require a "connecting" or "linking" mechanism whereby this can be achieved. That necessary connection *from the spirit* to the *soul, ethereal, astral* and *physical* bodies is provided by something called the "Silver Cord", mentioned in various spiritual works and The Bible. It is this connection that enables the spirit, through its **animating** power, to produce its earthly works as it **impresses its volition** on the *coverings* that *envelop* it, including the *physical* body; that which stares back at us from a mirror. [These last points provide the **major keys** to a full understanding of the complete death process!]

Note: Whilst it is the **power** of the spirit that **animates** the body, it is the *intermediary* function of the **brain** which supplies the **electrical impulses** that permit the end **physical motivation** – but nevertheless still under overall **command** of **the Spirit**!

In a broad sense, we can liken the "Silver Cord" to the umbilical cord that connects the growing foetus to the womb of the mother. As a very *basic* analogy, that cord provides life and warmth to the young life too, as well as nutrients to nurture the body. However, what it does not do after a specific point in pregnancy, is provide the *spiritual* life-force. The entry of an individual spirit into the foetus at the appropriate time assumes that role.

Because the concept and knowledge of the "Silver Cord" is crucial to understanding the "death process", some views about it from two of the main schools of religious thought offer interesting comparisons. *"Cruden's Complete Concordance to the Old and New Testament and the Apocrypha"*, is still highly regarded in the Christian world as an accurate and reputable publication even though the first Edition appeared as far back as 1737. The explanation of the "Silver Cord" in Cruden's work may perhaps still represent the fundamentalist Christian understanding about it today. From page 445:

> "By this, [the Silver Cord] commentators generally understand the pith, or marrow of the back-bone, which comes from the brain, and thence goeth down to the very lowest end of the back-bone, together with the nerves and sinews which, as anatomists observe, are nothing else but the production and continuation of the marrow. And this is aptly compared to a cord, both for its figure, which is very long and round, and for its use, which is to draw and move the parts of the body; and it is compared to silver, both for its excellency and colour, which is white and bright, even in a dead, and much more in a living body."

The above interpretation is obviously only a physical one concerned solely with the materiality of the body, for the wording of the text clearly refutes the idea of the Silver Cord being a connection between the physical body and the spirit. Compilers of more recent Concordances do not offer an interpretation of this "cord" aspect as does Cruden's. The actual connection, of course, must first be recognised and understood correctly in order to be able to explain it thus.

Eastern philosophical beliefs on the other hand have long held that the "Silver Cord" *is* the link connecting the soul to the body as a kind of "ethereal umbilical cord". The "Silver Cord" is also believed to link the various energy centres or "chakras" which are situated along the axis of the spine. While not physically visible, the "chakras" correspond to various nerve centres and organs of the body. It is the conduit or channel through which energy and the "life-force" pass to these centres during the course of our life on Earth. After death the cord is severed, thus allowing the soul to be released from the material body which, in turn, then decomposes into its original material elements.

Having established the main points of reference for our elucidation of this fascinating event, let us begin our actual journey into death by first examining the similarly reported phases of out-of-body experiences, as recorded and distilled by Dr Raymond Moody in his second book on this subject, "*Reflections On Life After Life*" (Pages 5-6):

> "A man is dying and, as he reaches the point of greatest physical distress, he hears himself pronounced dead by his doctor. He begins to hear an uncomfortable noise, a loud ringing or buzzing, and at the same time feels himself moving very rapidly through a long tunnel. After this, he suddenly finds himself outside of his own physical body, but still in the immediate physical environment, and he sees his own body from a distance, as though he is a spectator. He watches the resuscitation attempt from this unusual vantage point and is in a state of emotional upheaval.
>
> After a while, he collects himself and becomes more accustomed to his odd condition. He notices that he still has a "body", but one of a very different nature and with very different powers from the physical body he has left behind. Soon other things begin to happen. Others come to meet and to help him. He glimpses the spirits of relatives and friends who have already died, and a loving, warm spirit of a kind he has never encountered before – a being of light – appears before him. This being asks him a question, non verbally, to make him evaluate his life and helps him along by showing him a panoramic, instantaneous playback of the major events of his life. At some point he finds himself approaching some sort of barrier or border, apparently representing the limit between earthly life and the next life. Yet, he finds that he must go back to the Earth, that the time for his death has not yet come. At this point he resists, for by now he is taken up with his experiences in the afterlife and does not want to return. He is overwhelmed by intense feelings of joy, love, and peace. Despite his attitude, though, he somehow reunites with his physical body and lives.
>
> Later he tries to tell others, but he has trouble doing so. In the first place, he can find no human words adequate to describe these unearthly episodes. He also finds that others scoff, so he stops telling other people. Still, the experience affects his life profoundly, especially his views about death and its relationship to life."

Contained within the above report are some of the points we have thus far outlined. Note that the "Being of Light" communicated "non-verbally". We can thus assume that one's earthly language is of no importance at this point, and that communication is perhaps more via the spiritual intuition – a kind of "other-world telepathy". The obvious separation of the physical body from the non-physical is an especially clear point. In accordance with the knowledge we now have, we are able to recognise the reference to "moving rapidly through a long tunnel" as relating to the *drawing out* of the *non-physical* body *from* the *physical*.[6]

---

[6]This "long tunnel", in terms of its perceived length, does not refer to the length of the physical body as the soul-body exits the physical shell. It refers to an altered aspect of time, which has a vastly different reference value in that non-earthly sphere.

More importantly from the above report, however, was the requirement to evaluate the key phases of one's life; this aspect under the direction of a powerful Spiritual Being. Here can be observed the necessity for accepting the fact of ***personal spiritual responsibility for all ones thoughts, words and deeds***, exactly as The Spiritual Laws demand and which we must continually reinforce in this Work. In this regard, again consider the warnings of Jesus (Matthew 5:18):

> "...that until the heavens and the earth shall pass away, a single dot or hairstroke shall not disappear from the law, until all has been completed".

Consider, also, what we might regard as a further "spiritual" qualification of the above once more:

> "I tell you indeed, that you will not depart until **YOU** have ***repaid the very last farthing***."

> (Matthew 5:26, Fenton. Emphases mine.)

To be faced with the need to confront one's past life in the very early stages after one's earthly death may well presuppose the unsettling probability that the next stages of the process call for atonement and expiation in some way. That really is the inescapable reality, exactly as the above Biblical quotes clearly state, for the description from Dr. Moody's work ***does not explain the process of actually dying***. It merely describes *only the very first steps in just being "out of the body"*. In short, the person concerned has not died.[7]

Many researchers in this field have concluded that the feelings of love and well-being experienced at this time represent the *totality* of the after-death situation, but that is not the complete picture by any means. Through insufficient knowledge, they are not able to take into account the absolute and full outworking of this process – a process which can be only be understood with the knowledge contained within The Spiritual Laws of Creation.

Having determined that we must accept "personal spiritual responsibility" for our deeds, we need to draw the veil aside a little more in order to reveal the next step into earthly death proper. The actual happening is quite simple. Because the connection *between* the physical

---

[7]Some years ago I experienced the very first part of the death process i.e., I began to exit my physical body. A very sudden onset of acute and excruciating pain – from no *apparent* cause – began to rack my entire body internally and externally, forcing me to bed. The pain was so intense that I intuitively perceived I was actually dying. And because it was so sudden and not signalled in any way whatsoever, I also intuitively felt that even though experiencing great pain, the "unfolding event" was nonetheless occurring so that I might know the reality of what I had long accepted; that death could not possibly be the end of one's "actual life". Immediately thereafter I began to leave my body – through my head. In short, I watched my feet recede as I exited through the bed headboard and the wall behind it. At this point, I was pain-free. Whilst it was a singularly strange sensation, it was at the same time extremely fascinating for me. That is because the *primary purpose* of my life was/is to write *this* book you are now reading. Because it was still in basic manuscript form and proving difficult to publish at the time, I strongly petitioned – as I was exiting my physical shell – to: "Let me stay 'til I complete the work." Thereupon the exiting-process halted and I went back into my body – and back into the pain. However, something extraordinary then occurred. What I can only describe as a specifically-configured, gold-coloured, rotating "healing-force" materialised very clearly near the ceiling in a corner of the room closest to the bed. I intuitively knew that I would be "healed". And so it was. [I experienced this same effect sometime later in a hospital where, after minor surgery, the wound site had become infected. Fortunately, however, the few hours during the night that this "healing-force" was present was sufficient to reduce the infection which, over the next 24 hours, subsequently 'disappeared'.] With the help of a friend and colleague shortly thereafter, I was finally able to publish this and other similar works. Available at www.crystalbooks.org

and the non-physical parts of man is that of a *radiation process*, all that is required to effect a *complete* separation is for one or the other to become so debilitated as to not have **sufficient radiating strength** to hold itself **locked to the other.** We see this in severe illnesses, or during a long fast where the body can be considerably weakened.[8]

On the other hand, the "soul body" can also lose its "radiation-connection" to its physical counterpart such as in the case of giving up the will to live. So even where there may be no obvious physical reason for separation to occur, nevertheless, according to Spiritual Law, this must eventually take place if there is no *re-strengthening* of the necessary "connecting radiation" in such cases. Thus, as the radiation-attraction between the soul body and the physical body becomes progressively weaker, the point of separation is finally reached.

To clarify the process once more: Where a body has been forcibly destroyed, ruined by disease, or weakened by old age, and can no longer offer the **necessary strength of radiation sufficient to maintain a strong attraction between soul and body**, the soul must **sever itself** from its earthly body or covering.

That, quite naturally, is earthly death!

In terms of natural Law, which at the same time is Spiritual Law, it is simply the lawful process of *two species of matter,* once united on the Earth through a *mutually-attracting radiation,* but which must separate out again when one of the two *different species* can no longer fulfil its *attracting* role.

Now the soul, at the moment of severance, *draws the astral body*[9] *with it* away from the physical body. The soul needs to draw the astral body out of the physical shell because, unlike the physical body *at this particular moment* the astral becomes – but only for a very short while – the **next material cloak** for the Spirit. This phase of the death process is the *actual* exiting and departure from the physical shell where the soul **draws** the **astral body with it** out of **the physical body.** Since there was never a *fusion* as such, but only a *sliding into one another* – as with the example of a collapsible telescope – the soul simply **pulls the astral from the physical** as it strives to free itself from its former "material partner".

In doing so, the soul does not draw this astral body very far, because that body is still also connected with the physical shell. Moreover, the soul, which initiates the actual movement, needs to detach itself from the astral body too, so strives to get away from it. The astral body always remains near the physical body after the earthly departure of the soul. The further the soul moves away, however, the weaker the astral body becomes. The continuing detaching process of the soul eventually brings in its train the decay and disintegration of the astral body, which, in turn, immediately brings about the decay of the physical body too. This is the normal exiting process under the lawful outworking of The Spiritual Laws.

Even though this explanation of the *inviolable* death-process should be relatively easy to follow, particularly when viewed pictorially, as a further aid we can perhaps also consider the visible birth process to offer *some* understanding. At this time a separation also occurs between mother and baby where the new-born similarly seeks to initially strive out of, and away from, the mother's body. For it, too, is connected to its mother and to the placenta via its "life-cord", the umbilical, and must also "disconnect" from both. Whilst this may be regarded as a very crude analogy, the reader may find greater clarity to understanding the death process through this example, even though a kind of reverse view. However, the reader should not regard one process as perhaps being an exact mirror image of the other, though there are certain aspects which can possibly provide some enlightenment.

In Dr. Moody's description of just the "out-of-body" experience, the outworking of The Law of Spiritual Gravity is immediately evident, where the lighter, more mobile part – the soul

---

[8]The same Law operates here as in the process of amalgamation.

[9]In previous explanations we learned that the astral body is like the "prototype" of the physical.

body – glides away from the heavier, material body. It is important that this particular point be carefully noted. For whilst we have now described the death process, that is only with respect to a "normal happening", which is that for a soul who is quickly able to sever its connection or tie to its material body. Obviously the soul is still subject to The Spiritual Laws and must now follow its particular path into its new environment, into its new world. However, it can only embark upon its next journey when the "Silver Cord", that had once served as the necessary link between the "power source" of the Spirit and its material counterpart, is completely severed. In the same way, a baby cannot be completely free of its physical tie to its mother's body until its life-support cord is similarly cut.

We now enter the little understood, and perhaps less believed, area of **personal spiritual responsibility**. As the death process is subject to strict and firmly established Creation-Law, including that of The Law of Justice, what criteria governs the situation where a soul is not able to easily sever itself? And what does this mean for that soul body – that individual?

Whether or not a soul detaches itself quickly from the physical body will absolutely depend on *how it has lived its life on Earth*!

That is the short and blunt truth of the matter!

The spiritual nature of the individual human being is the decisive factor in this. We need to understand that it is not the teachings of any particular religion or belief that is decisive here, it is *how we are in our being, how we stand spiritually, individually*. The Law of Spiritual Gravity is a key aspect in our explanations now, for this Law operates in every sphere of Creation, and not just in an obvious way on Earth where its physical effects can be readily observed.

In a previous Chapter we explained this Law and its effects, and stated that everything we do, every thought we think and every action we take corresponds to a precise spiritual weight. Thoughts and actions of good are *spiritually lighter* than those that are not. Throughout our lives, therefore, we are naturally subject to all the different experiences that our personal choices will generate. The changing circumstances of them – but perhaps more particularly how we cope with them from an attitudinal standpoint, sometimes well, sometimes not – will all contribute to the final *specific spiritual weight* of our soul-body at earthly death.

A life of superficiality without concern for spiritual matters, or of seeking only the acquisition of material things to the exclusion of any elevating practices – even without necessarily evil intent – will ensure that the "Silver Cord" becomes darker and thicker precisely corresponding to the degree of superficiality or materialism lived. It thus naturally follows that a life of violence, crime and debasement, *regardless of the circumstances that might have brought it about*, will actually produce an individual "spiritually-heavier" than one who had not chosen to live such a path. This perceived effect has entered our language where we describe such persons as being or feeling "heavy". [e.g.; The well-known hit song: **"He ain't heavy, he's my brother."**]

Unfortunately for such people this "heaviness", with its associated and perhaps personally-desired intimidatory effect generating a tough, "untouchable status" on Earth, will likely set in place a very painful death experience. If no *genuine change of spiritual direction* is embarked upon before that time arrives, the effect of that "heaviness" on the "Silver Cord" is to darken and thicken it considerably, with serious consequences for that soul at earthly death.

Now, when the time comes for severance to occur, the "spiritually-darker and heavier" person with the correspondingly *thicker* cord will discover that this cannot be effected so easily. It may be very many days, perhaps weeks, before the Cord eventually begins to wither and disintegrate, thus finally setting the hapless soul free of its *now decomposing shell*. This particular example in the process clearly reveals the outworking of **The Justice of The Law** in the exercising of **our free will for evil or debased purposes**. Choosing an opposite lifestyle, however, especially one where *spiritual considerations* are a regular and normal part of one's life, will ensure that the "Cord" remains lighter.

It is important to reiterate that only ***our decisions are free***. ***The consequences***, however, ***are not***. They must be fully lived out under The Law of Sowing and Reaping. Thus the consequences for a soul who has lived a life without thought or care for any of the higher spiritual aspirations will mean an unnecessarily longer time tied to his physical body than need have been the case. Through the still-strong-attachment via his thicker and heavier "Cord", he will therefore feel ***all that the physical body undergoes in that time, including any autopsy, and perhaps cremation***. In longer-tied periods, ***even the decomposition process itself***. The actual moment of his release will have been precisely determined by The Spiritual Laws, in exact accordance with his "attitude and chosen lifestyle" during his life on Earth.

The exact same death *process*, however, offers a *vastly different experience* for a person who has lived a more noble life. His severance will be effected much faster and he will be quickly free of the shell. That is one reason **why *all*** the great Spiritual Teachers over the ages have constantly admonished mankind to always strive for the good.

> Those warnings were not the incoherent ramblings of *foolish old men*, or the strident fire and brimstone preaching of *doomsday prophets*, and should therefore ***not*** be ridiculed, mocked or ignored. Such *serious warnings* simply yet powerfully state **The Truth of The Eternal Laws!**

The effect of thousands of years of man's stubborn refusal to accept the Truth of it all has now brought us to the most serious point that mankind and this Earth have ever reached. And, whether alive or dead, we are well into the process of reaping the results of all our personal and collective choices. What will be experienced by humankind more graphically, however, is the exponential factor of much more in much less time.

With this new knowledge of the death process, and aside from the practice of autopsies, at what point can a person be safely pronounced dead? Some years ago, Dr. Lyall Watson wrote a book called "The Romeo Error". The subject matter was precisely about the difficulty in determining the exact moment of death. He recounted many instances where persons had been certified dead, even to the point where the early stages of decomposition had set in, and yet still returned to life. More harrowing were the experiences of the relatives of deceased where death certificates had been issued for the one apparently very dead, where funeral preparations and burial service were undertaken, and where the casket was duly consigned to the earth and the grave filled in. These particular cases recorded relatives requesting the exhumation of the deceased because of strong feelings and even dreams that indicated their loved ones were not actually dead at the time of burial.

Because of the need to convince appropriate authorities of the urgency in these cases – with official scepticism being an unfortunate time-barrier in such matters – subsequent exhumations did reveal persons "buried alive". Their short time awake was evident by the efforts they undertook to try to free themselves from their tomb. The most notable factors being the dishevelled arrangement of the clothing, and fingernails ripped from gouging the casket lid. Anecdotal reports also told of the look of frozen horror on the faces of the "now deceased". Moreover, Dr. Watson outlines the curious state of "Catatonia" in many of these cases where, in his opinion, the body appeared to be completely dead with no detectable or discernible life within it, yet still alive.[10]

Even today, with all the supposedly huge advances in diagnostic medical science, on rare occasions [as happened in a New Zealand hospital quite recently] medical authorities report bodies held in 'storage' awaiting autopsy have bled ***red blood*** when cut into – much to the very

---

[10]The "catatonic state" seems not to figure strongly in medical thinking today.

great surprise and *consternation* of medical staff. Explanation? **There is only one.** Such bodies, persons – *cadavers* – are not *actually* dead. They are still *there*, still *connected* to their physical shells.

Though it clearly does not accept or believe, the Medical Profession should nonetheless take urgent steps to learn about the crucial *purpose* of the "Silver Cord" – and thereby gain *real knowledge*.

The frightening situation of how one could possibly be accidentally buried alive surely begs the question how, and why? From the standpoint of The Spiritual Laws, and irrespective of what we believe or may *wish* to believe, whatever takes place on Earth is not solely the result of pure chance. It may be comforting to continually insist that such is the case, particularly when we might be personally affected detrimentally, but every event, every incident, even the most minute, *will have been brought about by a decision made by human beings somewhere in time.*

Indeed, it cannot possibly be otherwise for it is *we* who *cause* things to happen through our inherent spiritual ability to make decisions in the first place. As we need to continually emphasise, however, only our *decisions* are free, the *consequences* await to eventually be faced. So, if we are ever to make any sense of the *why* of the problems that beset us, a huge and fundamental leap into a *different* way of thinking must be made. A way of thinking that actually and finally accepts the absolute validity and unyielding nature of every single one of The Spiritual Laws of Creation, which return to us **every** consequence of **all** our decisions.

If, now, the question of "accidental" burial or any other *apparently* inexplicable human misfortune is considered, we should seriously consider the outworking of The Law of Reciprocal Action [*Sowing and Reaping*]. In such cases, might *that* have been the mechanism which had *"returned"* the reciprocal effect of an unfortunate decision made in the past – even if long distant – to the individual affected; a decision that perhaps once affected **another soul very detrimentally**? Perhaps a decision, therefore, which might require a similar kind of experience in order to expiate any such past deed.

To return to the existence of the "Silver Cord" and its purpose: Its vital function in the life and death of human beings brings into question the medical "wisdom" of organ transplants. In such undertakings it is vitally necessary to ensure that the organs are taken from a body very recently "presumed" dead, or conveniently pronounced "brain-dead", to ensure the "freshness" of the product. This means that the "donor" will almost certainly still be **attached** to the physical body and, depending on the density of the "Cord", **may well feel considerable pain at the removal of "his" organs**.

Viewed from the higher knowledge of Spiritual Law, organ transplants add little to the overall "life" of a person, as earthly death is merely a transitional phase in the total existence of an individual in any case. This is aside from the horrendous financial considerations of such "operations" of course.

The emotional turmoil associated with the thought of "losing loved ones forever" coupled with the Medical Profession's general disbelief in these matters has resulted in the propensity to want to extend physical life way past what should be a natural and desirable point at which to exit from earthly life. Consequently, this has changed the nature of how we relate to every other human being. Today we are all potential spare parts units. Of course, it is correct and proper to seek to extend life where possible, but surely not to the point where the lawful process of dying a completely natural death is actually hindered. Yet do we ever read of anyone dying of old age anymore? Hardly ever. Where death occurs in the very aged, medical protocol must always find the exact medical words to attempt to describe this completely natural process of ageing, even where it may logically be something as simple as plain organ deterioration.

The astute reader should now have little difficulty in recognising that the Silver Cord is the key to understanding how one can "return to life". As long as the cord is still attached to the body, the possibility exists for a return. In such a case, it is merely a question of the *re-strengthening* of the radiation-connection between the physical shell and the soul body which offers the potential for reconnection. The condition of the shell or corpse does not necessarily prevent such a reunion either, though a severely ravaged one will probably not allow for a reunion of any great length of time. As already noted, Dr. Watson records that even in cases where decomposition of the body had begun, people still returned to life. In all cases, however, the possible return of the "dead" or the inability to return will always be subject to strict Spiritual Law without any kind of arbitrary intervention.

9.2   Jesus — "Calling the Dead to Life"

The inviolable and thus *immutable* outworking of The Spiritual Laws in such cases permits a fascinating insight into *how* Jesus was able to call the "dead" back to life. What we should not lose sight of here is that Spiritual Law is also Natural Law; for it is **Creation-Law**! Indeed, The Spiritual Laws could not possibly be anything other than "completely natural". Thus the "miracles" that Jesus wrought were so wrought under the naturalness of the highest Spiritual Laws which He came to fulfil – as stated in Matthew 5:17, Fenton. We repeat:

> "Do not imagine that I have come to **abolish** the law and the prophets; I have not come to abolish, but to **complete** them."

It is unfortunate that the *followers* of all the great Teachers have invariably distorted the clear Truth of their original Teachings, probably more so with those of Jesus, Who came from out of The Living Law Itself. In His unequivocal reference to "fulfilling" The Laws, He firmly indicated that even He, as The Son of God, could not circumvent or overthrow The Spiritual Laws of Creation, but had also to submit to them. Thus even the "miracles" He performed were similarly subject to the strict consistency and inviolability of The Eternal Laws. The *miraculous aspect* of His work, however, was in the *acceleration* of the *healing effect* of the cures He wrought simply by virtue of the fact that He possessed the **Power** to bring that about.

This does not lessen the greatness of those miracles, however. Indeed, the very fact that He absolutely had to operate *within* The Law shows the sure certainty and naturalness of them whereby we human beings can also live in the supreme confidence and perfection of the same Laws. If, now, a reader may wish to use the argument that God, and therefore Jesus, could do anything without constraint from the very Laws which The Creator placed into Creation by virtue of being part of The Godhead, the very vital and critical point of the **"Perfection of God"** is called into question!

As we have stated in a previous Chapter: If we accept the premise that God is, and must be, Perfect by virtue of His Nature, then His Laws of Creation must also be similarly Perfect. The possible contention that a Perfect God would produce imperfect Laws is completely untenable, though it clearly reveals our human propensity to attempt to ascribe emotive human values to: **The Creator of All the Worlds!**

For *without* such Perfection in The Godhead and The Eternal Laws that have issued from It, the whole idea of Laws that *actually are* Eternal, inviolable in their "Perfection", and therefore *unchangeable*, becomes an absolute and illogical *impossibility.*

Therefore, the common belief that God can change His Laws at will in order to bring about a particular event, can only mean that The Law needing to be changed to effect such a thing was not perfect to begin with. Intimately connected with that assertion is the obvious further assertion of an imperfect God unable to put into place Perfect Laws from the very beginning. When we gaze at the night sky in awe and veneration and marvel at its incredible vastness, the idea of such imperfection and changeability cannot logically be considered – not even as a remote possibility.

Having clarified the key fact that it is not at all possible to alter The Spiritual Laws, let us now assess the "miracles" of Jesus with regard to the "dead". We can now easily understand that the soul-bodies of those He called back, *travelled back to the physical shell along the Silver Cord which had not yet been completely severed.* Whilst this is a lawful process, the key point here is that Jesus *possessed the power to do so.* In reiteration, issuing as He did from The Godhead – without which nothing could come into existence – He naturally and lawfully possessed the **Power** to **command** the souls to return.

Thus He clearly demonstrated the fact that death is only a transitory phase and that we should not fear it. However, a vital aspect of those particular "miracles" is not the fact that He *could* order the souls to return, but the *different manner* in which He *commanded* them to do so.

With the young maid who had recently died, He simply says:

> "My girl arise." Her breath thereupon returned, and she at once got up. And He gave orders for her to have something to eat.

> (Luke 8:54-55)

In the case of the young man from Nain who has been dead longer and is about to be buried, His command is stronger, more urgent, where He calls:

> "Young man, *I say to you,* Arise!"... the dead man sat up and began to speak. And He handed him to his mother.

> (Luke 7:14-15)

Finally, in the case of Lazarus who had already been in his tomb for four days, we read that Jesus, after ordering the cave-stone to be removed, first *prays for help,* before **commanding** Lazarus to rise. The Scripture states that '...He called *with a loud voice*':

> "Lazarus, come out!" He who was dead accordingly came out, swathed hand and foot with bandages, and his head wrapped in a napkin. Jesus told them, "loosen and let him walk".

> (John 11:42-44, Fenton all. Emphases mine.)

It is interesting to note that John the Disciple records Martha, sister of Lazarus, as objecting to the expressed intention of raising him from the dead when she stated to Jesus: "Master, by this time the smell must be offensive: for this is the fourth day." (John 11:39, Fenton.) The Disciples, who were also aghast at the thought of Jesus bringing back to Earth-life a man dead four days, protested to him to not be so foolish. He accordingly told them that with Lazarus, the Power of God through Him would be revealed for the world to see, and that they should not dare to oppose Him.[11]

Thus we see that in these three cases the longer the person had been dead, the *stronger the command required* by Jesus to effect a return, a clear indication of the relative "distances" the respective souls were from their bodies. As long as the "cord" is still attached the "dead" have the possibility of returning, which is the sole and lawful reason **why** Jesus **was able** to

---

[11]It is important to note that in each of the three respective cases, Jesus gave different instructions to the families of them. In the case of the young girl, whom we may deduce was formerly frail and weak, the order to give her food was probably to immediately re-strengthen the "radiation-connection" between her soul body and material body – which she had recently vacated and now re-entered.

bring this about, aside from *possessing* the Power to do so. Once the cord is severed, however, it is not possible for any return. Even though possessing The Power of The Divine, Jesus would *not* have been able to alter The Eternal Laws to achieve that, as He clearly pointed out!

His miraculous healings did not require a "Law change" either, as everything can only take place under the umbrella of The Spiritual Laws. It was simply a case of His Divine Power, which stands far higher again than The Spiritual, *accelerating* the normal process of healing by a very large degree so as to make it seem instantaneous, and thus miraculous. He intimated that humankind, too, would one day be able to achieve similar results once we had reached the appropriate level of Spiritual purity. The Bible narrative records that the Disciples also effected healing "miracles" *after* the Spiritual Ascension of Jesus!

According to the historical record, shortly after his resurrection, Lazarus left Palestine and the persecution of the Christians, and journeyed to Cyprus where he was ordained as Bishop by St Barnabas. Lazarus apparently lived there for a further 30 years and it is reported that he rarely smiled having seen the plight of the souls in the beyond. We should remember that he journeyed well past just the "out-of-body experience" of initial release from pain etc., into the actual state of earthly death where it is recorded that he spent four days in that "beyond" before being commanded to return to physical life.

The co-authors of "The Holy Blood and The Holy Grail" paint a rather more esoteric version of the fate of Lazarus. On page 361-362, they write:

> "If the 'beloved disciple' did not go to Ephesus, what became of him? If he and Lazarus were one and the same that question can be answered, for tradition is quite explicit about what became of Lazarus. According to tradition, as well as early Church writers, Lazarus, the Magdalene, Martha, Joseph of Arimathea and a few others, were transported by ship to Marseilles. Tradition maintains that - - Lazarus [died] at Marseilles after founding the first bishopric there."[12]

Now let us return to our own journey of discovery.

We have reached the stage where the soul-body is about to become free of its former "partner in earthly life". Firstly, however, we should return to the long, dark tunnel phase of the first stages of the death process to offer a more complete explanation of it. The subjects claimed that they felt "as if they were gliding through something dark and narrow, a valley, a dark shaft, a tunnel", and they used words like being "pulled out" in attempting to describe the sensation.

What is actually described here is the *striving away* of the ethereal soul *from* the astral body, the soul's pulling-out from the latter. At this moment of transition – during the striving away movement – the Spirit can no longer see through the eyes of either the earthly or astral body. Nor can it see through those of the ethereal soul body, which is not yet completely free. The Spirit therefore temporarily has the impression of darkness. We can liken this phase to that of being in a lift moving between two levels. Before we can look out again we must wait until the next one is reached.

The next stage is the emergence from out of this dark tunnel into the bright light of the next world. As previously stated, we can note some similarities in the birth process; in the striving away, the dark tunnel and the emergence into a bright new world. For, in reality, *earthly death* is simply *birth* into the ethereal world. This new, bright world for the soul is, however, still close to the Earth, but with a vastly altered time-perspective. Here, in this new, lighter world away from the constraints of the heavier physical body and the gross material Earth, everything is more mobile, more "speeded-up".

---

[12]It would seem that "tradition" has much to answer for.

For the departed one, this phase might be marked by much confusion, more so if he had paid no attention to this matter of death during his life. Now, in death, he discovers he has the ability to see and hear all that is taking place around him, but finds he is not able to make himself heard or felt. He sees the emotional anguish of those he left behind and strives to reassure them that he is not actually dead, that he lives. But he cannot! If those of his family members have the same attitude to death that he previously had, he will be forced to endure the emotional upheaval and non-comprehension of his kin that his death has produced. Because of this he may seek to make himself understood but, as he cannot with his "new soul-body", the only course open to him is to try to do so through the earthly organs of speech of the physical one he has very recently *vacated.*

His attempts bring about a renewed strengthening of the "cord" with perhaps a corresponding increase in feelings of pain, which he would recently have become free of. This effort on his part unnecessarily prolongs the death struggle which can last for days, and which his loved ones will anguish over. Thus his well-meaning attempts to offer solace to those around him actually only add more confusion for them, and sometimes fear. The feelings of anguish and loneliness for a soul who finds himself in such circumstances must surely be considerable. Far better if we all occupied ourselves with this vital question instead of pushing it away, as if that act might somehow keep earthly death away forever. Since knowledge empowers, it is far better to know than to not know!

The severing of the Silver Cord is not always easy. The Spirit-Author, Franchezzo, whose Dedication we included earlier in this Chapter, offers a sobering insight into this difficulty. After his physical death he sees, standing by his grave, the girl he loved. When she leaves he tries to follow her, but is unable to.

> "I strove with all my might to follow her. In vain, I could go but a few yards from the grave and my earthly body, and then I saw why. A chain as of dark silk thread – it seemed no thicker than a spider's web – held me to my body; no power of mine could break it; as I moved it stretched like elastic, but always drew me back again. Worst of all I began now to be conscious of feeling the corruption of that dead body affecting my spirit, as a limb that has become poisoned affects with suffering the whole body on earth, and a fresh horror filled my soul.

> Then a voice as of some majestic being spoke to me in the darkness, and said: *'You loved that body more than your soul. Watch it now as it turns to dust and know what it was that you so worshipped, and ministered and clung to. Know how perishable it was, how vile it has become, and look upon your spirit body and see how you have starved and cramped and neglected it for the sake of the enjoyments of the earthly body'.*"

(*A Wanderer in the Spirit Lands*, p.11
Bold emphasis mine.)

The Silver Cord, which in this case has thickened and become dark, binds the departed one very firmly to his physical body. Only after he has recognised the wrong of his earthly life, can he sever himself from his mortal shell. When the disintegration of the Silver Cord does finally occur, the departed one experiences the effects of **The Law of Spiritual Gravity** in its full manifestation. In accordance with previous explanations the soul is forced, through the consequential effects of its recently lived lifestyle, to then begin to "reap what it sowed". This is achieved under the outworking of the relevant Spiritual Laws where the soul is "propelled" to the particular plane which corresponds with its ethereal or "spiritual" weight.[13]

---

[13]In accordance with **The Law of Spiritual Gravity**, only on Earth can good and evil live side by side. On no other Plane of Creation is this possible.

Thus upon earthly death a separation takes place between all the departed. In accordance with that separation, they must then *occupy* the particular Plane that their ethereal weight has decreed for them and those of similar mind and propensity. Therefore souls will always find themselves surrounded by others of the same weight and essentially of the same nature. In this lies the Perfect Justice of The Eternal Laws, in particular the outworking of The Law of Attraction of Similar Species.

> And Man seeks his Long Home,
> And the Mourners will walk round the streets -
> *Ere the Silver Cord's loosed...*
> And Man goes to the earth that he was,
> And his Soul will return to the GOD Who gave it!

(Ecclesiastes 12:6-7, Fenton. Italics mine.)

9.3   The Nature of Hell

Much uncertainty surrounds this question of the nature of the place called "hell", or even if such a place exists or could exist. Some earlier philosophers postulated a duality of forces, i.e. a good and a bad one, and a light and a dark one. Such a view clearly presupposes that *two* forces must exist, and that there are *two* separate powers we can choose between or connect ourselves to. This belief is probably dominant in most cultures and religions today because, on the surface at least, it appears to be a reasonable one. The dark force, moreover, is invariably deemed to be the "creator" or "owner" of hell. The assumption or proposition that such a separate "dark force" exists has certainly been used often enough as a reason or excuse where horrific crimes have been committed. "I was told to do it" they say. "Voices from somewhere made me do it", and so on. The voices would be real enough, but their *origin* is the key consideration here.

St Augustine, a theologian who lived from 354 to 430 AD, was preoccupied for much of his life with what might be termed the "problem of evil": In essence where evil came from. For a time he was 'swayed' by the Stoic school of thought which held that there was no sharp division between good and evil. A major factor contributing to his quandary was Neoplatonism which espoused the view that all existence is divine in nature. A philosopher to begin with, Augustine had nevertheless long felt that there was a limit as to how far philosophy could go. It was not until he became a Christian that he found the peace he sought, a peace anchored in faith.
He wrote: "Our heart is not quiet until it rests in Thee."

Schelling (1775-1854), the leading Romantic philosopher, sought to unite mind and matter. He believed that all of nature in both the human soul and the physical reality was the expression of one Absolute or world Spirit. He saw this "world spirit" in nature but he also saw it in the human mind. He also accepted the idea of a development from earth to rock to "mind" governed by his "world spirit" beliefs. Schelling stated explicitly that "the world is in God". He believed that God was aware of some of it, but there were other aspects of nature which represented the unknown in God. This was the "dark side of God" in his view.

In reality, however, there is only *one power streaming through all of Creation*. It issues *solely from out of "The Creative Will of God"* and is completely *neutral*. Being, in essence, the "Living Power", it creates and sustains all life. However, in the case of we humans who are inherently endowed with the attribute of "free will" and who also stand in this power stream, we occupy a singularly consequential position, for we are like lenses. This "power" is *automatically refracted through us* precisely according to *how* we choose to use it and *where* we choose to direct it. Thus either for good, or for evil! This unstoppable free-will mechanism therewith ultimately determines our end-fate – through *how we choose* to live our lives.

So, whilst we **absorb** a *neutral power*, our free-will volition then *converts it* to whatever we choose – good or evil. Or, to word it differently, to either the correct principle or the incorrect principle. By this process we automatically "form" our environment thereby bringing in its train our personal reaping, the reaping of our society, our Nation and global family of Nations. Since all written history quite clearly attests to wars, blood and violence on the grandest possible scale, consider the *forms* <u>we</u> have created over thousands of years, and continue to do so. So because we *created* them, only through a fundamental change in attitude and way of being can we destroy them and become free.

Yet is there any move towards seeking to change the mostly dark forms of our free will volition? Generally speaking, no! How many on Earth are truly prepared to accept the reality of **The Law of Reciprocal Action**? Very few. Instead, we not only add to those forms but greatly nourish them in our selfish desire to "do what pleases us". In concert with "The Law of Attraction..." we are forced to reap more and more from that growing monster under the "Iron Law of Karma". Unfortunately, however, with additional burdens lawfully imposed via the aegis of the *whirlwind constant.*

The knowledge and outworking of Spiritual Law permits the concept of "hell" to be simply explained. The key thing to be understood is that it is **not an institution ordained and created by God**. It is composed of those levels in the world of the afterlife that we of humankind have created through giving full and unbridled rein to our evil dispositions over millennia. The rejection of *true* Spiritual ideals, and the gravitating toward material pleasures and vices – along with the natural accompaniment of evil activities – has brought about the formation of the "Planes of Hell". From there, its many and varied dark forms, under the outworking of **The Law of Attraction of Similar Species**, in their insidious nature go forth to further 'infect the world'. Down there, also, the darker like-minded are forced by Law to reside until such time as a genuine spiritual longing to be free of it all permits ascent for that individual under the outworking of The Law.

Humankind, therefore, is the landlord and owner of the place we call "hell".

Under the inter-related workings of all The Spiritual Laws, Perfect Spiritual Justice may be clearly discerned via those lawful mechanisms.

In striking contrast, the same process has also formed Planes of Light where like-minded souls enjoy the peace and beauty of the afterlife they have earned. Suffering and tragedy, therefore, are *not* willed by God. We bring that on ourselves via the same process, paradoxically, whereby we could enjoy continual peace and happiness, i.e. by the simple application of directing our free will toward the good.

The often bemoaned cry of "Where lies justice?" is quite clearly explained in the above discussion. If we consider the following Scripture, moreover, we can readily see that "Justice", down to its last ramification, is absolutely served. Perhaps not immediately on the Earth under human law, but most assuredly later under the Perfection of Spiritual Law! Through its outworking, we can more readily understand the following Scriptural quotes, key ones of which we have previously mentioned.

From Hosea 8:7; Hebrews 10:30; and Deuteronomy 30:19. (Fenton all.):

"And as they have sown only Wind, the Whirlwind alone shall they reap!"

"Yet we know who says PUNISHMENT IS MINE, I WILL REPAY."

"I place Life and Death before you, – the Blessing and the Curse! Therefore choose for yourselves the Life, – that you and your posterity may live!"

In each of the above Scriptures, the clear admonition to **choose** correctly is evident, and only with a free-will ability can we do so. Therefore all choices are ultimately ours and ours alone, and the automatic outworking of Creation-Law subsequently delivers to us the ensuing consequences.

There is one final question that remains to be addressed with regard to the *end-fate* of human spirits in terms of the *complete death-process*. That, however, is the subject of our next Chapter. For the moment we have arrived at the end of a basic explanation of this inevitable yet vital earthly happening. It is, however, a basic overview only. For greater understanding, the reader may wish to avail himself of *certain* other publications which offer more insight into the subject. The reader should note, however, that whilst there are *very many* books which *purport* to give correct explanations of the death process, in fact only a very few *actually* can. **And only <u>one</u>** – to which *this* book ultimately leads – **completely so!**

9.4   The Ramifications of Loud Wailing

Grieving is a natural facet of virtually all peoples at funerals. Some races, however, appear to inherently display a level of emotion that can sometimes border on unhealthy over-emotionalism. Whilst there will always be a normal and naturally-healthy level of grief for departed loved ones in particular, without the knowledge of the death process to guide us we could not ever have been sure of the **effect** that displays of very deep emotional grief and loud lamentations might have **on the very ones for whom we grieve**. Now that we do have clear and unequivocal understanding it behoves us, regardless of race, culture or tradition, to take cognisance of this knowledge, and begin to more fully understand the effects that our behaviour might have on the very recently departed.

We should therefore ask ourselves the question: *"What should we do to help those who are struggling to become free from the earthly body and associated ties?"* Given the huge amounts of emotion and stress invariably present at funerals, perhaps the more relevant question is: **"What should we not do** when grieving for the dead?" Equally importantly, **why** should we not do it? Even though a brief explanation is already offered in this Chapter, it is probably appropriate to re-define the relevant aspects again.

People who are present at a death bed should strive **not** to break out into loud expressions of grief! When the grief at parting is too strongly expressed, the person in the process of detaching himself from his physical body, or who may already be standing beside it in ethereal form, may hear or feel it and be emotionally disturbed by it. If he should then feel pity for those he left behind, a strong desire may awaken within him to say a few words of consolation. In his attempts to make himself **understood** to the grief-stricken mourners, his "associated struggle" binds him *more strongly* to his physical body.

Now, because of his renewed efforts to establish a closer connection with his physical body – *which is the only medium by which he is able to communicate* – the ethereal body, which was still in the natural process of detaching itself, *not only* re-unites itself *more closely* with the physical body, but will be *drawn back into it again*. Consequently, the pains from which he had already been delivered will be felt once more. When he next seeks to detach himself from his physical shell – and which he must inevitably do – it will be made more difficult and may last for several days. As previously stated this produces the prolonged, so-called "death struggle" which loved ones and relatives anguish over and which not only causes them more grief as they observe this process, but is also painful and difficult for the soul wanting to depart.

The blame for this unfortunate situation, as difficult as it may be to accept, lies solely with those who are unable to curb their emotions and who express it in loud wailing and lamentations of grief. *The natural course of development for that soul is thus held back as* **he** *struggles to cope with it.* From an earthly standpoint such behaviour is perhaps understandable. From that of the purely Spiritual, however, it is actually one of selfishness because the grieving ones are more concerned with *their loss* than for the lawful transition of their loved one into his next life, or for *his* emotional struggle as *he* observes *their* grief.

This quite unnecessary interruption of the normal process, even if only a weak attempt at concentrating on making himself understood, ensures that a new and *forced* connection occurs. Dissolving this unnatural connection again may not be so easy. Unfortunately, because **it** desired this reconnection itself, no assistance can be given. Moreover, so long as the physical body is still not yet completely cold and the "Silver Cord" – which may not necessarily tear for many weeks – is still intact, such "reconnections" can still be effected. *We should thus always consider the suffering of the dying one* ***first*** *and not the thought of our own loss.* The ideal situation for this serious event, therefore, should be one of absolute quiet, therewith offering the departing one the necessary dignity as should befit the importance of the hour.

These vital considerations should, at such times, induce each of us to seriously think about our own particular attitude; to ensure we are not remiss in this area. Would we want the experience of a painful death struggle? Clearly not! Unfortunately it is what we invariably visit upon those we *most care for* during **their** *death process*. We should therefore resolve to place our personal sense of loss in a secondary role and consider more the plight of our friend or loved one as **he** struggles to stand free of the shackles of the earthly body. More particularly if there has been a prolonged illness or a restrictive and painfully-debilitating accident. A quick merciful release from that should be our *primary* concern, and not our own personal wish to *hold him to us*.

To this end, it is important to clearly understand the ***differences*** that actually exist between a natural, ***emotional experiencing*** at such an event, and a situation where this aspect is perhaps ***unconsciously subjugated*** to a state of ***overwrought emotionalism*** brought on by the *collective*, emotional upwelling of the occasion. Even though the emotions are given to us to ***deepen*** every experience – irrespective of whether it be joyful or painful – there is a vast difference between the two positions in this case, even if, on the surface and to the onlooker, the grief may *appear* to be the same.

One is naturally healthy having a Spiritual foundation as its wellspring of understanding, whilst the other is basically earthly emotionalism. For **The Spiritual** knows only high, pure, cool objectivity, with Spiritual Love as its foundation. It is certainly not that which most people reveal at funerals. Therefore displays of *unnecessary emotionalism* have little affinity with true spirituality but, in its earthly manner, invariably focuses more on the person/s displaying it.

Only by accepting that **death is a far more serious and important occasion for the departing one** than it is for us, might we learn to leave behind the loud wailing and lamenting that has invariably accompanied death and funerals for so long. If we need to grieve – for it is recorded that **even Jesus wept openly at times** – we should replace loud lamentations with quiet, controlled, natural and dignified grief, thus offering the help of a quick release and peace and dignity to the one being farewelled.

Far better yet, we should strive to develop genuine understanding of the process and not display grief at all for, in Spiritual Truth, there is actually no need to do so! Earthly death being a "life-transition" process into the Ethereal Realm means that we should direct thoughts and words of encouragement and knowledge to the departed one to help him in his next and most necessary step. As we would no doubt want that also, we should remind ourselves once more of the following, appropriate words of Jesus, given from out of the Living Law:

"And as you wish men to do to you, do the same to them."

(Luke 6:31, Fenton.)

9.5 Death of a Soldier

For those who accept that life continues after physical death, a loved one's sacrifice in battle may be easier to deal with emotionally. But what of the actual sacrifice itself, the extinguishing of a life in battle for a particular cause? Where can we place that in spiritual terms, and are we able to? The simple answer is: "Yes"! There are spiritual effects for every soldier[14] in the ultimate sacrifice. So if death is the outcome in a just and righteous cause nobly and bravely carried out, the "after-effects" will be vastly different from those which "brutal adventurers" in an ignoble war will experience. A brief examination of relatively recent history can probably conclude that there will have been very many acts of noble sacrifice, by virtue of the need to stop the madness of megalomanic despots. What then spiritually happens for the soldier who bravely pays the ultimate sacrificial price?

In order to answer *this* question, we must refer back to our explanation of the Origin and nature of man. We know that the human spirit is an amalgam of a number of bodies telescoped, as it were, into each other, with each "body" corresponding to the nature and consistency of the particular Plane to which it belongs. From our Origins in The Spiritual Realm we are required to accept and occupy each appropriate body corresponding to, and consistent with, the nature of each Plane we must traverse on our journey downwards to personal self-consciousness on the Earth in the material world. At earthly death, the reverse process takes place whereby we discard each body at the height of its appropriate Realm or level, as we ascend on the journey home, assuming, of course, that we have earned the right to do so.

Connected with Spiritual Law and the Higher Realms are all the virtues, one of which is **heroism**. By virtue of its particular nature, its place of origin *can only be* in the Higher Planes. The gift of free will that is inherent in every human being means that in our chosen life-path, whether as an individual or even as part of a Nation, we can choose either the uplifting benefits of the virtues or the debasing, destructive energies of the vices. This means that certain activities will inherently have either uplifting or debasing qualities.

Now, whilst war may generally be regarded as destructive, particular elements within it or, more particularly, certain kinds of actions that war inevitably produces, *can* be connected to the higher virtues.[15] So, in the case of a soldier who recognises that his participation in a just war is necessary to preserve freedom, who carries out his duties with quiet efficiency, with objectivity for the cause and without hate for the opposing side, and who is killed during an act of heroism in the course of his serving, this soldier – in Spiritual terms – has released the virtue of heroism within him. It is thus connected to him.

This act of heroism in its **Spiritual Form**, through its release via an heroic act, is attracted upwards under **The Law of Attraction of Similar Species**, to its ordained place close to The Spiritual Realm of our Origin. This particular Plane of Creation to which we refer in this case is commonly alluded to as the "home of the gods" of many of the ancient cultures. It is that level which the Greeks, particularly, sought inspiration from to nobly emulate that loftier vision and apply it to every aspect of their society, including the military training of their young men. Their *spiritual* insight allowed them to "see" the activity and nature of the inhabitants there, such as the Elemental Lord Zeus, whom they erroneously believed to be a god. They

---

[14]The term "soldier" is used to describe the activity of all servicemen. Therefore the role of the sailor and the airman in war is the same as that of the soldier. They all inherently possess equal value.

[15]The Bhagavad-Gita offers a precise explanation in this regard, since its narrative is based on the duty and responsibility of a true hero and soldier, Arjuna, to his people, as instructed by Krishna.

named their "home" Mt. Olympus.[16] Thus every heroic act is connected to the essence of the natural power and nobleness of those "Elemental forces".[17]

It is from the noble volition of the Spirit – the real us – that heroic acts are generated. The "living form" of each heroic act is thus connected to its Origin in the Higher Realms. That *form* is "released" from the soul body of our noble soldier at his death in battle. It is drawn upwards to the topmost level of its ordained place where it is cared for until the day the "owner" of the heroic act – our soldier – might reach that point of his "spiritual ascent". If he does so it is automatically returned to him, since it was his alone. This he carries with him to the next level: The Spiritual Realm of his Origin and thus his *true* home. There it adorns him as a *spiritually-visible sign* of his noble sacrifice.

The ancient Nordic peoples also perceived the truth of this process and named that particular kingdom or level "Valhalla". This high "fastness" housed the "resting place" of their heroes killed in battle too. However, whilst they and the Greeks, among others, divined the existence of this Realm and the activity of the Beings therein, they had not reached a level of knowledge sufficient to fully understand the outworking of The Eternal Laws and the associated processes that determine the complete happening. Today we can fill those gaps with the relevant knowledge from particular Spiritual Works now available to us.

That is the *spiritual meaning* of a soldier's altruistic sacrifice in a just cause! Thus, whilst wars are a curse and a blight on mankind, they do provide opportunities whereby potentially-severe fate, returning to one under the outworking of **The Law of Reciprocal Action**, can be expiated by such an individual through deeds of great bravery. Therefore the common saying, "...better to be a live coward than a dead hero", does not actually occupy any truly Spiritual place. Cowardice, historically, has been reviled by most of the world's peoples, and the aftermath of various wars have seen known cowards executed.

Finally, the words of Jesus best explain the true meaning and greatness of what is termed, the "ultimate sacrifice", when He said:

> "Stronger love has no one than this, that one should lay down his own life for his friends."

> (John 15:13, Fenton.)

In such noble deeds the greatest Power in Creation is invoked, that of **The Power of Love**. This, however, is the Pure Love contained in true *spiritual* activity and is not the unfortunate distortion of base emotionalism produced by humankind's earthly interpretations and activities relating to this so crucially-important **Life-word**:

LOVE!

---

[16]The "formerly noble ideal" of the Olympic games has its origin here too.

[17]Even in the animal kingdom the inhabitants there will defend territory or young, to the point of dying for that cause.

10

THE SECOND DEATH

Crucial Imperative No 3:

That being more than just a physical body means we naturally and inherently possess *a separable entity* **within** the material form. And that *that* is the actual life-force, the animating core, that is actually *each individual*!

(Author.)

"The conqueror shall never be injured by the second death!"

(Revelation 2:11, Fenton.)

"Do not smile about it for it is true; Your thoughts, words and works are recorded in the 'Book of Life' **by none other than yourself**."

(*Heavenly Thoughts*, Karl May.
All emphases mine.)

The title of this Chapter may seem incredulous to many, more particularly perhaps for people who are uncertain or disbelieving of the nature and process of just the physical deaths we all see at various intervals during the course of life. So to state that there is such an event as a "second death" will surely cause considerable disbelief in the minds of many. Yet, just as we outlined the process of *earthly death* in the last Chapter, so can an explanation for a seemingly radical idea of a *"second death"* also be offered.

As with death in the *earthly* sense, the reality of the "second one" is equally as subject to immovable Spiritual Law. Indeed, only from that standpoint can it be so possible and be explained, by virtue of the simple fact that all things, from the smallest to the greatest, exist under Creation-Law. And neither does a "second death" notion clash with the Biblical statement wherein it states in Hebrews 9:27, Fenton:

"...it is appointed to men to die once..."

Quite obviously if there *was* such divergence, we could not logically have any allusions to such a thing as a "second death" in the first place. Yet we find in The Book of Revelation two other clear and unequivocal statements about it.

" ...over these the *second death* has no authority".

"...that is the *second death* – the lake of fire".

(Revelation 20:6 and 20:14, Fenton both.
Italics mine.)

Allusions to "second deaths" and "lakes of fire" may sound religiously crass to many living in our increasingly technological and computerised society strongly directed to the ethos of the "god-corporate" or the "god-academic". However, such *ostensibly* "archaic religious ideas" should be viewed as simply being "symbolic explanations" of **particular and very precise lawful processes and outcomes**! In any case, from the point of view of the Judaeo-Christian school of thought – upon which Western society is largely moulded anyway – we have at least established that the "second death" idea is very much "alive and well" in The Bible.

Moreover, the *Spiritual meaning* of the *conqueror* in the Biblical quote under the title heading of this particular Chapter should be understood to mean one who has succeeded in **conquering himself**! He has conquered **his own base weaknesses** and is thus far more spiritually mature and knowledgeable than "before the fact". His increasing spiritual awareness may also allow him to be more accepting of such an idea as "the second death". Establishing the Biblical fact of a "second death" therefore permits us the use of this foundation to assess the ramifications of how we might be affected by this "event". First, however, let us read the interpretation about it that Cruden's Concordance offers:

[2] "A separation of soul and body from God's favour in this life, which is the state of all unregenerated and unrenewed persons who are without the light of knowledge, and the quickening power of grace, Luke 1.79. This is *spiritual* death."

[3] "The perpetual separation of the whole man from God's heavenly presence and glory, to be tormented forever with the devil and his angels, Rev. 2. 11. This is the *second death.*"

(*Cruden's Concordance*, p.96)

If we accept that there is such a thing as a "second death", as The Bible clearly states, then we should expect that however it is brought about it can only be so under the strict outworking of Creation-Law. Since The Laws of Nature and scientific law both have their validity solely under the umbrella of those higher Spiritual Laws, let us approach this particular subject matter not from a purely "religious" perspective, but from the combined intermeshing of all the above Principles, as we did with the "first death".

In the current Biblical interpretation from Cruden's Concordance, *three* different kinds of deaths are noted. Yet The Bible does not appear to indicate anywhere that there are three in all. Cruden's mentions physical death, with which we are all familiar, and states that there is a "second death', and also a "spiritual death". Utilising The Spiritual Laws as the foundation for our assessments, we will show that, aside from physical death which all must experience, there is the **actual reality** of the "second death" to contend with. There are not two *different kinds* of *further deaths*, therefore, but only the final *secondary one*. This **'second death'** is thus **Spiritual Death**! Therefore we can safely conclude that any opinion to the contrary will be solely due to an incorrect Biblical interpretation on this particular subject.

But what *exactly* is a "second death" – if we have already "died" in the earthly sense? In order to find a starting point of explanation, we must first consider the differences between that which is eternal and that which is not. The earlier Greeks, Indians, Persians and Teutons shared a broad, common view that history is cyclical, with no beginning and no end. But in an "eternal interplay between birth and death", different civilisations rise and fall. This view, however, is not quite the "eternality" that we mean.

Let us compare that idea with the notion of Rene Descartes (1596-1650), a French philosopher and mathematician who rejected all previously held beliefs and built his own philosophy on the one premise he held to be indisputable, the existence of himself as a "thinking subject". This is signalled in his "personalised statement":

"I think, therefore I am."

As a "dualist" philosopher, Descartes believed that whilst there are two different forms of reality or substances – *thought* or mind, and *extension* or matter – he nevertheless maintained that *both substances* originate from God, because, as he correctly surmised, "...only God Himself exists independently of anything else". He thus came to the conclusion that man is a dual creature – of the mind, and of the body. Yet even though philosophically equating the mind with spirit, he apparently did not extend that thought to encompass *a separately-existing Spiritual Realm as the originating place of the Spirit.*

Sartre (1905-80), from his existentialist beliefs, thought that man had no eternal nature to fall back on, and it was therefore pointless to search for the meaning of life. Existentialism, in the philosophic sense, appears to represent the 20th Century's answer to all other philosophical beliefs of the past. It is therefore interesting to note the path that philosophy has taken. An early and strong acceptance of a *separable* soul or spirit before the birth of Christ became interspersed with diverging philosophic/religious views at varying intervals up to the present.[1]

In the century preceding Sartre's, however, another European philosopher had already rejected the values of Christianity. Friedrich Nietzsche (1844-1900), regarded the Christian ideal as "slave morality". In his opinion, both Christianity and traditional philosophy had turned away from what he termed "the real world", and instead directed their thinking towards "heaven" or the "world of ideas". He urged people to be "true to the world" and not to be seduced by any offers of "supernatural expectations".

In terms of an actual truth or a distortion of that truth, his reference to Christianity as being a "slave morality" could quite clearly be viewed as a "truth in itself" if, in the course of centuries, the original teachings had become so badly distorted that only rigid fundamentalism or a religion of fear was left. Without the vitality and vibrancy that only "Pure Truth" can offer, apathy, superficiality and non-understanding – with the obvious potential to lead into hypocrisy – may well then become the "way of that religion". Of course, this applies to all beliefs and teachings, and not necessarily religious ones.

As explained in the Chapter on our Origins, we know that Creation consists of two main basic parts, the Eternal and the non-eternal or Material. For human spirits, the Eternal part is that region of Creation from which we issued as *non-conscious spirit-seeds* on our journey down to the Earth in the non-eternal Material. For its part, the Material is that region to which the Earth and the physical universes belong and to which we journeyed in order to fulfil our ordained purpose to develop to a fully conscious state, thereby hopefully recognising both our Origin and our life's purpose. And, therefore, with the concomitant potential to *return* to The Spiritual Realm in the Eternal part of Creation as a completely purified Spiritual being.

---

[1]Perhaps we might now see existentialism and its general denial of the spirituality of man as the almost final excrescence of our lauding of intellectual prowess above all else.

For that is the *only* state in which we *are able* to return *home*!

In order to understand why there is a "second death" reality, there needs to be the *further* recognition that there is necessarily a "time-frame constraint" for all the Material Worlds of Creation. Creation-Law decrees that everything in those *material* worlds must inherently have a *finite* lifespan. The Eternal Realms, quite logically, do not. In our world of the Earth and physical universe, we can readily see vast numbers of diverse creatures and inanimate life-forms with varying life spans. From fractions of a second for sub-atomic particles, to hours for the most minute creatures, to days for some insects and on to years for those of the animal world. Man, as the only creature on Earth with an inner animating *spiritual core* and *free will*, has a life span of 70 odd years approximately. The great trees, though, can live for thousands of years.

Out in the vast tracts of the universe, however, suns and planets are born, live out their allotted life-span over billions of years and then disintegrate to be reborn as other celestial bodies aeons later. The far larger galaxies have a life span running into millions of light years.[2] Notwithstanding such incomprehensible measurements of distance and time, everything in the Material World nonetheless has its time of *birth, life and disintegration.*

The Material Part of Creation is therefore finite with a strictly ordained time of existence, after which it must also disintegrate back to its primordial components to be reformed into a new Material Creation. Such a time span is clearly difficult to comprehend, but it nonetheless behoves each of us to concern ourselves with this concept, for the disintegration of a whole part of the Material World cannot take place without huge and unimaginable dislocations and upheavals. Whole galaxies and universes would be absolutely convulsed in this process under the immensely powerful outworking of Creation-Law. Quite logically, therefore, whomever inhabitants this very small planet Earth can expect similar kinds of convulsions also, with a correspondingly large degree of dislocation and destruction *when that time arrives!*

We should clearly note, however, that disintegration of the Earth and its immediate inter-stellar environs is far in the future. What we have already explained in "Elemental Lore" is not the "Second Death process". It is the "cleansing of the Earth" of all spiritually-wrong works, along with their human architects and supporters. What may happen for very many, however, is that *continued* opposition to The Spiritual Laws even *after* earthly death, the "First Death", will set them on a course *towards* disintegration – the process of which we explain later on in this Chapter

Now, being of the Spirit in his inner animating core, and being of the Material in his *physical* body, man, in reality, **stands in both parts at the same time**. With his Origins from out of the Eternal Spiritual, he has the potential to return and reside there eternally. With his other foot in The World of Matter, however, he has an equal chance of remaining there tied, as it were, to it. The choice is his, and his alone. And therein lies the key to the understanding of the "Second Death".

In the granting of conscious life to humankind, and the accompanying formation of the Material Worlds for the many journeys man must make therein in order to spiritually develop and mature, The Spiritual Laws that govern this process also determine the total time of existence for this part of that World – in strict accordance, however, with The Creative Will. Thus this Earth, and therefore man on it, naturally has the exact same amount of allotted time – *in terms of its total existence in this part of the Material World.* At the close of that time-period, it will undergo its disintegration phase too, exactly in accordance with firmly established Creation-Law which then transforms the component pieces into a new part of the Material World in a vast,

---

[2]One light year is the distance a ray of light travels in one Earth year – approximately 6 million, million miles. Or more precisely – 9.4605 million, million kilometres.

humanly incomprehensible cycle of birth, life and disintegration over a similarly stupendous time-frame.[3]

It should be seriously understood that whilst such concepts of time are mind-boggling for humankind; in terms of Eternity under the aegis of The Creative Will, it is not even a "snap of the fingers". Our general inability to come to terms with such a concept owes itself to the fact that the human spirit, even though possessing the *potential* to live *eternally* as a self-conscious personality, was never inherently so. So it is important to remind ourselves that we will never be able to form a *knowing concept* of eternity. It will forever be beyond our grasp for we are merely "developed" beings only, and not "created" ones, as we have already noted.

Having thus established a basic framework of time through which the ramifications of the current subject can be further explored, let us continue our explanations. As previously stated, the precisely determined and ordained time of life for humankind *on Earth* is necessarily exactly the same as the far larger and clearly defined part of the Material World **to which the Earth belongs**. This fact decrees that *that* ordained time-span is naturally also the amount of time given over for our **spiritual maturation**. This aeons-long period nonetheless represents just *part* of our *total* existence.

As previously explained, also, the basic earthly concept of a *single lifetime* of birth, life and death is completely erroneous. One lifetime *hardly suffices* to gain even the *faintest* recognitions of *genuine* Spiritual Truth and its necessary and concomitant *life-experiencing*. Since it is barely possible to become spiritually mature in the course of just *one* lifetime, we are therefore able to designate a single-life time-period as being just a very small part of our *complete* existence. The greatest part of that totality is therefore spent in what we term the "beyond"; the Ethereal Realm.

Therefore, the totally erroneous 'Rest In Peace' notion [R.I.P.] that adorns millions of headstones to, *ostensibly*, give comfort to relatives of the deceased represents one of the greatest barriers to crucial life-knowledge for all peoples.

10.1   One Life! — or Many Lives?

This sub-Chapter returns us to the contentious question of a single-life concept versus a multi-life one. In terms of a "belief of conviction" about this particular concept/choice, what we determine for ourselves naturally affects every aspect of how we live our individual lives and how we relate to everything and everyone around us. The question of choice here is once again a **50 percent** one, but with the same **100 percent outcome**. Therefore, just as a personal choice over the question of "life after death" might logically presuppose a certain attitude and lifestyle in its *100 percent acceptance*, so might the question of "one life versus many" also produce a particular conviction as to one's perceived purpose and final outcome in life.

Yet the problem remains that if the *wrong 50 percent choice* is made – for whatever reason – that choice necessarily translates to being **100 percent wrong**, with all its attendant incorrect opinions and views. Around the truth of reincarnation, therefore, a wrong choice translates to a huge and consequential *reciprocal* effect under the outworking of Spiritual Law. Since we contend that it is not possible for the human spirit to acquire all the spiritual knowledge that it needs in *one* lifetime, we must therefore state our unshakeable conviction that the concept of

---

[3]We have correlated the findings of astronomical/cosmological science and Spiritual Law to more precisely detail the disintegrative processes. The explanations may be found in the sister-Book: "The Gathering Apocalypse and World Judgement" *What it Brings – Even Now – and Why*: Chapter 14; 'Science Supports the Judgement Process'.

multi-lives, or reincarnation, under the *immutable* aegis of **The Spiritual Law of Rebirth**, is the *only* correct 'possibility'.

Thus have we chosen our 100 percent outcome!

"Man is a spirit and his body is the dress, the clothes it wears while it is on the earth. Just as an earthman changes his clothes but remains the same person, so the human spirit changes his physical body in the process called death. But the spirit, the owner of the body, lives on after discarding the body.

Belief in reincarnation is simply the acceptance of the knowledge that a human spirit, in one continuous existence, is given the opportunity to come to the earth more than once. On each occasion, the human spirit takes on a different human body.

This simple concept is the key to the unravelling of many so-called mysteries, the explanations of the inequalities, apparent injustices and inequities that worry so many well-meaning people, and the understanding of some exceedingly important but difficult passages in The Bible. Reincarnation leads us to a conviction of *"the relative* **insignificance** *of tribe, race, and nationality"*, a conviction that is absolutely essential in moving mankind from its present-day chaos into a just and joyful social, political and economic order."

(*The Christian and Reincarnation.*
Stephen Lampe, p.1 Emphases mine.)

The Bible offers some interesting insights into the thought-processes of the people of the day, including the Disciples of Jesus, regarding this belief. In the story of the healing of the blind man, the question the Disciples put to Jesus regarding the reason why the beggar was born blind must clearly presuppose a belief and basic understanding that certain kinds of *suffering* can *only* be the result of a spiritual transgression *from a previous life.*

Note:

[An exceptional talent or genius in a particular field, such as that which child prodigies have historically displayed, can stem from the same process too. From the viewpoint of simple and 'clarifyingly-brutal' logic, it is ludicrous to believe that just a few short years of childhood would be sufficient to enable such a child to produce, for example, marvels of symphonic music, or solve mathematical problems of great complexity. Such a notion is simply *untenable* as a purely *empirical, earth-science, premise.*]

So, from the New Testament, we read:

His disciples accordingly asked Him: "Teacher, **who sinned**; **this man**, or **his parents**, in consequence of which **he** was **born blind**?"

(John 9:2, Fenton. Emphases mine.)

It is clear that the Disciples **would not have asked this question** if they did not believe that a man *could* be *born blind* as a *consequence* of a *previous sin* committed *somewhere else in time.* A sin, therefore, that could only have been committed in a previous life, **in order to be born blind.** Equally clearly, Jesus did not admonish them as fools for believing in such ostensibly "stupid beliefs". On the contrary, *in this particular case* He informed them that *"neither* the man *nor* his parents had sinned"*, but that **this man** was born blind:

"...in order that the workings of God may be displayed through him".

(John 9:3, Fenton.)

The obvious connotation from this discourse between Jesus and His Disciples is that reincarnation was a fact of life for them and, moreover, offered **exact reasons for hard misfortune** such as being *born* blind. Thus the puzzlement of the Disciples over this man's blindness was **not** about the truth or *otherwise* of reincarnation, but **which** of the **two** *possibilities* [the blind man or the parents sinning] in this particular case might have *caused* his blindness.

The Old Testament offers a number of relevant passages about reincarnation also, a few of which we can include here. In narrating his call to Prophethood, Jeremiah stated:

> Now the word of the Lord came to me saying, "Before I *formed you* in the *womb*, **I knew you**; and *before* you were *born* I **consecrated you**, and I **appointed you** a prophet to the nations."

(Jeremiah 1:4-5)

The case of the prophet Elijah is also worth analysing:

> "Behold, I will send you Elijah the prophet **before** the great and terrible day of the Lord comes."

(Malachi 4:5)

Whilst there might be uncertainty among some as to what the "great and terrible day of the Lord" refers to – the coming of Jesus, or to the Last Judgement of global humanity – there should be no uncertainty in the clear message that Elijah *would* be sent back to the Earth again. During the period of Christ's ministry, some Jewish people interpreted that particular prophecy in the sense of a reincarnation in that he would be born as a baby. Some therefore thought that Jesus was a rebirth of Elijah:

> And they said, "Some say John the Baptist; some Elijah, and others, Jeremiah, or *one of the prophets*."

(Matthew 16:14)

So here we have another strong reference that reincarnation was accepted by the people of that time as factual reality. In the context of multi-earth lives; if we follow this basic thread about Elijah further, then the reply by Jesus to His Disciples with regard to the identity of John the Baptist is especially revealing.

> "And if *you are willing to accept it*, **he is Elijah who is to come.** He that has ears to hear, let him hear."

Stephen Lampe notes that the translation in The Living New Testament Bible extrapolates this particular Scripture thus:

> "And if you are willing to understand what I mean, he is Elijah, **the one the prophets said would come.** And if ever you were ever willing to listen, listen now."

(Matthew 11:14-15. All emphases mine.)

The contentious question of reincarnation, at least for the many who subscribe to the generally accepted ideas of current Western philosophical and materialistic thought, has rarely been given the chance to be intelligently debated. It has invariably been dismissed as Eastern religious nonsense or, in the worst extreme view expounded by some Western/Christian Churches, as something evil stemming from, or having connotations to, Satanism. To be totally dismissive of an idea in such a highly emotive way might stem more from fear and ignorance rather than from rational, reasoned objectivity. Historically, the record of mankind reveals many instances of clinging to views that were clearly incorrect. Such an unfortunate stance does little to advance the cause of *real* knowledge for mankind.

Consider the "Flat Earth" theory held sacred by a blinkered and dogmatic Christian Europe for centuries. Much earlier, Greek mathematicians understood the truth of a spherical Earth. Socrates was killed because he "disturbed" his fellow citizens' "more conventional ideas" when he tried to light the way to "true insight". Consider, also, the trials of the English Doctor, Joseph Lister, [later Lord Lister], who for years attempted to enlighten his fellow doctors and surgeons to the fact that poor hygiene was actually causing the deaths of patients in operating theatres in British Hospitals. At that time, surgeons did not necessarily wash their hands before surgery, and neither was there a high priority placed on any kind of cleanliness of the operating tables or instruments. Gangrene and other infections were thought to be caused by *bad air*. Yet despite Lister's efforts to keep his new surgical rooms and instruments clean at the Glasgow Royal Infirmary, the mortality rate remained close to 50 percent.

From initiating a practice of spraying the air with carbolic acid without any real reduction in rates of post-operative infection, in 1865 he fortunately came across the germ theory of Pasteur. Utilising this knowledge and applying carbolic acid to instruments and directly to wounds and dressings, Lister reduced surgical mortality to 15 percent by 1869. His work in antisepsis met initial resistance, and even after demonstrating increasing levels of patient recovery through his simple procedure, it was not until the 1880's that his methods were finally accepted by the "medical establishment".

Gaarder, a latter-day philosopher and author of "Sophie's World', in analysing the philosophy of Seren Kierkegaard, a Danish philosopher (1813-55), noted Kierkegaard's belief that truth did not lie with the masses. His views suggested that "...the truth is always in the minority". And that "...the crowd is the untruth".

Such "lone voices in the wilderness" standing outside the "organism of the crowd" can sometimes launch huge changes in the consciousness of their fellow-men for the betterment of all. Of course, obvious physical changes cannot be so easily disputed in the same way that a physically intangible "idea" can. Like "unseen germs", reincarnation might be deemed to fall into that category. Nevertheless, many hundreds of millions of human beings over millennia have accepted reincarnation as fact. This could hardly be likened to a "lone voice" situation. The seeming problem in reincarnation for most Westerners appears to relate to the many differing views that are offered as explanations or as fact about it. Some, of course, are clearly so bizarre as to be completely untenable to even debate.

As with all aspects of life and death, however, even the smallest ramifications of reincarnation are subject to the strict and inviolable outworking of Creation-Law. The major difference between the respective religions of the Eastern and Western worlds is probably that of the **concept** of reincarnation. Present Eastern religions generally state that the purpose of one's existence is to strive for release from the cycle of rebirth and thereby finally merge with the "cosmic consciousness" and "become one with God". This is achieved, for the most part, by self-communion and meditation.

On the other hand, the three great Western religions of Christianity, Islam and Judaism all share the same fundamental idea that there is only One God, and that there is a distance between God and His Creation. With this view, man's purpose is to seek redemption from sin and blame. This is assisted by prayer and the study of the respective Scriptures, and perhaps certain austerities. The Christian Church has the added though dubious aspect of "faith and belief in the *physical* resurrection of Jesus".

Of course, not all beliefs of reincarnation share exactly the same views about it either. Arguably, perhaps the most difficult aspect for the Western intellect to accept is a particular notion which promotes the idea that we can return to Earth in a form *other than* human. Either for lessons of experiencing in a personal-wish situation, or being forced to in atonement under the "Iron Law of Karma": **The Law of Reciprocal Action.**

The reader will by now be familiar with the premise that only man possesses spirit as his "inner life-force". In a previous Chapter we outlined the reasons for this. In another Chapter we gave explanations as to why The Laws cannot be circumvented, including what we may regard as The Laws of Nature.

> Therefore, the inviolability of **Creation-Law** *absolutely decrees* thus: The notion that the ***cross-species transmigration of the human spirit*** into another and ***different*** kind of life-form might somehow be valid is not only ***completely impossible***; it is simply ludicrous.

The general thrust of life itself offers each 'group' the natural ability to procreate or otherwise produce its own, irrespective of however diverse that ability might be. For only with that "procreative reality" can any species exist. Any attempt to procreate outside/across the clearly-defined natural barriers which all species inherently possess, must ultimately fail.

One can quite easily observe this "naturally lawful fact" in just one group of creatures, in that of the animals. Even in those most closely related, such as the big cats for example, the inability to produce offspring between the different kinds should be regarded as clear proof of the inviolability of *any* transgression of Natural Law, regardless of any particular faith/belief-mode outlook. Thus in the case of a "liger" – a hybrid produced by the mating of a female tiger and a male lion; or a "tigon" – the offspring of a male tiger and a female lion – we note that all offspring from either union are sterile. It is the same for the mule, a sterile hybrid of a male ass and a female horse. "Mother Nature" will simply not permit cross-species tampering, for that is as it should be.

If that were not the case, and different species were able to cross-breed with any other kind, we would not have a clear, consistent classification of fauna as we now have. It short, it would be disastrous. However, this does not remove the opportunity for natural change or mutation *within* each species, because that is simply the process of continual *natural* development, an entirely different situation altogether. Therefore, according to the "Spiritual Rules" of the Creative process for all things, and as we have stressed previously: **Humans can only be re-born into human form!**

Rebirth, however, is not the same as that which Jesus alluded to in His enlightening statement when He stated to Nicodemus; (John 3:3, Fenton):

> "Most assuredly I tell you, that unless anyone is born from above, he cannot see the Kingdom of God."

That particular "birth" is a *spiritual* or *inner awakening* or *realisation* and does not, in any way, clash with multi-earth lives which are obviously *physical* births.[4]

---

[4]The reader who wishes to examine these same questions that have puzzled great thinkers and church leaders for centuries, and wish to be finally offered the explanations that eluded those erstwhile individuals, should examine the work, "The Christian and Reincarnation" by Stephen Lampe, (Millennium Press.) This well researched book, with much of the material culled from The Bible, will clarify many uncertainties for the serious seeker as to the validity and purpose of reincarnation, and will provide a disturbing challenge to those who might wish to scornfully dismiss the concept out of hand.

Now, since the idea of a "second death" necessarily travels into the area of multi-lives, it behoves the need to give sufficient explanation to this subject.

As a prime example, let us now examine just one particularly vital aspect of this subject from Stephen Lampe's work. It will offer the reader an explanation of how the early Church determined its final position on this matter of reincarnation. We should also recognise that there have always been, and there currently still are, a number of very eminent Christian Church leaders who have publicly stated their support for reincarnation, with the further far-reaching view that the concept **does not** contradict the teachings of The Bible.

As well, many eminent people from all walks of life believe it also, and recognise within it the inherent sense of *true* Justice which reincarnation *inherently encompasses*. Therefore, if we are to *fully understand* how there can be so many *apparent* social injustices and inequities amongst the world's peoples when we speak of absolute Justice contained within The Law, and how there can be a "Second Death" separate and distinct from being re-born "spiritually", then we must openly and objectively examine this matter of reincarnation/rebirth.

Since the generally accepted orthodox Christian view is to basically deny or refute the validity of such an idea, even with some of its leading clergy *accepting* of it, a need to define a starting point by which we might gain some insight into how the official Church position arose is vital.

Stephen Lampe offers clarification about it on pages 8-9 in Chapter 1 of his book, ("The Christian and Reincarnation"), entitled:

The Second Council of Constantinople (553 AD)

"The history of the official Church position on reincarnation is a very complex one. Many assume that the Second Council of Constantinople (552 A.D.) also called the Fifth Ecumenical Council of the church, condemned the teaching of reincarnation, but this assumption has been called into question by some competent church historians.

The Second Council of Constantinople was called by Emperor Justinian and convened on May 5th, 553 A.D. under the presidency of the Patriarch of Constantinople. However it was the Emperor, who had engaged in bitter [dispute] with Pope Vigilius, who controlled the proceedings. Even though the primary objective was to reconcile the churches of the East and West, the arrangements heavily favoured the East. It is reported that of the 165 bishops who signed the acts of the final meeting on June 2, not more than six could have been from the West. The request of Pope Vigilius for equal representation of bishops from East and West was refused. In protest, the Pope boycotted the meeting, even though he was in Constantinople, the venue of the meeting. However Pope Vigilius eventually accepted the decisions of the Council, an action that was not popular in the West, and which caused some dioceses, including that of Milan, to break off communion with Rome. Milan remained out of communion with Rome till the end of the sixth century.

Because of the protestations of Pope Vigilius, the Second Council of Constantinople did not open on schedule. While the assembled bishops were waiting Emperor Justinian ordered them to consider a subject (Origenism) that was not an item in the previously announced agenda. During this extra-conciliary session, fifteen condemnations (anathemas) proposed by the Emperor against the teachings of Origen (who had died three hundred years earlier in 254 AD) were approved. Apparently, one of the condemned teachings was the idea of pre-existence of the soul, and by implication, reincarnation. There is no evidence that Pope Vigilius, who was at the time protesting against the arrangements of the Council approved this action taken by Eastern bishops outside the formal sessions and before the opening of the Council. Thus, it is understandable that some Catholic scholars disassociate the Roman Church from the condemnations of the teachings of Origen, and therefore argue that the Roman Catholic Church has never really condemned the teaching of reincarnation.

Many otherwise knowledgeable Christians are unaware of the confusion surrounding the Second Council of Constantinople and the inconclusiveness and uncertainty of its decisions. For this reason, some imagine that they are obliged to uphold this ancient condemnation of reincarnation.

In any case Christians should appreciate that they should not necessarily consider themselves bound by decisions taken by some bishops more than 1,400 years ago. Did not the Church condemn Galileo's scientific support of the Copernican theory that the sun, and not the Earth is the centre of the solar system? And the ordinary Christians of that day of course dutifully joined Church officials in denouncing the Copernican theory. Christians at that time probably imagined that the idea which contradicts the Scriptures must have been put in the mind of Copernicus by Satan! Today some Christians, unfortunately, have a similar view of reincarnation."

One of the main points of interest regarding this important meeting was the fact that such an incredibly far-reaching and definitive decision could have been taken in a side issue separate from the main agenda. The either-or aspect of a one-life concept versus a multi-life one decided that day actually calls into question the very essence of much of Bible teaching, the cornerstone on which supposedly rest many of our beliefs and ideals.

For a few men, therefore, to cast the disturbing shadow of such a definitive decree down through the centuries surely smacks of religious machinations, particularly the edict issued against the Christian theologian, Origen, who believed in reincarnation. Among other things the edict stated that anyone who said or thought that the souls of men had had an earlier life (pre-existence) "...and were now incarnated in bodies ... would be anathematised"!

One might question the true motives of the Roman Emperor Justinian in *ordering* the bishops to consider condemning, among the other fifteen "anathemas", the concept of reincarnation. Perhaps the idea of being forced to face future lives to "reap what one sowed" – with the probability of some of those incarnations being lived out in less than favourable circumstances – was, in itself, considered blasphemous to one very much accustomed to living a life of great wealth and absolute power. The possibility of "inheriting" anything less than that must have been "anathema" to Justinian, since the line of Roman Emperors considered themselves to be divine and descended from the gods themselves.

So the very thought of reincarnation and atonement for an Emperor's possibly debased excesses needed to expunged from the day consciousness of the Empire in general. From the spiritual point of view, of course, no amount of legislation, debate or decree could have possibly altered the fact of The Law of Rebirth. Even the mighty Roman Emperor, Justinian, had to obey The Law.

Notwithstanding this decree, on page 11 of his Book Stephen Lampe observes that:

"Finally, Church historians point out that no papal encyclical against reincarnation has ever been issued – a point that should be of particular interest to Roman Catholics."

So for three hundred years before the Emperor Justinian declared it "anathema", **early Christianity embraced reincarnation.**

The knowledge of reincarnation was thus withheld from people. The truth about it would have given deeper meaning and greater significance to their lives on Earth and in the beyond – as it would today! We should therefore *expand, yet again,* our horizons to encompass the recognition that only *repeated* earth-lives offer the human spirit the means whereby it is *able* to accumulate sufficient experiences "of the spirit" to gain *true* spiritual insight as to its Origin and purpose. Multi earth-lives provide the necessary parameters whereby human spirits are gifted the opportunity to develop genuine spiritual *maturity.*

The intervals between incarnations should be regarded as a very necessary time of learning also, as the life experienced in the "beyond" will be a direct result of the *kind of life* lived whilst on Earth under the outworking of The Laws of "Sowing and Reaping", "Attraction..." and "Spiritual Gravity". Each further Earth-life, also strictly governed by The Eternal Laws, will bring the soul to the correct circumstances of family and race that it will need for its further maturing, either for its own learning, to provide the same for others in its new environment, and/or to expiate past misdeeds here.

Whatever the reason for an incarnation, it can only be in accordance with the strictness of The Spiritual Laws, so he will be justly placed in terms of circumstances and the requirement to experience that *which he once sowed.* A purification of the whole person is a necessary part of the overall learning process, provided, of course, that the path taken for this purpose truly aspires to "genuine spirituality". Even if this were not voluntarily the case, however, the same Laws would work on regardless, still bringing to that particular individual the consequences of previous decisions at the appropriate time.

Now, because our inherent free-will endowment determines what will return to us under The Spiritual Laws, this "constant-return" process takes effect whether we are on the Earth or in the "Planes of the beyond".

Thus we continually stand in the "reciprocal-effect mechanism" of all our past decisions.

Not necessarily the return effect of all at once but, nevertheless, in whatever is lawfully ordained for that particular point in time. In this lawful and completely inviolable process, **there is no escape!**

The fact that we generally vacillate between making good and bad decisions means we can naturally expect a life of changing fortunes. Therefore, some will always be better off than others at any given moment. Others will be worse off, simply by virtue of the reciprocal effect of The Spiritual Laws. That is the reality for all. Since changing fortunes are a fact of life for most people, the concept of repeated Earth-lives not only provides clear solutions to the worrying problems and trends current on the Earth, but allows an insight into the Wisdom and Grace of The Creative Will in granting humankind the opportunity to "make good" all past mistakes. We must do so in any case, if we are not to suffer potentially hard fate continually.

With regard to the changing fortunes of the numerous philosophical ideas throughout history, Kierkegaard, in fine contrast to what we affirm, believed that we are "...all unique individuals who only live once". He also attacked the reliance on ritual and dogma in Christianity, and what he thought was essentially the *empty faithlessness* of the adherents. He strongly felt they had to do more than just *believe* 'Christianity' is true. In his view, having a Christian faith meant following "...a Christian way of life". Kierkegaard, who rejected the basic thrust of "Hegelianism", also thought that the individual is "...responsible for his own life".

It is therefore imperative to "recognise the need" to make good one's transgressions. Once we have left the *relative protection of the physical body* at earthly death, it is too late to then lament the fact that we were too disbelieving, too superficial, too blind and stubborn to accept any view different to that which we personally wanted to believe. Because, there, in the far more *mobile* environment of the non-material world, all movement – even the effect of ones thoughts

– are "speeded-up" considerably. So, too, are the waiting reciprocal effects for the individual. Life in the physical body in the more ponderous world of the Earth at least allowed a "stay of proceedings", so to speak. Unless one were completely insane – in which case one could *not* be held spiritually accountable for one's actions[5] – one would surely wish to be treated with respect and kindness by one's fellow men. The admonition to: "...do unto others" is surely the most perfect advice ever gifted to man to prevent "hard yet lawful returns".

It is precisely the time spent on Earth that is crucial for correct decision-making, particularly at this point in the evolutionary development of this material part of Creation to which we and the Earth physically belong.

Now, from our explanations of the Death Process we know that lighter spiritual thoughts and deeds produce a corresponding lightness of the soul. Darker, heavier thoughts and actions produce the opposite under The Law of Spiritual Gravity. We therefore know that through personal choices, "heavier" souls will sink to the level corresponding to their particular "spiritual weight", there to live out their propensities alongside like-minded souls.

It is especially important to therefore understand that such levels *still remain* in the **Material Spheres**, even though *not actually* on **Earth**. All souls inhabiting these particular levels are therefore necessarily subject to whatever *finite* fate may befall them here. That is not the case with souls who gravitate to Higher, lighter, Planes, however. There, the more spiritually-enlightened thus more fortunate souls are not oppressed as are those in the darker regions; they who have surrendered their free-will choices to baser propensities. Unlike those ones, the souls who have earned the right to ascend to Higher levels are more easily able to *continually further ascend* to Realms of Light which are *above the pull of the Material World and its finite time*. Becoming sufficiently enlightened whilst on Earth so as to live correspondingly similar thoughts and deeds, guarantees an ascent into lighter Planes after earthly death.

The horizons of the inhabitants there are vastly more expansive than those who languish in the much more restrictive environment of the lower, darker planes. Partaking of the great joy and happiness that exists in the lighter Realms further imparts the natural wish to want more of the same, thus allowing still *further* ascent. The souls who have chosen the experience of the lower levels, set in place by their personal wish for the exact same things whilst on Earth, enjoy no such peace. Theirs is literally the torment of being preyed upon by others in the same way they once did. Yet, as formerly stated, The Law governing Grace gives even those sad ones the choice to leave their surroundings behind.

As a precursor to providing definitive explanations about the "second death", it is timely to examine more closely the "awakening" in the beyond of a previously *disbelieving soul* just released from his physical body. With such a soul, however, let us first re-visit the process and consider, once more, some of the things he may experience in the moments before burial when "friends" and relatives arrive to pay their "respects".

This usually difficult time invariably produces the whole range of emotional reactions in the psyche of the bystanders to the event. At such times, human emotions run the full gamut; from deep and genuine grief, to curiosity, to superficiality, sometimes to anger and sometimes to gladness at the death. However, what is generally not accepted is that the "departed" one *can still see and hear all that takes place around his "discarded shell"*. So one can easily imagine his reaction to eulogies and speeches in his memory or honour etc., particularly when those whom he believed he knew well whilst on Earth now perhaps reveal a different side to their character.

In some cases, he could well re-evaluate the relationship of those kinds of people. Sadly, it would be difficult to express gratitude to those who might now reveal genuine respect and

---

[5]Other karmaic events lead naturally and spiritually-logically to this condition; which we will not delve into at this stage.

friendship towards him, those whom he did not realise held him in high regard when he was alive. To all intents and purposes, however, his visitors – both the genuine and the superficial – believe him to be dead, and he has no way of proving to them that he still "lives".[6]

Because of the lawful outworking of The Spiritual Laws in this all-too-common situation, it should not be difficult to picture the anguish of the departed one as he follows the whole procedure of his own funeral even. Yet he is unable to offer clarification about his situation to those most affected. Thus we can relate to him as he attends the burial of his earthly shell, and empathise with him at the moment of greatest grief; when the casket is lowered! One can picture him in a state of great despondency and desolation at this time. After a while, tiredness would overtake him and he might find some solace in sleep.[7]

When this soul finally severs itself from its tie to its former physical body, (via the disintegration of the "Silver Cord" [described in the previous Chapter from the testimony of Franchezzo]), it will invariably find itself in a Plane closely corresponding to its previous state of "attitudinal-volition" during earthly life. If this had been one of disbelief or disinterest in "life after death" then, when he awakens, he will be surrounded by darkness. He will discover, however, that he is no longer connected to his physical shell. He is free, but in a strange and silent, oppressive darkness where he cannot even hear the sound of his own voice. And no matter what he may wish to believe about his situation, still the darkness presses in on him.

In its new and unfortunate surroundings, the soul *lives* as it did on Earth. For this is the *real* person except that he is, now, freed from his physical body. He experiences all the travails and joys in his soul-body in the same way that he experienced life in his physical one. He weeps, laughs, tires and sleeps. For his new world is just as real as the physical one recently left behind, purely because his new body is of the **exact same consistency as his surroundings**. Whilst his new body is not a physical one, it is not his spirit-body either for he is still very, very far from the genuine Spiritual Realm from where he originated. His spirit – **the real he** – is still the **inner animating core** of his **new** body. This "new body", however, is subject to the much faster vibration of the non-physical world of the "beyond" – his world at this time.

The effect of his "faster environment" will seed a strong urge to find out *why* than might have been the case on Earth, and he may seek answers *more desperately*. We can readily understand that the restless need to seek is borne of a desperation to find an explanation for his rather sad circumstances. But how to know exactly *what* to seek? He only knows that he **needs** answers to his plight. Yet to find an answer may take such a soul years, even decades or far longer, for time has a vastly different meaning outside the physical realm. Until such time as genuine yearning to be free wells up in the soul of one in this position, however, all he can look forward to is the continuing condition of dark uncertainty. So we can be sure that much inner searching would take place as he struggles to understand what had brought about his sorry plight. Hopefully his seeking will bring about the realisation that this, after all, must be the "other world" he refused to believe in!

Such an inner awakening for this soul must surely presuppose, at the very least, the *dawning* of the recognition of obviously still being alive, yet clearly **physically** dead. Even that realisation, however, may not be *sufficiently strong* to bring about a *change* in his surroundings. The simple wish for change must further develop into a *deep longing* from which springs a genuine

---

[6]The reader will recall the "Silver Cord" being a mediating connection to the earthly organs of sight and speech through still being attached to the physical shell. It is the special nature of the "cord" that makes it possible for the departed one to see and hear all that takes place around him. Despite this connection still permitting him sight- and sound-access to his recent world, he is nevertheless unable to make *himself* heard or felt by those still alive *because he no longer stands in a body of the same consistency as the material world* and therefore cannot "touch" anything of the Earth, including his loved ones.

[7]The reader may find this curious, but in the same way that the *physical* body tires through exertion, so will the soul-body.

petition for help, even if only a timid prayer at first. For such a longing is suffused with "the purer intuition born of desperate need".

Finally, with the entry of humility and submission into his soul through deep and genuine prayers for help, the outworking of Grace upon him and his surroundings takes effect because, now, a connection is established – albeit tenuous initially – with the Higher and lighter Spiritual Spheres of Love and Grace. Consequently for this soul, the darkness would then give way to a kind of twilight. He would experience a corresponding *lightness* in his *body* accompanied by feelings of soothing comfort. Now he can take stock of his surroundings and is better able to determine his next move.

The "lightening" of his surroundings also at last allows him a glimpse of a Light in the far distance. That far-away Light becomes a beacon of hope and a means of understanding his new world. It is the only point of welcoming focus. The Light comes no nearer to him but he intuitively knows that he must journey towards it, for he recognises that it will lead him out of his "twilight zone". Thus, gratitude and humility would begin to suffuse this soul as it senses more strongly the gift of Grace granted to it.

Humility, as an attribute and quality of the greatest power – Love – is a most necessary trait to develop if one seeks Spiritual ascent. To practise opposite traits such as arrogance and cynicism with regard to Spiritual Truth will ensure similar kinds of experiences for such believers as those outlined here. Whilst our example is basically that of the initial experiences of one soul in the Ethereal World of the "beyond", they could not be said to be those of a "bad" person, just one who had given no thought to his fate after earthly death. One who did not want to be "bothered with it".

In summary, anyone who in his Earth life refuses to acknowledge that there is "life after death", or that there is a concomitant requirement to one day render account for all that he has done and all that he has left *undone*, is blind and deaf when he finally passes over into the Ethereal World of the "beyond". Only for the time that he remains connected with his discarded physical body through the "Silver Cord" can he still partially observe events around him.

Once he is freed from his disintegrating physical body, this possibility is lost to him and he no longer sees or hears anything. Yet that should not be viewed as punishment. On the contrary, it should be recognised *as a perfectly natural consequence of his own attitude toward "life after death" whilst he lived.* Because he refused to "believe" – which is tantamount to "blindness" and "deafness" – he thus **forms for himself** his future ethereal environment which he must fully experience if, in the meantime, there is no change from his "disbelieving position" before his death arrives. After that transition, only a **voluntary change** in his soul will allow him to see and hear again.

The necessary condition for such a change after earthly death is the *desire of the individual himself* to **want** to change his circumstances. The time frame for this also solely depends upon him. It may take years or decades, perhaps far longer, but is the concern of the individual alone. The exercise of his personal free will brought him there in the first place, and can also release him from it – **if he** so desires. It cannot be forced upon him. The Light that the soul was finally permitted to see as a result of his inner change was *always there*. It was his *spiritual condition* that **prevented** him from seeing it. The **condition** of the soul thus determines **how** he sees it – whether strong or weak, or not at all!

The example we have outlined shows a soul experiencing the outworking of The Law of Reciprocal Action ['Sowing and Reaping'; 'Iron Law of Karma'] in stark relief. It received what it had wished, thus what it brought to itself in accordance with that wish, simply because it had refused to believe in the reality of "life after death".

What should be clearly and fully understood is: *The soul <u>cannot</u>, by any means,*

abolish the continuation of life for itself at "the First Death".[8]
The reason is perfectly simple, yet nonetheless final: _It [the soul] has absolutely_ <u>_no_</u> _jurisdiction over the lawful processes whatsoever!_

Disbelief of this fact cannot alter that lawful outcome by one single dot! This crucial knowledge should be regarded as the _key consideration_ as to how one should resolve to live one's life, for "death and life-after" <u>_is_</u> _the immutable reality_. Therefore, we should not introduce into our lives as _a way of life_ the aspiritual traits of cynicism, arrogance, ignorance or fear. In its stead, and from _true_ knowledge, accept the realisation that we simply cannot alter The Spiritual Laws to suit our personal wishes. A human soul, purely via his inherent free-will ability, can bring himself to either a dark region or a Light region in the Ethereal World.

Even if finding himself in the former, all that is required for him to ascend out of such a place is to generate a spiritually-pure volition of genuine humility in the recognition that he and _he alone_ was _responsible_ for the circumstances of his condition. With this first and most necessary step, he can begin the process of ascending out of the lower, denser, spheres of the 'beyond' to the Higher, lighter Planes far from the inexorable and ordained path of the Earth and its inter-stellar environs as _**they** track towards **their time** of disintegration and renewal_.

Now, if this is the position in which a relatively "decent" individual in the earthly sense would find himself after earthly death, how much more dire would the situation be for those whose earthly lives are given over totally to baseness? We would conclude that in their regions of darkness, there would probably not be any light to speak of! Now we may begin to understand why Jesus was so severe in His admonishing of those who were not prepared to change their ways, for He surely understood all of The Law in its strict and inviolable Justice.

The explanations offered here allow us to easily picture the fate of some past races, and perhaps even some present ones too. Members of races who live according to cultural traditions and beliefs that do not encompass any elements of Spiritual Law **_as it actually is_** may well descend to lower regions of darkness after earthly death, there to live out the reciprocal effects of their self-willed and self-chosen path.

So if even a relatively half-decent life brings about a sad and less than joyful outcome, it should remind each individual to carefully consider his attitude toward this inevitable event called death. Just as importantly for parents and society in general, _**the necessary schooling and explanations about it should be provided for the young**_, to thereby help to beneficially change the very nature of society itself. Via this recognition and educative method, we may perhaps even lessen the unacceptably high rate of youth suicide – _**suicide being a serious spiritual transgression**_.

Unfortunately, such souls as described in our example probably make up many, many millions on the Earth today. They have no wish to learn about God, spiritual things, or eternity, yet may be good and decent people. However, _**since**_ <u>_**The Law**_</u> _**has the final say in all matters human**_, the end-fate of those who are simply evil-minded speaks for itself. Far too many people are reluctant to even acknowledge that it just might be in their interest to think about their own time of exit from the Earth.

By contrast, what might be the experience of a person who _does_ believe in life _after_ death and thus recognises the need to live correctly _whilst_ on Earth? What might he experience upon awakening in the "beyond"? At the beginning of the previous Chapter we noted the plea of Franchezzo for humankind to awaken to the truth of life after death. And we further described the basic experiences of a soul who did _not_ believe. Here is an opposite account.

---

[8]The term, "First Death", in our explanations, does not mean just _one_ single death only in one's total existence. The term refers to the process of earthly death for _**each**_ incarnation; as opposed to the _**one single reality**_ of the "Second Death" for the very many who will experience it at some future point.

H. Dennis Bradley, an English poet who died in 1934, had promised to communicate after his death, if this were at all possible. Shortly afterwards he apparently did succeed. Through a medium he gave a good description of his experiences. What is interesting is the great difference between the kind of environment he experienced, and that of our previous example; of one who did not believe.

Bradley's narration follows:

> "The landscape in which we live is a great deal different from that of the earth. It is of a blessed purity and clearness. There is a tremendous amount of light, and nothing is grey or even dark.
> There is soil here too, as well as an ocean, trees and flowers, but everything is more beautiful and more wonderful than on earth.
> Even the plumage of the birds is more radiant and more colourful. But strangest of all are the flowers. They not only exude fragrance, but also emit delightful sounds which the physical ear cannot hear, and which are different for each kind of flower.
> There is no weariness here and no need for rest, instead one feels oneself overflowing with a wonderful strength. Time is of no importance. One is always busy; for there is a million times as much to learned as on earth.
> There are millions and millions of departed souls to be found here. The spirits can communicate with one another, even though they spoke different languages during their earthly lives.
> The ability to move from one place to another is also wonderful. It is not the same as on earth, for there are no physical bodies here. Even though I do have a form that could be compared with a body, it does not bind me.
> Here it is enough simply to wish to be somewhere, and immediately you are there. In the future it will probably again be possible for human beings still on earth and souls in the beyond to communicate. But for this it is necessary for the human being in simple trust to open the gates of knowledge which he has closed to himself by his lack of belief."

A few key points about Spiritual Law and Bible Scripture can be clarified from Bradley's description of his experiences in the level of the beyond he had *earned the right* to be in.

1. Note Bradley's description of the landscape in which he found himself; with the same physical features, in plants and fauna, as on earth. Just as we explained in the Chapter on our Origins. Naturally more perfect, however.

2. The soul of *our* example earlier in this Chapter, in being heavily burdened with non-understanding of the why of his plight, needed to rest. Bradley, and those of like spirit, animated by the purer surroundings of their higher, lighter realm, were filled with energising strength.

3. Note, also, the reference to "so much more to be learned there than on earth". In this statement lies the meaning of the Scripture: "And a thousand years are as one day." In other words, what would take a person a thousand years *to learn* in the heavy, ponderous physical realm of the Earth, would only need one day of **spiritual experiencing** in the higher Realms of Light.

4. Even though not possessing a physical body, the soul, with the spirit as its core, retains the bodily form as an envelope for the spirit. This "body form" is only shed if and/or when the entity ascends to the point of its Origin – The Spiritual Realm.

5. Bradley's recognition of man's paucity of spirit in closing himself to the knowledge he requires for the greater overview of the why of his very existence emphasises the crucial need for vital knowledge of the beyond. And thus how he [man] is *lawfully and irrevocably* connected to it.

6. The spirits "communicated with each other" even though they spoke "different languages while on earth". In that statement may be seen the key spiritual aspect of *the scattering of the languages* at the Biblical narrative of the building of The Tower of Babel – explained in Chapter on **"Language"** where we clarify exactly that point. It was not the different languages that proved the difficulty in communicating, one race with another, but the aspiritual forms that men had produced after "falling away", thereby severing the spiritual connection with their [our] origins. Thus, in the lighter, more "spiritually-alive" level of the "beyond" that H. Dennis Bradley had earned the right to be in after his earthly death, the *like-minded souls* there – remembering that The Law decrees that only here on Earth can good and evil live "side by side" – could *communicate easily.*

As a revealing-assessment of this *paucity of spirit* that strongly pervades the world today, perhaps we should collectively consider what has developed in the State education systems of some Western societies particularly. Over many years, that has taken the form of insidiously stripping away from schools the once regular practice of Biblical or religious instruction and prayer. Once there was at least a *basic* societal recognition of a Creator and inviolable Laws accepted by far more people than might accept such a view today. Instead, *officially*, we *solely* teach "knowledge of the genome", with which human science can play and spend millions of research dollars; all the while foolishly believing that **inanimate**, thus non-living, matter can somehow **will itself** to **animate itself**.

There is no single, magic *switch-on gene* that gives **life** to **physical** matter. We repeat: The genes in the many and varied physical life-forms on earth; at the **death** of those forms, **rot with them.** So where is the so-called *life-force* there?

In the present, religious or spiritual instruction "across the board" is generally deemed to be unimportant, even irrelevant – perhaps even a trampling on "human rights".

Stripped of its emotive or political implications, that is such a foolish and quite stupid term; as if any human being could produce the perfection of the universes and the earthly home we are permitted to live in. In the 21st century, all we still produce lots of is blood, war, terrorism, ethnic cleansing, human trafficking and exploitation, environmental degradation... Should one go on? Too many forces within our present societal infrastructure deem "religion" unnecessary for society's continuing function in these more supposedly *enlightened times of economic roulette on corporate earth...*

The blatant and dangerous **hypocrisy** of this "modern educational practice" is glaringly revealed as a false sham when these same societies are hit with disaster and tragedy.

Then we see the desperate prayers to GOD!

Even those who impose the new educational thinking upon society – the politicians and their servants – even they must bow to a clear truth and its concomitant recognition experienced by probably most soldiers placed in harm's way:

When the chips are down, everyone calls out for "THE MAN"!

Ferrar Fenton, from whose Bible we mainly quote, states in his Explanatory Note that one Professor Karl Behr of Munich insightfully argued for the retention of religion within the state or society if it was to survive. Fenton notes that on the Philosophy of History, Professor Behr observed:

"That the best-established doctrine of Historical Philosophy was, that all the power, prosperity, and mental energy of a Race or Nation sprang from and lived by its Religion; that *when its Religion ceased to be its Faith* – that is, its energising principle – *the intellect, power, vigour, and prosperity of that Race or Nation died away in proportion, and ultimately perished, both mentally and physically.*" [Emphasis mine.]

And Fenton further observes:

"...how he illustrated his doctrine by a wide survey and a series of illustrations from the history of all nations, Asiatic, African, and European, both Ancient and Modern, dwelling especially upon the fact that this Law of National Life did not depend upon any particular Religion, but was manifested by them all, Pagan, Jewish, Mohammedan, and Christian"?

(*The Holy Bible in Modern English.*
Explanatory Note, p.xi)

Fenton goes on to say that Professor Behr's doctrine "...did not urge a regard to that Law of History for any ecclesiastical purpose..." for he was not a professed member of any particular Christian Church. Professor Behr therefore emphasised it by a review of the Arabian Civilisation under the Kaliphat. What Professor Behr refers to as a "Law of National Life" is, of course, a Spiritual Law. His revealing insight offers clear reason for an acceptance and adjustment to The Laws for the betterment and, indeed, survival of our societies and Nations!

Therefore, teach religion as a step of faith to begin with, but teach "The One Law" for true knowledge and conviction for all!

10.2   Earthbound Souls

One issue that requires examination before finally exploring the actual meaning/process of the "second death" is that of how and why souls can become 'earthbound'. The term 'earthbound' is one with which many are possibly familiar but are perhaps not completely sure of the processes that determine the "binding". Even though much has been written about such situations there is little real knowledge as to why! The many recorded cases of hauntings, of poltergeist activity etc., even though true enough, do not give the full picture at all.

Poltergeist "energy", which anecdotal evidence claims produces "noisy" and perhaps frightening phenomena, will actually concern only a very small number of souls. The vast majority of the 'earthbound' continue their particular activities without earthly humankind being aware they are about. At various times the close presence of one may be "sensed", and people with clairvoyant or psychic ability can see them on occasions. With all processes and activities in Creation, however, the reason for the close presence of one will be subject to strict Spiritual Law, and will invariably be associated with land, a place or dwelling, or to a person or persons in that particular place. Or perhaps with an *activity* there to which the 'earthbound' one is drawn. There may be other ties but those outlined here will invariably hold the reason why.

In the first place, there should not be cause for fear if a poor 'earthbound' soul is recognised as being about, because the binding of one to the Earth is also a perfectly natural process. Many presently alive now may well find themselves tied to the Earth after their time of death too. Whilst we know that this should *not* be the normal process, nevertheless it is brought about once again by man's refusal to live correctly, i.e. according to Spiritual Law. The knowledge of that Law would help him to leave behind all pointless and unnecessary ties to the Earth. A few brief examples as to how such a sorry state can come about should offer some clarification of the process.

Let us examine the case, unfortunately quite common, where a questioning child is continually told by his parents that there is no such thing as "life after death". In the beginning the child may intuitively sense that there *is* life after death, or may have heard about it from school or in Church. Uncertain, he seeks confirmation of it from his parents, let us say his father. The father, perhaps through lack of interest in the matter, or even his own fear about it, dismisses the whole idea and *forcefully* imparts his view to the child. With continual reinforcement of this very incorrect belief, the child begins to doubt, until finally accepting the opinion of adults that there is no life after death.

However, the time comes when the father dies and, much to **his** horror and dismay, finds that death is not the end after all. The deep wish now arises within the father to impart the truth of this to his child, and this strong desire binds him to it. The child, unfortunately, can neither hear him nor sense his presence, for it now has the firm conviction that its father *has ceased to exist*. This conviction acts as *a completely natural and impenetrable wall between the child and the father's efforts.* Now the father must live the painful reality that, through misleading his child, there is the very real danger that he may take a path leading him further and further from the truth. Moreover, as the child grows into adulthood and gathers future generations around him, the same misleading error is passed on through them with the added danger of his child, *through **its** increasingly narrowing perceptions*, falling further.

Perhaps this is one meaning of the "sins of the father" visiting themselves upon successive generations. In any case, this forms the father's so-called "punishment" for misleading his child. In such circumstances, it would be extremely difficult for him to communicate to his offspring the knowledge that life continues on. Consequently, he will be forced to witness how his previous wrong idea is carried on down through the generations, and all as a result of his own disbelief. Unfortunately for him, he cannot be released until one of his descendants finally *recognises* the error and adjusts his life accordingly. Only then will the father be gradually released. And only *then* can he consider his own need for ascent.

A very typical and more insidious way in how one can be 'earthbound' is through the connection to cigarette smoking. It is a situation which impacts hugely and detrimentally on human health in two ways. Physically in the first instance, and spiritually in the second. An habitual smoker who dies takes over with him the strong craving to smoke. In its strength, it is actually a *propensity* which thus has a *connection to the "spiritual intuition"*, albeit only at its outermost edge. His propensity produces the need for gratification and he therefore seeks out smokers. There he is able to satisfy his craving because the changed nature of his "body" after earthly death enables him to enjoy **the inner sensations of smokers** to whom he is held.

If there is no stronger reciprocal effect waiting to bind him to any other place, the sensations he feels are, for him, generally pleasant ones. So such souls may not be aware that being tied to others on Earth through their propensity is actually a *self-imposed* punishment. This is also the case with drinking, so-called harmless recreational drug use and *aberrant* sexual desires. Given the heavy emphasis today on one's "right" to sexual gratification by any and all means, many might not consider this last a punishment at all. Yet any binding to the Earth prevents such souls from recognising that their "primary craving", which overshadows all else, is actually a punishment **stemming solely from their own aspiritual personal decisions and subsequent lifestyle whilst alive on Earth.** Consequently, the longing for something better, more noble and higher, cannot easily develop to become the main focus which would then free them from such base desires and uplift them.

Yet even if this main desire should reach a point where it begins to die away, other lesser desires – which a soul may still carry within – may then rise to take the place of the formerly-strongest propensity. The lawful requirement to "live it through" subsequently transports him to a place where the *lesser* desires can also be expiated. Eventually, with sufficient good will for his own ascent, he will finally succeed in clearing all the dross that had previously prevented any chance of release from his bind to the Earth. For only when the earthly sensations are gradually outlived or let go, associated with a longing for what is higher, purer and therefore more spiritual, can he steadily ascend. The variations here will be many but these few examples illustrate the *kinds* of circumstances that *can* allow a soul to become 'earthbound'.

The act of suicide can also produce very strong ties to the Earth for a soul that decides to exit Earth life by this means. With suicide, however, certain aspects in that individual's life will generally hold powerful sway prior to the deed. A stronger than usual emotional component, invariably seen as insurmountable, will help drive the thought toward suicide, so is often a powerful precursor to the final act. In concert with any problem that *appears* to have no solution, the inner strength of the one so assailed will ebb to a degree commensurate with the perceived degree of hopelessness of the particular situation faced.

However, notwithstanding the reason for such a desperate "solution", the very act of ending one's own life *prematurely* means that *that* soul has *rejected* the gift of life. A life, moreover, that *it* had petitioned for. Exiting before the fulfilment or completion of its life's purpose ensures that the soul is held to the particular level of "maturity" or experiencing attained up to that point in time. It therefore *'passes over' in an immature state*. Because of the very strong psychic/emotional "feelings" generated within and around a suicide, the site of the incident may become the strongest point of focus for it after death, and may thus bind the soul to that place for some time.

Since the outworking of The Laws demand spiritual fulfilment in *all* things, right down to the *smallest* ramification, this soul must then again incarnate on Earth to "catch up" with and then complete all that it did not attain to or fulfil previously. Because it personally chose to commit suicide as perhaps a seemingly-apparent **easy way out**, it will carry with it into its next life **the same unresolved aspect**. Only through recognising The Laws of Life and adjusting its thinking and activity to them, might it then *expiate* the previous unlawful deed to begin again its path of natural ascent. Its choice solely, however.

In the "strange but true" category, *sudden* and quite *unexpected* deaths, such as might occur in a random shooting, in war, terrorist bombings, an aircraft explosion etc., can happen so quickly that those killed *do not realise they are actually dead*. In a "normal" death situation, connection to its former cloak, i.e., the physical body, should provide a reference point for at least some level of understanding for the one recently departed. However, the complete disintegration or vaporisation of the body in an instant – not at all uncommon in increasing incidents of extreme violence today – may preclude that possibility. In such cases, the person affected is literally forcibly wrenched or ejected from the mortal shell in a split second, and thus stands alone and stripped of its now *virtually non-existent* earthly body.

10.2.1   The Earthbound Soldier

After the Second World War it was revealed that during The Battle of Britain, where *many young* Allied pilots were killed in air combat against the German Luftwaffe, a very senior RAF Commander from time to time worked with a medium to try to contact his dead pilots to help them leave the Earth. Anecdotal reports at the time strongly indicated that a number were "haunting" the Air Bases from which they had formerly operated. More especially in exploding fighters – but also in bombers – death came very suddenly and very quickly to very young men of incredible courage and daring, to "boys" who readily understood that their *life expectancy* in total air combat might only be a matter of minutes.

So for very young pilots now a world away from childhood, teenage years and families, the Air Base became their new "home". The Air Base was the place from which the battle was fought, but it was also a place of rest and *relative safety* between missions as well. It was the one "tangible anchorage" in a time of desperate uncertainty, where strong physical and emotional attachments of deep camaraderie and mutual respect would inevitably develop between skilled pilots and brave men. Men who understood they were engaged in a life and death struggle with an enemy bent on the destruction or enslavement of their homeland. Deriving from sheer psychological necessity to mask the seriousness of the struggle, the dire situation of the time drove pilots to adopt an almost cavalier approach to their task. For given the very high attrition rate, it was imperative to yet believe that one might nevertheless survive to the end.

Powerful *spiritual* forces bond servicemen in this kind of desperate yet noble struggle and sacrifice to the *utmost* degree. Even though rarely voiced by the men involved, that bond is actually **Love**! The Air Base and all that it contained thus represented the entirety of their life at the time, both in the machinery of war and in the intangible essence of enduring comradeship forged through necessary sacrifice for a just cause. Very significantly in this particular situation, however, it was the ***last earthly anchor point*** they would know before death overtook some of them. Therefore, to ***their*** "Base", ***their*** home and ***their*** fellow pilots, did some ***return*** after their personal sacrifice.

It thus follows that major battlefields will have more than their share of earthbound souls, as may any place of mass murder such as the German concentration camps of The Second World War.

Natural and man-made disasters, where large loss of life occurs, can also congregate their complement of souls. For all so earthbound, however, the onus is on each individual to determine *why* he is so bound, to work through that question, and the time necessary to become free. Correct recognition will then set him free to leave the Earth, as *should have been* the normal process to begin with.

It may sound incongruous to believe that one cannot know that one has died, yet that is the reality that some will inevitably experience.[9] Relatives or friends who possess some measure of *understanding* about the truth of "life after" should therefore consider helping their very recently departed to at least a similar measure of "knowing". And thus help them more easily transit the passage from the near-earth environs to their next ordained level of existence after the Silver Cord is severed. As formerly stated, the time to so explain it is in the days immediately after 'death'.

10.3   Hypnotism – a Spiritual Crime

The effect of this particular practice has resonance to the previous Sub-Chapter – "Earthbound Souls" – so is also important to visit at this point. Whilst its practitioners *can* be tied to souls on Earth, the more insidious effect of it is to become tied to lower levels of the "beyond" after earthly death. Hypnotism is a practice that certain branches of medicine – psychological, psychiatric and general etc., – use on a reasonably regular basis. Its use is ostensibly touted as being of great benefit for patients in certain categories of medicine. It is also regarded as an important crime-fighting tool by some law enforcement agencies in certain types of investigations.

A seemingly innocuous practice that *appears* to be of benefit to mankind in certain situations is, in truth, ***an extremely serious spiritual transgression*** – *for the hypnotist, particularly,* ***but for the one hypnotised too***. The spiritually-astute reader should recognise *why* this would be so. The *effects* of the *application* of hypnotism are so far-reaching that, *if fully recognised,* practitioners *in every current field of practice* would, in horror, ***immediately and voluntarily cease all such activities***. Why?

---

[9]In this regard, some films like "The Sixth Sense" *can* depict a certain measure of truth.

Because hypnotism *binds* the *personal and free will aspect* of the *human* subject to the *control* of the *hypnotist*!

And therein lies the *seriousness* of the transgression. It lies in the *binding* of the *spirit* of another human being. In other words, the one hypnotised is open to receiving whatever spiritually-adverse currents or forces that may wish to attach themselves thereto at that moment. That is because the **now open** subject is ***spiritually-unprotected***. It therefore cannot possibly resist, *and thus protect itself against, negative or even very detrimental and dangerous psychic forces which can easily approach the now-vulnerable individual.*

We should always be acutely aware of the following Biblical warning – which should not be foolishly or ignorantly dismissed as just simplistic religiosity:

> *"Because our fight is **not** against blood and flesh; but against the sovereignties, against the powers, against the commanders of the darkness of this world..."*

> (Ephesians 6:12, Fenton.
> Emphases mine.)

Even if used to relieve chronic pain, to help stop smoking or heal a bodily disease, any apparent subsequent improvement *resulting from* the "treatment" should be regarded as temporary alleviation. Since it has been the *spirit* that has been *bound*, and irrespective of the "condition" for which hypnotism might have been sought, what will be achieved will be more a "suppressive effect", but not *real control* of the problem or condition. Intervention by hypnotism is not any kind of ultimately beneficial panacea, for only with a free and *unhindered volition* can a human being take *full* control over its life-problems and destiny; a destiny or fate resulting primarily from its own decisions in any case.

Whilst the effects of being hypnotised are not at all helpful for the one hypnotised, the end result for the hypnotist is far more dire. Because he is the one who has *bound* the *spirit* of the other – and irrespective of the reason why – he is, *from that point on*, tied or *bound* to that other person. Forcibly binding the spirit of another through hypnotism *simultaneously binds* the hypnotist *to* his subject. And because *he* retarded the free development of that person, *he* cannot be released until *he* has helped him to advance as far as he would have done were it not for *his* intervention in the binding of that spirit.

The ultimate horror for all hypnotists after earthly death must surely be the realisation that they are inextricably-tied to *all* whom they once bound through hypnosis. For even after both have left the Earth the hypnotist must, by Law, also go where the spirits *he once bound* automatically go. Even to the lowest Realms of Darkness if need be, for *each* connecting tie to *all* whom **he** hypnotised must be redeemed, *one human link after the other*, but, however, from the lowest and darkest levels first. The hypnotist cannot ascend until the very last of his subjects has begun *their* ascent. Should any yet remain in the lower Realms; **he, too, will stay**!

In the light of this knowledge, consider how hypnotism is used in a comedic way in vaudeville and stage shows. Ostensibly all very hilarious, but ultimately foolish and dangerous in the extreme. As we state quite often, any transgression of The Spiritual Laws will always return the reciprocal effect. Not in accordance with human opinions, of course, but most certainly according to the full strength and Perfect Justice of: **Creation-Law!**

For what humanity <u>sows</u>, humanity <u>must reap</u>!

10.4   The Danger of Leading Astray

A similar fate awaits those who, in seeking followers through religious or "spiritual" activities, distort the Truth to such a degree that the followers are completely led astray i.e., *away from the direction leading to the possibility of spiritual ascent*. Good intentions hold no mandate here. Neither does it matter if the "leader" is trained in a Theological College, or holds an official position in a mainstream Church, promotes New-Age philosophy, or sets up a personalised, charismatic-type Church.

We should also include in this group "six-day creationists" with their strongly-promoted fundamentalism, and "geneticists" in the scientific field who similarly strongly promote their view that genes are the *singular* mechanism that produce and control *all* life. Even though perhaps sharing certain tenuous connections, both notions nevertheless together lead their supporters astray.

Religion and science, therefore, the two "strange bedfellows" that nonetheless **primarily** drive educational, cultural and social "imperatives" in Western societies, particularly, have the utmost responsibility to guide and lead *correctly*. Though encompassing a very broad-sweep umbrella, each camp will invariably produce only a relatively few "leaders" within who will set the basic agenda and overall direction for their respective "mass of believers". And despite the fact that there have been many dissenting voices within both Christian religion and science, the conjoined educational curriculum for Western Nations nevertheless steadfastly encompasses a more-or-less standard paradigm set by Universities and Theological Colleges. Upon the "agenda-setting individuals" or "boards" within the numerous "hallowed halls of learning" thus rests the greatest responsibility.

Writers, especially of so-called religious or scientific "truth", need to be absolutely aware of the inviolable outworking of The Law in this regard, for their writings can live on and continue to sway readers long after the authors have left the Earth. It was not without high purpose that one of the great Teachings specifically warned against the written word being used for wrong purposes; for those very words would stand with the author/s at the time of his/their Judgement. The incredible proliferation of so many books literally "churned out" in the millions stands as clear testimony to the use of the gift of language for, oftentimes, spurious purposes.

Of course, it remains the personal, free-will choice of any individual whether or not to accept a particular teaching, or follow a particular "leader". Notwithstanding that inherent truth, the historical record contains very many instances of so-called "religious leaders" who *actively* seek adherents. Not, however, to fulfil some kind of altruistic or spiritually-ennobled purpose, but to gain personal power, and/or political or financial advantage. Self-promoting egotism seems to be a common trait here. Therefore, even if, in the meantime, such "leaders" had come to the shattering recognition that they were wrong, those so 'pressured' by them must *similarly* recognise that error.

Two single books and one series of books, in particular hold literally millions – perhaps hundreds of millions – dangerously-captive in the spiritual sense. "The Holy Blood and the Holy Grail" and "The Da Vinci Code" are two books that lead readers away from The Truth about Jesus's association with the *true* Holy Grail! The reader should recall the explanations about that actual connection and what The Holy Grail really is, in the Chapter about His Life and Birth etc..

The line of books that, at this time, have probably led *more* Christians astray than any other is what is known as the "Left Behind" series; ten or so books that promote an ostensible end-time event called "the rapture". It is supposedly a phenomenon whereby all "truly believing" Christians will be suddenly "uplifted into the heavens" – whatever that means for believers.[10]

---

[10]Since that series is supposedly about the return of Jesus and the 'rapturing' of hundreds of millions

In summary, those who promote, teach and/or otherwise foment such shockingly-incorrect ideas about the how and why of Creation and human existence and thus lead people astray – i.e., away from Spiritual Truth – will discover to their horror upon their own death that they were *completely wrong*. For the many millions led astray, however; they, too, must accept *personal responsibility* for simply being *mindless* followers or believers. Recognition of how *wrong* were the 'teachings/doctrine' of the 'leader/s' **they** once believed in guarantees at least the *beginning* of **their** spiritual ascent *before that* of the particular leaders or teachers they formerly 'blindly-followed'.

For there, on the "other side" away from the *safer* environment of the Earth, the once "sure leaders" must wait until the very last *they* had led astray comes to recognition of their wrong decision and thus wrong path. Only then can they, the "leaders", begin their own ascent. In just the Christian Church alone – and deriving from the legacy of the murder of that so-called "trouble-maker", Jesus – how many well-meaning "church-servants" over centuries have preached sermons that badly distorted His Pure Teachings thus leading literally millions astray over that time? How many still do so today? For **everyone** on Earth, the warning out of The Living Law to be very sure of one's chosen path is simple, yet stark.

Narrow is the path, and <u>few</u> there are that find it!

10.5   The "Second Death" Process

First, the "cleansing process" of Earth and global humanity.

In the Chapter, "Elemental Lore", we described the "Elemental connection" between humankind's free-will attribute and the decisions that have accrued over millennia, and thus the resultant effect on our societies and the Earth itself. Brought about solely through our foolish refusal to heed The Spiritual Laws of Creation in the belief that we knew it better – that man could decide "the rules" with impunity – the impending destruction of man's mostly aspiritual works will carry along with it all who contributed to the whole insidious process; who thereby *accelerated* humankind's downward path.

Since it **is** the major part of global humanity who have chosen **not** to abide by the true Laws of Life, the "future reeling Earth" will provide the necessary power to effect, in the severest fulfilment, the degree of destruction required to remove the many at the "appointed hour". The curiously-termed "tribulation" for global humanity will therefore necessarily be the most destructive ever experienced in our long and bloody history. Global demographics, in terms of the very large numbers of the young, will play its decisive part in the emotional turmoil and anguish of families and societies at that inescapably-terrible time.

Despite the unfortunate "doomsday reality" of this impending Judgement, we should be under no illusion that **it is of our making**! So now, at this time in the spiritual and evolutionary development of mankind, our collective "karma" over millennia – which for the most part consists of dark, debased and degraded activities – is being returned to humankind with increasing strength and frequency under the lawful outworking of interlinked and inviolable Spiritual Laws.

It is the unenviable task of the "Elemental Beings", through the generation of increasingly severe effects of the world's weather patterns and catastrophic natural disasters, primarily, that "returns" a large part of this "payment" to us. It is thus in exact accordance with both the *individual* and *collective* Spiritual Volition of all humankind under the outworking of The Law of Reciprocal Action in the first instance.

We should be perfectly clear from the above explanations, therefore, that the "Forces of Nature" **will** bring about the "renewal" of the Earth under the outworking of the Natural Laws

---

of Christian believers, we will examine the whole idea in the later Chapter: **The Two Sons of God!**

which are, at the same time, The Spiritual Laws. We should thus strongly note a key point here; that these events will occur at the precisely ordained time, *"irrespective of the condition of the inhabitants"*.

The term condition in this case means the *spiritual condition*, or level of *spiritual maturity* of the inhabitants. Therefore, as we continually reinforce, since most of man's decisions for all his time on Earth have leaned more toward war, strife and degradation of his material home, we can expect that the collective reciprocal return of that volition will be severe and destructive, returning tenfold our original "choices", albeit in Perfect Justice. Unfortunately for humankind, however, under the aegis of the "whirlwind constant".

This lawful process marks the closing of all cycles – again activated by our free-will – for *earthly humanity in this Material Part of Creation*. In that context, what we have thus explained here will equate to the **"First Death"** process for the many who will be removed during the "scything" or "cleansing" of global humanity then.

The **"Second Death"**, however, is an entirely different proposition altogether, for that development leads to the actual "disintegration" of the very life force of each individual. The very many who will succumb to the "scything of global humanity" in the **"First Death"** reality we are all familiar with – and thus not enter into the next phase of humankind's ordained journey of "spiritual maturation" on a "cleansed Earth" – will set themselves on a course that will eventually take them through the process which brings about the **"Second Death"**. Thus that very large group of very intransigent, *departed*, humanity will, at the precisely-ordained future time, experience then the disintegration of their very "life force".

It is vitally important, therefore, to reinforce the fact that whilst the Grace of being able to "right past wrongs" is a constant promise, the time available for any such expiation is precisely that under which the material part of the world is ordained to exist as our physical home. At the end of that allotted time, everything that is part of that materiality or connected to it will go through its "natural disintegration process".

So unless we have reached a degree of spiritual maturity and inner purity **sufficient to take us above the pull of the Earth**, any human spirits who have not managed, or not bothered, to spiritually mature adequately enough **will be caught up in the disintegration too**. It should always be remembered, however, that this whole process is a completely natural and ordained one, even if difficult to comprehend in terms of reason or scale.

What is also vital to understand is that whilst the *Earth* is the obvious home of mankind in the *material* sense, and the *Ethereal World* holds transitional Planes for souls in the beyond, *both 'Planes' or 'Realms'* belong to the ***"non-eternal" Material Part*** of Creation. The true Spiritual Realm, as we now clearly know, stands far higher in **The Eternal**.

We now reach the point where we explain how the **"Second Death"** occurs. In order to fully understand the process and the Scriptural warning about it, we must again revisit the concept of reincarnation. It is a concept which needs to be recognised as, or likened to, a "school of learning". Thus, each Earth-life lived represents a class or stage in which our spiritual development can be furthered – **if we so choose**. However, we should not be so naive as to believe that each successive incarnation *automatically* places us on the next highest step. Whilst that may be a desirable idea, and one which has very many adherents in some religious beliefs, the reality is vastly different. In any case, the present state of humanity clearly testifies to the contrary. With each Earth-life, **we are given the opportunity to re-awaken – nothing more**. In **every** case, in **every** incarnation, we must **recognise the purpose for which we were born**, and *live accordingly*. Therefore, to this earthly school we must return a number of times.

The "extra classes" allow us more time to learn and to fulfil our spiritual purpose, thus helping our ascent. It is equally true, however, that one may *never* recognise the purpose for which one incarnates, irrespective of how many "classes" one might "attend". We would, thereby, naturally and consequently continually gravitate toward material or even evil pursuits. Such a life-path re-strengthens *unnecessary binds* to the Material World, *from which* one will need to strive harder to *break away* if one **truly wishes** to finally **ascend** out of the **inevitable and approaching chaos**. Irrevocably connected with **aspiritual** human endeavour and behaviour, that rapidly-approaching 'hour' signals to planet Earth's *Elemental Guardians* the *ordained time* for **Reciprocal "Creation-Law" resolution**.

Finally, after many "classes", examination day for *everyone* arrives. The result will determine whether one graduates from the "school" and achieves spiritual freedom, or whether one fails the "examination" and remains behind. With regard to we human beings currently in Material Creation, the examination is now due, with fewer opportunities for a "recount". This "reality" is mirrored in the increasing problems within societies, and in the enormous and rapidly increasing amount of *reaping in suffering* that we witness daily on a global scale. As previously stated, the length of time under which our "school" was ordained to run for is exactly that of the equally ordained time of life for this part of Material Creation to which the Earth, our "classroom", belongs.

The same process is also employed for the "collective reaping" of mankind, since **individual outcomes** are **simultaneously** being resolved within the parameters of the **collective happening**.

> Whilst a "second-death" concept necessarily represents a *finite* one – as must the life-span of each material globe – the *infinite* aspect of this incomprehensible process is characterised by a **Cycle of Creation** that is *Eternal*, thus *without end*. So a continuous **coming into being** of the star systems and universes contained within the Material World. Individual suns and planets **within** such systems simply undergo their time of **birth, life and disintegration** in this overall, *infinite* **continuity**.

That is because the Material part of Creation was firmly bound to the unalterable Laws of evolution and dissolution from the very beginning, in strict accordance with The Creative Will. This "Creative Will", of which The Laws of Nature are part, is the Power or Force which, in its activity, continually forms and dissolves worlds, exactly as can be observed in cosmological activity. We reiterate the key point of a previous statement; the reinforcement of our assertion that "The Laws of Nature" are inherent in "The Will of God". In other words, the "Elemental Forces of Nature", in their ordained purpose and activity, carry out The Eternal Will. Under the inviolable Law of Reciprocal Action [Sowing and Reaping], the "Elemental Beings" – both the large and the small – produce the reciprocal *effect* of mankind's decisions.

In the larger sense, it is an "elementally-wrought" process necessary for any particular part of the Material World that finally reaches the defining point of its life-cycle whereby its disintegration permits a further renewal for its continuing evolution. Each globe has its ordained time for this process. The key aspect contained within such lawful outcomes is the fact that the outworking of the Natural Laws precisely determines the point at which this disintegration process for each celestial globe must begin. Hence the reason why our own planet Earth cannot be exempt from this eventual and ordained outcome either.

As previously stated, what colours our situation most markedly is the fact that this "inevitable happening" will proceed at its precisely determined moment, **irrespective** of the **condition** of the **Earth**, or **its inhabitants** – i.e. **us**. And as we clearly know, the term condition in this case means the *spiritual condition* or level of *spiritual maturity* of the inhabitants.

Because such concepts differ vastly from standard scientific notions, and also from orthodox Christian teaching, *we will restate the key points once more.* We will, however, preface it with the relevant "Crucial Imperative" from Chapter 1!

Crucial Imperative No 5:

That because the physical Universe is a *material* expanse, it is therefore *not* without end. **It is finite!**

So, omnipresent throughout all of Creation is The Creative Will – out of which the Ethereal World of the 'beyond' and the Material World of the Earth Plane issued as one inter-connected Whole. In necessary reinforcement: From its earliest beginnings the Material Creation was thus inexorably bound to immutable Creation-Law, which also brought about evolution and disso-lution. And, as already noted, what we refer to as Natural Law, is, in reality, the *expression* of **The Will of God** in *Material Creation*! In its *expressionistic-activity*, therefore, it is continually forming and dissolving worlds, exactly as astronomers observe.

Thus; in concert with a time scale we humans can never ever comprehend, and a 'death' process that many would disbelieve anyway, it is *nonetheless* crucially important that we *rein-force for you* – scientist, theologian and layman – that you at least *strive* to understand this **key fact**: That in the Material World, *only the* cycle *of* Creation *is Eternal*. Not necessarily the life of individual component parts as a whole. Only in a *continuous* "coming-into-being, disintegration and re-formation" is the "great Cycle" **Eternal** and **without end**: thus **Infinite!**

It is therefore within this great and stupendous happening that all the many revelations and prophecies are fulfilled. Within this framework, also, there one day comes the last, i.e. the *final sorting out* for *each* material celestial globe. However, whilst this does not take place simultaneously in the whole of Creation, it is a process connected with that part of Creation which reaches the point in *its* cycle where its disintegration *must* occur, so that it can *once more* begin the process of *renewal* in the fulfilment of the Eternal Cycle.

It should be further understood that in strict accordance with the consistency of the Natural Laws, the exact point at which disintegration of each celestial globe must begin is precisely determined. Most importantly for humankind, therefore, the process of *disintegration* must develop at a very definite point in time.

So in accordance with **Creation-Law**, the Eternal Cycle drives every celestial globe irre-sistibly towards that crucial point, enabling its particular hour of disintegration to be fulfilled. However, as with everything in Creation, this actually represents simply a transformation – albeit a mighty one – which thereby provides the opportunity for further development.

Once this collective point of its ordained evolutionary development is reached, however, this Material part of Creation, along with the Earth and all its inhabitants, will be "ripe" for the "final sorting". That is the moment of our "either-or" – our final **50% Choice** and **100% Outcome!**

Either we are raised upwards to The Light if we have followed a spiritual path or, if we have become convinced that material or aspiritual considerations are more important or more valuable, *we are held fast to the World of Matter.* Thus, through our own personal desire to seek things other than those which hold true spiritual values, **we must then be drawn, with the World of Matter**, into *disintegration*: **Into spiritual death!**

And therewith is explained the meaning of The Second Death.

It is "Spiritual Death"! Equivalent to effacement from The Book of Life!

Long development over millennia from a non-conscious spirit-seed in The Spiritual Realm to its first incarnation onto the Earth plane permitted the newly-arrived human beings to subsequently reach the necessary state of personal self-consciousness, and then journey through the first stages of speech development. Continuing on through the era that we designate as early man, through the transitional stages of tribalism and thence into Nationhood and the world stage via many different incarnations, that long, often tortuous, path now finally nears its zenith.

This lengthy development to "personal self-consciousness" will unfortunately be terminated for those who, through their rejection of Spiritual Truth, are irrevocably drawn into the disintegrating process. They will therewith experience the piece-by-piece shredding of the *"ego of personal self-consciousness"* during the dissolution process of this part of the Material World to which we belong when *its* time of "renewal" arrives. Piece by piece, until the once "conscious" personality is reduced to an "unconscious" spirit-seed as it was at its beginnings. Reduced to the state of "spiritual death" – the "Second Death!"

For those who **do** ascend out of the chaos of disintegration and dissolution, the specific meaning of one particular Scripture in Revelation can be readily understood:

"...over these the second death has no authority"!

(Revelation 20:6, Fenton.)

In the closing segment of this Chapter it is important to clarify a key aspect of the human spirit's development to *spiritual self-consciousness* and the reverse process of its possible loss in the disintegration of the "Material World" in which it had developed to that self-conscious level.

We have identified that the "Spirit" originates from the Eternal Part of The Spiritual Realm and arrives in its first incarnation without yet having developed to the state of "personal self-consciousness". This can only be effected by that "spirit" in the "Material World", for it is its *personal experiencing in this **earthly** medium* that offers the mechanism for its necessary development to self-consciousness. Therefore, even though the *non-conscious spiritual part* of each human entity is originally of The Spiritual Realm, it can only *acquire* **personal** *"self-consciousness"* in its wanderings through the Material Realm, particularly whilst on **Earth!**

Therefore, the stripping away of its *spiritual* self-consciousness to the unfortunate condition of *spiritual death* can equally only occur during the *disintegration* of the *Material* part of Creation. For that is where it developed to its *self-conscious state* and to which the necessary "experiences" to obtain the requisite degree of "knowing" belong. This "stripping away" does not occur in the actual Spiritual Realm of Creation as the words may *seem* to suggest, for that is **not** the area where the human spirit is ordained to *develop* to personal self-consciousness and *gain knowledge* of The Spiritual. That particular "schooling" takes place in the various levels of the Material Realm, and naturally includes some time on Earth.

Thus it is The Spiritual Realm that the human spirit ascends to when it has gained *sufficient* spiritual purity and maturity to *earn* its place there. There in the Eternal Spiritual, secure in its eternal reality within the bounds of its original home, it can fulfil its complete spiritual potential – eternally!

The reality of the "Second Death" should not be equated with the beliefs of those who interpret this process as being similar to the attainment of "nirvana", the "desired" state of spiritual bliss expounded by some Eastern religions. Spiritual Law decrees that the human spirit is ordained to develop to **personal** *self-consciousness* only, which means it retains its ***individuality*** and therefore must render ***personal responsibility*** for all its activity. It was never ordained to merge with a collective "cosmic consciousness". This is a pleasant idea but does not at all accord with Spiritual Truth. The "either-or" **choice** here means **either** *individual spiritual life*, **or** *individual spiritual death*, in strict accordance with inviolable Spiritual Law. The choice once more, of course, is solely that of each individual alone.

There is one further important aspect of the "Second Death reality" to address at this crucial time in the Earth's and humankind's development. The words, "eternal damnation", are usually synonymous with fanatical "fire and brimstone" religion. Yet, in reality, it well describes the quite natural and lawful processes for any human spirit drawn into disintegration, for he <u>ceases to be personal</u>. From any standpoint, this must surely be the worst fate that could possibly befall any individual. For, as already stated, it is exactly synonymous with effacement from The Book of Life itself!

Moreover, this separation of *spirit* from *matter*, in itself also a completely natural process in accordance with The Spiritual Laws and now taking place under the aegis of The Creative Will, is the so-called "Last Judgement". This final 'sorting out' is necessarily connected with great upheavals and transformations but will be on a scale not previously known. The Book of Matthew (24:3, Fenton) offers a strong insight into just the *early stages* of the *complete process*. Those *now-stirring beginnings* are obviously connected with earthly humanity, and were given when the Disciples of Jesus asked Him what signs will portend "...the completion of this age" – our time now.

Verses 19 to 22 are particularly chilling in their portent.

> "But alas for those *with child* and those *who nurse in those days*! Pray, however, that your flight may not come during the winter, nor upon a Rest-day; for there shall *then* be widespread affliction, such as has *not been known* since the beginning of the world until now, no, nor will *ever* be known again. And if those times were not cut short, **not a man would be saved**; but for the sake of the chosen ones, those times will be cut short."

> (Matthew 19-22, Fenton.
> Emphases mine.)

Should we be modern, enlightened, intellectual human beings and mock such *unproven religious rantings* because our much-vaunted, *university-derived*, human science has now determined that "genes" are our life-force, and not such a thing as an *inner, animating* **spirit-core**? Scientifically impossible, and therefore nonsense, as *'earth-science' would surely determine it*.

Or should we use our *intuition*, which is *not* tied to *earthly* empiricism, to *therewith* recognise the obvious truth? That human genes and the processes they control affect *the physical body only* because they are *both* of *material* substance, and that therefore this scientific, so-called, *genetic life-force* **rots away with the body at its death**.

As with most Scripture in The Bible, the particular passages from the Revelation pertaining to the "second death" become far more clarified when assessed from the knowledge of **The Spiritual Laws of Creation**.

It would be a tragic mistake, therefore, to regard these explanations as just religious "fire and brimstone fanaticism" without any relevance to societal beliefs or norms today. The Prophets and Teachers of the great religious teachings understood this immutable point of The Law, for the Teachings they were called to give to peoples of specific lands and times in history were derived by their Spiritual insight and specific guidance; **from out of the very Truth Itself!**

The ordained 'spiritual cleansing' is certainly not that currently visited by the practitioners of certain religions against their own where they strangely believe that their 'murderous, evil activities' *do* fulfil that kind of ordination. Neither, therefore, are they pleasing to a Creator who is both Love and Justice absolute. Such 'mindless murderers' will not be permitted any kind of 'exalted place' in His proximity, irrespective of their terribly distorted beliefs to the contrary. Only with a belief in a 'one-life concept' can such appalling distortions exist at all.

The very fact that virtually everything is collapsing globally should be evidence enough that there is some exceptionally powerful *reaping* taking place now. We can be sure, therefore, that even what we observe daily is not yet the culmination – the final *collective reaping* – so to speak!

Consequently, it should be a simple matter to recognise that the Earth and 'its inhabitants' must surely be approaching a major and climactic point, simply because more is happening faster. The separation among men reveals itself more and more sharply every day as smaller and smaller splinter factions in religion, politics, or ethnic groupings, break away from parent organisations. Thus what had previously only manifested itself in 'opinions and convictions' now reveals itself more and more as intransigent positions, often marked by violence or the intimidatory threat thereof.

Therefore the present state of the world should be viewed with very great alarm and concern, with the urgent need to *seriously recognise* where we *actually* stand spiritually. In order to stand "right", however, we must exert the greatest strength to leave behind all base thoughts and activities, seek out Spiritual Truth and begin to live accordingly. If we do not, we are in danger of being chained to The World of Matter and eventually being drawn with it towards complete disintegration.

Cultural and ethnic traditions will also be placed under this immense pressure, and no amount of believing in one's 'ethnic spirituality', or one's indigenous right to it, will alter the actual and lawful outcome of this **unstoppable**, "separating force". All races must be absolutely sure that what they regard as 'high spiritual beliefs' *are truly so* according to The Spiritual Laws. It will not be enough to simply *imagine they are*. For the Eternal Spiritual Laws are not the least bit interested in the beliefs of any people and their imagined 'spirituality'. The Law will sift without favour and in complete objectivity – as it must in any case.

Yet, in the final analysis, that process will simply be the separating out of the opposing principles of Light and Darkness along with their respective adherents, irrespective of what ethnic or religious group they may belong to. For the end result is one of *individual and personal standing*, and **not** that of any *collective grouping*.

For those who strive for The Light, however, the *uplifting* attraction of this Spiritual Force will apply here equally as powerfully as with the *destruction* of all that opposes it. Thus those souls who hold more noble aspirations and goals will gradually become freed from the World of Matter, with the correspondingly greater opportunity to ascend more quickly to Planes of Light; to the home of all that is *truly* Spiritual. With that separation from the baser elements of humanity, the Judgement is fulfilled for them!
The correct knowledge now at our disposal enables us to shed light and clarity on much that was previously veiled in mystery and uncertainty.

We conclude this Chapter with a particularly relevant quote from Deuteronomy 30:19. [Emphases mine, Fenton.] The Scripture in its very wording *reveals the reality* of a "Second Death" *separate from* just the earthly death of the physical shell. What we are given here once more offers a final **50 percent choice** and **100 percent outcome**!

> "Bear witness to me, now, Heavens and Earth! **I place Life and Death before you, – the Blessing and the Curse!** Therefore *choose* for yourselves *the Life*, – that *you* and your posterity *may live*!"

11

THE "SEVEN CHURCHES IN ASIA": THE "REVELATION"

"Happy are the reader and hearers of this prophecy who observe its records; for the time is at hand."

(Revelation 1:3, Fenton.)

"If I have seen further than other men, it is because I have stood on the shoulders of giants."

(Sir Isaac Newton.)

Crucial Imperative No 5:

That because the physical Universe is a *material* expanse, it is therefore *not* without end. **It is finite!**

(Author.)

Thus far in this work we have examined The Laws of Life, our Origins, the processes of Death, the vital working of the Forces of Nature and the lives of the great Truth-Bringers; the Teachings of whom we were meant to heed. Since much of what we have looked at was meant to be examined and learned in the earthly environment, this Chapter appropriately offers ultimate insight into the wider *material* environment to which the Earth obviously belongs. It reveals the *limits* of the material parameters in which we live, and allows us to know our respective place within those far-reaching boundaries.

The truth that **Crucial Imperative No 5** inherently encompasses therefore sets boundaries on the otherwise humanly-incomprehensible immensity of the Material World:

That because the physical Universe is a *material* expanse, it is therefore *not* without end. **It is finite!**

The key focus of this Chapter is derived primarily from the knowledge in **The Book of Revelation**, for *it reveals* the wider *material environment* that the physical universes *actually represent*. Therefore, precisely centred on the un-fathomable vastness of that mind-numbing "amphitheatre"; as we reveal in a step-by-step process Sir Isaac Newton's "Plan of The World" we, the complete *human entity*, will nonetheless find <u>*our relative, physical, contextual place*</u> in the humanly-incomprehensible *material entity* of "space".

So crucial to knowing our *actual* place in the *greater* scheme of things centres on the question of who and what we actually are; i.e., the duality of man. Whilst we have answered that question earlier in the Work, in the context of this Chapter with its singularly-relevant topic for *all* of global humanity, we should revisit the question of where we, in our physical form, fit in the greater scheme of things. Are we little more than tissue, blood and bone entities animated by a computer-like brain with a heart-pump holding it all together; nothing more than that...? If so, what, then, is the end outcome? Just a hole in the ground with all *animating life-force* extinguished?

If space-scientists, especially, believe that; *why bother* with astronomy and cosmology at all? What would be the point; to learn about an immensity that is the greatest marvel in the *Material World* and at the end of it simply be *no more*? Why bother with studying the incredible marvel of the incomprehensible universe/s if that is the believed end-result? **Surely a pointless exercise in what would logically extrapolate to being an absolutely pointless career!**

No! The idea that death extinguishes our "life-force" is truly a "nonsense-notion". The huge industry now growing around the human genome and the overall genome mapping project is also ultimately just about *physical properties only*. The human-gene paradigm that science is all agog over now is therefore *not about* 'real life' at all. The human entity must understand this primary fact and yet deal with the greater and more crucial dimension of its true nature – **that of The Spiritual** – precisely as the present Pope has challenged science to open itself to.

Real life is therefore centred on our Spirit, the inner animating core within each of us, *upon which human genes have no bearing or impact whatsoever*. The opposite, however, is intrinsically correct. The spirit is the actual power and life-force within and thus ultimately drives *all movement and processes* concerning the physical body. The make-up and function of the very many genes that supposedly command all human life-processes, in the final analysis *all die with the physical body*.

On that very note for this particular Chapter, let us reacquaint ourselves with the key questions that the Documentary Channels continually resurrect. National Geographic queried *exactly* this question in two separate Documentaries: **"Birth of Life"**, and **"Human Ape"**. The associated and most relevant point asked was:
"How did *non-living* material come to life?"

The History Channel, too, sought the same kind of definitive answer in the series, **"How Life Began"**. It asked:
"Where did [this] life come from? What IS life, exactly?"

And in a *space* of perhaps *insightful prescience*, the Series further and crucially queries:
"Is it chemical, spiritual, <u>or a combination of both</u>?"

(All emphases mine.)

The same Documentary Channels also continually screen scientifically-updated programmes about 'space'. From various key universities, many experts in this field offer their particular level of 'expertise' to the documentaries – astronomers, cosmologists, astro-physicists, astro-biologists etc., etc.. What is most striking with regard to this group is the fact that a 'collective', across-the-board, academic notion has seemingly emerged from *their* study of the stars. Currently taught to 'space' students globally, the overall paradigm basically states:

1. That the 'creation' of the *physical* universe singularly provided, *on its own*, the building blocks for *all* life to emerge – including us.

2. That the increasing knowledge about the physical properties and make-up of the stars in the universe, including the various gases within it, therefore represents the greatest discovery of all for the human race.

3. And that, concomitant with such a view – now part of the educational-paradigm of earth-science – we, the 'complete' human entity, are thus constituted of star-material, solely. Stardust.

4. Within that strongly-promoted, so-called, "scientific reality", therefore; no place exists or can exist for an *inner animating core* which would also necessarily be the 'separable', *non-physical*, 'life-force' *within* and *for* the human entity.

For many astronomers and cosmologists it would seem; no belief in a **life-animating** 'soul' or 'spirit' most necessary for one's "ongoing existence". Just 'stardust'; i.e., atoms and molecules precisely configured – or perhaps *re-configured* – to form the tissue, blood, bones and organs necessary for physical earth-life, but which must then somehow **animate itself** so as to become a living, breathing, internally-pulsating, communicative, mobile human being. Shall we repeat the key question? We should!

"How did *non-living* material come to life?"

On the basis of that crucial question, let us once more note the so-called 'great scientific breakthrough' of 2010 by scientist Dr Craig Venter in *creating* 'artificial life' in a laboratory test tube. Reproduced here from **"Author's Note"**:
'The world headlines read: "Giant leap for science..." What does the word, *creation*, really mean anyway? In this case, of course, the building blocks required to *produce* this 'new life form' were already available to science. So it is not a question of truly **creating**, as such; but, with the aid of a computer, more *assembling* the various components – albeit to a precise configuration under strictly-controlled conditions.
To some degree in their crass sensationalism, the hype that journalistic jingoism gave to this new 'life-form' may perhaps have stemmed from envisioning all sorts of 'creatures' developing from *it*. However, in a Q. and A. session, Dr Venter quashed that 'possibility'.

Question: 'So is this new form of life a replicating, free-living organism.'

Answer: "That is correct, only it is free-living in the sense that it grows *in the laboratory* in a very rich culture media **so it wouldn't survive in the outside environment**. Given the right nutrients *in the laboratory* it is self-replicating on its own."

(All emphases mine.)

So this new thing will never even develop to the level of just a common garden slug – a real and mobile life-form animated by a real *life-force* – let alone anything higher. Human science can only *assemble*, not truly create. For we, ourselves, are simply a *species* of, and *in*, Creation!'

So on the basis of just reconfigured 'stardust' as the building blocks for 'life'; at the end of a lifetime of valuable furtherance of human knowledge, no 'form' that continues on. Just a black hole of nothingness where the very thought-processes that recently engaged with concepts which could not have been even imagined just generations ago are extinguished.

Gentlemen and women of space research: Sorry! Such a notion is not only untenable, it is really illogical. It is, in the final analysis, the ultimate *'nonsense-notion'*, for *inanimate matter* cannot possibly **animate itself**, regardless of what empirical science might determine as 'its truth'. Moreover, that is a *sure reality* which you will *all* discover to be *true* upon *your* exit from earth-life.

In a truly paradoxical twist for "star-dust only" astronomers, it is precisely the knowledge of the vastness of the material universes [plural] that is essential for the human entity to know in order for the realisation to "fully hit home" that *as incomprehensibly vast as what we will reveal further on, the unfathomable scope and scale of it all is nevertheless **just our physical home for our physical form**!* Only by that very sobering realisation can we gift to ourselves inner peace deriving from the fact that "home" truly is far above the Material Worlds. In Realms once known by earlier humankind to be sure fact – before being *intellectually relegated* to a "dustbin of derision" by the blinkered, intellectual constraints of empirical, thus "earthbound", science. So that far greater "space reality", which cosmology and astronomy have yet to recognise, we will *reveal in this Chapter from "The Revelation"*.

The Book of Revelation, by virtue of its seemingly enigmatic content, provides fertile ground for many interpretations, from the literal to the bizarre. That particular book is perceived to cover many prophetic aspects, though often *apparently* unrelated, and *ostensibly* without clear linkages. The Revelation, being part of that Book which is the foundation of Christianity – the be-all and end-all by their own admission for this particular group of global humanity – is nevertheless considered by many to be virtually impossible to understand logically.

Yet if the purpose of The Revelation **really was** to help **all** of humankind **understand** our 'reason for being' at precisely **this present time of our tenure in the Material World** what, then, must derive from either a wrong interpretation, or from ignoring it completely?

As we have stated elsewhere in this Work and repeat here, during his time with the Anglican Church the great mathematician, Isaac Newton, directed his monumental talent of genius to analysing The Bible, trying to discover the secret knowledge he believed lay hidden there. He further believed that some of the ancients – in particular the Greek mathematicians – had known this secret. If he could find it, he would know it too.

Astronomers and cosmologists, therefore: Do not place yourselves in the position of the Scribes and Pharisees of Jesus's time; they who sought religious/academic control over the masses. Remember His warning to *them*:

> "Woe to you, play-acting professors and Pharisees! because you lock up the King-dom of Heaven in the face of mankind; while you yourselves neither enter, nor allow those arriving to go in."

> (Matthew, 23:13. Fenton.)

Instead, open up to the all-encompassing **truth** of the **extent** of the physical Universes [plural] that your great "astronomy ancestor", Newton, *intuitively understood* to be factual reality. Though eluding him **then**; today, with the *immutable knowledge* of **Creation-Law** coupled with recent huge strides in cosmology, *you* can finally know: —

Isaac Newton's Plan of the World!

Two major points lay at the heart of Newton's unshakeable belief:

1. A rational God made a rational universe; and

2. All wisdom lay in the knowledge of numbers.[1]

Of special interest to Newton was The Book of Daniel with its mathematical time-line of prophecy. The Book of Revelation, however, was the primary Book of The Bible from which Newton sought his 'Plan' – from which we clarify the "7 Churches" mystery. The journey we need to take for this purpose has powerful echoes to Newton and his genius, for he provides the foundational-mathematics of astronomy which we will need to arrive at our conclusion. Why astronomy for that conclusion? For the moment we should let that reason be a "revelation" in itself. Since we have Newton as a man of the Church and a towering genius of science, he is surely the ideal companion for this august journey. Let us, then, not just take this man of spiritual and intellectual genius with us, but let us stand on **his** shoulders and discover the treasured goal that he could not find in his lifetime: **"The Plan of the World"**.

Because Newton believed that only *"a few natural laws apply to the whole universe"*, he regarded those natural laws **"as proof of the existence of a great and All-Mighty God"**. Since he was both a theologian and scientist vitally interested in apparently all things, including The Revelation, we would sincerely hope that modern-day scientists and theologians would want to journey with us too.

Any notion that states The Book of Revelation as being an enigma and therefore indecipherable, must thus presuppose that some of the greatest answers to life which lie in there might be too difficult to even attempt to understand. In our view that is an illogical and untenable position. After all, it is "The Revelation". By such statements, we reveal the actual level of our *non-understanding.*

As has been pointed out elsewhere in this book, the very fact that we are here on planet Earth must logically infer that we are **meant** to discover **all** the answers to our purpose for being. Otherwise it all becomes a rather pointless exercise: of either scientific contention deriving mainly from a theoretical-supposition basis, or religious contention deriving from differing interpretations of the many and varied beliefs awash across the globe. Unfortunately, ideas, theories, guesswork etc., do not provide *definitive* answers, a good reason why the admonition, "Seek and you shall find", should act as the impetus to really do so. This vitally-necessary *finding* of the final and ultimate answers to the questions to life cannot be achieved with the use of our intellect alone, however.

So for the complete understanding of this particular Chapter we must *strongly reiterate* that the purpose of the intellect is to facilitate, to the highest possible level, the material and technological undertakings that humans require for their sojourn and ongoing development in the *earthly environment.* The intellect possesses *no understanding whatsoever* of the many and far higher non-physical Realms of the incomprehensible total we sometimes too-loosely call Creation. That is because only the physical-body part of man is derived from the Material World. So also, therefore, is its closely associated aspects of intellectual-brain activity. Thus the "seeking" of final and complete knowledge must be driven by the *Spirit* – because it is connected to The Source of Life. Such seeking, however, needs a *clarified* intellect as its companion. In any case, no amount of intellectual or theological sophistry can change *what actually is.* So any religious or scientific pre-conceptions brought to bear here to attempt to discredit the true

---

[1]The reader will recall the term used in this book as not so much being the "knowledge of numbers" as **"The Law of Numbers"**.

meaning of the "7 Churches" question is, in the singular nature of things pertaining to Spiritual Truth, *immediately rendered irrelevant.*

Anyhow, it is well past the time that the true meaning was recognised. That essential recognition, as a vital part of the complete knowledge for humankind, permits critical threads to many of the key questions of life to be woven together to reveal a far larger picture than could *ever* be the case without this information. Moreover, it also provides the right structure, from the earthly viewpoint in this case, for the very necessary understanding of one of the previous Chapters:

Jesus: His Birth, Death and Resurrection!
— and also the next:

The Two Sons of God!

For Bible readers generally, but more particularly perhaps for Bible scholars, Theologians and the religiously learned of the Universities and Colleges of the world, the question of the "Seven Churches" or "assemblies or communities" in "Asia" or "Asia Minor" represents a curious and fascinating puzzle. The names of the seven "assemblies" – to each of which a Messenger of God delivers an address – are given as follows: Ephesus, Smyrna, Pergamos, Thyatira, Sardis, Philapelphia and Laodicea. And, just as The Revelation *seemingly* notes, they *were* communities which *did* exist in Asia Minor.

Ephesus: Ancient Greek city of Asia Minor, in what is now western Turkey, lying near the mouth of the river Ku-cuk Menderes. It was the site of the great Temple of Diana, one of the seven wonders of the world. It was destroyed by the Goths in AD 262.

Smyrna: Now called **Izmir**. City and port in western Turkey. At the head of the Gulf of Izmir, on the Aegean Sea, it is the commercial centre of the Levant.

(*Great Illustrated Dictionary*,
Reader's Digest; both.)

Pergamos: Now called **Bergama** in western Turkey. Once noted for its fabulous carpets; they were the most highly valued and probably woven with gold and silver thread. Nothing survives of these rich textiles because they were all burned long ago to extract the metal.

(Brittanica CD '97)

Thyatira: Now called **Akhisar**, a town in western Turkey, "... in a fertile plain on the great Zab River (the ancient Lycus). The ancient town, originally called Pelopia, was probably founded by the Lydians. It was made a Macedonian colony about 290 BC and renamed **Thyatira**. It became part of the kingdom of Pergamum in 190 BC and was an important station on the ancient Roman road from Pergamum (Bergama) to Laodicea (near Denizli). Its early Christian church appears as *one of the seven churches in the Revelation to John*".

(Brittanica CD '97. Italics mine.)

Also **Sardis:** Capital city of ancient Lydia, now a small village in western Turkey. When Lydia was absorbed into the Persian Empire following the defeat of Croeseus (c. 550 BC), Sardis remained the provincial capital of Asia Minor. It later became an early centre of Christianity – *one of the Seven Churches of Asia (Minor)*. Extensive excavations of the site have yielded the earliest known coins, dating from c. 700 BC.

Philadelphia: Now called **Alasehir**, also a town in western Turkey.

Laodicea: Name given to several cities built in Asia and Asia Minor by the Greek Seleucid Dynasty in the third century BC The chief one, Laodicea ad Lycum, near present day Denizli in western Turkey, was a prosperous market town on the Roman trading route from the Orient and an early centre of Christianity.

(*Great Illustrated Dictionary, R.D.*, Italics mine.)

Already now we have a strong *academic* view about what the "Seven Churches" *might* mean. Significantly, they were in a geographically very small area of present-day Turkey. In fact, the triangulated area encompassing the locations of those ancient "7 Churches", including the nearby island of Patmos and the area of sea between it and the mainland, amounts to something like 25,000 sq.km. The total area of modern Turkey is around 780,580 sq.km. The representative area of the "7 Churches triangle" is therefore only about 1/30th of that.

If we *carefully* read the introduction *prior* to the "messages" being given to the seven "assemblies" in Asia by the individual "Messengers" of God, then read the *actual* messages, and then finally the *explanation* about The One who has authorised the messages; a major problem immediately emerges if we hold to such a *small area of one small country on Earth*. The island of Patmos, where it is *believed* John the Disciple "received" The Revelation, is close by. So how do, or how might, the actual messages fit with such a scenario?

Each of the seven communities is addressed by its particular Messenger (a Guardian Angel) who calls the inhabitants to task for various transgressions against The Laws of Creation – The Laws of God – and warns the various 'assemblies' what will happen if they do not change their ways. Let us take just one message to one of the communities, and carefully note the **key** to understanding the **meaning** of that and the other messages.

11.1   The Vision in Patmos

> I, John,...was in the island known as Patmos. I became inspired on the Lord's day; and I heard a loud voice behind me resembling a trumpet blast saying: "What you see write in a book, and dispatch to the seven assemblies – to **Ephesus**, and to **Smyrna**" ... etc.. I accordingly turned to see the voice which spoke to me. And having turned, I observed **seven golden lampstands**; and **in the centre of the lampstands**, one like to the Son of Man... and **holding in His right hand seven stars**; and a sharp double-edged sword drawn from its sheath... "Write therefore what you have seen, what is, and what will come after these. The mystery of the **seven stars** which you saw upon my right hand, and the **seven golden lampstands**, *the seven stars are <u>Messengers</u> of seven assemblies; and the seven lampstands <u>are</u> the seven assemblies*."

(Revelation 1:9-19, Fenton.
Emphases mine.)

We have strongly emphasised the italicised parts of John's vision because they hold the key to understanding this *apparent* mystery, ***for it was reserved for this point in time in humanity's journey for it to be fully understood***. Verse 3 [quoted under the Chapter heading] offers a further connection:

> "Happy are the reader and hearers of this prophecy who observe its records; for the time is at hand."

The next key part is the text of the address to the first 'assembly' – **Ephesus**.

11.1.1   To the Assembly in Ephesus

To the messenger to the assembly in Ephesus write:

"Thus says the Controller of the seven stars by His right hand; **who walks in the centre of the seven golden lampstands**; I know your position, your industry, and your patience; and that you cannot endure those who are wicked; that you have put to the test those who have called themselves Apostles, and are not, and have found them false; and you have had patience and have suffered because of My Name, and have not failed. I have, however, a charge against you - that you have *forsaken your first love*! Remember, therefore, from where you have fallen, and repent, and practise your former works; failing which, and unless you alter your mind, **I will come and remove your <u>lampstand</u> from its place.**"[2]

(Revelation 2:1-6, Fenton.

Emphases mine.)

"From whence thou art fallen" refers to the over-cultivated intellect, which has pushed aside the spirit and caused it to fall, so that it can no longer, as before the Fall of Man, do "the first works", namely, keep awake the spiritual intuitive perception, and thus maintain the connection with God.

(*A Gate Opens*, Herbert Vollmann.)

The address to Ephesus continues on for a few more sentences, then there are the further, basically similar, addresses to the *other "assemblies" or churches.*

Now, if we accept, in the absolute literal sense, a scenario which declares that Messages from The Revelation were given to the named ancient 7 cities or 'churches' by "Messengers of God" in what is *now* western Turkey, then we might appear to have three possibilities. That in a past event [because the particular cities to which the names once belonged have either disappeared or are no longer known by their ancient names] the Messengers *did* appear to the people, and *did* deliver the appropriate messages. Subsequently the cities or communities *did* disappear so one *could* believe that they did *not* "change their ways" and thus suffered destruction. However, there is no known record of such visitations or warnings to those "churches" having taken place.

We note that the name Laodicea, alone, was given to *several* cities. That is surely problematic for a "Messenger" of God who is required to deliver a message of obviously great import to that particular "community". For messages at the behest of **The Almighty** cannot be superficial or insignificant.

That being the case, the question of *which* John received The Revelation is clearly important. There is a school of thought that accepts three different individuals: John the Baptist, John the Evangelist – the beloved Disciple of Jesus associated with the Fourth Gospel – and a John the Divine; believed to be the author of The Revelation. We, however, will embrace only two.

If we accept the view that **"The Revelation"** was received on the island of Patmos in the Aegean Sea by John the Disciple, we must logically accept that he was sufficiently "well-connected" to so receive such a powerful 'unearthly vision'. For such a **'Revelation'** could only come from **The One** *Enthroned* at the Height of **Creation**; thus **HE** with the greatest knowledge of **It**.

Notwithstanding the fact that *that* John was the "beloved of Jesus", such tidings of vital import must surely presuppose that only a very special individual – a greater one prepared over

---

[2]The italicised sentences in the whole discourse are vital for the reader to remember.

a long period of time perhaps – would be suitable for such a high task. Or was there a *second* John on *a Patmos*?

From Matthew 11:11, "A Gate Opens", by Herbert Vollmann; we read:

> Only one was found worthy to receive the great Revelation of past and future happenings: John the Baptist, of whom Jesus said, "Verily I say unto you, Among them that are born of women there hath not risen a greater than John the Baptist."

And from The Revelation of John, p 161, of the same Work:

> "Moreover, John received The Revelation not on the island of Patmos in the Aegean Sea during his earth-life, but after his earthly death – on the Isle of Patmos that lies in The Spiritual Realm, even above the Paradise of the human spirits. He passed it on to a human being on Earth *who was spiritually open for it,* and who translated it into earthly words. Thus the Book with seven seals, The Revelation of John, *was handed down to us.*"

Here we thus note that the "mansion" of John the Baptist [the "none greater"] lies far above human origins. Hence the reason, also, why *only he*, and not an ordinary priest at the time of Jesus, could baptise **The Son of God**.

Now, if it *is* believed that *John the Disciple* received 'The Revelation' on the island of Patmos in the 'Aegean', why did he not simply travel to each of the communities to deliver the messages? He was certainly close enough, would have been well respected in the communities, and therefore probably believed. Notwithstanding historical notations in some Bibles that John was *exiled* to Patmos because of his faith and in that case could not travel *from* there, his *followers* certainly could have. For we know that the four Evangelists had many. We note that the Apostle Paul journeyed to all those "churches" to preach, so they were certainly well-established.

Given that John was an especial and faithful 'servant' who would have regarded The Revelation as a singularly-important Message from God, he would surely have found a way whereby those clearly 'crucial messages' would have been delivered to the named communities. That is, of course, *if The Revelation really was about the "7 Churches" in existence there at that time.* There would not then be the need for messengers to descend into the physical part of Creation to utter proclamations.

The question therefore remains: Did those small cities warrant such an especial visit, and/or is it still yet to happen? But where are the names now? As we have noted, the cities, for the most part, no longer exist in their original form. Notwithstanding the fact that the overall region saw the birth of great religions – from where much recorded proclamation and prophecy is derived – such a notion nonetheless still focuses on a very small geographical area. And, moreover, on a part of the planet containing just a very small number of people.

The next question we might ask if we follow this improbable thread through is: What does it mean if it *was* fulfilled in some way, even though no record exists of powerful Messengers from on high visiting and proclaiming to whole communities? Surely the word would have gotten out and been recorded by someone, even if not by those in the actual communities who, however, would have experienced what would surely have been a stupendous event. After all, only a relatively few people saw the Star of Bethlehem and the "miracles" of Jesus. Fewer still saw Him in His *other-world body* prior to ascending to 'The Father' to become **One** again with **Him**! Yet all of that is accepted by many hundreds of millions today.

Can we not also accept that *if* such a major spiritual event *had* taken place *"seven times"* in such a small area, would not the whole of the known world have been "buzzing"? But — silence![3]

On this particular issue, then, uncertainty in 'theological treatises' and the like on the true meaning of the "Seven Churches in Asia-Minor" persists among the 'University-learned' and layman to this day. Again we ask the key question: *If* we accept the popular Christian view that John the Disciple received The Revelation on the island of Patmos but could not travel to the named "communities" by virtue of his exile there, why did not *others* close to him *deliver* the messages to the "7 Churches" after John *received* them?

We know that the Disciples were instructed by Jesus to a far greater level of knowledge than most human beings, even to *this* point in time. So having been instructed in the far greater expanse of Creation itself – *"In My Father's House there are many Mansions"* – the Disciples were well aware of impending future events because they had all been told in no uncertain terms **by The Son of God Himself** what would come upon humanity at the "completion of the times" – *our* **times** – and why! We can also know this if we wish to, simply because it was recorded by them, and we can read that forewarning discourse today in virtually any Bible.

However, even though the messages in 'The Revelation' were recorded "for all time", it was reserved *for a later time*, a future time – *our* **present time** – for its sure clarification and wider dissemination, when the true knowledge of Creation would be given to humanity as promised. Once recognised, that new knowledge could be more readily understood by present-day man through the twin Disciplines of **Science and Theology**. Thus, via the *relative* human dimensions of man in his *duality*, i.e., **Intellect and Spirit**.

Note:

[The astute and spiritually-aware reader will have well recognised by this point that under the perfect outworking of The Laws of Creation – in particular The Laws of "Rebirth" and "Reciprocal Action" – a point in time is set where all cycles previously unresolved between individuals and even whole peoples would need to be 'closed off'. In order for such 'closures' to be *fully understood* by all those "peoples" at that ordained time, however, the evolutionary path of humankind *should* have reached its zenith for all by then. That *"then"*, that zenith, is *this* present time. Therefore, the paths of religion, philosophy, science, and even the social order of all Nations and peoples, *should* have travelled a road of unfolding enlightenment founded on the great spiritual truths – given in a carefully-guided, step-by-step process through the line of Prophets and Truth-Bringers Called from Above – to culminate in this present time where *all* was ordained to be revealed.]

Hence the need for empirical scientists and 'religious theologians', particularly, by this time to have subjugated their singularly-egoistic positions *ostensibly* providing the *primary* truth for all of humankind, and recognise that both Disciplines had an equal part to play in leading

---

[3]Historically we know that the revolt of the Jews in 66 AD and the subsequent destruction of Jerusalem by Titus and his legions in 70 AD may have been initiated in part by the belief at the time that Jesus would return *shortly after His crucifixion* as the King/Messiah to inaugurate the millennium of peace and defeat the Roman oppressor. That this did not happen clearly shows that *that* interpretation by the religious leaders of the day was completely wrong. Indeed, they paid very dearly for that presumption with the wholesale slaughter of almost the entire population of Jerusalem. The legacy of that kind of great error continues on in theological circles today in the ongoing uncertainty about what The Bible actually states and means about Jesus ostensibly returning and bringing with Him an Apocalyptic Judgement and great destruction around this present time.

global humanity to complete and final knowledge of its true origin and purpose. Unfortunately, however, the window of opportunity for any kind of real accommodation in an harmonious and fully-knowledgeable working together to enlighten humanity has probably now closed.

And because it is primarily **untruth** that "educating-academia" have fed to the masses; at this decisive point in humankind's journey that task has now fallen to a few *radicals*, a few *"voices in the wilderness"*, to *reveal the errors* and thereby **proclaim for**, and **lead to**: **The All-Truth!** In concert with that sure proclamation, we herewith lead you, the reader, to the knowledge of:

11.2 Sir Isaac Newton's "Plan of The World"

So, if the messages were not actually for those ancient communities, what might it all mean? In order to understand this great question, a related one stands out as also being particularly important. It is the necessary understanding of where we, as human beings on planet Earth in the Material World, *actually stand* in relation to: **The Creator!**

> For **He** surely cannot stand in the same part of **His Material Creation** as we do;
> i.e., as a Presence or Power actually residing **in** the physical universes.
> **And neither does He!**

Yet there should be an inherent wish on our part *to want to know* where we do *actually* stand! Do we, upon earthly death, – as so many apparently believe – simply transit from Earth and be immediately in "paradise" and thus in the presence of God? That seems to be the general, broad belief of the three major monotheistic religions. We, however, already know the answer to that question. For if it *was* possible to be in The Almighty's immediate presence, if it *could* be so, then that would very illogically place Him quite close to we human beings of Earth. Yet our critical examination of The Book of Genesis and the *two Creations* clearly *negates* such a view of a close and convenient, personalised God. ***Simple logic should tell us that anyway.***

A connection between the "seven assemblies" and where we stand in relation to The Almighty might not be immediately apparent, or even seem logical. However, the ***true understanding*** of what the "7 Churches" ***actually means*** offers precisely that ***correct knowledge and relationship.*** The **correct** interpretation tells us what they [the 7 Churches or assemblies] **actually are** as a complete, **overall**, entity. And what it [each assembly] **is** in its singular, **individual**, form.

We have determined that this "mystery" is not solely a religious question only, and that *certain* Disciplines within the scientific "communities" as well need to think long and hard about what it all might actually mean. Since we contend that purely intellectual seeking alone – from either of the Disciplines of 'Science' or 'Theology' – will not permit any unveiling of the *true* meaning of the "7 Churches in Asia", we need to take the boldest possible step in order to "find". By *merging* the two Disciplines and using the clarified intellect guided by the spirit – as we have previously done with other key questions in this Work – we will achieve exactly that goal. We will, thereby, indeed discover a truly marvellous revelation; **the very revelation that Newton himself sought!** A revelation which is literally mind-blowing in its ramifications for science and for **all** religions, permitting the mind, intellect, soul and spirit to soar in exultant recognition.

> Therefore: If recognised and ***understood correctly***, the senses will reel before the ***true meaning*** of *"The 7 Churches in Asia-Minor"*. For it will "***completely***

shatter" all current scientific and theological ideas about the **actual** nature and **extent** of the universe/s *deriving from **either*** astronomy or religion.

It also reveals therewith the huge importance of The Revelation itself. The almost incomprehensible import of such a vastly overpowering, yet *spiritually-empowering,* extra-world view of where we human beings **actually stand** in Creation is virtually life-changing in that singular moment of **genuine recognition.**

To that end, the intuitive insights of **Pope Benedict XVI**, **Einstein** and even **Galileo** – we already have **Newton** with us – are exactly appropriate for this Chapter revealing 'Isaac **Newton's'** **"Plan of The World"**. More especially for singularly-focussed and perhaps hard-nosed cosmologists who might cross the path of this Work, the following *crucial insights* of one noted *theologian* and three of the **greatest foundational-scientists ever** offer an especial help for *present-day* cosmologists on **how** to understand **"The Revelation of the Cosmos"** — herein!

So between the three great *foundational space scientists* – never mind their many *other* great talents – we firstly have **Galileo** re-anchoring and thus rescuing the truth of the **Planetary System** from an egotistical and tyrannical 'religion' masquerading as the sole voice and representative of the profound and sublime Truth placed in 'its' care, yet which nonetheless cynically distorted that Truth for earthly ends. **Newton's** seminal discoveries emerge as *especially crucial* to the furtherance of 'space knowledge'. His **"Law of Gravitation"** allowed for further discoveries of great import. And, of course, **Einstein**; believed by some to be the greatest mind of all. His **"Theory of Relativity"** gave space-science especial keys to understanding much more about the cosmos than was previously possible.

However, whilst these *undeniably great scientists* ostensibly worked *solely* under the ethos of scientific-empiricism for their time, *present-day* scientists really need to recognise the clear fact that those three *especial men* obviously stood *way outside* the 'square box' of their contemporaries. For by virtue of the fact that they *were* so far ahead of their 'peers' – apart from the necessary empirical aspect of mathematics to prove their 'discoveries' – intuitional insight must have played a very crucial part in allowing them *in the first place* to *see* or *perceive* what others could not. It could be said, therefore, that their seminal discoveries and life's work *almost* placed them in the "lone voices in the wilderness" category.

From that necessary foundation and the amazing discoveries since; should we now say?:
Space! The <u>Final</u> Frontier!!! — [Exclamation mark/s!]

Or; as Newton has insightfully intimated *for* present-day cosmologists and 'space-science' and with which we unequivocally concur; should it rather be?:
Space? The Final <u>Frontier</u>??? — [Question mark/s?]

Specifically in concert with the great intuitive perception of Newton – and perhaps even *high spiritual guidance* in *his* case – [but also aided by Pope Benedict's spiritual insight] in this Chapter we reveal the final and greatest *space discovery* of all:
— **Sir Isaac Newton's "Plan of The World."** —
Whether believed or not, space scientists should at least be *intrigued enough* to *wonder* at what Newton was *really* searching for. Given the very radical nature of what we will now unveil – and as we have stated elsewhere in this Work – it is important to reiterate the nonetheless accepted fact that Newton **was not a deluded fool.** And no scientist today would dare label him deluded, at least not publicly.

So: Of the *two* possibilities about 'space' – and only **one** can be right – the *correct* position and thus the *greatest knowledge of all* about the **"cosmos"** equates to:
Space? The Final <u>Frontier</u>??? — [Question mark/s?]

"Modern scientific reason quite simply has to accept the rational structure of matter and the correspondence between *our spirit and the prevailing rational structures of nature as a given*, on which its methodology has to be based. Yet the question *why* this has to be so, is a *real* question, and one which has to be remanded *by the natural sciences* to *other* modes and planes of thought – to *philosophy* and *theology*."

(Pope Benedict XVI. Regensburg, 2004)

"Though religion may be that which determines the goal, it has, nevertheless learned from science, in the broadest sense, what means will contribute to the attainment of the goals it has set up. *But science can only be created by those who are* thoroughly imbued *with the aspiration toward* **truth** *and* **understanding**."

"Science without religion is lame, religion without science is blind."

(Einstein. Ideas and Opinions, p.42-3)

On the relationship between science and religion, Einstein notes:

"Intelligence makes clear to us the interrelation of means and ends. But mere thinking *cannot give us* a sense of the ultimate and fundamental ends. To make clear these fundamental ends and valuations, and to set them fast in the emotional life of the individual, seems to me precisely the most important function which religion has to perform in the social life of man. And if one asks whence derives the *authority* of such fundamental ends, since they cannot be stated and justified merely by reason, one can only answer: they come into being *not through demonstration* **but through revelation**, *through the* medium *of powerful personalities*. One must not attempt to justify them, but rather **to sense their nature simply and clearly**."

Though a very great mind in both the intuitive and intellectual sense, Einstein's sometimes almost 'tongue-in-cheek' quips nonetheless hold profound truths for a *perceptive* reader. For example:

"I never came upon any of my discoveries through the process of *rational thinking*."

(All emphases mine.)

Galileo: Regarded by some as the first true scientist. Upon his discovery and recognition that the Planetary Model Copernicus proposed was correct, he was forced to recant by the Inquisition. He is said to have muttered under his breath: "But it [the Earth] does move." Noting the Church's obsession to have Bible Scripture support Ptolemy's erroneous view of the Planetary System; anecdotally, Galileo evidently thought that whilst The Bible *was* 'the Word of God':

"...it was not a good astronomy book".

The huge strides made in astronomy since his death in 1642 would surely have astounded him – as it does modern man. However, notwithstanding all the marvellous discoveries since, Galileo was not correct in believing that astronomy was not in The Bible. As the overall thrust of this complete Work unequivocally states:
The Bible is a Primary Work of Foundational-Science! —

It was thus left to **Newton** to *seed in the minds of modern astronomers* the *golden key* to discovering the *final revelation* of the *true nature* of the cosmos. However, as the great man Einstein intimates, rational thinking will not do the job. Revelation and *spiritual intuition*, however, in concert with a *clarified intellect*, most certainly will.

As previously stated, since we have addressed the other key questions from a fundamentally different and far-reaching paradigm, this particular one, too, can only be logically understood by using the same method. However, because The Book of Revelation primarily reveals insights into vast **Spiritual** vistas and events that must necessarily *transcend* intellectual interpretations so, similarly – and by a considerable margin – must we also *vastly expand our human frames of reference* to answer and understand the meaning of "The 7 Churches in Asia Minor". For we contend, absolutely, that the premise we postulate is correct; that the question under scrutiny here is *not at all about earthly communities or churches*. The fact that those 'churches' did once exist has clearly confused the issue.

Where, then, might these places be? No satisfactory answer has publicly emerged from the Jewish faith, the Christian religions or the Institutions of Theology. In any case it is not about guesswork or theories, but about the knowledge of the outworking of **The Laws of Creation** and the concomitant knowledge of the *structure* of **The Creation** that has issued from the very outworking of those immutable Laws. Therefore, there *really is* a correct answer; there is *always* a correct answer! So what does that imply?

In summary, since we have concluded that the answer is *not connected* with the names of the "churches" in the stated general location of Asia-Minor on *Earth* in ancient times, the so-named "assemblies" must therefore represent something *entirely different*. That logically places *both* the communities *and* the delivery of each specific address by a "Messenger of the Lord" [the Guardian Angel of each assembly] *somewhere other than* the Earth, in a time *different to the times* when those *named* communities once existed.

Thus far we have sparred with possibilities and ideas about the meaning of the "7 Churches or assemblies in Asia-Minor". If, as we unequivocally state, the 'assemblies' are *not* on Earth – but nonetheless still exist – they would therefore *have to be*, quite logically, in the *World of Matter*. **For this is where "The Revelation" came *down* to; where we *live* in our obvious *physicality*.**

However, a seamless transition from current uncertain views to sure certainty in an instantly-recognisable answer is not a simple "fix" in this case, for it requires a huge and fundamental leap of truly gigantic proportions *into a completely new paradigm*. Moreover, it is not a paradigm that is simply and solely religious in nature and import. In reinforcement for this particular "revelation", *it also encompasses astronomy, astrophysics and cosmology on the most stupendous scale*.

Most unfortunately, however, a major problem preventing a wider outlook in the present lies with the so-called "academic elite" from the world of astronomy and cosmology. For *they* are the "experts" in their field, and only *they* are supposed to know. Notwithstanding how incomprehensibly vast the "known universe" is; nonetheless, it is the general inability of cosmologists to recognise that there is *much, much more to Creation than just the physical universe we see in the night sky* that effectively *suppresses* any wider vista. Since *they* accept and teach a *smaller* Material World than is *actually the case*, by educational default so, also, *must the greater mass of humanity*.

Despite having radio telescopes and the Hubble space telescope to now peer far further into the great expanse we euphemistically label 'space' – which concomitantly offers us truly marvellous and stunning images of ever new discoveries of the cosmos – *all of that does not even begin to get close to the actual nature and size of just the Material Part of Creation*.

*Astronomers and cosmologists, **as a global group**, do not yet know this to be the case.*

In an earlier Chapter, we stated that Creation and Evolution are necessarily one and the same. In reality, there is no separation. The old rivalries between science and religion are just that – rivalries. Rivalries based on the narrow parameters that each side promotes for its own edification. With regard to the question this Chapter examines, there is no actual separation there, either. Spiritual truth and earthly science were ordained to be *mutually inclusive under the parameters of **The Laws of Creation**.*

So, to arrive at the point of sure and conscious knowing about the meaning of the "7 Churches", we need to now extrapolate our present view of the physical universe/s upward and outward. Firstly from the immediate environs of our Solar System, and thenceforth undertake a mathematical journey into distances so vast as to be totally **incomprehensible**. Even the word itself does not nearly suffice to describe the immensity of just our "home galaxy", let alone the stupendous nature of what is *observable* beyond that; what science *believes* is the complete universe.

We have already explained the process of the formation of the various levels of Creation in broad outline. Now we need to do the same here, but solely with the *physical universes* of the *Material* part of Creation. In this case by using the mathematical unit of the 'light-year' as our measuring staff.

11.2.1 The 'Mathematics' of Cosmology: The "Big-Bang" and "Inflation" Model

We should seriously note that on the question of the very much vaunted 'Laws of Physics' – which can *supposedly* explain *all* events and processes – the current 'scientific mindset' centred on the *validity* of those laws, particulary in cosmology, *fail completely* when confronted by the 'perfectly natural' cosmological *reality-paradigms* of quasars and pulsars. The frightening raw power of a 'gamma ray burst' from an exploding star, along with the dreaded 'black holes' now known to exist at the center of most galaxies, add their astounding measure to what is really a totally inadequate 'human-scientific' struggle to even *begin* to understand such power.

Why should that be? Why should the mathematics of cosmology, which has answered many 'space questions' thus far, now fail in the face of those truly amazing spectacles? For astrophysicists, could it be nothing more than just "**The Error of Scientism**" we have previously quoted and reiterate further on in this Chapter? Has earth-science reached a point where it is simply 'outgunned' by cosmological processes far beyond any human empirical understanding at this time because *its* 'current' level of mathematics is completely inadequate for such an especial degree of elucidation of what must nonetheless be **perfectly natural processes** – albeit, however, on a truly gigantic scale?

As we have stated many times thus far, **The Spiritual Laws of Creation** alone hold the final keys to understanding the true nature of 'The Universe/s'. Earth-based university-mathematics, whilst necessary for most 'material' applications, are a very poor cousin to **The Law of Numbers**. It is thus the far *Higher Laws* which *entirely govern* all events and processes in "**The Creations**".

So let us examine the 'mathematics of cosmology' to begin with, and then travel far further with **The Law of Numbers** to learn the **"The Plan of The World"**; the 'secret' which Newton sought in the pages of that premier Foundational-book of Science: – **The Bible**. So:

One light-year represents the distance that light covers travelling in a vacuum for a period of one year – approximately 9.4607×10^{12} kilometres (5.878×10^{12} miles, at a speed of 186.000 miles per second).

Our journey starts, naturally, from Earth. It is the third planet revolving around a relatively small sun in a Solar System residing at the outer edges of a galaxy designated the Milky Way Galaxy. It contains 100,000 million odd stars to which the sun of our Solar System belongs. Even travelling at light-speed, sunlight takes 8 minutes to travel the 150,000,000 km before reaching us. The same light travels 5 more hours before striking the planet Pluto at the farthest edge of our Solar System. And 4.3 light-years later, or 40 trillion kilometres away, it reaches our nearest stellar neighbour, Alpha Centauri.

Our galaxy, a disc-shaped collection of stars with the Earth about a third of the way out from the centre, was once thought to be the entire universe until discoveries in the 1920s revealed a far greater expanse beyond it. Today we know it is only one of billions of galaxies. An observer looking at the Milky Way from Earth is actually looking edge-on into the Galaxy. In a broad-brush time-sweep, the Galaxy started to form some 10,000 to 14,000 million years ago, and its oldest stars are estimated to be perhaps up to 15 billion years old. Our sun takes about 230 million years to complete one journey round the centre. Our galaxy is about *100,000 light-years in diameter*.

Beyond the "Milky Way" can be located galaxies in every direction. We are part of a loosely bound cluster of some 20 galaxies called "the local group". From the centre to its outer boundaries is roughly 2,000,000 light-years – *4 million light-years across*.

The next larger formation we belong to is known as a "local supercluster". Clusters of galaxies – like armadas of ships – congregate in superclusters. The closest cluster to our local group is some 50 million light-years away, near the centre of our local supercluster. From the centre to its outer boundaries is roughly 75,000,000 light-years – *150 million light-years across*.

The only step left to take now with the present level of earthly knowledge derived from astronomy and cosmology, is into what is termed "the known universe" – the largest expanse by far. It is that of the farthest reaches of the universe which can be observed by the use of optical or radio telescopes. Our universe is stated to be isotropic in nature and form which means it looks the same in every direction. Quasars are the most distant objects observed. Each of the brightest quasars emits the energy of hundreds of galaxies from a volume far smaller than our Milky Way Galaxy. The furthest quasars are stated to be rushing away from us at 90% the speed of light. The "known universe" was, until quite recently, believed to be about *40,000,000,000 light-years across*. The most recent estimates to the *edge* of the universe, at least the visible part of it, places it at *100 billion trillion kilometres away*. Further recent estimates now puts the *size* of our universe at roughly *100 billion light-years across*.

So how did that vast, utterly incomprehensible expanse come into being?

The question of how the universe came into existence only gained real traction from the early 20th century. Notwithstanding Newton's crucial contribution to the science of astronomy, still relevant today – NASA acknowledges Newtonian physics as the foundation for its space programme – it was not until the larger telescopes and more powerful computers were developed that astronomers began to get a sense of how it might have begun and how it all might work. At this present time the 'Big-Bang theory' holds sway. Other ideas have been mooted and subsequently discarded. Various possibilities have encompassed an 'ever-expanding universe', the 'steady state' theory and an 'open universe' – whatever these terms *really* mean. Currently thought to have brought the universe into existence, the rather impossible-to-grasp sums of the "Big-Bang" explaining how it all began and developed, at the very least make fascinating reading.

On the question of the merits or otherwise of the 'Big-Bang', the reader must obviously decide for himself. Current thought on the how and why of the universe, even though able to now answer many previously unanswerable questions, is nevertheless still *solely-derived* from just an *empirical* paradigm.

As we have stated often, because the present level of "scientific learning" is not based on a **Creation-Law** foundation to begin with, it does not recognise – let alone even begin to take in – the far *greater* expanse of the *non-material* worlds. Science is therefore *unable* to derive final answers about the *physical universes* for, with its *present* level of knowledge, it can only engage with the 'singular universe' which the "Hubble" has mapped. Not possessing the requisite knowledge and thus recognition of the far greater and higher paradigm encompassing *all* the *non-material Realms* upwards to our Spiritual Origins, means that cosmological science has effectively shackled itself to a very constrained, solely-empirical, physical 'box'.

> We sincerely hope that at least *one* cosmologist *somewhere* will intuitively perceive the *Truth* of Newton's very sure recognition, and thus smash through the walls of *modern-day* cosmology's self-constructed and very myopic 'box'.

Notwithstanding our sure statements here; to explain the origin of the universe according to more recent analyses, the basic mathematics of the Big-Bang theory nonetheless proposes something called "The theory of inflation". It states that, "...the entire visible universe grew from a speck far smaller than a proton, to a nugget the size of a grapefruit, almost instantaneously, when the whole thing was 0.0000000000000000000000000000000001 second old." [Have I even quoted the correct number of zeroes here?]

> (Time, June 2001. Feature article –
> "How the Universe Will End")

According to the "inflation model" the incomprehensible immensity of the universe came from virtually nowhere in an *instant*. So small that you would have needed a microscope to find it. The inflation theory was proposed in 1979 by Alan Guth, then a junior particle physicist at Stanford University. It holds that within "...a fraction of a moment after the dawn of creation[4] the universe underwent a sudden dramatic expansion. It inflated."

The whole episode probably lasted no more than one million million million million millionths of a second – but it transformed the universe from something that could be held to something at least 10,000,000,000,000,000,000,000,000 times larger. According to Guth's theory, gravity came into being at one-ten millionth of a trillionth of a trillionth of a trillionth of a second. In a single moment, we were endowed with a universe that was at least 100 billion light years across. Feasible? Sounds impossible. For how can one individual second be logically and understandably carved up into such infinitesimal part-seconds? Anyway, who on this Earth can finally say?

It is interesting to note the opinion of other astronomers, such as Martin Rees.

> 'Martin Rees, Britain's Astronomer Royal, believes that there are many universes, possibly an infinite number, each with different attributes, in different combinations, and that we simply live in one that combines things in a way that allows us to exist... Rees maintains that six numbers in particular govern our universe, and that if any of these values were changed, even very slightly, things could not be as they are. For example, for the universe to exist as it does requires that hydrogen be converted to helium in a precise but comparatively stately manner – specifically in a way that converts seven one-thousandths of its mass to energy.
>
> Lower that value very slightly – from 0.007 per cent [sic, should be 0.7] to 0.006 per cent [sic, should be 0.6] say – and no transformation could take place; the

---

[4]Again this only refers to *just the Material Worlds*.

universe would consist of hydrogen and nothing else. Raise the value very slightly – to 0.008 per cent [sic, should be 0.8] – and bonding would be so wildly prolific that the hydrogen would long since have been exhausted. With the slightest tweaking of the numbers in either case, the universe as we know and need it would not be here.' [Figures clarified from "Seven Wonders of the Cosmos", p.200 (See Biblio.)]

(How to Make a Universe. Reader's Digest.
August, 2004)

What we thus clearly note here is a *perfected state* for life to be able to exist at all, and a stupendously huge "home", in the physical sense, for it to exist in. The Perfection of Creation overall surely precludes any notion that it all emerged by "accident".

The question of what might happen if we were *able* to travel to the edge of the universe and look beyond it is an interesting though perhaps ultimately pointless 'scientific quandary'. Nonetheless, Einstein's Theory of Relativity holds that the universe bends in a way that cannot adequately be imagined so we would, even after travelling in a straight line to the edge, eventually arrive back at our starting point. His theory suggests that space curves in a way that allows it to be boundless – ***but finite***. So the physical universe we see and *believe* we know **is finite!**

'Physicist and Nobel laureate Steven Weinberg explains that space cannot even properly be said to be expanding, because "Solar Systems and galaxies are not expanding." Rather, the galaxies are rushing apart. It is all something of a *challenge to intuition.* For us the universe goes only as far as light has travelled in the billions of years since the universe has formed. This visible universe – the universe we know and can talk about – is a million million million million (that's 1000,000,000,000,000,000,000,000) kilometres across. According to most theories, however, the universe at large – the meta-universe, as it is sometimes called – is vastly roomier still. According to Rees, the number of light years to the edge of this larger, unseen universe would be written not "...with ten zeroes, not even with a hundred, but with millions". In short, there's more space than you can imagine already without going to the trouble of trying to envision some additional beyond."

(How to Make a Universe, Reader's Digest.
Italics mine.)

To achieve the incredible expansion proposed by the "theory of inflation" – from an invisible speck to a structure billions of miles across in a fraction of an instant – the speed of light is very obviously totally inadequate. Einstein's Theory of Relativity, however, seemingly permits the mathematics to fit a "faster-than-light" possibility. From Time Magazine, June 2001: Feature article; "How the Universe Will End".

"An equally unsettling implication is that the universe is pervaded with a strange sort of "antigravity", a concept originally proposed, and later abandoned, by Einstein as the greatest blunder of his life."[5]

This force, which has lately been dubbed "dark energy", isn't just keeping the expansion from slowing down, it's making the universe fly apart faster and faster all the time, like a rocket ship with the throttle wide open. It gets stranger still. Not only does "dark energy" swamp ordinary gravity but an invisible substance known

---

[5] Adam Riess, a Space Telescope Science Institute astronomer, has seemingly helped prove that Einstein may have been right in the first place; a mysterious antigravity force that acts like Einstein's cosmological constant is evidently quite real.

to scientists as "dark matter" also seems to outweigh the ordinary stuff of stars, planets and people by a factor of 10 to 1. "Not only are we not at the centre of the universe," University of California, Santa Cruz, astrophysical theorist Joel Primack has commented, "...we aren't even made of the same stuff the universe is."

These discoveries raise more questions than they answer. For example, just because scientists know dark matter is there doesn't mean they understand what it really is. Same goes for dark energy. "If you thought the universe was hard to comprehend before," says University of Chicago astrophysicist Michael Turner, "...then you'd better take some smart pills, because it's only going to get worse."

From two fairly recent publications, we have noted and quoted the opinions and theories of some key academics in the field of cosmology and astronomy etc.. So it seems the "Big Bang" is the theory that is current, and ongoing research appears to support and strengthen it. Thus, from an infinitesimal speck, the huge and completely incomprehensible size and mass of the universe was, by cosmologists' reckoning, "suddenly there".

The key question that obviously arises is: How could this incredible mass emerge from virtually nothing? Even if we use a standard analogy of growth – say that of a human being where, at conception, the potential is simply that of a very tiny, fertilised egg but where the full potential unfolds to adulthood – it is on a scale that is easy to understand. What about a very tiny seedling which might grow to become an immense tree? That, too, is easy to comprehend. Not the 'Big Bang' scenario, however.

The physical form of the human being eventually dies, decays and reverts to its component parts; earth to earth, dust to dust – as will the giant tree. And the mass of the Earth, even with billions of creatures living and dying over aeons, remains the same. What about the total mass of *billions* of galaxies, each with their *billions* of suns, however? Can we really believe that *that* absolutely incomprehensible expanse could somehow explode out of something far smaller than a single dot on this page in the micro-millisecond time-frame proposed? Then very much later, in an equally incomprehensible future point in time, contract or implode, and squeeze itself back into something invisible, except through a microscope? It all seems too impossible, too strange, to *be* possible.

A "white dwarf" is surely a good example; a very small, extremely dense star where the atoms in it have been broken up and the various parts packed tightly together with almost no waste space so that the density rises to millions of times that of water. According to scientific calculations, a spoonful of white dwarf material would weigh many tons. Neutron stars, made up principally or completely of neutrons, have even greater density. Clearly, individual stars can be compressed to an incredibly small size. And in a black hole where not even light can escape, even more so. Multiply the total mass of literally *billions of* **galaxies** *worth*, however, and how do they fit back into that point of almost nothing?

Irrespective of what may seem to be theoretically correct from the point of view of earth-science, every event that occurs can only take place within strict and absolutely lawful parameters. Therefore, is the Big Bang theory correct? Deriving from theoretical analyses, empirical observations and mathematical calculations, is science right with regard to how it all came to be? Or has something critical been missed or not understood?

11.2.2   The "Big-Bang": A Problematic Theory

Thus far in this book, you, the reader, will have encountered concepts and explanations about the key questions to life that are vastly different to the standard educational fare fed to the student body of humankind. And in this Chapter you will have certainly noted the clear fact that this writer finds the present state of general cosmological theory centred on the Big Bang illogical, and therefore untenable.

For cosmologists and astronomers, mathematics must fit any proposed theory, otherwise the model must be 'tossed out'. Given the scale and time-frame of the life of the universe/s – unlike the mathematics required for architecture and engineering – 'cosmological maths' must enter a very *different* realm. The necessary expansion of theoretical analyses certainly allow for radical proposals here, but the associated mathematics must somewhere, somehow, have it all 'make sense' in order 'to make it fit'.

Again, unlike architecture, which – if the maths are wrong might see the building collapse – the 'mathematical playground' of the cosmos will not produce 'collapsed buildings' for astronomers. Nonetheless, if something is not correct, it is forever incorrect; or wrong!

As we must reinforce often, as long as astronomers remain locked to the notion that the be-all and end-all of human endeavour and existence is tied solely to just a Material-world paradigm, ***they will never ever arrive at the correct picture.***

> And therefore never recognise what the great scientist Sir Isaac Newton *intuitively* understood:
> That the universal reality of **"The Law of Numbers"** inherent in **"The Book of Revelation"** can – if present-day astronomers/cosmologists were *also* intuitively *open* to such recognitions – actually reveal for them and the earth-science of astronomy **The Truth** of **"The Plan Of The World!"**

In April of 2009, the Telegraph Group news agency featured a spectacular picture of the collapse of a huge star. The most distant object ever seen in the universe at 13 billion light years, it is so far away that its 'gamma ray burst of light' has taken almost the entire age of the universe to reach us. [Gamma ray bursts are the most luminous explosions in the universe and are the afterglow of dying stars.] Scientists believe the 'burst' was caused by a *massive* star collapsing and exploding at the end of its life, leaving a black hole. Yet we are told that the star which triggered this event, designated GRB 090423, was only 640 million years old.

Was this massive star 'unstable', and thus 'died young'? Or did it live out what would be a normal life span for such a large mass? Professor Edo Berger, from the Havard Smithsonian Centre for Astrophysics in Cambridge, Massachusetts, who also studied the burst, said:

> "We now have the first direct proof that the young universe was teeming with exploding stars and newly born black holes only a few hundred million years after the Big Bang."

In the ordinary course of processes cosmic we are told that a *small* star will live longer than a *massive* star. Simple logic would *seem* to suggest that the opposite would be the case. However, a larger body will burn off its *fuel supply* at a faster rate, thus leading to a 'short' life. Our sun has not only lived for 4.5 *billion* years and counting versus just 640 *million*, but will be around for a while yet. In that single fact lies the *key* insight into not only *why* our sun is the size that it is, but *therefore why* we *concomitantly inherit* a long time-span for life *down here*.

The long evolutionary processes we needed to undergo required a time-period commensurate with not only our *physical* development, but more importantly our *spiritual maturation*. Therefore, only a small sun could provide the time required. So, was it all a cosmic *accident*? Or did it come into being through **Divine Ordination** gifting us conscious life? Thus: **A Plan!** Deriving from the logical analyses throughout this Work, our unequivocal conviction embraces the latter.

On the question of a problematic 'Big Bang'; according to **Daniel Pendick**, Associate Editor of **Astronomy Magazine**, much evidence exists to support the 'standard model', such as the 'radiation afterglow' from the Big Bang, known as the cosmic microwave background

[CMB]. Maps of the CMB from the Cosmic Background Explorer [COBE] and, more recently, the Wilkinson Microwave Anisotropy Probe [WMAP] confirm a number of Big Bang cosmology predictions. However, trouble spots, such as the true nature of dark matter – the glue that binds galaxies together – remain. Strange patterns in the CMB challenge one of the foundations of the standard model, inflation theory. The 'standard model', moreover, requires innovative hypotheses 'to make it all fit'.

One of the strangest proposed is 'dark energy'. The notion of dark energy offered a ready explanation for accelerating cosmic expansion, yet 'creates nearly as many problems as it solves'. Lawrence Krauss, a theoretical physicist and cosmologist at Arizona State University, says:

> "When it comes to dark energy, we know that it exists, but we don't know anything about it."

> ("Is the Big Bang in trouble?"
> Astronomy, April 09. p.48)

Whilst WMAP's detailed picture of the CMB, the supernova observations, and 'various surveys of the distant universe have advanced cosmology at light speed', those discoveries did not get to the heart of the matter.

> "We've been so successful that the questions we're asking are so deep that they may remain unanswerable for some time to come – and maybe forever. We don't understand the model we have. It's completely inexplicable."

> (Krauss, p.48)

The concept of 'inflation' resolved fundamental theoretical problems for Big Bang cosmology. Blossoming into 'multiple versions', which according to science rests on a '*solid* foundation of *theoretical* physics' [surely there sits an amazing 'contradiction in terms'], there nonetheless remains an unresolved question. That is the question that this writer – who is neither an astronomer nor a scientist, and who has no 'letters' after his name – states cosmology must unequivocally answer: 'How do we know inflation really happened?'
Gary Hinshaw, an astrophysicist at NASA's Goddard Space Flight Center in Greenbelt, Maryland, and a member of the team that designed WMAP says:

> "The idea that there was a period of exponential growth is by far the best explanation we have of the current data. ... But the details of inflation, we have very little grasp of."

> (Hinshaw, p.49)

Theoretically, inflation generated ripples in space-time called 'gravitational waves', which would have left 'an imprint on the CMB'. Even if an 'imprint' were found, that might not be sufficient to 'dispel all doubt', according to Krauss.

> "The issue is not whether it is consistent with observations. ... The question is how to falsify it. What could you observe that would be *different* if inflation *did not happen*? It is a beautiful, natural explanation of everything we see, **but that doesn't mean it's right**."

> (Krauss, p.49. All emphases mine.)

The discovery of dark matter helps cosmologists understand how galaxies and galaxy clusters hold together. In fact, dark matter's gravitational influence keeps them from flying apart. However, whilst it fits the standard model, no one has yet found a particle of the stuff. An alternative to dark matter, called 'modified gravity theory', holds that gravity behaves differently 'out there among the galaxies'. Even though this theory accounts for some of 'the same observations as dark matter', it nonetheless faces a 'major hurdle': Einstein's general theory of relativity. Einstein's theory explains the universe more comprehensively than 'modified gravity' does.

'Astronomy' reports that data culled from the CMB support key aspects of the standard model, in particular a snapshot of the seeds of cosmic structure that evolved after inflation. British theoretical physicist, Stephen Hawking, 'proclaimed the COBE satellite's first glimpse of the CMB' as, [very *materially* and thus *very wrongly* in our *seriously unequivocal* view]:

> "...the discovery of the century, if not *all time*."

> (p.49. Italics mine.)

'But nothing is beyond question in the standard model. Since WMAP released its first set of data in 2003, scientists have found patterns in the CMB that seem at odds with the standard model'. 'If someone finds a one-in-a-million weirdness in the CMB – highly unlikely to be an accident – it might suggest something is wrong with inflation theory'.

> "The consequences are *potentially profound*. The large-scale alignments in the CMB might be *inconsistent* with *inflation*."

> (Hinshaw, p.50. Italics mine.)

So; what fills the 'empty' parts of space, the incomprehensible areas in-between the equally incomprehensible galaxies?

The standard model hypothesises 'dark energy' as the intrinsic "vacuum energy" of empty space. This notion postulates that as space expands, the density of dark energy [and its consequential 'repulsive-effect'] remains constant, while matter [and its gravitational pull] thins out. Cosmic expansion thereby speeds up. General relativity and quantum mechanics offer a mechanism for calculating the energy of empty space. Here we have one more example of impossible-to-understand numbers. The answer turns out to be 10^{120} more energy than astronomers have actually measured. That's the number 1 followed by 120 zeroes. Lawrence Krauss dismisses this quantity as "ridiculous".

At this point in Astronomy Magazine's article on the problematic "Big Bang" theory, further quotes from various theorists have resonance with the very thing we state must be taken into serious consideration by all scientists if they are ever to even get close to *really understanding* the 'space-time continuum' of the Material World in which we must reside for *part* of our *complete* existence.

To illustrate *our* point, 'Astronomy' notes that Krauss and other theorists find it *unsettling* that:

> "...the universe contains just enough dark energy to have allowed galaxies and other structures to form – and, coincidentally, human observers to exist."

Now why should the interesting term, *unsettling*, be used to describe what really should be easily recognised by *all* astronomers, cosmologists, astro-physicists – and whatever other names/titles this particular branch of 'human learning' deems relevant for its work – as the "created reality"?

In terms of the notion that dark energy actually exists, there appear to be only two possibilities:

- 'If there were just a *small* amount of dark energy, or none at all; the universe would have collapsed in a Big Crunch early in the expansion.'

- 'However, if dark energy matched the incredibly large proportion predicted by quantum physics, it would have expanded so rapidly that nothing more than a thin fog of matter and energy would fill the universe today.'

Quite obviously, we live in a universe exactly tailored and proportioned to support the myriad life-forms present on Earth. Here Astronomy uses another interesting term, *cosmic coincidence*, to explain why "...we seem to live in the best of all possible universes". The 'anthropic principle', invoked by some scientists to explain the 'odds stacked in our favour', states that '...the universe has the ideal amount of dark energy because we wouldn't be here to measure it if it didn't'.

> "If the amount of dark energy weren't that much bigger than what we measure, then there wouldn't be galaxies. And if there weren't galaxies, there wouldn't be stars; and if there weren't stars, there wouldn't be planets; and if there weren't planets, *there wouldn't be astronomers.*"

> (Krauss, p.51. Italics mine.)

Daniel Pendick of Astronomy Magazine writes:
'The anthropic principle's explanation for dark energy has the potential to shake the foundation of all physics.'

> "Physics is supposed to predict why things are and why they have to be that way. This would say they don't have to be that way at all. ***They just happen to be that way because <u>we're here</u>.***"

> (Krauss, p.51. Emphasis mine.)

Whether from a foundation of physics, 'cosmic mathematics', or from simple but ultimately more valuable "intuition" driven by "the spirit" within each of us; in that last sentence Lawrence Krauss has hit upon the *true reason* for the existence of the cosmos in the first place. We are not here by 'accident'. That is a truly ridiculous notion and a ***monumental error***. That idea, unfortunately too prevalent in 'earth-science', concentrates *valuable* academic thought and research on a *completely wrong paradigm* which can *never* find resolution – for it is *forever* wrong.

Chapter 2: – **"The Origins of Man: Genesis and Science Agree"** – explains why we are here and thus why we, the human entity, needed a material home for our physical component. Primarily, two words – or perhaps one hyphenated word – tells us why Lawrence Krauss is correct: **Free Will**; **Free-will!** Of all creatures in Creation, we, alone, possess the attribute of Free Will! That is why we seek answers to our reason for being. That is why we were seriously enjoined by Jesus, sent to Earth to show us the way home, to:
"Seek and you Shall find."

Free Will, however, means exactly that! We are *free* to *choose* a correct path of learning – one that *will bring* the *true* answers and thus *genuine enlightenment*; or we can *choose* to follow a path that is literally ***a dead-end in all respects***. Many scientific paths are already dead-ends before they start. In that regard, it is crucial for humankind to *get right* astronomy/cosmology, but in an *especial way* for a *most* especial *reason*.

At this time, that particular branch of earth-science correctly reveals the incomprehensible immensity of *our universe* in its *materiality*. However, what it does not do – and what really should be cosmology's next step and thus more crucial elucidatory purpose – is to *recognise* the connecting links which would offer that *especial* revelation.

For that to happen, however, *a fundamental shift in thinking must first take place within that scientific Discipline*. A paradigm shift – just to begin with – which encompasses a *greater* horizon than simply a *material* universe that astronomy *thinks* it knows. A *conscious* shift *into* the relevant *cosmological Creation-knowledge* would *bring* the requisite *recognition* that would allow the science to build *constant upon constant*. Thus *true knowledge* in place of the present, fractured state of that regime's 'guess-work reality'; trying to make things fit a particular theory or idea.

Astronomy Magazine gives an excellent example of differing ideas between the 'experts'. We quote the relevant segment verbatim:

11.2.3   "Lost in the Hubble Bubble."

'Some researchers have proposed to solve the problem by getting rid of dark energy entirely. It's theoretically possible to modify the standard model so that dark energy is not necessary to explain accelerated cosmic expansion. For example, Oxford University theoretical physicist Subir Sarkar and other researchers are investigating an alternative – the "Hubble Bubble" hypothesis. It holds that the local universe lies in a region of space with less-than-average density. It would expand at a faster-than-average rate relative to the space outside the bubble. If this is true, then accelerated cosmic expansion may be just a mirage caused by the assumption that the universe is homogeneous and isotropic on all scales.
Critics say the Hubble Bubble hypothesis is an example of stacking up "what ifs" until they add up to the desired answer.' Hinshaw says:

> "You can contrive models to fit the data without dark energy, ... but it then becomes
> a question of what is really plausible."

'Dark energy, he says, is the most plausible of all known possibilities. But Sarkar insists it's too soon to dismiss alternatives when confronted with something as bizarre as dark energy. He says:

> "The real universe looks more complex than the idealized standard model that
> makes us infer the existence of dark energy. ... And it's presumptuous to imagine
> that cosmology is basically sorted out. I think we have just started."

If we extrapolate just that division of opinion between two renowned and no doubt respected academics in their field to encompass all 'divisions of opinion' since the "Age of Enlightenment", what can we really claim as 'genuine' scientific progress; i.e.: That which no longer needs refinement but stands as an *absolute forever*? Not too much, one would have to say.

The April, 2009, edition of Astronomy Magazine also featured an article that offers an alternative to the Big Bang. Written by Paul J. Steinhardt; "**Why the universe had no beginning**" proposes the idea that instead of *one* Big Bang to explain the instant of creation and thus the beginning of the universe as we *believe* we know it, the *current* Big Bang was a *single* event in an *infinite* cycle. On page 33, he writes:

> "The cyclic model and the Big Bang model produce ... different pictures of the past
> history and future evolution of the universe. In the Big Bang view, the Big Bang
> marks the beginning of time, so the universe is only 13.7 billion years old. A period of
> inflation after the Big Bang sets the large-scale structure of the universe. Theorists

introduced dark energy to explain the universe's current accelerating expansion, but otherwise it serves no needed role. Once introduced, however, dark energy dominates the future of the universe. ...

In contrast, the cyclic view says 13.7 billion years represents only the time since the last bang and the creation of the matter and radiation we see today. The universe has had many such cycles – perhaps infinitely many – prior to the present one. And the true age of the universe is far more than 13.7 billion years.

The theory has no need for inflation because large-scale structure derives from events that lead up to each bang. ..."

Do *we* accept the notion that the material universe into which a myriad telescopes peer is *infinite*, thus in existence *forever*? No, we do not, for the **Material World** is a *"Work of Creation"*, in the same way that the **Higher Realms** are. The primary purpose of including the 'infinite cycle' theory here is to *strongly* illustrate – again *very* necessarily – the problematic nature of a scientific Discipline [cosmology] that does not possess a *'foundation of sure knowledge'* from which to conduct further research to gain greater insights. Such a 'scientific quandary' surely has resonance in the following obviously correct observation:

"Scientism, the aura of authority carried by scientists, has made us believe that knowledge obtained by scientists is the ultimate authority, that as we accumulate information, our capacity to understand, control and manage our surroundings will grow correspondingly. But the basic principle of scientific exploration contradicts this faith: knowledge comes from empirical observations, which are "made sense of" by hypotheses, which in turn can be experimentally tested. All information is open to being disproved. As Jonathan Marks has pointed out":
"...the vast majority of ideas that most scientists have ever had have been wrong. They have been refuted; they have been disposed of. Further, at any point in time, most ideas proposed by most scientists will ultimately be refuted and disposed of... Science, in other words, undermines scientism."

(Dr David Suzuki, *The Sacred Balance*, p.19)

If science is ever to reach the point of no longer 'undermining itself' with wrong theories, it must *first recognise* what is *inherently wrong* with 'scientism' – which very few scientists seemingly want to acknowledge as problematic at all. From *that correct recognition*, engage with and *embrace* the key 'human-entity pointers' that would facilitate the necessary transition from the present inconsistent state – which obviously reveals *uncertainty* in the *industry* – to one that *begins to open up* to knowledge that *mightily transcends* current astronomical *theories*.

To that end, they are:

- Our inherent free-will attribute.

- Which part of we, the human entity, possesses that free-will aspect.

- Where that free-will attribute comes from.

- How we acquired it.

- These points consequently *then lead* to the *knowledge* of the *true nature* of we, the human beings in Creation; and thus to:

- The *knowledge* of our *true* home.

In concert with those pointers, we restate perhaps the three primary "Crucial Imperatives" relevant to them:

Crucial Imperative No 2:

That we, the human beings of planet Earth, are not solely a physical entity, but also necessarily possess a *non-material* inner animating core: *For the physical **cannot** – and therefore **does not** – animate the physical!*

Crucial Imperative No 3:

That being more than just a physical body means we naturally and *inherently* possess a *separable entity **within*** the material form. And that *that* is the *actual* life-force, the *animating* core, that is *actually each individual!*

Crucial Imperative No 5:

That because the physical Universe is a ***material*** expanse, it is therefore ***not*** without end. **It is finite!**

In the final analysis, does it really matter what astronomy postulates as the true picture of the cosmos? Our purpose on Earth was always to recognise and strive to understand the **Universal Laws of Creation — Creation-Law —** by which we are enjoined to live. And to *thereby* recognise our Spiritual Origins – that place in Creation from whence we came – our ***true home*** – and to where we are meant to return. So the incredible amount of time and energy expended on trying to understand the physical universe/s, never mind the huge cost of it, may be ultimately wasted – ***if*** those particular scientists concentrate *solely* on just the single, material aspect.

Such efforts are nonetheless invariably lauded as possessing the potential to lead to some kind of *ultimate* knowledge, which is most unfortunate. For under current educational parameters – at least in the Western world anyway – generations of students, obviously numbering in the hundreds of millions, simply follow academic lines of thought which are *ultimately detrimental* to the *more necessary* 'deeper-seeing' paradigm.

That is not to say we should not study the stars and the universe, for such investigation really is the preserve of science. The truly intuitive scientist within that particular Discipline will understand that the gift of intelligence, which most scientists obviously possess, is exactly that; a gift. It is one, therefore, which should be employed for the purpose of studying and explaining the *connections between* the *transitory* material and *The Eternal* non-material; thus to *reveal and explain* the most powerful and profound *correlation* between that which is here in our *material* home-world, and that which exists *far above* the physical universes – **"the many mansions"**. As it stands today, however, science often appears to edify itself.

Science, and therefore scientists – out of themselves and ***through their work*** – should edify **The Creator** and **His Work of The Creations**. The very nature of scientific endeavour and discovery should bring about this recognition naturally in any case, particularly where the study of the cosmos is concerned. For:

> "When we consider thy heavens, the work of thy fingers,
> The moon and the stars, which thou hast ordained,
> What is man, that thou art mindful of him?"

(*The Gospel of the Essenes.*
E.B. Szekely, p 175)

Such clear wisdom from the ancient world has finally led us to the 21st century world of the Hubble Space Telescope, powerful radio telescopes and super-computers which help us better understand the make-up and behaviour of the *stars* within the 'incomprehensible' universe *we belong to*. Such wonderful aids, however, are yet still insufficient to provide final and definitive answers as to what the material universe **really is**.

The series of questions we asked regarding the impossible-to-understand numbers of the Big Bang 'inflation model', which mainstream cosmological science evidently claims is mathematically valid, should offer you, the reader, powerful food for thought for "digesting" the next and rather mind-blowing, *key part*, of this Chapter.

Does anyone *really* understand such 'space' distances? Notwithstanding the fact that present-day computer power can number-crunch very accurately, it all *seems* rather meaningless when many, many zeros are slotted behind a given digit and then perhaps to the power of another number for good measure. Nonetheless, such determined efforts to 'fix' the size of the universe has vital relevance to our understanding of the "7 Churches" question. A few quotes from various people and publications over past decades reveals the struggle to even try to begin to genuinely understand this thing known by millions of Star Trek fans, unfortunately *very wrongly*, however, as: **Space: The Final Frontier!** — [Exclamation mark/s!!!]

"My suspicion is that the universe is not only queerer than we suppose, but queerer than we *can* suppose."

(J.B.S. Haldane.)

"But what came before the big bang, and how will it all end? Billions of years hence, will gravity overcome the expansion and pull matter back into its primordial state – in a big crunch? And if the universe is closed, might another big bang follow, with another expansion? Or, as many astronomers now believe, will an ever-expanding, or open, universe end in a whimper, its galaxies scattered irretrievably, their star fires spent and cold? For now, the questions are the domain of the *philosopher* as well as the astronomer."

(*National Geographic Star Chart*, 1983.
Italics mine.)

"It may be that our universe is merely part of many larger universes, some in different dimensions, and that big bangs are going on all the time all over the place. Or it may be that space and time had some other forms altogether before the Big Bang – forms too alien for us to imagine – and that the Big Bang represents some sort of *transition phase*, where the universe went *from a form we can't understand to one we almost can*." ***"These are very close to religious questions."***
Dr Andrei Linde, a cosmologist at Stanford University, told The New York Times in 2001.

So what is the *true* nature and *extent* of the physical universes? Earth-science will surely say we may never ever know. The *greater knowledge* that lies inherent in **The Spiritual Laws Of Creation**, however, absolutely states we *can* know. Moreover, it is the Spiritual Duty and Responsibility of *every* human being to seek out this knowledge, exactly as the great scientist Isaac Newton sought. For in that most necessary first recognition lies the far greater recognition of how far we – the human beings of planet Earth in **Subsequent Creation** – *really are* from the **Very Source** of our life and *ultimate reason for being*.

11.3   The 'Revelation' of "The Plan of The World" The 'Meaning' of the "7 Churches"

With the huge strides made in the "science" of astronomy and cosmology wrought by the building and use of more and more powerful instruments to observe the great expanse *"out there"*, a fascinating paradox has seemingly emerged. It would appear that because the expanse of the, now, known universe is simply too incomprehensible to grasp, a point or limit in our brain-capacity to truly understand would inevitably be reached. So that any greater understanding would perhaps derive initially from the conjoined and expanding paths of philosophy and religion, but only reaching a complete and final picture with, and from, the knowledge of the actual **"Structure of Creation"** of which the *material* universes are, to emphasise once again, *the lowest and smallest part*.

If we now move a little closer to understanding the meaning of the "7 Churches" question proper, we should revisit the notion of what might happen if we *could* travel to the edge of the universe and look beyond it. To what, we may wonder?

> According to Einstein's Theory of Relativity, man could never reach that point because "...the universe bends in a way that can't adequately be imagined". Therefore we would, even after travelling in a straight line to the edge, eventually arrive back at our starting point because space curves in a way that allows it to be boundless – *but finite!*[6]
>
> "In short, there's more space than you can imagine already without going to the trouble of trying to envision some additional beyond."
>
> (*How to Make a Universe.* Reader's Digest,
> Emphases mine.)

That is **exactly** the purpose of this Chapter, however; to **recognise** that *'additional beyond'*. Therefore, since the science of astronomy/cosmology has seemingly not concerned itself with the great and key truths contained in certain religious writings, let us use the Spiritual/intuitive faculty available to the human entity to now finally explain and clarify – *for 'Science' and 'Theology'* – the true meaning of **"The Seven Churches in Asia-Minor"**.

To do that we need to return to, absolutely fittingly in this case, **The Book of <u>Revelation</u>**; in particular "The Vision in Patmos":

> I, John, ...was in the island known as Patmos. I became inspired on the Lord's day; and I heard a loud voice behind me resembling a trumpet blast saying: "What you see write in a book, and dispatch to the seven assemblies – to **Ephesus**, and to **Smyrna**"... etc.. I accordingly turned to see the voice which spoke to me. And having turned, I observed **seven golden lampstands**; and **in the centre of the lampstands**, one like to the Son of Man... and **holding in His right hand seven stars**; and a sharp double-edged sword drawn from its sheath... "Write therefore what you have seen, what is, and what will come after these. The mystery of the **seven stars** which you saw upon my right hand, and the **seven golden lampstands**, *the seven stars are <u>messengers</u> of seven assemblies; and the seven lampstands <u>are</u> the seven assemblies!*"
>
> (Revelation 1:9-19, Fenton.
> Emphases mine.)

---

[6]Here is a key understanding to the answer of the "7 Churches" question. The physical universe we see and believe we know is *finite!* [Crucial Imperative No 5: Chapter 1]

The key to understanding this *apparent* 'mystery' again lies mainly in the *italicised* words. The next key part is the text of the address to the first 'assembly' of **Ephesus**, which we shall quote once more.

> To the messenger to the assembly in Ephesus write:
> Thus says the Controller of the seven stars by His right hand; *who walks in the centre of the seven golden lampstands*; "I know your position, your industry, and your patience; and that you cannot endure those who are wicked; that you have put to the test those who have called themselves Apostles, and are not, and have found them false; and you have had patience and have suffered because of My Name, and have not failed. I have, however, a charge against you – that you have forsaken your first love! Remember, therefore, from where you have fallen, and repent, and practise your former works; failing which, and unless you alter your mind, *I will come and <u>remove</u> your <u>lampstand</u> from its place*."

> (Revelation 2:1-6, Fenton.
> Emphases mine.)

Here, too, the *italicised* sentences represent a *golden key* to the final and complete understanding of the meaning of the "7 Churches in Asia". And thus – in relation to the vast gulf and *humanly-unbridgeable distance* between we of Subsequent Creation and **The Almighty** [**"The Creator"**] – where we *actually stand* during the *earthly phases* of our complete existence.

We note that the address to Ephesus continues on for a few more sentences, then basically similar addresses are given to the other 'assemblies' or 'churches'. Notwithstanding the unequivocal stance we are postulating here, we nonetheless clearly recognise that the Messages *as they stand* certainly give the *impression* that they were/are addressed to the seven ancient cities of Ephesus, Smyrna, Pergamos, Thyatira, Sardis, Philadelphia and Laodicea.

For words like Jews, synagogue and Satan are used, along with the phrase, 'sons of Israel'. Moreover, we have mention of Balaam and Balak, names associated with ancient Asia Minor. Luther also cites the Nicolaitans, who are supposedly corrupting two of the "7 Churches". [It appears, however, that no one has really confirmed, historically, who they were.]

It must surely be known that The Book of Revelation possesses a powerful *spiritual dimension* that reaches *way beyond* the world of just 'Physical Matter' – the size and extent, alone, of which we 'earth-humans' will never ever be able to truly grasp. Therefore, the *actual reality* of that which Isaac Newton assiduously searched for must necessarily and inherently encompass a far greater expanse than the present, *nonetheless mind-boggling*, 'vista' currently accepted by science and Christendom. So we need to crucially understand that those particular and well-known terms used in the addresses must also relate to that *comprehensively wider view*. In this instance, then, the words used in the seven addresses similarly possess a far deeper and wider *spiritual* meaning; much more than would ever be the case here on earth.

Thus, a 'Jew' simply means 'a spiritual person', synagogue akin to a 'place/assembly of worship/ers'; and 'sons of Israel', a 'righteous group'. Satan – or the 'Being' Lucifer – affects the *whole* of **'The World of Matter'**, not just we *on Planet Earth*.

By way of example: If we now apply those 'spiritual' meanings to a small segment of just the addresses to Smyrna, Pergamos and Philadelphia respectively, a greater and wider vision arises; therewith permitting us to *actually perceive* Newton's: **Plan of The World!**

> "...and the insolence of those who assert themselves to be *Jews* and are not, but are,
> on the contrary, a *synagogue* of *Satan*." ....   [2:9-10]

"...because you have there some who are holders of the teachings of Balaam, who instructed Balak to place a stumbling-block before the *sons of Israel,*..."   [2:14]

"Therefore, I will give those of the *synagogue* of *Satan*, who assert themselves to be *Jews*, and are not, but lie;..."   [3:9]

(The Revelation. Fenton Bible.
Emphases mine.)

For humankind on Planet Earth in the World Community of Ephesus, however; our *ostensible cosmic reality* is that we live in a physical environment on a small and beautiful planet in an expanse so vast as to be totally incomprehensible. Because it *is* so vast, the obvious *assumption* that *could* be drawn is that the *visible* universe really is the *be-all* and *end-all* to our total existence.

If we track back to Chapter 2, however, we note that the Material World is purely for the purpose of developing to personal self-consciousness and maturation, both intellectually and spiritually. Whilst a good balance between those two aspects is essential for an harmonious working toward achieving necessary earthly goals, the *greater* responsibility of man was always to develop the Spiritual part within to the highest possible level attainable. And thereby *lead* the intellectual part.

A larger emphasis placed on developing the Spiritual part would have thus ensured that the connection to, and recognition of, our actual Spiritual Origins would *not* have been lost, and we would not need to struggle to understand the key questions to life such as we are addressing here. Therefore, the Material Worlds designated for the creature, **man**, to mature in should not be assumed to be just that which we *believe we know* and perhaps even *roughly* understand. For that would, indeed, be arrogance. From an extremely narrow, solely earth-oriented, viewpoint, earth-science prides itself in believing that it, alone, possesses the ability to solve the ultimate questions to 'life'.

Such a stance, however, represents a "delusion of denial", where the very sciences themselves become a kind of all-knowing god for their adherents. Such a belief logically states that there cannot be any other avenue open to mankind for those very answers which science believes *only it* can answer. To that end, let us *once more* revisit and perhaps brutally-reinforce a key truth.

"Scientism, the aura of authority carried by scientists, has made us believe that knowledge obtained by scientists is the ultimate authority, that as we accumulate information, our capacity to understand, control and manage our surroundings will grow correspondingly. But the basic principle of scientific exploration contradicts this faith: knowledge comes from empirical observations, which are "made sense of" by hypotheses, which in turn can be experimentally tested. All information is open to being disproved. As Jonathan Marks has pointed out":

"...the vast majority of ideas that most scientists have ever had have been wrong. They have been refuted; they have been disposed of. Further, at any point in time, most ideas proposed by most scientists will ultimately be refuted and disposed of... Science, in other words, undermines scientism."

(Dr David Suzuki. *The Sacred Balance*, p.19)

If, then, we are able to accept even just the *possibility* of Realms or regions that are *non-material* – the "many mansions" – and which therefore lie *far above* the physical universes, then we gift to ourselves the recognitory-acceptance that the physical-world part of Creation is, very logically, **far larger** than we could **ever** have even **supposed**. By that we do not mean just what we now know exists in *our* universe, but that a far *greater* reality *really does exist.* And, moreover, that the key to this stupendous knowledge has been with us *for a very long time.*

Since the 'Material World' that we know is the *physical* home of man, why should we assume that the *entity*, **man**, resides *solely* on planet Earth *in our particular universe*, and therefore nowhere else in the *complete physical expanse* we allude to? Such a view assumes that we know and understand more than The Creative Power Which permitted us conscious life. By such a belief, we actually limit ourselves to very narrow parameters of *so-called* great knowledge.

So, if the Messengers of God did *not* address seven *earthly* communities in the ancient world, yet nevertheless did, or will, address *"communities or assemblies of men"* upon the directive of the **"One like unto The Son of Man"**, that surely reveals the stupendous scale of the actual happening. A happening, moreover, *that could not possibly be confined to a very small part of one very small region of one very small planet.*

That being the actual reality of things here, we shall now simply take the boldest step and proclaim, here and now, *that* **Truth** that John, the receiver of **The Revelation** from a **Higher Sphere**, understood and passed on down to humankind *primarily for this present time.*

The very **Truth** that he received came from **The One by Whom** we came into being – **IMANUEL** – **The One Enthroned** – **The One Who Comes: The WILL OF GOD!**

He It was **Who** brought into being *the "seven homes of humanity"*: — *the "7 Churches"*. It is **He**, therefore, **Who**, [figuratively], *stands in the centre of the seven golden lamp-stands.*

And thus we note; "...**seven golden lampstands**; and in **the centre** of the lampstands, one like unto the **Son of Man**... and holding in **His** right hand *seven stars*".

So we are not only given *indications* of what the *seven golden lampstands* actually *are*, but also the *key* to the *meaning* of the *seven stars.*

Thus: "The mystery of the **seven stars** which you saw *upon my right hand*, and the **seven golden lampstands**, *the seven stars are* **messengers** *of seven assemblies*; and **the seven lampstands** <u>are</u> **the seven assemblies.**"   (All emphases mine.)

There lies the answer.

The *seven 'assemblies'*, which *are* the *'Seven Churches' in 'Asia Minor'* – in each of which *resides* a *"community of men"* – are the *seven golden lampstands* of **"The Revelation"**.

They are actually *seven universes* of roughly the *same size and configuration* as the *universe* in which <u>we</u> reside. *And in each an 'assembly' of men; of humanity.* We of planet Earth have our *physical home* in the *'universe'* or *'church'* called <u>*Ephesus!*</u>

The reader must clearly understand that these "lampstands" are not simply seven universes *within* the huge expanse of the cosmos visible to us via our radio and optical telescopes. No! Each universe or "church" is an incomprehensibly-vast rotating "island", *each a separate entity unto itself*: Each one similar to our own in mind-numbing size.

The seven universes together *rotate* in a huge *wreath-like formation* at the *lowest part of Creation*. The distance *between* each universe is naturally *greater than* the *diameter* of *each individual one*. We will therefore never be able to see the other universes and, quite obviously, never be able to travel to them, at least not by physical means.[7]

"The Revelation", however, permits us to *know* about the other '6 Churches'. The designation, "Asia-Minor" – used to describe the 'Material-Creation area' of the "7 Churches" – is simply a Spiritual one, as are the names of those '7 Churches'. Thus the "mystery" of the "7 Churches" is not a mystery at all.

The Bible — a Primary book of 'Foundational-Science' — provides the <u>cosmological</u> answer!

That is precisely why such a fundamental leap into a far greater level of knowledge was reserved for this particular time in our evolutionary development. For it is only within the last decades that we have had the ability to see our blue planet in its wholeness from a point outside of it; a picture free of all the superstition and ignorance of the past. As David Suzuki points out:

> "We have to recall the image of the planet from outer space; a single entity in which air, water, and continents are interconnected. That is our [physical] home."
>
> (Parenthetic addition mine.)

Just as that sublime vision has produced awe in many, so were we, via such technological aids as the Hubble space telescope, for example, meant to take cosmology to new heights in the recognition of the awesome greatness of just the vastness of the physical universe *alone*. The sheer and unfolding scale of it should thus have produced the *certain* recognition that what was being revealed, in the *physical sense*, could yet only represent the heaviest and therefore *lowest and smallest part* of Creation. [**Newton's Law of Gravitation!**] And that there was very much more beyond that 'small immensity'.[8]

That should have been a watershed recognition for humankind – especially cosmological science – recognising, *in humility*, that we are only "developed beings", far from our Creator. Yet even though we stand a very, very long way from The Source of Life, Its ever-present Grace permits us the *possibility* to eventually *leave behind* the confines of the material parts of Creation to return to our *true* home – our point of Origin in a far Higher Realm.

Since the purpose of this book is to offer *seriously awake people* explanations and answers to some of the major questions of life – thus some understanding of the *why* of the rapidly deteriorating state of humanity today; i.e., **"Global Societal Collapse"** – such a thing as an 'Apocalyptic Judgement' must inevitably surface with questions such as are raised in this Work. If so, a very telling *human* paradigm/question arises here. It is this:

> 'Why is it that we of the human race — who so desperately want to be rid of the bloodshed, violence and evil that permeates global societies and cultures with increasing ferocity; who long for a world where abject poverty and human exploitation is eliminated; and for a world that will not end up the nightmare we **all know** we are rushing headlong towards — obtusely refuse to accept the *only* mechanism that *can* bring about precisely that "better world"?'

And the answer?

---

[7]The same constraint applies to just our own galaxy, so it is not likely we will ever even journey to some of our "closest" star-system "neighbours". In any case, what would be the point of trying? Our true home is not "down here"!

[8]Had man not fallen "spiritually", the same degree of knowledge and insight would still have been his – and very much more besides – to enhance the mechanical and optical aids we have today.

'Quite simply: The *only* way that this desirable state *can* be achieved is through the **complete destruction** of the **very many** who **are** the problem!'

(Author.)

As previously stated, humankind was given a long period of time in which to learn and experience all that was necessary for the recognition of Spiritual Truth – the *primary* human responsibility. Refusal to do so logically presupposes that within *inviolable* **Creation-Law** parameters – which ultimately govern *all* processes, events and outcomes – there must come the inevitable day when 'the ferryman must be paid'. For all who refuse to accept and/or recognise such Truth, a period of 'cleansing' must therefore logically carry with it an appropriate level of apocalyptic accompaniment. Commensurate with that harrowing process – increasing at this very time – will be revealed the, then, rapidly-approaching cut-off point which will *precede* the final, inevitable, 'catastrophic-phase' for we of intransigent humankind.

Such a 'cut-off point' obviously represents the moment where there is no further time left to redeem or put right past transgressions. That opens the way for the final cleansing or "sorting-out" phase. After the "sorting-out" process comes the next phase – a time of harmonious peace no longer marred or harmed by what went before, i.e., that which *needed* to be *excised* and *removed.*

What happens, however, if the collective transgressions of a given 'assembly' of humanity in the *wider Material World* are so serious that there are no redeeming points whatever? What, then? If we look at the *key point* of the crucial message given for us here in Ephesus, it is very chilling in its clear import:

"Thus says the Controller of the seven stars by His right hand; who walks in ***the centre*** of the ***seven golden lampstands***; I know your position, your industry, and your patience; ... I have, however, ***a charge against you*** – that you have *forsaken your first love*! Remember, therefore, from where you have *fallen*, and *repent*, and practise your *former works*; failing which, and unless you alter your mind, ***I will come and remove your*** <u>***lampstand***</u> ***from its place.***"

(Revelation 2:1-6, Fenton.
Emphases mine.)

Remember that **each lampstand** is actually **one of the 7 great Universes** in which an "assembly of men" resides.

Now, since the whole of the Material World encompassing the "7 Churches" or 'universes' is the *lowest* and thus *smallest* part of **Creation**, the removal of one **lampstand** or 'Church' – as unfathomably vast as they are even individually – must nonetheless be understood to be a completely lawful and *simple* process for the *humanly-incomprehensible* Power which not only *produced* **them**, but very, very much more besides. For the 'assembly of men' in each, however, destruction on an unimaginable and truly apocalyptic scale which, however, is not imminent for Ephesus at this particular time on that gigantic scale.

What is stated here is the stupendous, constantly-recurring, 'renewal-cycle' of birth, life and disintegration that *all* the 7 great universes or assemblies – since the moment of Creation – must now undergo, but in a time-frame of cosmic proportions that could not ever be even imagined. Thus *finite* universes rotating through an *infinite* cycle of birth, life and disintegration.

We who reside on the tiny speck of the Earth in the great "universe-community" of Ephesus; do we even begin to recognise from whence we have fallen? Unfortunately we do not. More unfortunately, truly Spiritual aspirations are often derided and dismissed as irrelevant and of no consequence or importance for 21st century man. They were not considered all that relevant last century either.

And what was our first love with which we no longer bother? The love for **The Creator**, as stated in **The First Commandment**, or the love for one's neighbour? Not much evidence of either in today's world. There is, however, much love and adulation for our much-vaunted, *totally aspiritual*, intellect, precisely by which we *fail* to practise our former works – the far earlier spiritual ones. Carefully and craftily nurtured by the present, intellectually-derived, university-driven 'education system', only the adulation of human 'works' and 'achievements' by humans holds sway today. Even within global religions, the 'love of man' is far greater than **Love of The Creator**!

Clearly, then, our former works – which we are directed to once more practise – were better than those we produce now, before our spiritual fall and decline. Failing which, and unless we change our ways, our *lampstand*, the universe containing our earthly home, may well one day be 'removed'. In other words total disintegration of the *whole universe of Ephesus* at some designated future point. What is this, just religious ranting? Or is it the clearest warning yet that we could possibly receive to change our ways and begin living correctly according to **The True Laws of Life**: The Spiritual Laws of Creation? — <u>Creation-Law!</u>

The degraded and poisoned state of planet Earth today, along with the dysfunctional social order of most societies globally, clearly testifies to totally wrong thinking and wrong practices by we of the 'human assembly' of Ephesus. In terms of Perfect Justice, therefore, it would probably be the correct thing for most of humanity to be "taken out"! The inherent Perfection of Creation-Law would automatically achieve that in any case.

Since we have now reached a critical situation in just scientific terms – let alone any stronger effect from more powerful forces – it may only be a relatively brief matter of time before the "tipping-point" that earth-science states is very close now adds its particular measure to our "cup that [already] well and truly runneth-over". We, as stated unequivocally in previous Chapters, are presently rolling towards that cut-off point at a rapidly accelerating pace. Faster and faster to our self-willed destiny of "destruction and cleansing" for the greater mass, with perhaps survival for a few small groups and individuals scattered around the globe.

> "...for there shall then be wide-spread affliction, *such as has not been known since the beginning of the world until now, no, nor will ever be known again.* And if those times were not cut short, *not a man would be saved*".
>
> (Matthew 24:19-22)

> "And there will be signs in the sun, and moon, and stars; and upon the Earth *from fear, and apprehension of what is coming upon the world...*"
>
> (Luke 21:25-26)

In the same way that The Bible has permitted us the knowledge of the *extent* of the physical universes in the Material World, might we also find within that Work the same kinds of clear revelations with which we can understand the actual *Why* of our poisoned and degraded Earth? And thereby further reinforce our unequivocal premise that **The Bible** really is:
"A Primary Book of Foundational-Science!"

One especial Prophet of the Old Testament saw in visions what has already begun to happen. Isaiah, often referred to as the Great Prophet, proclaimed the kinds of events that have now not only occurred, but the outcome of which has forced earth-scientists to rewrite their 'theories' about the 'power' of Earth activity. For man's evolutionary journey to *true* knowledge, Isaiah saw in his time what we today know to be 'activity' associated with 'Plate Tectonics'.

'The "Earth" is utterly broken down, the "Earth" is clean dissolved, the "Earth" is *moved exceedingly.*

The "Earth" shall reel *to and fro* like a drunkard, and shall be *removed from her place.*'

(Isaiah 24:19-20, Fenton.
Emphases mine.)

How much of that chilling potential can we attribute to human decisions, societal attitudes and concomitant global activity? Isaiah certainly pulled no punches in identifying why. Bad human decisions will obviously produce bad outcomes, not only for human societies but for the planet as a whole. That is our present legacy and reality.

Decisions = consequences!

'The "Earth" mourns and fades away, the "World" languishes and fades away, the haughty people of the "Earth" do languish.

The "Earth" also is defiled under the inhabitants thereof; because they have *transgressed* the "Laws", *changed* the decrees, *broken* the everlasting covenant.

Therefore has the curse devoured the "Earth", and those that dwell therein are desolate: therefore the inhabitants of the "Earth" are burned, and few men left.'

(Isaiah 24: 4-6, Italics mine.)

What might modern-day scientists and 'empirical science' make of the above statements? Except for the relatively few who have broken out of the strait-jacket of 'empirical intellectualism', most would probably dismiss the whole idea of Bible prophecy – accurate enough to pinpoint future events of such catastrophic power sufficient to produce a "reeling Earth" – as religious rubbish. Ferrar Fenton's translation of just one line of Isaiah's vision [24:20] —

"And the Earth's foundations shake!"

— should strike a chord of serious warning for all scientists whose field of 'expertise' lies in anything even remotely connected with the Earth.

So: What does this *really mean* for the earth-scientist? More to the point, perhaps, should scientists take note of such prophecies, or be derisively dismissive of them? As we have already stated, what Isaiah was gifted to 'see' and give warning for future humanity was the ***vastly amplified activity*** of 'Plate Tectonics'.

When first mooted early last century, it was, of course, dismissed by the 'scientific establishment' as impossible nonsense. Now we all know **Plate Tectonics** to be "scientific fact". Surely a perfect example of **"The Error of Scientism"**. A "reeling Earth" which 'shakes its very foundation'? Is this impossible nonsense too? Not now! For this we also now know to be "scientifically feasible". How?

Earth-science and global humanity have the quite recent experience of knowing that *the whole Earth* can actually shake from just one, albeit very large but nevertheless, ***single*** Earth movement. The devastating and catastrophic experience of the Indian Ocean tsunami, Boxing Day, 2004, has surely shaken any scientific scepticism that such a thing was impossible.

In any case, what has *already occurred* a number of times in the past with obviously catastrophic consequences for the Earth could well happen again — a truly cataclysmic 'pole shift'. Such an event would *absolutely* fulfil Isaiah's vision.

A "reeling Earth" with mountains and islands 'moved out of their places' would certainly result from a 'pole shift'; with, of course, unimaginable and horrendous death and destruction. A similar, though perhaps *less destructive* outcome could also occur with multiple, simultaneous Earth-movements, or as a very rapid 'sundering' ripple-effect. The destruction and devastation wrought by Earth movements on that scale would produce tens, if not hundreds, of millions of lives lost. So the precedent for Isaiah's "shaking Earth" has now been experienced by 'science' and present-day humanity!

Should we hope that the Great Prophet's *harder vision* will not eventuate? Or has human behaviour and activity already proceeded too far past what is acceptable to The Laws of Life ..."because they [*we*] have **transgressed** the "Laws", **changed** the decrees, **broken** the everlasting covenant?"

Throughout this Work we have strongly stated **The Bible** to be "**A Primary Book of Foundational-Science**". From out of its **Book Of Revelation**, we have derived the cosmological answer to the meaning of "**The Seven Churches in Asia-Minor**". The clear visions of Isaiah depicting Plate Tectonic activity sufficiently strong to 'move the Earth' gives one more exceptionally clear and *scientifically-proven example* of the 'scientific validity' of **The Bible**.

The path we have traced, explored, analysed and explained in this Chapter marries the earth-science of astronomy/cosmology to Bible Revelation and Theology in a way that both transcends, illuminates and conjoins the respective views to provide the sure answer to the "**7 Churches**" question: Isaac Newton's "**Plan Of The World!**"

Therewith may we now know our 'place' when 'residing' in **The World of Matter**. And *thereby* 'begin to perceive' the **Immutable Truth** of the vast, *humanly-unbridgeable, distance* between we humans of just **Subsequent Creation** — and —

The Creator of <u>All</u> The Worlds!

11.3.1   An Astronomy Lecturer's Recognition

In order to more *fully understand* what has been *revealed* in this Chapter, I recommend that the lay-reader, particularly, find a reasonably comprehensive star-chart of the universe showing the journey of discovery from the Solar System to the galaxies, to groupings of galaxies, and so on to the known limits of the universe. [National Geographic have produced excellent charts over the years.] Then, using any mainstream Bible, apply the texts used herein to a visual examination of the star-chart and recognise the immensity of just our universe of Ephesus to begin with.

Then travel beyond that *in mind and spirit* into the area of Material Creation occupied by the other "6 Churches" or 'universes' and try to grasp the immensity of just the physical part, alone, of all that *down here*. Then strive to soar upwards into the *Non-Material Realms* of the *Eternal Part* of Creation, to one of the "many mansions in His Father's house"; that of our true home in The Spiritual Realm. From "there", look downwards and strive to picture the "7 Churches" or 'universes' rotating like a huge wreath very, very far below.

If the *spirit* is *truly awake* to the experiential-recognition that *can* occur in a *singular moment of profound insight*, such a *mind-numbing revelation* becomes a **spiritually-cathartic and life-changing event** for that individual.

*   *   *   *   *

The final word on this subject must go to a woman who lectured in astronomy at Auckland City Observatory in New Zealand, and who was at the same time also a devout Christian. Upon enquiring why I sought the 1983 edition of the National Geographic Star Chart, I asked how she reconciled the time-frame that cosmology accepts for the age of the universe with that of 6,000 years which many millions of Christians faithfully but *mistakenly* believe. She replied that *that* was not a contentious issue for her.

She again asked why I wanted the 'Star Chart'; the question of which I perceived to be a very 'leading' one. Intuitively, therefore, I asked her if she knew of the "7 Churches" in **The Book of Revelation**? She did. When made aware of the *true nature* of them, she asked – literally through a mask of what can only be described as something akin to "jaw-dropping, incredulity":

"Is that possible? Can it be possible?"

I stated to her that it was the only explanation which made logical sense [according to Inviolable and Immutable **Creation-Law**] and was therefore the *actual reality*. As both a lecturer in astronomy and a Christian with some knowledge of The Bible, she *immediately understood* the **full import** of such a concept.

A short while later she said – clearly after some very serious thought, however:

"Thank you for that. I've always believed we've tried to make GOD too small."

12

THE TWO SONS OF GOD

12.1   Introduction

In terms of "edit-speak", the idea of an Introduction for a Chapter is clearly not the norm. However, such is the *especial* importance of the subject here that we deem it necessary to 'change the rules', so to speak, with regard to this segment in the book *primarily* about **The Other Son!**

This Chapter, therefore, – indeed this whole Work – is specifically written to bring to the attention of the Christian Church, particularly, but global humanity as a whole – *including the world of science* – the knowledge of:

"The Two Sons of God!"

Now: Why would this book be constructed in such a way that the final Chapter examines perhaps the most contentious of so-called "Bible Mysteries"? Moreover, why would it be necessary to *include earth-science* in our elucidation about **The Two Sons Of God**? Would not such a subject be deemed by most to be solely a Christian/religious issue? So is it a "mystery" at all? Two thousand million odd Christians certainly seem oblivious to this quite stupendous reality. And the rest of global humanity ...? Well: In their myriad religions, sects, dogmas, doctrines and cults; would probably not be the least bit interested. There, however, in that very erroneous notion, the vast majority who would so reject would err terribly.

For the knowledge of **The Two Sons** [Parts or Extensions] of **The Creator** of *all* men is clearly revealed in <u>both</u> **The Bible** <u>and</u> **The Book of Esdras** in **The Apocrypha**. Therefore, from both these primary Works of Truth we will extract the very information that will reveal, elucidate and proclaim, the most *Crucial Imperative* for every human being on Earth *at this present time*.

Thus far in this Work we have looked at a number of contentious issues from the standpoints of science and religion. On this present subject, however, more from the Biblical/Christian perspective. Notwithstanding the requirement to source the relevant explanations from The Bible, a key question in this Chapter nonetheless has very serious resonance for scientists who single-mindedly strive to "prove" that the 'human genome' reigns supreme as "the life-force within". That key question obviously centres on "Creation versus Evolution".

As we have already noted, the History Channel seeks the same kind of definitive answer in questions such as:
"Where did [this] life come from? What IS life, exactly?" And:
"Is it chemical, spiritual, or a combination of both?"

Also, as we have formerly noted – and perhaps more crucially here – the National Geographic Channel asks:
"How did *non-living* material *come to life*?"

Should we regard these questions as scientific or religious – or both? As is the nature of the beast, there cannot possibly be two very different answers in diametric opposition to each other here. It is either one thing or the other. For very many who *are* interested enough to want to know, the issue is not at all clear-cut. We, of course, by simple and logical analyses of *both sides* of this really *unnecessary* debate, have already made our unequivocal determination.

So: What forces or processes *did* bring or *give life* to *inanimate* matter? Since we do not at all accept the completely illogical idea that *inanimate matter* can – *out of itself* – actually provide the *animating mechanism* to somehow *give life to itself* i.e., to inanimate matter; the only alternative that must necessarily be valid here is the existence of a **non-material** life-force to *so animate*. That being the most logical scenario; what form and/or process might facilitate such an amazing outcome? Paradoxically, *perhaps even perversely*, an outcome which permits us the reasoning intelligence to debate the yes or no of our very *reason for being*? Who or what, then, is *responsible* for that *animating life-force*? In other words, Who or What gave us, indeed permitted us, *conscious life*? Empirical earth-science would surely tend *towards* the **what**, whilst most religions would probably *state* the **Who**!

The purpose of this Introduction is not so much to revisit the Creation-process in any great depth – for we have already done so in Chapter 2: **"The Origins of Man: Genesis and Science Agree!"** – but to once more *elucidate* the *key point* that provides the definitive answer to the **Who** of Creation's *life-force reality*. Even though the whole of the Work states it clearly, this question of **The Two Sons [Parts] Of God** being the most **Crucial Imperative** for **all** of global humanity in **all** its diverse cultures, religions and scientific paradigms, means that an eluciatory analysis of **"The Two"** is paramount.

To that end, *and primarily for science in this case*, we will quickly notate explanatory Scripture from The Book of Genesis. Precisely because The Bible *is* a book of **Foundational-Science**, it really does reveal the processes *whereby* the animating life-force we all must necessarily possess in order to live is *gifted* to us. Inherent within that especial Work, therefore, is the *very clear* **Revelation of The Two**. And, moreover, **which** of **The Two** is **"The Who"** of the life-force for Creation. Reproduced more or less verbatim from Chapter 2 in *this* Work, the following Scriptures from Chapters 1 and 2 of "Genesis" *clarify the fact*.

> "Now the earth was a formless void. There was darkness over the deep, and God's *spirit* hovered over the water." [The Jerusalem Bible]

> "But the Earth was unorganised and empty; and darkness covered its convulsed surface; while the *breath* of GOD rocked the surface of its waters." [Fenton.]

The unequivocal reference to a **"Creative Spirit"** clearly shows that it was not God Himself Who Created the "heavens and the earth", but **He Who was with Him!** The very fact that it is so written reveals that the ancient writers of the original texts *understood this clearly*. We should readily understand, however, that Creation itself proceeded only *according* to **God's Plan**, under ***His Power and Authority***, but *through He* Who was *with* **GOD** as a *Part* of *Him.*

The Christian Church teaches that Jesus is the only Son [Part] of God. And that, therefore, the Creative Spirit must be Him. The following Scripture from John 1:1-3 can certainly be *interpreted* that way. [Emphases mine.]

> "The **WORD** existed **in the beginning**, and the **WORD** was *with* **GOD** and the **WORD** *was* **GOD**.
> <u>He</u> was present <u>*with*</u> **GOD** at the beginning.
> **All** came into existence by means of <u>***Him***</u>; and nothing came into existence apart from <u>***Him***</u>."

So we immediately see that ***at the time <u>when Creation came into being</u>*** there was not just **GOD** and the empty void, there was **Another** – <u>*with*</u> **GOD**! The key question here is:

Who was "<u>***He***</u> *Who was present* <u>*with*</u> **GOD**...?" Was '**He**' Jesus, as is perhaps currently accepted? Or was '**He**' the **Other**, to **Whom** we refer?

The obvious and key point that must be grasped here is that Whomever was *present **with* GOD** was there **at the beginning** [i.e., ***when Creation came into being***]. That is what must be seriously grasped from the Scripture. Moreover, the use of the personal pronoun **He** is a clear pointer as to *Who this particular One actually is*. As a second vital pointer to the answer, the Scripture also clearly states that; "...***the <u>Word</u> that was <u>with</u> GOD***..." was the "...<u>***He*** Who was present <u>*at* the beginning</u>." And that; "...<u>***all*** came into existence by means of <u>Him</u>!*"

To reiterate the key point of that particular Scripture again:

He Who was ***with* GOD** was **also** the ***Word of* GOD** too, and that **all** came into existence by means of **Him**! A mystery perhaps? No! Not a mystery at all because The Bible identifies **Who** that **"Other"** actually **Is**. Further on in this Chapter, we will *revisit* these exact points and, from **The Book of Revelation**, reveal and extend, *for science **and** religion*, the knowledge of **"Who"** of **The Two Sons Of God** was ***with* GOD** 'at the beginning'.

For 'genome scientists' once more, an insight into the 'two parts to man'. From Job 10:9-12, Fenton. [Emphases mine.]

> "Remember You made me from clay,
> That to dust You will make me return!
> And did You not curdle the milk,
> And fixed me together like cheese,
> Then clothed me with skin, and with flesh,
> And with bones and with muscles compact?
> And gave me my life and my reason,
> Then *last, **fixed my Spirit in me***?"

Crucial Imperative No 2:

That we, the human beings of planet Earth, are not solely a physical entity, but also necessarily possess a *non-material* <u>inner animating core</u>: *For the physical **cannot** – and therefore **does not** – <u>animate</u> the physical!*

The knowledge of "The Two Sons Of God" *could perhaps* be designated as the greatest "Bible Mystery" of all. As we earlier noted, however, not because it *is* a mystery, but because the Christian world, comprising close to one third of humanity, are completely *unaware* of this crucially important fact — or would probably refuse to believe it. For global Christendom, therefore, such a "blasphemous idea" would surely occupy the *not possible* category. Unfortunately, however, that denial *will bring* the severest "reaping" of all. Notwithstanding the too-long-held and appalling 'Christian-church distortion' of the 'sacrosanct tenet' which fiercely holds to "One Son Of God", we, on the other hand, will **state Truth** here.

So why is it important for global humanity as a whole to know this Truth? Are not all religions and beliefs regarded as having equal value today, for do not most also have gods too? References to "Sons of God" in the Christian sense would therefore be seen to have no apparent relationship with or to any other religious or cultural belief. However, even though ostensibly a "Christian subject", the, as-yet, *unseen ramifications for all of humankind* stemming from the question of non-recognition and/or denial of **The Two Sons of God** ultimately stands as **the** "Crucial Imperative" requiring unequivocal and timely recognition by **all** of global humanity.

The contentious nature of the subject matter in this particular Chapter will therefore obviously place it in direct opposition to the standard and long-held position of the mainstream Christian Churches. Why, then, have we gone out on a *seemingly* theologically-unassailable and therefore ostensibly-dangerous limb to proclaim unequivocally – and thereby directly challenge the stated position of the whole Christian world particularly – that there is not just one Son of God, **but Two**? If there has never yet been any *public* questioning of such a thing in the whole history of the Church, why bother now?

The answer is quite simple. As is the case of *all* the key questions in life; *either a thing is so, or it is not*! There is simply no other position that can be logically accepted. So must it be here. Therefore, **if** – *and the word **if** in this case is purely for the purpose of this immediate discussion* – there really is only One Son of God, Jesus, Who is to return and bring the Judgement and world peace etc., then the matter resolves itself.

This book would then hold the dubious position of not only being very wrong but, against all perceived scholarly wisdom and academic knowledge from virtually all the Theological Colleges and Religious Studies Departments of the great Universities of the world would, in a rather foolish exercise, expose the author of it to considerable public ridicule.

No one in their right mind, therefore, would seriously consider publishing a book that the academic world would mock if there were not some exceptionally powerful motivation to do so. An extraordinarily strong "courage of conviction" that seriously questioned the supposedly infallible view of the "experts" – those with Doctorates in Religious Studies and the heads of the major Christian Churches – would be required for this kind of challenge. And, of course, not to mention the almost two billion Christian faithful who would also surely brand such a view ridiculous, perhaps even heretical.

Nonetheless, historical examples of supposedly sacrosanct views of the Christian Church eventually being consigned to the rubbish heap of untruth are not at all uncommon. In any case, since the whole process is an evolutionary one, so will it ultimately be with this new recognition. And it will be sooner rather than later.

Tragically, past centuries have borne witness to the torture and execution of radical dissenters who dared to even question the "infallible", official, Church position. As we noted earlier, a perfect example of "foolish infallibility" centred on the Graeco-Egyptian mathematician and geographer Ptolemy (A.D. 90-168), who proposed an astronomical system, readily accepted by the Church, that placed the Earth at the center of the universe. In 1543, Polish Astronomer, Copernicus, published a description of the Solar System that correctly had the sun at the center.

This new and radical "truth", however, was unacceptable to the Church. Copernicus was forced to recant.

From a point of immediate and outright rejection on pain of death, an absolute Truth can be *held at bay* for hundreds of years, then perversely embraced and defended as 'immutable truth' *by the very same*. The Church, as we all now know, **was very wrong.**

"Ruling authorities" – especially religious or scientific ones – do not usually readily-accept radical ideas that challenge *their* status quo, *even if the 'insight' is true*. In such situations there are only two possibilities for the governing elite. Deny it and continue to cling, at all costs, to the established "well of truth" deriving from the particular religious and/or academic position/s concerned, **or admit to being wrong**. In this case only *one* position, *one* action, would possess truly noble greatness – and honesty.

The obvious ramification of what is proposed here is therefore brutally simple. It states that **everything** previously believed and understood about Jesus being the **only** Son of God, *is completely wrong*. And the pages of this Chapter, especially, show why that is the Truth of it. Yes, there *are* references in The Bible that *purportedly* state that Jesus will *return*, but they are far outweighed by the greater number of statements by Him *warning* that Another – **The Other Son Of God** – would Come onto the Earth! [**Son** actually means **Part**.]

A serious question arises for Christian readers who may cross the path of this analysis and derisively dismiss it as being impossible rubbish – those who will not bother to even consider it *as* a possibility; and that is:
"What must the outcome be **if** this **is** the actual Truth?"
In reiteration, the word **if** is **only** for the purpose of this discussion, for we are postulating **an absolute and inviolable premise** here!
The clear, *connective premise*, therefore, is that Jesus **will not return to set physical foot on Earth.** Hence the very sure Biblical warning that only the *few* – not the many hundreds of millions – would recognise.

In the final analysis, a denial of *any* Ordination of **The Living Truth** from out of **The Divine Will** – even the *smallest* aspect – must ultimately fall back on all who so deny. A denial of the magnitude of the Truth surrounding **The Two Sons of God** would be *especially severe*, for it is tantamount *to a rejection of*: **The Divine Will Itself!** The great and inviolable Law: **"What a man sows, that shall he reap"** would ultimately return *dire consequences* in this case.

This Work thus offers the chance for many to awaken to one of the *greatest errors* of Christian teaching. However, as we stated at the head of this Introduction, it is not only the Christian world that needs to awaken to this monumental error, but **all** of humanity – including science and scientists.

In terms of the present state of the world, the crucial recognition of **"The Two Sons of God"** provides the key to understanding **Why** so many Nations, societies, religions and cultures are rapidly failing now, and why that deterioration **cannot now be stayed.**

*　　　*　　　*　　　*　　　*

12.2   THE TWO SONS OF GOD

"Grace to you and peace, from **Him** who is, and who was **and who is to come**;
and from the seven Spirits who are before **His throne**;
__and__ from Jesus Christ,..."

(New American Standard Bible.)

"Blessing and peace to you from **the One** Who Is, Who Was and **Who comes**;
and from the seven Spirits which are before **His throne**;
and from Jesus Christ."[1]

(Revelation. 1:4-5, Fenton.
Emphases mine.)

"That one Scripture, *perhaps more than any other in the entire Bible and all related religious writings*, possesses the "Golden Key" to the clear reality of **The Two Sons of God**! It needs only to be read with *an open spirit* and without "religious fear" for the profound Truth of it to be *intuitively recognised*."

(Author.)

The Two Sons of God! An unusual heading. Perhaps even blasphemous. Should we designate it a statement, or a question? Standard Christian beliefs generally accept an approaching end-time of great tribulation and destruction and the concomitant need for there to be the return of Jesus to Earth to, *ostensibly,* fulfil the revelatory prophecies from Biblical Scripture. Even Time magazine, Issue 1 July, 2002, devoted their lead story to this growing belief. Yet the contention that there **is** Another **other than** Jesus will, in all probability, be dismissed as ludicrous and impossible by many. However, let us keep an open mind and follow this key thread to its particular conclusion.

If we broadly trace the line of Religious Prophets and Truth-Bringers and the teachings they brought to Earth at their particular time in history – Lao-Tse, Zoroaster, Buddha and Mohammed, Moses and the Prophets etc., – we find revealed therein a spiritual/evolutionary continuum that leads to a particular level of knowledge and insight. Though gifted with exceptional spiritual insight and guided strongly in their tasks, what they could not give was the *greater* encompassing knowledge of the *wider* Creation. For it is not possible for *any* human being to *inherently know* that level of knowledge.

Thus it was that Jesus, The Son of God, brought a *more complete* knowledge of The Truth than had yet been given to mankind up to that point. In fact He brought the whole of The Truth **living within Him**, but humankind was too spiritually closed to fully recognise His Sacred Mission or accept and absorb all that He brought. Even those closest to Him, those who received more instruction than any others – His Disciples; even they were not sufficiently spiritually-matured to understand all that He *could* have given them. Aware that the ruling Jewish Religious Authority actively sought His death and that the time He would need to *fully* instruct the Disciples on the complete knowledge of The Truth would be denied Him, He began to speak of the time in the future when that *could* happen *for* them.

---

[1]A key reason for the acceptance and promotion of Fenton's Bible by **"Crystal Publishing"** may be noted in the small example represented by that 'Scripture'. Fenton's hallmark trait throughout his translation is his clear display of greater reverence for **The Godhead** through regular and common use of **Capitals** when referencing **The Trinity**! This is not the case with other Bible translators. **"Crystal Publishing"**, in all its publications, unequivocally and unashamedly concurs with Fenton on this most crucial matter.

"I have still much more to tell you; but you are not yet able to bear it. When, however, the Spirit of Truth **Himself** comes, **He** will instruct you in all the truth:..."

(John 16:12-13, Fenton.
Emphases mine.)

So the time-line of the great Prophets and Truth-Bringers associated with the incarnation of Jesus onto the Earth plane reveal an almost evolutionary spiritual-knowledge path of Truth up to the present. And that is correct in its basic outline. The premise that this Work postulates absolutely unequivocally, therefore, is that *Jesus stands at the apex of Truth*, since **He Himself is a Living Part of It**. And He, as the **Part** thereof designated as not only **The Word** but also **"The Love of God"**, thus forever stands as:

One of The Two Sons of God!

If we did not state that reality as a living conviction in these pages, this Chapter would, of itself, be blasphemous. And would thereby serve to *corrupt* and *distort* the truth of:

The Living Word of God!

That we will not do since the purpose of this Work is to offer signposts to *the whole* of The Truth. The danger of denying that which is of The Living Truth Itself lies in the outworking of The Laws of Creation on those who so deny. That outworking rests completely and lawfully in The Law: *"What a man sows, that shall he reap."* Since there actually *are* **Two Sons of God**, a denial of this fact will ultimately visit its particular "reaping" too. Therefore, as we have designated Jesus as a Son of God and this Chapter is entitled, **"The Two Sons of God"**:

Who, then, is The Other?

12.3   The Revelation of "The Other Son"

As background to our bold claim: In a *very compressed* journey in time, we need to look at the path and impact of Judaeo-Christian beliefs on both the civilised and the New Worlds long *after* the time of Christ. The rise and fall of the many civilisations of the "Ancient World", particularly those written about in the Old Testament, ultimately prepared the stage for the Message of Jesus to begin its journey out into the world. Initially, of course, across and out to the borders of the Roman Empire, but thence to its future dissemination to the wider world through the later European Empires. The general religious foundation of the latter is basically derived from the Judaeo-Christian ethos as outlined in The Bible. However, its entry into the European psyche to the present time saw it undergo many upheavals resulting in huge differences in meaning from the original simple and pure Teaching of Its Bringer: Jesus.

The religious authorities were not content to simply accept the clear Truth He brought but chose, instead, to erect huge monasteries and "schools of learning", behind which doors they could dissect His original Teachings. As a result of this long process of analysis and debate, the once-clear meanings underwent change, some subtle, some far more radical. What finally emerged from that fermenting crucible of *intellectual religiosity* differs vastly from the *Spiritual original* given by Jesus. Not only that, but for a time was also removed from the ordinary people. Thus, what little the masses were permitted to have, even that was used to enforce and maintain religious power over them by the few.

The sorry history of mankind testifies to the fact that through very especial "Called Ones", **Divine Will** many times strove to seed the great Truths in men. Men, however, unfortunately and *perversely*, subverted them all to just religions and/or splintered offshoots of. For the most part, therefore, they became institutions of earthly power, wealth and *religious* subjugation.

This dark volition can be readily traced through the mad, religious fervour of the Dark Ages and the equally insane Inquisition. The wealth and excesses of the Papacy seeded the wonderfully enlightened protestations of the great spiritual scholar Martin Luther who, in 1520, launched the Protestant Reformation. His opposition to the, then, entrenched religious view found a kindred soul in the English King, Henry VIII. By the Act of Supremacy in 1536, Henry effectively formed a new English Church and broke with Rome.

Later, via exploration and colonisation, the gradual expansion and consolidation of the European Maritime Nations to the New Worlds was effected. Thus, along with the export of European ideas and some of their criminals, went the zealous missionaries and their Christian religion in its more or less final, distilled form.

Whilst that was obviously an expansion of the European Empires, it was not at the same time an expansion of Spiritual Truth. What was exported to the new lands was far *less* spiritual than the original pure Teaching. The religious madness of the Dark Ages and the Inquisition had ensured that certain ideas of religious rigidity, formulated as dogma during those long centuries of bigotry and cruel torture, were henceforth retained as inviolable tenets of the new religious thinking. That is what arrived in the New World to challenge and then, for the most part, subjugate the peoples to whom it was usually forcibly introduced.

However, even though the "religion" had lost much of the essence of actual Spiritual Truth it was at least, in many ways, far more enlightened than anything some of the Indigenous peoples of the New World possessed. Thus, in accordance with their "divine mandate" as they believed it to be – **and paradoxically probably should have been** – European explorers and Missionaries carried *their* version of The Word, once delivered Spiritually-pristine from out of the mouth of Its Bringer, to many parts of the Earth.

What arrived in those far-off lands was therefore not truly a correct *interpretation* of the Teachings of Jesus as recorded in The Bible. Religious scholars in great Universities and Theological Colleges today *still* argue and debate many points of religious disputation. Uncertain theoretical or theological argument should have no place in the dissemination of "The Living Word" given to humankind from One Whose Origin hailed from the very Source of that Word Itself! For any such wrong interpretation *must logically be* a dangerous transgression against the very **Creation-Laws** of **God**.

A radical statement concerning two Sons of God, then, would surely be described as too blasphemous to even consider, given that no past or present-day clergy or religious authority has *publicly* mooted this *possibility*. Yet, such radical assertions cannot be made without some relevant form of Biblical or Scriptural foundation to begin with. For that is the standard measure by which to anchor such a premise, at least in the world of Christian religion.

> In *this* book, however, *other* avenues – of *exceptional knowledge* and *clear Spiritual Insight* – immeasurably assist us in our *factual premise*.

Despite the clearly contentious nature of what we are saying, we nevertheless urge well-meaning Christians and Biblical scholars to be sufficiently open-minded to at least *objectively* examine this matter. We categorically state, however, that we do not, in any shape or form, seek approbation or approval from any said religious or Christian Authority or Church anywhere to state what we assert herein. For, in reality, the debates that still rage among the "religious-learned" are simply the final end-excrescence of that process begun so many centuries ago, even pre-dating the Church-theology of Medieval Europe.

The relative times differ vastly of course in that today we possess far greater scientific knowledge about much more of the world. Unlike the Dark Ages when the Church held absolute power, a non-partisan Police Force and Judiciary today protect citizens who might wish to challenge the religious status-quo. To have asserted then what we assert here now would surely have resulted in charges of heresy and blasphemy, and thus a death sentence – one invariably preceded by cruel torture to try to force a recant.

As with most questions, however, the obvious reality is – as we must state often – that *either a thing is so, or it is not.* Particular historical times and events can *never* alter *that* particular truth. So is it with our radical assertion. Either there *are* Two Sons of God as we unequivocally state, or there is only one – Jesus. If, as we assert, there are two, then that clearly poses huge and fundamental questions for all Christians – and not least for the time that is referred to as "The Final Tribulation".

Let us therefore once more consult The Bible and the key Scriptures within that clearly *reveal* and *validate* the Truth about **"The Two Sons of God"**. And from *that* Truth in Biblical Scripture exactly around this crucial recognition, let us intuitively strive to understand the *monumental portent* and *far-reaching ramifications* of this *reality.*

The starting point of The Bible is, of course, The Book of Genesis. The general Christian belief about it all would probably aver that Genesis *seemingly* states that **in the beginning** there was only **GOD**. Thus a **One God** Who has existed from Eternity, and the darkness of a formless void. Nothing else. No life save that of **He, The Creator**. Further to that 'idea', therefore, it would be fair to say that most Christians believe that **God Himself** 'created the world and all in it'.

Yet John, the beloved of Jesus, makes a fundamentally more profound statement in the very first Verse of *his* Book. We know from New Testament Scripture that John and the other Disciples – who all lived literally cheek-by-jowl with Jesus – were given the greatest amount of knowledge that men had yet received about Creation, life and The Law. Since their Teacher was **The Son of God Himself**, we should surely expect that certain passages written by at least *some* of the Disciples **might just carry within them** far-reaching insights of tremendous spiritual import for **all** of humankind.

For the world of Christianity in this case, however, spiritual import of a potentially explosive nature. Thus we read in John, the beloved of Jesus, Chapter 1, Verses 1-3:

> "The **WORD** existed **in the beginning**, and the **WORD** was *with* **GOD** and the **WORD** *was* **GOD**.
> **_He_** was present **_with_** **GOD** at the beginning.
> **All** came into existence by means of **_Him_**; and nothing came into existence apart from **_Him_**."

(Fenton Bible. Emphases mine.)

If we now analyse those passages with an open, objective and questing spirit and mind, we immediately see that **at the time _when Creation came into being_** there was not just GOD and the empty void, as Genesis might 'appear' to indicate. There was *Another* – **_with_** **GOD**! The obvious question automatically deriving from that crucial point must logically be:

Who was "**_He_** *Who was present* **_with_** **GOD**...?" Was **'He'** Jesus, as is perhaps currently accepted? Or was **'He'** the Other, to **Whom** we refer?

The key *insight* that must be grasped here is that *Whomever* it was that John referred to, was *present* **with** **GOD** '*at the beginning*'. Moreover, the use of the personal pronoun **He** is a clear pointer as to *Who this particular One actually is*. As a second vital pointer to the answer, the Scripture also clearly states that; "...*the **_Word_** that was **_with_** **GOD**...*" was the

"...*He Who was present 'at the beginning'*." And that; "...*all came into existence by means of Him!*"

To reiterate the key point of that particular Scripture once more:

He Who was *with* **GOD** was **also** the <u>Word</u> *of* **GOD** too, and that **all** came into existence by means of **Him**! Such a simple statement is surely clear enough to understand, for there is no mystery here. As we have previously and seriously stressed, The Bible identifies **Who** that **"Other"** actually **Is**. The knowledge of **Who** <u>He</u> is thus clarifies/elucidates many points of religious contention.

Now to *further strengthen* our premise that He "Who was with God *at the beginning*" was the same He Who created "all things", all we need do is go to Verse 2 of Chapter 1 in Genesis. For the purpose of comparison and evaluation, we will quote from three different Bibles:

> "And the earth was without form, and void; and darkness was upon the face of the deep. And the *spirit* of God moved upon the face of the waters."
>
> (King James Bible.)

> "Now the earth was a formless void. There was darkness over the deep, and God's *spirit* hovered over the water."
>
> (Jerusalem Bible.)

> "But the Earth was unorganised and empty; and darkness covered its convulsed surface; while the *breath* of GOD rocked the surface of its waters."
>
> (Fenton.)

The unequivocal reference to a **'Creative Spirit'** in all three differently-sourced Scriptures clearly shows that it was not God Himself Who Created the "heavens and the earth", but **He Who was with Him!** The very fact that it is so written reveals that the ancient writers of the original texts *understood this clearly*. Of course, we should readily understand that Creation itself nevertheless proceeded only *according* to **GOD's Plan**, under *His Power and Authority*, but *through He* Who was *with* **GOD** as a *Part* of *Him*.

A note of caution should be sounded here. We should not attempt to interpret the *complete Creation-process* as involving just the *Earth* and its immediate, *material* interstellar environs. A clearly stupendous happening of colossal and *humanly-incomprehensible magnitude* would thereby be brought down to a superficial level of human-earthly *non-understanding*. Fenton's sub-heading provides the vital spiritual insight: "The *First Creation* of the Universe by God..." For the word "earth" does not refer solely to our earthly home but is symbolic of a *far larger Spiritual Reality*.[2]

The same basic reference to that *Other* With God can be found in both our main Bibles of reference and, indeed, in virtually all the different Bibles. So the same Scripture of John 1:1-3 in the King James Version reads:

> "In the beginning was the **Word**, and the **Word** was *with* **GOD**, and the **Word** *was* **GOD**.
> The *same* was in the beginning *with* **GOD**.
> All things were made by *him*; and without *him* was not anything made that was made."

---

[2]See Chapter: "The Origins of Man: Genesis and Science Agree!" for detailed clarification.

The Jerusalem Bible (1985 edition) states it similarly:

> "In the beginning was the **Word**
> the **Word** was *with* **GOD**
> and the **Word was GOD**
> *He* was *with* **GOD** in the beginning.
> Through *Him* all things came into being
> and not one thing came into being except through *Him*."

In order to more completely clarify this issue we should very carefully note that whilst **He** of **The Word** was *with* **GOD**, both **He *and* The Word** – *as an inseparable Part* – were *also* **GOD**. Yet whilst **He** is **The Word**, and **The Word** *is* **GOD**, there is nevertheless a clear *demarcation* in the **'Divine Working'** *between* **He Who**, as the **Creative Will** *of* **GOD**, brought all things into being *through* **The Word**; – and **GOD** – out of **Whom He** of **The Word** <u>came</u>. Surely that is simple enough to understand...!

If we now track to certain other Bible passages where **Jesus** is similarly referred to as **The Word**, then *apparent* discrepancies do *appear* to develop. [Full clarification, however – given *by Jesus* to His Disciples – may be found in the following section **12.4: The Disciple's Confusion**. And in **12.5: "He" Who is "Enthroned"!**, further clarification from **The Revelation**.]

In *this* segment, from our two main reference Bibles, we will simply quote two Scriptures that have very unfortunately set in concrete for hundreds of millions the terribly erroneous belief of just **One Son**.

> "And the WORD became incarnate, and encamped among us – and we gazed upon His majesty, such majesty as that of a Father's only son – full of beneficence and truth."
>
> (John 1:14, Fenton.)

> "And the Word was made flesh and dwelt among us, (and we beheld his glory, the glory as of the only *begotten* of the Father,) full of grace and truth."
>
> (King James.)

> "No one has ever yet seen God; He has been made known by the only Son, Who exists in union with The Father."
>
> (John 1:18, Fenton.)

> "No man hath seen God at any time; the only *begotten* Son, which is in the bosom of the Father, he hath declared *him*."
>
> (King James. Emphases mine.)

Notwithstanding the *seemingly* ironclad meaning here, the word <u>*begotten*</u> in these particular Scriptures actually offers a pointer to the Truth of it all. For, *in this case*, **The One** who was *begotten* should not be regarded as **The One** who was *present* *from the beginning –* <u>*of Creation*</u>.

Begotten: Past participle of ***beget***; – *'to cause to exist'*.

The Scripture therefore stands *spiritually-correct*. Jesus *was* the *only begotten* **Son** – *after* **The Creation**. For it was not **He** – as **The <u>Love</u>** of **GOD** – that *was* or *is* **The <u>Creative Will</u> of GOD. He**, as **The Love**, however, was also **The Word** too. Thus: **He** was *that Part* of *The Word of GOD* that *had* to incarnate on earth 2,000 years ago, if humankind was not to *fall* utterly and irretrievably. — **WHY?** —

As far back as the eighth century B.C., the prophet Isaiah *foresaw* the path that we of Planet Earth *would take*. The present-day state of it and its global societies clearly shows a calamitous and *rapidly-deteriorating situation*.

> "The earth also is *defiled* under the *inhabitants* thereof; because they have
> <u>*transgressed*</u> *the laws*,
> <u>*changed*</u> *the decrees*,
> <u>*broken*</u> *the everlasting covenant*."
>
> Therefore has the curse devoured the earth,
> and those that dwell therein are *desolate*:
> therefore the inhabitants of the earth are ***burned***,[3]
> ***and few men left*.***"

(Isaiah 24:5-6, Fenton. Emphases mine.)

It was therefore necessary for there to be the entry onto earth of **One** stronger than the prophets that preceded **Him**. They, for thousands of years, had continually warned the so-called 'chosen race' to heed **The Law**; but they, a 'stiff-necked people', would not.

> Thus **Jesus** came, ultimately for *all* humanity. For only **He** could explain **The Law** — **CREATION-LAW** — and thereby show the way back to The Truth, because the knowledge He bore was *Complete* and *Living* ***within Him***.

As previously stated: Aware that the ruling Jewish Religious Authority sought His death, Jesus realised two crucial things:

1. That the time He would need to *fully* instruct His Disciples on the *complete knowledge* of The Truth would be denied Him.

2. But also that even *they*, who were *closest* to Him, did not have the necessary spiritual maturity to *fully understand* the deeper knowledge He brought – the knowledge necessary to stem the downward path of a rapidly-falling humanity.

From then on He began to speak of the time in the future when that *would* happen. He thus began to speak of **The Other** Who would one day *bring to earth* the **ALL-TRUTH**. [Precisely to which this and all other works of Crystal Publishing point, and in which *is* found the *confirmatory knowledge* of **The Two Sons of God**!]

In an **Act of Love** totally incomprehensible to we of Planet Earth, the ***begetting*** of Jesus by **The Creator** from ***out of Himself*** stayed the complete and utter fall of humankind at *that* time. Through that process – and in a time-continuum that we human beings cannot hope to ***ever even begin*** to understand – may be seen the *sequence* of the *step-by-step* establishment of **The GODHEAD**.

---

[3]The meaning of the term, '*burned*' – which continues to puzzle Bible scholars, theologians and scientists alike – is both clear and simple. We explain it in Section **12.6: Destruction by "Fire"**.

*   *   *   *   *

1. From Eternity: **GOD!** Alone.

2. At the *beginning* of the Creations: A *severance* of a **Part** of **Himself** as **The Creative Spirit** – **His Word**.

   "**All** came into existence by means of <u>*Him*</u>; and nothing came into existence apart from <u>*Him*</u>."

   Thus: **GOD** as a **Duality**!

3. After the disastrous 'Fall of Man': A *further* severance of a **Part** of **Himself** as **Jesus**: – **The Love of GOD** and **The Word of GOD** – to incarnate on earth to save a 'falling humanity'.

   Thus: **GOD** as a **Trinity**. **The TRIUNE GOD!**

*   *   *   *   *

Paradoxically for global Christendom in the first instance, but also for *all* religions and belief-systems and even science in the second; the *key* to so many 'problem-questions' ultimately centers on the *knowledge of*, and *about*, **The Two Sons**.

Unfortunately, however, the 'default setting' of global Christendom to any notion that clashes with the 'official doctrine' of *One Son only* is so locked in stone that even the most catastrophic events will probably not be sufficient for this *most necessary* awakening. Fear of change on the one hand, and absolute certainty of their *One Son only* interpretation on the other, will ensure – for the majority of Christians at least – that Isaiah's clear prophecy *will come to pass*.

Now, what of this *other* "**SON of GOD**"? We know that the Christian Churches – who *should* know The Bible – have always spoken of only **One** Son of God, Jesus! And that He, as The Living Word also, therefore brought the complete and final Truth to mankind. He, as a Part of The Living Truth Itself, certainly *brought "the whole"*, living, **within Him**.

Due to humankind's spiritual immaturity at the time, however, that consequential inability to receive The Truth *fully* from Him meant that the *writings* of those who were closest to Him – His Disciples – are *incomplete* with regard to the *whole* that Jesus brought to earth at that time. The obvious ramification that such an assertion must logically presume is that The Bible, therefore, *does not contain the whole*.

The Apostle Paul provides the relevant insight in his 'Letter to the Corinthians'. We should carefully note that the words of Paul were written *after* the Crucifixion, and *after* the Outpouring which, according to some religious "scholars", *was* the watershed event that *would lead them* [the Disciples] into "all-Truth". Thus the time when Jesus would send The Holy Spirit.

The Church thus broadly accepts the Outpouring of The Holy Spirit at Pentecost as the fulfilment of a key prophecy of Jesus i.e., "...to send the Helper, the Comforter, The Spirit of Truth after His departure". Jesus is recorded as stating, however, that The Holy Spirit "...will reprove the world of sin". The word, 'reprove', clearly means to reprimand, to admonish, to reproach. The Outpouring of The Holy Spirit, however, has not resulted in this event even two thousand years later.

It therefore unequivocally refers to that which this specific Chapter addresses. *It refers to the Coming of The Son of Man Who is also The Spirit of Truth/The Holy Spirit.*

Against this fact, some may cite the words of Matthew 12:32. (New American Standard Bible.):

"Anyone who speaks a word against The Son of man will *be* forgiven, but anyone who speaks against The Holy Spirit will *not be* forgiven, either in this age or the age to come."

The contention may thus arise that, as per the above, Jesus *seemingly* differentiates between The Son of Man and The Holy Spirit. Clearly, there are different ways of interpreting that Scripture. One could say that even if The Son of Man and The Holy Spirit are one and the same Person, speaking a single word against Him may be forgiven, but *continually speaking* against The Holy Spirit will not result in forgiveness. This clarifying interpretation becomes more plausible when one considers a different translation of the same Scripture from **Fenton**:

> "And if one gives expression to a thought against The Son of Man, it shall be forgiven him, but if one shall speak insultingly of The Holy Spirit it shall not be forgiven him, neither at the present time, nor in the future."

Here there is a clear difference between the phrase, "gives expression to a thought" versus "shall speak insultingly". The reader must spiritually-perceive and thus enter into the *true* sense of the words whilst understanding that the designations, Spirit of Truth, Holy Spirit and Son of Man – whilst seeming to be separate entities – are nevertheless: **One and The Same!**

We can perhaps better understand the *non-forgiveness* aspect of the Scripture which pertains to the title, "**The Holy Spirit**", if we relate it to that **Part** of **The Son of Man** which *is* **The Holy Spirit** *as* the **Creative Spirit** – **THE WILL** – *of* **GOD**. Thus **He** Who brought all things into being *through* **The Word**. We, also brought into being and gifted conscious life by the very same **Creative Spirit**, should therefore understand the strict requirement to not transgress the **Divine Commandment**:
"Thou Shalt Not Take The Name Of The Lord Thy God In Vain."
Thus, in reiteration: **He** of the **Word** Who was **with GOD** is also **He** Who **Is** **The Word** *of* **GOD**.

Notwithstanding the obvious Spiritual Power that must have been experienced by those present at "The Outpouring" at Pentecost, Paul states very clearly:

> "For we know *in part*, and we prophesy *in part*. But when that *which is perfect is come*, then that which is *in part* shall be *done away*."

> (1 Corinthians 13:9-10, King James.)

Fenton translates the same passages thus:

> "For we know *imperfectly*, and we teach with *imperfection*; but when the *perfect* arrives, the *imperfect* will *become useless*."

And The Jerusalem Bible says:

> "For our *knowledge* is *imperfect,* and our prophesying is *imperfect*; but once *perfection* comes, all *imperfect* things will *disappear*."

> (All emphases mine.)

Simple logic must lead us to the obvious conclusion that Paul could not have been referring to Jesus Himself as the *"part"* or the *imperfect,* for He, Whose Origin was The Divine, was *complete* in *Knowledge* and *Perfection.* In all of Paul's ministry, nothing to the contrary was ever so stated by him. In any case, it would be ludicrous to try to argue that the Teachings of Jesus – as The Son of God – could be *done away* with, *become useless*, or *disappear.* Paul certainly knew that, as did the Disciples.

For Matthew (24:35 Fenton, parenthetic addition mine) records Jesus stating in admonishing warning that:

> "The heaven and the earth may fade away; [*disappear*], but My Declarations [The Truth] will never pass away."

As previously examined, theologians and Bible scholars could be forgiven for believing that The Outpouring was, after all, the event where The Holy Spirit gave the "*complete and perfect*", the All-Truth, to the Disciples. For the strength of the happening was such that they all spoke in tongues and became seeing. Yet a simple analysis of it all points to a very different conclusion; a conclusion that Paul understood quite clearly. Therefore, if Jesus was not *"the part"* – and He surely was not the *imperfect* – then Who or what was Paul referring to? Who, therefore, would bring the Perfect, and when?

12.4   The Disciples' Confusion

The answer lies in the following Scriptures given by *Jesus* in reply to questions from His Disciples regarding the end-time. The singularly-strong aspect here is the clear statement that **The One to come** would instruct in *all* the *Truth*, meaning that Jesus had not done so. In other words, what He was *able to give for that particular point* in human spiritual evolution and have it at least basically understood, was just a *part* of the whole, *not* the *complete* thing.

In necessary reinforcement, this is so stated in John 16:12:

> "I have still much more to tell you; *but you are not able to bear it.*"

In other words, even though instructed by The Son of God Himself to a far deeper level of knowledge than certainly any other human beings to that time, the greater degree of understanding that humankind *still required* could not be imparted to the Disciples then. It was simply too much for them to understand or assimilate.
Therefore another, **The Other**, would have to come and bring *all* **The Truth**.

> "...because if **I** do not depart, the Helper will certainly not come to you; but when **I** depart, **I** will send *Him* to you. *He*, on *His* coming, will bring conviction to the world..." — — And also:

> "When, however, the Spirit of Truth *Himself* comes, *He* will instruct you *in all the truth... He Himself* will honour Me..."

> (John 16:7-8 & 13-14, Fenton.
> Emphases mine.)

The clear inference in all of these Scriptures is that the use of the personal pronoun, **He**, denotes an *actual* person in the same way that **Jesus** was an *actual person*. And, moreover, would be **The One** Whom *Jesus would send*, but only *after His* [Jesus's] *own departure*.

The "Second Coming of Christ" has been "accepted" as a non-negotiable event for centuries now by virtually all Christian groups. The ostensible sureness of that happening as espoused by Global Christendom, however, is clearly thrown into question if we assess particular Scriptural statements brutally-objectively. For *if* **The Other** *is* to come – the word-concept *if* only being used for the purposes of this discussion of this moment – such a crucial event must ultimately shake the very foundation of *all* religions and *all* science. In fact it would impact on every facet of what it means to be a human being resident in *Subsequent Creation* at this time. And whether one is on Earth or passed from it is irrelevant.

The quandary for the global Christian community of *if/should/when* centred on the *ostensible* return of Jesus and not any thought for the Coming of **The Other**, presupposes the probability that Christianity/humankind, in general disbelief anyway, will ignore it and continue to embrace, instead, totally different and therefore *wrong* concepts. The end result will surely not then be as Christians, particularly, might hope or imagine.

Whilst we may accept that Jesus indicated He would "return", He did not say where or how, or *precisely* why. In other words, in what "form" would such a "return" occur and for what purpose, given that **The Other** – the actual **Bringer of the All-Truth** – **would be here on Earth with that [His] All-Truth?** Is this another Bible mystery? No! Not with the complete knowledge contained *within* that **All-Truth**.

What we may deduce, therefore, is that *inherent* within the encompassing **All-Truth** which Jesus Himself stated would be brought to Earth by **The Other**, would be revealed the ***how*** and ***why*** of a very brief but nonetheless exceptionally spiritually-powerful, *non-physical*, "return" by Jesus! What we therefore now have is a **new knowledge** of a "dual working" of <u>Two Sons of God</u>. In this case, for a brief moment in time in order that **Divine Ordination** be fulfilled *for* earthly humanity. The very same of which, perversely, the *greatest majority* remain obtusely-oblivious to **The Event!**[4]

If we now look to The Revelation in Fenton's Bible, Chapter 1 Verses 4 and 5, (our defining introductory quote to this Chapter) we should singularly note, in strict objectivity, a further strong statement of differentiation between **The Two**.

> "Blessing and peace to you from <u>**the One**</u> Who Is, Who Was and <u>**Who comes**</u>; and from the seven Spirits which are before **His throne**; — **and** from Jesus Christ."

It is patently clear from the above Scripture that there is more than just one **"One"**. Moreover, the strongly denoted *separative-conjunction* **"and"** draws a clear line of demarcation between Jesus ***and*** — **The Other** – <u>**The One**</u> — "Who Is, Who Was and <u>**Who Comes**</u>"! This key Scripture reveals the fact very clearly for: "...the seven spirits are **before His Throne**..." And it is the throne of "**He Who Comes**..." Thus, in very necessary, repetitive-reinforcement in this crucial case: **The One Enthroned** – **is** – **The One Who Comes!**

He Who Comes, therefore, ***cannot possibly be*** **GOD, The Creator, Himself**, because it is **not** **"The Almighty"** **Who comes to Earth.** [*If it were even possible to begin with, the whole of the "Material Worlds" – in all its humanly-incomprehensible immensity – would be utterly consumed by His Power.*] For how could He possibly be The Eternal Mediator Who would thus have to, very illogically, stand as the link *between* humankind *and Himself*? That role belongs to The One appointed for the Task. The One "Who is, Who Was and **Who Comes**" – **The Alpha and the Omega** – **The Word of God Who exists: the All-ruler!**

> Therefore **The One Enthroned** is thus **"The One"** Who Comes as: **The Eternal Mediator, The Holy Spirit, The Son of Man.** He is that **Part** out of **GOD** Who Comes as **HIS Will.**

---

[4]You, reader, might be surprised to learn that a dual working *is precisely stated* in The Revelation. That particular Scripture, along with others of revelatory insight, is quoted further on in this Chapter.

Despite the crystal-clear logic of our explanations, we would yet be safe in commenting that the general, broad interpretation by many of the mainstream Christian Churches of the crucial message to John about "Who is to come" would teach that Jesus in the presence of **The One Enthroned** *would be interpreted* as Jesus in the immediate presence of **GOD** Who, of course, would naturally be Enthroned. However, as is brutally clear from the very logic inherent in the whole discourse, and which we will restate *again*: The One Who *is* Enthroned, is <u>also</u> *The One Who Comes*, so therefore **cannot possibly** be GOD! For "HE" is "**THE ALMIGHTY**" Who cannot *descend* to the $\overline{\text{Earth}}$, and is thus **THE ONE** Whom; "...**no man hath seen at any time**"!

Therefore, in logic brutal and clear, the *very fact* that the blessed recipient of this vision in the first place *could behold* The One *upon* The Throne, *automatically tells us* that He Who can be *seen* Enthroned *cannot possibly be* **THE CREATOR**. The One seen **Enthroned above All Creation** and designated as **The Lord** is the **Living**, **Creative**, aspect of **God**.

The entry onto the Earth of **The One Who Comes** with the complete and Perfect Whole of the All-Truth would thus ultimately fulfil the prophecies of Jesus and statements of Paul in that it would render any accumulated knowledge and belief, past and present, individual and collective, religious and scientific – *that did not perfectly accord with it* – irrelevant, and therefore useless. That is exactly the *"in part"* that shall be *"done away"*; and the *"imperfect"* that will *"become useless"*. It is when *"all imperfect things will disappear"*.

Thus it is actually for *this present era of humanity* with its concomitant spiritual and technological development that the **whole**, the **complete**, the **perfect,** was intended for. And the **One Who Comes** is **The One** *Who* would bring it. The same **Who**, as **The Spirit of Truth**, Jesus was to send. Moreover, the **All-Truth** that He would bring would speak *of* Jesus, as we have previously stated.

A very crucial message of Jesus to His Disciples clearly reveals the obvious fact that He is telling them about **The Other Son — Who is to Come**. The constant reference and emphasis in the personal pronoun here unequivocally shows that **The One** about Whom He is talking is not some vapourous or disembodied entity, but Someone – just as Jesus had to be – Who would be *present* in a *physical body on Earth*, BUT *at a future time*. The simple statement: **"He Himself will honour Me"**, tells it all very, very clearly.

> "I have still much more to tell you; but you are not yet able to bear it. When, however, the Spirit of Truth <u>Himself</u> comes, <u>He</u> will instruct you in *all* the truth: for <u>His</u> utterances do not proceed from <u>Himself</u>; but just what <u>He</u> learns <u>He</u> will declare, and the events that are coming <u>He</u> will announce to you.

<u>He Himself</u> will honour <u>Me</u>.

> ...because what <u>He</u> receives from <u>Me</u>, <u>He</u> will transmit to you. All that the Father possesses is Mine: that is why I said, 'It is of <u>Mine</u> that <u>He</u> takes and transmits to you.' Only a little while, and you will not see Me; and again a little while, and you shall see Me."[5]

(John 16:12-16, Fenton.
All emphases mine.)

---

[5]We may note in the last sentence the preparation for the Disciples of the impending event of His earthly death – "and you will not see Me" – and after "a little while" when He would rise in His non-earthly body, when – "you shall see Me".

The two thousand year time-frame since the time of Christ has permitted us the luxury of greater understanding and awareness of a far wider world than the people in His time could ever have known. Because of the greater level of overall knowledge now taught as a matter of course through scientific Disciplines, Institutions of "higher" learning and in the general education systems today, the presupposition should therefore be that we are now also sufficiently *spiritually* equipped to recognise this complete whole when it arrives. And thus similarly recognise **The Bringer** of it. **The Spirit of Truth; The Holy Spirit; The One Who Comes!**

Since it is *our present time* that is spoken of, the spiritual faculty within each one of us *should*, therefore, at least *intuitively* perceive that such an event is imminent – *or has possibly already occurred*. Yet, almost the whole of the Prophetic utterings of Jesus and the Prophets within the pages of The Bible clearly show that the majority of mankind *will miss the moment*; will *not be awake at the time*.

If we do *not recognise* in time, if we miss that moment, if we simply refuse to accept – *even if it should pass before us* – what happens then? If we stubbornly cling to what we presently believe out of fear of letting go, what will that mean for the one who has missed it, or for the one who is asleep? In turn, what will it mean for global humanity, *if the majority of the world's people – including, therefore, most Christians – are blind to the happening?*

Then, as we intimate, *if* there has not been sufficient recognition and spiritual growth and change in humankind:

"...all the tribes of the earth shall mourn..."

(Matthew 24:30, Fenton.)

"...then too all the peoples of the earth will beat their breasts..."

(Matthew 24:30, New Jerusalem Bible.)

Matthew, Chapter 24, offers key pointers to this question of whether Jesus was or is to return. For example, from verses 3-5:

Afterwards, when He was resting upon the Mount of Olives, His disciples approached Him privately, asking,
"Tell us when this will be; and what is the signal of Your presence, and the completion of this age." "Take care," said Jesus, in reply to them, "that none may deceive you. For many will come in My Name, asserting "I am the Messiah", and will lead many astray."

Verses 23 to 25 offer more indications.

Then if any should say to you, "Look! the Messiah is 'here', or 'there' do not believe it. For false prophets will make their appearance; and will give out great and terrible omens, so as to mislead, if possible, even the chosen. However, *I have forewarned you*."

Here Jesus surely indicates that many would pretend to be Him and that the Disciples would need to exercise the greatest possible degree of alertness and spiritual discernment when the time for the entry of The Son of Man onto the Earth arrived. That logically means that The Son of Man, The Eternal Mediator, *would be here when many false prophets would claim to be Jesus.* Historically, messianic claims are nothing new. It would be fair to say, however, that the 20th century probably saw the public emergence of perhaps more false messiahs than ever previously recorded. And, of course, many are alive and well in the 21st century too. So is He here? **If so, where?**

Matthew describes the key sign which will reveal the fact that The Eternal Mediator is – *or has already been* – on Earth. The following Scriptures not only add more Biblical weight to our premise, but they further illustrate the fact that Jesus does not refer to Himself in the first person but clearly infers that there really *is* Another.

> "...and then will appear the signal of the Son of Man in the sky. And **He** will send out **His** messengers – and they will collect all **His** chosen..."

> (Matthew 24:30-31, Fenton.)

Matthew, in 25:31, offers another powerful statement from Jesus in support of the **Other One**. Again, He *does not say* "**I**" will do this or that, but that the **Other One – He, The Son of Man** – will fulfil it!

> "But when the Son of Man appears in **His** Majesty, and all **His** angels with **Him**, then **He** will take **His** seat upon the throne of **His** Majesty; and collect all nations before **Himself**."

In that particular Scripture, as in many others, we would at least expect Jesus to say, "**I** will collect all Nations before **Me**." – if **He Himself** was to fulfil that role at the End-time. Yet that is not what **He** says, even though instructing and enlightening His Disciples as to what to expect then! Further Scriptural quotes clarify our premise:

> "...but the helper, the Holy Spirit, Whom the Father will send... **He** will teach you everything".

> (John 14:26)

> "When the Son of Man comes, however, will **He** find this faith upon the earth?"

> (Luke 18:8)

Further examples from The Jerusalem Bible provide more anchorage for our premise:

> "...proved by my going to the Father and your seeing Me no more".

> "I came from the Father and have come into the world, and now I leave the world to go to the Father."

> (John 16:10 and 16:28)

Despite the fact that we *can* find passages where Jesus *apparently indicates* He will return, it is **The Son of Man Who is to Come as The Eternal Mediator** – as Jesus clearly states. For too many other statements by Him show clear reference to the **Other** Whom **He** is to send. If it was unequivocally and absolutely certain that Jesus *was* **The One Who Comes**, then we would surely expect that *all* statements, references, Scriptures, inferences etc., would carry the "**I**" and not the "**He**" so clearly evident in so many places.

If it *was* so absolute, as Christian thinking today states so emphatically, then surely the men who were closest to Him – even though not fully understanding all that He gave them – would have written so in every case. However, that is not what we read, for that is not what they wrote. **For that is not what He told them in this case!** Why are we so emphatic about this exact aspect? Quite simple: A *very telling* point has been missed here. It is this:

The very fact that the Disciples did *not understand* Jesus on this issue, yet **nonetheless** **still** recorded the "**HE**" *more often* than the "**I**", must clearly presuppose that they really did *faithfully chronicle for posterity what they were told by Him — despite their non-understanding.* Otherwise, human nature being what it is, they would all have interpreted His words to replicate what *they believed* He meant; that The Son of God and The Son of Man Whom Jesus spoke about so often towards the end of His Ministry, were one and the same – i.e., **He**, their **Master**. Notwithstanding their confusion – and as we have noted in this Work – the Gospels nonetheless reference the "**HE**", The Other, *"Who is to Come"*, in many places.

We know there exists in Christendom the very prevalent *belief* that **The Bible** in its *entirety* is **The Word of God** given through *'inspiration without deviation'*. We also know that The Bible records Jesus as telling His Disciples they were *not ready* to receive all the knowledge **He** carried *within*, because they would not understand it. Should that not sound a note of warning to Christianity? We certainly think so. Why? For a very long time now global Christendom has conditioned itself to faithfully believe that The Bible provides an *absolute* and thus *non-negotiable* tenet: **One Son of God, Jesus**, Who is to return as "**The Eternal Mediator**". Yet that especial Work does not at all agree with what has now become a sacrosanct Church-ordination. So where lies the 'without deviation inspirational aspect' which must, by Christian definition at least, *never be questioned*?

An interesting yet problematic quandary for Christendom therefore rears its unwelcome head here, for the very Scriptures we quote and the obvious analyses and conclusions arising from them reveal a tenet that simply "does not stack up". So which parts of the relevant Scriptures, messages, writings, admonitions etc., should we accept – or ignore – in order "to make it fit"?

If Jesus really is to return as The Eternal Mediator, why did the Disciples not change their texts to read accordingly and thus use the **I**, solely, in their collective Gospels and writings? Moreover, why did all later translators and interpreters *also not change* that wording? Surely, in terms of human language, this is nothing more than very simple and basic grammatical expediency – for all languages must clearly differentiate between **I** and **HE**. If that were not the case normal discourse would be severely hampered, if not impossible.

Perhaps, on this most crucial issue, it really is a case of **The Divine Will** ensuring that *despite* so much *non-understanding throughout history*, The Bible actually does *"tell it like it is"* with regard to **The HE** Who is **The One** to set foot on Earth at the Divinely-ordained hour. Global Christendom *should* take *serious note* of the absolute truism proffered by the Danish philosopher, Kierkegaard:

'It is not the Truth that lies with the *masses*, but the untruth. The *crowd* is the 'untruth'.'

The validity or otherwise of the Four Gospels has been the subject of much scrutiny and debate by Bible scholars and theologians for centuries now. It is clear that the original writings, or perhaps more specifically the original words given to the Disciples from Jesus, underwent much change and editing through many translations, but also through the personal or religious bias of various scribes and translators. So we know that The Bible today is a heavily re-worked publication set in a more-or-less final form that powerful, and at times tyrannical, Church leaders – operating under the guise of spiritually-enlightened and infallible scholars – determined it should take. More recent researchers have seized upon this fact to call into question the actual validity of the Four Gospels of the Evangelists.

The co-authors of "The Holy Blood And The Holy Grail" make much of this to lend credence to their particular premise. It is surely impractical and illogical, however, to believe that the

Disciples of Jesus would report everything that transpired during their association with Him in *exactly* the same way. They were chosen *not* because of their *sameness* but because of their *differences.* They would therefore likely report events in the short yet hugely eventful Ministry of Jesus in historically volatile times differently from each other. Certain events would no doubt obviously impact more decisively on some than on others.

So the very fact that they apparently *did* report things slightly differently, with one or two clearly important events omitted from *some* Gospels, should not detract from the main and critical message ultimately contained *within the four Gospels.* Rather, it should be seen as a convincing insight into a much broader sweep of their overall connection and association with Jesus. Thus what they were tasked to pass on to the world.

Therefore, despite the obvious fact that the Evangelists were very different individuals from diverse educational and working backgrounds, The Books of the Four are *remarkably consistent* with regard **to what we are postulating here.** They no doubt made mistakes and perhaps did not report exactly all that transpired, and they clearly did not understand all that Jesus told them, according to *their* record of **His** statements. However, one could assume that if there were *huge* and *irreconcilable differences* and not simply minor ones in terms of what they were told by Jesus – or believed they were told, or grossly misinterpreted what they were told or heard – then we would surely see evidence of that in their individual writings.

That is clearly not the case, however. In fact the *consistency* with which references to **The Other**, obviously from Jesus Himself – *for where else could they have possibly gotten it from* – faithfully reproduced in the four Gospels by the four Evangelists clearly indicates, in our view, a singularly important aspect of what Jesus was trying to impart. And the four, in essence, recorded exactly that.

A strong example of what we contend can be found in Mark, [Fenton] Chapter 8, Verse 38.

> "If *anyone*, however, is ashamed of **Me** and of **My** teachings in this adulterous and wicked race, then will the Son of Man be ashamed of *him*, when **He** comes with the holy angels in the majesty of **His** Father."

In this example, Jesus does not say; "...when **I** come... in the majesty of **My** Father." as He surely would have if He was to fulfil that future role. Such statements reveal that Jesus knew He would *not* return to the Earth as the "Eternal Mediator", and that He knew Who *would.* He therefore prepared the Disciples, **and thus mankind through their writings**, to expect such an event.

A singularly important aspect of "His" Coming would require it to be strongly linked to the appointed time and thus to any indicative signs that *might* precede this event. As previously stated, the key requirement must surely be the **CRUCIAL RECOGNITION** that such an event was imminent. **Or perhaps had already taken place**, and thereby been **completely missed by most.**

Despite the sureness that the global Christian Church in its many guises confidently exudes about the "non-negotiable return of Jesus", the facts we outline here show that such a scenario *will* ultimately turn out to be **not the case**! The *actual reality* for the greater majority of humankind is very clearly spelt out in the Scriptural warnings from Jesus – He Who would send **The Other Who Is to Come.** As a further problem for such believers, any entry of The Eternal Mediator onto the Earth surely poses huge and fundamental problems for all Christian groupings that accept the validity of the return of "someone". For in the first place:

"Who will He come to?"

Since only cool, clear objectivity offers the key to a logical interpretation of prophetic Scripture, not emotive Christian religiosity, then we should well understand the obvious fact that the

All-ruler – the **Alpha** and the **Omega**, **The Eternal Mediator** – *must* and *will* stand far above such earthly ideas as diverse religious denominations. He therefore *will not*, and indeed *cannot*, ally Himself to any one group or Church. To put it bluntly, such a notion *is just plain silly*!

So, from the Disciples of Jesus, from those who lived with Him, who heard His Words and bequeathed their experiences to posterity, we offer a few more of His admonitions. Warnings to be fully awake and alert, to not get so bogged down in everyday worldly matters or pleasures that the spirit inside each of us falls asleep and misses the moment forever. Should this event not be recognised, that non-recognition will not stop the tribulatory effects that will be associated with it.

For the arrival of **The Son of Man** as **The Eternal Mediator** *heralds the beginning of the complete collapse of all distorted religious beliefs of the peoples of Earth, along with all wrong science.*

> "On account of this, be ready! because it may be that the Son of Man will appear at a time you do not expect."

> "Be you also ready; for it may be that the Son of Man will come at an unexpected moment."

> (Luke 12:40 and 44, Fenton.)

> "You too must stand ready, because the Son of Man is coming at an hour you do not expect."

> (Same Scripture – The Jerusalem Bible.)

> "Keep guard, therefore, for you know not what hour your Lord may come."

> (Matthew 24:42, Fenton.)

And in the parable of the ten thoughtless bridesmaids who were shut out of the wedding, Jesus admonishes and warns humankind to be alert and awake to this return.

> "Therefore keep awake; because you know neither the day nor the hour when the Son of Man will come."

> (Matthew 25:13.)

Paul's contribution to this reality is well stated in 1st Thessalonians 5:1-2.

> "But about the times and the seasons, brethren, there is no need for writing to you: for yourselves know well enough that the day of the Lord comes like a thief at night."

> (Fenton.)

Luke, 21:34-36 Fenton, gives a particularly strong warning about the crucial need to not miss the time or the moment. (Emphasis mine):

"But take care of yourselves, for fear your hearts should be loaded with debauchery, and drunkenness, **and business cares**,[6] and that day come swiftly upon you like a snare; for thus it will come upon all dwelling upon the face of the earth. Watch, therefore, at every season, offering prayer; so that you may be prepared to escape all the coming calamities, and take your stand in the presence of the Son of Man."

The Jerusalem Bible notates the same passages thus:

"Watch yourselves, or your hearts will be coarsened with debauchery and drunkenness and the cares of life, and that day will be sprung on you suddenly, like a trap. For it will come down on every living man on the face of the earth. Stay awake, praying at all times for the strength to survive all that is going to happen, and to stand with confidence before the Son of Man."

*   *   *   *   *

It is vitally important to understand **why** Jesus so strongly warned His Disciples to yet **prepare** for the **entry** of The Son of Man *at the end of the times*. Since He did not mean in **His** lifetime or even shortly thereafter – **because we have had 2000 years of history since** – *how, then*, could the Disciples watch and wait for such an event *if they all followed the natural path of life into earthly death as they obviously all did around that time?*

The answer lies in the overarching knowledge *inherent within* "**Creation-Law**" explained in Chapter 3: '**The Spiritual Laws: The Crucial knowledge**'. In this case, namely **The Law of Rebirth**. Therein lies the answer *immutability in concert with the spiritually lawful processes and inviolable outworking for all human beings that is the sure aftermath of the first death*, and the subsequent paths that **must** be taken **thereafter** – to either *life eternal*; or to the **Second Death**.

*   *   *   *   *

The warning to the Disciples to 'watch and wait' meant that they should be alert and awake to the signs which would herald the *arrival* of '**The Other**' far in *the future*. The clear admonition of Jesus to them of His words, "**I have forewarned you...**", was to prepare them for a future end-time of great confusion. **For at least some would need to be on Earth again, to stand in the presence of 'The Other'.** However, it was not just His Disciples to whom Jesus addressed the warning. It was to all of humanity then and now; for this time – today! For this is the era of **The Son of Man** and thus The Judgement for all!
A primary statement given by Jesus to His Disciples about the end-times indicates this clearly.

"Verily I say unto you, This generation *shall not pass away* till all be fulfilled."

(Luke 21:32 King James.
Italics mine.)

From The Book of Matthew, 24:34-35, Fenton:

"I tell you indeed, that this generation *shall not pass away* until all these arrive. The heaven and the earth may fade away; but My declarations will never pass away."

---

[6]Surely here is the greatest warning yet to the corporate world and its financiers, exchange-rate manipulators, share-market fanatics and all of similar ilk who elevate the *god-corporate* and the *god-financial* before all else. **"For what will it profit a man if he should gain the whole world and forfeit his life?"**[...lose his soul?]

Thus the generation of that time, those responsible for His murder, would all have to be back on the Earth to stand before the *Living Truth* of **The Son of Man**. Either to *pass into life* – *if* there had been sufficient "good works" for expiation of the deed since – or to *pass from life*; to pass away in the "second death", if there had not. All generations before and since would similarly be required to face their own individual wrongs, whilst in the same period also experiencing the destruction of all the wrong that humankind had collectively produced – to also either *pass from life* or *pass into life*.

One more warning – and one that surely applies to Western societies today!

> "And as in the days of Noah, so will also be the appearance of the Son of Man. For as they were, in the days before the flood, eating and drinking, marrying and giving in marriage, until the day arrived for Noah to enter the ark, and ***they would not understand*** until the flood came ***and carried all away***."

> (Matthew 24:37-39, Fenton.
> Emphases mine.)

This is that period. It *is* the time of that **prophesied fulfilment!**

> "And there will be signs in the sun, and moon, and stars; and upon the earth nations in despair, as when in terror of the roaring and raging sea; men expiring from fear, and apprehension of what is coming upon the world:..."

> (Luke 21:25-26, Fenton.)

Continuing on from that very necessary explanation, let us learn more about this singularly momentous issue. For if the full import of it is truly recognised and really understood, that recognition and understanding could then open a door that would greatly assist us *to pass into life*.

In this part of our revelation it is essential to stress the fact that The Bible regularly notes *two different references* to *two* particular **"Names"** and *two* respective **"Titles"** in various places within its pages. The general assumption has been that both contrasting titles referred to the same **One** – Jesus! Yet, firstly, we have the two different "Titles": **The Son of God *and* The Son of Man!** Secondly, we have the two different "Names" – **Jesus *and* Imanuel!** The Christian Churches, however, generally teach They are one and the same.

The Gospel of Luke, 1:31-32 and 35, offers a prime example of what we are saying. The message of the archangel Gabriel to Mary is very clear.

> "And listen: you shall conceive and give birth to a Son; and you shall give Him the name of **Jesus**."

> "...and therefore the holy result shall be called **Son of God**".

Conversely, Matthew's unfortunate mistake has bequeathed a legacy which has misled many successive generations to the present day. For in Chapter 1 he writes that prior to the birth of Jesus, Joseph, knowing he was not the father, was nevertheless directed by a messenger of the Lord to accept Mary as his wife. In Verse 21 Matthew states:

> "And she will give birth to a Son **and you shall name Him Jesus...**"

Then Matthew, perhaps out of his own beliefs and/or lack of sufficiently clear spiritual understanding, later writes:

"Now all this took place so that the statement of the Lord, as recorded by His prophet, might be fulfilled:
BEHOLD, THE VIRGIN SHALL CONCEIVE,
AND GIVE BIRTH TO A SON;
AND THEY SHALL CALL HIS NAME **EMMANUEL**,
which, when translated, means THE GOD AMONG US."

(Matthew 1:23, Fenton's Capitalisation.
Emphases mine.)

Joseph, however, *did not* name the child **Imanuel** but, in accordance with the *instructions* of the "messenger of the Lord", named Him **Jesus**.

Therefore, what should be understood here is the very crucial fact that whereas the *messenger* of **The Lord** clearly proclaimed **Jesus** as **The Son of God**; Isaiah [7:14] was the prophet who prophesied, and thus *proclaimed*, **Imanuel** as **The Son of Man: The Eternal Mediator!**

Matthew has very wrongly attempted to make two into one for the references relating to this truly 'dogma-shattering' revelation; in Chapter 1 of *his* Gospel are simply illogical. Had he received a personal visit from a messenger from Above who stated otherwise, Matthew would surely have written so. In quoting Isaiah he clearly does not recognise his own mistake, and neither have many since. He has therefore unfortunately bequeathed a huge error to posterity because his use of the Scriptures here make no sense. They serve only to confuse and cloud a very vital issue.

12.5 "HE" Who Is "Enthroned"!

To fully explain the meaning of this sub-Chapter, we need to now carefully examine particular Scriptures from 'The Book of Revelation' – that Book of which no word is to be altered – handed down to us by *the John* whom Jesus proclaimed as the "none greater among men". If we very carefully note the following references, we can readily see that there are, indeed: **TWO!** Chapters 4, 5, 6 and 7 state this reality. So, in Revelation 4:2, John observed:

"...a throne in the heaven, and upon the throne an Occupant".

We have already established that **The One Who Comes** is **Enthroned!** And in Revelation 4:9, those in attendance:

"...give praise, honour and thanks, to the Occupant of the Throne, Who lives for ever and ever..."

In Revelation 4:11, the very same state Who The Occupant is:

"You, our Lord and our God, are worthy to receive the majesty, and the honour, and the might; for You have created all things; and for Your purpose they were and are created."

He is therefore **The One *with* GOD** in the beginning, *through Whom* all things *came into existence* at the start of Creation.
John then saw a book:

'...upon the right hand of the Occupant of the throne'. It was written 'inside and outside' and '...sealed down with seven seals'. Then a strong angel proclaimed '...with a loud voice', "Who is worthy to open the book, and to break its seals?" 'And no one in the heaven, or upon the earth, or under the earth, was able to open the book, nor yet to gaze upon it'.

(Revelation 5:2-5)

John 'wept much', because '...no one was found worthy to open the book, or even to gaze at it'. Then he reports, 'But one of the elders said to me':

"Do not weep, see! the Lion out of the tribe of Judah, of the root of David, has succeeded in opening the book with its seven seals."

John then saw:

"...*between the throne and the four Beings*, and in the *centre* of the elders, *a Lamb* placed, as having been sacrificed..."

(Revelation 5:6)

In this momentous *revelation* from **The 'Book' of Revelation**, we have a Throne upon which an Occupant sits i.e., **One Enthroned**. And **Who** was *with* **GOD** and through Whom all things were made. In close attendance are what we might perhaps term "the whole host of the heavens", Angels, Elders, and Beings. Now, however, *we also have the Lamb*, Who is able to open The Book.

Who, then, is the Lamb?

The Lamb is clearly *not* the Occupant of the Throne, for the Lamb is *between* the Throne and the four Beings. And the Occupant of the Throne is the One Who both lives for ever and ever and yet Who has created all things – "for His purpose". But He is not:

The Almighty: GOD Himself!

"For no man hath seen God at any time."

(Emphases mine.)

Once again, the answer to Who is designated as occupying the Throne lies in the earlier Scripture in this Chapter:

"The **WORD** existed in the beginning, and the **WORD** was *with* **GOD** and the **WORD** was **GOD**.
He was present *with* **GOD** at the beginning.
All came into existence by means of *Him*; and nothing came into existence apart from *Him*."

The Revelation thus states the Occupant of the Throne to be the **'He'** Who was *present* with God 'from the beginning'. It is the same **He**, also, by Whom *everything* came into existence and, moreover, is *The One Who Comes*.
Because this issue is so vital to a correct understanding of revelatory prophecy – *and thus to the final fate of every individual on Earth* – let us once more ask the key question of the moment:

Who is the Lamb?

Whilst the designation, Lamb, would be regarded, grammatically, as a "which" and not a "who", the sureness of the personal pronoun, He, in this case reveals that *that* description clearly refers to a person. Surely, then, the *only* logical conclusion to draw is that **the Lamb is He, Jesus.** For if we do *not* acknowledge that as the Truth here, then we have a major problem with the following passages from The Revelation:

> *"And He [the Lamb] came, and **took it** [the book] **from** the right hand of the Occupant of the throne..."*

> (Revelation 5:7-8. Parentheses mine.)

The very word, *'from'*, is unequivocal in its **brutally-clear meaning**. Even with such clarity, however, there will yet be many who will refuse to "see"; who will refuse to acknowledge the Truth of our assertions. Paradoxically, they may well use the very book that we quote from to say it cannot be so. Indeed, they *must* use this same book, for the very many variations of Christian Church beliefs and interpretations derive their so-called *authority from* The Bible. And ultimately therefrom, also, their 'Christian mandates' which say to the faithful of all the *different, individual,* congregations: "Only *our* interpretation can be correct." Of course, all will rise or fall on exactly the interpretation clung to. So let us quote a few more Scriptural gems to further clarify the Truth of what we are saying.

Just as the host praised the Occupant on the Throne as being worthy to receive the majesty, honour and might, so do they now offer the same to the Lamb.

> "Worthy is the sacrificed Lamb to receive the power, and wealth, and wisdom, and might, and honour, and majesty, and celebrity!"

> (Revelation 5:12)

Both have now been **honoured equally** – as **separate Individuals!** For the next Verse very clearly illustrates this delineation between the Occupant of the Throne *and* the Lamb. The very words in Revelation 5:13-14, themselves so state it in the separative-conjunction — **"and"**!

> "To the Occupant of the throne **and** to the Lamb belong the fame, the honour, the majesty, and the might for ever and ever."

A far stronger message of warning about the Truth that this Chapter contains can be read in Revelation 6:16-17. Here the same delineation, but a very firm reference to a **dual working at the end-time**, as we previously stated.

> "Fall upon us, and *hide us* from the Occupant of the throne, *and from* the **displeasure** of the Lamb; for the great day of **their anger** is come – and *who is able to stand*?"

What do we understand the word, *their*, to mean? Even to the youngest English language reader it would obviously mean what it says. It means *more than one.*

> This simple and short, everyday English word must surely be *the single most important pointer* to finally showing that *there are*, indeed, **Two Sons of God!** What else could possibly be needed?

If this crystal-clear Scripture is *not* proof enough for the doubters, then all that is left to finally force an awakening within their ranks will be the very *sign* of the Son of Man Himself. Just as we clearly understand the meaning of the word, *their*, I am sure we also understand the meaning of the word, *"anger"*. Associated with the previous key word, *their*, this powerful Scripture *should*, therefore, **be the one that finally awakens mankind**! For who are **They** angry at? There can only be one group of creatures who would deserve such **Divine Wrath**. That is mankind on Earth! Who, indeed, can stand against **their anger**? But there is more:

> "The Salvation is from our God,
> Who sits upon the throne,
> **And from** the Lamb."

(Revelation 7:10)

As a final entry to this key issue, Revelation 7:14-17 offers the same truth. Here, John is addressed by one of the elders who asks him if he knows who the multitude are in "white robes". John did not know so asks who they are.

> "These are they", he proceeded, "who came out of great affliction, and **they** washed **their** robes, and made them white in the blood of the Lamb. Because of **this** they are before the throne of God, and day and night they serve Him in His sanctuary; and the **Occupant of the throne** protects them... because the Lamb having **ascended the midst of the throne** shall **shepherd them**..."

(Fenton. All emphases mine.)

This final reference to **The Two** from out of 'The Revelation' is interesting for more than the irrefutable Truth that there really are **Two Sons of God**. For in this particular example, we have a further clarification of very great import. Firstly, the **Occupant of the Throne** – Who therefore sits on it – **protects** the multitude who have cleansed *their* robes [*their* spirit] and made them white [pure] *themselves*. Jesus has not done it through His *acceptance* of death on the Cross. No, **they** have done it. They have achieved that state of grace by *living* His pure Teachings. And have therefore *earned the right* to, *metaphorically*, "stand before the Throne" and be forever protected by its Occupant.

Jesus, on the other hand, Who does not *occupy* the Throne – because He has **ascended** the **midst** of the **Throne** and therefore stands on the same level as **He** on **It** – nonetheless **shepherds** the throng. Here, also, a clear *dual* working, and one of *equal* Majesty, Power and Governance.

Notwithstanding such a clear statement about **their dual working**, we reinforce here again the especial and distinct demarcation between **The Two Sons of God**. This is defined by the fact that they possess *two different Names* – **Jesus** and **Imanuel**. And they have *two different Titles* – **Son of God** and **Son of Man**.

It is very simple to see, therefore, that they also have *two different Tasks* – for *two different Purposes*. **The Son of God**, Jesus, as The Word, also designated as **The Love of God** Who therefore works in Love, emphasised that He had '*not come to judge*'! (John 12:47)

The Son of Man as **The Will** *of* **GOD** does, however. The Will, moreover, is the *complete Will*. As we have already clearly explained, **The Son of Man** is thus **The Spirit of Truth, The Holy Spirit, The Eternal Mediator** – and thus **Justice of GOD**. It is **He** Who therefore *brings* the Judgement! Though a Judgement of **Divine Wrath**, it is a 'cleansing and sifting' nonetheless inherently imbued with the inseparable qualities of *Perfect Justice* and

Perfect Love. And therein lies *their Dual Working*: That of **The Two Sons of God** *in the Judgement.*

Yet even though there is *individual* working contained within those designated tasks, both 'Sons' are nevertheless **in God The Father**! And **God The Father** is **in Both**! Quite simply and clearly, therefore, **"The TWO"**, and **The LORD OF ALL**, comprise:

The TRINITY! The TRIUNE GOD!

In that **Divine Reality** — the outworking and understanding of which is forever denied to we human beings — may nonetheless be understood *the meaning* of the previous Scripture from Revelation 7:10; i.e., "...our God, Who sits upon the throne..."

'The One Enthroned' is that **Part** of **The Will** of **THE TRIUNE GOD** Whom 'John the Revelator' was granted to see!

As a further reference to **A Trinity**, the prophet Zakariah (4:1-5, Fenton), in the presence of a Messenger of The Lord, describes a curious vision which the Messenger interprets for him.

> The Messenger then turned to converse with me, and roused me like a man awakened from sleep, and asked me, "What are you looking at?" When I answered, I have been looking, and saw a lamp of gold, with a cup on its top, and seven lights on its seven uprights, with seven branches for the lights, that were on its top. Two Olive trees also stood one on the right and the other on the left.
> And I continued, and asked the Messenger who was conversing with me, and said, "Tell me, Sir, what are these?" The Messenger who conversed with me accordingly replied, and asked, *"Do you not know what these are?"* And I answered, "No, Sir!"

The Messenger then explained other things to Zakariah, but Zakariah insistently sought an answer to his question.

> But I continued and asked him, "What are those two Olives on the right and left of the lamps?" And I again enquired and asked him, "What are the two Olive branches that are on each side of the two golden feeders that extend from the golden standards?" And he replied to me asking, *"Do you not know what they are?"* When I answered, "No, Sir!" So he said, ***"Those are the two Sons-of-oil who stand near the Master of all the earth."***

> (Zakariah 4:11-14, Fenton.)

Taken all together, these explanations clearly point to a *major interpretative error* by the Christian Church and its many theologians historically. For the analyses herein really do clarify the Truth and Status of **The Trinity**. Certainly the *meaning* is clear enough; or should be for even the *basically-perceptive* reader. So the supposed *mystery* of **The Trinity** is not actually a mystery at all. Neither is it meant to be since we are enjoined by Law and **Divine Directive** to *seek* – and thus *find*!

Factually, we can certainly *know* what the *term*, Trinity, means. However, for we humans – who are merely 'developed beings' of the far lower level of **Subsequent Creation** – the 'mysterious' aspect associated with **The Divine Trinity** centres on the humanly-incomprehensible – thus *never-to-be-understood* – *concept* of: — **A**

<u>The</u> — "TRIUNE GOD"!

Human language cannot even *begin* to *express* such an 'idea', let alone somehow relate to **It** or engage with **It** meaningfully in *any* shape or form. Therefore, we must simply forever let such an *'overwhelming concept'* be the greatest "**Bible Mystery**" of all.

12.6   Destruction by "Fire"

In this Chapter we have endeavoured to use mainly **The Bible** as the key source for our revelations. We have also ventured into other areas to cull relevant and complementary knowledge to enhance our stated premise. In the closing stages of the Work it is timely to look at one especially vital aspect of **The Law**. For this *revelation* we will marry, from **The Bible**, part of **2 Peter** with part of "**The Book of Esdras**" from **The Apocrypha**.

The Books of **The Apocrypha** are not *officially* regarded as having the same degree of importance as the Books of **The Bible**. Whilst still an 'addition' or 'Addendum' to the Catholic Bible, the 'Apocryphal' Books were removed from Protestant Bibles by the British and Foreign Bible Society [primarily the Anglican Church] in the 19th century. Despite the unfortunate relegation of **The Apocrypha** to almost anonymity for probably the greater mass of global Christendom by the Church hierarchy, that body of work should nonetheless be *recognised* as being *absolutely essential* for a far greater degree of elucidation around certain key questions *in **The Bible*** that, at present, have no logical answers from Christendom; *as in the case of the question we address now.*

The Apocrypha, in concert *with* **The Bible**, provides the answer to it, thus giving a comprehensive picture of the whole by filling a knowledge-gap not so far addressed adequately by Christian theology. However, precisely because The Apocrypha is *officially designated* as a *lesser* work by Christendom overall, quotes from Esdras may be deemed to not carry the same authority as those from The Bible. Yet the two Books of Esdras not only provide the very answer to Peter's perhaps cryptic prophecy, but in it is *the most **powerful** and **relevant** spiritual insight and **revelation** for this very time* – for the Earth and **all** its peoples.

The question of "Destruction by Fire", long mulled over theologically, has now also been assessed from the scientific standpoint. From the earth-science perspective – and perhaps to a large degree from the theological side with regard to an Apocalyptic scenario – *destruction by fire* for global humanity tends towards such things as intense and widespread volcanic activity, a meteor impact, extreme drought, and perhaps prolonged solar activity.

Yet the *real answer*, whilst simple and straightforward, is ultimately *far more profound* for we human beings of Planet Earth than any notion which might suggest catastrophic events as being the *primary* driver for *destruction by fire*, and humanity *thereby* being *physically* burned. Though, of course, with certain natural phenomena, that is not just possible but very likely for some. Moreover, even for *very many* when such phenomena finally gives vent to its full power at *its* time of ordination. Now, whilst that will one day be a problematic reality for humankind, the distilled meaning of *'destruction by fire'* here means something **very**, **very different**.

The Book of Daniel is often used to mathematically calculate significant dates in a time-line of major events which many Christians believe reveals 'the time of the end'. Ezra, in our view clearly an important "apocalyptic prophet" in the mould of Daniel, offers a *singularly vital key* to the most crucial aspect of that approaching time; what exactly it is that will constitute the actual "force" of destruction and cleansing, and Who will bring it. Or, perhaps, **Who It was that might already have brought it!** Since we have earlier clarified the identities of both Jesus and Imanuel, the exercise we undertake now is to add considerably more weight to the outworking of **Creation-Law** for a rapidly approaching time of great upheaval.

The Prophecies of Daniel *might* have some relevance – in terms of a viable time-frame – *if* an **arrival** is still to be **expected.** However, if that has **already taken place**, in exact accordance with the many quotes already offered in this Chapter such as: "You know not the hour your Lord may come" etc., then the mathematical analyses from Daniel are logically *rendered irrelevant.* If, then, such a "return" *has occurred,* what we explain from 2 Peter and 2 Esdras equally logically fits that *possible* scenario.

Peter, towards the end of his life, offers advice to the growing numbers of Christians about what to expect at the end of the times. Fenton sub-titles Peter's discourse:

"The Irrevocable Word of God"

> "You should first recognise this, that during the latter times deceivers will come with deception, gratifying their own passions, and asking, "Where is the promise of His appearing? for since the forefathers went to sleep, everything continues the same from the beginning of the creation." For they willingly suffer to hide from them this reason, that by the intention of God the skies existed from of old, and the earth with water above and water below, arranged for the purpose of God, by means of which the then existing world perished, by the water having rushed down. But the *present earth and skies* are treasured up by His intention, '**reserved for fire**' at *a period of judgment and destruction of wicked men."*

> (2 Peter:3-7, Emphases mine.)

Peter's explanation of how and why the deluge at the time of Noah was possible on the scale intimated – of which there seems to be some scientific evidence – may offer some insight into understanding the "mechanics" of it. Obviously, a lot of water had to fall to achieve an inundation sufficiently large to destroy what was on *at least part of the Earth.* Equally obviously, the water had then to drain *somewhere* for the hills to reappear. It is not our intention to delve further here, but the reader may wish to contemplate on certain passages in Genesis that "seem" to complement Peter's explanation for the "deluge". As we have previously noted, the Disciples of Jesus received far more knowledge about more aspects of the world than any other men up to that time. The key point here now is Peter's statement:

> "...that the present earth and skies..." are "...**reserved for fire** at *a period of judgment and destruction of wicked men".*

The singular word **"fire"** provides the key to understanding what is not only to come, but what is *already occurring.*

What might we believe *fire* would mean in this case, however? Given that it will be a time of unimaginable desolation, we could perhaps envision a huge and fiery celestial object colliding with Earth. The Revelation does state that as an actual impending event in our probable 'near-future'. Or it could perhaps be an extremely large "coronal mass ejection" (CME) from the sun which reaches out and envelopes the Earth destroying [frying] all electrical and electronic components in everything on it; from power stations to aircraft to all computerised control systems affecting every single facet of our 'modern' world. [In 2011 NASA warned that increasing solar activity would peak sharply in 2012, with the possibility of exactly that kind of damage to global electronics that did not have the necessary shielding to protect the systems from the effects of the electro-magnetic blast/s from the sun. Modern electronics are not built to withstand such power-blasts, so will "fry" should NASA's prediction be correct.]

A massive CME that blasts the *whole Earth* would therefore effectively reduce all 'first-world' countries to 'third-world' status virtually *in an instant*, for it would cause *immediate* and *irreparable* damage to the computerised control systems that regulate every facet of our lives; even food production. The fact that all power stations would be 'knocked out' means that cities would simply cease to function – for many years. The inevitable result of such a scenario would be fear and panic, and thus anarchy.

So even though the word fire usually means flames, burning and heat, does it actually mean that here? From The Apocrypha, The Book of Esdras, Chapter 13, Verse 2, the prophet Ezra recounts a dream which is afterwards interpreted for him by the "Messenger of Light". The key to understanding the meaning of the "fire" that Peter alludes to – *and would no doubt have understood* – lies in the following relevant excerpts. Initially featuring the sea wherefrom a wind arose and stirred up the waves, Ezra's dream then showed the wind make something like the figure of a man emerge from the heart of the sea. That man then:

> "...flew with the clouds of heaven...", and wherever he turned his face to look, "...everything under his gaze trembled, and whenever his voice issued from his mouth...", all who heard it "...melted as wax melts when it feels the fire...".

After this Ezra beheld an "...innumerable multitude of men gathered together from the four winds of heaven..." to make war against the man who came up out of the sea. Ezra saw the "man" carve out for himself a great mountain and fly up onto it. But he was unable to see or recognise the region or place where it was. After that he saw that all who had gathered to fight him were "...much afraid, yet dared to fight". When the multitude rushed at him, "...he neither lifted his hand nor held a spear or weapon of war". But Ezra observed how he:

> "...sent forth from his mouth as it were *a stream of fire*, and from his lips *a flaming breath*, and from his tongue he shot forth *a storm of sparks*".

Ezra saw that all three were mingled together – "the stream of fire", "the flaming breath" and "the great storm". These fell on the attacking multitude and *burned them all up*. Nothing was left but the dust of ashes and the smell of smoke. After this Ezra saw the same "man" come down from the mountain and call to another multitude which was peaceable. In great fear Ezra awoke and besought an interpretation from the Most High. His petition was answered, and the key elements of the vision follow. The Messenger then spoke:

> "This is the interpretation of the vision. As for your seeing a man come up from out of the heart of the sea, *this is he whom the Most High has been keeping for many ages, who will himself deliver* **his creation**, and he will **direct those who are left**. And as for your seeing wind and fire and a storm coming out of his mouth, and as for his not holding a spear or weapon of war, yet destroying the onrushing multitude which came to destroy him, this is the interpretation."

The "interpreter" then tells Ezra that the time would come when:

> "...bewilderment of mind..." would come over those "...who dwell on the earth". And they would make war against one another, "...city against city, place against place, people against people, and kingdom against kingdom". "And when these things come to pass *and the signs **occur** which I showed you before,* **then my Son will be revealed**, whom you saw as a man coming up from out of the sea."

The next segment from The Book of Esdras provides the link with 2 Peter. The aspects of *primary significance* in this particular analysis are emphasised either in italics, in bold, underlined, capitalised, or varying combinations of all.

> "And when all the nations hear his voice, every man shall leave his own land and the warfare that they have against one another, and an innumerable multitude shall be gathered together, as you saw, desiring to come and conquer him - - -
> And he, my Son, ***will reprove*** the assembled nations for their **ungodliness** [symbolised by *the storm*], and will **reproach them to their face** with their **evil thoughts** and the **torments** with which they are to be **tortured** [symbolised by *the flames*], and will **destroy them without effort** by **THE LAW**." [Symbolised **by the fire.**]

> (Parenthetic additions and emphases mine.)

Here we have a clear pointer *linking* the warnings of **Peter** – thus from **The Bible** – through the clarified vision of **Ezra** – from **The Apocrypha** – to the outworking of **Creation-Law** on the affairs of mankind. Only *with* the essential contribution of the prophet, Ezra, can the *true spiritual meaning* of "**Destruction by Fire**" be answered logically. And *only* with the requisite *spiritual guidance* to *link* **The Bible** <u>*with*</u> **The Apocrypha** could we reveal that answer: An answer automatically mandated by the fact of the Perfection of **The Laws of Creation**, the explanations of which we are directed – thus graciously permitted – to offer in this and other Works of **Crystal Publishing**.

The crucial knowledge of **Creation-Law**,[7] deriving from and inherent within **Divinity Itself**, gives *back* to **The Bible** its proper place and status. The *terrible* and *inexcusable distortions* of the clear Truths in that especial Work – perversely clung to by blind millions – count strongly towards the impending *total collapse* of *all* facets of wrong *human* behaviour *and* endeavour. The associated destruction should be recognised as being produced by the *spiritually-lawful* **effect** of the *"fire"*; which is:

> "Whenever his voice issued from his mouth...", all who heard it "...*melted as wax melts when it feels the fire...*"

That is the key to understanding the effect of The Living Words of **The Law**! Whether written or spoken by '**The One**' – **The Son of Man** – Who brings 'the Complete': The '**Formed Word**' Proclaimed by **Him** is thus transformed into commensurate *real-time outworking* over the period of its ordained fulfilment in **The World of Matter**. And therewith is produced – under the aegis of **Inviolable Law** in Creation – the outworking of Peter's proclamatory *"destruction by fire"* upon our completely *aspiritual* global societies, cultures and religions. Quite obviously, therefore, very many of we – the *agglomerated* human race– will fully experience Peter's prophecy.[8]

Therefore, human works that comply *with* **The Law** will quite naturally prosper. Works that do not will suffer destruction. By this infallible measure we may recognise what is *true* to **The Law** and what is not. The '**fire**' of **The Law** thus unerringly produces the concomitant cleansing effect; [also **The Law**]. The powerful impact of *the storm, the flames* and *the fire* – which are all *already* strongly affecting mankind so detrimentally now – is solely the result of our intransigence, arrogance and stupidity in refusing to believe or accept **the one single and ultimate reality in the whole of Creation**. And that is:

---

[7]See Chapter 3: The Spiritual Laws of Creation: *The Crucial Knowledge for Humankind*; for detailed clarification.

[8]An 'agglomeration'. 2; a confused or jumbled mass. [Kierkegaard; "It is not the truth that lies with the masses, but the **untruth**. The **crowd** is the **untruth**."]

That only THE LAW — <u>CREATION-LAW</u> — reigns Supreme!

There is nothing else! Everything in all of the Creations was formed from out of **The Living Law Itself: From out of The Will of GOD – IMANUEL!** It is **He** Who thus brings **The Living Law**, which is the *'cleansing fire'* spoken of in The Book of Esdras.

Therefore *what we even now experience* is nevertheless still just the beginnings of the storm, the flames and the fire – **The Law.** Is His arrival imminent? Or is He already here? Difficult questions for most, but crucial for all! The appearance of the Sign of The Son of Man "in the sky" is the key to the fulfilment of the last events for an intransigent humanity. Since His Sign "appears in the sky", we can expect that it will be a powerful one. One, therefore, that cannot be missed, even by the obtuse.

Though what will it *actually* herald? That He is about to "descend on clouds", that He is about to be born, or perhaps to be revealed? Or perhaps it will state that He really **did** "...come like a thief in the night...", that only **the few** were awake, and that the world had therefore **missed The Event.**

Because His Sign is connected with Him, it will be visible to all human spirits in this part of "the world" and not just to those living on Earth at the time. Therefore, both the living and the physically dead will know that the Sign, **clearly visible to all then**, is here!

12.7   The 'Rapture'? A Distortion of Bible Truth!

The expected return of Jesus by one very large, mainly American, group of Christians involves, for them, the interesting notion that they, and they alone as a group from all humankind, will be "saved" by being "raptured". The concept of "The Rapture" as applied in this case takes the form of an event or process more fully formulated from earlier ideas mooted by an evangelical preacher, John Nelson Darby, who arrived in the U.S. in 1862. His minister, Cyrus Scofield, expanded the evangelist's ideas in the prominent Scofield Reference Bible.

Drawn from the Apostle Paul's seeming assertion that believers could or would be "lifted up to Christ in heaven", the idea of being "raptured to heaven" must presuppose that it is in the physical body since it all happens in an instant. That at least seems to be the general conviction of believers. However, we have already correctly concluded that according to The Almighty's Perfect and thus Unchangeable Laws – which accord with Perfect, natural, Laws derived from the higher Spiritual paradigm – *human physical bodies cannot be suddenly transformed and/or whisked away to sit on clouds or something similar.*

Even The Son of God Himself could not circumvent The Perfect Laws that He came to fulfil: "I come not to overthrow the Laws..."

As you, the reader, now know, The Chapter, *Jesus! His Birth, Death and Resurrection,* details the crucial "pre-discovery information" about where His body actually lies. It is secured in *a special tomb under Jerusalem.* It is a crucified body, **but without the legs broken.** We will once more note the prophecy about that key pointer:

> "The soldiers, therefore, came and broke the legs of the first, as well as of the other one crucified with Him; but when they came to Jesus, and seeing that He was already dead, **they did not break His legs.** And the eye-witness gives this evidence, and his evidence is truthful; and he himself knows that he speaks true, so that you may believe. For these events happened in order that the Scripture might be verified: *A BONE OF HIM SHALL NOT BE BROKEN.*"

(John 19:32-37, Fenton's Capitalisation. Emphases mine.)

Do Christians really believe that the **non-material** and therefore **Eternal 'Realm'** of what is so loosely designated as 'heaven' is some kind of jaunt *'just up there'*? Jesus told Pilate that His Kingdom was *not* of *this* world. And to His Disciples that He would *return to* The Father and they would see Him *'no more'*. How can it be that many millions will accept an idea that is an absolute impossibility according to the Perfect Laws of He Whose teachings of Perfect Truth those same millions *profess* to believe in and follow?

Phenomenal sales of the "Left Behind" series which promote the "rapture" concept and which have apparently sold somewhere around 50 million copies, clearly point to at least that many believers. Yet the sage observation of key Scriptures of warning should be made by all who wish to be "raptured":

> "I tell you indeed that you shall not depart until all has been fulfilled," – "Not one farthing shall be remitted you until *you* have paid fully."

And for the authors who have made millions of dollars but in the process of growing rich *already led millions astray now*:

"What does it profit a man if he gains the whole world and loses his soul?"

Should we designate the so-called "rapture" to be some kind of "Bible mystery"? After all, men prefer a mystery to Truth! No, it is not any kind of "Bible mystery" simply because the concept of "rapture", *as taught and believed by people in the Christian Church*, **is completely wrong**.

It is more an emotive concept ultimately derived from indulging human religious weaknesses. It does not exist and will not happen because the whole idea actually *opposes* all notions of necessarily **Perfect Laws** deriving from **The Almighty**. Disbelieving or dismissive Christians at this time of rapidly approaching "closures" will one day soon reel in shock and horror as the cold truth of these statements becomes brutally clear.

The rapid approach of the *end* of human foolishness, driven by increasing pressure from **The Light** Above, therefore means that all human concepts are exposed to the **Power** of that relentless *pressure*. In the case of the notion of 'The Rapture', its time of exposure and belief is perhaps at, or nearing, its peak. It has therefore gone through the necessary phase of revealing itself in its true nature; it has offered itself as a concept to those who have chosen it as truth; those choices have thus largely been made; and all that is left now is *its collapse at the appointed time*, **and therewith its demise.** There is therefore no further need to comment on what will almost certainly be:

The greatest non-event in human history!

12.8   THE PROCLAMATION!

The terribly wrong teaching of 'The Rapture' by the Christian Church pales into *insignificance* when compared with the *greatest distortion* of all; that there has only ever been *one* Son of GOD. The powerful outworking of **The Law** from ordained scriptural prophecy is perfectly proclaimed here in the Divine Warning:

"Vengeance [THE LAW] is mine, I will repay."

The Law will thus visit its terrifying reciprocity on *all* who subscribe to this *appalling distortion* of **The Living Truth!**

Everyone wants from their God a soft, enervating, vacillating, personalised, emotionally-satisfying, earthly brand of constant and all-forgiving love. Few there are who *really understand* that **Justice** is an *absolute* accompaniment of **The Love** of **The Divine!** Distorting the Truth from Above sets all who so distort it *against* that very Truth, and thus *against* its **Source:**

THE ALMIGHTY!

The knowledge about The Two Sons of GOD is, therefore, ***the most "Crucial Imperative" of all*** – for *all* humankind. This key Truth is not about being some kind of 'Christian truth', nor is it a point to be debated by so-called 'experts'. The religious scholars and leaders of *all* ethnic groups and cultures and *all* religions, no matter how derived, must face this Truth here, *now*, at this critical juncture in human history and evolution.

That evolution was never about the "human/chimp" split that occurred millions of years ago; that scientists have placed so much importance on. We have clearly refuted the totally incorrect *scientific obsession* surrounding that foolish belief in the Chapter: "The Origins of Man: Genesis and Science Agree!" So much wasted time and energy and research funding that would have been better spent examining subjects that could *really* benefit man.

The crucial recognition that we are not just a physical body solely is thus the key to understanding that the Earth is a place of "physical transition" only, and that our *actual* evolution was always meant to have been that of our *spiritual selves*, the *true* human being. However, just as primatologists, anthropologists and many other "...ologists" etc., have wasted valuable "spiritual-life" time pursuing something that was totally irrelevant for *real* human knowledge so, too, have the many "Christian scholars" also wasted the same kind of valuable "life-resource" in promoting completely wrong interpretations about what is the ultimate "Truth" given to mankind in The Bible:

The "Living Truth" of The <u>Two</u> Sons of GOD.

Religious scholars and ethnic and cultural leaders of belief-systems that ignore, disbelieve or outright oppose or condemn this Ultimate Truth will – **along with Christian Church leaders who also disbelieve or deny and thus lead astray** – live the full experience of the outworking of one of the very Laws that **One** of The Two Sons of GOD stated unequivocally He had "...not come to *overthrow*, but to fulfil."

Earth-science and all the great religions state that key Law in basically similar terms; *'The Law of Sowing and Reaping'*, *'The Iron Law of Karma'* – **'The Law of Reciprocal Action'.** We can quite rightly therefore say that *no* reasons or excuses exist anywhere in the total human science/religious paradigm whereby the outworking of that great Law – with regard to the Truth *about* **The Two Sons of GOD** – could *not* be recognised. Do we not see the effect of the increasing power of this Inviolable Law every day now?

The recognition of **The Two Sons** [i.e., **Parts or Extensions of GOD**] therefore represents the critical, spiritual evolutionary-step on the path to what is meant to be humankind's final goal – *our return home.* The recognition of this sublime Truth is thus also meant to be the same kind of evolutionary step that all leaders and teachers of all religious beliefs world-wide must make, **so that The Pure Truth of He Who gave us Life could be gifted to all.** The explanations in this Work will help lead the *serious* reader to that complete knowledge.

Throughout this Chapter we have alluded to the "possibility" that **The One Who Comes** *has already been.* Since He is to be expected at a time of great travail for the human race, we have striven to pique the curiosity and spiritual intuition of you, the reader, to seriously consider what we have stated here.

Because a statement about such an event would necessarily have to be proclamatory in nature, an absolute proclamation centred around **His Return** would therefore not be at all subject to intellectual analyses – *for such analyses would automatically be rendered irrelevant* **by The Event Itself!**

At the conclusion of this key Chapter and thus this Work, therefore, we unequivocally proclaim what is perhaps – for the Christian Church particularly, but mankind collectively – the greatest "truthful irony" of all:

Bible prophecy has been fulfilled, and "the world" has missed The Event!

Thus for all: – Bible Scholars, Popes, Archbishops, Presidents and Kings; politicians of *every* persuasion, scientists and writers, leaders of *all* Religions and Churches and of *all* ethnic and cultural Groups:

The "*Dual Working*" has therefore been fulfilled, and thus the key confirmatory-proclamation by **Jesus** that:

"He, Himself, will Honour Me!"

*   *   *   *   *

JESUS — The SON OF GOD –

– is thus **Honoured** in the **All-TRUTH** brought to Earth by:

IMANUEL — The SON OF MAN
— The ETERNAL MEDIATOR —

['GOD with us']

*   *   *   *   *

In the profound Grace of this knowledge, and in accordance with the Mandate to so proclaim, we herewith present our Proclamation:

The SON OF MAN has indeed come like a thief in the night and He has given to mankind HIS "Message" from out of "The Holy Grail"!

More decisively, however, we offer here:

HIS Admonition:

"You Can See It – If You Are Willing To See!"

Epilogue

The concepts and conclusions outlined in this book may represent a major challenge to some present-day cultural, philosophical, academic, medical, religious and spiritual beliefs. Notwithstanding that sure probability, under the aegis of **Creation-Law**, these same concepts are nonetheless inviolable.

As stated in the Preface, 'lone voices in the wilderness' who dare to challenge the status quo inevitably clash with the current academic thought of their particular generation. However, the historic, opposite inevitability is that each generation of academics must *re-learn* a basic Truth, especially with regard to the Spiritual Truths contained within the great religions: That it is not **The Truth** that lies "...with the masses", but the *untruth*, as Kierkegaard sagely notes. Historically, it is the lone voice or the small group that holds, *in lonely constancy*, to the kernel. Very often that lone voice or small group will not possess the requisite level of education or erudition which the 'Establishment' deems necessary for the retention, understanding and dissemination of such 'elevated concepts' as religious or Spiritual Truth.

Given this book's bold standpoint and associated challenge to long-held and sacrosanct 'Christian beliefs', the 'learned' from main-stream Christian-religious academia, particularly, will almost certainly and predictably ***wrongly*** determine the Work to be incorrect. It will even be labelled offensive by some, perhaps even by many. In the closing segment of this radically-important Work, I will therefore *again* remind all readers of Paul the Apostle's key statements to his followers. Accepted as a noted intellectual thinker and scholar by Christian academics throughout history and by many of the same today, let us once more take note of Paul's clear admonition to the academic elite of *his* time, and apply it to the *present*.

> "For, contemplate your vocation brothers: that not many philosophers, not many powerful, not many high-born – on the contrary, God has ***chosen*** the ***foolish of the world***, so that He might ***shame the philosophic***..."
> "Therefore none can boast in the presence of God."
>
> (1 Corinthians 1:26-29, Fenton.)

> "...how many of you were wise in the ordinary sense of the word, how many were influential people, or came from noble families? No, it was to ***shame the wise*** that God ***chose what is foolish by human reckoning***..."
>
> (The same from The Jerusalem Bible.
> All emphases mine.)

Since I have no academic mandate from a 'Theological College' or similar I will, for this Work – which greatly derives from The Bible and Teachings of Jesus – therefore accept without boast, the *greater mandate* from Paul, the appointed Apostle of that time.

If I therefore appear to be a 'lone voice in the wilderness', or a disturbing 'boat-rocker', then I count myself blessed and fortunate indeed for, historically, I stand in very good company. Presented to me via strong and clear inner urgings, the guidance to write this particular book for the academic world of science and religion is part of a series of books that, whilst directed to different groups, nonetheless contains the same *essential **core*** knowledge. For it is the knowledge that the "Crucial Imperatives" point to which underpin the purpose and content of this Work and others of "Crystal Publishing", [Booklet Series], which thus sets it apart from virtually all other Publishers/writers.

Whether what I have been *directed* to write is believed, accepted, mocked, reviled or offered any other view, is the concern of the reader alone. I have simply completed what I was *guided* to undertake, and what I clearly know I was meant to do. Quite obviously, *the free-will choice of each individual will ultimately determine how it is received.* As constantly stated throughout, all our life-path choices will always be determined by our personal, free-will decisions in any case. Thus the reader is free to accept or reject this Work too.

To that end, it is my sincere hope that readers who persevered to this point and whose spirits may now be agitated or unsettled, or perhaps seeking clarification about the current uncertain state of the world; may find the same "peace in knowing" – which I hope is *strongly* paralleled in this book – that I have experienced for some years now.
Particularly for those readers who may not have grasped the *full import* of explanations contained herein that really stand *well outside* current scientific/religious educational parameters, I would certainly recommend at least a second or even third reading.

For whilst this Work is relatively comprehensive in terms of *how* it mainly relates to Creation-Law and aspects of primarily Christian beliefs, it is, in the end, only a 'signpost'. A 'signpost', however, pointing the way to where ***all*** explanations of life – thus of Spiritual and scientific Truth and Law – can be found. So a 'signpost' pointing the way to that ultimate Truth which explains, and is also ultimately contained within:

The Spiritual Laws of Creation — Creation-Law!

That Truth is a particularly special, **Spiritual Work**, without which the explanations of global issues, racial problems, the environment and many other subjects – but more especially **Creation-Law** and *concomitant logical Bible interpretation* – could not have been offered here. It is the same Truth which allowed me to definitively and prophetically state what must happen to all societies worldwide in the Sister publication to this Work. Its Title is:

"The Gathering Apocalypse and World Judgement: What it Brings – Even Now – And Why!"

Chapter 14 therein: **"Science Supports the Judgement Process"**, is substantially derived from an Essay by Dr. Richard Steinpach titled; "***The Inconceivable – Here It happens***". His critical Essay [one of very many][9] describes ***certain key*** astrophysical processes which crucially *link* **Creation-Law** to stupendous *stellar events and processes*. That precise outworking has permitted a *complete and harmonious whole* to develop **between** the coarse material world we *physically* inhabit, ***and*** the finer non-material paradigm we must *transit* to *get here*, and then later *to leave*. Astronomers need to recognise and understand these lawful cosmological processes for they not only have a bearing on the *life* of the cosmos, but also on the *life* of every human being. In the final analysis, the attainment of that degree of knowledge and understanding is meant to be the great task and purpose of all earth-science anyway.

Dr. Steinpach's seminal writings bear unequivocal testimony to the *incontestable authority* of **The Source** from which we both derive the knowledge and insights for our respective publications.

---

[9]Dr Steinpach's writings are available in a number of languages and are published by the Stiftung Gralsbotschaft in Frankfurt, Germany.

That especial **Source** is precisely that which Jesus warned would come onto the Earth at the **End-Time** – **The All-Truth** [John 16] – that we of all humankind were to await and seek out at this very time. [*But of which it was also long-prophesied that only the few would find and recognise.*]

> "I have still much more to tell you; but you are not yet able to bear it. When, however, the **Spirit of Truth Himself** comes, **He will instruct you in all the truth**:...
>
> **He Himself will honour me**;..."

(John 16:12-14, Fenton. Emphases mine.)

<u>**Reader:**</u> Do not make the foolish mistake of believing that **The Spirit of Truth** here is some kind of filmy, amorphous wraith as the Christian Church *so very wrongly teaches*.
In final reiteration: There is the very sure 'Personal Pronoun': – **He!** And there is also the equally sure term: – **Himself!**

And, of course, the very telling sentence:
"He Himself will honour me;..."

Most unfortunately for well-meaning Christians, the non-recognition of the true nature of **The Spirit of Truth** by global Christendom coupled with their ongoing and terrible distortions of crucial Bible Scripture effectively means that 2,000 million [2 billion] so-called 'believers' have *missed the moment* – exactly as was prophesied. i.e., *"He shall come like a thief in the night..."* — *"Only the few would know..."*
So, what, exactly, *is* this most especial Teaching of **The All-Truth** that we have constantly alluded to throughout this book.

That crucial Work for humankind is:

The Grail Message

"IN THE LIGHT OF TRUTH"

by

Abd–ru–shin

As the author of a Work that offers deeper knowledge about the *true* meaning of Bible Scripture [and therefore from which we, in *this* book, elucidate the same for Bible readers especially] the name – **Abd-ru-shin** – might, at first glance, seem rather 'out of place'. Perhaps more so for 'Western Christendom', for that *especial Arabic name* translates to English as:

Son of The Holy Spirit.

So: Why an Arabic name? If you have read *this* book to *this* point, you will have well-noted the necessarily strong emphasis on the knowledge of **The Laws of Creation** throughout, including one that is problematic for many Westerners particularly: i.e., **The Law of Rebirth.** [You will also have noted in the Chapter on the life of **Jesus** the true meaning of **The Holy Grail** – the Origin of the very Life-Force for literally everything in Creation – and therefore why the word **Grail** is included in the overall Title of the Work: **IN THE LIGHT OF TRUTH.**]

Notwithstanding the full gamut of reactions from non-believers around the *concept* of "Rebirth", – from curiosity, to disbelief and rejection, to sheer vitriolic hostility; it is, nonetheless, an *absolute reality* under inviolable **CREATION-LAW**!

In this case, therefore, **Abd-ru-shin** – in His *first incarnation of that Name* – was an **Arabian Prince** who lived in the same time-frame as **'Moses the Law-Giver'** and the Egyptian Pharaoh, **Ramses II 'The Great'** (c.1300-1224B.C.) He was well-known to both, but *especially to Moses*. For the logically-minded, *astute* reader, therein lies a *clue* to a *stupendous connection*. To be *strongly associated* with two men who not only hold key places in human history but whose lives and activity influenced countless millions thereafter, obviously presupposes the probability that **Prince Abd-ru-shin** also held a key place then. And that is so!

So whilst there were many Pharaohs by the name of Ramses, only *one* was given the title: **The Great**! Once more for the *astute* reader, therefore; to be historically associated with *both* **Ramses the Great** *and* **Moses the Law-Giver** clearly reveals the importance of **Abd-ru-shin**.

The stupendous nature of the Work — **IN THE LIGHT OF TRUTH** — unequivocally testifies that sure fact to we of this present time.

Because there is no well-known historical record about **Abd-ru-shin**, it would be easy to simply dismiss this nonetheless *actual historical figure* as a fabrication.[10] However, in the context of the immutable **Laws of Creation**; just as we have unequivocally stated where the once-crucified body of **Jesus** lies [with the legs 'not broken'] – and the equally-sure fact that contrary to the collective opinions of hundreds of millions of believers He will not set physical foot on earth again – so, too, can we state what will one day be revealed as sure and irrefutable evidence of *this Man's* life on earth.

Murdered by a knife-wielding assassin – probably on the orders of Ramses – before He could *completely fulfil* His Mission for humanity *then*, the earthly cloak of **Abd-ru-shin** for that particular incarnation was placed in a Pyramid-tomb, now long-buried under desert sands. At the appropriate time, His tomb will one day be revealed. Then, however, the Christian Church, particularly – but *all* religions and belief systems ultimately – will have to contend with the hieroglyphic inscriptions on that especial tomb.

For the very last line of His story *then* reveals the completion of His Mission for humanity in the *20th century* as **THE ONE** Who was to come:

---

[10]The recent discovery of the so-called "heretic Pharaoh", Akhenaton, is a case in point. For daring to abolish Egypt's Priesthood and her many gods for a 'One God'; after his death his new temple city was destroyed, his image was effaced, and all references to him were expunged by succeeding Pharaohs. The Priesthood re-introduced the 'old gods' and Egypt sank into a dark age that ultimately led to her fall. Despite attempts to 'erase him completely', Akhenaton is now the most studied Pharaoh of all.

IMANUEL — THE SON OF MAN!

THE "WILL OF GOD":

— THE "SPIRIT OF TRUTH" —

— for the writing of The ALL-TRUTH:

"IN THE LIGHT OF TRUTH!"

Hence such a close association with **Moses** the **Law-Giver**, and thus the continuation of His Name and Title – **Abd-ru-shin** — from that time. Being **able** to write such knowledge in the first place very obviously means that **He** carries that highest of knowledge *Living* **within Him**. His Origin is clearly revealed in His Work.

Within that crucial Work, however, He states – as the *primary* consideration for all – to:

"Heed the Word, not the Bringer!"

...As should always have been done, as well, with the Teachings of Jesus – Who brought the knowledge of Creation and Divine Law to Earth *in a form understandable to believers then* – and with all others who similarly sought to *genuinely enlighten* earthly humanity... However, in the emotional stupidity that characterises we humans generally, we sought, instead, to *focus* on the 'Bringer/s'. The practice of elevating *them* to become the **focus** of the particular religion – rather than on **the Truths** they sought to impart – has resulted in the mess of religious intolerance and bloodshed we are burdened with today.

Whilst the thrust of this Work fulfils its major purpose elucidating precisely *why* **The Bible** is "**A Primary Book of Foundational-Science**", that vital knowledge cannot stand alone in grand isolation. For the very Laws which humankind have transgressed for millennia without thought or belief of future consequences deriving from those transgressions, now reveal their *inviolability* more powerfully with each passing day.

Yet science and religion still holds to its standard mind-set of *seeing only what it wishes to see*. In the impending "sorting out" process for all of humanity and its works, we *will* learn that we were, **by choice**, both *intransigent* **and** *blind*. We will also learn, unfortunately very severely now, that the "judging process" *we humans* have set in train and now rolling more intensively, **was not** – **is not** – visited upon us by **THE CREATOR**.

By placing His Perfect Laws —

Crucial Imperative No 6:

That there are certain and precise *Inviolable Laws* which govern *all life* and to which *all* human decisions and processes *are subject*. In their inherent Perfection these Laws are, in their perfect outworking, **Absolute**. And are therefore **Immutable**; and thus **Unchangeable**!

— into **His Creation**, we of humankind were gifted the perfect set of rules by which we *could* have produced an harmonious paradise on Earth. The present, final result is **crystal-clear** for all to see. For we, alone, are responsible for the tragic and long-failing state of earthly humanity. **The Almighty Himself**, being Perfect Love – but also Perfect Justice – has no need to, *and therefore does not*, actually judge humanity. Through the decisions we make for ourselves, **but under the aegis and outworking of His Perfect Laws**, we thus judge, **and pass judgement upon**, ourselves – as individuals and as a collective, global humanity.

In particular, moreover, under that decisive Law which unequivocally states in both perfect **Love** and **Justice**:

> **"For what a man sows, that will he also reap..."** [Gal.]

Since The Son of God warned that "...if the times were not cut short, not a man would be saved", and The Revelation itself indicates a hard mathematical outcome for the six thousand million plus presently alive on Earth: – "A third of a third of a third shall die." – **The Gift of Grace** may yet still offer a saving-grace mechanism for *some*.

The unnerving portent of those two indicators, *on their own*, show just how far the human race has *deviated* from the *correct path* we were *ordained* to travel, and how *serious* our collective transgressions over millennia *must actually have been* to now call in such destruction. Quite logically, therefore, only one outcome is certain. Complete destruction of *all they* who refuse, along with *all that* which refuses, to live by *true* **CREATION-LAW** — clearly explained for all of global humanity in the Work:

"IN THE LIGHT OF TRUTH!"

May you, reader, choose to seek out this most Exalted Knowledge, and therewith build within yourself *that* peace of spirit which must necessarily *accept*, yet objectively and compassionately *understand*, the increasingly disturbing and *seemingly* incomprehensible fate of suffering humankind on Earth today. Unfortunately, however, a fate brought about simply by our collective refusal to pay heed to **Creation-Law – Perfect, Immutable, Inviolable, Absolute** – in which we have our life and being.

Yet what of the many millions of deluded, often hate-filled, fundamentalists of every religious 'bent' who radically promote their particular belief as the so-called *only truth* for all? The necessary 'cleansing' that will finally *rid the world of them* will usher in – *for the few who are left* – the long-awaited **Millennium of Peace**.

For the 'spiritually asleep', and those who would mock and revile; two simple messages. One from **The Son of God**, Jesus, to one of His disciples who asked for leave to attend the funeral of a member of his earthly family — [Parenthetic additions mine]:

> **"Let the [spiritually] dead bury their [spiritually] dead."**

> — and 2 — Watch the nightly global News!

On an *individual* basis we can ameliorate, *at least for ourselves*, some of the *harder aspects* of the prophesied end-time for global societies. — Therefore:

> **"And acting nobly, we shall not suffer... So then, as we have opportunity, let us do good to all..."**

(Gal. 6:7-10, Fenton.)

The golden key to that more positive outcome will be best achieved by striving to understand the "Crucial Imperatives" – most especially that of:

THE TWO SONS OF GOD!

*   *   *   *   *

For all of **Creation** and **THE LAW** resides in **The Living Form** of:

*   *   *   *   *

THE TRIUNE GOD!

*   *   *   *   *

THE TWO SONS

— — and — —

*   *   *   *   *

THE LORD GOD!

*   *   *   *   *

Bibliography

1. The deeper knowledge in this book is derived from the Work: *"IN THE LIGHT OF TRUTH"* The Grail Message by Abd-ru-shin. 3 Volume Edition. Stiftung Gralsbotschaft Publishing Co., Stuttgart, Germany.

2. *A Gate Opens*, Herbert Vollmann, Composite Volume 1985, Stiftung Gralsbotschaft Publishing Co., Stuttgart, Germany.

3. Gralswelt (Magazine), Stiftung Gralsbotschaft Publishing Co., Stuttgart, Germany.

4. *The Holy Bible in Modern English*, Ferrar Fenton, Destiny Publishers, Massachusetts U.S.A. 1966 Edition.

5. *The Holy Bible, Authorised (King James) Version*, Eyre and Spottiswoode (Publishers) Ltd., Great Britain.

6. *The Jerusalem Bible, Reader's Edition*, First published 1968, Darton, Longman and Todd Ltd., London.

7. *The Apocrypha of the Old Testament*, Revised Standard Version, Published by Thomas Nelson and Sons Ltd.

8. *The Turin Shroud*, Ian Wilson. Penguin Books. First Published in U.S.A. by Doubleday & Company Inc., 1978. In Great Britain by Victor Gollancz, 1978. Revised [quoted] edition published in Penguin Books 1979.

9. *The Language of God: A Scientist Presents Evidence for Belief.* Francis S. Collins, M.D.,Ph.D. Published by Simon and Schuster Ltd., 2006.

10. *The Helmet and the Cross.* W. H. Canaway. Century Publishers, London. 1986.

11. *The Wisdom of Israel. [The Wisdom of Spinoza]*, Michael Joseph, London 1949.

12. *The Gospel of the Essenes*, The original Hebrew and Aramaic texts translated and edited by Edmund Bordeaux Szekely, Revised Edition, London, C. W. Daniel, 1976.

13. *A Wanderer In The Spirit Lands*, Franchezzo, Transcribed by A. Farnese, Progressive Thinker Publishing House, Chicago 1913.

14. *Cruden's Complete Concordance to the Old and New Testaments (and to the Apocrypha)*, Revised Edition, Guildford: Lutterworth Press, 1954.

15. *The Christian and Reincarnation*, Stephen Lampe, Millenium Press (UK) 1990.

16. *Building Future Societies*, Stephen Lampe, Millenium Press (UK) 1994.

17. *Heavenly Thoughts*, Karl May.

18. *Autobiography of a Yogi*, Paramahansa Yogananda, First published 1946, Random House.

19. *Man's Eternal Quest*, Paramahansa Yogananda, Collected Talks and Essays on Realizing God in Daily Life, Volume 1.

20. *Great Illustrated Dictionary Vol's I & II*, Readers Digest, First Edition, 1984, USA.

21. *The Concise Oxford Dictionary of Proverbs*, 1983 Edition, Oxford University Press, First Printing 1982, USA, New England Journal of Medicine.

22. *Reflections on Life After Life*, Raymond A. Moody, Bantam Books USA and Canada, 3rd Printing, 1978.

23. *The Soul – Whence and Whither*, Hazrat Inayat Khan, East-West Publication, 1984.

24. *Music Forms*, Geoffrey Hodson, The Theosophical Publishing House, Adyar, 1976.

25. *The Romeo Error*, Lyall Watson, London: Hodder and Stoughton, 1974.

26. *Ideas and Opinions*, Albert Einstein, Bonanza Books, New York, 1954.

27. *Philosophy History and Problems*, Third Edition, Samuel Enoch Stumpf, McGraw-Hill, USA 1983.

28. *The Nature Of The Gods*, Cicero, Penguin Classics, 1972 Edition, Translation by Horace C P Macgregor, Printed by Richard Clay (S E Asia) Pte. Ltd. Reprinted 1978, 1984.

29. *On the Speech of Neanderthal Man*, Philip Lieberman and Edmund S. Crelin, Linguistic Inquiry 2:203-222, Cambridge Mass., MIT Press.

30. *Sophie's World*, Jostein Gaardner, Phoenix House, Great Britain, 1996 Edition.

31. *The Atlas of the Universe*, Patrick Moore, Mitchell Beazley Publishers, London, 1981.

32. *Lifecloud: the origin of life in the universe*, Fred Hoyle and Chandra Wickramasinghe, 1978.

33. *The Life and Letters of Charles Darwin* (Editor - Frances Darwin), 2nd Edition, London: John Murray, 1887.

34. *The Mystery of Life's Origin: Reassessing Current Theories*, Charles B. Thaxton, Walter L. Bradley, Richard L. Olsen, Philosophical Library, 1984.

35. *Astronomy Magazine* Edition April, 2009. Kalmbach Publishing Coy., Waukesha, Wi. USA.

36. *Seven Wonders of the Cosmos* Jayant V. Narlikar. Cambridge University Press, 1999.

37. *Telegraph Group Ltd.*

38. *The Sacred Balance: Rediscovering our place in nature*, David Suzuki, Allen and Unwin, Australia, 1997.

39. *North American Indian Chiefs*, General Editor: Karl Nagerfeld, Tiger Books International, London. 1995.

40. *Native American Myths and Legends*, Editorial Consultant, Colin F. Taylor, New York: Smithmark, 1994.

41. *The Handbook of Unusual Natural Phenomena (Eyewitness Accounts of Nature's Greatest Mysteries)*, William R. Corliss, Arlington House, Crown Publishers, New York.

42. *Earthquake Information Bulletin*, 10: 231-33, 1978. Publisher; National Earthquake Information Centre (NEIC), (Rockville Md) Serial Publication, Bi-monthly, 1970-1985.

43. *Earthquakes and the Urban Environment*, Volume II, G. Lennis Berlin, Published Boca Raton, Fla: CRC Press, c 1980.

44. *Warm Earth Magazine, Number 41.* Warm Earth Publishing. Kenilworth Qld. Australia.

45. *None Dare Call It Conspiracy*, Gary Allen. Concord Press, Rossmoor, California. 1971.

46. *Montagu Norman*, John Hargrave. Greystone Press, N.Y., 1942.

47. *Conference Notes, U S Geological Survey Conference*, 10 Oct. 1976.

48. *Time Magazine 25th June 2001 Edition* (Feature Article: "How The Universe Will End")

49. *Readers Digest Magazine, Aug 2004*, ("How to Make a Universe", Bill Bryson)

50. *British Medical Journal.*

51. *Science Journal.*

52. *Economist.*

53. *Independent.*

54. *The Guardian Weekly.*

55. *As You Like It*, Shakespeare, Act 11.

56. *National Geographic Magazine.*

57. *National Geographic Star Chart*, 1983.

58. *National Geographic Documentary Channel.*

59. *Chief Seattle's Address on the Environment* Friends of the Earth.

60. *ASH (Action on smoking and health).*

61. *"Our World" The Savage Earth* – BBC Series (screened 1998).

62. *Discovery Channel.* "Earthquakes" documentary. Screened through 2002.

63. *History Channel.* "Crucifixion" documentary. Screened April, 2009; and series, "How Life Began". Screened through 2009.

64. *National Geographic Channel.* "Birth of Life" and "Human Ape" documentaries, 2009.

65. *Encarta* – Microsoft.

66. *"The Human Body"*, New Series Documentary, Part 1, Dr Robert Winston.

67. Brittanica CD '97.

68. CNN.

69. Bob Dylan music. "With God on our Side".

70. Dr. Alan Duggan. Researcher into "Male Health". Australia.

71. Professor Fiona Stanley. Australian Children's Advocate and "National Treasure".

72. Kathleen Quinlivan. Researcher, Canterbury University. New Zealand.

73. Rev. Gerald Hadlow. New Zealand.

74. "Larry King Live".

www.ingramcontent.com/pod-product-compliance
Lightning Source LLC
Chambersburg PA
CBHW080548090426
42735CB00016B/3180